SOCIAL PROBLEMS

SOCIAL PROBLEMS

BURTON WRIGHT
University of Central Florida

JOHN P. WEISS
Rollins College

Little, Brown and Company
Boston   Toronto

Copyright © 1980 by Burton Wright and John P. Weiss

All rights reserved. No part of this book may be reproduced in any form or by any electronic or mechanical means including information storage and retrieval systems without permission in writing from the publisher, except by a reviewer who may quote brief passages in a review.

Library of Congress Catalog Card No.: 79-88192

First Printing

Published simultaneously in Canada
by Little, Brown & Company (Canada) Limited

Printed in the United States of America

ALEX INKELES, Series Advisor

TEXT CREDITS

Table 2.3. From Robin M. Williams, Jr., *American Society: A Sociological Interpretation,* 3rd ed., Chapter XI. Copyright 1951, 1960, 1970 by Alfred A. Knopf, Inc. Reprinted by permission.

Table 5.5. From Stanley S. Surrey, *Pathways to Tax Reform: The Concept of Tax Expenditures,* p. 69. © Copyright 1973 by the President and Fellows of Harvard College. Reprinted by permission of Harvard University Press.

Table 6.1. From Peter I. Rose, *They and We: Racial and Ethnic Relations in the United States,* 2nd ed., p. 107. Copyright © 1974 by Random House, Inc. Reprinted by permission.

(continued on page 535)

PREFACE

This text is based on the premise that social problems arise because societies, as highly organized entities, are inevitably riddled with conflicts. This does not mean that we take a functionalist view and regard social problems as kinds of disequilibria. Rather, we see social problems as results of our efforts to organize complex social systems.

We do not believe that our social structure is sacred, to be protected at any cost. Change is necessary to solve, or at least alleviate, our major social problems. To achieve orderly and planned change, however, knowledge of the social structure and how it works is necessary.

Our book tries to provide some of this knowledge. While there are several excellent social problems texts available today, even the very best do not provide the organizing framework that integrates our text. Each chapter covers a social problem and includes an overview, introduction, historical overview, conceptual orientation (definition of the problem), objective dimensions of the problem (how the problem manifests itself), attempts at dealing with the problem, and prospects for future solutions. We have placed some stress on the social history of each problem. In this the text is unique, for it provides the student with a sense of history, something sociologists have resoundingly failed to do. We feel that knowledge of the past provides a superior foundation for analyzing social problems as they exist in the present. Also, in each section on attempts at dealing with the problem, we have introduced a concept borrowed from medicine, iatrogenic effects. It is used to denote a special type of latent effects, that is, new problems created in our efforts to solve other problems.

We have included at least two other areas that are mentioned only briefly in most other social problems texts. We provide extensive coverage of the largest of all minority groups — women, and a separate chapter deals with the problem of war. We are at a loss to explain why other texts have provided only scant coverage both of women, the minority group with the longest history of victimization, and of war, a condition that has caused misery and suffering throughout the ages.

In planning this text, we assumed no sociology background on the part of students. While sociology majors usually do take courses in social problems, the subject fits the category of "service course" very well, and attracts students majoring in other disciplines. At the same time it will benefit sociology majors, as a review of things they already know — or should know.

Several features in the text facilitate student learning. Summaries appear throughout the chapters to review major topics. Suggested readings at the end of each chapter provide references for additional research. A list of important words and terms at the end of each chapter identify key concepts. Each chapter also contains a number of discussion questions intended for class use. These questions enable students to use the knowledge gained in each chapter, and they also furnish a basis for lively and stimulating class discussions. An extensive illustration program expands text discussion further. Finally, a complete glossary is provided.

A student study guide provides key questions and items that will aid students in perceiving meaning. Also included in the study guide are two self-tests for each chapter. For the instructor there is a Teacher's Manual which serves as an excellent resource for test items and teaching aids.

We are indebted to our reviewers for their intelligent help and direction. More important, they chose to be direct in their criticism rather than tolerant of our feelings, and the result is a much better text. We wish to thank Alex Inkeles, Stanford University; Richard Minisce, Washington State University; John Williamson, Boston College; Howard Robboy, Trenton State University; and Gordon Lewis, University of Vermont. Thanks are also due to contributing authors Ida Cook, University of Central Florida, for her chapter on health, and John Washington, University of Central Florida, for his chapter on drugs and mental illness. We also wish to express our appreciation to Bruce Aldrich, University of Miami, for his unstinting help when this book was in the early planning stages.

We would be remiss if we did not acknowledge the remarkable assistance from those at Little, Brown and Company. We are greatly indebted to our sponsoring editor, Katie Carlone, for her continuing help and warm encouragement, and to her assistant, Sheryl Gipstein, for handling numerous administrative details with efficiency and good humor. We are most grateful for the generous support and assistance of our book editor, Tina Samaha, and for the very special skills provided by our copy editor, Dale Anderson, and our art editor, Tina Schwinder.

CONTENTS

**PART I
INTRODUCTION TO SOCIAL
PROBLEMS** 1

1 A GENERAL ORIENTATION TO
SOCIAL PROBLEMS
THE BIG PICTURE 3

    CHAPTER OVERVIEW 4
    INTRODUCTION 4
    DEFINING SOCIAL PROBLEMS 5
    Observable Conditions 7
    Subjective Analysis 9
    Solvability 11
    Influential People as Catalysts 13
    *Organized Efforts to Solve
       the Problem* 16
    Summary 17
    WITCHCRAFT AS A SOCIAL
      PROBLEM 17
    FILTERING AND DISTORTION 19
    Physiological Sources of Error 19
    Social Sources of Error 20
    Beliefs 20
    The Information Chain 22
    Summary 24
    CONCLUSION 24
    IMPORTANT WORDS AND TERMS 24
    QUESTIONS FOR DISCUSSION 24
    SUGGESTED READING 25
    NOTES 26

2 SOCIAL STRUCTURE
*THE BREEDING GROUND OF
SOCIAL PROBLEMS* 29

    CHAPTER OVERVIEW 30
    INTRODUCTION 30
    MODELS OF SOCIAL PROBLEMS 31
    The Organic Analogy 31
    *The Functionalist and Conflict
       Perspectives* 32
    Modern Functionalism 33
    Summary 33
    THE SOCIAL STRUCTURE:
    INTERACTION AND PARTS 34
    Social Interaction 34
    Social Institutions 36
    Summary 38
    VALUES 39
    Values Defined 39
    Values and Social Problems 40
    Summary 44
    NORMS 44
    Mores 44
    The Function of General Norms 45
    Types of General Norms 47
    Laws 48
    Summary 49
    SANCTIONS 49
    The Necessity for Sanctions 50
    Sanction Incongruence 50
    Summary 51
    STATUSES AND ROLES 51
    The Male Status and Role 52
    Status, Role, and Mental Illness 52
    Status Lock 53
    Summary 53

SOCIAL DISORGANIZATION 53
   Defining Social Disorganization 53
   The Relativity of Social
      Disorganization 54
   Organization as a Cultural Universal 55
   Summary 55
CONCLUSION 56
IMPORTANT WORDS AND TERMS 56
QUESTIONS FOR DISCUSSION 57
SUGGESTED READING 57
NOTES 58

PART II
INSTITUTIONAL PROBLEMS 61

3 THE FAMILY
CROSS CURRENTS OF EMOTIONALITY 63

CHAPTER OVERVIEW 64
INTRODUCTION 64
CONCEPTUAL ORIENTATION 65
   Definitions 65
   The Normal American Family 66
   Summary 67
CROSS-CULTURAL AND HISTORICAL
   OVERVIEW 68
   Cross-Cultural Evidence 68
   Sex Roles in American Society 69
   Summary 72
OBJECTIVE DIMENSIONS OF THE
   PROBLEM 72
   Education and Sex Roles 73
   Women in the Labor Force 74
   Contraception and Abortion 75
   Marriage Rates 78
   Divorce Rates 79
   Birthrates 81
   Fertility Among Single Women: The
      Problem of Illegitimacy 82
   Violence in the Family 83
   Summary 85

ATTEMPTS AT DEALING WITH THE
   PROBLEM 85
   Ideological Responses to the Problem 86
   Iatrogenic Effects 88
PROSPECTS FOR SOLVING THE
   PROBLEM 89
IMPORTANT WORDS AND TERMS 92
QUESTIONS FOR DISCUSSION 92
SUGGESTED READING 92
NOTES 93

4 WORK
ALIENATION, DISAFFECTION, AND EXPLOITATION 97

CHAPTER OVERVIEW 98
INTRODUCTION 98
HISTORICAL OVERVIEW 99
   The Impact of Technology on Work 99
   The Effect of the Industrial Revolution 102
   Summary 102
CONCEPTUAL ORIENTATION 103
OBJECTIVE DIMENSIONS OF THE
   PROBLEM 106
   The Changing Relationship between
      Education and Jobs 107
   Job Satisfaction 109
   Wages and Employment 111
   The Influence of Work on Health 112
   Women in the Labor Force 114
   Unemployment and
      Underemployment 115
   Summary 116
ATTEMPTS AT DEALING WITH THE
   PROBLEM 117
   Management Strategies 117
   Labor Unions 118
   Government Action 120
   Iatrogenic Effects 122
PROSPECTS FOR SOLVING THE
   PROBLEM 124
IMPORTANT WORDS AND TERMS 126
QUESTIONS FOR DISCUSSION 127
SUGGESTED READING 127
NOTES 128

5 POVERTY
TRAPPED IN A VICIOUS CYCLE 131

    CHAPTER OVERVIEW 132
    INTRODUCTION 132
    HISTORICAL OVERVIEW 132
        The Poor in Europe 132
        Poverty in the United States 134
        Summary 135
    CONCEPTUAL ORIENTATION 136
        Defining Poverty 136
        Summary 139
    OBJECTIVE DIMENSIONS OF THE PROBLEM 139
        Children 140
        The Elderly 141
        Blacks 142
        The Impact of Poverty 142
        Summary 145
    ATTEMPTS AT DEALING WITH THE PROBLEM 145
        The Government's Approaches 145
        Reevaluating Government Welfare Programs 146
        Negative Income Tax Plans 148
        Iatrogenic Effects 149
    PROSPECTS FOR SOLVING THE PROBLEM 151
        What Will It Cost? 151
        Who Will Pay? 154
    IMPORTANT WORDS AND TERMS 157
    QUESTIONS FOR DISCUSSION 157
    SUGGESTED READING 157
    NOTES 158

6 MINORITIES
A WORLD OF ILLOGIC AND REDUCED OPPORTUNITIES 161

    CHAPTER OVERVIEW 162
    INTRODUCTION 162
    CONCEPTUAL ORIENTATION 163
        Minorities Defined 163
        Visibility 164
        Prejudice 165
        Discrimination 170
        Ending Minority Group Status 172
        Summary 174
    HISTORICAL OVERVIEW 174
        Power and Authority 176
        Women as a Minority 177
        Blacks as a Minority 178
        Summary 181
    OBJECTIVE DIMENSIONS OF THE PROBLEM 181
        Females 182
        Blacks 185
        Other Minorities 190
        Summary 194
    ATTEMPTS AT DEALING WITH THE PROBLEM 195
        Militance and Affirmative Action 195
        Iatrogenic Effects 196
    PROSPECTS FOR SOLVING THE PROBLEM 197
    IMPORTANT WORDS AND TERMS 198
    QUESTIONS FOR DISCUSSION 198
    SUGGESTED READING 199
    NOTES 200

7 THE YOUNG AND THE OLD
AGE STRATIFICATION 203

    CHAPTER OVERVIEW 204
    INTRODUCTION 204
    CONCEPTUAL ORIENTATION 205
        The Relationship between the Problems of Youth and Age 206
        Support of Age Roles by Players 206
        Summary 207
    CROSS-CULTURAL AND HISTORICAL OVERVIEW 207
        Anthropological Conclusions 207
        The Impact of the Industrial Revolution 209
        Summary 214
    OBJECTIVE DIMENSIONS OF THE PROBLEM 214
        Delinquency: The Failure of Socialization 214

Socialization: The Balanced Perspective 216
Socialization for Retirement 218
Myths About Aging 219
Summary 222
ATTEMPTS AT DEALING WITH THE PROBLEM 225
Iatrogenic Effects of the Educational System 225
Iatrogenic Effects of Social Security 225
PROSPECTS FOR SOLVING THE PROBLEM 226
The Problem of Youth 226
The Problem of the Aged 227
The Future of Life Cycle Problems 228
IMPORTANT WORDS AND TERMS 231
QUESTIONS FOR DISCUSSION 231
SUGGESTED READING 232
NOTES 232

**PART III
PROBLEMS OF DEVIANCE 235**

8 CRIME AND JUSTICE
LAWBREAKERS IN A FLAWED SYSTEM 237

CHAPTER OVERVIEW 238
INTRODUCTION 238
CONCEPTUAL ORIENTATION 239
The Value of Achievement 239
Informal Norms and the Law 239
The Lawbreakers 240
Summary 241
CROSS-CULTURAL AND HISTORICAL OVERVIEW 241
Crime in Preliterate Societies 241
The Social Consequences of Population Growth 242
Criminal Justice in England 244
Toward a Professional Police Force 246
Summary 249

OBJECTIVE DIMENSIONS OF THE PROBLEM 249
How Much Crime? 249
The Criminal Justice System 251
Political Aspects of Crime 258
Summary 261
ATTEMPTS AT DEALING WITH THE PROBLEM 261
Biological Theories 261
Psychological Theories 262
Sociological Theories 264
Iatrogenic Effects 268
PROSPECTS FOR SOLVING THE PROBLEM 269
IMPORTANT WORDS AND TERMS 270
QUESTIONS FOR DISCUSSION 270
SUGGESTED READING 271
NOTES 272

9 HUMAN SEXUALITY
CHANGING STANDARDS AND BEHAVIOR 275

CHAPTER OVERVIEW 276
INTRODUCTION 276
HISTORICAL AND CROSS-CULTURAL OVERVIEW 277
The Ancient Heritage 277
The Christian View of Sex and Morality 279
Cross-Cultural Perspectives 282
Summary 283
CONCEPTUAL ORIENTATION 283
The Meaning of Sexuality in American Society 284
The Sexual Revolution 285
Summary 288
OBJECTIVE DIMENSIONS OF THE PROBLEM 288
Extramarital Sex 289
Homosexuality 290
Prostitution 293
Pornography and Obscenity 294
Paraphilias 296

  Rape 298
  Summary 300
 ATTEMPTS AT DEALING WITH THE
  PROBLEM 300
  New Attitudes 300
  Iatrogenic Effects 302
 PROSPECTS FOR SOLVING THE
  PROBLEM 304
 IMPORTANT WORDS AND TERMS 306
 QUESTIONS FOR DISCUSSION 307
 SUGGESTED READING 307
 NOTES 308

10 PERSONAL PATHOLOGY
*ESCAPE BY MENTAL ILLNESS
AND DRUGS 311*

 CHAPTER OVERVIEW 312
 INTRODUCTION 312
 HISTORICAL OVERVIEW 313
  Perceptions of Mental Illness 313
  The Long History of Drugs 315
  Summary 318
 CONCEPTUAL ORIENTATION 318
  Problems in Defining Mental Illness 318
  The Medical Model 319
  The Sociocultural Model 322
  The Operational Model 323
  Escape by Drugs 324
  Summary 324
 OBJECTIVE DIMENSIONS OF THE
  PROBLEM 325
  Who Are the Mentally Ill? 325
  Alcohol 327
  Tobacco 331
  Sedatives 332
  Illegal Drugs 333
  Summary 335
 ATTEMPTS AT DEALING WITH THE
  PROBLEM 336
  Treating Mental Illness 336
  Treating Alcohol Abuse 337
  Treating Drug Abuse 338
  Iatrogenic Effects 338

 PROSPECTS FOR SOLVING THE
  PROBLEM 339
 IMPORTANT WORDS AND TERMS 340
 QUESTIONS FOR DISCUSSION 341
 SUGGESTED READING 341
 NOTES 342

**PART IV
PROBLEMS OF OUR CHANGING
WORLD 345**

11 POPULATION
*GROWING NUMBERS AND
SHRINKING RESOURCES 347*

 CHAPTER OVERVIEW 348
 INTRODUCTION 348
 HISTORICAL OVERVIEW 350
  The Neolithic Revolution 350
  The Industrial Revolution 352
  Summary 354
 CONCEPTUAL ORIENTATION 354
  Fertility and Mortality 354
  The Scarcity of Resources 356
  Summary 358
 OBJECTIVE DIMENSIONS OF THE
  PROBLEM 358
  Population Growth in the World 358
  *Population Growth in Developed
   Countries 361*
  Summary 364
 ATTEMPTS AT DEALING WITH THE
  PROBLEM 364
  *The Eufunctions of Zero Population
   Growth 364*
  Iatrogenic Effects 365
 PROSPECTS FOR SOLVING THE
  PROBLEM 368
  Factors Tending to Reduce Fertility 368
  Factors Tending to Increase Fertility 371
  A Look Ahead 375
 IMPORTANT WORDS AND TERMS 376

QUESTIONS FOR DISCUSSION   376
SUGGESTED READING   377
NOTES   378

12 THE CITIES
A STUDY IN SENESCENCE   381

CHAPTER OVERVIEW   382
INTRODUCTION   382
HISTORICAL OVERVIEW   383
   The Rise of Ancient Cities   383
   American Cities   384
   Summary   386
CONCEPTUAL ORIENTATION   386
   Changing Patterns of Urbanization   387
   Demographic Changes   388
   Summary   389
OBJECTIVE DIMENSIONS OF THE PROBLEM   389
   Race and Politics in the American City   390
   City Financing   391
   Education   394
   Employment   397
   Housing   399
   Summary   400
ATTEMPTS AT DEALING WITH THE PROBLEM   401
   The Changing Federal Role   401
   The Structure of Current Welfare Programs   402
   Employment and Education Programs   403
   Iatrogenic Effects   405
PROSPECTS FOR SOLVING THE PROBLEM   407
IMPORTANT WORDS AND TERMS   410
QUESTIONS FOR DISCUSSION   410
SUGGESTED READING   411
NOTES   412

13 HUMAN ECOLOGY
ORGANIZED DESPOLIATION   415

CHAPTER OVERVIEW   416
INTRODUCTION   416
CONCEPTUAL ORIENTATION   417
   The Ecological Perspective   417
   Ecological Concepts   418
   Summary   420
HISTORICAL OVERVIEW   420
   The Beginning of Human Destructiveness   420
   American Destructiveness   421
   Ideology and Environmental Damage   423
   Summary   424
OBJECTIVE DIMENSIONS OF THE PROBLEM   425
   The Scope of Pollution   425
   Air Pollution   426
   Water Pollution   429
   Pesticides   432
   Other Forms of Pollution   433
   Summary   434
ATTEMPTS AT DEALING WITH THE PROBLEM   435
   Different Views of the Problem   435
   Environmental Groups   437
   The Politics and Economics of Technology   438
   Attempts at Increasing Public Awareness   440
   Iatrogenic Effects   441
PROSPECTS FOR SOLVING THE PROBLEM   444
IMPORTANT WORDS AND TERMS   446
QUESTIONS FOR DISCUSSION   446
SUGGESTED READING   447
NOTES   448

14 HEALTH
PRESCRIPTIONS AND PROSCRIPTIONS   451

CHAPTER OVERVIEW   452
INTRODUCTION   452
CONCEPTUAL ORIENTATION   453
   Medical Sociology   453
   Summary   456
HISTORICAL OVERVIEW   456
   The Origins of Medicine   456

Medicine in the Middle Ages 457
Modern Medicine 459
Summary 460
OBJECTIVE DIMENSIONS OF THE PROBLEM 461
Systems of Health Care 461
Health Care in the United States 462
Medical Professionals: The Non-Western Perspective 468
Summary 469
ATTEMPTS AT DEALING WITH THE PROBLEM 469
Iatrogenic Effects 469
Alternative Medical Perspectives 474
PROSPECTS FOR SOLVING THE PROBLEM 476
IMPORTANT WORDS AND TERMS 478
QUESTIONS FOR DISCUSSION 478
SUGGESTED READING 479
NOTES 479

15 **INTERNATIONAL CONFLICT** *SOPHISTICATED WEAPONRY AND STONE AGE MENTALITY* 483

CHAPTER OVERVIEW 484
INTRODUCTION 484
CONCEPTUAL ORIENTATION 485
The Nature of Human Aggression 485
War in Primitive Societies 486
Defining War 486
Summary 487

HISTORICAL OVERVIEW 487
Primitive and Early Warfare 488
Modern Warfare 488
Summary 490
OBJECTIVE DIMENSIONS OF THE PROBLEM 492
Technological Advances 492
Contemporary Military Organization 493
The Military-Industrial Complex 494
The Military Budget 496
Worldwide Arms Expenditures 500
The Economics of Defense Procurement 502
Summary 503
ATTEMPTS AT DEALING WITH THE PROBLEM 503
American Ideology and International Conflict 504
The Rise of Anticommunism 505
America and Vietnam 506
Iatrogenic Effects 507
PROSPECTS FOR SOLVING THE PROBLEM 509
The Domestic Structure 509
The Superpowers and the International Community 510
The Role of the United Nations 511
Summary 512
IMPORTANT WORDS AND TERMS 513
QUESTIONS FOR DISCUSSION 513
SUGGESTED READING 513
NOTES 514

SOCIAL PROBLEMS

PART I
INTRODUCTION TO SOCIAL PROBLEMS

1 A GENERAL ORIENTATION TO SOCIAL PROBLEMS
THE BIG PICTURE

CHAPTER OVERVIEW

INTRODUCTION

DEFINING SOCIAL PROBLEMS
Observable Conditions
Subjective Analysis
Solvability
Influential People as Catalysts
Organized Efforts to Solve the Social Problem
Summary

WITCHCRAFT AS A
  SOCIAL PROBLEM

FILTERING AND DISTORTION
Physiological Sources of Error
Social Sources of Error
Beliefs
The Information Chain
Summary

CONCLUSION

IMPORTANT WORDS AND TERMS

QUESTIONS FOR DISCUSSION

SUGGESTED READING

NOTES

Man is born unto trouble, as the sparks fly upward.

Job 5:7

i have noticed that when chickens quit quarreling over their food they often find that there is enough for all of them i wonder if it might not be the same with the human race.

Don Marquis, *Archy and Mehitabel*

CHAPTER OVERVIEW

In this chapter, we tackle the difficult task of defining social problems. Some people believe that a social problem is simply any harmful or adverse condition. But there is more to it than that.

We present the five criteria that a condition must meet to be defined as a social problem, and discuss each principle. For a condition to be a social problem it must have observable evidence; people must subjectively analyze the evidence; the condition must be judged a problem and considered solvable; some people must catalyze action against the problem; and society must take organized action to solve it. To study how these principles apply to a real condition, we analyze a social problem, witchcraft. Of course, witchcraft is not a social problem now, but it was for nearly three hundred years. Because we can now look at witchcraft objectively, it illustrates the complexities of social problems and the social factors underlying these problems and their definition as problems. Finally, we will discuss how distortion affects people's judgments of objective conditions.

INTRODUCTION

The prophet Job was correct in observing that our species is born unto trouble. Archy the cockroach was equally correct in his observation: some of our problems might be solved or alleviated if we behaved in a more civilized fashion. Job's description of the human condition and archy's prescription for bettering it are both part of defining social problems.

To most of us it sometimes seems that the world has never been in such deplorable condition. On all sides, we see crime, poverty, discrimination, corruption, wars, famine, overpopulation, pollution, violations of human rights, economic disruptions, disintegrating families, alienation, mental disorders, drug addiction, sexual misbehavior, and so on, endlessly.

People wonder what brought the world and humankind into this condition. There are many answers to this question. Some people root their answer in something called basic human nature. Robert Ardrey explains violent crimes by saying that "man is a predator whose natural instinct is to kill with a weapon."[1] Ardrey goes further. He claims that war is inevitable, because humans, as primates, have "instincts demanding the maintenance and defense of territories; an attitude of perpetual hostility for the territorial neighbor."[2]

But can we really explain adverse social conditions like war as the result of instinct? Some years ago, it was believed that our species had an instinct for almost every variety of behavior. For example, William Mc-

Dougall, a psychologist writing in the early twentieth century, saw humankind as a repository of every imaginable instinct.[3] If we are to accept the beliefs of McDougall or the more recent and far more sophisticated arguments of Ardrey or Konrad Lorenz, an animal behaviorist, it would be fruitless to pursue the topic of social problems any further. Humans would be beyond redemption because they were helplessly in the grip of powerful, inherited behavioral patterns. But we cannot escape the responsibility for our problems quite so easily. Some modern social scientists maintain that *Homo sapiens* (our species) has no instincts of importance.[4]

The fact is that human problems are mostly social. That is, the behavior of people in groups produces social problems. It follows that if we produce our own problems, we ought to be able to solve them. But how?

Today, as in the past, there are numerous ideas on how to remedy social problems. One small but vocal group of social scientists sees the only hope for humankind to lie in the radical alteration of current social structures. To explain why such extensive change is required, Robert Perrucci and Marc Pilisuk assess the position of modern society:

> Rather than a society that is essentially healthy while beset by particular problems, we see a society whose very patterns of successful adjustment are causing severe and widening strains in accommodating to new and different circumstances.[5]

Perrucci and Pilisuk are correct in a general way, and offer us an important bit of sociological insight. Virtually all patterns of successful adjustment exact a price. For example, our society encourages us to strive for success, and many achieve it. However, success is defined by nonsuccess and while there are winners, there must be losers. A large group of perennial losers in our society are called the poor, and they constitute a social problem.

But Perrucci and Pilisuk go further in their analysis. They condemn modern society:

> This is a death culture. It contains no visions of a better life for its citizens. It stimulates no human impulses in its people. It develops no sense of common purpose or challenge that results in a reaffirmation of life.[6]

We can sympathize with Perrucci and Pilisuk's indignation. But if this is a death culture stimulating no human impulses, where did these writers get their humanitarian ideals? Clearly, understandable indignation has bred logical incongruence.

We disagree with any general condemnation of society, particularly those expressed emotionally. Understanding of social problems is not found in rhetoric, however dramatic and engaging, it is found in objective analysis. We agree with Perrucci and Pilisuk, and others, that much needs to be changed in our own and other societies. But a more dispassionate approach to the changes is in order. Before beginning this approach, we must first explain precisely and at length what is meant by a social problem.

DEFINING SOCIAL PROBLEMS

Many thinkers, from Plato in the fourth century B.C. to Karl Marx in the nineteenth century A.D., have envisioned an ideal society. The utopia they imagined would be marked by perfect harmony and be free from social problems. Such a perfect society is pleasant to contemplate, but it can never be achieved. Problems exist in all societies; no society could be entirely free of social problems.

Consider crime, as Emile Durkheim did:

> Imagine a society of saints, a perfect cloister of exemplary individuals. Crimes, properly

called, will there be unknown; but faults which appear venial to the layman will create there the same scandal that the ordinary offense does in the ordinary consciousness. If, then, this society has the power to judge and punish, it will define these acts as criminal and will treat them as such.[7]

Durkheim is saying that the misbehavior of saints would be regarded as trivial by the rest of us but not by other saints. Crime is not simply a matter of committing a criminal act. Certain behaviors are regarded as criminal because society defines them as criminal, that is, the definition of crime is subjective and varies from culture to culture. The same is true of social problems. These are defined by a society.

This text will analyze the dynamics underlying several social problems as well as the efforts to deal with them. This means we must investigate the definition of social problems. Why has crime been considered a social problem for millenia but poverty, a condition of equal antiquity, become one only recently? Racial discrimination has a very ancient history, but only occasional voices were raised against it in the past. And pollution did not just come about recently. The Thames River in England has been one long sewer for centuries. Only in the 1970s was it made clean enough for game fish to live in it. Why, then, has pollution only recently been defined as a social problem?

The definition of a social problem is a group process. Identifying problems is a matter of *collective definition*, involving a continuous interaction within a group. It involves five major elements:

1. an observable set of conditions — something that can be seen, reported, and discussed
2. subjective analysis of the conditions — people thinking about what they have seen or heard
3. defining the condition as a problem, and feeling that the problem can be solved
4. active involvement, particularly in the definitional stage, of persons able to influence others, who attempt to involve the general public in their concerns
5. some organized efforts, successful or not, to deal with the condition

The first two elements are common to many conditions; it is the final three that are crucial to defining a condition as a social problem.

The behavior of people in every society produces social problems, although what is perceived as a social problem differs from culture to culture and from century to century. Blacks relaxing in a park in Johannesburg, South Africa, are solemn witnesses to the cruelty of segregation, a condition recognized as a social problem only in modern history.

To make this clear, let us consider each element in some detail.

Observable Conditions

Observable conditions provide a foundation for defining social problems. There is not now and there never has been a social problem that lacks observable conditions or empirical evidence of its existence. Defining poverty as a social problem is based on the observation that in all societies various people and groups have life-styles that are less desirable than those of other persons or groups. Let us look at a social problem on which there is a considerable amount of data available.

Some people are alarmed by the number of people in the world and the number expected in the future. Based on census figures, we know what the population of the United States was and is. By projecting these data we can estimate future population growth.

The population explosion is a function of two variables: birthrates and death rates. Migration, another variable, no longer has a significant effect on population in this country. It also seems that increased longevity is not too important for future predictions, although it appears that the average life span will increase slightly until about the year 2020 and then level off.[8] This means, then, that if birthrates are high and death rates low, population goes up.

Figure 1.1 forecasts population changes using three projections based on different possible birthrates. As of early 1979, it appears that actual growth may fall somewhere between Series W and Series V. As can be seen, even with a low fertility rate of 1.7 there will still be a substantial increase in population by the year 2000. This growth in itself is not a problem. After all, the population has been growing for centuries without being seen as harmful. However, the situation is graver now. What is growing is an already large population, and this growth puts pressure on our capacity to provide enough food, jobs, and living space for everyone. People now see population growth as increasing poverty, and others say it will cause rises in crime rates and the incidence of social disorder. As a result, overpopulation is defined as a social problem.

Let us look at another social problem, witchcraft. At first glance, this appears ridiculous. Witchcraft is a social problem? People today (or most of them, at any rate) understand that witchcraft and sorcery do not exist, so how could witchcraft be a social problem? In other words, what are the observable indicators of something we know to be illusory? Marvin Harris, an anthropologist, enlightens us:

> I suggest that the best way to understand the cause of the witch mania is to examine its earthly results rather than its heavenly intentions. The principal results of the witch-hunt system (aside from charred bodies) was that the poor came to believe that they were being victimized by witches and devils instead of princes and popes. Did your roof leak, your cow abort, your baby die? It was a neighbor, the one who broke your fence, owed you money, or wanted your land — a neighbor turned witch. Did the price of bread go up, taxes soar, wages fall, jobs grow scarce? It was the work of witches. Did plague and famine carry off one-third of the inhabitants of every village and town? The diabolical witches were growing bolder all the time.[9]

Today we have similar observable indicators. We see inflation and unemployment, natural disasters, and outbreaks of disease. Cows on modern dairy farms sometimes abort, as do human females. The difference

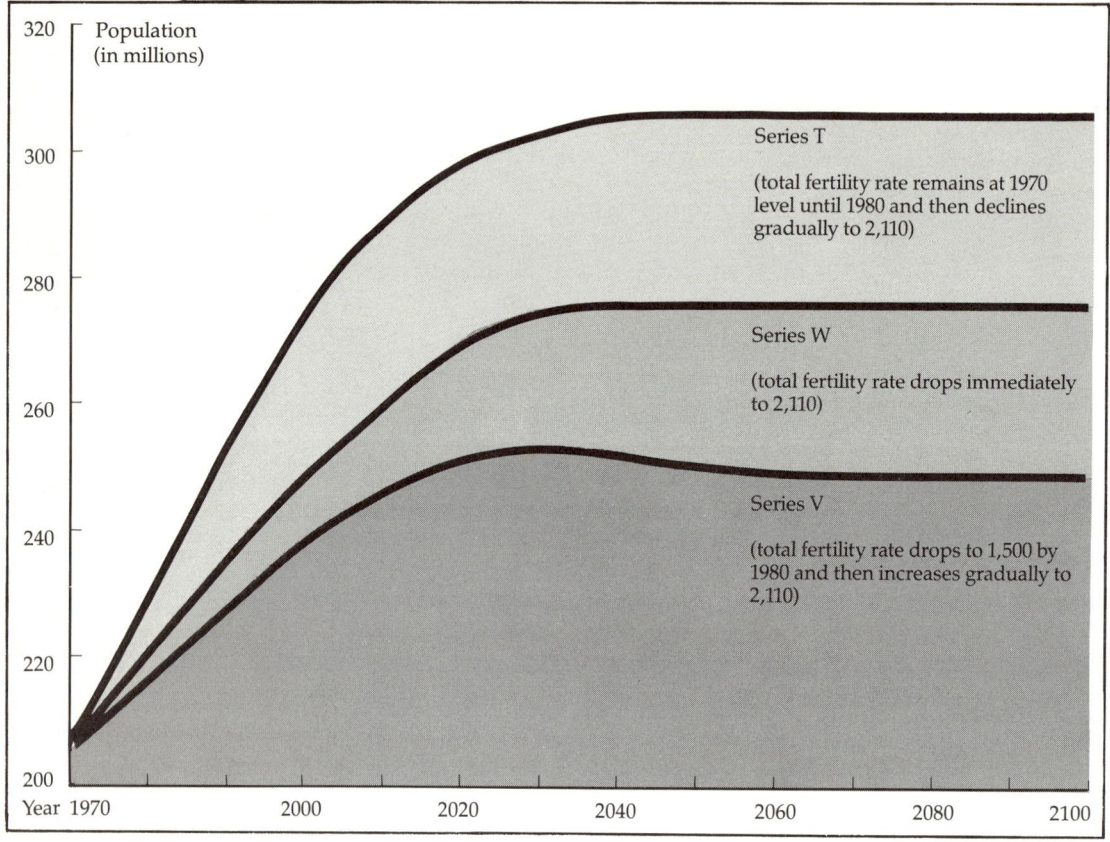

FIGURE 1.1 Population Projections for the United States

Source: Current Population Reports: Population Estimates and Projections, Series P–25, No. 480 (April 1972) (Washington, D.C.: U.S. Government Printing Office, 1972).

is that modern economists do not attribute economic difficulties to witchcraft, and veterinarians and physicians seek the causes of spontaneous abortions in physiology not the occult. When witchcraft was a social problem it was "a phenomenon that, for centuries, gripped the minds of men from the most illiterate peasant to the most skilled philosopher or scientist, leading to torture and death for hundreds of thousands."[10] But now we have more objective explanations for the phenomena previously said to be caused by witchcraft. We see witchcraft as a myth, and as a result it cannot be defined as a social problem.

We are now ready to state the first principle of defining social problems:

All social problems are based on observable conditions. No social problem can ever be entirely the product of mythology or group hysteria. There must be signs — objective indicators — providing evidence for the existence of a social problem.

That these conditions are objective means there can be no dispute of their reality. Overpopulation is a problem only as long as people agree that the population is rising and resources are limited. Witchcraft was no longer a problem when people stopped seeing disasters as the work of witches. But objective conditions do not define social problems alone. People define social problems, which brings us to the question of subjectivity.

Subjective Analysis

All objective conditions undergo *subjective evaluation*. A factory chimney belching black smoke into the air is certainly objective; we see and smell the smoke. But what is it an objective indicator of? An environmental protectionist would say it showed pollution. But the factory owner, the stockholders, and the executives and workers employed in it might see the smoke differently. To them, it constitutes an objective indicator of a factory busily at work making useful things, bringing employment to the community and profits to the stockholders. An objective indicator of a serious social problem to some is a sign of economic well-being to others.

To understand why these perceptions differ, we can look at theories of behavior. A serious weakness of some theories of learning is the implicit assumptions that organisms, including humans, respond somewhat mechanically to *stimuli* from the environment, agents that affect our senses. Given the right rewards or reinforcement for behavior, some psychologists tell us, behavior can be controlled. In general terms, they are correct. Various animals can be taught behaviors not in their native repertoires. Raccoons do not normally play basketball, but psychologists have taught some to.[11]

But these psychologists overlook something crucial to understanding social problems. What they ignore is analogous to what R. P. Cuzzort, a sociologist, calls "black-box problems":

> problems given to students in electronics who observe the electrical energies going into and coming out of a mysterious black box — they must determine what is in the box on the basis of this information. So it is with society.[12]

In the study of human behavior, Cuzzort's black box is the human brain. All of us undergo *socialization*, learning directly and indirectly from family, school, friends, and church, what our culture's values, norms, and beliefs are. Our brains, as a result of socialization and our own experience, are filled with all sorts of knowledge. This knowledge includes many things, including the values, norms, opinions, and beliefs of our culture. This means that what we see and hear and feel is perceived, weighed, judged, and evaluated on a cultural basis (see Figure 1.2).

Environmental stimuli that we receive and are aware of are subjected to our individual black boxes. The interpretation of these stimuli is very much a matter of what is in these black boxes. A sixteenth-century person who saw elderly women picking herbs and followed by black cats would see them as witches plying their black arts. To a modern person, the same women would simply be elderly women who like herbs and cats. These different judgments are a function of subjectivity caused by socialization, and do not necessarily accurately reflect the stimuli.

This discussion leads to our second principle of social problems:

> *The analysis of indicators of observable conditions and their definition as indicators of a social problem is a complex, subjective process in which external stimuli are covertly changed or modified in accordance with learned cultural traits and individual experience.*

Most people assume that their descriptions of a condition are reasonable facsimiles

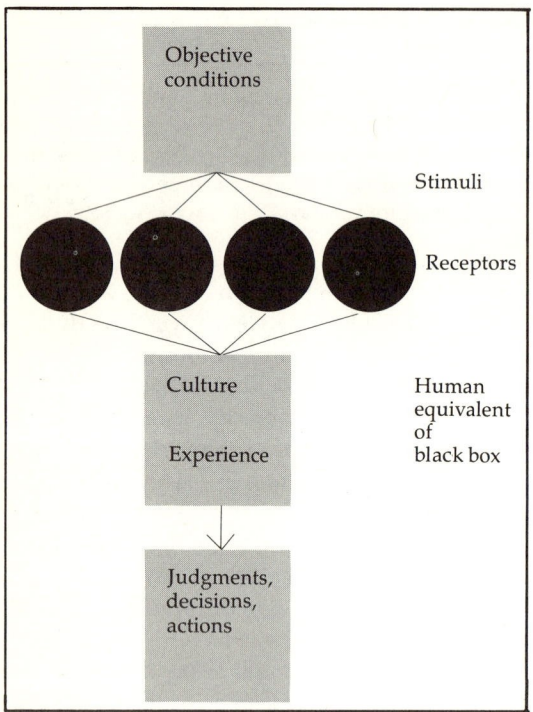

FIGURE 1.2 The Judgment, Decision, Action Paradigm

of the conditions. Obviously, our perceptions of the world must be somewhat correct for us to survive. Most of us, for example, are fully aware of the difference between a car standing still and one traveling seventy miles per hour down a street. Our awareness of the difference saves our lives: we avoid crossing the street when we see the moving car. But social conditions are more complex than crossing the street, and the accuracy of our perceptions is less clear. To understand social problems we must realize the inescapable fact that powerful subjective elements determine our perspectives, and that this subjectivity is strongly influenced by *culture*. In fact, culture is perspective. One part of culture, language, "actually defines experiences for us by reason of its formal completeness and because of our unconscious projection of its implicit expectations into the field of experience."[13] For example, our language tends to dichotomize our thinking. Things are right or wrong, moral or immoral, safe or dangerous. Because of language it is difficult for us to grasp the many variations between extremes. For example, we tend to categorize as immoral an individual who has committed a minor sexual offense. Yet this same individual may be a model of propriety in all other areas of his or her life.

Is it possible to become more objective, or better yet, do perspectives change as culture changes? The answer is yes. Not too many years ago, venereal disease was viewed as punishment for illicit sexual intercourse. But today, most of us recognize that neither the microorganism causing syphilis nor the one causing gonorrhea selectively infect only those guilty of adultery or fornication. In medicine we have become more objective, and have learned how specific germs or behaviors lead to disease or ill health. But our culture has not become completely objective.

Among the Andamanese, who live on islands in the Bay of Bengal, boys and girls are permitted to experiment sexually prior to marriage.[14] Even though our society is more permissive today than it used to be, such experimentation is still considered a social problem. In respect to sex, there are considerable differences among modern societies. In modern Denmark the sale of sexually explicit materials is perfectly legal. Yet in a number of other countries, including the United States, the continuing litigation surrounding the sale of pornography shows that pornography is a social problem. People of the United States have found it difficult to overcome a long history of cultural disapproval of such material. Socialization has created the subjective judgment that such material is harmful.

Solvability

The third element of a social problem is conceptualizing or perceiving a condition as a problem. The condition must be seen as disadvantageous and undesirable. Furthermore, it must be seen as solvable: a problem is something to be solved.

Defining a large number of conditions as social problems is relatively new in human affairs. For example, for many centuries, sex roles were accepted as givens. Men and women filled the required roles without thinking that there might be something wrong with them. Yet today, many people view sex roles with concern, or even alarm, seeing them as injurious to society and to the individuals who fill them.[15] Why this change?

Most modern social problems represent conditions that have existed for thousands of years, although some — pollution, for example — are more severe now than in the past. Our ancestors accepted most of these as natural conditions of life. A significant reasons for this acceptance was a set of attitudes called *fatalism*, "the belief that an outcome, whether desirable or undesirable, will occur regardless of individual striving."[16] Even though people saw these conditions as harmful, they were not social problems because people did not believe that they could do something about them.

But this fatalism is no longer prevalent. The most singular general change of relatively recent times is in this attitude. "Modern [people] are usually confident that something can be done about most of their problems, particularly the technical ones."[17]

People in modern societies are problem oriented. Instead of accepting adverse conditions with a shrug of the shoulders, people view them as problems to be solved. It follows that a rejection of fatalism will cause a great many more conditions to be defined as social problems. A paradox of our times is that the large number of social problems is a sign of social health.

An equally significant change in attitude is increased sensitivity not only to conditions that adversely affect us personally but conditions that affect others adversely as well. Further, we have a considerable advantage over our progenitors in defining conditions as problems. That advantage is the *knowledge explosion* that has taken place in recent times. The extent of this explosion is made dramatically clear by John Diebold,

A social problem can be solved only if people see the condition as problematic and have confidence in their ability to handle the situation.

who points out that "half of the scientific research conducted in [the] United States since the republic was founded has been crowded into the last eight years; 90 percent of all the scientists who have ever lived in the history of mankind are alive today."[18]

Whatever the reasons (increased sensitivity, greater knowledge, an orientation to problems), modern people define many situations and conditions as social problems that previously people accepted as something to be endured. Alexis de Tocqueville described this when he wrote:

> The evil which was suffered patiently as inevitable seems unendurable as soon as the idea of escaping from it crosses [people's] minds. All the abuses then removed call attention to those that remain and they now appear more galling. The evil, it is true, has now become less, but sensibility to it has become more acute.[19]

Another aspect of this change in attitude is greater faith and confidence that problems can be solved. Earthquakes, typhoons, tidal waves, and droughts are natural phenomena that have brought death, injury, disease, and suffering to countless millions. In the 1970s, earthquakes have leveled Managua, Nicaragua, and Tientsin, China, and hurricanes twice devastated the Gulf States of this country. While the aftermath of natural disasters are temporary adverse conditions, typhoons, earthquakes, and floods are not defined as social problems.

As late as the seventeenth century, periodic plagues seriously decimated Europe, but plagues were not considered social problems. Today, diseases of all kinds are lumped together under the general social problem of public health. The difference between natural calamities like earthquakes and natural calamities like plagues is that nothing can be done about the former. But in the past century or more, doctors and scientists have developed the germ theory of disease, the theory that diseases and infections are caused by microorganisms. As a result, we are confident that we do not need to suffer illness and disease in the same way that we must submit to the ravages of earthquakes and hurricanes. The difference between something that is accepted, such as the weather, and something that is to be dealt with, such as a disease, is a matter of faith and confidence. Faith springs from adequate knowledge and the confidence that this knowledge can be applied constructively.

Modern societies are characterized by considerable confidence in human ability to deal with a wide variety of problems. Americans appear to take it for granted that if enough time, money, and effort are expended, virtually all problems, social or otherwise, can be solved. It is conviction, confidence, and faith that move people to attempt to deal with social problems. Whether or not people do solve the problem is irrelevant as far as the definition is concerned. What matters is the conviction that the problem can be solved.

If success in alleviating or solving the problem were a required part of the definition of social problems, then we would have few problems, because few are solved. Certainly it is desirable for problems to be solved, but in terms of defining them, all that matters is that some efforts are undertaken. These efforts are germane to the study of social problems, as readers will see in the following chapters. What sociologists maintain is that there must be "consensus that there is a problem and that something can be done to alleviate it."[20] As stated in the beginning, defining a condition as a social problem is a group effort, requiring the *consensus,* or general agreement, of a society.

We now have the third principle of social problems:

> To be a social problem, a condition must be seen as disadvantageous and there must be general faith and confidence that the problem can be remedied or alleviated.

Let us again emphasize that this confidence in our ability to solve social problems has helped create the large number of social problems we now have. Many conditions now viewed as problematical were accepted in the past as being the way things were. Sadly, much of the time, money and effort expended by Americans to solve our current social problems have not produced very much in the way of tangible results. Worse yet, some efforts to cure problems have exacerbated the problems or created new ones.

Influential People as Catalysts

The defining of social problems, like some chemical reactions, requires catalytic agents. That is, the process of identifying a condition as a social problem must be begun by some person or persons. If society as a whole is to agree that a condition is a problem, those people need to be influential.

Over the centuries, the work of many individuals has served to identify and define social problems. The Gracchi brothers, who lived in the second century, B.C., were social reformers in Rome; Wendell Phillips (1811–1884) was a leader of the antislavery movement; Susan B. Anthony (1820–1906) and Lucy Stone (1818–1893) were leaders in the women's suffrage movement; and Marie C. Stopes (1880–1958) established Great Britain's first birth-control clinic. There have been recent examples, too, who may be more familiar, including Rachel Carson, whose *Silent Spring* was instrumental in starting the ecology movement; Paul Ehrlich, whose *Population Bomb* alarmed us about overpopulation; and Michael Harrington, whose *The Other America* reawakened us to the existence of poverty.

The people just mentioned were not the only ones to perceive a certain condition as a problem. But these persons are important because, by their writing, speeches, or actions they aroused and unified some segment of public opinion. In so doing, they began the definition of a condition as a social problem.

An excellent example — perhaps the best example — of the function of these influential people is in the crusade against alcohol conducted by a relatively small but highly organized group of people. These individuals, formed in groups like the Women's Christian Temperance Union (WCTU), saw drinking as a serious social problem, which they thought could be solved by making the use of alcohol illegal. Organized protest against alcohol began in the early nineteenth century, but the movement had to struggle for almost a hundred years before succeeding. Finally, however, they convinced a significant number of Americans to agree with them. Their activities culminated in the passage of the Eighteenth Amendment to the Constitution in 1919. This prohibition amendment made the sale and consumption of alcoholic drinks illegal throughout the United States. But the government found enforcement of the law impossible, and opposition to it grew. It was finally repealed in 1933.[21] Alcoholism remains a social problem,

The actions of the members of the Women's Christian Temperance Union in praying outside saloons may not have changed the drinking habits of the patrons, but in the aggregate these and other dedicated persons were able to swing public opinion sufficiently to bring about passage of the Eighteenth (Prohibition) Amendment.

but prohibition will probably not be tried as a remedy again. Despite the failure of prohibition, the dry crusade illustrates the fact that a few individuals properly organized can not only identify a condition as a social problem, but manage to put into operation their remedies as well.

For an individual or a small group of individuals to succeed in establishing a condition as a social problem, there are three requirements. First, their views must be disseminated widely enough to reach a substantial number of other people. Second, they must have credibility, be believable. Third, the focus of concern must be on matters congruent with prevailing values, norms, and information.

The first two points may seem obvious — although we will discuss the first in greater detail shortly — but the third may not be so clear. Individuals and groups have probably tried thousands upon thousands of times to establish some condition as a social problem, but they succeed only if their definition fits society's perspective. Remember that defining a condition as a social problem involves subjective judgment. For example, wife and child abuse is now regarded as a social problem. But any effort to make husband abuse a social problem would probably not be successful, because it would contradict society's views of the relative strength of men and women. Similarly, a number of people have attempted to make technology, as such, a social problem. Jacques Ellul, René Dubos, Hannah Arendt, Herbert Marcuse, and others, oppose technology and economic growth, arguing that they have human costs. But it will be difficult for them to convince a technological society that its basis is a social problem.

But once they take a stand congruent with society's values, how do these individuals and groups succeed in convincing society that a condition is a problem? An important cause underlying the proliferation of social problems in modern societies is the mass media. Modern mass media have vastly increased the amount of interaction possible between these influential people and the rest of us. Ignorance and limited human interaction reduce the number of social problems. Owing in considerable part to the growth of television, radio, newspapers, and magazines, we now perceive many more conditions as problematical than in the past —

Bumper stickers are a form of mass media which can be influential in attracting the public's attention to current or possibly new and as yet unidentified social problems.

this is the information explosion mentioned earlier. But can we be confident that the mass media present objective reality, describing the world as it really is?

No. The mass media do not convey to the public a very objective description of the world. This is true for three reasons. First, as became clear from our earlier discussion, no one perceives reality completely objectively — the mass media are no different. But the other two reasons are themselves peculiar to the media: first, a few individuals control the media and determine what information is carried; and second, in the United States, the mass media are commercial and coverage is dictated by the profit motive. The media attempt to attract viewers and readers by presenting the shocking, the unusual, and the bizarre. Even if it could overcome the problem of subjectivity, any newspaper or television station that attempted to present an objective, factual account of our society would not attract many viewers, listeners, or readers. The end result of fully objective reporting would be bankruptcy, a condition commercial enterprises seek to avoid.

Social problems have proliferated in modern societies not only because there is now more knowledge, but also because this knowledge is widely disseminated. But what gets disseminated is determined by those who control the media and those who have access to them — politicians of major parties, high-budget advertisers, and well-known public figures. Defining a condition as a social problem and efforts to solve it are more likely when influential individuals or groups recognize the condition as problematical. For society to define a condition as a social problem, it must be persuaded by influential people. In modern society those people are the politically and economically powerful.

We can now state the fourth principle of social problems:

To be defined as a social problem, a condition must, initially at least, be considered as one by individuals or groups having credibility, author-

ity, and influence, in the form of access to or control of the mass media. They use this access to convince a sizable segment of the population that the condition is a social problem.

Organized Efforts to Solve the Problem

To claim that a condition is a problem and do nothing about it is to see it as something to be accepted. Complaints about the weather fall into this category. Unless a substantial number of people in a society are involved in or support organized efforts to alleviate an adverse condition, it is not a social problem. This does not mean that all members of society must be behind the efforts to remedy a problem. In most cases, those concerned about a problem constitute only a segment of the public. But for the condition to be a problem, the segment concerned must be engaged in some cooperative efforts to solve the problem.

Let us briefly consider a modern social problem: poverty. Our own society is among the most affluent in the world, yet poverty still exists in the midst of all this plenty. But our failure to end poverty is hardly because of any lack of organized effort. Organizations, public and private, work diligently against poverty, but they have not been able to erase it, or even alleviate it. In fact, it seems likely that the current massive expenditure of time, effort, and money will continue in the future. As long as these efforts do continue, poverty will be a social problem, even if the efforts are unsuccessful. The only way poverty would lose its status as a social problem would be if we ceased all efforts to solve it.

We have now come to our final principle of social problems:

For a condition to be a social problem, there must be organized, large-scale efforts to alleviate or remedy it, regardless of the effectiveness of the efforts.

The social problem does not end with efforts to solve it, however. The attempted solutions change conditions, creating new situations. A similar phenomenon occurs in medicine. When doctors prescribe medicine to cure a patient or alleviate his symptoms, the medicine often has additional effects. Because human bodies are complex organisms, a medicine that helps one part of the body may in fact harm another. For instance, the birth-control pill, which helps prevent conception, can also contribute to high blood pressure. For another example, the chemotherapy used to treat cancer can induce nausea. These undesirable side effects are called *iatrogenic effects*, which means they are caused by the physician in the efforts to cure the patient. Iatrogenic effects are a special variety of latent effects—unintended and often unrecognized consequences of specific actions or behaviors. While latent effects, however, need not be harmful and may in fact be eufunctional, iatrogenic effects *are* harmful. Further, iatrogenic effects may be anticipated, as is the case with chemotherapy, or they may be the unexpected result of appropriate or inappropriate treatment.

Societies, like human bodies, are complex structures of interrelated elements. Every change in one component affects other components as well. When people try to solve one problem they can create another. For example, if a government were to decide to end its participation in a war and disband its army, it would be producing unemployment. What would all the soldiers do for work? While one could argue that unemployment is a lesser evil than war, it is nevertheless an evil. In trying to solve one problem, the government has created another. In each chapter, after outlining the various attempts that have been made to solve a problem, we will discuss the iatrogenic effects of these attempted solutions. We must consider them also, for they become part of the problem.

Summary

All social problems begin with some observable conditions. However, the larger portion of defining a condition as a social problem is cultural and subjective. This does not mean that social problems are fanciful; even witchcraft had its objective aspects. Indeed, witchcraft is particularly useful in illustrating the process of defining social problems, because it shows clearly the cultural and subjective factors involved in such definitions.

WITCHCRAFT AS A SOCIAL PROBLEM

Witchcraft is comparable to modern social problems, like water pollution. Water appears to be clean and drinkable but microscopic examination reveals it to be swarming with dangerous microorganisms. We take the word of experts and do not drink the water without purifying it. Similarly, people of earlier times had their experts warning them about witchcraft. "St. Augustine, whose influence on subsequent Christian thought was unequaled, affirmed the reality of magic, which he argued could be performed only with the help of demons."[22] He was the influential person, whose ideas were widely disseminated throughout the clergy and through them to the laity.

With the spread of this idea, witchcraft became a social problem. As we mentioned earlier, objective indicators of witches and witchcraft were found in disease and famine. People believed in the existence of witches because they were told to by authorities, Saint Augustine and the clergy. And people had faith and confidence that the problem could be solved — God could triumph over the devil. Finally, a great deal of continuing action was taken to solve the problem. Witch hunting — the attempts to solve this social problem — was at its height roughly from the early fifteenth through the mid-seventeenth centuries. Thousands of persons were tortured and put to death during this period. Modern people would call these actions cruel and foolish, but the hunters and slayers of witches hardly had a monopoly on either cruelty or foolishness.

We have grown wiser with the passage of time. We know now that disease isn't caused by witches, but by infection; poor crops aren't brought on by a curse, but by the lack of fertilizer. But it is important to remember that witches and witchcraft were as real to the people living in these centuries as pollution and poverty are to us today. The reality of witchcraft is seen in the steps they took against it. Laws were written prohibiting the practice of witchcraft and establishing punishments for those convicted of it. "In 1563, the British Parliament passed an 'Act Against Conjurations, Enchantments and Witchcraft' (5 Eliz. Cap. 16) — also known as the 'Elizabethan Witchcraft Act.' "[23] And as is the case today, the mass media were active in forming public opinion and gaining general acceptance of the definition of witchcraft as a social problem. As Ronald Seth states:

> The majority knew all about witches and how they operated and were kept well-informed of all developments by the sensational journalists of the times, the pamphleteers who after every great trial produced lurid accounts which sold like hot cakes in the streets.[24]

(It would seem that modern journalists behave to some extent like their predecessors.)

In the fifteenth and sixteenth centuries, witchcraft was a social problem because it was thought to be the direct cause of evil and disease. The solution to the problem was torture and death to witches, as in this public hanging in Scotland in 1678.

Witchcraft differs from modern social problems in one significant fact: it came to an end. In the eighteenth century "witchcraft ceased to be legally prosecuted.... The rationalism of that time rejected the objective existence of sorcery and witchcraft, and the witch trials were attributed to errors of superstition and fraud."[25] But that difference points up an important principle. Since social problems are virtually unsolvable in any absolute sense, the conditions basic to their definition will always remain. Any change in their status will be definitional. That is, the conditions will only cease to be social problems in the same way they became social problems — by a change in definition. Because conditions were no longer seen as evidence of witchcraft, it was no longer a social problem.

The importance of definitions creates difficulty, for definitions depend on judgment, and judgment is subjective. It is these *definitional errors* that must be avoided. As we have seen from the example of witchcraft, people can define conditions as social problems that are not problematical at all. In some cases, problems are seen to lie in symptoms rather than in causes. For example, it has been and still is stated by some people that poverty causes crime. The obvious solution would then be to eliminate poverty, thus automatically doing away with crime. But people do not commit crimes only to avoid starvation — many white-collar criminals are quite well off. Eliminating poverty would not solve the problem.

A great many conditions are defined as problems through irrationality. The failure to apply objectivity to human affairs is responsible for much human misery. Some people disagree, feeling that objectivity diminishes human experience. But a comment by Marvin Harris is germane:

> Various prophets of the modern "counter-culture" even blame the inequities and disasters of recent history on too much "objectification." One of them claims that objective consciousness always leads to a loss of "moral sensitivity," and thereby equates the quest for scientific knowledge with original sin.[26]

The critics Harris describes fail to recognize that the objectivity they deplore may not be objectivity at all, but *rationalization,* self-serving pseudologic. For example, business people argue that pollution controls are undesirable because they restrict profits, and claim that they are being rational. Some people maintain that strict drug laws and severe punishment will end drug abuse, and fervently insist on their objectivity and rationality. Similar justifications are advanced by persons who place bombs in public buildings with the naive expectation that society will be brought down and all social problems solved in one fell swoop. But claiming rationality and objectivity does not demonstrate it.

What is needed is true objectivity, an effort to see conditions as they really are, shedding the blinders put on us by socialization. The definition of various conditions as social problems appears to focus on symptoms rather than causes. For everything defined as a social problem, we should strive for objectivity by asking: are we getting at the cause of some adverse condition or are we dealing with symptoms? We need to remember the example of witchcraft. If people could assume that witchcraft was a social problem, we too — despite all our sophistication — might be in error sometime. The error can arise in our perception of conditions or in our definition of a condition as a problem. The errors differ in magnitude — some are trifling, some considerable. But because subjectivity is involved, distortion takes place, and with distortion lies the possibility of error.

FILTERING AND DISTORTION

As we have tried to make clear, social problems are not defined by conditions but by people. This means that human perceptions and judgments may not accurately portray objective conditions. Generally, group perceptions could not be wildly in error, otherwise our species could hardly have survived. Nonetheless, there are built-in sources of error that make it virtually impossible for even the most careful scientific observer to be 100 percent accurate. And for the rest of us, who do not employ the scientific method, the probability of error is considerably enhanced.

Physiological Sources of Error

Sociologists are principally concerned with social errors, but it is instructive to realize that our physical equipment for receiving and processing stimuli by no means conveys all of reality to us. We are all subject to *physiological error.* For example, some wavelengths of light are more effective to us, that is, we see better under some light conditions than others. The same is true of hearing; the limits in humans are roughly between 20 and 20,000 cycles per second. Frequencies above or below these limits are not heard by humans.

Our physiological equipment is not only limited but also can make mistakes. In vision, for example, light rays impinge on the eye and cause chemical changes to occur in the cones and rods of the retina. These chemical changes stimulate nerves, which carry impulses in the form of electrical energy to the occipital cortex of the brain, which, with other parts of the brain, interprets these impulses. The opportunities for something to go wrong in this complex process are considerable. What we see or hear is not a precise replica of what is out there, but what our physiological equipment permits us to see or hear.

We generally assume that what we see is what really is, but that assumption isn't accurate. And if that is the case in the physical world, it is even more so in the social world. The limits and distortions on our physical perceptions are minor compared to those on our social perceptions.

Social Sources of Error

As we become socialized, each of us learns part of the culture of our society — we say part because no one ever knows all the culture of a society. Part of what we learn is our culture's _values_. Values differ from culture to culture, but all cultures have values, which "provide . . . individuals with bases for making judgments or selections from or on a wide range of objects, persons, situations, and behaviors."[27] These values are social facts, and greatly affect social problems.

When we see conditions or behaviors, we do not simply see them. We judge them as well. Our judgments are, to a considerable extent, a function of the culture we have learned. Individuals who have been socialized to value free enterprise probably do not objectively analyze government regulation of business. They judge it as interfering with and injurious to free enterprise, and thus resist it. In contrast, others hold strongly to the value of equality and may support the same regulation because it restricts the power of selfish elites. To some people, government regulation is a social problem. To others, the social problem is the selfish elite who must be regulated.

Culture pervades all life and influences perceptions. Americans have a pronounced _cultural trait:_ they emphasize the positive. Unpleasant realities are modified so that they will be less unpleasant or, if that is impossible, simply ignored. In the mid-1970s, with mounting evidence that the supply of fossil fuels was nearing exhaustion, Americans continued to drive large, low-mileage automobiles. Implicit in their behavior was the notion that the negative information was wrong and that the supply of fossil fuels was inexhaustible.

As the 1970s came to an end, however, it seemed that the limits on the availability of fossil fuels began to be recognized as a social problem. But the positive continues to be emphasized. Some people maintain that additional supplies of fossil fuels will be found. Others claim that by the time fossil fuels run out, we will have developed alternative sources of energy.

Beliefs

Beliefs also play an important role in defining social problems. Many people believe that the modern family is a social problem, but they differ in the definition of the problem.

Different people have different beliefs about the definitions of social problems. Demonstrators for and against abortion show their conflicting opinion of the issue: Is the social problem the failure to permit abortions or the failure to prohibit abortions?

William J. Goode, an authority on the family, sees the family as important. It "releases people from older family rigidities, and contributes to the development of the society and economy which in turn yield more opportunities for its members."[28] To Goode the apparent *changes* in the family are the problem. But others see it differently. They believe that the family is outmoded, useless — in the words of Barrington Moore, "a relic of barbarism."[29] To them, the family is a social problem because it continues to exist. The point is that beliefs affect perceptions. Everyone sees that the divorce rate is rising. Those who believe in the family's importance are disturbed by this sign of its disintegration; those who see the family as outdated applaud this sign of its collapse.

Not everyone agrees that any given condition is a social problem. But total agreement is not a requirement for defining a condition as a social problem.

All organized efforts to solve or alleviate a social problem meet with resistance. For example, many Americans define drug abuse as a serious social problem. This group obviously includes many legislators, for most states have antidrug laws. Yet those who see no real harm in marijuana perceive the real social problem to be government interference with individual freedom. These people resist efforts to regulate their behavior, and even try to change the laws.

There is never unanimity of opinion with respect to a social problem, but why? A good part of the answer lies in the *information chain*, the way we learn about conditions.

The Information Chain

In modern societies, very little information is firsthand. Only a small number of persons

FIGURE 1.3 The Information Chain

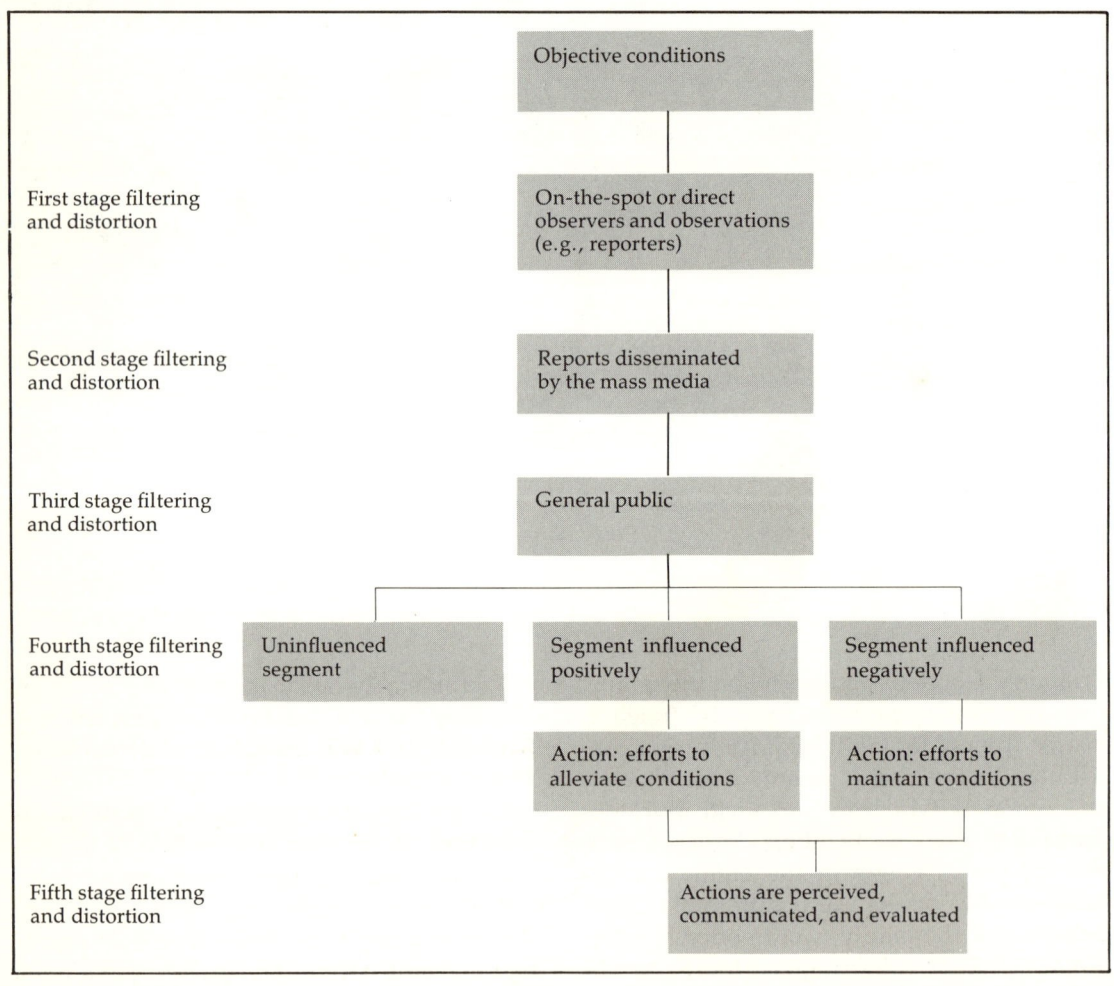

have ever witnessed a bank robbery, brain surgery, or experiments with lasers. But most of us know about these things or can easily find out about them. Sometimes our knowledge is secondhand, but more often it is third- or even fourthhand. This distance is important, because every link in the information chain, from observing conditions to making the final definition, involves changes, however minor, in the information.

Figure 1.3 illustrates the information chain and shows filtering and distortion through five stages. The model is simplified, but it does indicate that a social problem is not simply a matter of observing an adverse condition and quickly agreeing on what needs to be done about it. There is room for many disagreements, considerable controversy, and much error as information moves along the chain.

Consider the social problem called drug abuse. The initial observation was the fact that some citizens were using drugs, ranging from cocaine to marijuana. Those who observed drugs being used saw it differently, depending on their beliefs. Some saw drug use as a legitimate way to escape from the frustrations and disappointments of life. Some were not alarmed by drug use, seeing little difference between using alcohol, an accepted drug, and other drugs. But others viewed drug use as leading to degeneracy, crime, and the eventual ruin of society. These were the people with influence — politicians, police, and some scientists — who transmitted their views to the mass media.

Mass media reports, as we stated, tend to reflect sensationalism and sensational interpretations. Obviously, human degradation and the possible collapse of society make dramatic reading, listening, and viewing. As these were the views that were most profitable to report (those that would sell the most newspapers) and as they were held by those people with access to the media, they were the reports that were broadcast. As these dire predictions were disseminated to the general public, reactions varied. Some people were indifferent and others were concerned that attempts to stop drug use infringed on human freedom and constitutional rights. But perhaps the most widespread reaction was alarm at drug use, leading to attempts to put a stop to it.

The reason for filtering and distortion lies in the subjectivity of perception and in the considerable *heterogeneity* found in societies. This heterogeneity is not chaos: there is some evidence that our society possesses a common core of values.[30] But these values are interpreted differently by different groups and individuals. And although there are societywide institutions that socialize most individuals similarly, there also exist different socialization pressures varying by social stratum, ethnic background, family, peer group, school, and religion. Obviously, then, we cannot expect full consensus on any social problem. True, we are taking many kinds of action to alleviate a considerable number of social problems — crime, pollution, poverty, drug abuse, pornography, littering, and discrimination. But these actions do not indicate that all or nearly all citizens see things the same way. What these actions do mean is that there is some consensus among those persons and groups in a position to implement their viewpoints, such as legislators. Because legislators in our society are somewhat responsive to the electorate, they may still believe that they are reflecting the public will in passing some laws which, in themselves, are an effort to alleviate or cure a social problem. But they may be in error as illustrated by the Eighteenth (prohibition) Amendment to the Constitution.

Summary

Sociologists do not decide what social problems are, societies do. The sociologist's task is to look at those conditions defined as social problems, study their origins, review efforts to correct or alleviate them, and examine the controversies raging around them. Why does one segment of the population see drug use as a serious social problem and another group perceive those objecting to drug use as the problem? Why do some people deplore the apparent decline of the family, and others approve it? These questions constitute important matters for sociological analysis and explanation.

CONCLUSION

It would simplify our lives if all social problems were a matter of societywide consensus. Remedies could then be easily sought and effectively applied. But the real world is not like that. We must deal with things as they are, not as they should be, keeping in mind that things as they should be — ideals and values — are the root of all social problems.

Dealing with things as they are is different from accepting things as they are. Problems, whether individual or social, will not go away because we wish them to. Nor can they be solved by intuition or irrationality. To deal effectively with our modern social problems, we must know them as they are and understand how they got started. We must also understand the forces in society that not only function to cause problems but also to maintain them.

In the following chapter, the origins of social problems will be sought in the structure of society. The word *social* is intended to mean that all the problems we call *social problems* are the result of human interaction. Since human interaction takes place within social structures, an understanding of social structure is a prerequisite for any full understanding of social problems.

IMPORTANT WORDS AND TERMS

beliefs	definitional errors	information chain	socialization
collective definitions	fatalism	knowledge explosion	stimuli
consensus	heterogeneity	observable conditions	subjective evaluation
culture	iatrogenic effects	physiological error	values
cultural trait	influential people	rationalization	

QUESTIONS FOR DISCUSSION

1. Can you name a human instinct? Be prepared to defend your position and demonstrate that the behavior in question is not the result of learning.

2. As we all know, many young couples today are living together without having been married. Does this behavior constitute a social problem? If so, to whom and why?

3. Are there any signs that we are beginning to regard death as a social problem? What are these signs, if any?
4. There is some evidence to indicate that a surprising number of husbands are physically abused by their wives. Why, then, has husband abuse not become a social problem?
5. If the mass media were controlled by the government, and their messages were no longer influenced by the profit motive, would we receive more objective accounts of adverse conditions and social problems as they really exist in this country? Why or why not?
6. How well are we doing in our efforts to solve such social problems as drug abuse, crime, pollution, poverty, and pornography? Review each problem and see if you think that we might be doing better. If you do not agree that one or more of the conditions mentioned is a social problem, defend your view.
7. Every city in this country has its psychic readers, mediums, and spiritualists, and a few people who claim to be witches. Why do we not regard such persons as being a social problem? Or do we, in some minor way?
8. Is any modern social problem solvable in an absolute and complete sense? If you cannot think of one, why did you come to this conclusion?
9. *Time* magazine (November 14, 1977) carried a feature article highly critical of American secondary education. If this is a social problem, what are the symptoms and what are the causes?
10. Which is the social problem — big business or government regulation of big business? Do you understand why you answered as you did?
11. Is the American cultural trait of emphasizing the positive a factor in creating social problems? Explain your reasoning.
12. Why can we always count on some individuals and groups to resist all attempts to alleviate or cure any social problem?
13. Most experts consider alcohol use to be a far more serious problem than the use of marijuana. Yet a large segment of the general public takes a serious view of marijuana and a very lenient view of alcohol use. Why?

SUGGESTED READING

Frederick Lewis Allen, *Only Yesterday: An Informal History of the 1920s* (New York: Harper and Row, 1959).

In highly entertaining prose, the author tells us about Prohibition and makes clear the end results of this "noble experiment." The sociological implications of this book are important for legislators and citizens. As Allen makes clear, it is simply futile to pass a law to solve a social problem when substantial proportions of the society do not accept the condition as a problem. Allen's book discusses the iatrogenic effects of the Eighteenth Amendment, including corruption of law enforcement, increased consumption of alcohol, and the growth of organized crime.

John Diebold, *Man and the Computer: Technology as an Agent of Social Change* (New York: Praeger, 1969).

A considerable source of alienation in modern societies is the belief by some that technology, including computers, are dehumanizing society and turning us into so many punch cards. It is instructive to read these essays by John Diebold, in which he counters this view. Diebold clearly sees technology as humankind's servant rather than master.

Marvin Harris, *Cows, Pigs, Wars and Witches: The Riddle of Culture* (New York: Random House, 1974).

Marvin Harris is one of those rare social scientists who is also a superb writer. Professor Harris's principal theme is that much if not most human behavior has some utilitarian base. If we look hard enough and intelligently enough we will find the real — and often sensible — reason for actions that superficially appear counterproductive and irrational. For example, Professor Harris explains, among other things, why Hindus refuse to kill and eat cows even though people are starving. This book is particularly useful in aiding the understanding of social problems because it makes clear how culture has a filtering and distorting effect on our interpretation of events and conditions.

NOTES

1. Robert Ardrey, *African Genesis* (New York: Dell, 1961), p. 316.
2. Ibid.
3. William McDougall, *Social Psychology*, 13th ed. (Boston: Luce, 1918).
4. See John Beatty, "Taking Issue with Lorenz on the Ute"; Edmund R. Leach, "Don't Say 'Boo' to a Goose"; and Omer C. Stewart, "Lorenz-Margolis on the Ute," all in Ashley Montagu (ed.), *Man and Aggression* (New York: Oxford University Press, 1968).
5. Robert Perrucci and Marc Pilisuk, *The Triple Revolution Emerging: Social Problems in Depth*, 2nd ed. (Boston: Little, Brown, 1971), p. v.
6. Ibid., p. xxiii.
7. Emile Durkheim, *The Rules of Sociological Method*, 8th ed., trans. Sarah W. Solovay and John H. Mueller, ed. George E. G. Catlin (New York: Free Press, 1938), p. 69.
8. Bureau of the Census, *Current Population Reports: Projections of the Population of the United States by Age and Sex, 1975 to 2000 with Extensions of Total Population to 2025*, Series P-25, No. 541 (February 1975). (Washington, D.C.: U.S. Government Printing Office, 1975), pp. 4–5.
9. Marvin Harris, *Cows, Pigs, Wars and Witches: The Riddle of Culture* (New York: Random House, 1974), p. 237.
10. Jeffrey Burton Russell, *Witchcraft in the Middle Ages* (Ithaca, N.Y.: Cornell University Press, 1972), p. 1.
11. Jerome Kagan and Ernest Havemann, *Psychology: An Introduction* (New York: Harcourt, Brace and World, 1968), p. 62.
12. R. P. Cuzzort, *Humanity and Modern Sociological Thought* (New York: Holt, Rinehart and Winston, 1969), p. 27.
13. Edward Sapir, "Conceptual Categories in Primitive Languages," in Dell Hymes (ed.), *Language in Culture and Society* (New York: Harper and Row, 1964), p. 128.
14. Elman R. Service, *Profiles in Ethnology* (New York: Harper and Row, 1963), p. 53.
15. See James Harrison, "Warning: The Male Sex Role May Be Dangerous to Your Health," *Journal of Social Issues*, Vol. 34, No. 1 (1978), pp. 65–86.
16. Marvin Harris, *Culture, Man, and Nature* (New York: Crowell, 1971), p. 594.
17. Gerhard Lenski, *Human Societies* (New York: McGraw-Hill, 1970), p. 411.
18. John Diebold, *Man and the Computer* (New York: Praeger, 1969), p. 7.
19. Alexis de Tocqueville, *Democracy in America* (New York: Vintage, 1954), Vol. I, p. 272.
20. Arnold M. Rose, "Theory for the Study of Social Problems," *Journal of Social Problems*, Vol. 4, No. 3 (1957), p. 190.
21. For accounts of the dry crusade and the Eighteenth Amendment, see George E. Mowry (ed.), *Fords, Flappers, and Fanatics* (Englewood Cliffs, N.J.: Prentice-Hall, 1963), pp. 89–120.

22. Russell, *Witchcraft in the Middle Ages*, pp. 56–57.

23. Ronald Seth, *Children Against Witches* (New York: Taplinger, 1969), p. 27.

24. Ibid., p. 21.

25. Russell, *Witchcraft in the Middle Ages*, p. 28.

26. Harris, *Cows, Pigs, Wars and Witches*, p. 6.

27. Burton Wright, John P. Weiss, and Charles M. Unkovic, *Perspective: An Introduction to Sociology* (Hinsdale, Ill.: Dryden, 1975), p. 103.

28. William J. Goode, "The Family as an Element in the World Revolution," in Peter I. Rose (ed.), *The Study of Society* (New York: Random House, 1967), p. 538.

29. Barrington Moore, *Political Power and Social Theory* (Cambridge, Mass.: Harvard University Press, 1958), p. 160.

30. On American values, see Robin M. Williams, Jr., *American Society*, 3rd ed. (New York: Knopf, 1970), ch. 11, and Burton Wright, "An Exploration of the Domain of Values and Value Change Through the Use of Projective and Semi-Projective Techniques," paper presented at the Annual Meeting of the Southern Sociological Society, Atlanta, April 14, 1973.

2 SOCIAL STRUCTURE
THE BREEDING GROUND OF SOCIAL PROBLEMS

CHAPTER OVERVIEW

INTRODUCTION

MODELS OF SOCIAL PROBLEMS
The Organic Analogy
    Homeostasis: Organic and Social
    Pathology and Social Problems
The Functionalist and Conflict Perspectives
Modern Functionalism
Summary

THE SOCIAL STRUCTURE:
    INTERACTION AND PARTS
Social Interaction
    Social Interaction Is Symbolic Interaction
    Social Facts
    The Development of Social Interaction
    Culture, Irrationality, and Social Problems
Social Institutions
    The Functions of Institutions
    Institutional Interrelationships
Summary

VALUES
Values Defined
Values and Social Problems
    Traditional American Values:
      A Study in Contradictions
    The Relationships Between Values
      and Social Problems
Summary

NORMS
Mores
The Function of General Norms
Types of General Norms
    Technicways
    Alternative Norms
    Systematic Nonconformity and Norms
      for Breaking Norms
Laws
Summary

SANCTIONS
The Necessity for Sanctions
Sanction Incongruence
Summary

STATUSES AND ROLES
The Male Status and Role
Status, Role, and Mental Illness
Status Lock
Summary

SOCIAL DISORGANIZATION
Defining Social Disorganization
The Relativity of Social Disorganization
Organization as a Cultural Universal
Summary

CONCLUSION

IMPORTANT WORDS AND TERMS

QUESTIONS FOR DISCUSSION

SUGGESTED READING

NOTES

We seek the truth and will endure the consequences.
Charles Seymour,
president of Yale University

The human eye with all its warps and astigmatisms, can yet be trained to see more clearly than it does at present.
Kai T. Erikson,
"Sociology: That Awkward Age"

CHAPTER OVERVIEW

Prior to beginning a serious study of social problems, it is essential that students have a basic knowledge of social structure, that is, how societies are constructed and how they function. One cannot study social problems without certain background knowledge. To do so would be akin to trying to understand diseases without knowing body chemistry and bodily functions.

We begin by reviewing a simplistic but often used model of society — the organic analogy. Following this, we discuss modern functionalism, or neo-functionalism, the model used throughout this book.

We then move on to a discussion of the essential parts of the social system: (1) social institutions, (2) values, (3) norms, (4) sanctions, and (5) statuses and roles. We conclude by analyzing the concept of social disorganization. This discussion is somewhat detailed for an important reason. Too often social problems are dismissed as being the result of disorganization. However, disorganization is not at the root of most of our problems, but rather organization is — and a very high degree of organization at that.

We have attempted to be as objective and empirical as possible in our discussion of social structure. Sometimes, it has been necessary to point out some painful and unpalatable truths. But we must accept these unpleasantries as the consequences of such an approach. Unfortunately, our species has developed numerous ways of concealing the facts, particularly unpleasant ones. We act like the ostrich, who is reputed to bury his head in the sand at the approach of danger. This behavior may make him momentarily happier, but it also exposes him to greater danger.

Though our perceptions are imperfect, this does not mean that we can never see the world as it actually exists. An important function of all science — social, natural, and physical — is to help us perceive the world more clearly. We have been acting like the ostrich far too long, and as a result have many problems. Had our predecessors behaved differently, confronting problems instead of avoiding them, perhaps we would be beset by fewer problems today.

INTRODUCTION

Social problems do not occur spontaneously. They are caused. Each social problem has its own set of antecedent circumstances and causes. Sometimes we must dig deep to find those causes, and usually we find a number of them interacting, not just one alone, and these causes can be found in our actions. Harmful and undesirable conditions are usually brought about by human behavior. The exceptions are natural disasters, such as hurricanes and earthquakes, but as we have seen, such calamities are not defined as social problems.

There are causes not only for the conditions defined as problematical, but also for the perceptions underlying the defining process itself. As we saw in Chapter 1, socialization strongly influences our attitudes, and those attitudes determine judgments. Most of us would view a devastating earthquake as extremely undesirable. But some people, devoutly religious and dismayed by the wickedness of the world, may consider such a natural disaster as beneficial, seeing it as a just punishment for our collective sins. Human conditions and how humans interpret these conditions are the stuff of which social problems are made.

While the following chapters will deal with specific causes of specific social problems, we must first grasp the general causes underlying all social problems. Further, we must see what it is that maintains social problems, that is, why they go on relatively unchanged year after year. In this chapter we discuss the general cause of social problems, the social structure. But before discussing the social structure, we wish to review two models of social problems. One is the organic model, a commonly held but far too simplistic view of society. The other is the analytical model we use in this text.

MODELS OF SOCIAL PROBLEMS

The Organic Analogy

To sociologists, the *organic analogy* refers to the comparison of human societies to biological organisms. As we all know, organisms are living creatures having highly differentiated organs; humans, for instance, have hearts, lungs, livers, brains, and so forth. Obviously, our lives depend on each organ functioning reasonably well. If an organ fails, the result is serious illness or even death.

It is not stretching things too far to compare modern societies to these organisms, for they are marked by similar dependencies. Each of us is dependent on thousands of organizations and people for the goods and services we require or desire every day. For example, imagine a massive, lengthy trucking strike. How would goods reach the shelves of supermarkets? Where would we obtain the gasoline our cars need? How would we get back and forth to work, assuming there was work to do? When we use the organic analogy, we are apt to compare social problems to illnesses. The truckers' strike, shutting off the flow of food and energy, may be called a breakdown in society's circulatory system. But such comparisons lead to serious error and misunderstanding. Although the analogy applies in part, it is not completely true. Societies are not organisms in the strictly biological sense.

HOMEOSTASIS: ORGANIC AND SOCIAL

Homeostasis refers to an organism's tendency to maintain a relatively constant internal environment. When we are well, our body temperature is approximately 98.6° Fahrenheit. Organisms, in order to stay alive, must maintain a somewhat constant internal equilibrium. Some departures from homeostasis are brief and not injurious — exercise, for example. But prolonged departure from homeostasis can mean illness and threaten the survival of the organism.

Societies must also maintain some kind of internal equilibrium, but this equilibrium is not as strictly required as it is for living organisms. Social problems are not illnesses likely to cause the death of a society unless cured. Societies have suffered from adverse conditions and still survived for long periods of time. The Eastern Roman Empire persisted for some twelve centuries in spite of being afflicted with many serious problems, particularly powerful external enemies.

PATHOLOGY AND SOCIAL PROBLEMS

Attempting to explain social problems as illnesses afflicting basically healthy societies is grossly inaccurate. An important reason for this is that social problems are not merely adverse conditions. Social problems are rooted in conditions that serve useful and important functions for societies. That is, social problems are not completely undesirable. Most of us wish to eliminate poverty, but what would a complete disappearance of poverty do to society? Modern Switzerland has virtually no poverty among its natives, but for this reason, native Swiss cannot be found to perform many menial but necessary jobs. As a result, Switzerland has found it necessary to import foreign labor. In effect, the Swiss are finding the poor necessary for their society to function.[1]

Social problems may be the result of some useful or necessary operations or they may serve desirable purposes for some people or both. For example, some manufacturers produce chemicals we use. They also provide thousands of jobs for workers all over the country. But at the same time, they contribute to the social problem of pollution. For an example of the second group, again using pollution, the exhaust from cars pollutes the air, and it would be advantageous to all to reduce the amount of exhaust. Yet the automakers resist efforts to change car design, which would require expensive retooling of their plants.

It is attractive to liken social problems to illnesses, but if social problems are to be really understood, such a comparison is misleading. We cannot vaccinate against social problems. To get a better understanding of social problems, let us turn to the model we will use throughout the text.

The Functionalist and Conflict Perspectives

Some years ago, sociology was divided into two different schools: structural-functional theory and conflict theory. The former perspective stated that societies primarily tried to maintain equilibrium; it downplayed or ignored the significance of conflict. In contrast, conflict theorists saw the principal factor in societies to be conflict. For example, Lewis Coser maintains that "a flexible society benefits from conflict because such behavior, by helping to create and modify norms, assures its continuance under changed conditions."[2]

It is unsatisfactory to study social problems from either a strict structural-functional or conflict perspective. The fact that various social problems persist over time appears to support the view of equilibrium maintenance. At the same time, social problems and social change involve a considerable amount of conflict. Fortunately, it is not necessary to choose between these two positions. A realistic examination of human societies reveals that they are all marked by both equilibrium and conflict. Further, all societies experience greater or lesser degrees of social change.

The approach used in this text can be best described as *modern functionalism* or *neofunctionalism*. This theoretical position recognizes that equilibrium, conflict, and change are common to all societies. Inherent in this approach is the effort to examine human interaction as objectively as possible and to avoid, as much as possible, making value judgments on social problems. Of course, we cannot be completely free of value judgments, however hard we may try.[3] But the closer we come to being objective, the better are our chances of seeing problems as they actually are.

Modern Functionalism

Modern functionalism interprets the results of human interaction and behavior in terms of consequences, not merely for those immediately concerned but for society as a whole.[4] Consequences that appear efficient or beneficial are called *eufunctional*. Outcomes that are adverse or inefficient are called *dysfunctional*. Beneficial and adverse are defined in terms of the society's immediate and long-term survival and growth.

While assessing consequences is marked by some subjectivity, it is possible to make such judgments reasonably objective. The first step toward that goal is to use data that are as objective as possible. Someone claiming that the air is polluted cannot support that claim with a photograph. She must use instruments to measure the amount of pollutants in the air and demonstrate experimentally that such a quantity is injurious.

In addition to objectifying data, we must use all that pertains. It is not enough to say that the world is experiencing a population explosion. We need to look at the best data on the rate of population increase and the availability of resources. And we must go beneath the data to examine the causes of the great increase in the number of living humans. Some of these causes are actually beneficial. As we pointed out in Chapter 1, overpopulation is a function of the birthrate and the death rate. The birthrate now exceeds the death rate because of many technological advances. Improvements in medicine and in the standard of living have dramatically cut the death rate for children. Similarly, better medical care has increased the normal life span. Clearly these are social goods. Fewer children die, people are healthier throughout their life, and they live longer. Yet these goods have created a social problem. With more people living, we are confronted by overpopulation. In other words, some actions that have eufunctional consequences can also have dysfunctional consequences.

Summary

The modern functionalist or neofunctional approach to social problems is not easy to follow. We are tempted to look for simple causes and simple solutions to complex problems. For example, it is common to blame juvenile delinquency on parents or an inability to read on teachers or pollution on greedy industrialists. But no social problem can be dismissed this easily.

Social problems have complex causes because they originate in a complex entity, the social structure. Their origin in the social structure means that all social problems are things we do to ourselves. Of course, most people do not realize this, and some who do recognize it do not care, or continue acting on the basis of narrow self-interest. To understand how to avoid such behavior, we must proceed to our discussion of the social structure and its parts. But keep in mind that a discussion of these parts as discrete units is artificial. While we can identify and analyze the separate parts of the social structure, they actually function together; they are highly interrelated and interdependent.

THE SOCIAL STRUCTURE: INTERACTION AND PARTS

Arnold Rose, a sociologist, defines sociology as "the science of interaction among people and of the effects of this interaction on human behavior."[5] This definition is useful for the study of social problems. It is interaction among humans that created social structures and societies, which make it possible for us to survive, and also created our problems.

Social Interaction

Social interaction is no spontaneous, unique, accidental, random phenomenon. It is, for the greater part, composed of behavior showing much regularity; it lacks spontaneity and is highly predictable. If human interaction were random and unregulated, there would be no science of sociology, for all sciences depend on predictability and regularity in what they describe. A science of unique events is impossible.

These festive Louisiana Cajuns in masquerade engage in social interactions unique to their ethnic culture. Patterns of interaction within any society must be implicitly understood and expected by the society's members. Without this predictability, there would be no science of sociology.

SOCIAL INTERACTION IS SYMBOLIC INTERACTION

The most significant human invention is language. Without it, there would be no societies as we know them, and very possibly no humans. What we call our mind "is the presence in behavior of significant symbols."[6] Without mind and complex significant symbols there would be no social problems. Of course, humans without language, if they existed, would probably experience adverse conditions. But like gorillas and chimpanzees, they would be incapable of recognizing adverse conditions and of defining them as problematical. The reason is clear. Recognizing adverse conditions and defining them as social problems is a purely symbolic act. Dealing with social problems, whether successfully or not, is a symbolic matter.

Because all human interaction is symbolic, it is important to remember that our symbols tend to be imprecise. Much symbolic interaction is blurred around the edges and we frequently do not fully understand what others mean, although we think we do. When a young man tells a young woman that he loves her, what does he really mean? Does he wish to love, honor, and cherish her until death? Or does he want to spend some time with her in bed?

In reading the following pages, remember that we are making and using symbols. Even our concept of reality is constructed out of symbols. Disagreement and consensus arise out of symbolic interaction. Sometimes people view a condition that we see as problematic as no problem at all, or even as desirable, but we shouldn't be surprised. We need to remember the inexactness of symbolic interaction.

SOCIAL FACTS

The regularities we observe in human interaction reflect social structure. Social structure is inferred from observations of human interaction. *Society* refers to a group of people acting in similar ways because they share a common culture.

We do not see societies directly, but that does not mean that societies are unreal. Although we cannot see social structure, nearly all of our behavior is in accordance with our society's social structure, with what Emile Durkheim called *social facts*. Durkheim did not mean "that social facts are material things but that they are things by the same right as material things although they differ from them in type."[7]

Social facts, the various parts of the social structure, compel behavior. In Durkheim's words:

> Institutions may impose themselves upon us, but we cling to them; they compel us and we love them; they constrain us, and we find our welfare in adherence to them and in this very constraint.[8]

An example of the truth of Durkheim's words can be found in the letters to the editor section in newspapers. Some of these letters express regret and worry at what the writers see as a loss of morality, the decadence of modern life, and the falling away from the good ways of the past. Clearly, these letters express a love for social institutions, although some may also show a profound misunderstanding of the inevitability of social change.

THE DEVELOPMENT OF SOCIAL INTERACTION

Large, modern organizations or bureaucracies are the result of planning and rationality. The criterion of efficiency is used to evaluate the various operations of these organizations. Leaders try to have all the functions of the bureaucracy work smoothly together. Societies might have fewer problems if they, too, had been rationally designed. But of course rationality has little part in the development of society.

Most of culture is not and never has been the product of logical, empirical, objective planning. There are exceptions — as we said, large organizations are planned to a considerable degree and they are a cultural concept. But this principle is true of a culture as a whole. We do not know how culture got started, other than to say that it had to develop out of human interaction. However, it seems clear that elements of a culture were added to the culture because they appeared to work. People adopted an innovation or invention, material or nonmaterial, when it appeared to accomplish something important, useful, or desirable. Development occurs the same way today. For example, tolerance in sexual matters is not brought about by a governmental directive or a presidential recommendation. Instead, it develops slowly as people find it a more satisfying or useful attitude in their interactions.

While modern society does attempt rational social planning, most of our culture has deep roots in the past. This means, in part, that change comes slowly. The implications for social problems are clear. Social problems tend to persist because they rest on culture — on the ways people have done things for many years.

CULTURE, IRRATIONALITY, AND SOCIAL PROBLEMS

Modern people are horrified at the idea of human sacrifice for religious purposes. But given certain cultural beliefs, human sacrifice not only appears logical but necessary. Among the Aztecs of Mexico "the principal function of the 5000 priests living in the Aztec capital was to make sure the end of the world came later than sooner. This could be assured only by pleasing the legion of gods believed to govern the world. The best way to please the gods was to give them gifts, the most precious being fresh human hearts."[9]

Lest we smile at the naiveté of the Aztecs and their priests, remember that in the 1960s and 1970s, the United States fought a war in Vietnam and sacrificed some 55,000 young Americans using rationalizations without much better logic than those used by the ancient Aztecs. Another modern example is the firmly held belief that the use of marijuana can be prevented by passing laws against it. The failure of Prohibition should make people realize that morality cannot be legislated, but many refuse to see that.

The point is that culture, which directs our behavior, does not have to be rational. Cultural traits can direct behavior that is illogical, that can adversely affect human lives, that is potentially or actually harmful to members of society, or that is not even particularly efficient. To become a part of culture and be retained, it is only necessary that a particular trait satisfy enough people.

We turn now to examine the integral parts of the social structure, with particular emphasis on how structure functions to produce certain conditions and later define them as social problems.

Social Institutions

While all cultural traits are important to any society, "the principal institutions of a society use a considerable proportion of its resources and form the society's most conspicuous structural features."[10] There is some confusion about what is a *social institution*, but the following offers a good definition:

> *A social institution is a complex of values, statuses, roles, and norms organized around some functions considered important to society.*

THE FUNCTIONS OF INSTITUTIONS

Robin M. Williams, Jr., a sociologist, provides us with an excellent description of the general functions of social institutions:

> Institutions regulate the modes of meeting important, recurrent situations such as birth, death, marriage, acquiring economic goods, dealing with power relations, maintaining social consensus, and training the young, and at the same time help ensure that these situations will recur. By defining problems and approved solutions in certain ways, any particular institutional structure channelizes human experience along certain lines and ignores or prohibits other possibilities. It is a truism that the problems or evils in any society result partly from its most venerated institutions.[11]

Table 2.1 provides a list of the nine major modern social institutions and their principal functions. A brief look at this table may lead you astray because it makes the institutions seem neat, straightforward, and efficient. But they are not so in reality.

There is a considerable gap between ideal functions of social institutions and the way they actually function. As Williams pointed out, social problems are partly the result of social institutions. An essential function for all societies is the socialization of the young. In modern societies, the family performs part of this function along with other social institutions, particularly education. But how well do they do the job? Not perfectly, as can be seen by looking at Table 2.2. Part of socialization is to teach people what society's rules are and how to obey them. But as this table shows, almost 475,000 arrests were made of persons fifteen years of age and younger in the United States during 1977. And the actual number of crimes performed by young people was even higher, as the *Uniform Crime Reports* reflect only reported crimes.

TABLE 2.1 Major Institutions and Their Principal Functions

Institution	Functions
Family	To provide for legitimate sexual access and procreation; to socialize the young; and to provide support (economic and psychic) and protection for all members
Religion	To furnish answers for metaphysical questions (Why are we here? What happens after death?); to provide a system of ethics and morality; to legitimate marriage; and satisfy desire for group activities
Education	To prepare the young for full, effective membership in society as adults; to prepare persons of all ages for certain activities, particularly economic; to enrich intellectual life and support intellectual endeavors
Economy	To provide for the production, transportation, and distribution of goods and services needed or desired by members of society
Politics	To control and provide for the acquisition of and use of authority, especially as related to government and the state
Science	To promote and direct empirical research; to socialize those aspiring to be scientists into the ethics and techniques of science; and to make available the results of research and thought
Recreation	To provide for the use of leisure time
Art	To promote artistic endeavors, such as music, painting, and literature
Military	To be prepared to apply force for defense, offense, or both in the interests of the state

TABLE 2.2 Total Arrests by Age

Offense	10 and under	11–12	13–14	15
Criminal homicide				
Murder and nonnegligent homicide	14	21	180	258
Manslaughter by negligence	7	8	27	38
Forcible rape	53	176	852	748
Robbery	503	1,997	7,809	7,597
Aggravated assault	1,062	2,266	7,064	6,430
Violent crime	1,632	4,460	15,905	15,033
Percent distribution	.4	1.2	4.1	3.9
Burglary	9,369	19,393	58,862	47,099
Larceny-theft	22,655	49,002	116,453	78,248
Motor vehicle theft	455	2,152	16,120	18,030
Property crime	32,479	70,547	191,435	143,377
Percent distribution	2.0	4.4	12.0	9.0
Total violent and property crimes	34,118	75,015	207,367	158,448
Percent distribution	1.7	3.8	10.4	8.0

Source: Federal Bureau of Investigation, *Uniform Crime Reports: Crime in the United States, 1977* (Washington, D.C.: U.S. Government Printing Office, 1978), p. 180.

INSTITUTIONAL INTERRELATIONSHIPS

Crime or any other social problem is not the result of the failure of one institution. It is easy to blame juvenile delinquency on the family or the schools or both. But other institutions play a part as well. Politics establishes laws that define certain behaviors as delinquent or criminal, but fails to deter such behavior. The economy provides attractive, portable, and expensive items, which make theft profitable, but fails to discourage theft effectively.

It is virtually impossible to find a social problem produced or defined by only one institution. Drug use seems to be a problem affecting only recreation, but laws are passed against marijuana, so politics is involved as well. The development of cars seems to involve the economy only, but it also affects politics, the family, and recreation. Military action may appear only to affect the military, and perhaps government, but in fact it also touches the family. To turn to an earlier example, Prohibition, on the surface, affected only recreation, but it also involved religion, politics, the family, and the economy — five out of nine institutions.

Summary

These examples demonstrate a point made earlier: it is not only the failure of institutions that causes problems, but sometimes their proper functioning. If the military responds to an attack it is doing its job, but the family is disrupted nevertheless. All social institutions perform necessary and useful functions for societies. At the same time, their operation can produce adverse conditions, sometimes by impairing the function of another institution. No institution ever meets the ideal model of performance. It is this gap between the ideal and the reality that, in good part, serves to identify adverse conditions and define them as social problems.

VALUES

When people speak of American values, they are understood to mean that most Americans hold certain values. But if this were true and the United States had a single value system, there would be more agreement on social problems than actually exists. As we discussed in Chapter 1, individuals or groups seeking to correct what they see as social problems are invariably opposed by other individuals or groups, who view the reformers as the social problem.

Why is it that people do not agree on what constitutes a social problem? These disagreements are a function of values. Values provide the motivation for life, and much of its zest, but they are also the source of many of our difficulties. What, specifically, are values?

Values Defined

It is difficult to find a good analogy for values. Some say that the relationship between society and values is analogous to that between mariners and stars. Mariners use the position of stars to tell them fairly accurately where they are on the seas. But this analogy is false. Values lack this precision. They cannot tell us exactly what to do. Rather, they provide general directions for societies, groups, and individuals. There is another difference between values and stars. Stars give objective information, but values are subjective, judgmental. As Peter Senn says:

> A value proposition is one that involves the idea of "good," "should," "ought," or similar terms. Questions like "Is peace good?" or "Should we eliminate poverty?" must be answered in terms of an ethical, moral, or value system.[12]

Values are important in the study of social problems because they are involved in one of the principles in defining conditions as problems. Conditions are problematical only if they conflict with values. Whether one is concerned about poverty, alarmed by pollution, in favor of abortion, opposed to the use of marijuana, or afraid of the military-industrial complex is a matter of values.

If values were innate or instinctive, there would be no conflict over values. We would all have the same values and our societies, like ant societies, would be marked by industry, harmony, no social change, and boredom. But values are not instinctive, they are learned, and the specific values of any individual are a matter of that person's socialization and particular experience. Out of the variety of possible values, individuals only have some — these are their *held values*. When people with differing held values meet, conflict can occur. Since people differ in their held values, it follows that they will also differ in whether or not they perceive some observable conditions as indicating a social problem.

A difficulty in the scientific study of values is that the learning of values is largely an unconscious process. Humans are generally unaware of their own values. Asking people about their values is unsatisfactory, because they cannot easily say what their values are. We can best define an individual's values by observing how the person acts in given situations. Rather than ask someone what his values are, we ask him what he does. We find out that he wrote his legislator in support of a bill permitting prayer in public schools, that he contributes money to a group opposed to abortion, and that he regularly attends religious services. These facts give us some idea of his held values.

Values are highly resistant to change. Because they are learned early in life and are held unconsciously, they are "relatively enduring orientations toward goal objects of a social system or subsystem as distinguished from relatively transitory postures such as attitudes and opinions."[13] For example, individuals and groups who value the principles of democratic participation will not easily adjust to authoritarian rule. Similarly, those individuals and groups who value more authoritarian leadership will find it difficult to adjust to democratic participation.

Although they are unconsciously held, values are just as real as physical objects. They are social facts, as Durkheim defined social facts: they compel behavior. Our reactions to a wide variety of persons, events, and subjects are a function of our values. The road map we use to guide us on our trip is real; similarly, the values we use to guide us in our life are real. But remember, this does not mean that values are a map — they are general guides for conduct, not exact direction markers. They are, however, as real as a map, even if we cannot touch them.

We acquire values unconsciously, as we are socialized, and are usually unaware of our own held values. Nonetheless, values guide both individual and group behavior.

Values are unconsciously learned and held general guides that provide people with the bases for judging and evaluating situations, conditions, groups, and individuals, as well as providing for the selection of goals.

Let us add that an individual lacking in values is impossible. When we say, as we often do, that someone lacks values, we really mean that she doesn't have ours.

Values and Social Problems

Values influence individuals and groups to define certain conditions as social problems. Other persons and groups, holding different values, are indifferent to the same conditions or perceive them as desirable. This means that while values are important to defining social problems, they can also interfere with solving those problems. They "obstruct solutions to conditions defined as social problems because people are unwilling to endorse programs of amelioration which prejudice or require abandonment of their cherished beliefs and institutions."[14] Widespread agreement that a given condition is a social problem indicates that most people share similar values on that particular point.

We do not know what all the major American values are, but we know many. Let us now consider how some of these values relate to social problems.

TRADITIONAL AMERICAN
VALUES: A STUDY IN CONTRADICTIONS

In the beginning of the section on values, we pointed out that all Americans do not hold to a single value system. There are many differences, by class, region, religion, and ethnic group. Nevertheless, some values — the traditional American values — are commonly held. But it is not enough to prepare

Our values help determine what we view as social problems. This advertisement, which appeals to such traditional values as hard work, efficiency, and self-reliance, implies that today's educational system is fraught with social problems.

a list of these values, for such a list conceals the dynamic interaction among values. The reason is that these values are often contradictory. For each value, there is invariably a reciprocal or opposite that is just as much a value.

Table 2.3 lists the major traditional American values and the opposite or reciprocal value for each. In comparing these opposed values, we can see how values produce social problems. For example, equality is opposed by achievement and success. Valuing achievement and success promotes competition and produces both winners and losers. As a result, we have a substantial number of persons who have not competed successfully, and some who have not competed at all. Their nonsuccess, and the success of others, produces poverty, which is economic inequality. Because this conflicts with the value of equality, we define poverty as a social problem.

Equality is also opposed by racism and related group-superiority themes. Equality identifies and defines the social problem of minorities and provides efforts to end discrimination. But at the same time racism acts to maintain discrimination. For another example, progress has blinded many people to pollution. A final example concerns moralism, conformity, and individualism. The first two values operate together to identify, among other things, sexual deviance as a social problem. In contrast, individualism motivates people to maintain that sexual behavior is a personal matter of no concern to society.

THE RELATIONSHIPS BETWEEN VALUES AND SOCIAL PROBLEMS

Values and social problems do not exist in a simple one-to-one relationship. In the first place, social problems involve the conflict between the values of those who see the condition as a social problem and the values of those who don't. But the lack of one-to-one correspondence is true in another sense. Just as social problems involve more than one institution, they also involve more than one value, and sometimes those values are contradictory.

To show how this is true, let us look at Figure 2.1, which illustrates the major values supporting the problem of racial minorities. As you can see, minorities are placed in an undesirable position in society because of racist attitudes and the value placed on conformity. When the society also values achievement and success, as ours does, and minorities' efforts to succeed are thwarted from the start by society's actions based on the other values, adverse conditions are created. These conditions become defined as a

TABLE 2.3 Traditional and Opposing American Values

Traditional American Values	Opposing or Reciprocal Values
Achievement and success	Noncompetition
Activity and work	Leisure
Moral orientation	Tolerance
Humanitarian mores	Self-aggrandizement
Efficiency and practicality	Philosophical withdrawal
Progress	Equilibrium
Material comfort	Ascetism and self-denial
Equality	Achievement and success
Freedom	Control
External conformity	Individualism
Science and secular rationality	Sensing and feeling
Nationalism and patriotism	Brotherhood of all men
Democracy	Authoritarianism
Individual personality	Conformity
Racism and related group superiority themes	Equality

Source: The traditional American values are from Robin M. Williams, Jr., *American Society*, 3rd ed. (New York: Knopf, 1970), ch. 11.

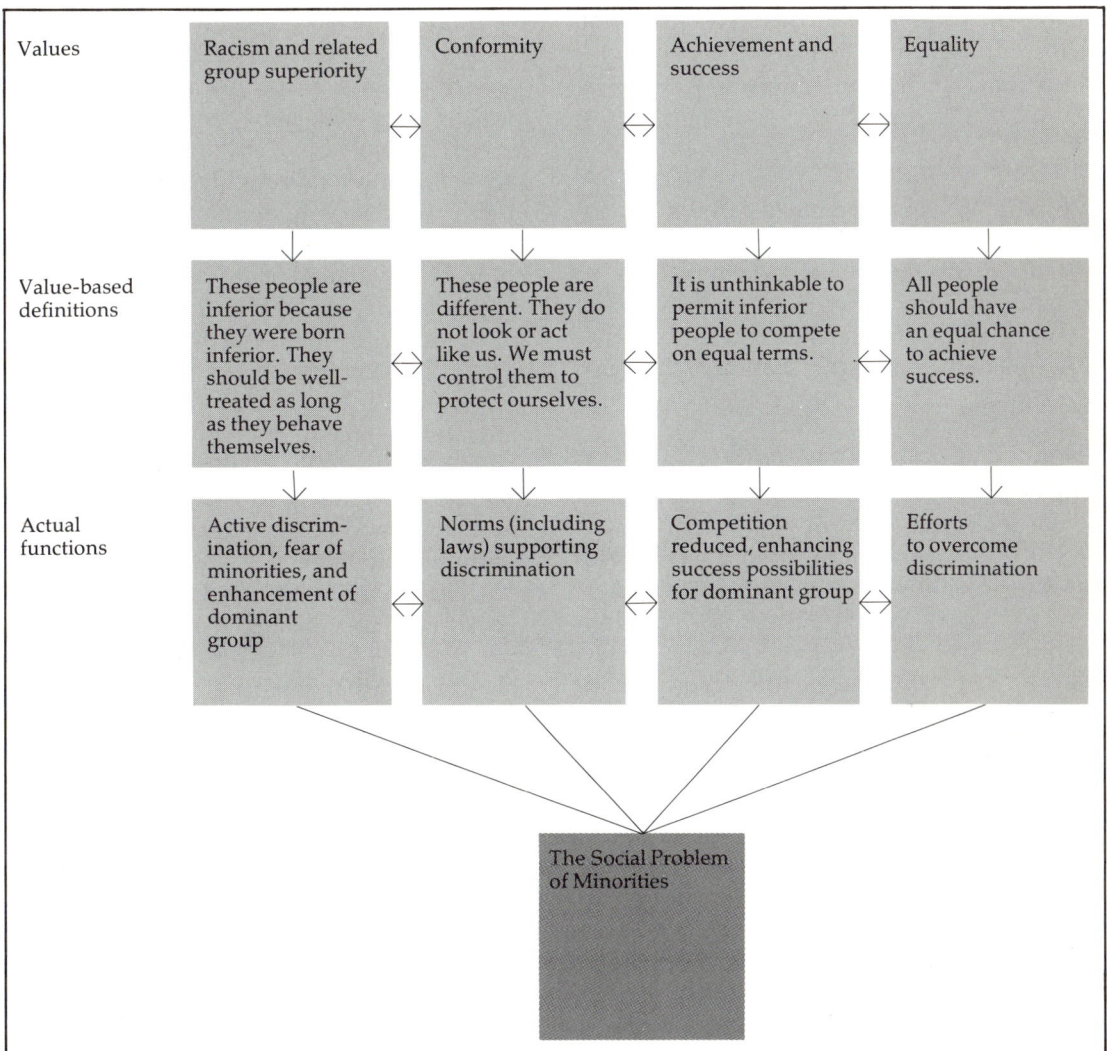

FIGURE 2.1 Values and the Social Problem of Minorities

social problem because society also values equality, which is clearly being violated.

This figure also indicates the rationalizations and perceptions that originate in these values. People who only hold one of the values listed — those who favor conformity, for instance — will not see the position of minorities as a problem. Those who believe strongly in equality will. But both groups will rationalize their values, and will perceive conditions according to their values. That many rationalizations of behavior, including discrimination, are illogical is beside the point. What matters is that they exist.

That makes them real, makes them social facts, and they must be taken into account if discrimination is to be understood.

Summary

Values, along with the other parts of the social structure, interact to produce, maintain, worsen, or alleviate social problems. This interaction is continuous, fluid, and dynamic. If values and other parts of the social structure function to maintain stability, they also function to produce social problems and conflict.

This appears to say that chaos reigns. It would be easy to dismiss modern social problems as the result of poor organization, and it is certainly tempting to do so. Philip M. Hauser says modern society is "characterized by dissonant cultural strata — by confusion and disorder."[15] But Hauser is correct only in part. Underneath this seeming confusion is a great deal of organization — some of it the direct cause of our problems. To make this clear, we now turn to a discussion of norms, statuses, and roles.

NORMS

"Societies require a system of social control. And . . . there must be a system of rules . . . to define right conduct."[16] Sociologists call these rules *norms*, which are:

> Rules or patterns for behavior, defining what is expected, customary, right, or proper in a given situation. They are guides to what a person must, may, or should think, do, and feel.[17]

A large proportion of norms produce desirable consequences. Complex, modern societies require many norms to work efficiently. But organization and efficiency, or the norms underlying them, do not necessarily produce good consequences. The Nazi Gestapo was well organized. Discrimination against minorities has always existed, but because society is now more highly organized, it can put discriminatory practices into action more thoroughly. Indeed so thoroughly is discrimination organized that it entails the cooperation of the very groups being discriminated against.

To some degree, then, all social problems are produced by behavior that is in accordance with existing norms. Norms can be double-edged. Our social rules produce organization, which benefits us. Societies could not run without them. At the same time, however, social problems are produced and maintained by norms, as they are by institutions and values.

Norms have their roots in values. We establish norms to ensure that values will be maintained. But we all know that there are some norms that must not be violated and others that can be broken with considerable impunity. Why? It would appear that there is a good deal of inconsistency with respect to norms. But the truth is that norms are somewhat like events in our lives: some are important, some are routine, others are trivial.

Mores

Of the various types of norms, mores are the closest to values and therefore of greatest importance in defining social problems. Reece McGee defines mores as

> customs which a given society values so much that conformity with them is widely accepted as being important to the society itself; failure to observe them is disturbing to others and will be reacted to by them.[18]

Mores have a sacred quality; violations of

them are condemned and violators may be severely punished. Examples of widely held mores are the prohibitions against murder, incest, and treason. Even some behaviors that would be called manners are governed by mores. For example, laughing at a funeral service would be highly offensive to most of us and we would react strongly to someone who did.

Though all societies have mores, particular ones are by no means universal. To use an extreme example, ritual cannibalism of slain enemies was once widespread in Polynesia. In contrast, one of our most powerful mores is against the eating of human flesh. In fact, this prohibition extends to the eating of some other species as well. Few modern Americans would willingly and knowingly consume fried cat or roast dog, even though these animals, along with our own species, are perfectly edible.

Mores express in behavioral terms a society's values, which are general, diffuse, and unconscious. They also direct attention and channel perceptions in such a way that various conditions are defined as social problems. The value of reverence for life establishes various mores, including ideas of the proper behavior at funerals and prohibitions against murder. We pay attention to the observance of these mores, and if we see frequent violations we define them as constituting a social problem.

There is no question that our perception of differences between observable conditions and our ideals, defined by values and mores, cause strong emotional reactions. In Chapter 1, we noted that an essential part of the definition of a social problem is action taken to alleviate or solve the problem. Emotion is a key factor in bringing about that action. Without emotions there would be no social problems and mores serve an essential function in the arousal of emotion: actions violating our mores make us worried and angry and arouse us to action.

The Function of General Norms

The term *general norms* is not in common usage. However, much that is important about norms is hidden when we lump all social rules together under one heading. To differentiate, then, we use *general norms* to refer to social rules not having the force of mores that nevertheless control and direct human behavior. General norms prescribe and proscribe behavior, that is, they tell us what to do and what not to do. They produce and maintain orderliness and predictability. But like mores, values, and institutions, norms also produce and maintain conditions that come to be defined as social problems. Let us see how general norms contribute to and define a social problem.

All societies have norms governing suitable behavior for people of various age groups. In our society, it is considered proper for adolescents to behave with considerable vitality, venturesomeness, mischief, and even some rebellion. While living up to these norms, however, some young people go too far and find themselves defined as delinquents. We can speculate on what might happen to the amount of juvenile delinquency if the norms for adolescents were to change. If young people were expected to be responsible, prudent, and hard-working, we can hypothesize that there would be less delinquency.[19] Apropos of the foregoing, the popular fad of streaking of several years back was largely confined to the young. Generally, this nude frolicking was viewed tolerantly. But what would have been the reaction to middle-aged persons, perhaps two or three senior male and female professors cavorting naked across the campus? At the least, they would have met with severe disapproval from their peers and suggestions that they needed psychiatric help.

Figure 2.2 illustrates how norms prescribe behavior for adolescents. Sometimes young people follow the norms laid down for them too well; then other norms define that behavior as deviant. This results, in part, in defining youth as a social problem. A principal difficulty faced by adolescents is learning the boundaries of norms, that is, just how far they can go and stay out of serious trouble.

FIGURE 2.2 How Norms Help Define Youth as a Social Problem

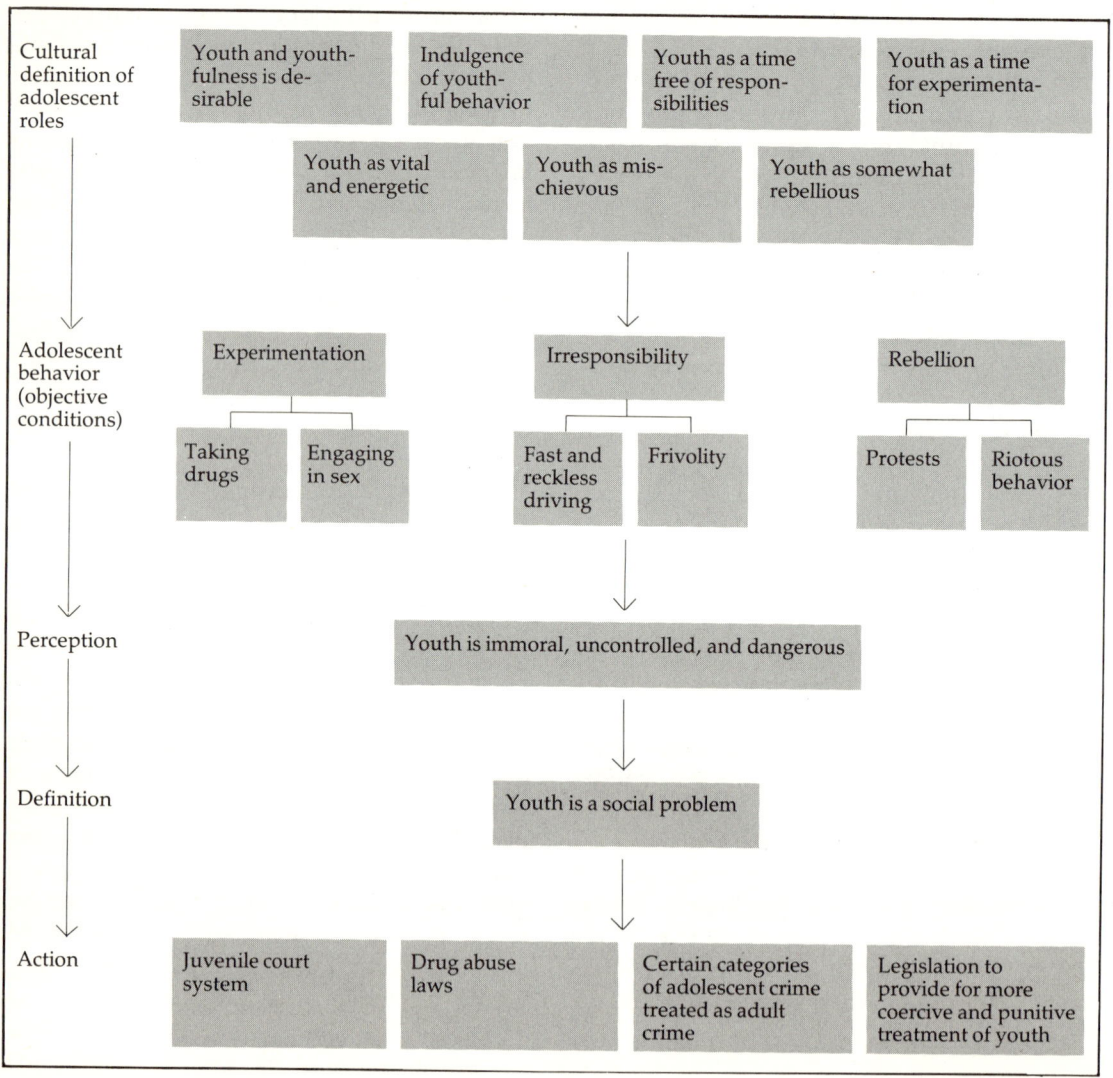

Some disruptive youthful behavior is the result of testing the limits of norms.

Types of General Norms

There are three types of general norms: (1) technicways, (2) alternative norms, and (3) norms for breaking norms. All three come in two forms: formal and informal. Formal norms are explicitly stated rules for behavior, laws for example. Informal norms are more general rules, which we all understand by observing the way society functions, rather than by hearing direct statements. It should not be thought that formal norms are the more powerful means of social control. To a considerable extent, all of us are controlled by the informal norms prevailing in those groups to which we belong, such as families and closest friends.

TECHNICWAYS

One variety of general norms is called *technicways*, meaning "simply the skills or habits associated with some material utilitarian object. Most job skills in modern industrial society are technicways."[20] We have broadened this definition somewhat to include all the directions for making things and accomplishing tasks having primarily utilitarian goals. Obviously then, technicways are productive of the vast amounts of goods and services we enjoy. But technicways also function to produce social problems, pollution being the prime example. Because technicways become habits and have utilitarian justification, they are difficult to change, even if they are harmful. Consider as an illustration the practices of sea-going ships.

It is necessary, from time to time, to perform an operation called pumping bilges, which removes the water that accumulates inside the hull through small leaks and condensation. Because bilge water is far from clean, containing oil and mineral residues, most seaports now have strict regulations forbidding the pumping of bilges while in port. However, once at sea and out of sight of land, ship captains order the bilges pumped. This would be insignificant if only a few ships did it, but multiply this by the thousands of ships that sail, and it is clear that the pumping of bilges is contributing to the pollution of seas and oceans.

The technicways specifying the pumping of bilges are eufunctional. The excess water inside ships' hulls must be removed. But they are also quite dysfunctional in terms of water pollution.

ALTERNATIVE NORMS

Adamson Hoebel described *alternative norms* as "the patterns that exist where several different norms apply to the same situation. A permissible range of choice and leeway is available."[21] This variety complicates life and anyone who means to stay out of trouble requires considerable cultural information. Let us consider an example in which formal official norms conflict with informal alternative norms to produce deviance.

People working for the United States government are required by law to report cases of attempted bribery. The mere offer of a bribe is a penal offense. Yet in at least one government agency, minor officials are reluctant to report bribery attempts because such reports add to the workload and make it difficult to settle cases. In fact, for these reasons, most minor officials in the agency ignore bribery attempts.[22]

SYSTEMATIC NONCONFORMITY AND NORMS FOR BREAKING NORMS

Permissible alternative ways of doing things are common and highly useful, because they provide for elasticity and some autonomy. Equally common are complexes of norms that go beyond mere elasticity and provide for behavior contrary to established norms. This systematic nonconformity has been described as "institutionalized evasions of institutional rules."[23] That is, norms for breaking norms are part of culture and provide for regular forms and kinds of deviant behavior.

Let us consider an example of the foregoing. There are formal norms prohibiting discrimination, but there are also informal norms allowing discrimination in hiring and promotion, thus maintaining the social problem of minorities. A well-qualified woman applying for almost any high-level business position is operating under a severe handicap: the informal norm permitting discrimination breaks the formal norm forbidding it. Males, who hold most high-level positions, are fully aware of the informal norms supporting discrimination against women. The woman will probably not get the job, but she will never be told that she was not chosen because of her sex. The reason given will be that the successful applicant, a male, was better qualified.

A more common example concerns driving automobiles. Many motorists habitually drive well over posted speed limits — until they see a patrol car. When they do, they promptly reduce their speed to something approximating the legal limit. The norm for breaking a norm is that one can drive somewhat above the speed limit until one sees a patrol car.

Laws

Can laws, like other norms, cause, maintain, or even worsen social problems? Unfortunately, yes. Many people believe that the way to deal with adverse conditions is to pass laws against them. Sadly, this attempt is usually not successful. We say sadly because life would be greatly simplified if passing laws could solve our problems.

Laws are formal norms, but they are not necessarily institutionalized norms. That is, some laws, even many, are not supported by culture. For example, some laws prohibit commercial activities on Sundays, but people can still find stores to shop in.

This discrepancy exists because many laws are attempts to enforce *pretend rules*. These rules are "standards . . . honored in the spoken word, but breeched in customary behavior. . . . This sets the difference between *real culture*, what people actually do, and *ideal culture*, what they say and believe they should do."[24] To illustrate the difference, let us look at sexual behavior. All American states have laws to regulate sexual behavior. Common throughout the fifty states are proscriptions against fornication, or sexual intercourse outside marriage. Many kinds of sexual activity within marriage are also prohibited, such as cunnilingus and fellatio. These laws represent ideal norms, but they have not been institutionalized — they are not strictly followed or enforced. A considerable variety of sexual behavior is widely practiced and condoned by alternative, informal norms, which are institutionalized or part of the culture.

Laws based on ideal norms serve to create and worsen social problems in two ways. First, they are either not enforced or are enforced capriciously. For example, laws against prostitution are enforced against prostitutes but not against their customers. Second, the lack of observance of such laws creates disrespect for all laws, encouraging other kinds of deviance. These laws supporting ideal culture are called *mala quia prohi-*

bita, or "bad because forbidden." The phrase means that the behavior is bad only because the laws says so. In contrast, *mala per se* ("bad as such") laws prohibit actions that are undesirable in themselves. As Johannes Andenaes explains:

> In the case of *mala per se,* the law supports the moral codes of society. If the threats of legal punishment were removed, moral feelings and the fear of public judgment would remain as powerful crime prevention forces. . . . In the case of *mala quia prohibita,* the law stands alone; conformity is essentially a matter of legal sanctions.[25]

A dramatic example of the problems arising out of laws representing ideal norms but at variance with real norms was the Eighteenth Amendment to the Constitution, which instituted Prohibition in 1919. This amendment forbade the manufacture, sale, transportation, and use of alcoholic beverages throughout the United States. Genuine public support in the form of institutionalized norms was lacking. As a result, the law was flouted.[26] To supply the thirst for illegal liquor, a network of bootleggers sprang up, the beginning of organized crime. Also, there was widespread corruption of police departments and the judiciary from 1919 to 1933. This corruption, coupled with the obvious fact that a billion-dollar-a-year industry flourished outside the law, did much to create disrespect for the law, which persists. Although the Eighteenth Amendment was repealed in 1933, the disrespect for the law and the power of organized crime show that the social costs of Prohibition are still being paid.

As we can see, deviance has been worsened by a failure to recognize that there must be public support for any law if it is to be enforced. A law that is in opposition to institutionalized norms invites violations and increases deviance. Antimarijuana laws provide an excellent current example. In the words of Albert K. Cohen:

> Much that is deviant can be largely attributed to efforts, some of them nobly motivated, to control deviant behavior. For example, efforts to prevent the consumption of liquor and narcotics and to prevent gambling have fostered the growth of large-scale criminal organizations for the provisions of these goods and services, and those organizations in turn have contributed to the corruption of politics and law enforcement. In short, that which we deplore and that which we cherish are not only part of the same seamless web, they are actually woven of the same fibers.[27]

Summary

Norms are a society's standards of behavior. Values are general statements of what a society treasures; norms are specific expressions of these values in terms of everyday behavior. Norms are the guideposts of life, they tell people how to behave, which makes social interaction easier. But norms benefit society as well as individuals. They not only embody society's values, they also make the smooth functioning of society possible. For smooth functioning to occur, society must enlist another set of social facts to enforce obedience to norms: sanctions.

SANCTIONS

Sanctions are that part of the social structure that directly serves the interests of social control. A *sanction* is either positive, a reward, or negative, a punishment. No system of norms could function without sanctions. A well-known example of sanctions to college students is the grading system. This system ensures that good performance is rewarded with high grades and ineffective performance is punished with low grades.

The Necessity for Sanctions

Sanctions are necessary for a reasonably orderly society. "There is no known society that does not make some definition of deviance and utilize sanctions, both positive and negative, to keep deviance within bounds."[28] If there were no sanctions, there would be no way society could ensure that people behave in accordance with norms.

Every society has a wealth of positive and negative sanctions. We are all aware of formal, legal sanctions, such as a prison sentence. But we are probably less aware of the enormous power of informal sanctions, the small rewards and punishments we use every day in attempting to control the behavior of others. Who can doubt the power of a smile or a frown to influence our actions. In thinking of the power of informal sanctions, remember what Andenaes said about *mala per se* laws: even "if threats of legal punishment were removed, moral feelings and the fear of public judgment would remain as powerful crime prevention forces."[29]

This seems straightforward, but there is a problem. The fact is that positive sanctions are also given for behavior defined as deviant. In fact, a host of positive sanctions underlie virtually every social problem.

Sanction Incongruence

Middle- and upper-class norms emphasize such traits and behaviors as order, compromise, cooperation, and a reliance on rationality and science. Individuals from all classes who conform to these norms expect to receive positive sanctions, those who do not conform expect to receive negative sanctions. This makes good sense, and creates rewarding lives for middle-class persons. But how about lower-class individuals? They are victims of *sanction incongruence*. These people live in a society ruled by middle-class values and norms. But as they live under different conditions, working-class and poor people have subcultures emphasizing different norms, as noted by Walter B. Miller:

> What the law defines as delinquency and crime is not a matter of a deviant youth group or even youth subculture but, rather, represents the values and norms of the lower-class subculture. This lower-class subculture emphasizes such values as excitement, pugnacity, autonomy, and reliance on the operation of fate or chance.[30]

The plight of lower-class persons, particularly adolescents, is clear. If they violate the norms of the dominant group, they will be punished. But they are also likely to be punished if they do not live up to the norms of their subculture. To worsen the situation, lower-class youths are expected to violate middle-class norms, and thus receive close attention from and harassment by police.

As a result, lower-class youths are in a bind. Obedience to the dominant middle-class norms keeps them out of trouble with the law, but alienates them from their peers. Obedience to the norms of their subculture wins acceptance from their peers, but because of intensive police surveillance, they will probably be caught. Middle-class people do not have this conflict; it is easier for them to be virtuous. They are rewarded for following the norms of their own class.

The discrimination against minorities is also buttressed to some extent by sanction incongruence. For example, some members of dominant and minority groups might wish to associate socially with members of the other group. But if they do, they invite the imposition of negative sanctions. Or take the case of employers. If they refuse openly to employ persons on the basis of race, religion, or ethnicity, they invite legal sanctions. But if they do hire on an open and fair basis and, as a result, employ minority-group members, particularly in upper-level positions, they may invite negative sanctions from some employees, and even from the community. It is very difficult to win a court case against discriminatory hiring. Because of this, the informal negative sanctions of the community probably outweigh the formal sanctions of the legal system.

But even the higher classes are not immune from norms and sanctions promoting and maintaining social problems. For example, the corporation president is charged with making profits for his company. If he seeks only profits and ignores the problems of waste disposal and pollution, he is likely to run afoul of new laws regulating these matters. On the other hand, should he install expensive antipollution and waste-control systems, profits are reduced and he may lose his job, an extreme negative sanction. In most cases, the corporation president will attempt to steer some middle course and avoid negative sanctions from both stockholders and the law. The result of such action is to delay effective pollution control.

Summary

To ensure control of individuals' behavior, societies have sanctions that enforce compliance with norms. Everyone is familiar with such formal sanctions as prison sentences for breaking the law. Most of us are also aware of the informal sanctions created by the groups we belong to — the names we are called for not doing what our peers want us to do. Formal sanctions apply technically to society as a whole, to all its members, although they may not always be enforced against privileged members. But the informal sanctions vary according to our position in society and how we are expected to behave, that is, according to our status and role.

STATUSES AND ROLES

"A status is a cultural category by which all of us are defined."[31] All humans have various *statuses*, for example, boy, girl, man, woman, black, white, lawyer, welder, rich, poor. Some of these are *ascribed*, that is, assigned to people somewhat automatically — examples include boy, girl, black, and white. Others are *achieved*, or earned, including lawyer, welder, rich, and poor. Ascribed statuses are assigned to us by others; achieved statuses are earned, presumably by our own efforts.

All statuses have a group of norms that define them. These norms are called a *role*, which means a pattern of behavior reflecting the duties, rights, and obligations of a particular status. There is no such thing as a status without a role, and vice versa.

Socialized humans know their own statuses and roles and those of others. Thus we know what behavior is expected of us and what to expect of others. As a result, statuses and roles make social interaction easier and less confusing; they give us rules to follow. But recognizing their necessity should not blind us to the fact that they contribute to social rigidity, that is, resistance to change. While they promote order and help us know how to relate to each other, statuses and roles

Statuses may be either achieved or ascribed. The president of the United States earns achieved status presumably by public service achievements in the political arena. On the other hand, the Prince of Wales, here at his 1969 investiture, acquires his ascribed status purely by accident of birth.

simultaneously contribute to the establishment and maintenance of social problems, just as institutions, values, norms, and sanctions do. Let us consider a few examples, keeping in mind the pervasive power of statuses and roles. They "influence almost every kind of decision from the choice of a car to the choice of a spouse."[32]

The Male Status and Role

In Latin America, surrounding the status and role of male is the mystique of *machismo*. Part of this mystique emphasizes the importance of male virility, judged by the number of children a man fathers or is presumed to have fathered. The more children a man has, the greater his virility. Since machismo is valued so highly, this judgment is earnestly desired by many men. Obviously, then, machismo functions to make males resist birth control. For a male to support birth control would be to attack an important source of his personal identity and worth. Thus, the norms of male role contribute to the creation and maintenance of the social problem of overpopulation.

In many societies, the concept of maleness includes such behavioral norms as pugnacity, courage, and hard-headedness. A man willing to compromise, able to see another's point of view, and reluctant to use force, risks being classified as soft and his maleness becoming suspect. A reading of the famous *Pentagon Papers* shows that the way the male role is defined in American society played a part in the United States involvement in Vietnam, particularly the build-up of American military power in that country. For several years, those who advocated attempting to make peace or arriving at an understanding with the North Vietnamese were regarded as soft, and their counsels went unheard.

Status, Role, and Mental Illness

Status and role are also relevant to the problem of mental illness. As Thomas Szasz, a psychiatrist, observed, certain deviant behaviors are labeled "mental illness," which is then specified as the cause of the behavior.[33] Illness is a status with an associated role, the status ascribed, ordinarily, by psychiatrists. The consequences of being so labeled are serious. Many employment applications ask if the applicant has ever been in a mental hospital or under psychiatric treatment. Obviously, answering yes to this question is not likely to aid the applicant in being hired. Unfortunately, these labels are rarely questioned, and sometimes they are misapplied.

The problem is caused by a norm of the psychiatrist's role. These professionals are the final authority on mental health, and are expected to make an authoritative diagnosis. To live up to their role expectations they are forced to make such a diagnosis even when they are far from certain. If they did not, they would lose status as professionals. Imagine what would happen to a psychiatrist who refused to diagnose a case coming to his or her attention on the grounds that he or she could not be sure.

Status Lock

Our statuses and roles lock us all into certain normative behaviors. This *status lock* functions, in part, to create and maintain social problems. The male who considers it a sign of weakness to drive at the speed limit contributes to highway accidents and death tolls. The female locked into the traditional role of women in our society and staunchly resisting efforts to end discrimination makes the ending of such treatment less likely.

We stay locked in our statuses because we do not know how to act otherwise. We insist on fulfilling roles and resist efforts to change them. We wish to act in the way that is familiar, to follow the path of least resistance. It follows that the alleviation of some social problems, perhaps many, is difficult, because it requires changes in statuses and roles that people are unwilling to make.

Summary

Statuses and roles reflect the norms of behavior, which in turn express society's values. These roles establish proper modes of social interaction — they contribute to social institutions. Each of these social facts, from institutions to roles, is resistant to change; all combine to create social structure. You can perhaps begin to see now why we said that social problems are created not by disorganization, but by organization. But to demonstrate this more clearly, let us look directly at the concept of social disorganization.

SOCIAL DISORGANIZATION

What does social disorganization mean? Most of us believe that we know disorganization when we see it, but do we? Some of us equate social problems with disorganization. But is this correct?

Defining Social Disorganization

Frank Scarpitti states that *social disorganization* "occurs when a specific aspect of the social system fails to fulfill adequately the social objectives of all groups and their individual members, relative to standards that groups and individuals share for that system."[34] This definition is based on the idea that any failure to meet objectives constitutes disorganization. Scarpitti's definition does not help us to understand social problems. It assumes that social problems are the result of social disorganization, which comes from the failure to establish a society that meets its members' standards. But a failure to establish an ideal society does not constitute social disorganization. Our species will probably never establish an ideal society. One reason, of course, is that it would be impossible to get any number of humans to agree on what constitutes an ideal society.

Assume that social disorganization is the underlying cause of social problems. If so, all we have to do to end social problems is to get organized. But is that the answer? Scarpitti defines social disorganization as present when a system does not adequately meet the needs of its members. But adequacy is defined by humans. One doubts very much that all members of any society would define their life-styles as adequate.

The problem is the same one we've encountered before: human perceptions. Society appears disorganized because people see their positions as inadequate. But differing perceptions are not evidence of disorganization. People's perceptions are subjective, but an objective look at society shows that inadequate life-styles are necessary to the functioning of society. Getting organized will not solve our problems. We already are organized, and we already have problems. What is need is a change in organization.

The Relativity of Social Disorganization

When we describe some condition as disorganized, it must be relative to some other condition, which is or appears to be organized. That is, we need benchmarks. Whether an activity appears organized or disorganized is a function of one's knowledge of and previous experience with the activity. To the uninitiated, the floor of the New York stock exchange appears greatly confused and extremely disorganized. But to the experienced stockbroker, it is highly organized. The middle-class person driving through an urban ghetto sees disorganization, but his impression is in error. Ghetto dwellers are extremely well organized to deal with the special problems they face in eking out some kind of existence, just as suburbanites are well organized to deal with their special problems.

In sports, Englishmen watching an American football game for the first time are doubtless confused and, as a result, perceive confusion. The same is true of an American seeing rugby played for the first time. Nevertheless, both games have strict rules that are followed in matches. The point is that we should not assume that any condition, including a social problem, represents disorganization. Such an assumption can be made only if the person making the claim has thorough knowledge of the condition. Such a claim can be valid only if it is based on objective analysis, but such analysis often disproves such claims.

Deviance is often regarded as representing social disorganization. While some deviant behavior may cause or precipitate temporary disorganization, deviant behavior "is not *ipso facto* disorganization."[35] Deviant behavior is found in all societies, it is part of the social structure: remember Durkheim's insight that even a society of saints would have crime. Deviant behavior is absent only in ant societies, not in human ones.

Riots appear to constitute severe disorganization. Yet, as sociologists have found:

A riot is not "all hell breaking loose," but a complex sociopolitical process. Patterns not apparent on the surface characterizing different forms of riotous behavior can be uncovered through systematic analysis and do shed new light on the rioting phenomenon.[36]

This finding is consonant with the *emergent norm* theory of Ralph Turner. Crowds, even rioting crowds, are governed by norms, just as other groups are. The collective behavior evidenced in crowds is guided by some definition of the situation; appropriate norms emerge and the action taken is in accordance with these norms.[37] As many television newscasts illustrate, student demonstrations around the world show similarities, indicating organization and the existence of norms providing rules for such demonstrations.

Organization as a Cultural Universal

If there are any cultural universals, at least one of these is organization. By *cultural universal*, we mean a trait common to all cultures and societies. Wherever and whenever humans congregate for any length of time, they interact symbolically and some kind of organization always emerges.

This organizing tendency does not invariably or even usually result in efficiency. Human organizations meet only one criterion: they work well enough; they get the job done. Out of this criterion emerge many conditions that come to be defined as social problems because humans are dissatisfied and see discrepancies between what ought to be and what is.

We do not totally reject the concept of disorganization. It does have limited applications. But in analyzing social problems, focusing on social disorganization obscures real causes. For example, a substantial proportion of the work force in any modern society depends for its existence on a continuing supply of criminals. If there were no criminals, lawyers, police officers, prison guards, and parole officers would be out of their jobs. As you will see in Chapter 8, modern societies are organized in such a way as to guarantee that the requisite number of persons will be recruited annually into a life of crime. It is not social disorganization that causes crime, but social organization.

Social disorganization does not explain any continuing social problem. It requires very complex organization to maintain such problems as old age, sexual deviance, mental illness, and overpopulation. None of these are caused by disorganization although some of their effects are disorganizing.

Summary

In concluding this section, it is important to emphasize that no individuals or groups planned or plotted to bring out our problems. Much of social structure is the result of trial-and-error learning. When people are confronted with a problem, they try various responses until they find one that works. A response that works is rewarding, tends to get learned, and, if repeated often enough by a number of people, becomes a cultural trait, a part of the social structure. But we should remember that what is eufunctional can also be dysfunctional, as Robert Merton points out:

> Far more useful as a directive for research or analysis would seem the provisional assumption that persisting cultural forms have a net balance of functional [desirable] consequences either for the society considered as a unit or for subgroups sufficiently powerful to retain these forms intact by means of direct coercion or indirect persuasion.[38]

In other words, social problems directly or indirectly benefit various individuals and groups. In spite of some people's concern about problems, powerful groups are able to resist efforts to bring about change. Powerful interests and expensive lobbyists attempt to influence all legislatures, from the state to the national. Just as influential people are needed to define a social problem, influential people resist the solving of it. We will not be able to understand social problems by focusing on disorganization. We must concentrate on social organization.

CONCLUSION

Social structure generates our problems, but grasping this fact is not enough. To complain about modern society and insist that it be drastically altered will not solve problems, even if such a drastic alteration were possible. To come closer to understanding social problems we must develop an understanding of the dynamic relationships characterizing them. Such knowledge can be applied to finding ways to solve our problems and to evaluate solutions being tried.

Empirical analysis of attempts to solve problems can reveal four distinct possibilities. First, we may see that what is being done is sound and should be continued. Second, we may find out that present measures will probably not have any effect. Third, we may come to see that a given social problem may not, in the light of current knowledge and resources, be solvable at all. Last, we may realize that what is being done is actually making things worse rather than better.

How do we, for example, evaluate India's attempts to solve the problem of overpopulation in the face of its decision to invest millions of dollars in developing an atomic bomb? It would seem that overpopulation should take priority over developing atomic weapons. Is it possible that some societies are so organized that some social problems cannot be dealt with at all? Any objective sociological analysis must consider that a possibility.

This pessimistic view is probably not true. As a species, we are remarkably adaptable. If there is a solution to a problem, humans are likely to find it — eventually. But if we are to solve our problems, we must take a different perspective than currently prevails in American society. Hiding our head like the ostrich or searching for the answer in social disorganization will not help. We can only do something constructive if we understand the social forces causing and supporting social problems.

IMPORTANT WORDS AND TERMS

achieved status
alternative norms
ascribed status
dysfunction
emergent norms
eufunction
general norms
held values

homeostatis
ideal culture
mala per se
mala quia prohibita
modern functionalism
mores
neofunctionalism

norm
organic analogy
pretend rules
real culture
role
sanction
sanction incongruence

social disorganization
social fact
social institution
society
status
status lock
technicways

QUESTIONS FOR DISCUSSION

1. Most of us claim to be against sin. But does sinful behavior benefit or bring enjoyment to people other than the sinners? Think carefully before you answer this question. If you answer yes, who benefits or obtains enjoyment?
2. If an important human organ ceases to function, the person concerned may die. But what about society? Would a part of society failing in its functions also kill a society? Why or why not?
3. Imagine that poverty were suddenly eliminated in the United States. Would this result in new problems? What?
4. We are opposed to human sacrifice for religious purposes. Now a serious social problem in this country is the heavy toll of death and injury on the nation's highways. Are we, in effect, sacrificing people who are killed on the highways? To what or whom are we making this sacrifice?
5. Universities are fairly rational, but also contain irrational elements. You should be able to think of a few. For example, are intercollegiate athletics, particularly football, partly irrational?
6. Without looking at your text's discussion of values, sit down and try to make a list of your own values. Was it difficult to come up with twelve to fifteen values? Why?
7. Is it possible that both pro- and antiabortionists hold the same or similar values? Explain.
8. Do the norms for classroom behavior vary from professor to professor or are they generally the same? If you answer no, provide an example or two.
9. Your text says that in order for discrimination to be practiced, minority group members must themselves cooperate. This seems unreasonable, but is it? Explain.
10. The *Uniform Crime Reports* indicate that the number and proportion of arrests decline sharply with advancing age. Could this decline have anything to do with the roles of adolescent, young adult, middle-aged, or old persons? Explain your reasoning.
11. It has been said that all crime is political. What is the meaning of this statement?
12. Most students are opposed to cheating on examinations. Yet very few students will report cases of cheating that they have personally observed. This involves norm incongruence. What norms are involved and why are they incongruent?
13. The mass media commonly report crimes. Can such reporting actually serve as a reward for the criminals? Explain.
14. Which is harder to play successfully — the male or female role? Why?
15. Look over the table of contents of this text. Are any of the social problems covered caused chiefly by social disorganization? Support your answer logically.

SUGGESTED READING

SYDNEY ANGLO, *Machiavelli: A Dissection* (New York: Harcourt, Brace and World, 1969).

In this chapter we emphasized that sociologists ought to describe things as they are, not as we like them to be. But this can get people into difficulty, nowhere better illustrated than in the life and writings of Niccolo Machiavelli (1469–1527). The word "Machiavellian" has crept into the English language as a synonym for political cunning and bad faith, but the Florentine thinker and writer has been widely misunderstood and wrongfully maligned. Machiavelli's crime was to describe politics as he saw it. Believing that the ideal was the real, many people were disturbed (and still are) by Machiavelli because he made it quite clear that political reality is a long way from the ideals. Sydney Anglo's treatment of Machiavelli is sympathetic. He makes it clear by his own writing and judicious use of quotations that Machiavelli was, in many ways, a competent early sociologist. For some interesting history of an exciting era and, more important, for an example of a shrewd and enlightening sociological analysis of Renaissance politics, this is the book. After reading it, the student might ask whether politics has really changed since Machiavelli's day.

AMITAI ETZIONI, *The Active Society* (New York: Free Press, 1968).

The trouble with virtually all models of an ideal society, from Plato's *Republic* to Marx's classless society, is that they simply wouldn't work. Professor Etzioni, however, presents a model of an ideal society that might come into being some day. He defines an "active society" as one which controls itself and which is responsive to the needs of its members, as modern societies are not. We do not recommend this book for everyone.

The language and thinking are sophisticated. But the superior student should be able to read it with interest, profit, and, quite possibly, a surge of optimism about the future.

DANIEL BELL, "America as a Mass Society: A Critique," in W. Richard Scott (ed.), *Social Processes and Social Structures* (New York: Holt, Rinehart and Winston, 1970), pp. 538–548.

Daniel Bell's analysis is a refreshing antidote to jaundiced writing about modern socities. If one believes that all our social problems arise out of an essentially sick society, then further attempts at analysis cease. We will never know what really causes and maintains social problems, much less how to deal with them. Professor Bell, in this short article, puts things back in perspective.

NOTES

1. Herbert J. Gans, "The Positive Functions of Poverty," *American Journal of Sociology*, Vol. 78, No. 2 (1968), pp. 275–289.
2. Lewis Coser, "The Functions of Conflict," in N. J. Demerath III and Richard A. Peterson (eds.), *Systems, Change, and Conflict* (New York: Free Press, 1967), p. 309.
3. Alvin Gouldner, "Anti-Minotaur: The Myth of a Value-Free Sociology," *Journal of Social Problems*, Vol. 9 (Winter 1962), pp. 199–213.
4. Robert K. Merton, *Social Theory and Social Structure*, enl. ed. (New York: Free Press, 1968), pp. 100–101.
5. Arnold M. Rose, *Sociology*, 2nd ed. (New York: Knopf, 1965). p. 3.
6. Charles W. Morris, "G. H. Mead's Theory of Individual and Society," in Edgar A. Schuler et al. (eds.), *Readings in Sociology* (New York: Crowell, 1974), p. 171.
7. Emile Durkheim, *The Rules of the Sociological Method*, 8th ed., trans. Sarah A. Solovay and John H. Mueller, ed. George E. G. Catlin (New York: Free Press, 1938), p. xliii.
8. Ibid., p. liv.
9. Marvin Harris, *Culture, Man, and Nature* (New York: Crowell, 1971), p. 554.
10. Fred E. Katz (ed.), *Contemporary Sociological Theory* (New York: Random House, 1971), p. 6.
11. Robin M. Williams, Jr., *American Society*, 3rd ed. (New York: Knopf, 1970), p. 38.
12. Peter R. Senn, *Social Science and Its Methods* (Boston: Holbrook, 1971), p. 37.
13. James A. Robinson and Richard C. Snyder, "Decision-Making in International Politics," in Herbert C. Kelman (ed.), *International Behavior* (New York: Holt, Rinehart and Winston, 1966), p. 447.
14. Richard C. Fuller and Richard R. Myers, "The Natural History of a Social Problem," *American Sociological Review*, Vol. 6 (June 1941), p. 320.
15. Philip M. Hauser, "The Chaotic Society," in James A. Inciardi and Harvey M. Siegal (eds.), *Emerging Social Issues* (New York: Praeger, 1975), p. 27.
16. Gerhard E. Lenski, *Human Societies* (New York: McGraw-Hill, 1970), p. 30.
17. Mavis H. Biesanz and John Biesanz, *Intro-*

duction to Sociology, 2nd ed. (Englewood Cliffs, N.J.: Prentice-Hall, 1973), p. 73.

18. Reece McGee, *Points of Departure* (Hinsdale, Ill.: Dryden, 1972), p. 31.

19. The authors are indebted to Donald Larrick, Ohio State University, for the insights underlying this analysis.

20. Biesanz and Biesanz, *Introduction to Sociology*, p. 67.

21. Adamson E. Hoebel, "The Nature of Culture," in Paul E. Mott et al. (eds.), *Sociological Perspectives* (Columbus, Ohio: Merrill, 1973), p. 148.

22. Peter M. Blau, "Unofficial Norms," in Marshall M. Meyer (ed.), *Structures, Symbols, and Systems: Readings on Organizational Behavior* (Boston: Little, Brown, 1971), pp. 78–93.

23. Philip K. Bock, *Modern Cultural Anthropology* (New York: Knopf, 1969), p. 109.

24. Hoebel, "The Nature of Culture," p. 150.

25. Johannes Andenaes, "The General Preventive Effects of Punishment," *University of Pennsylvania Law Review*, Vol. 114 (May 1966), p. 957.

26. For some illuminating background material on Prohibition, see George E. Mowry (ed.), *The Twenties: Fords, Flappers and Fanatics* (Englewood Cliffs, N.J.: Prentice-Hall, 1963), pp. 89–120.

27. Albert K. Cohen, "The Study of Social Disorganization and Deviant Behavior," in Lewis A. Coser and Bernard Rosenberg (eds.), *Sociological Theory: A Book of Readings*, 3rd ed. (New York: Macmillan, 1969), p. 592.

28. Adamson E. Hoebel, *The Law of Primitive Man* (Cambridge, Mass.: Harvard University Press, 1954), p. 127.

29. Andenaes, "The General Preventive Effects of Punishment," p. 957.

30. Walter B. Miller, "Lower-Class Culture as a Generating Milieu of Gang Delinquency," *Journal of Social Issues*, Vol. 14, No. 3 (1958), p. 11.

31. McGee, *Points of Departure*, p. 72.

32. Gerhard E. Lenski, *Power and Privilege* (New York: McGraw-Hill, 1966), p. 37.

33. Thomas Szasz, "The Myth of Mental Illness," *American Psychologist*, Vol. 15 (February 1960), pp. 112–118.

34. Frank R. Scarpitti, *Social Problems* (New York: Holt, Rinehart and Winston, 1974), p. 8.

35. Cohen, "The Study of Social Disorganization," p. 594.

36. Margaret J. G. Abudu et al., "Black Ghetto Violence: A Case Study Inquiry into the Spatial Patterns of Four Los Angeles Riot Event-Types," *Journal of Social Problems*, Vol. 19, No. 3 (Winter 1972), p. 408.

37. Ralph Turner, "Collective Behavior," in Robert E. L. Faris (ed.), *Handbook of Modern Sociology* (Chicago: Rand McNally, 1964), pp. 389–392.

38. Merton, *Social Theory and Social Structure*, p. 86.

PART II
INSTITUTIONAL PROBLEMS

3 THE FAMILY
CROSS CURRENTS OF EMOTIONALITY

CHAPTER OVERVIEW

INTRODUCTION

CONCEPTUAL ORIENTATION
Definitions
The Normal American Family
Summary

CROSS-CULTURAL AND HISTORICAL OVERVIEW
Cross-Cultural Evidence
Sex Roles in American Society
Summary

OBJECTIVE DIMENSIONS OF THE PROBLEM
Education and Sex Roles
Women in the Labor Force
Contraception and Abortion
Marriage Rates

Divorce Rates
Birthrates
Fertility Among Single Women: The Problem of Illegitimacy
Violence in the Family
Summary

ATTEMPTS AT DEALING WITH THE PROBLEM
Ideological Responses to the Problem
Iatrogenic Effects

PROSPECTS FOR SOLVING THE PROBLEM

IMPORTANT WORDS AND TERMS

QUESTIONS FOR DISCUSSION

SUGGESTED READING

NOTES

Nature intended women to be our slaves. . . . They are our property; we are not theirs. They belong to us just as a tree that bears fruit belongs to a gardener. What a mad idea to demand equality for women! Women are nothing but machines for producing children.

Napoleon (attributed)

That man was wrong who said the British Empire's fall began when it was declared unlawful for a man to beat his wife. The real problem was introduced when his wife and daughters began to read.

Emily Hahn, *Once Upon a Pedestal*

CHAPTER OVERVIEW

In this chapter we examine some problems facing the American family. Since the end of World War II, family structure has been affected by many changes, including new ideas about marriage, a rising divorce rate, a dramatic decline in birthrate, and a changing role for women. We analyze these trends, first describing the American family structure and discussing sex roles in our society and others. This point is important because it is largely women's rising educational and employment levels and their changing expectations that are causing the vast changes in marriage, divorce, and birthrates. After outlining these changes statistically, we turn to consider various solutions offered for the problems facing the family.

INTRODUCTION

Every day the mass media tell us in some new way that the American family is in trouble. The divorce rate is rising rapidly — in California it is supposedly already over 50 percent. And it is going up fastest among people who have been married 20 years or longer. About a million legal abortions are done each year, sending the birthrate below the replacement level. Almost 50 percent of all adult women work at least part time, a parameter that implies, among other things, many children are being cared for largely by people other than their parents. And the women's liberation movement seems to be putting down most traditional ideas about how men and women should deal with each other. The family seems to be facing a major crisis and some observers think it may be so seriously weakened that it can never fully recover.

These changes arouse strong feelings in people, especially those who grew up in a different world, where many things young people take for granted today were almost unknown. Nice people did not live together before marriage then, or have sex outside of marriage, and if an abortion was necessary people never admitted to having it, and no one talked about abortions in public. Whether these changes are for the better and what their long-range effects will be is still not clear. To find out, we need to study the family as sociologists have; then we can understand the major structural changes occurring in the American family.

CONCEPTUAL ORIENTATION

Many sociologists study family life from the institutional approach, which focuses on how institutions provide the norms for members of a society. Sociologists taking this approach argue that institutions find ways of creating the kind of individual needed to maintain the current way of doing things. This is accomplished through socialization, by which new members are taught the right way to behave, and through social control, by which deviants are brought back into line.

The institutional approach, however, does not mean that social structures have total domination over the members of a society. Socialization is never perfect, and social control, especially as it is exercised by the family over its members, has grown weaker in the past generations. People are now freer to work out new and different life-styles. Some sociologists see the basic institutions of a society as coexisting in a high degree of harmony and stability, called equilibrium, but we find this emphasis on equilibrium one-sided. Change and conflict are also basic social processes, and it is clear that they, not stability, characterize family life in the United States today.

We see social interaction as the product of a variety of interrelated structural influences. Change in one area sets in motion forces that change other areas as well. With this approach in mind, let us turn our attention to some concepts and definitions we will be using. We will then examine the basic forms of the American family.

Definitions

While it may seem unnecessary, the first term we must define is the family. The problem of defining the family has perplexed anthropologists for years, primarily because of the enormous variations in family structure found in human societies. We will be focusing on the American family, though, and take a useful definition from William Stephens, who sees the *family* as:

> a social arrangement based on marriage and the marriage contract, including recognition of the rights and duties of parenthood, common residence for husband, wife and children, and reciprocal economic obligations between husband and wife.[1]

Stephens has based his definition of the family on the associated concept of marriage, which he defines as:

> a socially legitimate sexual union, begun with a public announcement and undertaken with some idea of permanence; it is assumed with a more or less explicit marriage contract which spells out the reciprocal rights and obligations between spouses and between the spouses and their future children.[2]

These two definitions help clarify some of the confusion in the way these words are sometimes used. They also point out why many conditions in today's families are defined as problems. For example, the idea of permanence is seen as being undercut by divorce. And many people are asking what the legitimate demands are that one spouse can make on the other, especially since so many women are now in the labor force. These definitions will serve as a point of orientation from which we can examine the problems facing contemporary family life.

In looking at a social structure like the family, the sociologist uses a few basic conceptual tools, which we outlined in Chapter 2. Particularly important are norms, roles, and statuses. Roles not only prescribe how a person should behave, they also oblige the person to behave in acceptable ways. When group members perform according to their roles, they expect others to also. Along with roles, a person always has a position within the group, called status. We both play roles and hold statuses at the same time, for the two are different sides of the same coin.

In looking at the family, we immediately see the kinship statuses of husband and wife, parent and child, brother and sister. The average American assumes that the family is limited to these few roles and statuses, but a study of families in other cultures shows that the American family is unique in this respect. In other cultures, families include a broad range of kin, with many holding statuses we don't even have words for. This diversity throughout the world calls into question our own assumptions. Is there really a normal American family, from which all deviant forms can then be measured?

The Normal American Family

In the "Leave It to Beaver" television series of the mid-1950s, the normal American family was presented as consisting of a "regular guy" father (Ward Cleaver), who commuted to work each day; his wife (June), who stayed at home and took care of the house and children; an older brother (Wally), and finally Beaver, a boy of almost eleven around whose activities the series revolved. They were white, lived in an affluent suburb, were obviously of Anglo-Saxon descent, and lived apart from any other relatives. Roles were clearly defined: Ward was to provide for the family and June was to manage the home. While Ward's influence usually prevailed and June and the boys deferred to his judgment, the family was characterized by a certain degree of egalitarianism. The boys were in the process of learning the role they would play when they grew up. There was never any serious conflict, because all shared a definition of appropriate sex roles. The family also was happy, largely because its general expectations were consistently met.

In contrast to the television programs about the family in the 1970s, this picture from the fifties creates a certain nostalgia. But this kind of family, while presented as the ideal to Americans for many years, was not the way most families were actually structured. Important class, racial, and ethnic differences have made the fifties' television family an unreal picture for most Americans. Studies done over the past fifty years indicate that no one set of characteristics is common to all American families; recognizing this is an important element in our analysis.

American family forms have varied primarily on three dimensions. The first is the range of kin included in the family. A family including interaction only between parents and children is said to be *nuclear*. If other kin, like grandparents, aunts, uncles, and cousins, are part of the interaction pattern on a day-to-day basis, the family is said to be *extended*. Most American families are somewhere between these two poles. Although for residence purposes the majority are nuclear, other kin often live nearby and are part of the family's daily life. Most families have never been totally isolated from all kin, even though the trend over the past fifty years has been in that nuclear direction. (This movement has contributed to other problems of our society, as will be seen in Chapter 7.)

Another set of differences among American families has been the nature of the ties organizing the family. Our definition of the family stressed the importance of marriage, but this has not been the tie binding most of the world's families in the past. If the primary tie is marriage, the family is said to be *conjugal;* but if the tie is based on blood relationships the nature of the bond is quite different and is called *consanguinal.* For most immigrant families who came to America after the 1880s, the ties were primarily consanguinal.

Every society has both sets of ties, but since the end of World War II, the conjugal bond has been replacing consanguinal ties for most Americans. Some observers see this as the heart of what is wrong with American families, arguing that the emphasis on the conjugal bond and the growing isolation of the nuclear family weaken important interpersonal bonds. For this reason, many communes were established that attempted to eliminate conjugal bonds altogether. Studies of racial, ethnic, and class variations in family structure all emphasize the greater importance of consanguinal ties, but for most middle-class Americans these bonds appear to grow weaker with each passing year. In recent years, with the rising education and mobility of the population, conjugal ties have assumed more importance. This fact is central to understanding the issue of divorce today, for divorce ruptures conjugal ties but not necessarily consanguinal ones.

One final dimension along which American families vary is in their decision-making and authority structure. Traditionally, observers like Alexis de Tocqueville, who wrote his impressions in the 1830s, have seen egalitarianism as more prevalent in America than Europe. However, the control over decision making varies widely in American families, again by racial, ethnic, and class factors. The white upper-middle class family may allow *egalitarianism,* with decision making shared by husband and wife. The vast majority of American families, however, are more *authoritarian,* although the dominant figure can vary. In some black families, the female is clearly the head of the household, whereas in many working-class ethnic families the male dominates, as was comically portrayed by Archie Bunker in the television series "All in the Family." This issue of decision making is crucial for understanding the characteristics of those people who have been the staunchest supporters of the movement for greater equality for women. They have been well-educated women from white middle-class families, trying to carry their egalitarian structure to other segments of the population, but since most people do not live in this kind of family, their message has often fallen on deaf ears.

Summary

The family — as it is in America — is a social arrangement based on marriage. Nevertheless, American families vary greatly. Most Americans do not live in isolated, egalitarian, nuclear families. The growing importance of the conjugal tie needs to be stressed, because some observers see it as central to understanding the strains felt by contemporary families. Family structure is organized around roles and statuses and all families use age and sex criteria to organize the activities of the family unit. Obviously, when notions of appropriate sex roles change, as they have for American women, assumptions about family structure will be greatly affected.

To gain some perspective on what is at issue, let us see how sex roles have been defined in other societies and throughout our own society's history. We will focus on women's role because much of the conflict within the family has grown out of changes in that role. This does not mean that men's roles should be ignored, nor that their roles are not problematic. But men have not been subject to the controversy and conflict many women now face in their daily lives.

CROSS-CULTURAL AND HISTORICAL OVERVIEW

Each day the world is invaded by hordes of naked little barbarians who threaten any society's established way of doing things. These babies need to be tamed by socializing them into acceptable roles and into the prevailing value system. To some extent preliterate societies have to divide up the tasks that need to be performed, and one common division, however arbitrary, is along sex lines. For centuries men have been the hunters, while the women stayed at home to cook, garden, and tend the children. Among many preliterate societies all activities are organized through the family, which conditions young children to take on traditional ways. As the societies develop and become more technologically advanced, these roles may change with circumstances — but because socialization supports the status quo, they will also persist.

When we speak of the biological differences between the two sexes, we speak of *male* and *female* characteristics; when we talk about the behavioral differences between the two sexes, we label these characteristics as *masculine* or *feminine*. The latter concepts refer to *gender identity*, defined by all societies according to the ideas they have about how males and females should behave. Gender identity is an abstraction formed out of the roles a person is expected to play on the basis of his or her sex. In other words, *sex roles* serve as the basis for gender identity for the individual members of any society.

Many people believe that basic biological differences between men and women inevitably lead to the sex roles we find common in most societies. While the French have a saying, *vive la difference,* to indicate that men and women are wonderfully different in their biological make-up, the social outcomes of these differences have had profound consequences in both males and females. To test that assumption, we will compare the roles in our society with those found in other parts of the world. If sex roles seem uniform, the argument that they are based on biology — that there are natural sex roles — would be strengthened. But if considerable variation is found in sex roles, the biological differences must be less important than the culture that defines and develops sex roles.

Cross-Cultural Evidence

The noted anthropologist, Margaret Mead, was deeply interested in the question of the origin of sex roles. Through her work with three different primitive tribes on the island of New Guinea, Mead was made aware of how personality traits and temperament — behavioral characteristics — become associated with biological differences.[3] Mead studied how sex roles were structured among these three tribes, all living in the same general area. Each society had sex roles with a great deal of consistency within each tribe, but together the three showed extreme variation.

In one tribe, the Arapesh, both men and women showed similar characteristics, with both sexes nonaggressive, cooperative, and responsive to the needs of other people. We would call these traits feminine, but both men and women of the Arapesh possessed them. In the Mundugumor the two sexes were also highly similar in personality and temperament, although in this case both were ruthless and aggressive like a violent male in our culture. Interestingly enough, a third society was found with roles in reverse of ours. Tchambuli women were dominant and rather impersonal, while men were less responsible and more emotionally dependent.

From these three examples, Mead concluded that while male and female are biological categories, the concepts masculine and feminine are *psychosexual* categories largely unrelated to any consistent biological basis. Males could display feminine personality and temperament, and females masculine traits. Mead's work remains central to our understanding of the issues covered in this chapter. Masculine and feminine behavior, psychosexual concepts, are defined by cultural conditioning. Work by other anthropologists supports Mead's conclusion. Another group, the Manus, assumes that only men enjoy playing with babies, while the Toda believe housework is too sacred to be done by women. The Arapesh insist that women's heads are stronger than men's. Every culture has seized on the conspicuous biological sex differences, but how they use these differences varies greatly.

Men and women are differentiated in all cultures and each sex has certain roles to which it is expected to conform. Most anthropologists reject the Freudian idea that "anatomy is destiny," the argument that biology determines behavior. They also reject the idea that social behavior is carried and transmitted biologically by genes. Anthropologists' work shows the enormous malleability of humans and the extreme importance of cultural conditioning in producing psychosexual differences. Most social scientists agree that any behavior or personality differences between the two sexes are creations of the culture into which each new generation is born and then socialized.

The evidence provided by anthropology about the variations in sex roles in different cultures can be augmented by examining how sex roles have changed in our country since its founding over three hundred and seventy years ago. In this review we will focus on changes in women's roles, because it is their roles, not men's, that are changing now and these changes are having a tremendous impact on the family.

Sex Roles in American Society

In their attempts to gain greater equality, many women today are looking back at the way they have formerly participated in our culture. In doing so, Janice Law Trecker noted the sexism inherent in the basic motivations of the men who first settled our country: "Early in our history, enterprising groups of English gentlemen attempted to found all male colonies. The attempts were failures, but the idea of a society without women appears to have held extraordinary appeal for the descendants of the early colonists."[4] These colonizers felt women to be inferior to men, an assumption that had been codified into British common law. Women's physical and intellectual inferiority to men was taken for granted by early settlers. They felt that God had created a superior being, man, and an inferior one, woman.

Even those settlers who felt women were needed for a colony to succeed did not give them much credit. Women were not to be trusted to manage family finances and were thought incapable of any real mental activity. Emily Hahn summarizes the attitude of these men: "The delicate little brain of a woman, if over taxed, was likely to give way entirely. Such was the fate of Mistress Anne Hopkins of Connecticut who spent too much time reading and writing. As a result, said Governor John Winthrop in his *History of New England*, she went insane."[5]

By 1776, when the Declaration of Independence was signed, there had been much debate in the colonies over the education of girls. Little by little men came to agree that girls, too, should have some education outside the home. For the well to do, girls were taught in finishing schools. However, until almost 1830, there was little real interest in educating any women to use their intellectual capacity, and until the Civil War very few women were as well educated as the average man. The desire to improve women's standing centered on the push for more education, which has a familiar ring today. In 1833 Oberlin became the first American college to admit women, but this didn't mark a dramatic shift in attitude. The college was meant to educate women to be good wives and mothers. The writing of the 1830s indicates that there was little real challenge to the idea that women were primarily interested in home and family, leaving men to carry out the duties and responsibilities outside the home.

During the 1840s another development had an impact on the beginning of a full-scale women's rights movement. The movement for the abolition of slavery was growing and some women took the lead in this fight. However, participating in the same groups with male abolitionists was impossible, for women were barred from membership in some of the leading organizations. Women were forced to organize their own abolitionist groups, but their experience with organizing benefited them greatly. Perhaps the most important event concerning the rights of women to happen in pre-Civil War America occurred in 1848 at Seneca Falls, New York, where a meeting led by Elizabeth Cady Stanton and Lucretia Mott represented the first serious attempt by women to question their place in society. This meeting had a tremendous impact by focusing on the civil rights denied women and on the psychological oppression of women by men. It brought together for the first time about three hundred women who

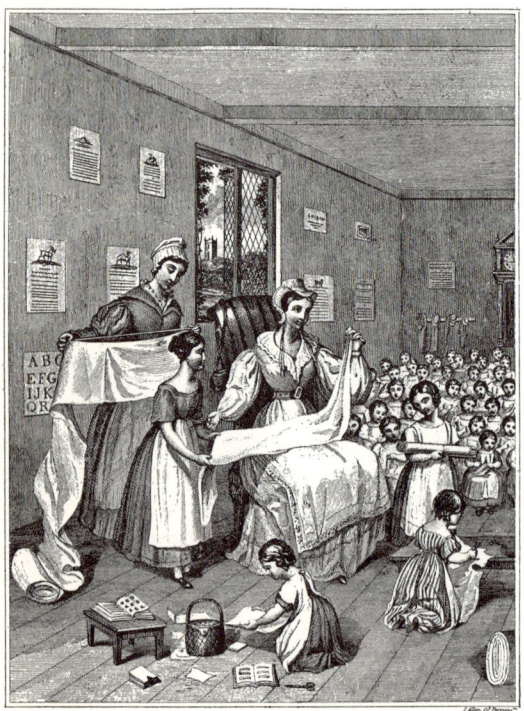

Girls were schooled to be ladies in the 1840s, and sewing was obviously an essential skill to be mastered. Ironically, education can be both a means for perpetuating existing sex roles and a tool for changing them.

suddenly realized they were not alone in their central concerns.

In changing the Constitution after the Civil War, the Thirteenth Amendment was passed abolishing slavery. The Fourteenth Amendment, outlining the rights, privileges, and responsibilities of the newly freed slaves, used the word male in the Constitution for the first time. The Fifteenth Amendment forbid the denial of the right to vote by race. But to the great disappointment of the women who had worked for abolition, no amendment gave women the right to vote. Laws prohibiting women from holding property, forbidding them to sue in court, and giving husbands sovereign rights over his wife and children all were changed. Opportunity for education also increased, as many women's colleges, like Smith, Vassar, and Wellesley, were founded in the 1860s and 1870s. But women were still denied rights. The politicians deserted the women who had been instrumental in winning freedom for blacks. Again and again, women were told "this is to be the Negro's hour," that they would have to wait for suffrage.

Women organized themselves into the National Women's Suffrage Association (NAWSA) to get the vote, seeing the lack of *suffrage* as the symbol of their oppression. In 1875 women got the Supreme Court to hear a case on the constitutionality of their exclusion from voting. The women argued that the Fourteenth Amendment gave the right to vote to all citizens, including women, but the Court turned them down and said it was constitutionally permissible to limit the right to vote only to men. A woman's suffrage amendment was introduced into every session of Congress from 1878 on, and women also fought for the vote in the states, but progress wasn't rapid, even during the early 1900s. In 1920, however, after parades were organized and mass demonstrations conducted (with women being arrested and thrown in jail for their protests), the amendment giving women the right to vote was finally ratified.

As the battle for the vote was being fought, women began to enter fields previously denied to them. This movement was accelerated after suffrage. They went to school, got an education, and became active in professions. In 1930 more women got Ph.D. degrees than ever before. After World War I, in addition to greater educational and occupational opportunities, emancipation took other forms. Greater freedom for women produced the "flapper" image of the 1920s; women's sexuality, suppressed under long skirts and stiff corsets for generations, came out into the open. The average woman was now freer to do things done only by prostitutes in the past — to smoke, wear lipstick, show her legs in public, and travel around unchaperoned.

World War II brought about an enormous change in women's roles. Women poured into the defense plants where they became mechanics, lathe operators, and inspectors, all jobs held formerly only by men. "Rosie the Riveter," the pretty girl working at an important man's job, was part of the wartime propaganda used to stimulate production. The stigma of women working in unfeminine jobs was quickly and effectively erased — but its effect was hardly long lasting. When the men returned from the war, women left the plants to return home and begin families. In fact, many were turned out from jobs they had held for years in order to make room for returning male veterans.

The divorce rate in 1946 hit a peak as many marriages made during the war fell apart. Returning GIs remarried, moved to the suburbs, and started raising families.

The baby boom began in 1946 and continued until about 1961, when the birthrate finally began to taper off. During these fifteen years, women lost much of the ground gained during the 1940s. They were again defined by the traditional roles of wife and mother, something many women (although by no means all) eagerly embraced after their stint in the war plants. But by the early 1960s grumblings were being heard from some discontented housewives, who found suburban life empty, boring, and meaningless. In 1963, Betty Friedan published *The Feminine Mystique,* articulating the way many modern women felt and analyzing their exploitation in a male-dominated society. The latest round in a three-hundred-year struggle for equality had begun; the modern feminist movement was born.

The mass media soon jumped on this attempt, calling it "women's lib" and showing women burning their bras and marching around protesting everything from housework (called "shitwork" by the protesters) to the Miss America pageant. The movement was subtly ridiculed by the mass media, which was to be expected from the male-dominated news organizations. As data show, institutionalized discrimination kept women out of publishing, newspaper work, and radio and television journalism. It is not hard to understand why women's rights activists were labeled and mocked: the reaction to feminism was a defensive maneuver by an industry long guilty of the very discrimination being decried.

Conditions are somewhat better now: the media's treatment of women's claims is more favorable, as is the attitude of society as a whole. Nevertheless, the progress made is not complete. Symbolizing the frustration of those advocating equality is the failure of the nation to ratify the Equal Rights Amendment (ERA) to the Constitution, which would prohibit sex discrimination just as the Fourteenth Amendment prohibited racial discrimination. The amendment was passed by the Senate in October 1971 and was quickly ratified by many states, but the approval of three more states has been needed and missing since 1975. Despite the efforts of women fighting for its passage, no end to the stall seems in sight.

Summary

Cross-cultural evidence on the formation of gender identity and the changes in women's role in the United States both help us understand why many features of the American family are now seen as problematic. This information also shows why definitions of the problem differ, even if the evidence for its existence is the same. The definition depends on the social characteristics of the person doing the defining. Men bring a different perspective than women and older people make different comparisons than younger people. As with all problems, those confronting the family are based on value conflicts, changing norms, and differences in definitions by a variety of groups. Still, we can analyze a few issues that many agree are the most problematic. It is to these issues that we now turn our attention.

OBJECTIVE DIMENSIONS OF THE PROBLEM

We have stressed changing female sex roles and the feminist movement because they are having an enormous impact on the family. Any social institution involves people's expectations about how things should be done and how they and others should behave.

Over the past decade, women's expectations about themselves, their place in society, and their role in marriage have changed. These changes are the result of changes in society: they stem from rising education levels of women, their greater participation in the work force, the general concern for human rights, the liberation of female sexuality (for more on this factor see Chapter 9), and the greater availability of birth control.

Sociologists recognize that access to resources in one institution strengthens a person's position in another. This is true for women now. With more power as a result of working and education and more control over their reproductive lives, women can back up their claims for greater equality in the family. These changes in society have contributed to changes in the frequency of marriage and divorce and in the birthrate.

Two other problems connected with the family are not as clearly related to these trends. The number of illegitimate children being born is growing, seemingly taking away the family's primary function of providing for and socializing society's new members. Also, great concern is felt over the abuse of spouses and children, reflecting perhaps the failure of the family to function properly. While these two problems cannot be traced to women's changing position, they certainly constitute grave problems facing the American family.

Education and Sex Roles

Though males and females differ biologically at birth, in potential for social behavior they do not. People formerly believed that sex differences in behavior are based on biology, but research has shown this belief to be of dubious validity. But if biology is not the reason, what is? As shown by our discussion of Margaret Mead's work, current research stresses cultural conditioning as the cause. Children are socialized by social institutions, and in the process they learn what sex roles they are allowed or required to play. As children develop language they develop ideas about themselves, including their gender identity. This, the basic meaning of being masculine or feminine, is defined by their society.

In any society, learned sex-role definitions and expectations result in different self-images for men and women. Mirra Komarovsky has made insightful additions to our understanding of how *social learning* accomplishes this differentiation. She reviews how young boys and girls are socialized:

1. Pressures are exerted on girls to select girl's toys and to be more restrained, sedentary, quiet and neat in their play than their brothers or boys in the neighborhood.
2. Social pressure is exerted upon girls to be gentler and more emotionally dependent than boys.
3. They are given fewer opportunities for independent action and those came later than was the case for their brothers.
4. Daughters of the family are held to a more exacting code of filial and kinship obligations.
5. The risks of the traditional upbringing reside in the failure to develop in the girl independence, inner resources, and that degree of self-assertion which life will demand of her.[6]

Over the past decade, the feminist movement has rejected these stereotypes and exposed women to alternative ways of thinking about their role in American society. Feminist ideas have not affected all segments of the population equally, but have had their greatest impact on well-educated, middle-class

TABLE 3.1 Educational Level of White Females 25 Years and Older, 1960–1976

	High School	1–3 Years College	4 Years College or More
1960	29.2%	9.5%	6.0%
1970	39.0	10.1	8.6
1976	41.2	12.8	11.6

Source: Bureau of the Census, *Statistical Abstract of the United States, 1977* (Washington, D.C.: U.S. Government Printing Office, 1977), p. 136.

and upper-middle-class women. As Table 3.1 clearly shows, the educational level of women has been rising since 1960, with the percentage of women completing college almost doubling. It has become increasingly hard for these educated women to accept the traditional norms that force women to be dependent, passive, and overemotional while men alone possess such valued attributes as independence, ambition, self-assertiveness and creativity.

In addition to their efforts to end economic and legal discrimination, feminists have tried to change attitudes toward women. Knowing that sex roles are learned in childhood, they have sought to solve the problem at the source by changing socialization. As a result, a growing area of concern is the presentation of men and women in school books. Accused of being particularly *sexist* (portraying women unfavorably) are elementary reading books, in which

> Women are portrayed almost exclusively as housewives doing household chores. . . . Mothers wear aprons most of the time, they sport funny hats, they go shopping, and they tend to children, but they NEVER WORK. (At a time when more than one-half of all women, including mothers, are working.) Most books

seen have stories in which an old or young female who has done some foolishness is rescued by a male (young or old) or a bunch of males.[7]

History books and other reading materials have also been criticized by women's groups because they portray women unfavorably. Many books have been accused of ignoring the contributions of women, making them invisible in history, the arts, and other areas. Women's groups argue that including women in the books will help overcome some of the sex-role stereotypes learned by young children. In response to the concern over sex-role stereotyping many publishers are revising their texts to make them less objectionable.

Women in the Labor Force

Although increases in education have helped launch an ideological attack on sex-role stereotypes, more important changes are the result of the increase in the number of women working, because this change affects all classes in society. Among the many changes in the roles women are playing in society, none is more important than their greater involvement in the labor force. Approximately 35 million women sixteen years of age and older were employed in the United States in 1977, with 26 million working full time and 9 million working part time. They comprise about one-third of all full-time workers and about two-thirds of those who work part time.[8] Almost two-thirds (65 percent) hold white-collar jobs, compared to only about 42 percent of the employed males. Of the almost 83 million American women sixteen and older, 48.5 percent are considered to be in the labor force while 51.5 percent are not. Of those not in the labor force, about 80 percent are housewives and the rest would be considered unemployed. In 1977 about 3 million more women were employed outside the home than were housewives. These figures show a dramatic rise in the number of working women, which more than doubled between 1947 and 1977, increasing from 32 percent in 1947 to the 48.5 percent noted above.[9]

A pattern emerges when the work patterns of white male and female workers are compared by age. Female participation in the labor force starts off at about 45 percent for sixteen to seventeen year olds, increases to two-thirds for twenty to twenty-four year olds, and drops to about 60 percent for twenty-five to forty-four year olds. It continues to decline for women over forty-five, reaching only one-third for those sixty to sixty-four. White male employment rates start off higher and consistently run higher. For twenty-five- to fifty-four-year-old males the participation rate is 95 percent, and about fifty-five it is 75 percent until age sixty-five.[10] Women's work patterns are shaped by and tied to family responsibilities. Women tend to drop in and out of the labor force, depending on the demands made on them by their husbands and children. This leaves them open to economic exploitation more than men's work patterns do.

Numerous studies have shown that women who work do so to ensure that the family obtains necessities, rather than to provide luxuries. Most women work either to supplement a low wage earned by the male head of the household or as the sole support of themselves and their families. As Tristen Amundsen noted in 1971:

> We find that 7.8 million of the married working women have husbands who earn less than $5000 yearly and over half of these have children under the age of 18 at home. Work for them is a compelling necessity. For the single female workers, 6.5 million in all, it is almost without exception the need for money that drives them into the job market.[11]

In addition to women who must work to supplement male income, almost 6 million female workers are divorced, separated, or widowed and must work not only to support themselves but also to provide for their families. A large number of working women (2.5 million) have total incomes below the government's established poverty level, yet these women have an average of two children dependent on them for all support. Almost two-thirds of the women who work do so out of financial necessity. Of the one-third remaining, the majority have husbands with incomes below what the government defines as comfortable. Clearly it is only a few women who work primarily for self-gratification or to obtain luxuries. The vast majority work to lift themselves and their families out of poverty; without their efforts the total number of poor people would be two or three times what it is now.

Contraception and Abortion

Another social change that has had an effect on women, and thus on the family, is the greater availability of birth control. Surprisingly, as recently as the mid-1960s, it was still illegal to sell contraceptive devices without a prescription in some states. Fifteen years later contraception is no longer a highly emotional issue. A 1976 survey of women between eighteen and twenty-four found 75 percent reporting that they expected to have two children or less; only about 45 percent expected to have two children or less in 1967.[12] Acting on that desire, more women than ever are practicing contraception. More importantly, the less effective forms of birth control such as condoms are being used less frequently; and the more effective forms such as the pill and intrauterine devices (IUDs) are being used by an increasing number of women.[13] For example, in 1965 about 65 percent of white married women used some form of contraception. By 1973 (the year the latest data was gathered), the pill was being used by about 35 percent of all white married women, and by about 65 percent of white married women between fifteen and twenty-four. These findings contrast the results from 1965, when only about 24 percent of all white married women used the pill, and only about 51 percent of those between eighteen and twenty-four did.

In addition to contraception, abortion is now being used by an increasing number of women to avoid bearing children they do not want. Abortion is part of a complex set of legal, social, and moral issues that have been marked by much change in the past ten years. The first antiabortion laws were passed in 1828, with the proclaimed intent of protecting the lives of both mother and child. The argument made sense. At the time all operations were hazardous because they were so unsanitary. It was only around the mid-1800s that doctors began washing their hands before an operation, and many did so only reluctantly. Once proper sanitary measures were adopted legal abortions presumably would have been safer, if they had been allowed.

Up until 1970, however, abortions were illegal. In many states it was only possible to get an abortion in cases of rape or incest or if the mother's life was in danger because of the physical or psychological complications of having a child. This led many women who could afford it to two psychiatrists to verify that they might commit suicide if an abortion were not granted. Those who could not afford to sidestep the law in this way were forced to have an unwanted child or have an illegal abortion, a dangerous business. Before abortions were made legal in New York in 1970, an estimated 10,000 women died from abortion-related causes every year. The exact figure is hard to determine with any accuracy for, as with all deviant behaviors, the incidence is underreported because of the social and legal stigma involved. It has been estimated that about one out of every hundred women who got an illegal abortion died as the result of it. These illegal abortions punished the lower classes. Of these abortion-related deaths, about 80 percent of those reported in New York City were either black or Puerto Rican women. The abortion death rate was about eight times greater for black women than for whites.

In 1970 after much turmoil and controversy, New York state passed a law legalizing abortion. This occurred after much protest, including a suit brought by about 300 women against the New York Attorney General to discourage him from further enforcement of the abortion statutes. These women, led by Florynce Kennedy, a black woman lawyer, started the "Great Abortion Suit" and used as their motto "Women of the world unite, you have nothing to lose but your coat-hangers!"[14] After much testimony, and many delays and appeals, these women won their case in 1970. Soon afterward the state legislature legalized abortion, with other states following.

The actual number of abortions performed each year has not been accurately tabulated until very recently because up to 1970 the vast majority were performed illegally. According to the latest data available, in 1975 over 1 million legal abortions were per-

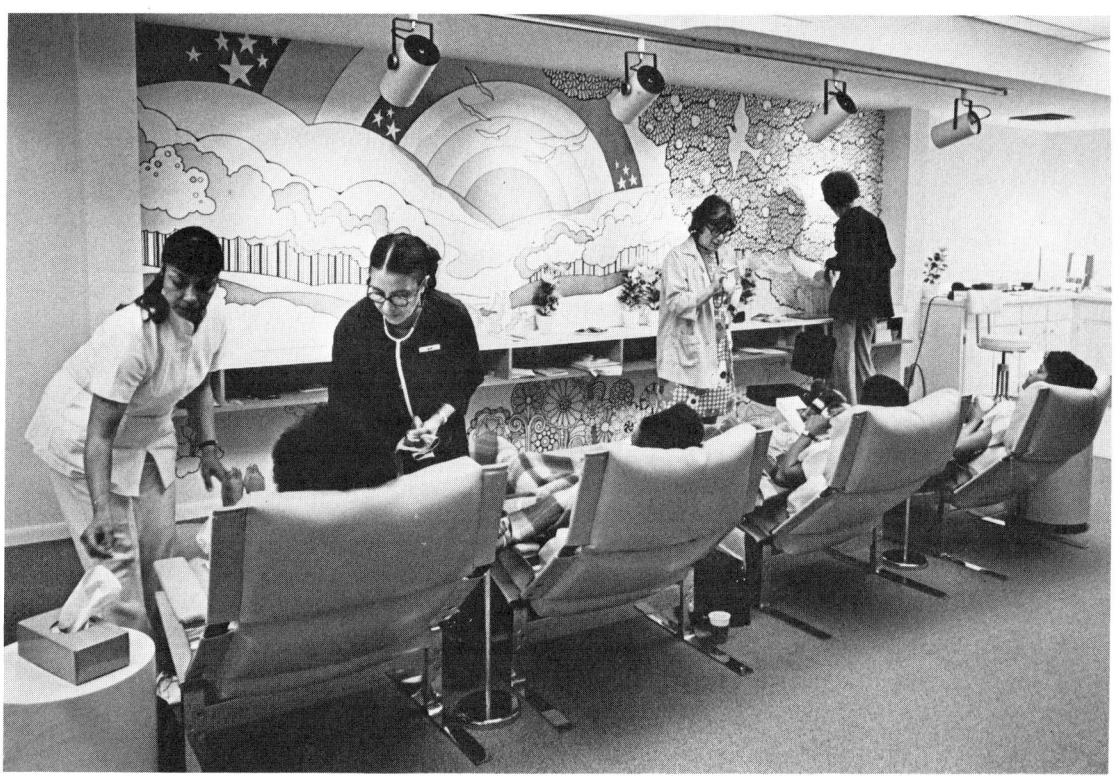

Legalizing abortion has not eliminated the psychological and social complications involved in terminating a pregnancy. Therefore, many abortion clinics, like the one shown here, include intensive counseling as part of their service.

formed in the United States. New York and California led the rest, and accounted for about one-third of all abortions performed in the country. In 1975, 331 abortions were done per 1,000 live births; in New York City there were 1,138 abortions per 1,000 live births, and in Washington, D.C., 1,115 abortions per 1,000 live births. Abortions are occurring at an increasing rate and the total number is rising rapidly, going from 742,500 in 1973 to 1,034,000 in 1975. The group that has the most abortions are unmarried women, who accounted for between 60 percent of all abortions in Mississippi to almost 81 percent of those done in Maryland.[15]

Today most state laws follow the guidelines established by New York, although requirements do vary. But some provisions, like the one requiring physicians to perform abortions, are being challenged by women's rights groups. These groups feel that this requirement is unnecessary, pointing out that the training of midwives to be used in child delivery is proceeding rapidly in some cities and that abortion is a much simpler procedure than childbirth. European practice shows that expensive hospital beds need not be tied up for abortions, yet mandatory hospitalization too was written into many state laws. And the question of whether abortions should be permitted later than the first trimester (12 weeks) is still hotly debated inside and outside the medical profession.

The issue that perhaps created the biggest stir with the women's rights groups involved the requirement that a woman obtain her husband's or parent's permission before getting an abortion. The state laws involving consent have been declared unconstitutional, but the issue raised by the consent question involved reexamining the roles women should be expected to play in society. As the feminist Lucinda Cisler states:

> Since her basic function has been to bear children whatever "extra" achievements the culture and the economy have allowed her to pursue, anything that alters social control over her reproductive capacities is deeply and fundamentally threatening to societal and individual psyches; different reproductive roles are the basic dichotomy in humankind and have been used to rationalize all the others. Without the full capacity to limit her own reproduction a woman's other freedoms are tantalizing mockeries that cannot be exercised.[16]

Modern feminists see a woman's right to decide for herself if she will bear a child as the cornerstone of all other rights. The conflict over who will have the power to say whether a woman may have an abortion strikes at the heart of the issue of sexual equality. It is for this reason that abortion, the most commonly used birth control method in much of the rest of the world, has generated the controversy it has in recent years.

Marriage Rates

It is clear that these changes outside the family have had a major impact on marriage. The feminist movement, the growing number of working women, and the greater availability of birth control have affected women's decisions to marry or remain single, the expectations they bring to marriage, and whether they decide to have children or not.

As a result of these changes the percentage of married persons in the United States has been steadily declining during the past twenty years. In 1955, 76 percent of all males eighteen years of age and older were married, and 72 percent of all females in this age group were. By 1976, this had declined to 72 percent for males and to 66 percent for females.[17] Since 1959 the percentage of persons ever married has declined each year, with the greatest decline coming among women younger than twenty-five years and those older than sixty-five. But this decline is only about 0.3 percent a year; it hardly looks like people are abandoning marriage in wholesale numbers, as some alarmists would have us believe.

While the percentage of people who will ever marry has decreased a little, a large change has occurred in the number of people living together as unmarried couples, or *cohabitation*. In 1977 almost 2 million Americans were cohabiting, an increase of 83 percent in seven years.[18] Largely because of this, the median age of first marriage increased from 1975 to 1976 by more than one full year for males, to 23.8 years, and by almost one-half year for females, to 21.3 years.[19] The age composition of couples cohabiting has also changed, with the greatest increase among young people where the man is under twenty-five. Nevertheless, while cohabiting is on the increase, only 7.4 percent of all couples living together are unmarried; this hardly indicates a major revolution in living arrangements. There does seem to be a change in how cohabitation is viewed. In a 1977 CBS News poll, 82 percent of the men between eighteen and twenty-nine and 69

In the 1950s, observers of this scene could reasonably assume that newlyweds were moving into their first apartment. Today, with the increasing numbers of cohabitors and the growing acceptance of cohabitation, that assumption is hardly automatic.

percent of the women said cohabitation was acceptable. And from recent studies it appears that about 40 percent of the couples living together will eventually marry each other. Rates of cohabitation also have been found to be about three times higher among the divorced than among those persons who have never married.

It appears possible to make several conclusions. While there has been a dramatic increase in cohabitation, most young people remain conventional in their ideas about heterosexual relationships. By the time people reach thirty to thirty-four years old, over 90 percent of the females and almost 90 percent of the males are married. This represents virtually no change since 1960. The greatest changes have occurred in the eighteen to twenty-nine age group; once age thirty is reached, people settle down into more traditional patterns. There is a danger in saying this: it may not be the case when the current group of teenagers reach thirty and living together seems to be more than a fad. With its high level of acceptance, cohabitation will probably increase in the future.

Divorce Rates

With the changing role of women, society is shifting away from the idea that a wife is under the rule of her husband. Demands for equality based on the changes outlined above are reflected in the divorce rate, which has been rising rapidly. In 1976 the United States led the rest of the world with a *divorce rate* of five per thousand population, a threefold increase in the rate during the past one hundred years. The divorce rate hit its peak in 1946, dropped off rapidly to a low point in the mid-1950s, and has been on the rise in each successive year.

But this crude divorce rate is misleadingly small; a more significant statistic is the number of divorces per marriage. In 1976 Paul Glick and Arthur Norton, demographers with the Census Bureau, found two divorces for every five marriages in the United States. They arrived at their numbers in this way:

1. of each 100 first marriages, 38 will end in divorce
2. of the 38 pairs of divorcees, three-fourths, or 29, will remarry
3. of the 29 new marriages (for both men and women), 44 percent, or 13, will become redivorced

4. of the 100 men and 100 women who first married, there will be 38 plus 13, or 51, divorces, and 100 plus 29, or 129, marriages and remarriages
5. 51 divorces after 129 marriages means that at current rates 40 percent of all marriages will end in divorce[20]

While the divorce rate is going up, the rate varies for different groups. Social factors like age at marriage, race, and educational level make major differences in the probability of any particular person being divorced. At present rates, 30 percent of the marriages of women college graduates will end in divorce. Women now in their late twenties who were married between ages fourteen and seventeen have a 72 percent probability of divorcing. Among blacks the rate for both sexes age eighteen and older is about 25 percent higher than for whites, reflecting the fact that blacks tend to marry younger and have a lower average education than do whites.[21]

If divorce is seen as a problem, certainly more people view it as problematic if children are involved. In 1975 an average of about one child was involved in every divorce, but as Figure 3.1 shows, this is much lower than it was in 1965. This decline is partly a product of the decreasing birthrate in general and partly a result of changing views on illegitimacy. In the past a couple usually got married when the woman became pregnant, but the marriage often ended in divorce. Now the marriage is less likely to occur, so the child won't be involved in a divorce. Even with the decline, in 1976 only two-thirds of all children under age eighteen were living with both natural parents. For blacks the figure was only 45 percent. And since 1960 the proportion of children under eighteen who are living only with their mother has doubled. Based on the work of Glick and Norton, it looks as if almost half of all children born in 1977 will end up spending some time in a one-parent family before they reach eighteen.[22]

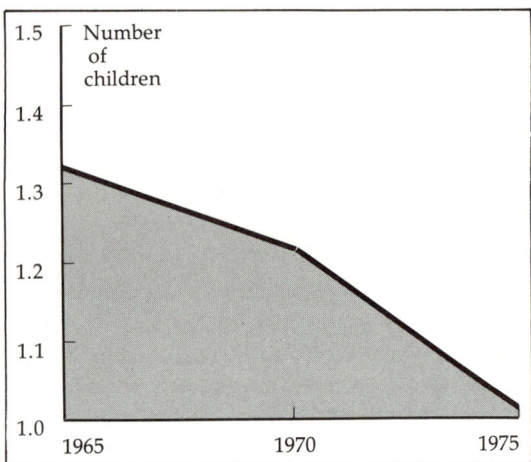

FIGURE 3.1 Children Involved Per Divorce, 1965–1975

Source: Bureau of the Census, *Statistical Abstract of the United States, 1977* (Washington, D.C.: U.S. Government Printing Office, 1977), p. 74.

Although divorce is on the rise, is there really as much cause for alarm as some observers think? Others think not. As John Scanzoni noted: "Clearly if better than 98 percent of the married women (and men) do not seek divorces in any given year, there seems little indication of mass dissatisfaction with marriage or *wholesale rejection* of it as a viable institution."[23] Increased personal freedom, the feminist movement, the decline in the influence of religion, and general liberalizing of attitudes are all reasons for the increased divorce rate. We would emphasize that changes in women's opportunities in society and in the availability of divorce are also responsible.

For example, changing opportunities in the employment of divorced or separated women have contributed to the increase. Women no longer need to depend on men for economic support. This is quite a change over earlier periods, such as the early 1800s:

> When romance went sour or when marriage and motherhood were threatened by a husband's drinking, open infidelity, gambling or some other form of improvidence, women who depended completely on men began to think about their position and wonder if independence might not be better. Thinking was as far as most of them got.[24]

Now women are able to get jobs and support themselves; knowing this makes divorce a more realistic alternative for them. Another change regards the question of children. In years past people endured marriages that were unsatisfactory, often rationalizing their decision on being necessary for the good of the children. This is seen as less of a problem now, first because of the decline in the birthrate, second because people are now more likely to view an acrimonious marriage as more harmful to a child than a divorce.

Recent changes in divorce laws have also altered the nature of divorce. In the past, women were awarded alimony because of their assumed inability to support themselves. Alimony rights were considered an extension of the husband's duty to support his wife, a duty he undertook at the time of the marriage. The issue of alimony is closely related to the question of the allowable grounds for divorce, and there have been important changes in this area as well. In the past divorce was granted only to one spouse because of the misbehavior of the other. Some states still reflect this earlier view of the purpose of alimony as punishment of the male for misconduct in the marriage. But in many states now the courts are taking a different view of divorce and are conducting *no-fault divorces,* in which they do not attempt to pin the blame on either partner. However, if the divorce is contested by one partner or if children are involved, the courts may still make a judgment of guilt, even if that judgment is not officially recorded.

More rights and increased opportunities for women have altered their traditional rights in divorce. Divorce now carries less stigma for either party and reflects a greater equality for the two sexes before the law. Greater equality does not cause people to divorce each other, but these changes do make obtaining a divorce easier for men and women.

Birthrates

The family has as one of its main purposes the reproduction of the population. Many people are disturbed that it seems to be performing this function less well than before. In the past fifteen years, the crude birthrate — the number of births per thousand population — has fallen by almost 25 percent (see Figure 3.2).

Again, this crude rate may not indicate the magnitude of the change. More revealing is the annual fertility rate of women: the number of children born per thousand women. For women eighteen to twenty-four years old, the rate of 3.6 in 1960 had dropped by 1975 to only 1.7, a decrease of more than 50 percent. The Bureau of the Census indicates that young women are expecting to have fewer children and are doing so. In 1976 the average number of births expected of married women eighteen to twenty-four years old was 2.1; in 1960 it had been over 3.0.[25] This change represents a drastic de-

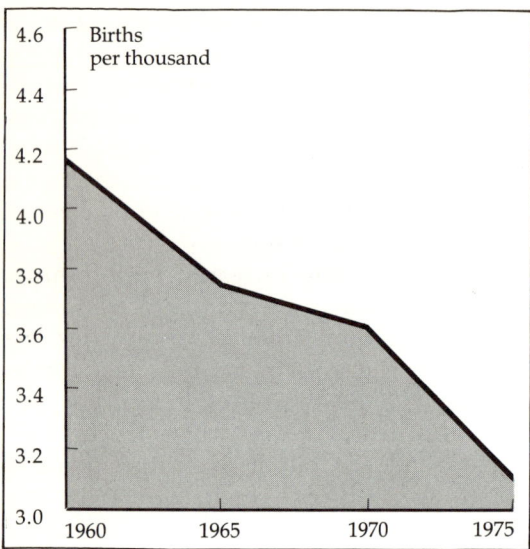

FIGURE 3.2 Live Births in the United States, 1960–1975

Source: Bureau of the Census, *Statistical Abstract of the United States, 1977* (Washington, D.C.: U.S. Government Printing Office, 1977), p. 74.

crease over past rates. In 1880, for example, the average woman expected to have seven children during her lifetime. As a result of this decline, the birthrate is now at its lowest point in the nation's history.

Demographers are always skeptical about whether or not to expect a new baby boom, but many feel that low fertility rates will be a long-term trend. Several factors account for these low rates. First, as we pointed out earlier, women now have effective means to prevent unwanted births because of better contraception and widely available abortion. Secondly, the greater educational attainments of women and their greater participation in the work force have changed their expectations.

Fertility Among Single Women: The Problem of Illegitimacy

Even though more women who do not want children are using contraceptives and resorting to abortions, a contradictory trend is also apparent. More children are being born to unmarried women. It used to be that reproduction was limited to the family and severe penalties were incurred for illegitimate births, but today more and more children are being born to unmarried women and the stigma is largely disappearing. In 1950, about 4 percent of all live births were to unmarried women; in 1975 about 14 percent were. Particularly alarming to many observers of this trend is the growing number of teenage pregnancies. In 1950, 22 percent of all these births occurred to women under nineteen years of age; in 1975 about 41 percent did.

Studies indicate that about 1 million teenagers are becoming pregnant per year, and approximately 600,000 of these will give birth to their babies. Clearly, not all of these young girls are unmarried at the time they give birth, but surveys show that 75 percent of the pregnancies were unwanted. Nevertheless, about 90 percent of the teenage mothers end up keeping their babies, with many of them eventually going on welfare because they cannot support themselves and their children.[26]

Studies have shown that social class and education correlate with whether births are wanted or not. In a study done in 1973, married and unmarried black and white mothers were compared to see what percentage of total births were unwanted. About two-and-a-half times as many black mothers, who had lower socioeconomic status, had unwanted children (28 percent) as did white mothers

(11 percent). And as Table 3.2 shows, the higher the educational level the smaller the percentage of unwanted children. As can be seen from this table, women who have never gone to high school bear on the average 1.3 more children than do women who have four years of college or more. And women with the least education bear about three-and-a-half times as many unwanted children as do those with the most. While birthrates of wanted children also decrease with education, it is interesting to note that after high school the number of unwanted children drops off significantly. In bearing unwanted children, the big split is between women who graduate from high school and those who do not. This split isn't surprising, though: many teenage pregnancies involve the mother dropping out of high school before graduation.

Violence in the Family

Another problem now confronts the family, which is considerably harder to study and the causes of which are more difficult to determine. In recent years there seems to be a great upsurge in the amount of spouse and child abuse reported in the popular press. While it could be that the actual incidence of such abuse is increasing, we cannot be certain. It seems that the increased coverage does not reflect a real rise in incidence, but is the product of a greater concern for the problem, a greater willingness to talk about the problem in public, and a greater effort being made to deal with it. In many cities these problems are now being dealt with in new ways by the police, whereas once these incidents remained hidden from view.

Stories abound in daily papers detailing how wives were beaten by their husbands for twenty years or how parents put their children in boiling water to punish them. But these accounts as evidence about trends or even the actual magnitude of the problem are seriously open to question. In many cases, the law has just recently been changed to allow the police and family service agencies to intervene. Previously, parents were more or less free to do anything to their children short of actually killing them. And until recently a wife had to swear out a warrant against her husband before the police could act in any capacity except to call an ambu-

TABLE 3.2 Percentage Unwanted Children and Total Births per Mother by Education, 1973

Education	Unwanted Births	Total Births	Unwanted Births	Total minus Unwanted
Less than high school	16.5%	3.48	.57	2.91
1–3 years high school	17.9	2.96	.53	2.43
4 years high school	11.1	2.46	.27	2.19
1–3 years college	9.7	2.38	.23	2.15
4 years college and over	7.4	2.18	.16	2.02

Source: Bureau of the Census, *Statistical Abstract of the United States, 1977* (Washington, D.C.: U.S. Government Printing Office, 1977), p. 62.

lance. Changes in city and state laws have brought the problem of abuse out into the open, but we have no way of knowing if the problem is getting worse or is about the same. In fact, some observers feel the problem may be diminishing, arguing that with liberalized divorce laws women are freer to leave an intolerable home situation.

Even with the inadequacy of the available data, a few things can be noted about family violence. The vast majority of cases of spouse abuse involve the husband beating the wife; and although alcohol does not cause family violence, it is regularly associated with it. It was formerly thought that only lower-class people engaged in spouse and child abuse, but present data show that while the problem still seems to be concentrated among working-class families, it is also prevalent in the middle and upper-middle classes. However, the middle and upper-middle classes are better able to keep their deviance out of the public eye because of the way police, judges, and the court system treat them.

Recent legal changes giving children some rights in the family are beginning to have an effect on child abuse, protecting children from the almost unlimited power parents formerly enjoyed. For some years, animals were better protected from abuse than children. In 1871 a child was being abused by her adoptive parents and church social workers were unable to get the courts to take any legal action against the parents. They finally appealed to the Society for the Prevention of Cruelty to Animals, on the grounds that the girl was a member of the animal kingdom and that her treatment should therefore be considered under laws against animal cruelty. The courts agreed to this, and removed the child from her parents.[27] To make such an appeal unnecessary in the future, concerned people formed the Society for the Prevention of Cruelty to Children.

Since 1871, a number of societies have been formed to protect children. Nevertheless, the issue of children's rights, especially

Little is known about the causes and the extent of child abuse in the United States despite the fact that it is one of the most appalling social problems related to the family. Looking at this battered infant, it is distressing to think that only a century ago such cruelty was not even illegal.

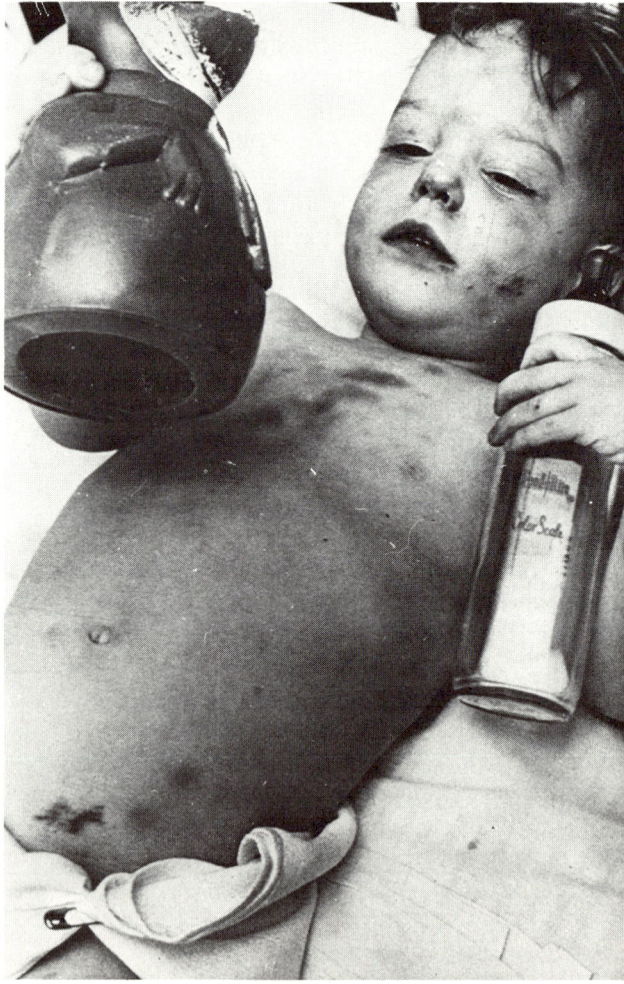

with regard to family violence directed against them, continues to this day to be sadly neglected. In 1961 the American Academy of Pediatrics conducted a program dealing with the problem of child abuse and awarded a grant for studying the problem. With the grant the American Humane Society found 662 cases in a single year; 27 percent of these cases involved fatalities and many more of the abused children suffered permanent brain damage.[28]

"Spare the rod and spoil the child" has long been central to the beliefs of many parents. Unfortunately, some parents are unable to distinguish discipline from violence. Like all other problems, violence in the family is rooted in the structures of society where power and access to resources are differently distributed to certain groups. The abuse of children by their parents is no exception to this basic tenet. Child abuse occurs regularly in a large number of American families. Only in the past decade has consciousness of the problem of children's rights grown, but we still know little about child abuse. From the available data, we can say that, like spouse abuse, child abuse is not limited to any particular class. Although most studies have found it more frequently among the lower class, as with most other forms of deviant behavior, a class differential is created in large measure by how the agencies of social control choose to deal with the problem. Abuse in the middle class is underreported, in the lower class it is overreported.

It has also been determined that mothers are more frequently the child abusers than fathers. As with many other problems, a vicious circle becomes established: parents who were abused as children often become child abusers. In addition, abused children are often the product of unwanted pregnancies. In this case the parent is striking out at a concrete source of family stress — the child no one wanted.

Summary

We have just examined those areas of family life which have been undergoing rapid change within the past decade. While other factors are contributing to these changes, we stress the changing role of women in our society. In all areas women are being given greater control and power over their lives, which makes them more equal but also creates conflicts with traditional sex roles. Women's changing expectations and the widespread use of contraceptives and abortion are causing a drastic decline in the birthrate. Divorce rates are up, marriage rates are down, and more people are living together without being married. Women are getting more education and entering the job market in increasing numbers. Many writers look at these facts and conclude that a crisis is confronting the American family. What they believe the family should be like determines what they see as the essential problem, and also how they wish to solve it. It is to these attempted solutions that we turn now.

ATTEMPTS AT DEALING WITH THE PROBLEM

As with many other social problems, governments at all levels have attempted to deal with the problems facing the family. But in this area in particular, many people feel the government has intensified or even created the problems by its actions. These critics point to the laws making divorce easier to obtain, those making abortion available on demand, and those undermining traditional sex-role patterns in education and other fields. In the past quarter century, numerous laws have been passed and court rulings issued, all increasing the personal freedom available to men and women. Once this freedom was granted, people took advantage of it rather than submit to traditional ways. In no area has this been truer than in the range of issues discussed in this chapter.

Ideological Responses to the Problem

The debate continues over whether we need to increase individual freedom further or repeal some of the liberal legislation of the past decade. Best symbolizing the fury of this controversy is the question of abortion. Many people have formed "right-to-life" groups to pressure state legislatures to keep old abortion laws or repeal more liberal ones. The arguments of these antiabortion groups go back to the idea that the main purpose of sex is reproduction. A major tactic is to equate abortion with murder. These groups condemn abortion as "killing a life to be," "killing someone before he takes his first breath," "taking the life of a human being," or "depriving someone of the privilege of living." Those who support the more liberal laws see the issue as one of choice. They argue that a woman should be allowed to choose whether or not she wishes to have a child.

This argument demonstrates the importance of beliefs to social problems. Each side is using basic moral principles to justify its own position and to undermine those of the opposition. What we see is the confrontation of widely conflicting ideological viewpoints in which people believe deeply and sincerely. These viewpoints form the basis for their definition of the problem and what course of action they see as necessary to solve the problem.

The different ideological positions on the problems facing the family are all based on beliefs about how and why the sexes differ. One major school of thought reflects the position stated by Sigmund Freud that "anatomy is destiny." This theory holds that the biological differences between the sexes produce the differences found in behavior. Although much anthropological and scientific research tends to disprove biology as the determinant of behavior, many people still hold this view. And of those who do, many oppose the movement to make women equal with men in employment, sexuality, education, and other areas. To these people, establishing equality for women would require ripping the social fabric and would put the family in a deeper crisis than it now faces. Such equality would be unnatural, as Helen Lawrenson notes:

> When a woman falls madly in love with a man she *wants* to wait on him and please him and be bossed by him and make a home for him and bear his children. Anyone who says otherwise is talking rubbish. Women's Lib members who for whatever personal reasons find this idea loathsome are bucking nature.[29]

Other people wish to maintain the status quo because they think women are in a better position the way society is currently structured. They argue that any change in the role of women would mean losing advantages women now have over men. They point to the new divorce laws that no longer guarantee alimony, saying that as a result women lost their privileged position. Similarly, these people object to laws ending the almost automatic grant of custody of the children to the mother. These people back up their view with the following data:

1. Women control over 85 percent of the buying power in the country.
2. Women control almost 60 percent of the listed securities.
3. Women have title to almost three-quarters of the suburban homes.
4. Women own more than 50 percent of the money.
5. Women live, on the average, seven years longer than men.[30]

Not wishing to lose this advantageous position, many women see the women's liberation movement, abortion reform, increased rates of premarital sex, and liberal divorce laws as threats that take away advantages. They feel that any changes designed to promote equality for women will result in more exploitation, taking away still more advantages.

For virtually every point presented above, a set of counterarguments is set forth by women demanding equality. Advocates of equality often base their arguments on a different view of the origin of sex roles. These people do allow that physiological differences have an influence on behavior, but rather than saying that biology determines behavior, they stress learning as the most important influence on the development of masculine and feminine character traits in any culture. These writers make the distinction we made earlier, between the psychosexual characteristics of masculine and feminine and the biological categories of male and female. They find psychosexual development to be primarily the result of learned experiences and not derived from some basic male or female nature founded on biological differences.

Rather than perceiving the home as the place where a woman can act out her natural, biological instincts, then, many women rebel at the prospects of marriage and childrearing. There have been numerous analyses of what radical feminists call "the politics of housework," with the result that many women are disavowing any interest in cooking, cleaning, and the other menial chores associated with being a housewife. Other women declare that a successful marriage requires that these chores be shared by husband and wife. Many women want childcare centers to be provided by the state or by employers, to make it easier for mothers to achieve through the same channels available to men.

Feminists argue that since cultural conditioning determines sex roles, there is no reason not to change them to make women equal and allow them more opportunities. They also point out that over the years society has changed, and changing sex roles could benefit society as a whole, and not just women. A strong and rigid division of labor by sex may have made sense in a preindustrial society, where the male's greater physical strength made him more fit for certain tasks. But in our society, with much of the heavy physical work being done by machines, human intelligence and creativity become the most important criteria for many jobs. Society suffers from a great loss of talent by systematically excluding over half of its members from full participation in economic and political institutions.

Perhaps the most notable attempt to gain equality for women has been the Equal Rights Amendment (ERA) to the Constitution. The bill was first introduced in Congress in 1923, but it took forty-nine years for Congress to agree that "Equality of rights under the law shall not be denied or abridged by the United States or by any State on account of sex."[31] In October 1971, the House of Representatives passed the amendment 354 to 23; in March 1972, the Senate passed it 84 to 8. Hawaii was the first state to ratify the ERA, and was followed by twenty-one other states in 1972. But in the following years, only thirteen more did, leaving the amendment three states short of the thirty-eight required. The ERA cause has suffered so badly that three states have voted to rescind their earlier ratifications, although there is much legal debate over the constitutionality of such an action. In 1979, ERA supporters got an extension of three years (in addition to the normal seven years) for ratification. No other amendment has required even four years for ratification, indicating clearly the lack of consensus on this issue. Whether thirty-eight states will ever ratify this amendment, regardless of the new deadline established, remains to be seen.

A number of questions about the ERA have been raised, especially by those groups who feel that women are losing their favored place in society. ERA opponents claim that with ratification women would be eligible to be drafted and serve in combat on an equal footing with men and would lose their rights to alimony and child custody in divorce settlements. At the extreme, some anti-ERA leaders have charged that if the amendment were ratified, men and women could no longer enjoy the privacy of separate public toilets. Others oppose ERA on the grounds that it is unnecessary. They feel that women have sufficient protection under the law already.

Despite the feeling that women have sufficient protection under existing law, and despite the failure to ratify the ERA, laws increasing opportunities for women have been passed, especially in the area of education. Particularly important was Title IX of the 1968 Education Act, which forbade discrimination by sex in schooling. Common practices were declared illegal, for instance, schools can no longer stop both sexes from playing on athletic teams together, nor can they bar students from taking a course on the basis of sex (schools have prohibited girls from taking shop courses and boys from home economics courses). These new laws also prohibit different pay for male and female teachers. To enforce the law, Congress made noncompliance mean the loss of federal money.

As attempts to change the law have gathered momentum, the number of women's rights groups has also grown sharply. Probably the foremost is the National Organization for Women (NOW), formed originally by Betty Friedan and others in 1966. It is basically a civil rights organization dedicated to "bringing women into full participation in the mainstream of American society, exercising all the privileges and responsibilities thereof in truly equal partnership with men."[32] NOW, primarily composed of liberal white middle-class women, generally fights for what it wants within the system. Its successes are considerable. It has helped airline stewardesses fight against being forced into retirement when they reach age thirty-five or get married and it has succeeded in persuading newspapers to stop segregating jobs into male and female categories in their want ads. Changes in the abortion laws and sex discrimination in education have also been two of their more successful campaigns.

Iatrogenic Effects

In Chapter 1, when we outlined how a condition is defined as a social problem we mentioned that there must be efforts to solve the problem. We also pointed out that those attempted solutions often introduced new problems, just as medicine taken to cure an illness in one part of the body can harm another part of the body. These bad side effects — called iatrogenic effects — are found to result from actions taken to create equality and free people from traditional sex roles. For example, many groups have complained that the family is undercut by the availability of contraception and the right to abortion. Further, many women feel that they were the losers when sentencing laws were changed. Some states had provided unequal sentences for the same crime, depending on whether it was committed by a man or a woman. This practice has been overturned as unconstitutional and now both sexes face equal sentences. Changes in the law cut two ways and may have positive and negative consequences depending on one's point of view.

For another example of how change is a double-edged sword, let us look at day care. Depending on one's perspective, day-care centers are an asset or a liability. Those that favor day-care centers see them as a way of helping working women meet their job and family responsibilities. Those who oppose them claim that these facilities do not provide the affection and individual attention young children need. Opponents also fear that increasing the availability of day-care centers will entice more women to use them, thus increasing the number of women in the labor force and further weakening the traditional family structures. With increasing government aid to these facilities, many opponents see the crisis facing the family worsening.

Some people argue that changes in sex roles will have other negative effects. These people point out that the rate of population increase has been reduced so much that the population is no longer reproducing itself. Some people believe that our capitalist economy requires constant population growth to remain viable; they fear that a long-term population decrease will create serious problems. The declining birthrate has already created economic problems in the baby-food industry and in the elementary schools; these people anticipate further dislocations. Others are afraid that with more people living longer, the social security system could go bankrupt unless more young people enter the labor force. According to this argument, the young are needed in increasing, not decreasing, numbers.

As women become more assertive of their rights, some people think they jeopardize males' identity to the point of fostering male insecurity. The frailty of man's identity has long been ridiculed by many feminists, usually with good reason. But in comparing unmarried men with unmarried women, a number of features stand out. Only about half as many single men hold professional jobs as do single women, and single men are about eight times as likely to demonstrate neurotic symptoms as single women. They are also about 60 percent more likely than women to suffer from various psychological disorders (including depression) and twenty times more likely to become inmates in prisons or mental institutions than married men. While these statistics do not prove the frailty of the male identity, they suggest that family life may be more important to men than it is to women. Certainly examining the serious problems men have in exerting their masculinity in modern society must be part of understanding the dilemmas inherent in changing something as basic as one's sexual identity.

PROSPECTS FOR SOLVING THE PROBLEM

In this chapter, we tried to show how changes in women's sex roles have had an effect on the American family. It is impossible to talk about the one without the other.

As standards for sex roles have been gradually changing, greater freedom of choice has been allowed for people of both sexes. Laws increasing the availability of contraceptives and allowing abortion on demand have decreased the relationship between sexual activity and reproduction.

Women today are focusing their demands on basic problems, especially control over reproduction. The reason is clear. A woman's decision to have children affects, perhaps even determines, every other aspect of her life. Many women feel unable to accept additional responsibility in a job because doing so might interfere with being a mother. Unfortunately, women who are determined to achieve and build a career must do so on the same terms as a man. At this time, this requires a certain inflexibility of schedules and full-time devotion to one's occupation or career (although there are promising changes in these areas). Meanwhile working women may get some help at home from their husbands, but running the home is still perceived as their responsibility. If the husband is involved with a job or career of his own, he may refuse to share the burden of keeping the house and raising the children. Until recently, the alternatives for most women have been clear: be a fulltime housewife and mother or a fulltime childless careerwoman.

A major problem is that men have been socialized into roles that complement women's traditional roles, but not their new ones. Their reluctance to change creates major stumbling blocks for equality. Perhaps the greatest contribution of the latest round in the women's rights movement has been the attempt to treat the roles of both men and women as problematic. Today's concern over sex roles pays attention to men's problems created by their roles, as well as to those of women.[33] Recent studies of college males have shown more and more men are willing to accept some ideas of the women's movement, but many refuse to accept any changes in their roles. Recent studies have shown that men, even well-educated ones, want much the same home life their fathers enjoyed a generation ago. This finding fits nicely with other research. In Sweden and Russia, for instance, where female equality has gone significantly further than in the United States, men are still unwilling to give up their traditional advantages.[34]

Again, the problem is the way males are socialized. Our society, with its emphasis on achievement through competition leaves lit-

The women's rights movement has spurred sex role changes for men as well as for women. Just as women are moving into traditionally male positions in the labor force, so are men accepting more responsibility for the managing and care of the home and children.

tle room for genuine human concerns to be expressed, especially by men. People must be managed and manipulated for larger organizational goals. Inexpressive men and those trained to falsify emotion fit in nicely with the prevailing social organization. Socialization for success means males must sell themselves by developing the marketplace personality. They must learn to think of themselves as objects to be sold, like a car. The result of this socialization is that people see each other as objects to be manipulated.

Because of this socialization, achieving equality between the sexes is difficult. The pressure exerted on men to achieve success in their work, as numerous plays and novels have shown, has had a disastrous effect on family life. Men systematically neglect their families in the pursuit of occupational achievement. The man who complains about how his job is hurting his family life is suspect in our culture; many who work overly hard to get ahead rationalize by saying they do it for the good of the family. Before there can be equality between the sexes and before marriages can become more democratic, our society needs to redefine success. The structure of work in our society is a major obstacle to the reorganization of sex roles. Women cannot change their roles by themselves; men must change theirs too.

With sex roles so highly structured by economic forces outside the family, it appears unlikely that much change will occur here until attention is paid to economic and political issues. In business there is considerable discussion about shorter work weeks, more flexible work schedules, paternity leaves for fathers, day-care centers for mothers, further automation, and a host of other reforms. If handled properly, many of these could result in greater role flexibility. Today the potential for solving some of these problems seems to be increasing. In our view, changes on this level must accompany the pressures for change on the private and individual level.

What consequence will these changes have on family structure? Suppose men learn to become more expressive toward women. This could result not only in improved relationships between husband and wife, but between men and all women. As barriers to sexual activity outside marriage are reduced, the frequency of extramarital and premarital sexual affairs might increase. If these affairs lead to greater marital instability, would the effect be equally liberating for both partners? Would better interpersonal relationships ever materialize? The answer is uncertain.

We are beginning to realize that family stability involves a series of matters that mean the meeting of some human needs at the expense of neglecting others. At present the family is a volatile institution, and people are uncertain which needs to meet and which to sacrifice. In the future relationships and marriage will not be dictated by custom, tradition, or even law. What is taking the place of tradition is the basic right of individuals to decide for themselves how they want to structure their relationships. As with all steps toward greater freedom for the individual, liberation from tradition makes human happiness more possible. But it also increases our ability to make tragic mistakes, because we lack a consensus on definitions of appropriate behavior.

Today sex and reproduction have become two different things. As a result, the future may see a drastic departure from the regularized and highly patterned sex roles and family structures of the past. Whether any of these changes will solve the problems of the family is hard to estimate, but in fifty years we should at least know more than we do today. That in itself may represent progress.

IMPORTANT WORDS AND TERMS

cohabitation
conjugal family
consanguinal family
divorce rate
egalitarianism

Equal Rights
  Amendment
extended family
family
feminist movement

fertility rate
gender identity
marriage
nuclear family
no-fault divorce

psychosexual
sexist
sex roles
social learning
suffrage

QUESTIONS FOR DISCUSSION

1. From what you have read in this chapter, do you think the American family is disintegrating? Support your answer by citing evidence from this chapter and from other things you have read.
2. Some people have argued that the rising divorce rate is a good thing. Do you think so?
3. Abortion is a very controversial issue. What factors need to be considered in working out a personal position on this issue? a societal position?
4. "The problems of aging in America are directly related to changes in family structure." Why?
5. The greatest changes seem to be occurring in the female sex role. Why?
6. The Equal Rights Amendment is a short and simple statement. Why has its passage aroused such controversy?
7. If the ERA is finally ratified, what changes could we expect to see within five years? within ten years?
8. Some advocates of day-care centers say such facilities could easily be added to the public schools. What do you think of this idea?
9. Economic factors affect family life. What economic changes need to be made if we are to improve the quality of family life in America today?
10. Cohabitation is becoming more widespread each year. Do men and women think the same way about this issue? If not, what are the major differences between them?

SUGGESTED READING

JOHN SCANZONI, *Sexual Bargaining* (Englewood Cliffs, N.J.: Prentice-Hall, 1972).

Scanzoni looks at the viability of the institution of marriage, and has an excellent discussion of the meaning of the rising divorce rate. He discusses the differing expectations people now bring to marriage as sex roles change. The role of conflict in marriage is examined, and Scanzoni concludes that conflict can be positive if it leads to a change in the relationship. Scanzoni also looks at the future of marriage, concluding that people continue to need the relationship that marriage provides.

JOYCE ASCHENBRENNER, *Lifelines* (New York: Holt, Rinehart, and Winston, 1975).

This short book about black families is written by a cultural anthropologist. Aschenbrenner presents the culture of the black family in a nonevaluative way, so that when readers finish the book, they understand the meaning of behavior within its cultural context. To the anthropologist, many behaviors we would label deviant fit in with kinds of problems blacks face in their daily lives. Aschenbrenner shows that the black family is organized around a different set of cultural values, that it provides for many of the needs of its members, and that it is an adaptive cultural response to the needs of blacks living in America. This book will help readers better understand some fundamental weaknesses in the white family, because of the contrast Aschenbrenner provides.

ROBIN MORGAN (ed.), *Sisterhood Is Powerful* (New York: Random House, 1970).

While Morgan's book is not new, it contains many articles not found elsewhere and many selections are valuable because they are controversial. Homosexuality, abortion, rape, and work are discussed from a feminist perspective, which will challenge the reader's way of thinking about these problems. Even if the reader cannot accept the points made, they will provoke him or her to think about feminism in a way the mass media never would.

WARREN FARRELL, *The Liberated Man* (New York: Bantam, 1975).

As a new women's movement is growing in this country, this book makes clear that there are also the seeds of a new men's movement. The author addresses himself to a vital question: what costs do men incur from the way their roles are now structured? Farrell looks at various institutions — including the army, sports, and the schools — to see what problems these institutions create for males. While this book does not suggest any solutions, it effectively argues that it is not easy to be a male in American society. The book should go a long way toward raising the consciousness of men.

SUSANNE STEINMETZ AND MURRAY STRAUS (eds.), *Violence in the Family* (New York: Harper and Row, 1974).

For those interested in the subject of violence among people who are supposed to be close to each other, this book is a welcome addition to our scant knowledge. The editors have pulled together a series of readings about child and spouse abuse, organizing the articles around a series of central questions. While they provide some insight into the problem, they show us that we still know very little about the issues involved in understanding violence among family members. These articles raise serious questions about the way family relationships are structured, and get rid of many myths surrounding the issue. For those readers interested in counseling work or for those who simply want a better understanding of this sensitive subject, this book is the best to date.

NOTES

1. William Stephens, *The Family in Cross-Cultural Perspective* (New York: Holt, 1963), p. 5.
2. Ibid., p. 5.
3. Margaret Mead, *Sex and Temperament in Three Primitive Societies* (New York: Morrow, 1963).
4. Janice Law Trecker, "Women in U.S. History, High School Textbooks," *Social Education* (March 1971), p. 249.
5. Emily Hahn, *Once Upon a Pedestal* (New York: Crowell, 1974), p. 7.
6. Mirra Komarovsky, "Learning the Feminine Role," in Edwin Schur (ed.), *The Family and the Sexual Revolution* (Bloomington: Indiana University Press, 1964), pp. 213–223.
7. Marcia Federbush, *Let Them Aspire*, 4th ed. (Pittsburgh: Know, Inc., 1973), p. 4.
8. Department of Labor, *Employment and Earnings, January 1978* (Washington, D.C.: U.S. Government Printing Office, 1978), p. 144.
9. Ibid., p. 137.
10. Ibid., pp. 24–25.
11. Tristen Amundsen, *The Silenced Majority* (Englewood Cliffs, N.J.: Prentice-Hall, 1971), p. 9.
12. Bureau of the Census, *Statistical Abstract of the United States, 1977* (Washington, D.C.:

U.S. Government Printing Office, 1977), p. 82.
13. Ibid., p. 62.
14. C. Dreyfus, "Women's Lib Hits the Courts," in Sookie Stambler (ed.), *Women's Liberation* (New York: Ace Books, 1970), p. 61.
15. *Statistical Abstract, 1977*, p. 63.
16. Lucinda Cisler, "Unfinished Business: Birth Control and Women's Liberation," in Robin Morgan (ed.), *Sisterhood Is Powerful* (New York: Random House, 1970), p. 258.
17. *Statistical Abstract, 1977*, p. 74.
18. Population Reference Bureau, *Population Education Newsletter*, Vol. 7, No. 1 (January 1978), p. 1.
19. *Statistical Abstract, 1977*, p. 74.
20. Population Reference Bureau, *Interchange*, Vol. 7, No. 1, p. 2.
21. Ibid., p. 2.
22. Ibid., p. 2.
23. John Scanzoni, *Sexual Bargaining* (Englewood Cliffs, N.J.: Prentice-Hall, 1977), p. 14.
24. Hahn, *Once Upon a Pedestal*, p. 121.
25. *Statistical Abstract, 1977*, p. 60.
26. For a good discussion of how illegitimacy is related to family structure see Joyce Aschenbrenner, *Lifelines* (New York: Holt, Rinehart, Winston, 1975).
27. Samuel Rodbill, "A History of Child Abuse and Infanticide," in Suzanne Steinmetz and Murray A. Straus (eds.), *Violence in the Family* (New York: Harper and Row, 1974), p. 175.
28. Ibid., p. 178.
29. Helen Lawrenson, "The Feminine Mistake," in Robert Antonio and George Ritzer (eds.), *Social Problems* (Boston: Allyn and Bacon, 1977), p. 281.
30. A. H. Kamiat, *Feminine Superiority* (New York: Bookman Associates, 1960), pp. 93ff.
31. Caroline Bird, *Born Female* (New York: Simon and Schuster, 1969), p. 179.
32. Morgan, *Sisterhood Is Powerful*, p. xxi.
33. Warren Farrell, *The Liberated Man* (New York: Random House, 1975).
34. See Edmund Dahlstrom, *Changing Roles of Men and Women* (Boston: Beacon Press, 1971).

4 WORK ALIENATION, DISAFFECTION, AND EXPLOITATION

CHAPTER OVERVIEW

INTRODUCTION

HISTORICAL OVERVIEW
The Impact of Technology on Work
The Effect of the Industrial Revolution
Summary

CONCEPTUAL ORIENTATION

OBJECTIVE DIMENSIONS OF THE PROBLEM
The Changing Relationship Between Education and Jobs
Job Satisfaction
Wages and Employment
The Influence of Work on Health
Women in the Labor Force
Unemployment and Underemployment
Summary

ATTEMPTS AT DEALING WITH THE PROBLEM
Management Strategies
Labor Unions
Government Action
Iatrogenic Effects

PROSPECTS FOR SOLVING THE PROBLEM

IMPORTANT WORDS AND TERMS

QUESTIONS FOR DISCUSSION

SUGGESTED READING

NOTES

Work really includes all or nearly all human activity. Birth, marriage, death, means work for the midwife, priest, and undertaker. One could even say that sex means work for the prostitute.
Clifton Bryant, The Social Dimensions of Work

For the many there is a hardly concealed discontent. The blue collar blues is no more bitterly sung than the white collar moan.
Studs Terkel, Working

CHAPTER OVERVIEW

The chapter begins with a review of history, outlining the evolution of ideas about work and pointing out the main features of work in modern society. These features were created in the Industrial Revolution, which changed the nature of work and was the cause of many problems for the worker. Our critique of work in American society focuses on the role of technology and, following the lead of Karl Marx, on how the capitalist methods of production structure work. To show how technology and capitalism affect society, we examine contemporary problems in the workplace, concentrating on job satisfaction, health and safety hazards, discrimination against women, and unemployment. We analyze the failure of both government and unions to improve working conditions, concluding that their failure is due to a reluctance to bring about major changes in how work is structured. Finally, we assess prospects for the future, emphasizing that using our rapidly advancing technology in different ways holds the key to improving the general condition of American workers.

INTRODUCTION

As doomed prisoners neared Auschwitz, the gigantic Nazi concentration camp, they were welcomed by a large sign over the gate saying *Arbeit Macht Frei,* or "work shall set you free." For the millions who died behind the barbed wire, the irony of the phrase became all too suddenly apparent. The jobs prisoners were forced to do provided a sadistic caricature of the work done outside the camps. Yet this Nazi effort to use work to help break the human spirit shows how important work is to Western life. In the twentieth century work has become part of humankind's search for the meaning of existence. Work has become an essential act of self-definition, an activity through which personal identity is both developed and reflected.

The work we do influences us in a number of ways, so much so that many people actually *become* the roles they play at work. Their identity cannot be separated from those activities that occupy so large a part of their waking hours. For many, work consumes them both physically and emotionally. The vast majority of Americans say they like the work they do. Many say they would work even if they did not need the money, although they admit that they might not keep their current jobs. But what of the dull, boring, routine jobs people perform, year in and year out? Have they adjusted to the repetitive and meaningless tasks confronting them every Monday morning? Or do they deceive themselves into believing they are really happy, partly because they have no other choice? And what about the millions of unemployed, cut off from earning a living?

These problems are the subject of this chapter. In discussing them, we will focus on the answers to three questions that are central to understanding problems associated with how work is structured. These questions are:

1. How have work roles changed since the Industrial Revolution?
2. How is work currently structured in American society?
3. How satisfied are Americans with the work they do?

To answer these questions we must first understand the history of work, to know how present conditions came to be. We must also learn about different ideas people use to define and discuss work. It is to an examination of these areas that we now turn our attention.

HISTORICAL OVERVIEW

The Impact of Technology on Work

Social change theorists today maintain that *technology* is the organizing principle of society and the driving force behind social change. To demonstrate the basis of this principle, we will discuss how technology has affected the structure of work throughout history. To do that job thoroughly, we must begin at the beginning, but that confronts us with a problem: prehistoric societies left no written records. The artifacts and monuments remain, but the ideas behind ancient societies are often hard to construct from what is left.

Still, some of the record can be filled in by archaeologists. From them we learn that ancient *hunters and gatherers* lived in small bands continuously on the move in search of new sources of food, and we learn that population growth was extremely slow. But other than this, we know nothing directly about societies existing before 4000 B.C. There is another source of knowledge, however. We can also learn from social anthropologists, who study societies existing today that have a similar level of technology, such as the Bushmen of the Kalahari Desert in southern Africa and the Aborigines of the Australian outback. From these two sources — the work of archaeologists and social anthropologists — we can draw some conclusions about how these ancient peoples lived.

In those ancient societies with a low level of technology, people were hunters and gatherers formed in small groups. Daily activity consisted primarily of performing tasks necessary for survival. Work was done, but it seems impossible to differentiate work roles from other roles needing to be carried out. There was no such thing as an occupation, as we would understand the term today; people simply gathered food and hunted animals. As George Ritzer has said, "to work was to live, for if one did not work or was not successful in gathering enough food and providing sufficient warmth and shelter, then one died."[1] Based on the analysis of language spoken by primitive people in today's world, there appears to be no word to convey what we call work. As Walter Neff has noted, "work appears to be such a natural activity akin to breathing or existing that it does not require a distinctive term to describe it."[2]

Yet hunting and gathering were not done equally by all members of the group. Daily activity was differentiated by age and sex. Young children helped their mothers in gathering whatever useful material was located in the area while the mature men who were physically able carried on the hunt. All societies appear to have used age and sex to divide up the daily tasks, but labor was probably not differentiated further. All men were expected to play pretty much the same role, even though there must have been a wide range of variation in their hunting skill. And among the women, all mature females were expected to bear and rear the young, one factor determining which tasks they were to perform, for gathering interfered little with that activity. Another characteristic of these primitive societies was the lack of an economic surplus. They produced only what was needed for survival.

The next stage in social evolution was begun by the technological change allowing the development of settled agriculture. These highly productive *agricultural societies* were located on the banks of rivers, ensuring themselves a constant supply of irrigation water and of rich earth, as each spring the floods came, deposited soil, and receded. Here the great ancient civilizations were born and produced for the first time the form of social organization called cities. Even these ancient cities had a high degree of division and specialization of labor, especially in comparison to what had existed before. The growing differentiation of work roles was made possible by an agricultural surplus, allowing major advances to be made in technology as a result of invention, innovation, and sharing ideas with other civilizations. The economic surplus was not large enough to permit many persons to be freed from the land, however, and the vast majority of work was still concerned with farming and with a new land-based practice, raising domesticated animals. Nevertheless, some people were freed from the demands for agricultural labor, and a new form of differentiation began to take place based on emerging institutions concerned with governing the masses of agricultural workers. These evolving social institutions were structured around various occupational roles and included priests, scribes, tax collectors, weapons makers, and soldiers, whose roles had now become full-time jobs.

These changes in occupational specialization, occurring about 3000 B.C., spelled the end of the dominance of the communal and egalitarian hunting-and-gathering societies. Work in the agricultural societies was characterized by the use of human and animal muscle power and a lack of sophisticated mechanical devices. Because the work needing to be done was unpleasant and based on a growing differentiation in social power, *slavery* and other forms of forced labor became widespread. Military conquests produced new legions of subjugated peoples, the major part of the work force in the ancient world. It is easy to see how agricultural work began to take on a negative connotation, with the jobs of warrior, priest, and scribe receiving greater prestige.

The nomadic ancestors of the Greeks developed an effective military organization and overran the Greek peninsula between 3000 and 2000 B.C., subjugating the people living in the area. Not only did all heavy agricultural work fall to slaves; gradually even tasks related to education, manufacturing, and trade did as well. By the time the city-states were fully established, Greek citizens were freed from the need to labor at all. Under these conditions, they developed the idea that work is inherently degrading to the individual. As Neff concludes from his discussion of work in classical Greek society: "The Grecian example provides us with the classic case of the conditions under which work acquires totally negative meanings. . . . It is not work itself which is degrading but the power relationships and social structures which surround it" that make it so.[3] Work always occurs in a social context: it is structured by the prevailing value system. As the Greek example makes clear, the subjective meaning of work varies greatly, based on the power one group has over another.

The pattern of dependence on slave labor continued until the Middle Ages, when slavery was replaced by the *feudal system* that spread throughout Europe in the wake of the disintegration of the Roman Empire. The *serf* was not a slave owned by his lord, but was involved in a social hierarchy resting on obligations derived in part from Christian teachings. Serfs had obligations to their lords to support them with food and work, but lords also had obligations to protect their serfs and govern them properly. In some attitudes the change was not great. Feudal lords still disdained the work done by their serfs and they felt their status freed them from the need to engage in demeaning manual labor. But feudalism was not a regression of civilization; the pattern of ancient slavery had now been broken and the basis for a new social order was set in motion.

One seed of this new order was planted by the monasteries, where monks' rules required them to work. This elevated manual and intellectual labor to the status of a religious duty, for work was seen as a way of serving God, of disciplining the soul, and was not done for material gain. Rather than being degrading, it was seen as ennobling the person who performed it. Based on this religious conception of work, the monasteries of the Middle Ages became major productive enterprises, as well as important religious institutions.

In the eleventh century, economic activity revived, and by the year 1300 *guilds* were established as the organizational form to structure productive handwork. The guilds established a hierarchy within a craft, with ranks assigned to workers based on skill. Because higher levels could only be attained by years of work, the older workers enjoyed highest rankings. The major rankings, from bottom to top, were apprentice, journeyman, and master craftsman. Guild workers owned their own tools, were committed to their craft for life, and derived much satisfaction from the accomplishments of their labor. Their work was highly valued and they took much pride in it and their degree of independence.

By the time of the Protestant Reformation, in the sixteenth century, the meaning of work had been transformed. The most widely held theory attributes the final stages of this change to the Reformation itself, particularly to the Calvinist sect, which is said to have created the values underlying the modern religion of work. Calvinists believed in predestination, meaning that God had determined who was and who was not going to heaven. People could do nothing to influence their fate, not even work their way to salvation. However, Calvinists thought there were signs of who was saved and their creed stressed the need to avoid indulging in wordly pleasures. As a result, they concluded that the lazy or self-indulgent person was receiving a sign that he was not saved; he who lived a disciplined and thrifty life full of hard work at least could hope that his self-control was a sign of being saved.

This set of beliefs had major social consequences, as Max Weber established in *The Protestant Ethic and the Spirit of Capitalism*. Weber argued that the unintended consequences of Calvinism were to support and guide the growth of *capitalism*. In a capitalist system, profits from an enterprise are not consumed, but are plowed back into the enterprise, where they are used to create greater profits. Work becomes elevated to a religion of its own, the *Protestant work ethic*, which controls the behavior of worker and capitalist alike. Weber's ideas have been accepted by some social scientists and debated by others. Another theory is that modern ideas about work were first expressed by the twelfth-century biblical scholar Joachim.[4] Regardless of who is established as the originator of our ideas, it is clear that by the time the Industrial Revolution began the meaning of work had profoundly changed.

Work had become central to the philosophy of Western society and contained several notions quite alien to former times. Work was seen as part of the way the world could be perfected. It became man's duty to work, while in return he was relieved of his anxiety about the meaning of life. Work came to be a behavioral imperative implied in the concept of the Protestant work ethic, and had lost virtually all its earlier negative connotations. Occurring as this did along with other social changes, particularly with the growth of science and the breakup of the feudal order, the stage was set for the radical transformation of society we now call the Industrial Revolution.

The Effect of the Industrial Revolution

Technology has been the dynamo of historical change. It acted as such a force in England beginning in the eighteenth century, and across the entire Western world in the nineteenth. Rapid advances were made in the application of scientific findings to the manufacture of goods, setting in motion other changes having wide ramifications for views about work. One of the first changes was the substitution of inanimate forms of energy for muscle power. Along with this came the increased use of machines to manufacture products in less time. People also developed machines that could produce uniform parts for a product: each nail was exactly like every other nail, meaning that each nail could replace every other nail. This *interchangeability of parts* meant that goods could be mass produced, although mass production required breaking production down into smaller and smaller tasks.

Once this was done, workers no longer started on the product and labored to complete it. Instead they might work on only one thousandth of it, other workers completing their own parts in successive order. There is nothing strange about this manufacturing process by today's standards, but at the time it necessitated rapid and major change in the way work was structured. Highly skilled craftsmen were unable to compete with the new production techniques, as mass production allowed quality goods to be produced in greater quantity than could ever be done by hand. But the craftsman wasn't the only loser, the worker lost too. The central characteristic of guild work, a sense of craftsmanship, was lost with the advent of the factory system. Similar changes displaced farmers. The increased mechanization of agriculture freed masses of workers from tilling the land and harvesting its crops. They had little choice but to stream toward the rapidly expanding industrial centers. Increasingly, standards were set by machines, workers no longer owned their own tools, their skill was no longer valued, and pride in their work was no longer possible. Workers fed, tended, and repaired the machines that could work faster than humans at greatly reduced cost.

Summary

In primitive hunting-and-gathering societies work was divided by age and sex, but the entire community shared both the labor and what was produced. Egalitarianism ended with the beginning of settled agriculture, which introduced job specialization, an economic surplus, and rigid status differences. Work was characterized by slavery and degradation for centuries, until the Middle Ages when, with the rise of guilds, the stigma was removed from work by the value placed on a high level of craftsmanship. The importance of work was heightened by the Reformation, which elevated work to a religious duty. But then the Industrial Revolution struck. Mass production was introduced, and pride of craftsmanship was lost, and workers were forced to work on small discrete tasks instead of on entire products. As the parts became interchangeable, so did the workers. With a tremendous surplus of labor, wages fell to pitifully low levels. Faced with this situation, working men made many efforts to improve their lot. Since many of these were based on the ideas of Karl Marx, it is to his writings that we now turn.

CONCEPTUAL ORIENTATION

Karl Marx, born in Germany in 1818, was one of the intellectual giants of the nineteenth century. Marx thought that the economic system structured a society, and central to his ideas about economics was his *labor theory of value*. He argued that the determinant of the value of a manufactured article is the amount of human labor going into it. This is not only true of products like cars. Oil in the ground or trees in the forest also have no value until a human worker transforms them into usable form. Labor creates value and the value of a product is only the result of the labor that went into it.

Marx then analyzed capitalism, to see what determined the selling price of a manufactured object. He concluded that the selling price reflected an object's social utility as determined by the market structure. However, instead of the *proletariat* (the workers) receiving the rewards for their labor in creating the object, the *bourgeoisie* (the owners of the factories) kept part of the selling price as their profit. Profit is the owner extracting *surplus value* from the workers, and is claimed as legitimate reward for ownership in a capitalist system. For Marx, however, the means of production had been created by the labor of past generations, so profits should go to the workers and not to the owners. When the laborer is paid less than the actual value of his work, he is suffering *exploitation*. In essence, the bourgeoisie steal a portion of the worker's labor and use it to maintain their luxurious life-style. The greater the profit, the more successful the owner is; but to Marx, the greater the profit, the bigger the thief the owner is.

This system is dangerous, however. The bourgeoisie cannot expect the proletariat to allow their labor to be stolen so easily. To keep workers in a position where they can do nothing to stop their own exploitation, the capitalists oppress them. *Oppression* can take many forms, but most often it consists of keeping the workers from realizing that they are being exploited and convincing them that profits are a legitimate reward for ownership. The bourgeoisie do this by controlling the agents of socialization, thus teaching the proletariat its values, by convincing him of the legitimacy of the pattern of ownership and control exercised over the workplace.

A final concept of importance to the Marxist perspective on work is *alienation*. In capitalism, work is organized so as to yield the maximum profit to the owner of the enterprise. To maximize profit, work is organized in the most efficient way. If a product can be made at lower cost by breaking it down into many smaller tasks and assigning a worker to do only one, then that is how work will be organized. This form of organization creates problems for the workers. They have no say in how the tasks will be broken down and are powerless to say how many tasks they can and should do, for that is determined by the criterion of technical efficiency.

The result of this organization is the typical assembly line: workers are unable to interact with each other and are almost totally isolated from human contact during the work day. They perform the same mechanical task thousands of times a day without stop. These conditions engender what Marx called alienation, by which he meant a sense of isolation, powerlessness, and loss of control. This alienation not only marked how people view their work, but their whole life, for Marx believed deeply that the meaning of human existence was found in work.

Marx was outraged by the exploitation and alienation of workers, but saw hope. He believed that people make history and that they can improve their lot by changing their society through collective action and conscious effort. Of course, these ideas threaten capitalism, for they suggest a different rationale for human existence than the meanings offered by our culture. American society is dominated by economic institutions and by the related quest for material gain and reward in the form of consumer goods. Society recognizes the threat that Marx represents: the public schools do not teach that a society can have any other guiding principle than capitalism, and its drawbacks are not pointed out. Only after high school do we get an inkling of the issues involved in the organization of society. By that time, since getting a college education is part of attaining an elite status in America, this knowledge produces little change. This was foreseen by Marx, who thought that leaving public education to the state would allow the system to legitimize itself and provide a labor force properly conditioned to be bought off by the rewards of the system.

Marx feared that, as the result of this socialization, workers would not want to change the system or organize to overthrow the bourgeois. Instead, they would feel that they could make progress within capitalism. His most famous work, *The Communist Manifesto,* warns European labor leaders not to settle for less than a full-scale revolution.[5] To do so would mean to permit the continuation of an economic system organized to exploit the workers. He feared that workers would settle for increased prosperity within the system, as long as they believed that they could live like the bourgeoisie. Marx called this the *embourgeoisment of the proletariat* and saw it as a betrayal of the revolution. In retrospect, he was proved right.

Karl Marx was concerned about alienation through exploitation; another founding father of sociology was concerned with alienation based on the increased use of bureaucratic work structures. Max Weber, whose ideas we discussed earlier, was alarmed by the impact he felt bureaucratic structures were having on work and workers. Weber summarized his attitude toward the increasing use of bureaucracy:

> It is still more horrible to think that the world could one day be filled with nothing but those little cogs, little men clinging to little jobs, and striving towards bigger ones — a state of affairs which is to be seen once more . . . playing an ever increasing part in the spirit of our present administrative system. . . . This passion for bureaucracy as we have heard it expressed here is enough to drive one to despair.[6]

But what was Weber describing? A *bureaucracy* is a highly organized hierarchy in the form of a pyramid. In such a structure, orders come from the top downward and information flows from the bottom upward. Each person has a specific function ordered by the rules, and the chance to exercise personal initiative is limited because of the rules. Bureaucracies are efficient in accomplishing large-scale tasks and in coordinating large numbers of workers doing diverse jobs. But along with that advantage, they transform each worker into a minute cog in a great machine, with only the few at the top able to see the end product or the accomplishment of the organization's goals.

The increasing use of bureaucracy contributes to the alienation of workers from their work. But what is this work? Is work the woman in a primitive society gathering berries and roots? Is it the medieval craftsman weaving a tapestry? An early mill worker feeding the carding machine with wool? Or the modern lawyer arguing for his clients? What do all of these activities have in common? We have been discussing work as if we all knew what was meant, but we need a clear definition. *Work* is:

> *purposeful mental or physical human activity, entailing the expenditure of energy at some sacrifice of pleasure.*

Work does not include all human activity, but those tasks done in pursuit of external rewards. People labor to gain a whole series of rewards, including money, power privilege, and status. As the sociologist William Torbert commented:

> People labor [work] not only at jobs but also at schools, with their family or at dances, depending upon the extent to which in any of these situations they strive for goals which do not directly express their exploratory impulse.

Tension characterizes labor, for labor involves the repression of the rhythm of the self and a rechanneling of the self's energies — the energy of the exploratory drive — to the service of external rewards.[7]

It has often been said that work is something people do for money that they wouldn't do if they weren't being paid. While this oversimplifies the nature of the rewards available in modern society, it expresses what we mean. Work involves disciplining and controlling the self and participating in structures that call on people to perform tasks for which they are rewarded. In our money-based economy, the reward most people work for is income. This is not to minimize the other rewards derived by workers — such things as power and status — it is just to say that for most people these are secondary to the money involved.

Two related concepts are also important. We have said that work involves some sacrifice of pleasure, some suppression of personal desire. Another activity allows for the expression of those desires — that activity is leisure. Leisure does not mean lying in a hammock drinking beer. Rather, *leisure* is:

> *definite human activity based on an attitude of freedom used for developing one's individuality, and improving one's understanding of the world and of the self in relation to the external world.*

As you can see, leisure has different purposes than work. In work, the individual could perform socially useful tasks that he finds totally meaningless. Work produces tension and mental or physical weariness in workers, which must be relieved so that they can work efficiently again. For this purpose, workers are given free time to rest and engage in *recreation*, which is:

> *human activity designed to reduce the tension of work, which does not involve the expression or*

One of the primary motivations for working is income, which in turn determines purchasing power in the marketplace. Americans are tireless consumers of both essential and nonessential goods, and we take our buying seriously, as is witnessed by these bargain hunters in a San Francisco shop.

development of the self or increase a person's understanding of the world.

Leisure, on the other hand, involves personal exploration. In leisure, a person's goals are to her individuality, self-expression, and further understanding of the world; producing a socially useful product is not the main purpose of her activity. The difference between work and leisure creates the strain between the individual goals and societal goals — this is the strain Marx saw as the fundamental and inherent conflict in capitalism.

OBJECTIVE DIMENSIONS OF THE PROBLEM

Marx and Weber have shown where we should look for work-related problems in modern society. Marx tells us to look for the exploitation of workers and at their alienation, based on the monotony and small scope of their tasks. Weber also tells us to expect alienation resulting from the bureaucratic structure of economic enterprises. Using these concepts, we will analyze work in our society, showing how their predictions have come true. We will find alienation in the lack of job satisfaction, in exploitation in wages, in questions of worker safety, in discrimination, and in unemployment. These problems are inherent in capitalism and are a direct result of our values, which emphasize primarily the material rewards for work. Today many of our problems also arise out of the application of our technology. A major question facing modern society is whether we can use our more sophisticated technology to structure work so people can produce a socially useful product and achieve greater self-fulfillment at the same time. Technology can free workers, but is it doing so? Many answer this question by pointing to the rising educational level of the American work force, saying that greater educational attainments show that high technology demands higher skills. Let us see if this is true.

The Changing Relationship Between Education and Jobs

A whole new array of jobs has been created by our changing technology. In 1900 the largest group of workers was farm laborers. By 1940 the largest group was industrial workers, composed primarily of semiskilled machine operators. By 1960 the largest group was professional, managerial, and technical workers.

Many people assume this means that the jobs now demand more training. Common wisdom is that *automation* — the use of machines to perform tasks previously done by people — increases the need for education: educated workers are needed to run the machines. But in fact it appears that the educational attainment of the population has risen faster than the skill levels demanded by these shifts in the job market. Numerous studies have shown that the effect of automation, when combined with the increased bureaucratization of work, has been to *reduce* the level of technical skill required in many new occupations. There has been a dramatic increase in the number of *white-collar jobs* (professional, managerial, service, and sales work), but this has not meant an increase in the skill level required for them. In fact, the largest increase in white-collar work has been in clerical work, where skill requirements continue to be relatively low.

As Harry Braverman has clearly shown, much of the change thought to have taken place is simply the result of the redefinition of occupational categories.[8] He compares data for 1900 with those for 1970 and demonstrates that almost exactly the same proportion of people are employed in what could be called the manual working class (see Table 4.1).

The largest shifts have been a decline in the nonfarm laborers and an increase in the number of operatives, but Braverman traces these shifts to a change in the classification of occupations by the Bureau of the Census. He goes on to show that the increase in skill level demanded by jobs is largely imaginary; any skills a worker needs can be picked up

TABLE 4.1 Percentage of Laborers in the Manual Working Class, 1900–1970

	1900	1970
Craftsmen, foremen, and kindred	10.5%	13.9%
Operatives and kindred	12.8	17.9
Nonfarm laborers	12.5	4.7
	35.8	36.5

Source: Harry Braverman, *Labor and Monopoly Capital* (New York: Monthly Review Press, 1974), p. 427.

quickly on the job. As Charles Silberman, an editor of *Fortune Magazine*, has said: "A detailed manpower survey by the New York State Department of Labor, for example, revealed that approximately two-thirds of all the jobs in existence in the state involve such simple skills that can be — and are — learned in a few days, weeks, or at most months of on-the-job training."[9]

Braverman also questions the assumption that higher skill levels are required for white-collar occupations like clerical and sales jobs. Like many other industrial sociologists, he points out that white-collar work has greater prestige than *blue-collar* work (skilled, semiskilled, and unskilled manual labor). But that does not mean that such work requires greater skills. The greater prestige is simply created to convince the white-collar worker that his job is better than the manual laborer's. As Braverman states:

> The worker may remain a creature without knowledge or capacity, a mere "hand" by which capital does its work; but so long as he or she is adequate to the needs of capital the worker is no longer to be considered or called unskilled. It is this conception that lies behind the shabby nominal sociology in which sociologists find upgrading in the new names given to classifications by the statisticians.[10]

Braverman's argument is convincing, but some changes in the labor force have created a need for higher skills. Since World War II, the number of people engaged in producing services has rapidly increased, and the number engaged in producing goods has decreased. By 1980 over two-thirds of the labor force will be employed in this area. Transportation, the wholesale and retail trades, real estate, insurance, and government work are all areas of increasing employment where a more highly educated labor force (with the right social and behavioral skills) is desirable. This is not true of all jobs in these fields. Truck drivers, receptionists, or sales workers do not necessarily have jobs demanding higher skills than factory workers. Nor does more education ensure better performance. Researchers have also attempted to evaluate the effects of education on the performance of workers. In one study Ivar Berg looked at the effect of education on a series of job-related issues.[11] He found that education was directly related to turnover, absenteeism, productivity, and supervision ratings in a wide variety of occupational settings. That is, the higher the education, the higher the turnover rate, the more absenteeism, the lower productivity. Other researchers have found the same thing. Yet the educational demands for many jobs are being increased as the general educational level of the population rises. This forces people with

One dramatic change in the labor force over the past three decades has been increased employment in service-producing industries — transportation, entertainment, health, recreation, retailing, and so on. Two-thirds of all workers, including the staff at this restaurant, are now engaged in providing services.

a college degree to drop further down the occupational structure in the competition for jobs.

Well-educated workers do obtain the better paying and more attractive jobs, but apparently not because their education trained them for the job. Instead, they are hired because employers are using education as a sorting and filtering mechanism to control access to the occupational structure. Schooling cultivates such behavioral characteristics as discipline, conformity, and punctuality, and cancels out such undesirable traits as rebellion, creativity, and unorthodox beliefs. The ability to work easily under supervision and to sit quietly at a desk, which contribute to success on the job, also lead to success in education.

While education does provide the socialization needed for large-scale bureaucratic organizations, it also has created on the part of many young people demands which the work experience is not designed to provide. Numerous studies have shown younger workers with advanced education are the ones most likely to be dissatisfied with their jobs. The paradox of the above situation is that while the better educated workers have the behavioral characteristics employers desire, they also make some demands from their work most employers are not prepared to meet. Combined with an ever-increasing competition for the better jobs based on rising educational levels, it becomes hard to argue that a college education by itself any longer guarantees entrance to the best range of jobs available in our society.

Job Satisfaction

Marx and Weber introduced the key problem of work: the degree of job satisfaction. Much research has been done on this issue, producing often contradictory results. Based on many of the studies of the past twenty-five years, it would be inaccurate and unfair to say that most working Americans are dissatisfied with their jobs. Studies done by the Survey Research Center of the University of Michigan and the National Opinion Research Center asked people "How satisfied are you with your job (or your work)?" As Table 4.2 shows, those answering "very satisfied," "somewhat satisfied," and "fairly satisfied" predominated (the percentages combine the totals for these three answers). When the above data is broken down by age, younger workers (those under age thirty) show somewhat less satisfaction than those over thirty. And on the variable of race, white workers were a little more satisfied than blacks, but there was basically no relationship between educational level and job satisfaction.

However, data like these are not very useful, because it is hard to tell what the respondent is reacting to in this kind of interview. Other attitudinal measures have been devised to determine satisfaction. One involves asking the respondents if they would want their son or daughter to enter their occupa-

TABLE 4.2 Percentage of Workers Expressing Job Satisfaction

	Survey Research Center		NORC	
	1969	1973	1975	1976
Male	88%	91%	90%	87%
Female	81	89	87	87

Note: The totals combine three favorable answers: very satisfied, somewhat satisfied, and fairly satisfied.

Source: Bureau of the Census, *Statistical Abstract of the United States, 1977* (Washington, D.C.: U.S. Government Printing Office, 1977), p. 398.

tion. The vast majority of American workers hope their children will go into some other job. Obviously, these data contradict the other studies.

But these indirect questions are faulty too. The issue of job satisfaction is too complex to be measured by simple questions. Instead of relying on these public opinion polls, industrial sociologists have gone into factories in attempting to measure dissatisfaction and alienation. These studies have problems too. Factors outside work greatly influence how workers feel about their jobs. If there is a recession, workers who were once dissatisfied with their jobs may now be glad just to have them. And after a new union contract has been signed, workers may reconsider their previous dissatisfaction. Because of this, many industrial sociologists feel that it is impossible to measure worker satisfaction without considering the worker's whole life. With these cautions in mind, let us examine what some research has shown.

Back in the 1930s a series of studies on worker motivation and productivity were undertaken by a group of researchers from Harvard University.[12] Initially the researchers tried to see how varying the illumination level affected productivity. They realized that the chief factor increasing productivity was not their manipulation of lighting, but their concern for the welfare of the workers and the amount of attention workers were receiving from these experiments. What the researchers had done was to remove the group under study from the bureaucratic organization of the Western Electric Company and transform it into a small and autonomous work group whose members rotated tasks among themselves.[13] As a result, worker productivity increased dramatically.

This landmark study, completed over forty years ago, has not had a marked impact on the organization of work. Businesses still use bureaucratic structures to organize work, for to move from this model would mean questioning the basic premises of our economic structures. Given how our society is organized, with power highly concentrated and used to increase profits, nonbureaucratic structures would create too many problems for those in control. Democracy has not come to the workplace in America; bringing it in would challenge the whole pattern of power, wealth, and privilege in American society.

The early 1950s saw the next important study of worker alienation, when C. Wright Mills, a sociologist at Columbia University, outlined his concern for some of the changes occurring in the job market.[14] Mills undercut the widespread optimism about the changing emphasis from manual blue-collar jobs to white-collar ones. He showed that the workers doing office work, while rescued from dangerous and heavy manual labor, were nevertheless dissatisfied, confronted by dull, repetitive, and meaningless paper shuffling. The strategy of solving worker alienation by making all workers white-collar was seriously in error, based on Mills's findings. But, again, the important findings of a study of work were ignored. Since Mills wrote, many Americans have become even more convinced of the superiority of white-collar work. The irony is that blue-collar jobs surpass white-collar work on the most important scale in our society — income. Plumbers, electricians, and others with strong labor unions often make three times what many clerical or sales workers do. In many places, plumbers make double what starting public school teachers can, and many union carpenters, welders, and laborers make more than a new Ph.D. working in a college or university. Not only are many white-collar jobs plagued by the boring work Mills described, but they are also less rewarding than the lower status jobs.

In 1955 Eli Chinoy published another classic study, which described the frustrations of blue-collar workers.[15] He showed that the single overriding concern of many automobile assembly-line workers was to get off the line and start a business of their own. But with the high rate of failures for small businesses, many workers found themselves back in the factory, where the work at least paid relatively well.

Arthur Kornhauser also studied auto assembly-line workers and worked out an index to test the men's adjustment to their jobs. He found that the percentage of workers who enjoyed good mental health increased steadily up the occupational hierarchy. Kornhauser concluded: "The influence determining occupational mental health differences among factory workers are to be found in the jobs themselves and their associated life conditions."[16] The relationship between the job characteristics and the workers' level of mental health was not due to differences in their background before hiring or to personality factors. Regardless of their background, workers with low-skill jobs had negative feelings about themselves, anxieties, tensions, and a sense of futility. These were the feelings Marx had noted more than one hundred years earlier. Even though assembly-line workers are comparatively well paid, they hold their jobs and themselves in contempt. Any satisfaction these workers have with their lives comes almost solely from off-the-job experiences.

A widely acclaimed study of how workers feel about their jobs was recently published. This was not a statistical study, but a collection of interviews with people in a multitude of occupations. Though it is risky to generalize from these comments, the book offers valuable insight into how people feel about their jobs. Their detailed, honest comments give us a depth of understanding statistical studies cannot supply. The book is hard to summarize, but author Studs Terkel attempts it when he says: "This book being about work is by its very nature about violence to the spirit as to the body . . . it is above all about daily humiliations. To survive the day is triumph enough for the working wounded among the great many of us."[17] In these few words, Terkel tells us what the book meant to him. He had investigated a wide range of jobs, from hooker to factory owner, and was disturbed to see how much people have to adjust to the requirements of their jobs. In almost every case Terkel found that what has meaning for the worker is not the work itself, but the extrinsic rewards like power and money. From his long and thorough report, it is clear that we are a long way from achieving the kind of work that people would want to do for the sheer enjoyment of it. But the question we need to answer now is whether the rewards they receive are even enough.

Wages and Employment

Before we can say whether workers are exploited, we need to find out what determines their wages. While it may seem easy to determine the extent of worker exploitation, it would be necessary to know the following for each product American industry turns out:

1. the cost of the raw material
2. the cost of the equipment needed to produce it, prorated out over its useful life
3. the amount represented by the workers' labor
4. how necessary other costs (packaging and advertising) really are

But finding out these costs is not easy. In fact, according to Ralph Nader, production costs are among the most closely guarded secrets in industry. The reason is that if consumers and workers knew what production costs were, they would be outraged at how little they were being paid as workers and how much they were forced to pay as consumers. Still, based on his investigations, Nader claims to know that a spark plug costs General Motors only seven cents to produce, that seat and shoulder harnesses cost $3.50, and that the engine of a full-size Ford costs only $70. On each item, the selling price shows about a tenfold increase over the production cost.[18]

Nader's figures may be wrong, but we cannot say, and that is because he was right in his first charge: American companies keep these costs secret. They also manage to confuse production costs with other costs. For example, many companies discard perfectly usable machinery, abandon profitable locations, or mount expensive and unnecessary advertising campaigns simply to avoid having their profits taxed by the federal government. What appears to be an easy problem to analyze becomes impossible, because the records of American corporations are not open to the public. Of course, this is part of what private enterprise means, but it is also part of the strategy for maintaining the credibility of our economic system. Companies withhold information from workers and consumers to be able to manipulate them in the workplace and the marketplace.

Although we cannot say if wages are fair in terms of production costs, we can judge wages by other standards. Using 1967 dollars (to discount for inflation), the wages of workers in all private nonfarm industries increased about 70 percent in the past eight years, with the greatest increases occurring in transportation and public utility and the least in the wholesale and retail trades. In December 1976, workers producing durable goods were averaging $5.78 an hour; those producing nondurable goods averaged $4.89.[19] Gross average weekly earnings for industrial workers was $257.75 in 1976, but that is partly the result of inflation. Based on 1967 dollars it was only $151.15, amounting to about a $20 per week increase over ten years, or an increase of about $2.00 per week per year. During the same period (1967–1976) the consumer price index rose from 100 to 170.5, meaning that it took 70 percent more money to buy the same goods as in 1967. In other words, wage inflation has just about kept pace with price inflation.

Another way the government tells us how well the worker is doing is to compute annual costs for a family of four living at three different budget levels. For the urban worker living in a metropolitan area in the fall of 1975, these costs were $9721 for the lower budget, $15,638 for the intermediate budget, and $22,940 for the higher budget.[20] Yet in the same year the median income for all American families was only about $14,000, which falls in between the lower and intermediate budgets. And about 33 percent of the families in this country have incomes at or below the low-budget figure, while about 58 percent have incomes below the minimum for the intermediate budget.[21] Like Alice in Wonderland, most workers have to run faster each year just to keep from falling further behind.

The Influence of Work on Health

We have already examined the way jobs influence the mental health of employees in our discussion of job satisfaction. But observers are also concerned with the physical health of American workers, and many studies have been done. One of the first, by Carey McCord in 1948, found that, because of their jobs, train dispatchers had a life expectancy of only 50.1 years.[22] Dispatchers had to make approximately five decisions a minute in the course of an eight-hour day. With that many decisions to make, many of them involving life-or-death situations, it is not surprising that heart disease was identified as the single greatest factor in their deaths. Today, more than thirty years later, air traffic controllers suffer the same problem, as a result of similar stress.

Other stressful jobs also lead to increased levels of serum cholesterol, thus increasing the risk of heart disease. Studies have also indicated that low levels of job satisfaction are related to elevated cholesterol levels and thus to increased heart disease. A wide variety of job stresses have been related to coronary heart disease. In other studies, the degree of job satisfaction was found to be one of the strongest predictors of longevity, better even than a physical exam by a doctor or a measure of tobacco usage.[23] Peptic ulcers have been related to high levels of job-related responsibility and to increased levels of interpersonal tension and conflict.[24]

As is well known, industrial chemicals are also hazardous. Asbestos, kepone, cadmium, and mercury have caused diseases and illnesses in many workers whose jobs require their use. Until recently, however, when workers in these occupations got sick, company doctors told them that nothing was wrong with them or that whatever was wrong did not result from their job. A common disease among coal miners, black lung, affects thousands of men, who are forced to retire prematurely. And more recently we have become aware of the problem of brown lung among the nation's quarter million textile mill workers. Exposure to cotton dust

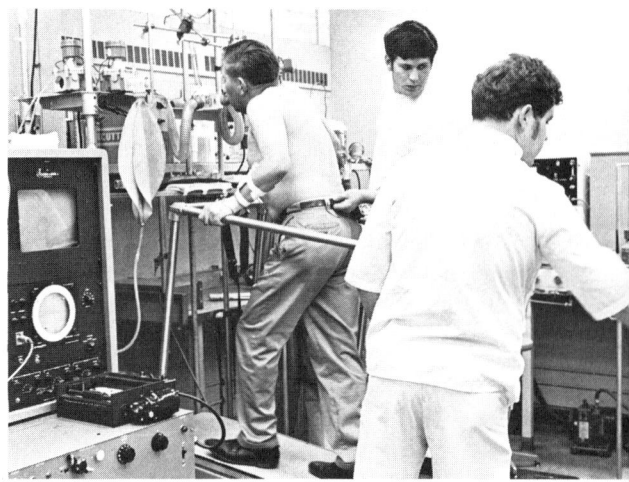

Many jobs and job conditions are detrimental to the physical health of workers. In this Appalachian clinic, a coal miner's blood, heart, and respiration are examined for black lung, a deadly disease caused by years of inhaling coal dust particles.

over long periods of time apparently has a similar effect to coal dust. These hazardous conditions are regulated by law and should not exist, but enforcement is not always strict. The levels of cotton dust in North Carolina plants of the J. P. Stevens Company were twelve times what the federal standard allows. Even though the company has been cited for these violations many times, nothing has been done to correct the situation.

Industrial accidents are also a major source of injury and death for many workers. The National Safety Council estimates that over 15,000 workers die on the job each year while another 2.2 million suffer disabling injuries. Industrial accidents rose 26.7 percent from 1960 to 1970, largely because of unsafe working conditions attributable to an attempt to cut costs by factory owners.[25] Illnesses are obviously much harder to detect. Many occur only after long periods of time on the job and often a worker has switched jobs several times since having the one that caused the problem. For these reasons, data on occupational illness are far harder to rely on, but one study cited in congressional reports estimates about 400,000 job-related illnesses per year, resulting in as many as 100,000 fatalities. The conclusion is inescapable that American workers face many hazards on their jobs.

Women in the Labor Force

According to the latest government figures, since 1950 the proportion of women in the labor force has climbed from about one-third to just one-half. Middle-aged women were largely responsible for the increase between 1950 and 1965, but since then the largest gains have been among women under thirty-five. There has been a dramatic increase in the number of working women from twenty-four to thirty-five; their rate of participation went up 14 percent in twelve years, to stand at 59 percent in 1977. Almost two thirds of these women (64 percent) are married, live with their husbands, and have children under eighteen. Add on those women in this age group who have children under age eighteen and are divorced or separated from their husbands — an additional 10 percent — and about three-quarters of working women from ages twenty-four to thirty-five have major family responsibilities in addition to the demands at work.[26]

Many studies have shown that when women work they are faced with what could be labeled as *role overload*. Instead of having the husband take on an increased share of the duties and responsibilities of running the home and taking care of the children, most women have to handle both sets of responsibilities with little help from the male. This may be a product of male chauvinistic attitudes, but it is also probably tied to the distribution of power within the family based on the income earned by the husband and by the wife. In 1975, the wife's earnings accounted for only 26 percent of total family income in general, and it was only 39 percent in those families where the wife worked full-time. More will be said about this later.

Of course, part of the reason for this income differential is that women have traditionally held lower-paying jobs. To correct this imbalance, efforts have been made to find women employment in fields other than the traditional ones. People generally feel that great strides have been made, but the data tend to contradict this, as Table 4.3 and Table 4.4 show. Women still dominate the traditional female occupations and do not appear in significant numbers in the traditional male occupations.

TABLE 4.3 Percentage of Women in Traditional Female Occupations, 1977

Occupation	Women
Librarian	83%
Registered nurse	97
Elementary-school teacher	84
Nursery and kindergarten teacher	99
Sales demonstrator	96
Bank teller	90
Bookkeeper	92
Secretary	99
Telephone operator	95
Dressmaker	98
Private household worker	97
Waitress	90
Dental assistant	98

Source: Department of Labor, *Employment and Earnings, January, 1978* (Washington, D.C.: U.S. Government Printing Office, 1978), pp. 153–154.

TABLE 4.4 Percentage of Women in Traditional Male Occupations, 1977

Occupation	Women
Architect	3.4%
Engineer	2.7
Dentist	2.9
Sales manager	3.7
Mail carrier	9.5
Carpenter	.9
Electrician	.2
Plumber	.5
Auto mechanic	.9
Fire fighter	.4
Truck driver	1.3
Police	3.8

Source: Department of Labor, *Employment and Earnings, January, 1978* (Washington, D.C.: U.S. Government Printing Office, 1978), pp. 153–154.

While many changes may be occurring, the data show that the pattern of sex-role stereotyping in the job market is still followed. It must be admitted that many occupations formerly closed to women are now actively recruiting women employees, but the illusion of progress disappears with a look at the data. While there are many reasons for this, recent research indicates that a major cause is male hostility toward women who step outside their more traditional roles. This is even true in academia, which has long prided itself on being more liberal than other fields. Despite this self-image, studies show that out of more than 2,500 colleges and universities the number of women college presidents rarely exceeds 110. Of these, 110 women, over 80 percent are in Catholic women's colleges, leading one commentator to suggest, "If a woman wanted to become a college president, she had ought to become a nun first."

Sex discrimination does not end with job placement. Studies show that the starting pay of women and the rapidity of their advancement are both less than for males doing the same job. With the number of women in the labor force growing at a steady rate, this is an area of key concern, and it would seem to be of greater concern than discrimination by race. Women of both races earn significantly less than their male counterparts, with the difference relatively constant for the past thirty-five years. White women make only about 60 percent of a white man's earnings, black women about two-thirds of what a black male does. And according to the data, white women earn significantly less than black men. In the market place, sexism seems stronger than racism.[27]

Unemployment and Underemployment

The Bureau of Labor Statistics defines *unemployment* as follows:

> Unemployed persons comprise all persons who did not work during the survey week, who made specific efforts to find a job within the past four weeks, and who were available for work during the survey week (except for temporary illness). Also included as unemployed are those who did not work at all, were available for work and (a) were waiting to be called back to a job from which they had been laid off; or (b) were waiting to report to a new wage or salary job within thirty days.[28]

This definition determines how the government gathers unemployment statistics. In light of that, a few things should be noted. If a worker gets so discouraged in looking for work that she no longer actively seeks out jobs, she is no longer considered as unemployed. Obviously, then, the number of unemployed as stated in government statistics will always be low. A useful supplement to this measure would be the number of people suffering *underemployment*. This would include:

1. people who work part time when they want to work full time
2. people whose educational level greatly exceeds the demands of the job they do
3. people who are working for wages so low that they work full time but still make less than enough money to live above the poverty line

As an indicator of the employment problems facing certain groups in our society, underemployment is far better than the unemployment rate. In many cities the underemployment rate has traditionally been about three times the unemployment rate. However, these statistics are not kept regularly, so to pursue the problem we must look at the government's unemployment statistics (see Figure 4.1).

A major contributing factor to the rise of the rate in the first half of the 1970s was government policy. The economic strategy of the Nixon and Ford administrations, focusing on cooling off the inflation rate, allowed the number of unemployed persons to increase dramatically. Inflation was seen as a more serious problem than was unemployment. While the number of unemployed has risen greatly in the past decade, so has the number of people employed, which reaches a new high almost every time the data is gathered. Nevertheless, the unemployment rate reached a high of 8.5 percent in 1975 and stands at about 7.0 percent for 1978.

This general rate — as bad as it looks with the recent increases — obscures the serious impact of unemployment on certain groups (see Table 4.5). Unemployment rates also vary by occupational group. As of December 1977 white-collar workers had an unemployment rate of 3.9; for blue-collar workers the rate was 7.3. It was highest for nonfarm laborers within the blue-collar category (10.6 percent) and lowest (2.5 percent) for managers and administrators within the white-collar group.[29] These data show clearly that the unemployment rates vary greatly within the population; to talk of the general rate is to overlook the problems confronting certain groups in society.

Summary

Armed with the analyses of Marx and Weber, we have investigated work in our society to determine whether problems exist. They do. Work is still unsafe and unhealthy and many people are still unable to find jobs. Workers are dissatisfied with their work. Data even show supposed improvements to be illusory;

FIGURE 4.1 Unemployment Rate, 1967–1976

Source: Department of Labor, *Handbook of Labor Statistics, 1977* (Washington, D.C.: U.S. Government Printing Office, 1977), p. 108.

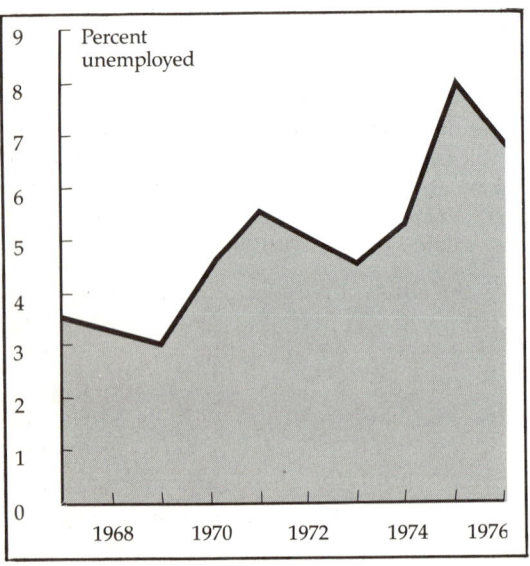

TABLE 4.5 Groups with Highest Unemployment Rates, 1977

Group	Unemployed [looking for full-time work]
Females [16 years and over]	8.0%
Black females	7.1
White females	13.6
Blacks [16 years and over]	12.4
Black females	13.6
Black males	11.5
Teenagers [16–19 years old]	18.2
Black female teenagers	42.3
Black male teenagers	37.6
White female teenagers	16.8
White male teenagers	14.4

Source: United States Department of Labor *Employment and Earnings, January, 1978* (Washington, D.C.: U.S. Government Printing Office, 1978).

higher levels of education do not mean better jobs and women are still discriminated against. These problems have persisted, but not because no one has tried to solve them.

ATTEMPTS AT DEALING WITH THE PROBLEM

It would be unfair to say that in the past quarter century workers have made no gains. They have. Many strenuous jobs have been mechanized or have been eliminated by automation. For example, robots are now being used in some plants to weld the frames of cars together, eliminating the human element in this unpleasant job. Workers have achieved some degree of job security. They have cleaner plants to work in, better ventilation, and most toilets in workers' rest rooms now have doors on them. They have more relief time on their shifts and many plants provide food. Cost-of-living increases are built into many contracts, as are more liberal retirement plans. In the auto industry, workers can retire at age fifty-six and new agreements contain the provision for working thirty years and then retiring, regardless of age. And many companies are giving their workers fringe benefits like offering stocks or profit-sharing. These changes have all benefited workers, and discontent has been kept at tolerable levels. Yet, as we saw in the last section, objective conditions indicate that there are problems in the workplace. Three groups have tried to solve these problems, in different ways. Employers have tried to lessen discontent and increase satisfaction; unions have tried to improve working conditions and compensation; and the government has fought for greater worker safety, more employment, and an end to discrimination. We will now see how these attempted solutions have fared.

Management Strategies

As is often noted, American workers are the best paid in the world, especially when their wages are calculated in terms of the number of minutes or hours on the job needed to buy consumer goods. Obviously, we live in a consumer society, where the relationship between increased prosperity and happiness is constantly preached. For many this formula seems true, and prosperity is a major reason that most people say they are satisfied with their jobs. As we have shown, such reports are suspect. Under scrutiny a lot of the satisfaction proves superficial, yet for many people a larger paycheck can compensate for dissatisfaction. The beauty of the American system of work is that it is not required to function perfectly, but only well enough to keep things structured as they are.

For example, many of the hippies of the late 1960s refused to engage in work as it was structured in American society. As children of middle- and upper-middle-class families, they had always lived in material comfort, something most of the parents had had to work hard to achieve. They were not motivated by the satisfaction of material needs but demanded meaningful and nonalienating work. When their demands were not met, many dropped out. Their places were taken by the sons and daughters of blue-collar workers, who still wanted to increase their level of comfort. The system continues to work for people like this, whose expectations can be met simply with a nice paycheck. And as long as there are enough of these people available, the system does not have to respond to pressure for change.

Along with increasing wages, companies have also motivated workers to perform by encouraging a system of status differentials and privileges on the job. Workers are given the opportunity to move through a status hierarchy that is largely meaningless in terms of the way the work is organized. With each increase in level comes a more prestigious title, some additional corporate privileges, and some increase in pay. However, the nature of the work does not necessarily change, nor does the promotion mean increased creativity or control. But this status hierarchy works because it gives the impression of mobility within the organization and it divides the work force into groups who do not see themselves as having common interests or identity. Status groupings in American society have been used very effectively to prevent class consciousness from developing, and with many more workers now in white-collar jobs, status differentiation has increased.

Labor Unions

As mentioned in our discussion of the ideas of Karl Marx, labor unions were at one time thought to be the key to improving the conditions of working people. They have not been so. Unions have not organized a sufficient number of workers to pressure for changes in the system. They never included more than about 25 percent of the labor force at their peak and today they comprise only 22 percent of the work force.[30] Since 1968, the percentage of the work force in unions has fallen steadily. Union activity has also decreased. There were about 5,000 work stoppages by unions in 1975, with slightly over half involving the issue of wages. The range of union issues is now smaller. Problems of plant administration (23 percent), union matters (11.6 percent), and job security (5.1 percent) were the most frequent problems involved in stopping work.[31] In the early part of this century, unions were politically active in ways they no longer are, as they would stop work over a wider range of issues. As prosperity has risen, union demands have seldom touched basic issues like job satisfaction, racial or sex discrimination, or unemployment. And to add irony to their role, the AFL-CIO broke tradition and supported a Republican, Richard M. Nixon, in the 1972 presidential election, and then found themselves confronted by the highest unemployment rates since the end of World War II. Nevertheless, today unions and management both agree that the satisfaction of the worker can be best attained if wages are raised high enough.

Many early unions were clearly Marxist inspired, and set welfare goals for their members that went far beyond the workplace. Many attempts to build a better society have been begun by radical union leaders motivated by a belief that socialism was the answer to working peoples' problems. In their minds, until the workers own the means of production, workers' lot would never improve significantly. What happened to these attempts is an interesting story, involving political repression and government support of illegal practices by factory owners, but to oversimplify, in addition to such tactics these movements failed because workers' demands for wage increases have been sufficiently met over the long run to keep them at work, generally unresponsive to radical appeals. The owners were able to grant higher wages because of changes in technology and changes in the organization of work. The result is that the owners of the means of production have retained control of the plants, have increased their own wealth, and have paid what appear to be higher wages. Higher wages do not necessarily mean less exploitation, for often new equipment allows a higher wage to be paid while rates of exploitation remain constant. Today American unions have essentially bought the viewpoint of management, seeing any wage increases as tied to increasing productivity.

Many observers have noted that this places the worker in the middle, caught between the union and management, both of whom share the objective of increasing his output. Unions have also become quite protective of the jobs they control access to, and have as a result lost their desire to unionize the entire labor force. White males comprise the vast majority of union members and some critics charge that unions are not interested in recruiting blacks or females.

Unions have also been unconcerned about increasing their membership in the South, although this has changed recently. A major

Strikes are powerful tools used by labor unions against management to bring about better wages, hours, working conditions, or benefits. These Kentucky coal miners were part of the nationwide 1977 strike that crippled the country for several winter months.

attempt is now being made to organize textile workers, many of whom are blacks or women, which has engendered a bitter struggle with the J. P. Stevens Company, a major cotton producer with 45,000 employees and $1.5 billion in net sales.[32] Stevens has resorted to illegal measures to defeat the union and keep its wages as low as possible. Stevens has violated the law on many occasions and has defied the courts after being cited for those violations. Ironically, given the way the tax laws are structured, even if Stevens pays a large fine or has to pay an army of lawyers to defend its actions, the company is able to claim these costs as a legitimate business expense and avoid paying taxes on this part of its profits.

As the second largest textile chain in the

nation, Stevens is particularly important to organize, and the battle between business and union is on. The company has liquidated all its unionized plants in the North and acquired dozens of smaller firms in the South where not a single employee is covered by a union contract. Many observers feel that Stevens's practices show how all wage laborers would be treated were it not for unions. Therefore they see Stevens as a test case, with much at stake. Like the lettuce and grape pickers in California, textile workers have had to fight even for the right to have a union represent them. The opposition unions still meet, combined with the declining percentage of the work force that is unionized and with labor's unwillingness to push for wide changes in the structure of work, mean that the hope unions once represented for the betterment of workers is somewhat diminished.

Government Action

The government has intervened in the economy to solve three of the problems we've discussed: sex discrimination, worker health and safety, and unemployment. In each area, the reason for government action was a perception that industry and labor were not willing to solve the problem if left to themselves. The latter two issues have been the subject of government action for some decades, but the question of sex discrimination has been taken up only recently. In trying to reverse the traditional low status of women in the work force, the government has supported *affirmative action* programs, which are company plans to recruit women for nontraditional jobs. Court rulings and legislative action have combined to try to influence companies to open opportunities up for women. But despite government economic and legal pressure to institute such programs, the position of women is not markedly improved, as was shown in Table 4.3 and Table 4.4.

The government also has moved into the area of worker health and safety, although the situation was somewhat different. Whereas it seemed that unions were not going to pressure industry to end sex discrimination, unions have focused on worker health and safety ever since they were first formed. As recently as 1977 these issues were central to a protracted strike. The coal miners' strike of that winter was as long and bitter as it was partly because of miners' resentment over the dangers to their lives

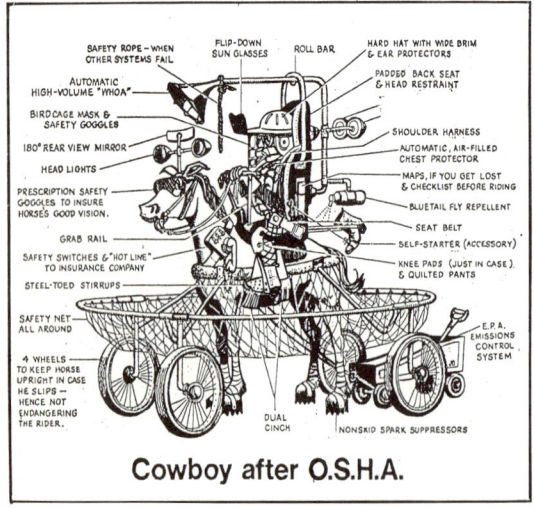

The Occupational Safety and Health Administration (OSHA) is responsible for improving worker safety, but it has been attacked for too much bureaucracy and too little inspection and enforcement. This view of a cowboy after an OSHA investigation ridicules OSHA's paperwork approach to correcting hazardous working conditions.

presented by the coal companies' safety violations. Wildcat strikes are often called on the spot, in this industry and others, when a worker is killed or injured on the job, and many of the traditional hatreds of the workers come out at this time. But while unions have done a great deal, because the vast majority of the American labor force is not unionized, the federal government has had to act. The agent for federal action is the Occupational Safety and Health Administration (OSHA), established in 1970.

Unfortunately, OSHA's record to date has not been impressive. OSHA has concentrated on improving worker safety, but it has done little. The rate of serious injuries in manufacturing rose 2.3 percent in the first five years of its existence. At best there have been modest gains in some areas, partly because enforcement is so weak. In 1976 OSHA inspected fewer than 2 percent of the 5 million workplaces it could have. This kind of effort cannot be expected to yield major results. Even worse than this failure is the fundamental mistake the agency made in deciding on its focus: "performance has fallen short of ambition. . . . OSHA's failings to date should not be surprising since it focused on the wrong problem, safety on the job, instead of occupational health and then employed the wrong tool, direct regulation, rather than an incentive approach."[33] As was stressed earlier, worker health is a far more serious problem than are accidents on the job, and the sources of illnesses are very hard to do something about. As anyone coping with a problem often does, the government, in creating OSHA, did what was easiest to do first. Perhaps in time the real health problems facing workers will be faced, especially in their psychological and social dimensions. But to date this has not been done.

A similar misconception has plagued government efforts to end unemployment. As we noted earlier, unemployment rates are highest among blacks, teenagers, women, and laborers. These facts have been known for years and several strategies have been tried by the government to alleviate the problem. However, as with all other social problems, the solutions tried were based on how the problem was analyzed and what was taken to be the real issue. There are three ways of looking at the problem of unemployment, all based on one's understanding of what determines wages in our society:[34]

1. Orthodox economic theory states that the determinant of wages is the worker's productivity, which can be increased by education or training. Unemployment is the result of workers not being productive enough.
2. Dual market theory stresses that the job market is broken down into a primary sector, where the good jobs are, and a secondary sector, involving jobs that are low-paying, menial, or of short duration. Unemployment is the result of discrimination on the part of the employers, who stereotype workers according to their social group.
3. Radical economic theory stresses the total organization of labor in a capitalist system where workers do not have a sense of being members of the proletariat. Instead, workers identify with their own occupational group and do not try to organize all working people to pressure all employers for increased jobs and wages. Unemployment results from capitalist society's inability to marshall the resources needed to give everyone who wants to work a productive job.

The government has consistently followed the first perspective, ignoring the possibility of any other approach, thus dooming its intervention.

Steps taken to deal with unemployment are more fully discussed in the chapter on the central cities (Chapter 12), because most recent government efforts have been aimed at the hard-core unemployed living there, but a few points can be made here. There is growing concern over the costs to American society of an unemployment rate of about 7 percent. Unemployed workers do not pay taxes, but the benefits they receive come out of government revenues. In addition, one side of the debate over rising welfare costs insists that recipients work, even if the government itself must employ them. And others in the government are genuinely concerned over the effects of chronic unemployment on the individual. But all attempted solutions avoid a restructuring of work. Instead, the government has concentrated on identifying those who can work — those not too young, too old, or with small children — and has designed federal programs to help them.

The most notable effort has been the Job Corps. Based on orthodox economic theory, it has meant instituting worker education and training programs, with the greatest emphasis on teaching literacy, simple math, and some marketable skill. As you can see, this effort is largely a duplication of effort necessitated by the failure of public schools. And while there have been some successes based on this program, the problem of discrimination has not been addressed. The problem with unemployment is not the shortage of skilled workers, but the shortage of good jobs available to all groups. The Job Corps has done nothing to address this issue, since it is based on different assumptions.

The Humphrey-Hawkins bill, being considered by Congress, affords a contrast. As originally written, it provided that the government would step in and create jobs for anyone willing to work if private industry did not supply work. This strategy obviously flies in the face of society's ideology, which holds that the private sector is to provide work in accordance with the needs of the market structure. But this bill shows what can happen when the government departs from its orthodox view. First introduced in 1975, the bill has been so watered down that it no longer expresses a new approach to unemployment. The government will return to its old stand-by policies: trying to expand the economy by granting tax breaks to corporations that purchase new and more productive machines and create jobs, and to consumers to spur consumer spending. In the past these strategies have produced a slowly but steadily increasing gross national product, and have resulted in more people than ever before being employed. Still, they have not provided jobs for the hard-core unemployed.

Iatrogenic Effects

While there have been major attempts to better the conditions of the American worker, there have also been some unintended and unanticipated harmful side effects, the iatrogenic effects that accompany attempts to solve all social problems. Higher wages and increased fringe benefits have largely killed the willingness of workers to demand changes in the nature of the work they do. The American worker today finds that industry's increased productivity has increased his access to the consumer goods industry produces. Any sense of working-class consciousness that may have existed has been all but eradicated by the post-World War II prosperity. Prosperity has more firmly established the legitimacy of the capitalist economic system in the minds of most workers, especially those who were adults or grew up during the Depression.

Increased educational opportunities for younger Americans have been made available, on the premise that higher educational levels would be necessary to fill tomorrow's jobs. This has not been the case. With so many college graduates around, the educational requirements of many jobs have simply been increased, using education as a sorting device. While it is true that who goes to college cannot be accurately predicted on the basis of class background, who graduates from college still can be. Rising levels of education have eliminated the poor and minority groups from a chance at the better jobs in a more sophisticated fashion than ever before. No longer are race and ethnic or class discrimination needed to keep the wrong people directly out of the good jobs; formal education does this very nicely. For many people at the bottom of society, opportunities are decreasing rather than increasing.

In addition, many college graduates have come to expect that their education will get them better jobs, but that hasn't been the case either. Today we find college-educated people working at all sorts of menial jobs, with some Ph.D.'s driving taxis. Although it can be argued that education is good for its own sake, it is probably true that many of these underemployed people become bitter. Essentially those who do not get good jobs were lied to when their expectations were raised too high. This partly accounts for the finding that more educated workers are not as productive as workers with less education. The phenomenon is so widespread today that industry is speaking of the over-educated American. Increased wages and fringe benefits will not meet their demands for jobs allowing greater freedom, creativity, and self-control.

Government programs designed to ensure prosperity in order to reduce unemployment have also not worked as they should have. Given tax breaks to buy new machinery, many firms have bought highly automated systems, which wind up displacing workers. Today the unemployment rate is about twice as high as a decade ago, partly as the result of increased automation. As wages have increased, many companies have moved faster on automation because of the savings in wages it represents. And as the federal minimum wage is raised, in an attempt to help workers at the bottom of the wage structure, many employers lay off some of those workers whose wages they feel they can no longer afford. Government action cuts two ways and keeps the unemployment rate high, at least for certain groups.

In the area of worker safety, OSHA has not only failed to affect great improvement, it has increased antagonism toward government involvement with the workplace. There seems to be a growing bitterness toward government regulations and control, an unanticipated result that could have drastic consequences. Many people who once favored government attempts to solve social problems are now backing off from this view, seeing OSHA as an example of the inevitable failure of such a policy. Because government programs and the funds to support them are dependent on attitudes, a wholesale shift toward the negative created by antagonism will cause the programs themselves to suffer. OSHA is a prime example of this backlash against increased government involvement.

Government safety regulations have combined with high wages to produce another problem. American corporations have moved to foreign countries, where workers are not in a position to demand that the work be safe, rewarding, or well paid. The multinational corporations are the newest form of colonialism where, in the name of profit, foreign workers are exploited because their labor is cheap. At the same time, American jobs are lost. For example, like many other electrical companies, Zenith has moved its manufacturing operations outside the United States; as the result of the government safety standards, so have the major asbestos companies. Tin miners working for American controlled companies are reportedly making about thirteen cents an hour and in other areas the wage rate is well below what the American worker could demand. All of this, of course, creates additional problems for American workers, and not just those who lose their jobs. As more companies go overseas, the nation's balance of payments deficit increases, driving up the cost of importing foreign goods. As a result of this trend — as well as other factors — the American dollar recently has reached its lowest point since the end of World War II, with its lower value also contributing to inflation.

A final set of problems revolves around action against discrimination. While affirmative action is being challenged by suits charging such programs institute reverse discrimination, other court rulings have held mandatory retirement ages as discriminatory. Many companies offer early retirement as an incentive to get older workers out of the job market so they can be replaced by younger ones who can be paid less. These programs are not endangered, and some people will take advantage of them, although most workers still prefer working to losing the benefits their jobs offer in money and as an outlet for their energies. But by outlawing mandatory retirement, these court decisions may create unemployment among younger people, as the turnover rate in jobs slows down.

PROSPECTS FOR SOLVING THE PROBLEM

The way work-related problems will be dealt with in the 1980s depends on the economic conditions prevailing at the time. Obviously, this is difficult to forecast with any certainty. With a severe depression, unemployment rates would rise and many workers would be glad simply to have jobs, even if they were unsatisfying or monotonous. But assuming normal economic conditions, a number of things can be said about the issues presented in this chapter.

The most important comment is that, while the role of government is crucial, we feel there will be little if any push from the federal government for improvement in many of these programs. In the past decade, government social programs have grown at astounding rates and are now costing hundreds of billions of dollars each year. To meet the cost of these, the federal government relies on tax revenues from individuals and American corporations. No profits to tax means no funding for social programs. Many in business are complaining about the taxes they already pay, and many are arguing that taxes reduce their incentive to be more profitable. This is an important point: it means that both government and corporations are committed to enlarging profits. If Marx was right and profit does mean the retention of surplus value by the owners and the exploitation of workers, it seems unlikely that workers will get a larger share of the returns from their labor.

Another source of change in the workplace could be the unions, but they are also unlikely to play such a role. American unions are in a far different position from European ones, which have a greater sense of class consciousness. In some European countries a general strike is often called in order to remind everyone just how dependent they are on the work other people do. But with the American unions accepting the need for higher productivity for the worker to be paid more and the corporations to maintain high profits, it does not appear that unions are going to be a force for major change. Ironically, in the Great Depression of the 1930s, union demands went far beyond what they had been in the prosperous 1920s. The unions began to challenge the nature of the capitalist system itself. Because the system was unable to supply jobs or goods for so many people, their cries for change fell on receptive ears. This demonstrates a fact of American society; as long as the capitalist system delivers on its promises of material prosperity, it can ward off cries for change. Worker demands for better paying jobs and more interesting work all occur in good economic times, for in the bad times most workers simply want not to be unemployed. In better economic times when they are making more money and are able to buy the latest consumer goods, worker demands for change usually focus primarily on higher wages. This is especially true in times of high inflation rates, such as the post-Vietnam years.

The American economic and political system has always stressed individual social mobility, usually from the working class into the middle class. Our ideology of social mobility sees the question as one of individual desire: if a person fails to make the grade, he is at fault. Clearly one aspect of American capitalism has been to give the appearance of mobility to millions of workers while keeping power and control structured as they always have been. An examination shows that the distribution of income and the pattern of ownership of corporate assets have changed little during the past fifty years. A very few people own the majority of the stocks and bonds of American corporations.

The big change has come not in the pattern of ownership but in how control is maintained. A managerial class has been created — and rewarded — to keep the pattern of ownership intact. This managerial class has no sense of itself as part of the proletariat because its work is different from that done by the working class a hundred years ago. But this does not mean there has been a real shift in power, at least in the ownership of the means of production. What there has been instead is rising prosperity, with the worker and the manager both cut in on a piece of the action in order to keep the system viable. As a result, the average American knows that the system works for him; it meets those demands he was educated and indoctrinated to have.

With the economic structure unchanged, the worker faces problems that still can be solved in ways other than the traditional increase in wages. Many observers feel that such an improvement would be shortening the work week. Others contend that, with the pattern of recreation that has developed in American society since the end of World War II, more free time might not benefit the worker at all. But as we stressed in our original distinction between leisure and recreation, it takes workers some time to unwind from their jobs and make the shift required to use their free time as leisure and not simply as recreation. With more time off, workers may be able to make that shift more easily. They would then be using their time for leisure and not simply as recreation. Of course, this can cause problems too. Workers could develop their individuality to such an extent that they grow increasingly dissatisfied with their work. This is all speculation, however. It has never been tried on a large scale involving a wide range of different occupations. But it is clear that work conditions workers in certain definite ways and that this conditioning helps to keep them working. Anything that interferes with this conditioning must have some consequences on how workers view their jobs.

Another frequently discussed solution to the problems with work has been the increased use of automation. This approach has worked well in a number of different industries and has eliminated much of the backbreaking work of years past. However, it does not appear that higher technology will bring major benefits to workers, at least not in the near future. Automation is developed and introduced only if economic incentives allow its cost to be paid for out of increased profits. The technology exists to improve the structure of working conditions on a large number of jobs, but because the economic incentives are lacking, it has not been introduced. We now realize that technology is not free from social control; it is shaped by the values and needs of the people with power in our society. They will use it in their interest as long as they have the power to do so.

We believe that technology could be used to revolutionize work in American society, but it will not until democracy is brought to the workplace. Democracy will challenge the power and control within the corporation and in society in general. While we give lip service to living in a democratic society, much research by social scientists clearly shows that we do not. Special interest groups, especially the corporations, have greatly influenced government and subverted the meaning of democracy. This has important implications for the problems of the workplace, for true democracy is in our view mandatory if work is to change significantly. Technology is developed, channeled, and directed only in terms of the prevailing power structures. Its impact on the workplace could be enormous, but it will be used only to increase our material comfort, not to make work more meaningful. Only democracy in the workplace can change that.

IMPORTANT WORDS AND TERMS

affirmative action
agricultural societies
alienation
automation
blue-collar worker
bourgeoisie
bureaucracy
capitalism

embourgeoisment
   of the proletariat
exploitation
feudal system
guild
hunters and gatherers
interchangeable parts
labor theory of value

leisure
oppression
proletariat
Protestant work
   ethic
recreation
role overload
serf

slavery
social mobility
surplus value
technology
underemployment
unemployment
white-collar work
work

QUESTIONS FOR DISCUSSION

1. Of the people you know who work for a living, how many would work at the same job if they did not need the money? at a different job? at no job?
2. Could a corporate manager earning $35,000 a year be exploited by the company he or she works for?
3. In America today, who makes up the proletariat?
4. Every job has many dimensions to it (money, status, power). Which is the most important to you and why?
5. Why do people work at unpleasant and boring jobs?
6. Is the Protestant work ethic alive in America today? How do you know?
7. From the people you know, how many use anything they learned in school on their jobs? How much have they needed to learn on the job?
8. Analyze this statement: "The better the job, the less it should pay."
9. The government has often allowed the unemployment rate to rise while fighting inflation. Is this a good idea in your mind? Support your answer with facts.
10. Should there be a strong relationship between the amount of schooling a person has and the status of a job he gets? Why?
11. What can be done about the underemployment of black youths in urban areas?
12. "A woman who works should split the household and child-care chores with her working husband equally." Present the pros and cons of this statement.
13. Do you think we need more or less government regulation of the workplace? Be specific, and indicate the areas where more or less regulation is needed.
14. Discuss the pros and cons of this statement: "The government should give a job to anyone wanting to work."

SUGGESTED READING

STUDS TERKEL, *Working* (New York: Avon, 1974).

Like the other things Terkel has written, in this book he lets people talk, this time about their jobs. The result is an impressionistic book covering a wide range of jobs, which gives good insight into how people feel about their work. The bitterness many employees feel about their jobs is balanced by the sense of accomplishment reported by others. Terkel gives us more data than we can possibly digest, but this book has the advantage of presenting its findings in narrative form; and while it is very long, it is fun to read, and can be read selectively.

GEORGE RITZER, *Man and His Work* (New York: Appleton-Century-Crofts, 1972).

This book takes a sophisticated look at work, emphasizing how occupations develop in relation to changes occurring in the social structure. A major focus is on the drive for the professionalization of an occupation as a means of securing greater rewards for those in the job. Ritzer also looks at situations where people in a number of different occupations must work together and analyzes the frictions that arise; he also examines how they are resolved. This is an important book for those interested in the changes and conflicts occurring in the workplace.

FREDERICK THAYER, *An End to Hierarchy! An End to Competition!* (New York: Franklin Watts, 1973).

Our economic structure is organized bureaucratically. In addition, we use competition for status to motivate people. In this provocative book, Thayer discusses the assumptions underlying these two ideas. He shows each to be based on false premises. Thayer feels we pay too high a price — in dissatisfaction with the quality of life — by using these mechanisms to structure work. He is committed to putting our belief in democracy into practice and, like some other social theorists, sees democracy as being systematically undermined by the use of bureaucracy. His chapter on the absurdities of economic competition is one of the most exciting parts of a most provocative book.

WILLIAM TORBERT, *Being for the Most Part Puppets* (Cambridge, Mass.: Schenkman, 1973).

Like Thayer's book reviewed above, and as can be seen from its title, Torbert's monograph is controversial. Torbert examines how our values are undermined by how we organize work. In his analysis he studies problems in implementing our democratic ideology. He uses alienation in a political sense and in terms of the work people do as the focus for his concern. Torbert is very much concerned with how work has become divorced from leisure, the activities that help a person grow and develop. He also sees the way people now get to spend their free time as forcing them to "recreate" the energy necessary to go back to work. This book will cause you to question your values and think about work from a different perspective.

DAVID GORDON, *Theories of Poverty and Underemployment* (Lexington, Mass.: D. C. Heath, 1972).

David Gordon has written this monograph from the perspective of political economy, showing how the analysis of unemployment depends on the analyst's ideology. More important, he shows how different assumptions provide both alternative definitions of the problem and alternative solutions. Gordon is critical of past efforts to combat poverty through employment training programs for minority and lower-class people; he feels they have been based on false assumptions and that explains their failure. Gordon suggests we look at our economic institutions and the structure of work from a different viewpoint, based on different assumptions. This book is difficult, but important for understanding why so many of our efforts have not solved the problems of unemployment or of poverty.

NOTES

1. George Ritzer, *Working-Conflict and Change* (Englewood Cliffs, N.J.: Prentice-Hall, 1977), p. 3.
2. Walter Neff, *Work and Human Behavior* (New York: Atherton Press, 1968), p. 52.
3. Ibid., p. 63.
4. See Robert Beam, "From Millennium to Malaise," *Modern Age,* Vol. 22, No. 1 (Winter 1978), pp. 54–63.
5. Karl Marx, *The Communist Manifesto,* trans. Paul Sweezy (New York: Monthly Review Press, 1968), pp. 45–49.
6. Max Weber, "Some Consequences of Bureaucratization," in Lewis Coser and Bernard Rosenberg (eds.), *Sociological Theory* (New York: Macmillan, 1976), p. 362.
7. William Torbert, *Being for the Most Part Puppets* (Cambridge, Mass.: Schenkman, 1973), p. 64.
8. Harry Braverman, *Labor and Monopoly Capital* (New York: Monthly Review Press, 1974).
9. Ibid., p. 433.
10. Ibid., p. 447.
11. Ivar Berg, *Education and Jobs: The Great Training Robbery* (Boston: Beacon Press, 1971).
12. Fritz Rothlisberger and William Dickson, *Management and the Worker* (Cambridge, Mass.: Harvard University Press, 1939).
13. For an interesting discussion see Frederick Thayer, *An End to Hierarchy! An End to Competition!* (New York: Franklin Watts, 1973).
14. C. Wright Mills, *White Collar* (New York: Oxford University Press, 1951).
15. Eli Chinoy, *Automobile Workers and the*

American Dream (Garden City, N.Y.: Doubleday, 1955).

16. Arthur Kornhauser, "Toward an Assessment of the Mental Health of Factory Workers," *Human Organization*, Vol. 21, No. 1 (Spring 1962), p. 46.

17. Studs Terkel, *Working* (New York: Avon, 1975).

18. Speech delivered at University of Colorado, 1971.

19. Department of Labor, *Handbook of Labor Statistics, 1977* (Washington, D.C.: U.S. Government Printing Office, 1977), p. 188.

20. Ibid., pp. 270–275.

21. Ibid., p. 349.

22. Carey McCord, "Life and Death by the Minute," *Industrial Machine*, Vol. 17, No. 10 (October 1948), p. 28.

23. James House, "Effects of Occupational Stress on Physical Health," in James O'Toole (ed.), *Work and the Quality of Life* (Cambridge, Mass.: M.I.T. Press, 1974), p. 151.

24. Ibid., p. 160.

25. Albert Nichols and Richard Zeckhauser, "Government Comes to the Work Place," *Public Interest* (Fall 1977), pp. 39–40.

26. Department of Labor, *U.S. Working Women: A Data Book* (Washington, D.C.: U.S. Government Printing Office, 1977).

27. Department of Labor, *Working Women*, pp. 34–36.

28. Department of Labor, *Employment and Earnings, January 1978*, p. 181.

29. Ibid., pp. 20–23.

30. Department of Labor, *Handbook of Labor Statistics*, p. 293.

31. Ibid., p. 305.

32. Jerry DeMuth, "Brown Lung in the Cotton Mills," *America* (March 18, 1978), pp. 206–208.

33. Nichols and Zeckhauser, "Government Comes to the Work Place," p. 39.

34. For a detailed look at these perspectives see David Gordon, *Theories of Poverty and Unemployment* (Lexington, Mass.: D. C. Heath, 1972).

5 POVERTY
TRAPPED IN A VICIOUS CYCLE

CHAPTER OVERVIEW

INTRODUCTION

HISTORICAL OVERVIEW
The Poor in Europe
Poverty in the United States
    The Poor in the Cities
    The Depression and Government Response
Summary

CONCEPTUAL ORIENTATION
Defining Poverty
    An Absolute Definition of Poverty
    A Relative Definition of Poverty
Summary

OBJECTIVE DIMENSIONS OF
    THE PROBLEM
Children
The Elderly
Blacks

The Impact of Poverty
Summary

ATTEMPTS AT DEALING WITH
    THE PROBLEM
The Government's Approaches
Reevaluating Government Welfare Programs
Negative Income Tax Plans
Iatrogenic Effects

PROSPECTS FOR SOLVING
    THE PROBLEM
What Will It Cost?
Who Will Pay?

IMPORTANT WORDS AND TERMS

QUESTIONS FOR DISCUSSION

SUGGESTED READING

NOTES

In every crucial area — food, housing, education, and other social responsibilities — the United States provides its worst off citizens only a percentage of what they desperately need.
　　　　　　　　　　　　Michael Harrington, *The Other America*

The number of persons in poverty started to increase again in 1970 and has not declined since then. There is some evidence to believe that the real incidence of poverty is higher than the poverty statistics would indicate.
　　　　　　　　　　　　Select Committee on Nutrition
　　　　　　　　　　　　and Human Needs, *Hunger 1973*

CHAPTER OVERVIEW

In America, each new generation, much to its surprise, finds widespread poverty in the midst of general prosperity. Because the prosperity is so real, the poverty seems impossible; the result is disbelief in the number of poor people. In this chapter, we show that such disbelief is misplaced. We describe who the poor are, what mechanisms account for their poverty, and what has been done to help them. We use a structural analysis of social inequality to account for poverty, dismissing the theory of the culture of poverty, which blames the poor. With this structural emphasis in mind, we show that only basic changes in social organization can remove the problem of poverty.

INTRODUCTION

Discussing poverty, especially in the 1980s, is a bizarre task for most Americans. For many, the idea that a sizable part of the population is living at or below the officially established poverty level is difficult to grasp. But a closer look reveals the existence of this other America, where deprivation and hunger must be faced daily. But only recently has the poverty existing in our country come to be considered as a social problem.

The catalyst for this definition was Michael Harrington, whose book, *The Other America,* pointed out the existence of widespread poverty in the midst of plenty.[1] Prior to 1962, when the book was published, several widely used social problems texts did not even refer to poverty in American society.[2] To understand why this attitude was prevalent, it is necessary to see how poverty was defined and coped with in the past. We will then examine current definitions of the problem, analyze what causes poverty, and look at the effectiveness of recent attempts to solve it.

HISTORICAL OVERVIEW

The Poor in Europe

The general affluence characteristic of America since World War II has been unknown in history. Previously, only small elites were as well off, but generally societies had great differentials in wealth and power, with most people eking out an existence. Of the billions of people who have ever lived, the vast majority have lived in what we would today call an impoverished condition. Until the twentieth century, life expectancy at birth was under thirty years and food was periodically in short supply. People's lives were restricted by two ecological limits that eighteenth-century economist Thomas Malthus outlined in his essay *On Population:* disease and famine.[3]

These poor people did not all starve and die. Some managed to survive on their own, and others received public assistance, for every society has made some provision for the poor. For our purposes, the most important provisions were those of the early modern age, because they formed the basis for modern arrangements. In the Middle Ages, the church, acting from its Christian duty, assumed responsibility for helping the poor. However, in the late thirteenth century, some people began to see problems in granting this aid. Because resources were limited and poor people too numerous, laws were passed restricting eligibility for help.

The first major public relief systems in Europe were the result of mass civil disturbances that erupted in the sixteenth century as part of the transition from feudalism to capitalism. Because the death rate had dropped, population was growing rapidly during this time; along with this population growth came a noticeable increase in the number of beggars. And, during periods of crop failures and natural disasters, hordes of peasants entered cities demanding food, thus threatening the social order. Something needed to be done, and the solution chosen has more or less been continued to the present.

The problem and the solution are typified by events in Lyons, France. In 1531 mobs of starving peasants overran the town, causing mass panic. The problem was wrestled with for three years, when the rulers finally concluded that aid to the poor should no longer be a religious function but would become the responsibility of the government. First the government wished to monopolize poor relief, so begging was prohibited. To enact its program, a list of the needy was compiled and those who qualified for aid identified. Standards for giving out food and money were codified and the sick were sent off to hospitals where free treatment was provided. Criteria were established to distinguish the worthy poor from the unworthy and a policy of keeping track of the progress of the poor was begun along with efforts to rehabilitate them. As you can see, many features of a modern welfare system were present in these programs.

Such relief systems, while designed to aid the poor, tended also to reinforce the system of wage labor, by helping to overcome the lack of fit between the needs of the labor market and the availability of the labor force. Included in these efforts across the continent were poor laws that forced the unemployed to work when work was offered, no matter what the wage. The poor became pawns.

These systems continued in effect, with only minor changes, for over two centuries, but then the rapid growth of the population and the Industrial Revolution rendered them inadequate. During the nineteenth century, this lack of fit had become increasingly serious. Many who had been forced off the land could no longer be absorbed into the urban work force, and remained in the countryside as vagrants. Others migrated into the cities and crowded into shacks and hovels. As a result civil disorder spread. To cope with these disturbances, relief systems expanded; but they were designed to discipline the idle masses, trying to make them fit into the labor market or at least trying to prevent a revolt of the poor.

Poverty in the United States

In the United States this nineteenth-century crisis was not as acute, but still existed. The country's vast territory offered great opportunity for geographical mobility. Individuals could overcome poverty by picking up and moving on. The result was to decrease the number of poor temporarily, but more important, this westward expansion added a new dimension to ideas about poverty. Many Americans came to see poverty not as the result of the economic system's failure to supply work, but as the lack of individual initiative and desire to work.

THE POOR IN THE CITIES

Even with the great opportunity to move on in search of a better life, large masses of poor people could not do so and remained trapped in eastern cities. Although the chance for mobility remained even into the twentieth century, the cities were beginning to be clogged by the poor in the 1840s and 1850s. Historian Arthur Schlesinger, writing about the cities in the mid-nineteenth century, comments that optimism about the opportunities the frontier provided overlooked the realities of life for these urban poor: "For the increasing numbers of urban wage earners the so-called safety valve of the frontier failed to work. 'The Wilderness has receded,' declared an Eastern observer in 1840, 'and already the new lands are beyond the reach of the mere laborer, and the employer has him at his mercy.'"[4] Attempts were begun to aid the poor, including a concerted attack on slum housing. There were also attempts at social welfare based on the application of so-called scientific principles of charity, including the establishment of settlement houses, playgrounds for poor children, and the like.

At the end of the nineteenth century the situation worsened. A new flood of immigrants poured into the country. Because they spoke a different language and dressed and behaved in different ways, they were discriminated against. They were employed in unskilled and semiskilled jobs. With only the

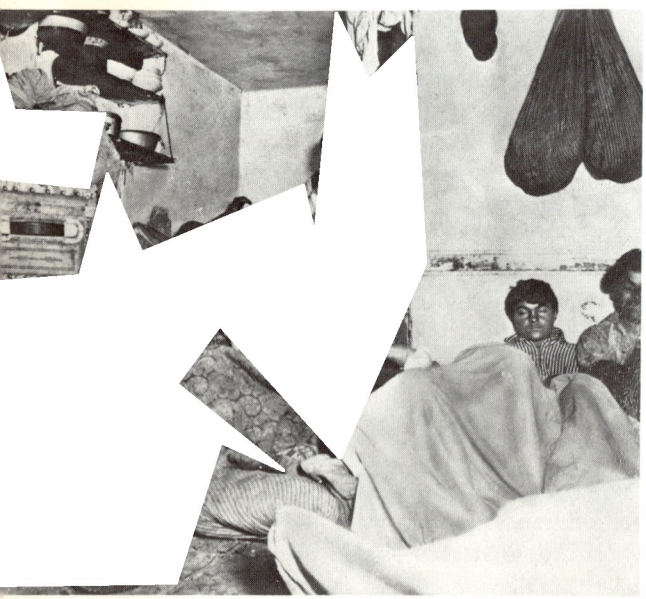

At the end of the nineteenth century, American cities were flooded with immigrants looking for a new life but finding that their poverty relegated them to squalor. Poverty, however, was not always perceived as a social problem; the plight of these immigrants sheltered in a New York City tenement would have been blamed on their being foreign rather than their being poor.

simplest training, they could be put to work in factories and sweatshops. Their pay was low because they were unskilled, uneducated, and unorganized. Most had no choice but to live in the squalid, rundown slums, where they could at least be close to others of their own nationality. Their problem was seen not as their poverty, but as their foreign ways.[5] Although it was widespread, poverty was not perceived as a social problem to be systematically attacked through concerted governmental action.

THE DEPRESSION AND
GOVERNMENT RESPONSE

A basic change in American ideas about poverty began in the year 1929. The economic disaster called the Great Depression threw large numbers of people out of work, including able-bodied, hardworking, and successful people, many of whom were without work for the first time in their lives. The result of the unregulated workings of the capitalist system, the Depression created a massive threat to the existing social order. Something had to be done.

Ideas about work and aid to the poor had to change. It became impossible to explain away the widespread poverty on the basis of people's unwillingness to work. People wanted to work but could find none. By 1935 unemployment was so widespread that more than 20 million people were getting some sort of relief. More important, the government had to defuse the growing unrest among what had been the most loyal part of the population. The government relief efforts of the 1930s changed the basic economic institutions only enough to quiet massive discontent. While institutions were being altered, the government gave aid to people, but it was cut back as soon as the discontent with the system lessened.

As the efforts of the Lyons city government in the 1530s and of the United States government in the 1930s illustrate, throughout history welfare has been given at those times and to those groups who make trouble for the established order. This does not mean that the humanitarian rhetoric accompanying this aid has been totally false. In many cases, aid has been given out of real concern for the people involved. This is especially true of aid to the very poor, and explains why welfare has been continued — on however small a scale — after the Depression ended. Nevertheless, it becomes clear that throughout history these efforts were also seen as a way of keeping more widespread discontent from developing. More will be said of this when we discuss recent welfare policy.

Summary

This brief historical overview has indicated how the conditions of and attitudes toward poverty have evolved. In the early modern era, with the change from federalism to capitalism, laws were passed giving aid only to those persons who could not work. Over time, European laws went so far as to make poverty a crime and to place the poor at the mercy of anyone willing to offer them work. Poor laws and relief efforts based on them were actually in the interest of the groups with power. This was the inheritance to which the United States added an ideology: poverty was the result of personal failure. Many of these attitudes toward the poor changed drastically during the Depression, however, when people saw poverty as a direct result of how society was organized. Relief efforts were then aimed at controlling discontent and civil disorder; they were withdrawn when the unrest subsided. Since then poverty was almost ignored. World War II brought prosperity back and the postwar period was so affluent that people forgot about the poor, until they were reminded in the 1960s. A sizable proportion of the population still lives slightly above, at, or below the poverty line. Before we discuss the characteristics of these people and efforts to solve the problem, we must find out how large a proportion of the population are categorized as poor. That requires defining poverty.

CONCEPTUAL ORIENTATION

Defining Poverty

Our discussion of contemporary ideas about poverty and recent statistical trends begins with a seemingly straightforward and simple question: how many poor people are there in the United States today? In the early 1960s, Michael Harrington pointed out that because they were ignored, the poor were largely invisible, but before too many years passed they had been rediscovered in massive numbers by economists and sociologists. During the sixties, although affluence was taken for granted, many authors set out to define what was meant by poverty in America. But no consensus was reached, and there were almost as many definitions as there were people doing the defining. Daniel P. Moynihan concluded from a seminar of poverty experts held in the late 1960s that "there was no common understanding as to the nature of poverty or the process of deliberate social change."[6] Part of the disagreement stemmed from the fact that poverty was a multidimensional problem, with different elements emphasized. The most useful delineation of these dimensions comes from Arthur B. Shostak, who finds seven separate dimensions of *poverty* — the problem of unequal distribution of rewards. These are:

1. income
2. wealth
3. education
4. services
5. self-respect
6. cognitive skill
7. occupational status[7]

People living at the bottom of society do not have access to these rewards, although most middle-class people take them for granted. Shostak argues that each dimension is interrelated with the others. He points to the work of other sociologists, which shows that low income concentrated in an area usually leads to a low tax base, which leads to inadequate schooling. Inadequate schooling then decreases the students' prospects of adequate income in the future. They will then suffer from low income, reducing the tax base in their area, thus impairing education and restricting the chances of another generation. A vicious cycle is created.

Clearly, one's location in the social structure determines to a large degree one's life chances. Even though the many dimensions of poverty are interrelated, we must begin by focusing on only one element. The one we choose is not only the one that many feel is most important, but also the factor that has been the subject of the most disagreement: the distribution of income.

AN ABSOLUTE DEFINITION OF POVERTY

Income distribution figures express the proportion of families earning various levels of income for a given year. Once we know what these figures are for a particular period, we can ask several questions. Where should we establish a cutoff point, below which we say people live in poverty? What have been recent trends in statistics on the number living in poverty? What have been the results of the attempts to reduce inequities in income distribution?

Answering the first question means establishing *an absolute definition* of poverty, a fixed point that marks the *minimum subsistence income*. Attempts at defining this minimum income level have been seriously undertaken by the government since the early 1960s. According to Herman P. Miller in *Rich Man, Poor Man:*

> One report found that in this, the richest of all countries, forty per cent of the families live in poverty and deprivation. In fact, that is the title of a study published in 1962, *Poverty and Deprivation in the U.S. — The Plight of Two-Fifths of a Nation*. This is no phony Communist propaganda nor the wild charges of a radical reformer. These are the hard-boiled statistical facts proposed by Leon Keyserling, chief economic counselor to President Truman and former head of the Council of Economic Advisors.[8]

Given the prosperity of the late 1950s and early 1960s, it seems odd that Keyserling would find 40 percent of the families of our country to be poor. After all, President Franklin D. Roosevelt had estimated only one-third of the nation was poor, and that was during the height of the Depression. The point of this difference is important. The level at which the *poverty line* is drawn is all important in computing the percentage of people who fall below that line and who are thus said to be living in poverty.

This does not mean that the poverty line can be arbitrarily established. Defining a reasonable limit requires painstaking work. Some of the pioneer work on this for the government was done by Mollie Orshansky of the Social Security Administration. Without going into all of the details of how Orshansky arrived at her conclusions, the government defined the poverty line in 1965 to be $3,225 for a family of four.[9] By 1976 this figure had jumped to $5,815. Table 5.1 shows how many people the government thought lived below its definition of the poverty line.

The total number of Americans living in poverty has dropped from 39.5 million in 1959 to 25.0 million in 1976, a decrease from 22.4 percent to 11.8 percent. The poverty line went from $2,973 to $5,815, due to inflation. At the same time, however, the median income for all families rose from $5,417 to $14,958. In other words, in 1959 the poverty level was 55 percent of the median income, while by 1976 the government had reduced the figure to only 39 percent of median income. By making the poverty level proportionately lower, the government can theoretically eliminate as much poverty as it wants to. But those living with inadequate income

TABLE 5.1 Trends in Poverty 1959–1976

Year	Persons in Poverty (millions)	Percent of Population	Poverty Line	Median Family Income (current dollars)
1959	39.5	22.4	$2,973	$ 5,417
1966	28.5	14.7	3,317	7,500
1970	25.4	12.6	3,968	9,867
1971	25.6	12.5	4,137	10,285
1972	24.5	11.9	4,275	11,116
1973	23.0	11.1	4,540	12,051
1974	23.4	11.2	5,038	12,902
1975	25.9	12.3	5,500	13,719
1976	25.0	11.8	5,815	14,958

Source: Bureau of the Census, *Statistical Abstract of the United States, 1977* (Washington, D.C.: U.S. Government Printing Office, 1977), p. 453.

levels are no better off just because government statistics say so.

The lack of fairness of this definition is not its only weakness. As an absolute standard it is also deficient. If one accepts the government figures as they are, they still do not tell the entire story. Remember that poverty is a multidimensional problem. There are many ways poor people are deprived — in absolute terms — that do not appear in these figures. For example, if the poor tend to go to inferior schools, how much does this cost them in dollars per year? Whatever the amount, it never shows up in government figures.

Again, however, the worst failing of these statistics is the unfairness of the definition of the minimum income — after all, income is considered the most important dimension of poverty. To get a better idea of how many poor people there are, then, we need a better idea of the relative position of people. To do that we need to study *income distribution*.

A RELATIVE DEFINITION OF POVERTY

To find a *relative definition* that takes into account the position of various groups on a scale of income we must compare the income share of those at the bottom to that of those at the top. With complete income equality, the top 20 percent of people would get 20 percent of the income available, and the bottom 20 percent would get 20 percent also. As Table 5.2 shows, that is hardly the case.

As you can see, in 1976 the top 20 percent of the population received 41.1 percent of the income available, about twice what they should have gotten under conditions of complete income equality. Conversely, the 20 percent at the bottom received 5.4 percent of total income, about one-quarter of what they would have gotten with equal distribution.

TABLE 5.2 Percent of Income Received by Each Fifth of the Population

	1950	1960	1970	1976
Lowest fifth	4.5	4.8	5.4	5.4
Second fifth	12.0	12.2	11.9	11.8
Middle fifth	17.4	17.8	17.6	17.6
Fourth fifth	23.4	24.0	23.8	24.1
Highest fifth	42.7	41.3	40.9	41.1

Source: Bureau of the Census, *Statistical Abstract of the United States, 1977* (Washington, D.C.: U.S. Government Printing Office, 1977), p. 449.

This means that the people at the top got about eight times the income of the people at the bottom. Those in the middle are closer to the proportion they would receive with income equality than are the extremes, but the two groups nearest them, while not as wide of the mark as the extremes, are still getting a disproportionate share. The bottom two-fifths get about one-sixth the total income available while those in the top two-fifths get about two-thirds of what is available. Contrary to many people's expectations, income distribution has not changed much in the past quarter century. In fact, it hasn't changed much since 1929. The question of income distribution affects the definition of the poverty line, although first we need to discuss the *median family income* — the point on the income distribution scale at which 50 percent of the families earn more and 50 percent of the families earn less. A percentage of this median income can be used as the cutoff line for poverty. Here is where attitudes toward income distribution come into play. The percentage chosen as the cutoff point depends on the values of the person doing the choosing. If income equality is highly valued (as it is in Sweden) the cutoff point might be

TABLE 5.3 Distribution of Families at Various Income Levels (in 1976 dollars)

Year	Under $3,000	$3,000– $6,999	$7,000– $9,999	$10,000– $14,999	$15,000– $24,999	$25,000+	Median Income
1955	12.0%	21.2%	21.4%	26.8%	15.3%	3.4%	$ 7,850
1960	9.4	18.7	17.0	27.9	21.0	6.0	9,393
1965	6.8	16.1	14.2	26.0	27.3	9.7	12,552
1970	4.8	13.3	11.9	22.7	32.3	15.0	14,465
1976	3.9	14.2	11.8	20.3	32.0	17.8	14,958

Source: Bureau of the Census, *Statistical Abstract of United States, 1977* (Washington, D.C.: U.S. Government Printing Office, 1977), p. 440.

established at 80 percent of median income. If a 50 percent or lower figure were selected as the poverty line, the person would have opted for a society permitting sizable differentials in income. So that the reader can see what would be the result of setting the cutoff point at various levels, Table 5.3 shows the percentage of families at various income levels and also shows the median income. The table is used this way. In 1976, for example, the median family income was $14,958. If we chose two-thirds of this figure as the most desirable proportion, the poverty line would be $10,000. That would leave about 30 percent of all American families below the poverty line: about 17 million of the 56 million American families. This is a far cry from the 11.8 percent that the government says is living in poverty, using their limit of $5,815 for a family of four.

Summary

Poverty is largely the result of the way income is distributed. Despite widespread belief in the ease of social mobility, there have existed and continue to exist large income differentials. These income differentials are seen by more and more sociologists as the generators of all the other problems associated with poverty. Rejecting the old belief that some lack of personal initiative is keeping the poor in poverty, sociologists emphasize situational factors, such as discrimination and the problem of the vicious cycle: poverty reduces access to rewards, which limits opportunities for escaping poverty, which further reduces access to rewards. It is because groups are systematically kept in poverty — and not because individuals fail and thus fall into it — that we can identify the factors that cause poverty.

OBJECTIVE DIMENSIONS OF THE PROBLEM

Most Americans still believe that social mobility is available and that hard work is the key to it. While the faith in mobility may be misplaced, the emphasis on work is accurate, in a sense. The ability to find work is central to escaping poverty. Remember our discussion of unemployment in Chapter 4. We will find that those groups that are chronically unemployed — the young and blacks — are among the largest segments of the poor population. Keep in mind that the demographic characteristics of the low income groups can overlap. For example, many poor people are both black and young. These people face more than one handicap in trying to get a job. To begin our discussion of the demographic characteristics of the poor, we will accept the government estimates of poverty that use an absolute level. We have already shown the numerous problems involved in defining poverty this way, but we will use it more for convenience because all other government poverty statistics are based on that definition.

Children

The single largest group of poor people in our society is children, who comprised 40.4 percent of those in poverty in 1976. In light of their numbers and their inability to do anything about it — the young are too young to work and teenagers cannot find jobs — the treatment of these children is a tragedy of twentieth-century America. These poor children, faced with shortages of food, shelter, and clothing, are being deprived during their formative years of their basic needs. Many of these children, when they reach eighteen, will enter the labor force and begin to earn income. But many others will be unable to escape poverty, and will be trapped in the vicious cycle we've spoken of.

Acknowledging this problem of the vicious cycle, many people trying to alleviate the problem of poverty say that the cycle is worsened by the excessive fertility rates of the poor. Table 5.4 shows the actual figures. As the table shows, the fertility rate for the poor is quite a bit higher than for the nonpoor. Women at the poorest levels have almost one child more than the more affluent. These statistics can also be broken down by race to see if the relation between income and the number of children holds true. It does. For both white and black women the fertility rate is higher among the poor. From this we can conclude that there is a differential between the fertility rate of the richer and the poorer as well as between the rates of blacks and whites. In fact, we can say that poverty is a more significant factor. The dif-

Poverty has a tendency to imprison its victims for life. This welfare mother and her family of nine have just been evicted from their one-bedroom home. Continually deprived of adequate food, shelter, and clothing, these children are locked in a world of poverty that makes their future precarious at best.

TABLE 5.4 Average Number of Children Born to Women Ever Married Fifteen Years Old and Older, 1970

	Average Number of Children	Differential
Black and white combined		
Total	2.51	
Income above poverty level	2.40	.80
Income below poverty level	3.20	
White only		
Total	2.45	
Income above poverty level	2.37	.67
Income below poverty level	3.04	
Black only		
Total	3.02	
Income above poverty level	2.68	1.05
Income below poverty level	3.73	

Source: Bureau of the Census, *Low Income Population, 1970* (Washington, D.C.: U.S. Government Printing Office, 1973), pp. 143–150.

ferential for blacks and whites is .57; the differential for the poor and nonpoor is .80. The differences shown in these data, taken from the 1970 census, are confirmed by studies using data from 1975, although the birthrate for all groups is dropping.[10]

The Elderly

The second largest group of poor people in this country is also an age group: the elderly, those age sixty-five and older. The problems of the elderly are discussed fully in Chapter 7, so we will restrict our discussion here to the problems of their poverty. In 1976, families with the head of the household sixty-five years old and older constituted 13 percent of all families living in poverty; more significantly, the number of elderly individuals comprised 37 percent of the poor, reflecting the isolation of the elderly. Government estimates said that one of every six elderly people lived in poverty. As expected, the elderly derive a much smaller proportion of their income from work, since most do not hold jobs. The result is a median income far below the median for the whole population. In 1974 the median income for white families was $13,271 while for black families it was $7,807. Among those sixty-five and older, family income was $7,518 for whites and $4,874 for blacks.[11]

If we break the poverty data down by race, we find that while 13.8 percent of elderly whites live in poverty, 36.4 percent of elderly blacks do. Using sex as the variable, we find that the percentage of elderly males is 35 percent while the proportion of females is 65 percent.[12] This is because of the differential in life expectancy between males and females. Both of these data breaks show that demographic characteristics overlap: the bad position of blacks and women is compounded by the disadvantages of age.

The plight of the elderly was summed up by Dr. Robert Butler, the new director of the National Institute on Aging, in 1976. Dr. Butler pointed out that the average elderly person has $75 a week to live on, and people over sixty-five commit 25 percent of the suicides committed each year.[13] Dr. Butler also estimates that one-third of the elderly are at or below the poverty level (compared to the government's estimate of one-sixth). This is the most disturbing statistic, for as of 1974, 10.3 percent of the population was elderly, and that proportion is expected to double by 2050.

Blacks

Another large poverty-stricken group is blacks. It surprises many people, who think that the largest group of poor people is blacks, but in fact among the 25.0 million poor in the country in 1976, 16.7 million (or about two-thirds) were white. Contrary to popular impressions, about twice as many white people live in poverty than do black in absolute numbers. But the proportion of each race living in poverty tells a different story. In 1976, about 30 percent of blacks were poor, whereas only about 9 percent of whites were.[14] In other words, proportionally a little more than three times more blacks live in poverty than do whites. One major factor contributing to this high proportion is the high number of black families headed by women. In 1976, of the black families living in poverty, 1,122,000 were headed by females while only 495,000 were headed by males. About 60 percent of poor black families had a woman as their head, another example of how double discrimination worsens a group's position.[15]

The Impact of Poverty

Now that we have discovered who the poor are, we must determine what effect poverty has on them. We've made mention of one effect in connection with the elderly (the greater likelihood to commit suicide), but there are other damaging effects as well. Robert Strauss, in his "The Problem of Conceptualizing Poverty," points us in the right direction when he says: "Poverty encompasses the bulk of low status members of society who are economically poor, often disenfranchised, undereducated, carrying high risks for morbidity, and burdened with a stigma which is extended at birth to each new member."[16] Poor people lack more than money. They also lack the means to participate fully in American society. The poor not only have inadequate income, they do not have political power, adequate schools, adequate housing, or adequately met health needs.

Poverty is not simply the failure to satisfy material goals. It also entails restricted access to the cultural goals of the majority of Americans. Some sociologists have taken this fact and stated that as a result the poor lose faith in their ability to do much about their lives. Low education, low income, poor housing, and inadequate health care are seen as both causes and consequences at the very same time. These writers contend that this self-defeating worldview influences the behavior patterns, attitudes, and values of the poor to create what has been called a *culture of poverty*. The culture of poverty has not been applied to all the poor: the elderly, who often live alone and who are scattered and isolated, are not included. Rather, the concept applies to those racial and ethnic groups that live in communities, such as blacks and Chicanos. The culture of poverty refers primarily to those values that govern the responses of the poor as they learn to live with deprivations. For example, research shows that when people are deprived of the income to secure adequate housing, they do not value the places where they have to live. Because of ethnic, racial, and class discrimination, the poor spend proportionally more and get far less for their housing dollar than do the more affluent. Housing market discrimination thus becomes a reality to which the poor must adjust, which can result in a lack of care for their residences.

Writing on the culture of poverty has tended to play up the role of both defeatist values and the structure of the family, as the socializing agent transmitting those values in maintaining poverty as a way of life. Let us examine these elements to try to determine if this concept helps us to understand the essential aspects of the problem of poverty.

Much of the writing done about the culture of poverty assumes that the values of the poor differ from those of the middle class. That assumption is suspect, however, as Eleanor Leacock has written:

> Social scientists are human beings which means social and cultural beings whose needs, desires, fears, and persuasions must impinge upon their work in various ways. By definition middle class, their scientific calling does not automatically make them immune to ethnocentrism when looking at members of the lower class. Since the vast majority of social scientists are white, their attempts to achieve understanding across black-white lines are also subject to the chauvinism embedded in our culture. When viewing black members of the lower class, we must examine their claim to objectivity with a particularly critical eye.[17]

Not only is middle-class ethnocentrism at issue; some research assumptions are open to question. Researchers often assume that the interaction they observe in a limited situation represents the total range of lower-class attitudes and behavior. Of course, that is absurd. It only shows part of the total range of values and attitudes held by lower-class people. Second, researchers tend to assume that the groups they have worked with are truly representative of large segments of some undefined lower-class. Third, they have often interpreted the observed behavior in reference not only to middle-class moral standards but also in terms of the functions such behavior would have in a middle-class setting. They label a behavior as deviant, ignoring the fact that what they see as dysfunctional using middle-class definitions may be eufunctional in the lower class. These three facts have led to a number of erroneous conclusions by most authors working on the culture of poverty.

This becomes clear if we turn to the part of the culture of poverty that has aroused the most controversy, the idea that the poor do not really want to work. Many claim that the poor would rather live off welfare than take the initiative to better themselves through work. If the poor would only go out and get jobs, the argument goes, they would have access to the income necessary to become part of the middle class. A study published in 1972 has done a lot to help clarify this controversy over welfare and attitudes toward work.[18] Leonard Goodwin interviewed over 4,000 persons, many of them welfare mothers and their children, to test a number of hypotheses about the supposed unwillingness of the poor to seek and hold employment. He concluded that the view of work held by any group is complex and that simplistic statements do not do justice to the range of issues involved.

All groups of mothers, whether on welfare or not, gave equally high ratings to the work ethic. They did, however, show wide differences in their belief in their own ability to secure work. Women who had been on welfare for a considerable amount of time lacked confidence in their ability to obtain and hold a job. The key difference between the two groups was not what would have been predicted by the culture of poverty thesis. This insecurity could not be attributed to the receipt of welfare per se. Rather, Goodwin traced this insecurity to situational factors: (1) the mothers' lack of education (the average was only about nine years of school); (2) the fact that they will earn little more than the minimum wage; and (3) the presence of three or more children she needs to support. To quote Goodwin, "These findings do not support the position that there are cultural differences (differences in basic goals or values) between the poor and non-poor with respect to work."[19]

But according to the culture of poverty, this insecurity should engender deviance in children. Is that the case? In looking at the sons of those families Goodwin reached similar conclusions. Rather surprisingly, the welfare sons were more similar to the non-welfare sons than they were different. As Goodwin comments, "The important conclusion to be drawn is that teenage males who have spent virtually their entire lives on welfare have certain positive orientations toward work. Having no working parent in the home — neither mother nor father — has made the sons' identification with work no weaker than that of sons with working fathers."[20] Goodwin did find that, like their mothers, welfare sons are less confident about their ability to ensure success in the job market; they also saw less stigma attached to accepting welfare if they were unable to get work than did nonwelfare sons.

The relationship between the values people place on work and their receipt of welfare is not as simple as some have portrayed it. The values held by the poor correspond closely to those held by other groups in our society. More research is needed to understand the way the poor differ from the majority of Americans, but that done until now tends to disprove the hypothesis that there is a culture of poverty.

Writings on the culture of poverty have also not done justice to the variety of responses individuals can make within a particular setting. Conflicting desires and values are often at play within any one person, and the way these are evoked often depends greatly on situational factors. Eleanor Leacock gives us a valuable insight when she says, "Interviews with black high school youth, some from extremely poor homes, who were taking part in a school boycott gave testimony to the exhilaration they experienced when doing something together toward improving the situations they had found so demoralizing."[21] The poor often find themselves powerless and they react to this by developing mechanisms, including an "I don't care" attitude. But when they can affect the outcome of events, they are ready to take an active role.

A final problem with the culture of poverty thesis is the danger that concern over this concept may distract attention from the real issue. Estelle Fuchs expresses the view of most social scientists when she dismisses the culture of poverty and emphasizes the lack of income. People systematically deprived from an adequate income face, as our definition stressed, problems in meeting their needs. As Fuchs points out, focusing on the culture of poverty

> detracts from an examination of the crucial structural characteristics of American life. Factors such as unemployment and low income are problems with which the poor must cope. These problems stem from the structure of the total economic system in which the non-poor play a dominant role. It is this larger structure that determines conditions to which the poor must react.[22]

Summary

Poverty still exists in the United States and hits certain social groups much harder than others. The majority of poor people are poor because they are either too young or too old to be employed. The remainder are poor because of racial and sex discrimination. After the young and the old, the next largest segment of the poor is the working poor, largely female heads of households who have jobs but cannot make enough money to rise above the poverty level. From these data we see that most poverty is related to problems that certain groups of individuals with certain social characteristics face in entering the job market. Obviously, creating jobs will not solve poverty. Many of the poor on the welfare rolls are either too young or too old to work or already working.

ATTEMPTS AT DEALING WITH THE PROBLEM

The problems of living in poverty have faced humankind for thousands of years. In places like India millions live in the streets without any shelter and beg for their daily survival. Obviously American poverty is not of this order, but the poor in this country still face deprivation relative to the rest of the population. But with the prosperity of the postwar era, attitudes about the poor have changed greatly. Because of such great prosperity, many of the poor feel more deprived than before, even though their own living conditions may have improved absolutely. A basic and important change has also occurred among the rest of the population. Enormous prosperity today has caused well-off people to argue that poverty cannot be tolerated.

The Government's Approaches

One government strategy in the postwar period to eliminate poverty has been to increase general prosperity. Much government policy has followed the *trickle-down theory*, which holds that increased assistance to business will increase profits and increased profits will allow the benefits to trickle down to all levels of society, including the poor. For example, the government chooses to lose revenue by giving tax breaks to corporations for the depreciation of equipment, thinking that these tax breaks will help businesses increase production. With this increase, more jobs will be created, meaning that the income of those people living below or near the poverty level will increase. But as we saw, while the poor do receive more money today than they did twenty-five years ago, they receive almost exactly the same proportion of the income available as they did then. The increased general prosperity has not helped the poor. The trickle-down theory has been shown to be wrong.

With the publication of Michael Harrington's *The Other America* in 1962, people were awakened to the extent of poverty. The studies of poverty that were soon generated produced data similar to those we've looked at, all of which pointed to the failure of the trickle-down theory. The progress indicated by government statistics was illusory. Increased affluence thrust more expensive consumption patterns on the poor by creating new necessities. For example, the poor needed a telephone more than they had needed one in 1950. And as residential and employment patterns have changed — as jobs have left the cities, where the poor live — the automobile has become a necessity for employment.

The government began to recognize the great extent of poverty and the need to do something about it. The Democratic administrations of 1960 to 1968 began to define poverty in relative terms and saw it as the failure of the economic system, not the failure of individual initiative. Many programs were instituted under President Lyndon Johnson's Great Society plan. The government pumped millions of dollars into these attempts to combat poverty, which included increasing welfare benefits and aid to education and instituting job training programs. But these solutions were largely abandoned after 1968, when a Republican president was elected. Richard Nixon perceived the problem of poverty differently than Lyndon Johnson had. Campaign rhetoric reemphasized the image that the poor were unwilling to work and government statistics again relied on the absolute definition of poverty. Using that standard, the government was able to say that fewer and fewer people were under the limit, but that was a definitional error, as we saw on pages 137–138.

The difference in policy became apparent with President Nixon's handling of another problem. He inherited a steadily rising inflation rate, which he determined was a more dangerous problem than poverty. But in his efforts to combat inflation he made the poor's position worse, creating a recession that saw unemployment jump from 3.5 percent in 1969 to almost 10 percent by the early 1970s. Unemployment not only created more poor, it diverted resources from programs that could have helped the poor. As Nixon's antiinflation emphasis was continued by President Gerald Ford, the 1970s saw little effective action directed against poverty. In his two years in office, President Ford vetoed more than sixty bills passed by a predominantly Democratic Congress, many of which were aimed at broadening welfare efforts for poor people. Many of the programs begun in the late 1960s are still awaiting action by the government and many others, like those set up by the Office of Economic Opportunity, have been allowed to die.

Reevaluating Government Welfare Programs

When social scientists began studying poverty in the sixties, they also began to criticize the government's efforts to alleviate the problems of the poor. These criticisms increased in the seventies, as the government rejected the systemic causes of poverty and again emphasized individual failure. They were based not only on the realization that poverty needs to be defined relatively, but also on a new perspective on government efforts to relieve poverty. The new perspective came from looking at all society's welfare expenses, defining *welfare* as all income, commodities, or services not derived directly from work. They found, surprisingly, that the poor are not the only group to receive welfare. In fact, middle and upper income groups benefit more than the poor do. Let us examine the welfare efforts directed at these two groups, since they are directly related to the ideology of welfare programs in general and the problem of a lack of adequate funds to aid the poor.

The dominant American ideology of individualism continues, as it has in the past, to reject the idea of government aid to the poor, fearing that it might lead to a welfare state. Of course this attitude can change when it is to one's benefit. As we saw, during the Depression, the middle class demanded government aid when employment became difficult. Since the Depression, many groups

Assistance programs benefit both the rich and the poor, but not in proportion to their needs. These Mexican-American farm workers, landless migrants, may receive a few hundred dollars a year in aid. The farm owners who hire their cheap labor, however, may receive thousands of dollars annually in government subsidies.

have lobbied for government assistance. To make this assistance more acceptable to the public, it is not referred to as welfare; thus the stigma that ideology attaches to such aid is avoided. These programs are welfare as we have defined it, but they simply aren't called that. Names are invented to disguise these programs and allow representatives in Congress to vote for them without fear of getting their constituents all worked up about new and costly welfare programs. Camouflage by name substitutes the words "compensation," "parity," "insurance," and "tax deduction" for the term "welfare." Of course, the efforts to meet the needs of the poor are still called welfare.

The result of these assistance programs is a vast amount of money being spent on the nonpoor. The cost of these programs can be seen by looking at the Farm Subsidy Program. Larry Casalino has studied the crop subsidy program and compared it to welfare efforts for the poor, concluding that:

> Ronald Reagan, Richard Nixon and other politicians throughout the country have been very successful in persuading people that welfare is

a major problem. They never mention the fact that federal crop subsidy programs cost the taxpayer more than all federal, state, and local welfare programs combined. Welfare is a problem for taxpayers — welfare for the rich.[23]

In California's Imperial Valley, five hundred large growers received $12 million in farm subsidies in one year. This worked out to an average of $24,000 each. At the same time the ten thousand landless poor living in the valley received less than $8 million dollars in welfare, about $800 each. Government subsidies to growers include federal grants for water and research, tax shelters, and price supports. It all adds up to an enormous welfare effort on the part of the government.

To put government welfare aimed at the poor in perspective, it is necessary to look at all programs benefiting the well-to-do, which have been called *wealth fare*. It has been estimated that the total government effort to aid wealthy people amounts to at least $100 billion per year. This takes the form of direct subsidies and tax breaks, including these:

1. loss in revenue through lower tax on capital gains: $8.7 billion
2. investment tax credits: $8.7 billion
3. homeowners' deductions for interest and property taxes: $11.7 billion
4. revenue lost because property is underassessed and undertaxed: $16.3 billion[24]

In addition, there are huge revenue losses to the government because of the way the tax laws are written. Intangible property like stocks, bonds, and patents are not taxed in the same way as is tangible property. And losses because the property held by churches and private schools is tax exempt run into the many billions. All this represents welfare aimed not at the poor but at middle- and upper-income Americans.

Based on these facts, almost all the literature recently written on welfare by social scientists has been somewhat critical of how postwar welfare programs for the poor have actually worked. Some minor attempts at welfare and tax reform have been attempted, but most have not gotten to the heart of the problem. A new series of proposals had been made, based on the idea of a guaranteed annual income and on redistributing income through tax reform or the negative income tax. Let us examine these proposals.

Negative Income Tax Plans

A *negative income tax* is a tax credit given to each citizen. Depending on the person's income, she would either be able to keep some or all of it or would apply it to the tax bill she owed to the federal government. Essentially, this program would use the Internal Revenue Service to distribute money to poor people. The amount received would depend on the number of poor people in a family, its earnings, and its tax bill. This simple system would replace the huge bureaucracies that administer welfare programs now, and proponents claim that having the Internal Revenue Service deal directly with the poor would result in great savings. Another benefit of the plan, according to its proponents, is that the poor will be allowed to choose how they wish to spend their money, rather than having services provided to them by a welfare agency.

Many different plans have been proposed, but Christopher Green outlines the three points all these plans have in common:

1. a guaranteed income that varies with family size
2. a tax rate or rate applied against a tax base

3. a break-even level of income, where tax liability equals the allowance guarantee[25]

The levels chosen for each of these variables differ drastically from one proposed plan to another, but they all work the same way. If, for example, the guaranteed minimum income for a family of four was set at $4,000 (variable 1) and a tax rate of 50 percent (variable 2) is applied against a family's income (including the guaranteed government allowance), the break-even point of income (variable 3) for this family is $8,000. In other words, at $8,000 of income the family owes no taxes and would receive no government allowance. With an income under $8,000, they would receive an income supplement; with an income above this figure, they would pay taxes. The minimum income and the tax rate determine the break-even point.

We chose a tax rate of 50 percent to build a strong incentive to work into such a program. If no one in the family were able to work, the family would still receive the basic allowance of $4,000. But if a family member took a job, even a low-paying one yielding $3,000 per year, the family would be better off. The income would bring the family's total to $5,500 ($4,000 plus 50 percent of $3,000). This leaves the family better off than they would have been if the person did not work, even though the work was only for low wages.

This program, with lower administrative costs and greater benefits going directly to the persons in need, would benefit both the working poor and those who are unable to secure "adequate" employment because of age, race, sex, or illness. Thus many of the problems inherent in the highly bureaucratized current system are avoided. This program also would encourage work, which many criticize the current system for failing to do. Such a system would be difficult to introduce, because it would also entail the end to wealth fare, and the well off will hardly vote for such a change. But one thing we need to consider is, if such a plan were implemented, what effects would it have?

Iatrogenic Effects

Attempts to solve the problem of poverty, like attempts to solve all social problems, have had iatrogenic effects in the form of new problems. To understand these effects, though, we must first understand the functions of poverty. In many ways our society is set up to use poor people to the basic advantage of the more affluent. In his recent book *More Equality*, Herbert J. Gans points out the functions that the poor perform to benefit the rest of society.

1. They serve as human subjects in the training of medical personnel in free clinics.
2. They serve in the lower ranks of the military and fight wars.
3. They provide a group that lower-status people can use to show their superiority.
4. They serve as consumers of used but not yet worn-out cars, appliances, and television sets.
5. They do the most menial and boring jobs.[26]

If we end poverty who would fulfill these functions? The answer involves changes in the stratification system most Americans would rather not see.

The major effect of implementing such a program would be to achieve the redistribution of income — as we saw, the unequal distribution of income is the best measure of poverty. Under the more liberal and far-reaching plans, the wealthy will begin to bear a greater share of the tax burden. Of course, this would not represent a basic change in the system of taxation we already claim to have. American ideology has long supported the idea of the rich paying a greater proportion to their income in taxes and a progressive income tax system has been set up on this basis. However, through the use of allowances, exemptions, and other tax loopholes, the system has been subverted. So in reality, what we are talking about is implementing the ideals and spirit of the current tax system. In his writing, Gans points out how changing to a negative income tax will affect the well off:

> The resulting losses in tax receipts would have been made up by more affluent people, particularly those who earned money from capital gains and other tax preferred sources. For example, a family of four with a $27,500 income, half of which was derived from capital gains, would have been paying almost $5,500 in taxes as compared with $3,150 now; a similar family with a $100,000 income from the same sources, $33,000 instead of $24,300.[27]

Obviously these people will not gladly pay more taxes, and will try to prevent the adoption of this system. But if it is instituted, we can see that the redistribution of income will have other effects. There could be some short-run disruptions in our economy. A few examples of what readjustments might be required will show why. First, many of the more prestigious private colleges rely heavily on donations made by rich and powerful alumni to make up for operating deficits. These contributions now pay up to half of the cost of going to one of these colleges. If these contributions were no longer tax deductible, some colleges might be seriously affected. Many are already running into a deficit, and to reduce this source of income may cripple them. Also tax deductible are contributions made to the Boy Scouts, the Heart Fund, the American Civil Liberties Union, and these would also be affected. This could mean the end of some charities that are widely recognized as benefiting society.

Another area to be affected would be the financing of bond issues for schools, libraries, turnpikes, and other government expenses. Bonds to finance these vital services are usually sold at reduced interest rates but the interest they pay is tax exempt. Well-off people buy these bonds to reduce the impact of the progressive income tax structure. With the present system, it is perfectly legitimate for a person to have an income reaching millions of dollars per year and still pay no taxes at all if this income is derived from tax exempt bonds. Whether this tax-exempt status should be abolished or not is hotly debated in Congress. Those who argue for keeping the current system say that government's ability to finance projects will suffer with any change. Opponents usually agree, but feel that the current way of doing business has proven too costly in terms of lost government revenues.

Another major effect of increasing the tax burden of the well off has to do with savings. Research has shown that people with high incomes save proportionally more of their income than do people at the bottom or middle levels. This is because their discretionary income (that remaining after the purchase of necessities) is considerably greater and by choice they save a certain proportion of it. With less discretionary income — because of higher taxes — they may save less. As a result, savings banks will have less money available to loan to middle-income people in the form of mortgages. This would hurt the building of new homes and the financing of others, creating problems for the housing industry.

Another effect of increasing the tax burden of the wealthy and transferring this income to the poor would be to increase inflation. The income the poor receive would be immediately spent on meeting their basic needs in food, health care, and housing. But without an increase in the supply of these services, greater demand would drive prices up. While this might seem farfetched, it is precisely what has already happened in the field of health care. Along with Medicare and Medicaid, government payment of health care for the poor, has come a rapid rise in health care costs at a rate approaching 20 percent per year. Some attribute this increase in part to the greater demand created by the government support. Whether similar effects would accompany a negative income tax remains to be seen.

A final problem created by the redistribution of income could be the effect on people's motivation to work hard in order to get ahead. Most Americans see the fruits of hard work to be an increase in income. With income redistribution, this incentive would be partly removed and, as Gans noted, people would not wish to share their hard earned wealth.[28]

The question is whether the cost of closing tax loopholes and reducing tax shelters and deductions for the wealthy will exceed the general social benefits of doing so. Since the number of wealthy people is fewer than 2 million, while the number of poor exceeds 20 million, it would appear that the social costs of continued poverty would be out of all proportion to the benefits of maintaining our current distribution system. But the question is not quite that simple. The current system has general benefits, as well as benefits only for the wealthy, as we have seen. These benefits will also have to be considered in evaluating a plan to eliminate poverty.

PROSPECTS FOR SOLVING THE PROBLEM

Two major questions about solutions to social problems always arise: how much will it cost and who will pay? This is especially true of strategies to eliminate poverty because, as we have stressed, poverty today is connected to the structure of income distribution. The tax structure, despite the ideals it is built on, perpetuates the basic inequality of American society by allowing subsidies for the rich. Our assessment of the prospects of eliminating poverty must then focus on the willingness of people at middle and upper levels of income to implement a system that could work to their disadvantage. Before we can assess their willingness to pay this cost, we must determine what the cost will be.

What Will It Cost?

At present the federal government spends about 56 percent of all its total outlays for programs in the field of social welfare. This amounted to about $200 billion in 1976 at the federal level and was augmented by $133 billion at the state and local level for a combined governmental welfare expenditure of about a third of a trillion dollars.[29] This included, however, social insurance programs, public aid, health and medical programs, veterans' programs, and housing. Many of these do not benefit only poor people. It is virtually impossible to tell how much of this goes to the poor and how much benefits the remainder of the population.

These programs have been increasing in their costs quite rapidly in the past decade both in terms of actual dollars spent and as percentage of the gross national product. In 1950 social welfare expenditures were 8.9 percent of the gross national product and 37.6 percent of total government outlays. In 1976 these figures had increased dramatically to almost 21 percent of the Gross National Product and almost 60 percent of total government outlays.

The cost of income transfer programs depends on the limits set for the three variables (the guaranteed minimum income, the tax rate, and the break-even point), and what social services are provided in addition to these programs. While there seems to be a great deal of support for the idea of such a program from both liberals and conservatives, once details are discussed all similarity in their position ends. The conservative proposals have placed the minimum income for a family of four at around $1,500 and made the tax rate on additional earned income 50 percent, setting the break-even point at $3,000.[30] Of course, this income locks a family into poverty. Conservatives support this plan because it promises to clean up the welfare mess and may save the government money in welfare costs. They also like the fact that these programs mean less government interference in people's lives.

Some of the conservative programs include other benefits, particularly food stamps. This would help, for over 10 million people are now receiving this form of aid. Conservative economist Milton Friedman would like to phase out other government assistance programs like Head Start and Job Corps, which he feels have not been effective in dealing with the problems of the poor. The cost for the conservative programs (such as the Nixon Family Assistance Plan and Friedman's Negative Income Tax Proposal) was put at about $2 billion a year above what the federal government was then paying for welfare. This, of course, amounts to a very small percentage of the total federal budget of almost $530 billion, which includes enormous expenditures for defense, highways, farm crop subsidies, etc. The conservative position also favors these income transfer programs because it sees them as part of an overall cut-back in the intervention of the federal government in the lives of people. Other proposals would entail cutting back on government services as the negative tax program is implemented and becomes effective.

The liberal position is best demonstrated by the proposal made by the President's Commission on Income Maintenance and on an alternative to this plan proposed by economist James Tobin. For the President's Commission, the minimum income was to be $2,400 for a family of four; for the Tobin proposal it was to be $3,200.[31] Both almost double what the conservative program proposed. Each of these liberal proposals has a tax rate of 50 percent on additional earned income, with break-evens of $4,800 and $6,400, respectively. The additional cost of the President's Commission program would be $6 billion, while for the Tobin proposal it would be over $17 billion. Clearly, as the program increases benefits, the cost goes up.

In 1974 President Ford drafted a bill in keeping with Tobin's proposal. His ideas contained elements of both conservative and liberal proposals. There was to be a basic cash payment of $3,600 to a family of four if there was no other income. This cash payment would be supplemented by the federal government, depending on the family's

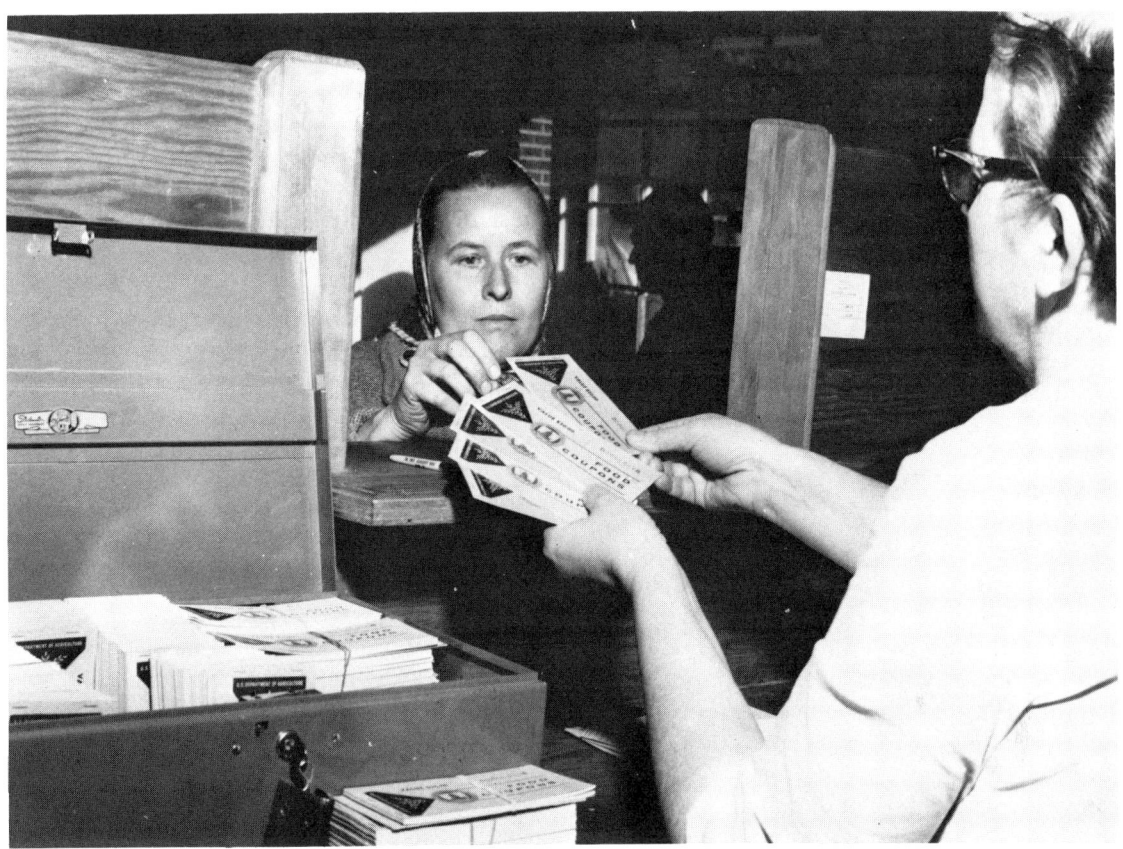

Flagrant abuses in the food stamp program have resulted in funding cutbacks and eligibility restrictions. Nevertheless, this program remains one government benefit that meets the needs of the poor directly. It hardly works to eliminate poverty itself, but it can alleviate the burden of poverty.

needs, up to a maximum of $7,200. There was no provision for any restructuring of the income tax system. While many details of this plan were unspecified, a few are known. It did call for the elimination of traditional forms of welfare, such as food stamps and aid to families with dependent children. This was in keeping with the desire to reduce the large sums of money now being administered by the welfare bureaucracies at the local, state, and federal levels. Total costs for the Ford proposal were difficult to assess because not enough of the details had been worked out.[32]

The government itself presents some statistics indicating in part what might be required to bring everyone now living in poverty up to the poverty line. Using the officially established poverty line and then looking at the deficit for every individual living in poverty, they have established an aggregate income deficit, the money needed to bring up the income of all persons now living in poverty. In 1975 this amounted to almost $16 billion. Any proposal to eliminate poverty would cost at least this much, but probably would be more, for three reasons: (a) administrative costs to implement a new program; (b) the need to continue to attack other problems still facing the poor, like inadequate health care and education; and (c) an unrealistic setting of the poverty line. Distributing $16 billion to all those living in poverty to bring them up to the poverty line will not be enough.

Who Will Pay?

Many lower-middle and upper-middle income taxpayers worry that these proposals will increase the number and cost of welfare programs, thus cutting down on their own disposable income. Concern about taxes became widespread in the late 1970s. Citizens in many towns turned down new school bond issues, sewer and library expansion programs, and a host of other general welfare programs. The revolt of the middle class taxpayer at a time of increasing inflation is hardly surprising. Since the middle class makes up the majority of voters, any attempt to eliminate poverty must be tied to tax reforms to win their favor. Such reform can be found in closing tax loopholes, such as ending homeowners' deductions for mortage interest and real estate taxes and eliminating the tax-free status of state and municipal bond interest. Table 5.5 shows the increase in the tax burden people at different income levels would face. As can be seen, people at all levels would have their taxes increased, but the wealthy would pay a greatly increased share. The key question then comes

TABLE 5.5 Percentage Increase in Taxes with Closing of Tax Loopholes

Income group	Increase in taxes
Under $3,000	18%
$3,000 to $5,000	16
$5,000 to $10,000	17
$10,000 to $15,000	22
$15,000 to $20,000	23
$20,000 to $25,000	24
$25,000 to $50,000	28
$50,000 to $100,000	45
$100,000 to $500,000	73
$500,000 to $1,000,000	98
Over $1,000,000	96

Source: Stanley S. Survey, *Pathways to Tax Reform* (Cambridge, Mass.: Harvard University Press, 1973), p. 69.

down to the politics behind tax reform. Will those people who benefit most from the current tax structure be able to marshall enough power to block reform? Change will undoubtedly take place, but it may turn out to be piecemeal, like so many attempts in the past. These piecemeal attempts give the illusion of attacking the problem but do not challenge the inequality that the tax structure allows.

One thing the poor have consistently failed to do is to take direct political action to implement their demands. Such action has been made difficult by the way political representation has been structured in this country. Although this is changing somewhat, as the cities become more and more the places where the poor live, but even that change isn't enough. While the poor may make their demands felt for increased services and expenditures at the local level, the resources for poverty programs come from the federal government. It is only at this level that the resources exist to eliminate the poverty of the over 25 million Americans the government acknowledges to be poor.

There will undoubtedly be resistance to large-scale tax reform, but just as unquestionable is the need for it. While the number of poor people has declined in the past several decades, the number of rich people has dramatically increased. Perhaps the largest increase has been in the number of upper-middle-class persons, roughly defined as those having incomes of $25,000 or more for a family of four. As the number of these people grows, the problem of expenditures within our society has changed greatly. Many of these families now have two or more new cars, swimming pools, expensive stereo equipment, boats, campers, and other luxuries not even available a generation ago. These consumer items are costly but become part of the life-style that increased personal income has made possible. The growing difference between the well off and the poor is reaching a critical point, where choices must be made. In 1974, more second homes for upper-income people were being built than were low-cost units for the poor. In other words, eliminating poverty comes down to a question of national priorities. Do most Americans, especially those with the power to implement their desires, want to live more luxurious lives or would they prefer to eliminate poverty?

This is one of the hard choices confronting Americans. Pressure to change the tax structure and to implement some of the more liberal income readjustment schemes, if it materializes, will probably be based on the following factors. Americans have an ideology that stresses everyone getting an equal chance in life to show what he or she is worth. Most Americans probably do not believe in complete equality between people, but would nevertheless support more equal and open opportunities. With such a large percentage of the poor being children, this would entail many changes in the welfare efforts aimed at this group. Yet in areas affecting children, like education, there are paradoxes in policies and attitudes. Americans want equality for all, but at the same time they want to pass on the power and privilege they now have to their children. Equality of opportunity hardly ever means equality of outcomes to most Americans. A key issue in understanding the conflict in American society is the extreme class, racial, and ethnic heterogeneity of our population.

Starting as a nation of immigrants with many different racial and ethnic backgrounds, this nation has moved steadily in the direction of less ethnic heterogeneity. But race, which is related directly to poverty, is still a source of heterogeneity as are class divisions. If one looks at the distribution of income over time, as we did earlier, class differences do not seem to be diminishing, even though more and more Americans are living in greater luxury than ever before. The implications of this general decrease in ethnic heterogeneity are hard to judge, but a look at the Scandinavian countries may provide a glimpse into America's future.

Unlike the United States, these countries have had a long history of ethnic homogeneity. Based partly on this and on their prosperity, these countries have tried to lessen the impact of social class in determining one's life chances. Essentially this has meant reducing the gap between rich and poor, mainly through taxation at the upper levels and the provision of government services (like free health care and low-cost housing) at the lower levels. These nations have largely eliminated poverty in an effort to implement a more egalitarian society. Beginning with little ethnic heterogeneity made this job easier, but it was their dedication to remove inequality that made them so successful.

With the progress made by these countries have come economic changes. Their tax rates are among the highest in the world and much of industry, which would be in private hands in our country, is owned and run by the government. The ideology of these countries no longer stresses the chance to become rich, but rather how prosperity can become general, thus ensuring peace and harmony. On almost all indices of what it means to live in a civilized society (low infant mortality rates, low murder rates, long life expectancy) these countries are at or near the top of the list. Whether they can serve as models for the United States is, of course, open to question. But at least they represent one place where Americans interested in solving the problem of poverty can see how alternative strategies are working.

We have tried to outline some of the factors that need to be considered in developing a strategy to eliminate poverty. There still exist many myths about how the poor differ from the rest of the population in their abilities and life-style, but social scientists are gathering more data to show that these are but myths. The groundwork is being established for some basic changes. As prosperity has increased in our society, the discussion of rights basic to living in America has changed, and it will continue to change in the future. The rapid changes are shown in the current debate over national health care, an idea that could not have gathered much acceptance decades ago. When we reach the point of agreeing that everyone is entitled at birth to the means of securing a decent existence, we will have taken an important first step in solving the problem of poverty.

In the meantime, attempts can still be made and will revolve around the issue of social inequality. There seems to be a growing awareness of the necessity to establish some sort of income or standard of living as a floor, below which people will not be forced to live. This represents a real change in attitude in the past generation and is based partly on postwar prosperity. As prosperity has grown, no middle-income person has had to choose between his own prosperity and helping those living in poverty. As long as prosperity continues, people will probably be willing to pay greater attention to the needs of the poor.

But planning for a continuously growing gross national product also contains some basic fallacies, as Chapter 13 on ecology points out. The solution to solve some problems often creates problems in other areas. Because of this particular conflict at some point Americans will have to decide what exactly they mean by their belief in equality. The answer will determine whether we take steps to reduce and eliminate poverty or whether we continue to allow the present structure perpetuating inequality to exist. Most Americans would favor the elimination of poverty if someone else pays for it and if their own relative position could be maintained, but if we mobilize the resources to eliminate poverty all will have to pay. This is the dilemma that makes it hard for Americans to decide whether to do something about poverty or to continue on with business as usual.

IMPORTANT WORDS AND TERMS

absolute definition of poverty
culture of poverty
Great Depression
income distribution
median family income
minimum subsistence income
negative income tax
poverty
poverty line
relative definition of poverty
trickle-down theory
wealth fare
welfare

QUESTIONS FOR DISCUSSION

1. What priority should the elimination of poverty have in the United States during the current year?
2. Would you be willing to reduce your standard of living by 10 percent, if the United States could thereby eliminate poverty? By 20 percent?
3. Should the United States government employ anyone wanting to work? Defend your answer.
4. What dimensions should be considered in defining a family as poor?
5. Do you think the United States should be described as a welfare state for the rich? If not, how would you describe it?
6. What do you think is the income level for a family of four that should be considered as the poverty line?
7. How many poor people do you know personally, and what makes them poor?
8. Some people feel the poor are lazy and do not want to work. How would you counter this charge?
9. Imagine a society where everyone has the same income. What would motivate people to work?
10. "Welfare programs are not designed to eliminate poverty, only to perpetuate it." Do you agree or disagree?
11. How much income difference is needed in America to keep our system working?
12. Some people have suggested that poor people should not be allowed to have children. What do you think about this?
13. The elimination of poverty could be a top American priority. What do you think would have to be sacrificed to make it so?
14. "It is harder to be poor in the United States than in other countries like India." Do you agree? Why or why not?

SUGGESTED READING

HERBERT GANS, *More Equality* (New York: Random House, 1974).

This is one of the most thought provoking works on the issue of equality. Gans looks at the incentives Americans work for and questions what changes in these would be required if greater equality came about. His section on the functions of the poor is one of the better parts of the book, and he raises many questions that must be considered in any discussion of a stratified society. Gans's work is an important commentary on the issues that need to be confronted by a general strategy to eliminate poverty.

LEONARD GOODWIN, *Do the Poor Want to Work?* (Washington, D.C.: Brookings Institution, 1972).

Goodwin's book is based on extensive research he did on the relationship between welfare and the desire to work. It has often been argued that welfare kills the incentive to work, but Goodwin's data show that this is untrue. His conclusions are important to anyone wanting to be informed about the effects the welfare system has on the poor.

DAVID GORDON, *Theories of Poverty and Unemployment* (Lexington, Mass.: D. C. Heath, 1973).

Most of the poor live in poverty because they do not have jobs or have only low-paying ones. Gordon looks at three different approaches to two related questions: what are the determinants of wages in American society and what are the causes of unemployment in this country. He shows that economists have made different assumptions about both issues and he also shows that the solutions to both poverty and unemployment are almost totally dependent on the ideological assumptions that affect the definition of the problem. While this book is quite heavy reading, Gordon brings together a lot of conflicting ideas about what should be done about the problem of poverty. His work is invaluable to anyone wanting to understand what has gone wrong with past governmental efforts to eliminate poverty.

JONATHAN TURNER AND CHARLES STARNES, *Privilege and Poverty* (Pacific Palisades, Calif.: Goodyear, 1976).

The authors present the ingredients needed for understanding the distribution of wealth and income in the United States. They first describe the distribution of wealth and income, but they go beyond that to explain the dynamics that produce a high concentration of wealth and an inequitable distribution of income. They focus on how government produces wealth fare for the rich and a smaller welfare effort for the poor. The most important part of this book is the connection it makes between the role of government aid to the rich and the relative lack of aid to the poor. Because poverty must be seen in the context of income distribution, this book is must reading.

FRANCIS PIVEN AND RICHARD CLOWARD, *Regulating the Poor* (New York: Random House, 1972).

In this work the authors present a view of the welfare system in keeping with the one developed in this chapter. They trace the historical uses of welfare, and have an especially good section on the Depression. They make a very good case that the rationale behind any government welfare effort is to maintain social order and commitment to the status quo. Anyone who reads this work will never again think that the primary role of welfare is to help eliminate poverty.

NOTES

1. Michael Harrington, *The Other America* (Baltimore: Penguin Books, 1962).
2. Two of these texts are Russell Dynes et al., *Social Problems* (New York: Oxford University Press, 1964), and Paul Horton and Gerald Leslie, *The Sociology of Social Problems* (New York: Appleton-Century-Crofts, 1960).
3. Thomas Malthus, *On Population* (New York: New American Library, 1951).
4. Arthur Schlesinger, "The City in American History," in John Palen and Karl Flaming (eds.), *Urban America* (New York: Holt, Rinehart and Winston, 1972), p. 35.
5. See John Higham, *Strangers in the Land: Patterns of American Nativism, 1860–1925* (New York: Atheneum, 1963).
6. Daniel P. Moynihan (ed.), *On Understanding Poverty* (New York: Basic Books, 1969), p. 19.

7. Arthur B. Shostak, *Privilege in America* (Englewood Cliffs, N.J.: Prentice-Hall, 1973).

8. Herman P. Miller, *Rich Man, Poor Man* (New York: Crowell, 1964), p. 58.

9. Mollie Orshansky, "Counting the Poor," in Louis Ferman et al. (eds.), *Poverty in America* (Ann Arbor: University of Michigan Press, 1969).

10. Bureau of the Census, *Current Population Reports*, "Consumer Income: Characteristics of the Population Below Poverty Level — 1975," Series P-60, No. 106 (Washington, D.C.: U.S. Government Printing Office, 1977), p. 58.

11. Bureau of the Census, *Statistical Abstract of the United States, 1977* (Washington, D.C.: U.S. Government Printing Office, 1977), p. 456, and *Statistical Abstract of the United States, 1975* (Washington, D.C.: U.S. Government Printing Office, 1975), p. 397.

12. *Statistical Abstract, 1975*, p. 403.

13. From Lloyd Shearer, "Intelligence Report," *Parade Magazine* (August 22, 1976), p. 4.

14. *Statistical Abstract, 1977*, p. 454.

15. Ibid., p. 453.

16. Robert Strauss, "The Problem of Conceptualizing Poverty," in Thomas Weaver and Alvin Magid (eds.), *Poverty: New Interdisciplinary Perspectives* (San Francisco, Calif.: Chandler, 1969), p. 11.

17. Eleanor Leacock, *The Culture of Poverty — A Critique* (New York: Simon and Schuster, 1971), p. 18.

18. Leonard Goodwin, *Do the Poor Really Want to Work?* (Washington, D.C.: Brookings Institution, 1972).

19. Ibid., p. 52.

20. Ibid., p. 68.

21. Leacock, *Culture of Poverty — A Critique*, p. 15.

22. Estelle Fuchs, "Education and the Culture of Poverty," in Weaver and Magid (eds.), *Poverty*, p. 165.

23. Larry Casilino, "This Land Is Their Land," *Ramparts* (July 1972), pp. 33–34.

24. For a more extensive discussion of this issue, see Jonathan Turner and Charles Starnes, *Inequality: Privilege and Poverty in America* (Pacific Palisades, Calif.: Goodyear, 1976).

25. Christopher Green, *Negative Taxes and the Poverty Program* (Washington, D.C.: Brookings Institution, 1967).

26. Herbert J. Gans, *More Equality* (New York: Vintage, 1974), pp. 102–126.

27. Ibid., p. 154.

28. Ibid., pp. 149–174.

29. *Statistical Abstract, 1977*, p. 316.

30. For a good review of this issue, see David Gordon, *Problems in Political Economy* (Lexington, Mass.: D. C. Heath, 1971).

31. James Tobin, "Raising the Income of the Poor," in Kermit Gordon (ed.), *Agenda for the Nation* (Washington, D.C.: Brookings Institution, 1968).

32. *Statistical Abstract, 1977*, p. 316.

6 MINORITIES
A WORLD OF ILLOGIC AND REDUCED OPPORTUNITIES

CHAPTER OVERVIEW

INTRODUCTION

CONCEPTUAL ORIENTATION
Minorities Defined
Visibility
Prejudice
   The Dynamics of Prejudice
   The Social Consequences of
      Ascribed Characteristics
   Ethnocentrism and Racism
Discrimination
   De Jure Discrimination
   De Facto Discrimination
   Cooling-Out
Ending Minority Group Status
   Separatism
   Assimilation
   Integration
   Pluralism
Summary

HISTORICAL OVERVIEW OF THE PROBLEM
Power and Authority
Women as a Minority
Blacks as a Minority
Summary

OBJECTIVE DIMENSIONS OF THE PROBLEM
Females
   Discrimination in Work
   Discrimination in Education
Blacks
   Discrimination in Work
   Discrimination in Education
   Discrimination in Housing
Other Minorities
   Chicanos
   Jews
   Puerto Ricans
   Orientals
   Indians
Summary

ATTEMPTS AT DEALING WITH THE PROBLEM
Militance and Affirmative Action
Iatrogenic Effects

PROSPECTS FOR SOLVING
   THE PROBLEM

IMPORTANT WORDS AND TERMS

QUESTIONS FOR DISCUSSION

SUGGESTED READING

NOTES

We hold these truths to be self-evident; that all men are created equal; that they are endowed by their creator with certain inalienable rights.

The Declaration of Independence

All animals are equal, but some animals are more equal than others.

George Orwell, *Animal Farm*

CHAPTER OVERVIEW

All of us suffer occasionally from garden-variety discrimination. We do not like this but we accept it as being a fact of life. In this chapter, we are considering a different kind of discrimination. We will discuss illogical, unjust, and undemocratic, systematic discrimination against some people simply because they belong to a minority group. First we will explain how a person is defined as belonging to a minority group, how that status is maintained, and what are its results. We will then discuss the history of minorities, for discriminatory treatment of various groups has existed since history began. We will look at how present-day minorities were first given lower status and will discuss their efforts to improve their position.

This discussion will lead us to the present. In covering the objective dimensions of minorities today, we will focus on two minorities, women and blacks, because they have organized the most to change their status. Space limitations prevent a detailed discussion of other minorities. However, it should be emphasized that this omission does not mean that the situation facing Chicanos, Indians, Puerto Ricans, Jews, or Orientals is not serious. And we will not discuss the elderly, another minority, for they are treated in another chapter. After seeing what conditions face minorities, we will review what has been done to better their position and assess the prospects for solving this problem in the future. Happily, we can be more optimistic with this problem than with others.

INTRODUCTION

Inequality is a pervasive condition of social life. Humans may be created equal but that equality holds true at no time in human life, except perhaps when people vote in democratic elections. Even before birth there is inequality. Embryos in the uterus do not enjoy equality, if for no other reason than that mothers differ in health. And inequality is the key matter with respect to abortion; both pro- and anti-abortionists accept inequality, though a different kind. The proabortionists maintain that it is a woman's right to decide whether or not she will carry an embryo to full term. Thus, the mother is superior to the child. In contrast, antiabortionists contend that, once conceived, the embryo has a right to be born regardless of the mother's desires. In this case, the unborn baby takes precedence. So it is throughout life. The child is subordinate to parents and teachers, most adults are to employers, and employers are to boards of directors and stockholders. Even the president is subordinate to the electorate — at least hypothetically.

Most of the time most of us accept this inequality. We resent specific instances of personal subordination from time to time but, by and large, we recognize that inequality is something we cannot change and most of us adjust with varying degrees of good grace. Some kinds of inequality are acceptable and accepted largely because we do not see a current subordinate position as necessarily permanent. One facet of the American dream is that by hard work, diligence, and motivation any one of us can improve our lot in life. If we fail to do so, the blame lies not with our social system but with ourselves. Or, put another way, many Americans hold that those who remain subordinate do so because they are unwilling to work hard, they lack ambition, or they are poorly motivated. Although it is not completely true, it is believed that people are not prevented from upward mobility.

This chapter, however, is concerned with a different kind of inequality. Some people are prevented from being upwardly mobile. They do not have low status because they lack motivation or ability but are kept in such a station. Such individuals are members of groups called minorities. All societies, from the simplest to the most complex, have at least one minority group. Larger societies have several; the United States has eight clearly identifiable minority groups: women, blacks, Chicanos, Indians, Puerto Ricans, Orientals, Jews, and the elderly.

Because of how our society is organized and functions, few of us have equal opportunities for upward mobility. But members of the majority or dominant group — white males — do not see this. If a white male fails to move upward, he and most others blame the individual. What has caused much of the ferment over minority group status in recent years is that minority group members no longer accept their inability to succeed as a personal matter. They see that their difficulties are a function of discrimination. Their position has not improved because the dominant group has not come to see this and still defines failure as a personal problem.

CONCEPTUAL ORIENTATION

Superficially, the concept of minorities seems simple enough: some people are mistreated because of their racial, national, or religious origins. If the problem were that simple, it would be far easier to solve. But it isn't that simple. To study minorities, we need to determine why certain groups are chosen to receive unequal treatment, how they are actually treated, and what the results of that treatment are. Indeed, it is essential first to understand what sociologists mean when they use the term minorities.

Minorities Defined

The word *minorities* connotes numerical inferiority and, therefore, is apt to be misleading when we study minority groups. Let us consider sociologist Louis Wirth's definition of a minority:

> A group of people who, because of their physical or cultural characteristics, are singled out from the others in the society in which they live for differential and unequal treatment. . . . The existence of a minority in a society implies the existence of a corresponding dominant group with higher social status and greater privileges. Minority status carries with it the exclusion from full participation in the life of the society.[1]

It should be noted that Wirth's definition says nothing about the numerical size of a minority. The examples of Rhodesia and the Republic of South Africa show that a relatively small minority (in both cases, whites) can dominate a vastly greater number and proportion of persons of another race (in both cases, blacks) and exclude them from full participation in the society. In addition to these two examples, there is no known society that does not exclude roughly half of its members as a minority group. This group is females.

How is it that minority groups acquire their position? How does the dominant group achieve superiority? There are three typical ways that this status is created: conquest, immigration, and possession of power. *Conquest* means that an outside force comes into a country and seizes control. The means of the conquest can be military strength and technological superiority, as with the whites in South Africa and Rhodesia, or economic power, as with the domination of the United States over many Third World nations. *Immigration* can also be a source of minority group status, when a people enter a new country — voluntarily or involuntarily — and is treated as a minority group, with low-status jobs, poor living conditions, and limited opportunities. This was what happened to Orientals and blacks who came to the United States. The third method of creating a minority group is for one group to acquire and exercise power over a group already present in society. The best example of this possession of power is male subjugation of females.

But in each of these three cases, if a group is to be treated as a minority, it must be identifiable. That is, unless people know that a person (or persons) is a member of a minority group, they cannot practice discrimination.

Visibility

As a whole, humans resemble each other very closely. We have no difficulty in distinguishing members of our species from members of other species. But as we all know, there are also differences among humans that can be easily perceived. For example, the usually darker skin of black people or the epicanthic fold in the eyes of Orientals is readily apparent. Thus, if either blacks or Orientals are a minority group, it is easy to identify people as black or Oriental. Identification must be easy because the dominant group has to make sure that it doesn't discriminate against any of its members. The only way to ensure that is to make sure that the minority group members are clearly different. Sometimes the dominant group creates this difference. Jews in Nazi Europe looked like Germans, Poles, Austrians, or Danes — like the other people in the countries they lived in. To make it easier to identify the Jews, the Nazis made them wear yellow armbands.

As we can see, visibility is not just a matter of natural physical appearance, but can be created by the dominant group. It can also be created by the minority group in their ethnic traits, which are then used by the dominant group as identifying traits.

Ethnicity refers to common cultural traits of some aggregate of persons. Ethnic aggregates or groups are set apart from the rest of the society in which they live on the basis of certain cultural traits they hold that differ from those of the rest of society. When these traits are visible, they can be used to identify the group as a minority. Ordinarily, the more readily distinguishable traits are language, dress, and mannerisms. Identifiable racial groups can also have distinguishing ethnic characteristics. For example, in Chinatown in San Francisco, some persons still wear Oriental garb and speak English with a decided accent or not at all. Some blacks speak *black English,* a variant on standard American English.

Ethnicity is easier to understand when we consider what has happened to the descendants of the waves of mass immigrants who came to the United States in the latter half of the nineteenth century and the early decades of the twentieth. Although most came from European countries with a similar cultural heritage, there were some cultural differences. As a result, they had visible cultural traits and suffered some discrimination and exploitation. For example, there were strong anti-Irish feelings in the midnineteenth century and prejudice against Italians at the turn of the twentieth. With the passage of time, the immigrants — but more likely their descendants — began to speak and dress like the dominant group. By the third generation, these descendants could not be distinguished from the majority group. In fact, many became full members of the dominant part of society. For some, however, discrimination remains a fact of life. Last names are still used to identify certain ethnic and religious groups. People with names that indicate Italian or Irish origins may suffer discrimination because people assume that their religion is Roman Catholic and there has always been some anti-Catholic sentiment in the United States. While the Irish and the Italians have largely been successful in removing prejudice and discrimination, those who maintain that blacks ought to follow their example miss an important point. The Irish and the Italians, along with other European immigrants, were white; they could become invisible by adopting the dress, speech, and manners of the dominant majority. But blacks cannot change their skin color. They remain identifiable and are still easy victims of prejudice.

Prejudice

Prejudice is a rigid, emotional attitude often based on inadequate data, characterized by stereotyped thinking and involving a tendency to respond negatively toward certain identifiable groups or members of these groups. Prejudice does not involve any overt action or behavior, although it may serve as a stimulus to behavior. As it is an attitude, it is a hidden or covert characteristic, which people may or may not reveal to others.

Prejudice is emotional, it involves feelings. These feelings are negative and are often revealed in the words used to describe a group. After the Japanese attacked Pearl Harbor, strong prejudice against them existed in this country. The Japanese were described as cunning, crafty, wily, slippery, shifty, treacherous, evasive, and underhanded, all obviously undesirable traits. Such negative connotations are also attached to the word *black*. For example, blacken, blackguard, Black Hand, blackleg, black magic, blackmail, and Black Mass. Of course, the word *white* can also be used emotionally and negatively, as in white flag, white elephant, white feather, white-livered, and white plague.

THE DYNAMICS OF PREJUDICE

Prejudice comes from the Latin *prejudicum* — meaning a preceding judgment, a judgment before the facts are gathered. All of us continually make preceding judgments based on our attitudes, but prejudice is dif-

166 MINORITIES: *A World of Illogic and Reduced Opportunities*

Prejudice is an attitude not an act, but it certainly may lead to action. Prejudice against blacks continues to incite violence despite and often because of forced integration. These policemen have created a barricade between rock and bottle throwing blacks and whites at a South Boston beach.

ferent from ordinary attitudes. Attitudes can be changed. "Typically, attitude change comes about through receiving new information about something that induces a change in the evaluative belief component. The change in the belief component, in turn, tends to bring about corresponding changes in the feeling and action-orientation components."[2] But prejudicial beliefs and attitudes are not so readily changed. The misjudgments and misconceptions underlying prejudices are defended, often vigorously, by those who hold them. Information contrary to prejudices is either ignored or altered to make this information congruent with the prejudices. In short, prejudiced persons are not troubled by facts, either because they do not become aware of them — all of us can shut out things we do not wish to hear — or because they twist them around to make them support prejudices.

Prejudiced people manipulate information all the time. Suppose that in a small town we have two businesspersons — Mr.

Smith and Mr. Fein. Mr. Smith is white, male, and Protestant. Mr. Fein is white, male, and Jewish. If Mr. Smith succeeds in business, it is because he is hard-working, intelligent, and well-motivated. If Mr. Fein likewise does well, it is interpreted as the result of his cunning in business, because a common belief is that Jews make money in sly, devious, shady ways. If Mr. Smith is constantly involved in community activities, it is because he is a public-spirited citizen. Should Mr. Fein give of his time and money for worthy community causes, it is because Jews are pushy. Should Mr. Smith fall into bankruptcy, it is seen simply as bad luck for a good man. When Mr. Fein becomes bankrupt, people assume that he will manage to make a bundle out of the failure.

THE SOCIAL CONSEQUENCES OF ASCRIBED CHARACTERISTICS

An important component of prejudice, then, is the unfavorable characteristics attributed to minority group members. All minority groups have a considerable number of negative characteristics arbitrarily assigned to them. For example, the stereotype of blacks is that they are happy-go-lucky, shiftless, careless, childlike, dishonest, sexually permissive, and incapable of taking a full and equal place in society. Ascribed characteristics have three social consequences: (1) they support and rationalize prejudice; (2) they enhance the egos of the dominant group — it is gratifying to most people to have others upon whom they can look down as inferiors; and (3) they keep the minority group down, for they are frequently accepted by minority group members as being accurate. Fortunately, this latter consequence is less true today. The slogan "black is beautiful" reflects a healthy rebellion against the black stereotype and marks efforts at changing the perceptions of blacks and whites.

ETHNOCENTRISM AND RACISM

Ethnocentrism is a kind of prejudice, a belief that one's group and its members are superior to other groups and their members. All groups are ethnocentric to an extent; all wish to believe that their society is best. But some societies — and some individuals in every society — go beyond ethnocentrism to racism. *Racists* firmly believe that their race is inherently superior to all others. Racists often call on science, or pseudoscience, to justify their beliefs and throughout history elaborate systems, detailing the superiority of the devisers' race, have been constructed (see Table 6.1). But racism is not the same as ethnocentrism or as prejudice. Rather, it is ethnocentrism in its most virulent form. Ethnocentrism must be seen as a continuum with racism at its extreme, as shown in Figure 6.1.

Some members of all races are racists. For example, Hiroshi Wagatsuma, a Japanese, provides us with what is held by some Japanese to be an accurate portrayal of whites:

> The image of a Caucasian with white skin, deep-set eyes, wavy hair of a color other than black, a tall, stout, hairy body and large hands and feet, seems to evoke in many Japanese an association with "vitality," "superior energy," "strong sexuality," or "anormality," and the feeling that Caucasians are basically discontinuous with Asians.[3]

While this description may seem flattering, it isn't. White skin is not particularly valued by the Japanese, as its association with anormality shows, nor are such physical attributes as hairy bodies or large hands and feet. As for strong sexuality, this trait is frequently attributed by dominant groups to minority groups. Bluntly put, the racist perspective on visible differences is that the characteristics of his group are superior to those of other groups.

TABLE 6.1 Racism in Science: The Linnaean Classification of *Homo Sapiens* into Four Racial Categories

English Category	Latin Category	Linnaeus's Description of Mentality
African	Afer niger	Slow and negligent; cunning and capricious
American Indian	Americanus rufus	Tenacious, free, and easily contented
Asiatic	Asiaticus luridus	Haughty, stern, and opinionated
European	Europaeus albus	Lively, creative, and superior to all other racial types

Note: Carolus Linnaeus, born Carl von Linné (1707–1778), was a Swedish botanist and taxonomist and is considered the founder of the binomial system of nomenclature for all plants and animal species and the originator of the modern scientific classification of animals and plants. His classification of our species, however, was woefully inadequate and revealed profound ignorance and racism.

Source: Peter I. Rose, *They and We: Racial and Ethnic Relations in the United States*, 2nd ed. (New York: Random House, 1974), p. 107.

Deep-seated racist attitudes on the part of whites are well illustrated by the following excerpt from *The Autobiography of Malcolm X*:

> Somehow, I happened to be alone in the classroom with Mr. Ostrowski, my English teacher. . . . He told me, "Malcolm, you ought to be thinking about a career. Have you given it any thought?"
>
> The truth is, I hadn't. I never have figured out why I told him, "Well, yes sir, I've thinking I'd like to be a lawyer." Lansing certainly had no Negro lawyers — or doctors either — in those days to hold up an image I might have aspired to. All I really knew for certain was that a lawyer didn't have to wash dishes as I was doing.
>
> Mr. Ostrowski looked suprised, I remember, and leaned back in his chair and clasped his hands behind his head. He kind of half-smiled and said, "Malcolm, one of life's first needs is for us to be realistic. Don't misunderstand me now. We all here like you, you know

FIGURE 6.1 A Continuum Model of Ethnocentricism

| Complete acceptance of all out-groups | Mild concern about out-groups: sees differences, but generally indulgent | Feelings of superiority but also indulgence toward out-groups | Serious concern about out-groups plus some hostility, fear, and suspicion of out-groups | Great hostility toward out-groups, with hatred, deep suspicion, and marked fear, plus a readiness to restrict activities of out-groups and out-group members |

Among the outspoken proponents of racism is the white supremacist National Socialist Party of America. The Nazis' paramount and highly visible position is white superiority especially over blacks and Jews.

that. But you've got to be realistic about being a nigger. A lawyer — that's no realistic goal for a nigger. You need to think about something you can be. You're good with your hands — making things. . . . Why don't you plan on carpentry."[4]

Such expressions of racism, however kindly they are meant, demean the individual they are directed at and doubtlessly infuriate him as well. The preceding quotation helps us to understand the rage Malcolm X felt in the latter years of his life.

These comments do not accompany only racism. Other minority groups are subjected to similar bigotry, even if they are not members of a different race. Some years ago a highly intelligent woman, then a college student, was told by a professor that her ambition to be a certified public accountant was unsuitable for a female. This comment and that of Malcolm X's teacher reflect what prejudice leads to: the limiting of educational and professional opportunities that we call discrimination.

Discrimination

Discrimination is the effective barring from full participation in society of members of identifiable groups on grounds that are totally irrelevant to such participation.[5] An important thing to remember is that discrimination does not always accompany prejudice. As Table 6.2 shows, there are four possible combinations of these two elements.

Discrimination involves action across a society. It is found in all major social institutions — the economy, politics, education, and others. It has two principal components: (1) attempts to render it difficult or impossible for minority group members to compete with the majority; and (2) social values, norms, and customs that emphasize for both groups their differential status. As an example of the first, we have the separate but highly unequal white and black school systems found in the Deep South for many years. The second has many examples, such as the separate toilets and drinking fountains for blacks and whites found at one time in the South.

DE JURE DISCRIMINATION

Discrimination comes in two forms. *De jure discrimination* is legal discrimination. Until recent years, the so-called *Jim Crow* laws in the South gave the force of law to many discriminatory practices, including prohibitions against blacks voting, denial of their right to trial, and prohibitions against *miscegenation,* or interracial marriage.

Today in the United States, there is no de jure discrimination; such laws have been declared unconstitutional and removed. Organizations and individuals, private and public, can no longer legally discriminate against

---

TABLE 6.2 Four Possible Combinations of Prejudice and Discrimination

Combination	Characteristics
Nonprejudiced nondiscriminator	She upholds strongly such values as equality and democracy. She refuses to discriminate against any person or group on the basis of race or ethnicity. She openly makes her views known and acts consistently with her values.
Nonprejudiced discriminator	He has no prejudices but discriminates against persons or groups on racial or ethnic grounds because everyone else does or to avoid conflict with other persons who practice discrimination. This type is sometimes referred to as a fair-weather liberal.
Prejudiced nondiscriminator	She is prejudiced against persons or groups on racial or ethnic grounds, but does not practice discrimination because of social pressures or fear of the consequences.
Prejudiced discriminator	He is highly prejudiced against groups and individuals because of race or ethnicity. He openly admits to being highly prejudiced and practices discrimination when possible.

Source: Adapted from Robert Merton, "Discrimination and the American Creed," in Robert M. MacIver (ed.), *Discrimination and the National Welfare* (New York: Harper and Row, 1949), pp. 99–126.

persons or groups on the basis of race, sex, religion, ethnicity, or age. Blacks, women, Jews, Chicanos, and other minorities are to be accorded an equal opportunity with the dominant group (white males) not only for specific positions but generally for upward mobility.

Unfortunately, making discrimination illegal has not ended it, although it has been reduced somewhat. To understand why this has been the case, we must discuss the other kind of discrimination, de facto discrimination.

DE FACTO DISCRIMINATION

De facto discrimination means discrimination actually taking place, legal or not. De facto acts of discrimination are now against the law but are in accord with, and governed by, powerful informal norms. As our discussion of norms in Chapter 2 showed, passing a law will not automatically bring about a change in behavior. Laws like Prohibition or current laws against marijuana will not change behavior because they lack popular support and are opposed by powerful informal norms. There is, without a doubt, much cultural support for laws attempting to curb discrimination. At the same time, however, there is a good deal of cultural support for discriminatory practices.

The legal problem is to prove discrimination, but that is very difficult to do. Discrimination still exists in hiring, but how can a minority group prove it? When a job position becomes available, minority group members apply. Now, if the organization is dominated by white males, what are the chances of a minority applicant being selected for a particularly desirable post? Obviously, they are not very good. However, the company would not admit that it did not hire a woman because she is a woman. And even if the five men who decided whom to hire did admit this to themselves, they would tell only each other. The woman would not hear the discussion and thus would not be able to prove her charge of discrimination in court.

COOLING-OUT

Discrimination, like prejudice, is reinforced by inculcating in minority group members a belief in their own inferiority. Some years ago, sociologist Burton Clark used the phrase *cooling-out* to describe how the educational system is organized so as to cause students to acknowledge that their scholastic failures are not the fault of the system but are the result of the student's own shortcomings.[6]

Clark's concept sheds light on the continuance of discrimination and on the fate of efforts to reduce or eliminate it. Minority groups and their members frequently accept the evaluation made of them by the dominant group. That is, they come to believe that they are inferior. This acceptance serves a cooling-out function; it reduces the likelihood of action to end the discrimination.

Today this is much less the case. Substantial numbers of minority group members have become aware that race and ethnicity do not determine native aptitudes. The system no longer cools off minorities as it once did, because scientific evidence shows that intelligence, motivation, and various aptitudes are distributed roughly the same among minority group members as they are among white males. And in conjunction with court rulings forbidding de jure discrimination have come other rulings demanding efforts to redress the inequalities created by past conduct. As the late comedian Oliver Hardy used to say to his partner, "You've gotten us into a pretty pickle this time, Stanley!" Assuredly, we have gotten ourselves into a "pretty pickle" by our long-standing, previous discrimination against minorities.

These efforts to atone for past failures are termed by some *reverse discrimination*. They argue that just as people should not be barred from participation on the basis of sex or race, neither should they be guaranteed a job. These people — generally white males — argue that schools and employers are now in a position where they must accept minority group members simply because they belong to a minority. This difficult question will be discussed in detail at the end of the chapter, when we consider efforts to solve the problem of minorities. For now, we should consider these efforts at bringing minority group members into full participation in society as one of the four ways of ending minority group status.

Ending Minority Group Status

Minorities are segregated. *Segregation* means the separation of ethnic, religious, or racial groups in such areas of life as schooling, places of residence, and work. This separation can be voluntary, but it usually isn't. Rather, it is forced on the minority group by the dominant group. Segregation does not mean that the dominant and minority groups have no social interaction at all — that is separatism — it means that any interaction that does occur is limited and strictly regulated by formal and informal norms. Minorities trying to end their status as minorities have four choices: separatism, assimilation, integration, and pluralism. The first and last maintain that cultural differences exist now and always will, although their conclusions based on this principle differ; the middle two hold that differences exist but can be removed. The four alternatives form a continuum based on their reaction to cultural differences. Separatism sees the differences as irreconcilable and possibly generating hostility; assimilation sees the differences as removable, but prefers the dominant culture to the minority one; integration sees the differences as removable, resulting in a new single culture valuing both dominant and minority cultures equally; and pluralism sees the differences as largely irreconcilable but as valuable expressions of human variety.

SEPARATISM

Separatism means the complete separation of minorities from the dominant sector of society. The demands of the Black Muslims epitomize the aims of separatists. They "advocate the complete rejection of the white man's culture and seek to separate themselves physically from the white man."[7]

Some blacks, including the Black Muslims, argue for the establishment of separate territories for blacks and whites within the geographical boundaries of the United States. Although they are sincere in this argument, the practical barriers to this arrangement are so formidable that the idea is wholly impractical. A more common way to bring about separatism is to move one group to another territory. An example of such an arrangement is Liberia, an African nation founded in 1822 by the American Colonization Society as a colony for freed American slaves. It is an interesting commentary on our species that present-day Liberia, ruled by the descendants of those freed slaves, has a minority group that is discriminated against. The native population is subject to the rule of the descendants of the immigrants.

Conceptual Orientation 173

The goal of Black Muslims, shown here at their national convention, is absolute separatism from the dominant white culture of the United States. They believe their inspiration and calling to that end are divine and thus irrefutable.

ASSIMILATION

Assimilation means the minority group must adjust to the dominant or host culture. That is, the onus for change is on the minority group, which must change and become culturally similar or identical to dominant group members. Booker T. Washington held this perspective and maintained that blacks needed to prove themselves through education and hard work as being ready for full acceptance in white society. Today, few members of any minority group accept assimilation as a means of adjustment. As we stated, assimilation downgrades the value of the minority culture and insists on its removal. As this culture is abandoned, minority status hypothetically disappears as minority groups make themselves indistinguishable from the dominant majority.

INTEGRATION

Integration means the coalescing of different subcultures into a new culture that is a harmonious, single culture. Once the new culture is formed, members should be culturally similar and indistinguishable from one another and live under equality. Integration differs from assimilation in that both dominant and minority cultures are valued.

A considerable proportion of minority groups' efforts toward ending segregation has been in the direction of integration. The *black middle class*, for instance, now holds white-collar positions in what were formerly all-white industries. They believe that it is possible to compete with whites and that barriers to black participation can be broken down.[8] This black middle class is opting for integration, which seems likely to be what a majority of black citizens desire: "They do not want to be separate and equal or separate and superior. They want what is constitutionally guaranteed and are willing to fight to get it."[9]

PLURALISM

With *pluralism,* all different groups in a society retain their identities and distinctive subcultures but are coequal with all other groups. In a pluralistic society, there are no dominant or minority groups, simply different groups.

A significant move for pluralism in American society is being made by American Indians. In recent years, "native Americans have moved from retreatist, religious, and mystical movements to the political offensive as evidenced by two contemporary elements of what might well be called the 'red power movement.' These are the National Indian Youth Council (NIYC) and the American Indian Movement (AIM)."[10] As evidenced by court suits, Indians are also taking the economic offensive to recover land they claim was taken from them by fraud and theft. But what is particularly important about these attempts at organization is the underlying theme. Indians are trying to establish their right to live according to the norms of their culture and not have to give in to the dominant white culture. They want land back so that they can live on it as they choose.

Actually, we already have a kind of pluralism in urban areas. In many American cities, there is a Little Italy for the Italians, a Chinatown for the Chinese, and other sections inhabited by persons of such backgrounds as Polish and German. These communities have been able to carry on their traditions unmolested for many years, producing a variety of behavior for city dwellers. Also, there has been a considerable revival of interest in ancestry and pride in ethnic background brought about in part by the civil rights movement. In addition, the showing of "Roots" on television in 1978 and 1979 did more than cause black Americans to become interested in their ancestry. Other groups also began to investigate their origins and feel proud of their contributions to American life.

But though many in this country are hyphenated Americans, this society is not truly pluralistic. In a pluralistic society all groups exist in a coequal, democratic fashion. We can hardly claim that we have achieved this ideal today.

Is pluralism possible? Frankly, we do not know. Historically, there is no evidence that it has ever been tried. The problem may be that when different groups exist in a society, they are in a competitive situation and competition requires losers as well as winners. If there is competition, minority groups — the losers — are likely to emerge.

Summary

As we have seen, the concept of minorities is far from simple. Figure 6.2 presents a model of what has been discussed in this section. Minorities have their origins in such things as conquest, immigration, or the possession of power. Their visibility plays a role. When a group is placed at a disadvantage by either conquest or immigration, visibility of that group — either physical, ethnic, or both — leads to prejudice. Prejudice causes the dominant group to ascribe undesirable characteristics to minority group members. Categorizing a group of persons as innately inferior justifies exploitation and discrimination, which further buttresses the fear, dislike, and repugnance of minorities by the dominant group. The result is inequality.

At this point, many will wonder how this applies to women. They surely constitute a minority group, but do males fear or dislike them? We cannot be certain that women are not feared or disliked by more than few supposedly dominant males. Imagine if women competed on absolutely equal terms with men for jobs. If this were to occur in the United States, what proportion of males would hold high positions both in private industry and government employment? The obvious answer makes it clear why women could be feared or disliked. They threaten men's superior position.

HISTORICAL OVERVIEW

Minorities existed before the beginning of recorded history: slavery was a well-estab-

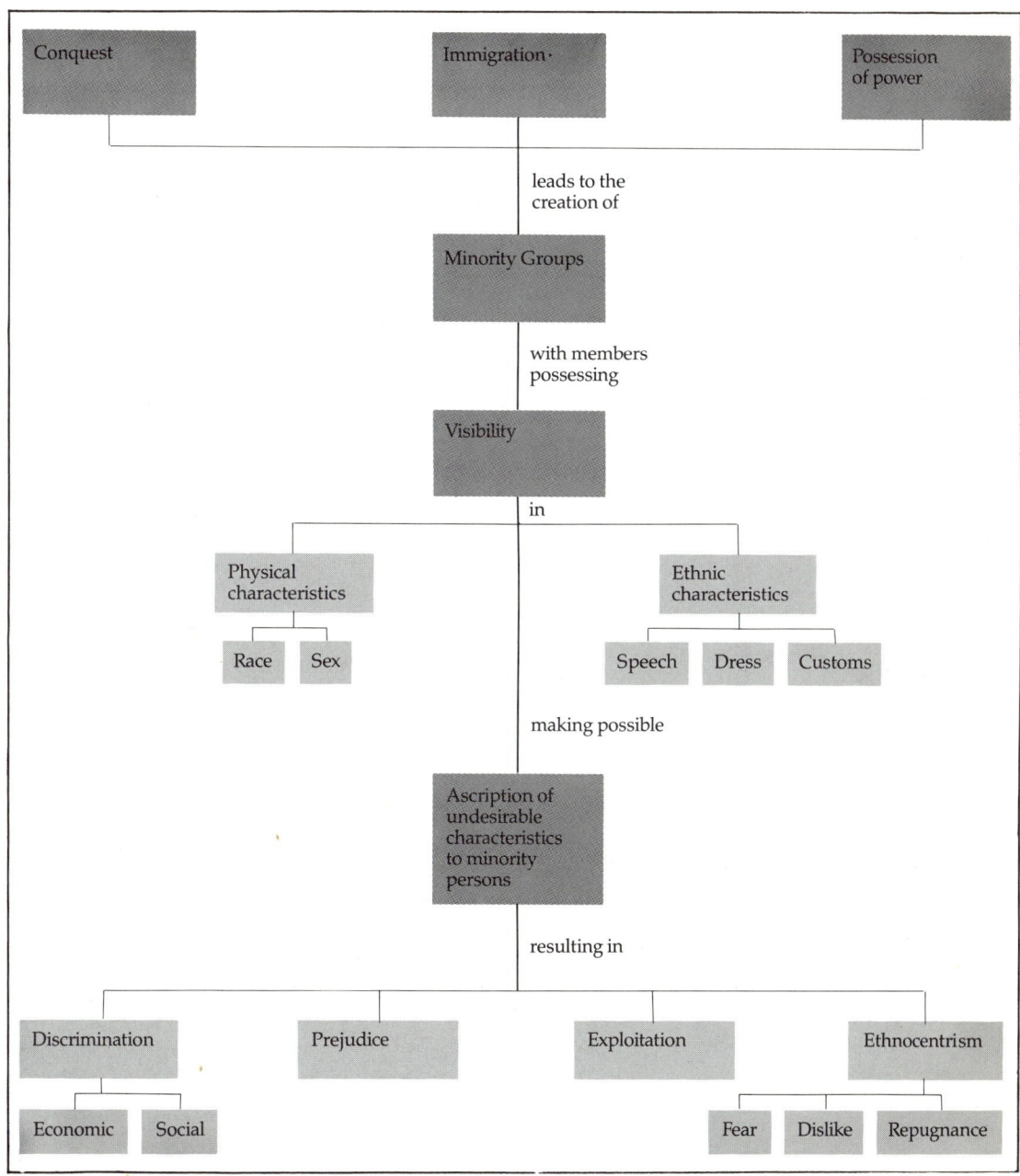

FIGURE 6.2 A Model of the Dynamics Underlying the Status and Treatment of Minorities

lished practice in some societies by 4000 B.C. "By early historic times slavery was a foundation of ancient industry and a potent instrument in the accumulation of capital. Bound captives, presumably doomed to servitude, are depicted on some of the oldest figure documents . . . from Mesopotamia, and are as ancient as scenes of battle."[11]

Slaves have constituted a minority group for many centuries, but there are varying conditions of servitude. A *slave* is a person whose services are under the control of another or others and who cannot voluntarily and unilaterally end that control in a legal, lawful fashion. With minority groups the situation is similar. The crux of the matter is not so much control by others as the lack of power to end domination by others. Minorities are similar to slaves in their lack of power to change their status. The dominant group has the power to impose its will on the minority and has the authority to make its actions legitimate.

Power and Authority

Power is the ability to impose one's will on another. Power is coercive, meaning it often involves physical force or threats of force. But it can also use other means, including economic control.

Contrary to what some people believe, power is not the basis for governments or the existence of minority groups. On the basis of mere power alone, no government could maintain itself for long. Power alone could not compel minority groups to accept discrimination. Something far more important than power is required — authority. *Authority* supports power by making it legitimate, worthy of obedience. Legitimate power operates with the consent of those subjects to it.[12]

Power alone is inefficient in the long run, because it requires enormous resources and vigilance to maintain. Without authority power needs great amounts of coercion. In contrast, authority is efficient because it means voluntary obedience. Those subjected to power with authority accept it as just, right, and proper.

It is authority that creates and maintains minority group status. No system of discrimination can be long maintained unless those subject to it accept it and grant it authority. And it is citizens, not governments, who grant or withdraw authority.

To see how power and authority work to maintain minority status we will look at a group that is not now a minority. The fourteenth century marked the end of the Middle Ages and the beginnings of the Renaissance in Europe. In this century, a small proportion of the population, the first and second estates (the nobility and the clergy), led lives of considerable autonomy and luxury. The third estate was the bourgeoisie, people of some substance. The great mass of the people were in a fourth category, the peasant.

The *estate system* was not completely closed. Vertical social movement was possible. Over several generations, noble families could lose their standing, representing downward mobility. And it was also possible for enterprising peasants to move upward in the social system, representing upward mobility.[13] But on the whole, escape from the peasant class or even the third estate was difficult. The nobility prevented any encroachments on their privileges by others. For example, sumptuary laws were established, which laid down rigid dress codes for people depending on their station in life. "Proclaimed by criers in the country courts and public assemblies, exact gradations of fabric, color, fur trimmings, ornaments, and jewels were laid down for every rank and income level. Bourgeoisie might be forbidden to own a carriage or wear ermine, and peasants to wear any color but black or brown."[14]

Although the third estate and the peasants were numerically superior to the first and second estates, both were minority groups. While the bourgeoisie had some political power in the towns, the peasants had virtually none. Occasional rebellions by the peasants, such as the Jacquerie of 1358, were short lived and ruthlessly put down. How is it that this great mass of people tolerated almost total subjugation from a smaller group? The answer is the same reason that minority status is maintained in modern societies. The status was supported by law and beliefs and the supports for the estate system are almost identical with modern-day supports for a system of minorities. Two powerful supports both then and now are the force of tradition and authority. *Tradition* reflects people's tendency, when they are socialized into a system, to accept that system, however onerous its workings. The tradition is built on the base of society's values and ideals; since people know no other values, they support the traditional ones. And these values are built into the power structure. Because all societies socialize their members into accepting the existing political structure, people accept it and grant it authority. Because it has authority people accept its distribution of power. At all times and in all places, the basis for the existence of minority groups is differential power. The nobility and the clergy were organized and had military power to enforce their commands. We need to remember that power always involves organization. Within limits, organized groups can generally prevail over unorganized aggregates. Until minorities learn this lesson of the necessity of organization, they will remain as minorities.

Women as a Minority

History does not help us much in determining what caused women to be established as a minority group. We can only speculate, aided by whatever evidence is available. Evidence from anthropology indicates that by the start of recorded history, women already held minority status. Humans first formed into bands or tribes and it appears that these groups had a division of labor that led to women becoming a minority group. Women would bear, nurse, and care for children. Because of this primary responsibility, they could not range far from a camp or settlement in search of game. Further, males are equipped for hunting by their greater strength and speed. Where the possession of power depended on size and muscular strength plus skill in the use of weapons, dominance was accorded to males. As anthropologist John Beattie observed, "In the most simple societies it is still true, as it was in pre-twentieth century Europe, that the human world is 'a man's world.' "[15]

The paradox is that although male labor (hunting) is valued more it is neither assured of success nor the major source of food. For example, among the Tiwi of Australia, hunting is the far more prestigious occupation, yet most of the food supply comes from gathering. Tiwi women, like the slaves in the pre-Civil War South, constitute the more important labor force but are exploited because of their minority status.[16] Similarly, women in twentieth-century America are not ordinarily paid for being homemakers, although their work enables society to function. Modern women and Tiwi women are sisters.

Also among their sisters are the billions of women who ever lived, for women have been a minority not only in the prehistoric hunting and gathering societies similar to the Tiwi and not only in modern America, but everywhere in between. Their position has fluctuated from being deplored as the cause of sin to being exalted as semidivine, but at all times their rights have been largely denied. Modern patterns of sex roles, while built on these ancient patterns, are largely the product of industrialization. The status of women changed dramatically when economies shifted from an agricultural to an industrial base. Families ceased being both production and consumption units, becoming largely just consumption units. Women began to work outside the home in increasing numbers. Children, no longer economic assets as helping hands on the farm, became economic liabilities; and families voluntarily limited their numbers of offspring. The declining birthrate and the resultant smaller family size have freed more and more women to take up full-time employment. The pattern of women having fewer children and working outside the home has increased to the present (see Figures 6.3 and 6.4).

These changes and others, such as increased education for women and gradual acceptance of them into the labor force, led to widespread dissatisfaction with traditional roles. This discontent was channeled into the women's movements of the nineteenth and twentieth centuries outlined in Chapter 3. The important point to make here is that women continued to be suppressed and their rights abused until they began to organize. Although the struggle was not easy, and is not over, women have achieved significant victories because they got together to fight against their minority status. The same is true of another American minority, blacks.

Blacks as a Minority

The first blacks came to this country early in the seventeenth century, like many whites, as *indentured servants*, laborers who contracted to work for a specific term (generally three to seven years) and then became free. However, by the mid-seventeenth century, the growing agriculture industry created an ever greater demand for cheap labor. The evolution of slavery is complex, but can be boiled down to two facts. Slaves were a cheaper and steadier labor force than indentured servants and black indentured servants, not white ones, became slaves, solely because they were black. American slavery was a racial phenomenon. Gradually slavery caught hold and by the middle of the eighteenth century, slavery was legalized in all American colonies. Although some colonies in the North soon repealed such laws, slavery remained legal in the South, where it was more prevalent and more economical. Slavery was legal in the South until the passage of the Thirteenth Amendment to the Constitution after the end of the Civil War in 1865. Contrary to what many people believe, President Abraham Lincoln's Emancipation Proclamation did not free the slaves in 1863; the constitutional amendment was required.

For a brief period after the end of the Civil War, the rights of blacks were in the ascendancy. By 1870 more than a million blacks had the right to vote. And they exercised that right, voting into office blacks and their Republican allies. But the legal measures giving blacks equality were made effective by the presence of federal troops in the South, which ended with the Hayes-Tilden Compromise to settle the disputed election of 1876. Federal troops were then withdrawn from the South and blacks were unprotected. It did not take southern whites long to institute measures that segregated the South, with whites in one caste and blacks in the other.

A *caste system* may have numerous castes, as in India, or only two, as in the United States. But all such systems have four char-

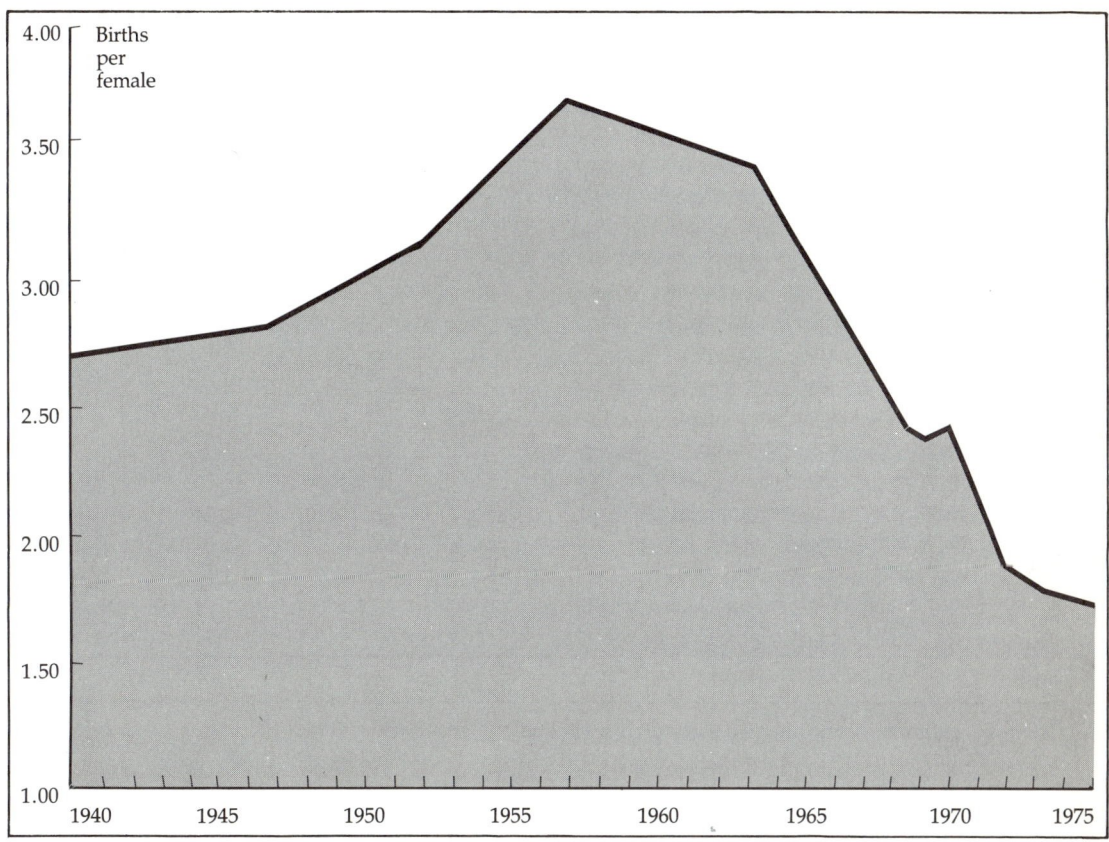

FIGURE 6.3 Fertility Rate for U.S. Females, 1940–1975

Source: Bureau of the Census, *Statistical Abstract of the United States, 1977* (Washington, D.C.: U.S. Government Printing Office, 1977), p. 56.

acteristics: (1) caste membership is by birth; (2) membership is permanent; (3) marriage is *endogamous* (caste members can only marry other caste members); and (4) the division of labor is based on caste.[17] In the South, blacks were segregated from whites in all public places, interracial marriage was forbidden, and blacks' opportunities to reach higher education and better jobs were nonexistent. Black life was regulated by the Jim Crow laws mentioned earlier, which restricted activities from riding streetcars to voting.

These laws were mostly passed in the 1890s and this decade and the one following marked the low point of black rights since the Civil War. But blacks slowly began to organize, despite the restrictions on their activities, and in 1909 formed the National Association for the Advancement of Colored People, a significant event because the organization's black and white members marked the first union of blacks and white liberals since the pre-Civil War antislavery movement. With this increased power and a grow-

180 MINORITIES: *A World of Illogic and Reduced Opportunities*

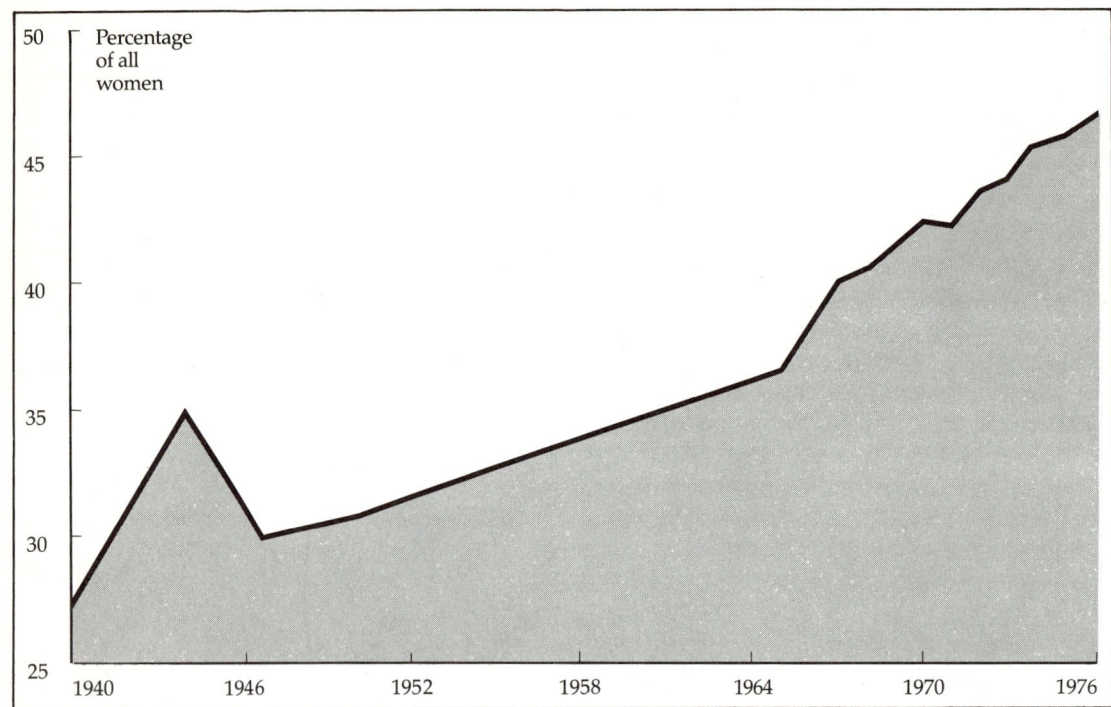

FIGURE 6.4 Women Working as a Proportion of Female Population, 1940–1976

Source: Adapted from Bureau of the Census, *Statistical Abstract of the United States, 1977* (Washington, D.C.: U.S. Government Printing Office, 1977), p. 391.

ing organization, blacks were gradually able to win more of their rights. The major breakthroughs have come since World War II, however. First came President Harry Truman's 1948 order to desegregate the armed forces. Then came the 1954 Supreme Court decision that struck down the segregation prevalent in schools in the South.

But perhaps the most significant event in the civil rights movement was the simple determination of Rosa Parks, a tired black woman going home from work, who refused to give up her bus seat to a white man. That night Dr. Martin Luther King, Jr., met with friends and was elected president of a group calling itself the Montgomery Improvement Association. This group initiated a bus boycott that marked a change in tactics in the civil rights movement, a switch from court battles to *nonviolent protest*. Such tactics were followed in marches all across the country throughout the sixties. These marches to secure the end of segregation were buttressed by efforts in Congress to pass legislation guaranteeing black rights, a landmark in this push being the Voting Rights Act of 1965, which prohibited the denial of voting rights.

The civil rights movement had its origins in the gradual development of a consensus among blacks that the system lacked the authority to maintain the caste system. In this determination blacks were joined by liberal whites. The civil rights movement withdrew authority from the state governments, leaving political authorities with only raw power, the use of force. In turn blacks demonstrated that they had power in the large numbers who participated in their marches and in the economic distress caused by their boycotts. And this power was supplemented by the power and authority of the federal government. Again, it was organizing that made possible the success of the civil rights movement.

Summary

We have seen that minorities have existed since before recorded human history, although in modern Western societies, minorities are shrinking in size relative to the total population. From ancient times through the Middle Ages to today, the greater mass of people, slaves, and commoners, constituted a vast part of the total population but were still minority groups. With greater prosperity and general equality, the Western democracies limit the opportunities of fewer people.

These minorities are becoming more restive, less likely to accept their status. History shows that minority status is difficult to change. It rests upon a solid foundation of tradition, authority, and socialization. But change is possible. When the minority organizes and challenges authority successfully, minority-dominant relations will change, as they already have in this and other countries.

Let us now look at the conditions of the American minorities and see why they are dissatisfied and whether they are organized to effect change.

OBJECTIVE DIMENSIONS OF THE PROBLEM

How large is the problem of minorities? That is, how many people are minority group members? The data in Table 6.3 show that minorities are no small matter. We should note that some minority group members are doubly jeopardized because they belong to more than one minority group. This is true of elderly women, for example, who suffer discrimination for being old and for being female.

But is this discrimination genuine? Some argue that minorities — women and blacks, say — do not suffer at all. If minorities were a purely hypothetical construct, then we would expect no evidence of discrimination. When we obtain objective data on minority groups we would see no significant differ-

TABLE 6.3 Population of Minority Groups in the United States

Minority	Estimated Number	Proportion of Total Population
Females	110,199,000	51.2%
Blacks	24,763,000	11.5
Chicanos	6,590,000	3.1
Jews	6,115,000	2.8
Puerto Ricans	1,753,000	0.8
Orientals	1,026,000	0.5
Indians	792,700	0.4

Source: Bureau of the Census, *Statistical Abstract of the United States, 1977* (Washington, D.C.: U.S. Government Printing Office, 1977), pp. 25, 27, 30, 33, 50.

ences between minority groups and the dominant group in employment, median incomes, years of schooling, or housing. We will now look at existing minorities to determine whether discrimination actually exists in present-day America. We will focus on women and blacks because they are the largest groups, with the most data available.

Females

A good many people of both sexes would deny that women are a minority group. Certainly women are not segregated from the dominant males. Indeed, males show some eagerness to mingle socially and otherwise with females. And many maintain that, far from being suppressed, women are a highly privileged group, protected, looked after, and possibly coddled. What this argument ignores is that while male protection of women is ego-enhancing for males, and for some females, it has an opposite effect on other women. Many women resent the implication of being indulged and protected — the implication that they are incapable of looking out for themselves and need a male to take care of them. Many women find this condescension infuriating. And while it is true that women are not segregated from men, this attitude reveals how they are a minority, for this is precisely the attitude taken by dominant sectors of societies toward minority groups. Minority groups are always seen as somewhat incompetent and requiring protection and guidance.

If women were incapable of caring for themselves, they should be incapable of performing some tasks. But if one is objective, it is difficult to find a single occupation or profession in modern society for which females are by nature less well-equipped than males. The argument that females do less well in some school subjects, such as mathematics, has been verified by national testing only for fifth grade and up, when it is believed girls have learned that they are not supposed to do well in mathematics. The cause is not a lack of natural aptitude. Rather, it is that females have been socialized to believe that they cannot do as well as males. As W. I. Thomas, a sociologist, observed many years ago, "If people believe certain things to be real, then they are real in their consequences."[18] Nowhere is the truth of Thomas's words more clearly shown than in the performance of males and females on certain tasks.

DISCRIMINATION IN WORK

Do women suffer discrimination in terms of employment opportunities and pay? Let us see. The Bureau of Census has grouped jobs into eleven job families. These are aggregates of occupations which share certain similarities. For example, they group together such professions as law, medicine, and dentistry, because they resemble each other more closely than they do such occupations as lathe operator and electrician.

Table 6.4 compares the eleven job families according to the proportion of males and females employed in each. As this table indicates, women have gained in seven out of eleven of the job families. Does this mean that job discrimination against women is weakening? In such cases as professional, technical, and kindred workers, where the increase is large, the answer seems to be yes. However, what appears to be a significant increase in other cases merely reflects the fact that more women are entering the labor force. If job discrimination against women is lessening it is doing so very slowly. And the higher proportion of women than men in

TABLE 6.4 Occupational Families by Sex, 1960 and 1975 (in thousands)

Occupational Families	1960				1975				Percentage Change	
	Male	Percentage	Female	Percentage	Male	Percentage	Female	Percentage	Male	Female
Professional, technical, and kindred workers	4,766	7.2	2,703	4.1	7,481	8.8	5,276	6.2	+1.6	+2.1
Managers, officials, and proprietors	5,968	9.1	1,099	1.7	7,162	8.4	1,729	2.0	−0.7	+0.3
Clerical and kindred workers	3,145	4.8	6,617	10.1	3,355	4.0	11,773	13.9	−0.8	+3.8
Sales workers	2,544	3.9	1,680	2.6	3,137	3.7	2,323	2.7	−0.2	+0.1
Craftsmen and supervisors	8,322	12.7	222	0.3	10,472	12.4	501	0.6	−0.3	+0.3
Operatives	8,617	13.1	3,333	5.1	8,971	10.6	3,885	4.6	−2.5	−0.5
Nonfarm laborers	3,471	5.3	82	0.1	3,777	4.5	357	0.4	−0.8	+0.3
Private household workers	30	0.05	1,943	3.0	30	0.04	1,141	1.3	−0.01	−1.7
Service workers, except private household	2,814	4.3	3,236	4.9	4,370	5.2	6,116	7.2	+0.9	+2.3
Farmers and farm managers	2,667	4.1	109	0.2	1,492	1.8	102	0.1	−2.3	−0.1
Farm laborers and supervisors	1,552	2.4	848	1.3	985	1.2	358	0.4	−1.2	−0.9

Source: Adapted from Bureau of the Census, *Social Indicators, 1976* (Washington, D.C.: U.S. Government Printing Office, 1977), p. 377.

such categories as clerical work and private household work clearly shows that a sex-based division of labor remains a significant characteristic of American society.

Comparing the incomes of those working full-time, the data also show that economic discrimination against women still exists. In 1976, the median income for women working full-time was $8,312; for men it was $13,859. Not only is the gap large, it is widening. In 1965, the difference between the median incomes of men and women was only $3,502. It

184 MINORITIES: *A World of Illogic and Reduced Opportunities*

had widened to $3,744 by 1970 and was up to $5,574 by 1976.[19]

Although the data do not demonstrate this directly, part of the increasing difference between the median incomes of working men and women arises from the fact that growing numbers of women are entering the work force. Since a substantial proportion of these new workers are taking jobs at lower levels, their yearly incomes tend to depress the average for women as a group. Nonetheless, women are still underpaid. Even those engaged in the same occupation as a male often receive lower salaries. We can conclude that discrimination still goes on against women.

DISCRIMINATION IN EDUCATION

Women are doing well insofar as obtaining a high school education is concerned. The proportion of females in the high school age group who graduate from high school has been higher than that of males in the same age group for every year since 1950.[20] However, discrimination is still a fact of life with respect to higher education, a more important statistic, since attending a college or university is voluntary (whereas a certain amount of high school attendance is compulsory) and also entails a family decision on how to spend family money (whereas high school is free). Table 6.5 shows us that the gap has narrowed between the number of baccalaureate degrees awarded to men and women in the century since 1876. However, the gap still remains out of proportion to the number of males and females in the population, roughly fifty-fifty. This may change in the last two decades of this century, with women achieving parity with men. One contributing factor to change is the growing number of older women returning to college. These are women who are going to college for the first time, or who left college before graduating, or who are pursuing an advanced degree.[21]

Graduate school discrimination against women seems to be decreasing if we look at the awarding of master's degrees. In 1975,

TABLE 6.5 Baccalaureate Degrees 1876 to 1976

Year	Total	Male		Female	
		Number	Percentage	Number	Percentage
1876	12,005	9,911	82.6	2,094	17.4
1886	13,097	10,731	81.9	2,366	18.1
1896	24,593	20,076	81.6	4,517	18.4
1906	32,019	25,215	78.8	6,804	21.2
1916	45,250	31,852	70.4	13,398	29.6
1926	97,263	62,218	64.0	35,045	36.0
1936	143,125	86,067	60.1	57,058	39.9
1946	136,174	58,664	43.1	77,510	56.9[a]
1956	309,514	198,615	64.2	110,899	35.8
1966	551,047	328,853	59.7	222,194	40.3
1976	988,000	558,000	56.5	430,000	43.5

[a]The higher percentage of females receiving baccalaureate degrees in this year reflects the effects of World War II.

Sources: Adapted from Bureau of the Census, *Historical Statistics of the United States: Colonial Times to 1970*, Part 1 (Washington, D.C.: U.S. Government Printing Office, 1975), pp. 385–386; and Bureau of the Census, *Statistical Abstract of the United States, 1977* (Washington, D.C.: U.S. Government Printing Office, 1977), p. 160.

women earned 44.8 percent of all these degrees. However, women are receiving a much lower proportion of doctoral degrees — only 21.3 percent of the 34,086 degrees awarded in 1975.[22] Further, some areas of graduate study remain largely closed to women, such as engineering, business and management, the physical sciences, and theology. In other areas, notably education and the social sciences, women are earning more degrees but still fewer than men. Even in education, in which women earn more baccalaureates (73.3 percent) and master's (62.2 percent), they still lag well behind men in doctorates (30.8 percent). The result is that men have a considerable advantage for moving into top-level positions in education, as in the rest of academia. In fact, women are underrepresented on college and university faculties. And again, the situation is worsening. From 1932 to 1966, the proportion of women on faculties decreased from 28.9 percent to 22.2 percent.[23] While women are improving in getting high school diplomas and baccalaureate degrees, they are still discriminated against in the competition for advanced degrees.

In education as in work, in spite of modest gains, women remain a minority group. Again, we must remember than even with greater participation by women in work and education, there is a more important area that must be changed for any progress to be made. That is traditional sex roles. Some of the inequities we have seen are not solely the result of deliberate exclusion of women. Many women are excluded from certain choices by what they are taught. They have been socialized to believe themselves unsuited for certain occupations. As Elizabeth Janeway expresses it:

> "Why should I bother to study this science or tackle that subject?" an intelligent girl may still ask herself. She is encouraged by the very situation in which she finds herself to let inertia take hold and say, "I needn't bother learning that, I'm only a girl."[24]

Blacks

By blacks we mean those persons who are identified by others as black, identify themselves as black, or as it usually is, both. People with black ancestors who consider themselves as white and are so viewed by others are, for all sociological purposes, white. Any other definition of black American is sociologically irrelevant. Legally, of course, even this definition is inappropriate, for in hiring, in schooling, or in housing there should be no difference between the way blacks and whites are treated. Has the legal end to discrimination meant the actual end of discrimination?

DISCRIMINATION IN WORK

As Table 6.6 makes clear, discrimination against black males in jobs still occurs. Black males are underrepresented in white-collar positions and overrepresented in the less prestigious and lower paid blue-collar, semiskilled, and unskilled jobs. Additionally in all but one occupational group, the median incomes of all males is higher than that of black males. Although not shown in Table 6.6, the relative positions of black females is the same as black males or worse, showing the double jeopardy of belonging to two minority groups.

Even in terms of employment, blacks suffer, as we pointed out in Chapter 4 and as Table 6.7 reveals. Plainly, black workers are more likely to suffer unemployment than white workers. The difference between the proportion of blacks in the total population (11.5 percent) and the proportion in the work force in 1976 (10.8 percent) may appear insig-

TABLE 6.6 Black Males in Occupational Families and Comparative Median Incomes, 1970 (in thousands)

Occupational Family	Male Total	Black Males	Percentage of Total Males	Median Male Income	Median Black Male Income
Managers, officials, and proprietors[a]	5,386	125	2.3	$11,277	$7,439
Sales workers[a]	3,378	88	2.6	8,451	5,425
Farmers and farm managers[a]	1,357	38	2.8	4,822	1,749
Craftsmen and supervisors[a]	10,530	657	6.2	8,172	5,920
Professional, technical, and kindred workers[a]	49,455	4,304	8.7	7,610	5,194
Clerical and kindred workers[a]	3,748	342	9.1	7,265	6,157
Operatives, except transport[b]	6,835	851	12.5	6,730	5,582
Transport equipment operatives[b]	2,954	422	14.3	6,903	5,431
Service workers, except private household[b]	4,010	668	16.7	5,100	4,359
Farm laborers and supervisors[b]	848	151	17.8	2,570	1,862
Private household workers[b]	38	19	50.0	1,891	1,945

[a]Black are underrepresented.

[b]Blacks are overrepresented.

Source: Adapted from Bureau of the Census, *Statistical Abstract of the United States, 1977* (Washington, D.C.: U.S. Government Printing Office), pp. 407–409.

TABLE 6.7 Number and Percent of Employed Persons by Race (in thousands)

Race	1960	1970	1974	1975	1976
White	58,850	70,182	76,620	75,713	78,021
Black	6,927	8,445	9,316	9,070	9,464
Percent black of all employed	11.7	10.7	10.8	10.7	10.8
Percent black of total population	10.5	11.1	11.4	11.5	11.5

Source: Adapted from Bureau of the Census, *Statistical Abstract of the United States, 1977* (Washington, D.C.: U.S. Government Printing Office, 1977), pp. 30, 407.

nificant. In terms of human beings, however, it amounts to more than a half million unemployed persons.

Blacks are more often unemployed. When they are employed, black workers are underrepresented in the higher-paying and more prestigious positions. And at almost any level, black median income is below that of whites. Whether they come from poor families and have little education or from mid-

While blacks remain victims of discrimination in employment, more and more qualified black men and women are moving into professional ranks. Black women must struggle to overcome the dual burden of being both black and female, but many of them, like this television reporter, are winning the battle.

dle-class families and have considerable education, blacks still receive lesser rewards than comparable whites. "Black men have experienced a perverse sort of egalitarianism — neither the disadvantages of lower socioeconomic origins nor the advantages of higher social origins and education weigh as heavily in the status attainments of blacks as they do in those of whites."[25]

DISCRIMINATION IN EDUCATION

The more education black persons have, the greater their median income. But white median income surpasses black median income at all educational levels. Blacks and whites who have only a first through seventh grade education or who did not graduate from high school show little difference in annual incomes. Having a high school diploma, some college, or four or more years of college, however, makes a considerable difference in income for both blacks and whites.[26]

Table 6.8 shows the differences between blacks and whites at seven levels of education. These findings can be summarized as follows:

1. More blacks delay their education two or more years than whites.
2. Black males have a higher level of high school non-attendance than do white males, but white and black females are equal.
3. Blacks are considerably less likely to complete high school than whites.
4. Blacks are less likely to complete college than whites, but black females are more likely to do so than black males.
5. While a high proportion of both whites and blacks are working at jobs for which they are overqualified by a high school education, blacks are more likely to be doing so than whites.
6. Black males with a college education are more likely than white males to be working in a job for which they are overqualified, but black females are less likely to be overqualified for their jobs than either white males or females.
7. For those who have completed college, white males have higher median earnings than black males, black females, and white females, but black females are earning more than are white females.

TABLE 6.8 Comparing Whites and Blacks on Seven Indices of Educational Accomplishment, 1976

Criteria	White Males	Black Males	Difference	White Females	Black Females	Difference
Delayed education (two or more years for 15–17 year olds)	10.7%	23.0%	+13.0%	7.0%	15.0%	+8.0%
High school nonattendance	5.0	7.0	+ 2.0	6.0	6.0	0
High school completion	87.0	74.0	−13.0	86.0	74.0	−12.0
College completion	34.0	11.0	−23.0	22.0	11.0	−11.0
High school overqualification[a]	44.2	67.2	+23.0	49.0	56.1	+ 7.1
College overqualification[b]	44.7	55.0	+10.3	45.4	41.3	− 4.1
Earnings for college-educated persons (in thousands)	$15.2	$12.3	−2.9	$8.1	$9.9	+1.8

[a]Working at a job for which a high school diploma is not necessary.
[b]Working at a job for which a college degree is not necessary.

Source: Adapted from Commission on Civil Rights, *Social Indicators of Equality for Minorities and Women* (Washington, D.C.: U.S. Government Printing Office, 1978), pp. 6–24.

TABLE 6.9 Changes in Indices of Educational Achievement for Whites and Blacks, 1960 and 1976

	White Males			Black Males			White Females			Black Females		
Criteria	1960	1976	Difference[a]	1960	1976	Difference[a]	1960	1976	Difference[a]	1960	1976	Difference[a]
Delayed education (two or more years for 15–17 year olds)	18.0%	10.0%	+8	23.0%	13.0%	+13	10.0%	7.0%	+3	25.0%	15.0%	+10
High school nonattendance	18.0	5.0	+13	21.0	7.0	+14	12.0	6.0	+6	23.0	6.0	+17
High school completion	69.0	87.0	+18	41.0	74.0	+33	70.0	86.0	+16	42.0	74.0	+32
College completion	20.0	34.0	+14	4.0	11.0	+7	9.0	22.0	+13	6.0	11.0	+5
High school overqualification	40.2	44.2	−4	70.2	67.2	+3	33.4	49.0	−15.6	65.1	56.1	+9
College overqualification	42.7	44.7	−2	58.8	55.0	+3.8	29.0	45.0	−16	41.4	41.3	+0.1
Earnings for college-educated persons (in thousands)	$6.8	$15.2	+$8.4	$4.5	$11.7	+7.2	$1.7	$8.1	+6.4	$2.8	$9.9	+7.1

[a]A plus sign indicates improvement; a minus sign retrogression. Improvement does not mean a higher number, but better achievement. Thus a drop in the number who did not complete high school, while a decrease in numbers, is in fact an improvement.

Source: Adapted from Commission on Civil Rights, *Social Indicators of Equality for Minorities and Women* (Washington, D.C.: U.S. Government Printing Office, 1978), pp. 6–24.

De facto discrimination of black people in education remains an unpleasant fact of American society. But we need to know if the situation is improving, whether changes have occurred and in what direction. Table 6.9 compares white and black educational achievement from 1960 and 1976 on the same seven indices. Here we see a somewhat different picture:

1. All groups show a drop in delayed education but blacks have improved more than whites.
2. High school nonattendance has generally decreased but the decrease was greater for blacks than for whites.
3. High school completion is up overall but more so for blacks than for whites.
4. College completion is up for the population as a whole but whites are doing better than blacks.
5. For high school overqualification, blacks improved considerably, whereas whites retrogressed.
6. College overqualification has improved somewhat for blacks, worsened somewhat for white males, and become a major problem for white females.
7. With inflation, college graduates should be earning more in 1976 than in 1960, and this is the case. However, black males have not done as well as white males, with the gap between them widening from $2,251 to $2,841. However, black females have done better than white females.

Without a doubt, there are notable improvements for black citizens in the area of education over the recent decade and a half. It is difficult to explain the last two findings, however. The widening income gap between college-educated white and black males could occur because black males are willing to work for less to obtain entry into higher-level jobs. The fact that black males are less likely than white males to be working at a job for which they are overqualified by a college education lends credence to this hypothesis. But while these findings are encouraging, and black males and females are gaining, they still lag behind whites in access to higher education. Until this gap is closed, we can only conclude that discrimination against blacks remains a feature of our society.

DISCRIMINATION IN HOUSING

Since 1960, the black population in central cities has been steadily growing, increasing from 9.9 million to 13.8 million persons as of 1975.[27] The 1970 census shows that 81.3 percent of all blacks lived in cities, compared to 69.6 percent for whites.[28] This brings up the question of the quality of their life. Even the most casual trip through any metropolitan area shows that there are considerable differences in housing, from mansions in affluent suburbs to overcrowded flats in ghettos. There is economic segregation in urban areas, but is there also racial segregation?

While we do not have complete evidence on racial segregation, we do know that all major American cities have neighborhoods that are predominantly black. And racial segregation appears to be the explanation for another finding: economic class is not as much a determiner of place of residence for blacks as it is for whites. In a study in Chicago Brigitte Erbe determined that "high income blacks are much less isolated from low income blacks than high income whites are from low income whites."[29] Erbe concludes that middle- and upper-class blacks live in closer contiguity, on the average, with lower-class blacks than do lower-class whites with their own race.[30] Although it is now unlawful to segregate housing on the basis of race, housing segregation obviously continues.

How do blacks compare on other indices of housing equality or inequality? Table 6.10 shows that blacks lag behind whites in nearly all areas of housing and associated indices. Blacks are much less likely to own their own homes than are whites. More black households lack all or some plumbing facilities. Black residences are more likely to be overcrowded than white residences. Black households are less likely than white households to possess refrigerators, clothes dryers, freezers, and air conditioners. White households are more likely than black households to own one automobile and considerably more likely to have two or more. Fewer black households earn incomes in the higher brackets. Some 25.8 percent of white households have an income of $15,200 or higher, contrasted with 9.2 percent of black households.

It appears that black and white differences are breaking down, although slowly. Much of the credit for these changes must go to blacks who organized and campaigned for change vigorously. As Peter I. Rose, a sociologist, has written, "Such activities did more to bring about changes in the status quo than all the pious platitudes from segregated pulpits or the admonitions of the specialists in urban affairs and poverty."[31] As we observed earlier, minority groups will remain minorities only so long as they acquiesce in discriminatory treatment. Once they organize they can throw off their status.

TABLE 6.10 Comparing Blacks and Whites on Housing and Associated Indices

Indices	Blacks	Whites
Owner occupied	43.0%	67.0%
Lacking some or all plumbing	10.0	3.0
Overcrowding		
1.01 or more persons per room	11.5	4.2
1.51 or more persons per room	3.4	0.6
Household owning appliances[a]		
Refrigerator	73	81
Clothes dryer	16	52
Dishwasher	4	24
Home freezer	23	33
Television (one or more)	93	96
Air conditioning	26	51
Automobiles[a]		
One	39	49
Two or more	18	36
Household with income of $15,200 or higher[a]	66,900	16,213

[a]Total households in thousands

Source: Adapted from Bureau of the Census, *Current Population Reports*, "The Social and Economic Status of the Black Population of the United States, 1974," Special Studies, Series P-23, No. 54 (Washington, D.C.: U.S. Government Printing Office, 1975), pp. 135–139.

Other Minorities

Females and blacks comprise the largest minority groups in the United States today, but there are other minorities as well, including Chicanos, Jews, Puerto Ricans, Orientals, and Indians. We will discuss each of these groups briefly, keeping in mind that generally speaking the discrimination we have shown to exist against women and blacks subjugates these minorities as well. With this as a given, we will focus on the actions these groups have taken to organize themselves to secure their rights.

CHICANOS

Chicanos, or Mexican Americans, numbered over 6.5 million in 1977 to comprise 3.1 percent of the population. That they are discriminated against is unquestionable. The discrimination they suffer is compounded by the language problem. Although a large proportion of Chicanos are bilingual, speaking both Spanish and English, English is generally their second language and is sometimes a handicap.

Like blacks, Chicanos have been and are organizing to better their conditions. An early reform organization, La Alianza Hispano Americana, was founded in 1894. After World War II, numerous other organizations were started, including a Mexican-American veterans' organization, the GI Forum, the Mexican-American Political Association, the Political Association of Spanish-Speaking Americans, and the Mexican-American Youth Organization. The more recent organizations have taken a more forceful stand. Such groups as the Alianza Federal de Mercedes, formed in 1963 by Reies Lopez Tijerina, and the National Farm Workers Association, formed in 1962 by Cesar Chavez, have had much success adapting the blacks' tactics of nonviolent protest and using unionization to assert the rights of Chicano workers.

Earlier Chicano groups emphasized assimilation, but that has changed in recent years. Many Chicanos now stress the maintenance of their cultural heritage. Establishing an effective Chicano movement nationwide may be difficult for, though there are many Chicanos, they are only a small proportion of the population. However, the emphasis on Chicano culture will probably increase group cohesion and with greater organization Chicanos can anticipate more success in establishing their rights in the Southwest, where they form a significant segment of the population.[32]

JEWS

Although Jews have clearly gained in many respects, there is no question that anti-Semitism still afflicts the over 6 million Jews in the United States. There are obstacles to Jews' access to some jobs, educational opportunities, and certain residential areas. But any discrimination against Jews tends to be carefully concealed because the Jewish community is highly organized and takes swift action when a case of discrimination is uncovered. This only means that discrimination becomes more subtle and harder to detect.

The major issue confronting the Jewish community, now, however, seems to be the question of what part they should take in American life. Today a majority of Jews probably favors pluralism rather than assimilation. German Jews, who were assimilated to some extent in their society, paid a fearful price for their failure to organize effectively in the face of the rise of Nazism. There is also a fear that, even if assimilation does not endanger Jews' lives, it may lead to the loss of their special culture and traditions. Nonetheless, the forces of assimilation are powerful: it is difficult to maintain Jewish identity in a Christian culture. It may be that with time the distinctions between Jews and non-Jews will begin to blur. If so, this greater assimilation should at least yield one benefit to Jews. Traditional barriers to certain occupations, to intermarriage, and to clubs and residential areas should lower.

PUERTO RICANS

Somewhat over half of the 1.7 million Puerto Ricans in the mainland United States live in New York City. They suffer from some of the same discrimination blacks are subjected to, and, like the Chicanos, their situation is worsened by language problems. In this regard, Puerto Ricans, some 80 percent of whom are white, face problems similar to those encountered by early twentieth-century immigrants from Europe. Like those who came from Europe, Puerto Ricans came seeking a better life. Like those who came from Europe, they suffer prejudice and are confronted by the difficulty of functioning in a new society that demands that they learn a foreign language. Once they overcome this problem Puerto Ricans may be better off than blacks, for many of them need not confront the additional obstacle of race.

Puerto Ricans have been slower to organize for political action than Chicanos. Nonetheless, they have made some beginnings. In Boston, the Emergency Tenants Council has been active in bringing rents down. La Comunidad Latin, a Puerto Rican citizens' group in Chicago, has brought pressure for new and better schools in that city.

As the second and third generation of Puerto Ricans grow up, some will probably leave New York for other parts of the country. Others will return to Puerto Rico, as many do now. In time, some large proportion of Puerto Ricans may well assimilate into the mainstream of American society and become part of the dominant group. Indeed, some already have done so.

ORIENTALS

The United States has over a million persons of Oriental ancestry, with people of Japanese and Chinese descent predominating. The Japanese have assimilated better than the Chinese. Except in Hawaii, the Chinese generally live in ghettos, although this concentration into Chinatowns tends to be voluntary rather than forced.

The degree to which Americans of Oriental ancestry suffer discrimination is difficult to assess. Certainly, they were discriminated against in the past. Chinese Americans were cruelly taken advantage of in the West toward the end of the nineteenth century and shortly after the entrance of the United States into World War II, Japanese Americans were rounded up and placed in "relocation centers" that were concentration camps. Not only were these people deprived of their liberty, they were also forced to sell their property at rates well below actual values. In spite of this, many young Japanese enlisted in the Armed Forces during World War II and a regiment composed largely of Japanese Americans fought with conspicuous valor in Italy during the war. It seems now that such overt discrimination is past — certainly it no longer occurs on such a vast scale. But there are undoubtedly many isolated instances of Orientals having their rights denied.

Neither the Japanese nor the Chinese have organized effectively for political action. Although members of both groups help each other and communities are close-knit, they seem to prefer being left alone. An exception to this took place in 1970 when some Chinese students, mainly in New York and California, joined with Puerto Ricans and Chicanos in a Third World organization that, among other stands, opposed the Vietnam War.

INDIANS

This country's treatment of its almost 800,000 Indians, or native Americans, is a dark chapter in American history. At the time Columbus discovered America, it is estimated that there were about one million Indians living in what is now the continental United States. That this population has actually decreased in almost 500 years shows how forcefully Indians have been suppressed. With the relentless westward expansion of whites in the eighteenth and nineteenth centuries, Indians were either killed or despoiled of their lands and the survivors penned up on reservations. The reservations were inevitably bleak and located in areas not coveted by whites. Of course, if the land proved valuable later the Indians were moved off their reservation too.

Jurisdiction over Indians has belonged since 1836 to the Bureau of Indian Affairs (BIA), which significantly was originally part of the War Department. The BIA was transferred to the Department of the Interior in 1849, but that has not meant peace for Indians. The BIA has made many policy changes over the years, but has yet to find a solution to the Indians' problems. For the most part, thanks to the Dawes Act of 1887 and the Wheeler–Howard Act of 1934, the bureau has functioned to a considerable extent as a land administering agency.

Under the Dawes Act, or the General Allotment Act, tribal holdings were divided among individual Indians. The result was chaos. Millions of acres of Indian land were lost to unscrupulous whites and tribal authority and the Indian tradition of collective ownership was subverted. In addition, no effort was made to train Indians to use the land, so they benefited little. Though the plan was obviously a failure, it took the BIA almost fifty years to draw up and gain passage for an alternative. The result, the Wheeler–Howard Act (or Indian Reorganization Act) of 1940, recognized the existence of tribes and tribal organizations and gave these limited authority over their own af-

Complicated legal suits over Indian land claims and natural resource rights are somehow a fitting result of the United States inconsistent, incomprehensible, and often inhumane treatment of native Americans.

"There's a Mr. Scudding-Cloud outside, sir, who claims <u>he</u> owns the mineral rights under our Milwaukee regional office."

fairs. This act served to negate to some extent assimilationist policies by recognizing the integrity of Indian organizations and the rights of Indians with respect to their own affairs.

That this plan has not been a success either is evident from the condition of Indians today. Although available data are meager because the Bureau of the Census frequently lumps Indians together with "other races," we know that Indians suffer the same problems afflicting other minorities — only the problems are more aggravated. The following list summarizes how badly off Indians are:

1. Indians have the lowest median age of any racial group in the United States. Two things contribute to this: a high fertility rate and a high death rate.
2. Indians have the highest proportion of unemployed of all racial groups.
3. Indians have the lowest median income of all minority groups.
4. Indians have an infant death rate of 32.2 per 1,000 live births, compared with 26.4 for the United States as a whole.
5. The Indian traffic accident death rate is over four times that for the general public.
6. The Indian death rate from tuberculosis is eight times the national norm.
7. The Indian suicide rate is twice that for the rest of the American population.
8. The Indian homicide rate is 3.3 times the national average.
9. The Indian incidence of alcoholism is 6.5 times as high as any other group.
10. Indian children fall below both national norms and all other minority groups on a standard test.
11. Indians contract nutritional diseases far more often than other Americans.[33]

There is no question that the current condition of most American Indians is deplorable; it is equally clear that this condition is the result of continued exploitation, apathy, greed, ignorance, and neglect. In recent years, there have been some improvements, but considering the long road still to be traveled, these gains are unimpressive. As with other groups, the principal thrust for change must come from the Indians themselves. Indians are organizing, but they have a special problem. Although they are viewed by whites as a single cultural group, most Indians see themselves as members of a tribe rather than as Indians. Until some kind of pan-Indian movement becomes widespread and tribal differences are forgotten, future progress will be slow and uneven.

Summary

We have seen that the American ideal of full equality has yet to become a reality. American society is dominated by one group: white males. More than half the total population belongs to minority groups, with females alone accounting for half. Over 50 percent of American society has limited economic opportunities. The result for these groups is poor housing, poor education, and few and undesirable jobs. The result of this discrimination is the organization of the various groups to secure for themselves the rights that the Constitution guarantees them, but that white male domination denies them. Women, blacks, Chicanos, and Jews have all organized to end discrimination, with varying degrees of success. Orientals have done less, and Puerto Ricans and Indians are beginning to gather together to ensure their rights. But as we will see in the next section, the frustration of denied rights has offered another solution than peaceful protest, and these more militant efforts have caused white males to react.

ATTEMPTS AT DEALING WITH THE PROBLEM

In the preceding sections, we have discussed in passing the major method of solving the problem of minorities. We have stressed the vital importance of minorities organizing and working actively themselves for change. Some gains have been made for all minorities, and organization is generally responsible. But others have been frustrated by the slow pace of change that organized protest leads to, and have tried two other methods. In the late sixties, the call was for *militance,* a hard-line stand for the use of force to effect change or for separatism. In the late seventies, the method is to fight in the courts to secure *affirmative action,* or active recruiting of minority students and workers in schools and businesses. Both efforts have been perceived as threats to dominant members of society, who have reacted.

Militance and Affirmative Action

Force and threats of force have been most prominent in the black struggle for equality — although the civil rights movement was overwhelmingly nonviolent, force has played a greater role in the black movement than in the women's movement or the Chicano movement, for instance. While black calls for violent overthrow of white domination are now rarely heard, such voices were loud in the late sixties. The justification for these calls came in 1970, when black activist Angela Davis declared that "the first condition of freedom is an open act of resistance — physical resistance, violent resistance."[34] Certainly Davis had a good deal of historical evidence to back up her words, including the American Revolution.

The movement for equality of minorities has involved violence. The mid-sixties riots in such cities as Los Angeles and Detroit were widely reported and did much to communicate blacks' refusal to accept further delay in ending discrimination. Of course, these riots were not orchestrated events with the purpose of demonstrating a political stand, as Davis and others have called for. Rather, they were spontaneous outbreaks of rage against specific and local acts of discrimination. What they accomplished — besides speeding up government efforts to improve cities and better the condition of blacks — was to lend credibility to the statements of militants like Angela Davis. After these riots, when whites heard some blacks demand the organized use of violence to end discrimination, they believed that blacks could indeed organize to commit violence.

Another kind of militance was the separatism demanded by some black groups in the late sixties. The major advocates of such a policy were the Black Muslims, although this group has subsequently changed its stand and no longer insists that black and white cannot live together. This change marks a general abandonment of militant tactics, as minority groups have come to recognize that the major gains of the civil rights movement came from the nonviolent protest of Martin Luther King, Jr.[35] And minorities have returned to another successful tactic of the civil rights movement: fighting in court.

Minorities have successfully challenged many previously well-entrenched discriminatory practices in court to establish their equal right to employment. The court battles of the late 1970s have focused not only on such issues as equal pay for equal work, but on the question of affirmative action, asking for an equality of placement. Under this policy, a proportionate number of people hired and promoted or admitted to specialized education must be from minority groups. In effect, this orientation demands group rights in order to compensate for previous injustices. And advocates of affirmative action — which has so far been a policy pursued primarily by women and blacks and not other minorities — maintain that at first more than a proportional number of minority group members should be hired or admitted to school, to make up for past discrimination. Once the proper percentage of women, for example, is attending a college it will be appropriate for the college to admit men and women in roughly equal numbers. But until then more women than men should be admitted.

As minority group members see it, the only way to prevent de facto discrimination is through the imposition of minority quotas. They argue, justifiably, that unless schools and businesses are forced by the power and authority of the courts to end discrimination they will not do so. Affirmative action, and even the imposition of rigid hiring quotas, is seen as an essential short-run tactic to compensate for decades of lost opportunity and as a means of attaining adequate representation of minority group members in positions formerly closed to them. Future opportunities of any significant magnitude depend in part on this base being established quickly.

Iatrogenic Effects

Both the militance of the late sixties and the push for affirmative action in the late seventies have acted according to the laws of social physics, which say that for every social action there is an equal and opposite reaction. In both cases the reaction can be termed a *backlash;* like a whip snapping the whipper from behind, these tactics have caused further problems for minorities.

First came white fear of black violence. As pointed out, the riots of the 1960s convinced whites that black threats of violence were something to worry about. But the result was not positive. Although some effort was made to remove the conditions that caused a call for violence, more prevalent were repression and alienation. Just as airline hijackings by terrorists led to the annoying inspection of passengers, black urban violence led to greater police surveillance. In addition, attitudes became polarized. Calls to violence and for separatism supported the views of white racists, who replied that blacks should be sent back to Africa. Perhaps worse, these extreme tactics alienated the liberals and the government, who had supported the black drive for equality.

Gradually this support returned, as militant demands were withdrawn during the course of the seventies. But while minority groups received moral support for their return to court tactics, this approach also drew new opposition. Some members of the majority group have come to view affirmative action not as a proper atonement for past discrimination, but as *reverse discrimination*, simply transferring unfairness from the minority to the majority. These people do not see affirmative action as fair, arguing that since minorities were first subjugated long ago by people who are now dead, there is no reason why they should be made to pay now. Of course, this ignores the fact that these people did benefit from the protective "white only" policy. The deliberate exclusion of minority group members from many occupations greatly enhanced job opportunities for whites. But it is also true that this policy contradicts American liberal ideology, which maintains that success be judged according to individual background and skills. Liberals are torn between wanting to support a policy that insists that fairness be done to minorities and wanting to avoid a rigid quota system that may not reward talent. Of course, these liberals may also be trying to protect their own privileged position.

Are some people really threatened by affirmative action? The answer is that of course they are. As women move toward greater equality in the world of work, males who would previously have attained high positions will no longer do so because of competition from well-qualified women. White ethnics feel threatened on economic grounds by competition from people who hitherto were the last hired and the first fired. Jews are also threatened. Currently they are overrepresented in many professions, including law and medicine. If affirmative action is widely adopted and quotas are instituted, fewer Jews may be able to get into certain professions.

Resistance to affirmative action is mounting and will probably become more pronounced in coming years. Already we have had court suits filed by whites arguing that they were denied advancement because of racial discrimination. For example, in the celebrated case of Alan Bakke, a white medical school applicant sued for admission on the grounds that he had been rejected on a racial and therefore discriminatory basis. The net effect of the backlash has been to promote divisiveness in American society and to weaken social cohesion. But the pressure for affirmative action on the part of minority groups will not end until they are assured that they will no longer suffer discrimination, that desirable jobs or admission to higher education will be gained solely on the basis of personal merit and qualification. This assurance will take a long time to develop.

PROSPECTS FOR SOLVING THE PROBLEM

Discrimination against minorities has gone on for centuries and antedates written history. There are powerful supports for maintaining conditions of discrimination against minority groups. For one thing, it is advantageous to the dominant sector. And minority group members themselves support discrimination when they acquiesce in it and behave as they are expected to behave. We can hardly overestimate the consequences of being socialized into minority status. Keep in mind that some of the most vocal and active opponents of the Equal Rights Amendment are women.

Today no minority group in this country passively accepts minority status. On every front, groups are organizing to reduce discrimination or end it altogether. But these efforts would be less than fruitful were there not traits in American society favoring them. For example, we now know that discrimination is illogical. More and more people accept the scientific evidence that there are no significant differences between the races that have any bearing on an individual's capacity to take a full place in our society. Also important are the values of American society. The emphasis on the equality of humans gives authority to efforts to end discrimination. It is difficult for us to understand the vast changes that have taken place in American society or how this society compares with others. But because of our society's progress so far and its values, we can be sanguine about the eventual disappearance of minority groups.

Of course, this may be overoptimism about one's own society, but other people see our chances of ending discrimination as equally good. Jean-François Revel, a distinguished French journalist and author, has done an exhaustive study of the United States and its institutions. He has concluded that this country is leading a new revolution — a peaceful revolution with great and positive implications for the rest of the world. Revel describes this society as

> a revolutionary universe, characterized by the demand for equality of sexes, races, and age groups; by the rejection of the authoritarian relationships on which rest all societies that have been stratified by force and despotism; by the transformation of directed culture into productive culture; by the rejection of nationalism in foreign policy; by the realization of the outdated character of the "authority of the state," constituted without sufficient participation by the people and exercised under conditions that allow an abuse of power to a degree that has become intolerable; and by an insistence on economic and educational equality.[36]

IMPORTANT WORDS AND TERMS

affirmative action	cooling-out	indentured servants	power
assimilation	de facto discrimination	integration	prejudice
authority	de jure discrimination	Jim Crow laws	racist
backlash	discrimination	militance	reverse discrimination
bilingual	endogamous	minority	segregation
black	estate system	miscegenation	separatism
black English	ethnicity	nonviolent protest	slave
caste system	ethnocentrism	overqualification	tradition
Chicano	immigration	pluralism	visibility

QUESTIONS FOR DISCUSSION

1. Do all members of the dominant groups in our society have equal opportunities for success, however success is defined? Why or why not?
2. Explain why a prejudiced person does not necessarily practice discrimination and an unprejudiced person sometimes does.
3. Discrimination is against the law in the United States, but it is frequently practiced without penalty. Explain some ways in which de facto discrimination can be practiced without running afoul of the law.
4. Is there — in this country — any real hostility between the sexes? If you answer yes, do you think that the fact that women are a minority group has anything to do with this hostility?
5. Look over the description of a caste system and decide whether or not a caste system still exists in this country. Be able to defend your answer.
6. Many minority group persons, particularly blacks, reject assimilation as a practical means for ending discrimination. Why?
7. Quite a few people in our society cannot see

that women constitute a genuine minority group. Do you feel that such people are correct or incorrect? Be able to support your answer.
8. Can you think of any jobs in modern society for which women are innately unqualified, either physically or mentally? What are they?
9. Do you believe that we will eventually or even ever reach a time when all occupations and professions show a roughly equal proportion of men and women working full-time in this country? Why or why not?
10. Why do you think that black persons are predominantly urban dwellers in the United States?
11. Do people of the Jewish faith suffer discrimination to the extent that black people do in this country? In your view, is it sociologically correct to categorize Jews as a minority group today? Why or why not?
12. Which do you believe is more likely to take place in this country over the next half century — a move toward integration or a move toward pluralism? Justify your answer.
13. Can affirmative action really be made to work? Justify your answer.
14. Do *you* see our modern American society as truly representing a peaceful revolution? Why or why not?

SUGGESTED READING

AMERICAN INDIAN POLICY REVIEW COMMISSION, *Report on Indian Education* (Washington, D.C.: U.S. Government Printing Office, 1976).

On the whole, government reports tend to be tedious reading. This is a happy exception. For those who wish to read a complete account of the activities of the Bureau of Indian Affairs as well as other facets of Indian life, this report is fascinating and instructive.

FRANCES ANNE KEMBLE, *Journal of a Residence on a Georgian Plantation in 1838–1839,* ed. John A. Scott (New York: Knopf, 1970).

Frances Anne Kemble was a famous English actress who was married to a southern plantation owner and slaveowner. Her account of the two years she spent on her husband's plantation provides a graphic account of what slavery and slaveholding were really like. As the reader will see, Frances Kemble was a woman of high intelligence, wit, humor, and compassion. Upon completing her journal, readers will feel privileged to have known this woman, even if only through the pages of her journal.

JEAN-FRANÇOIS REVEL, *Without Marx or Jesus: The New Revolution Has Begun*, trans. J. F. Bernard (Garden City, N.Y.: Doubleday, 1970).

Americans are highly critical of themselves — it is almost a national sport to denigrate our society. Revel's book is a welcome antidote to the words and writings of those who see nothing good in American society. This latter-day de Tocqueville made an in-depth study of this country, its people, and its institutions and sees in us a genuine but peaceful revolution, which will ultimately change all the peoples on earth.

PETER I. ROSE, *They and We: Racial and Ethnic Relations in the United States,* 2nd ed. (New York: Random House, 1974).

While the author is sympathetic toward minority groups, he does not permit his sympathies to interfere with presenting an excellent sociological analysis of racial and ethnic relations in this country. The fact that this book is scholarly should not frighten readers. It is written clearly and lucidly. Moreover, the author makes his points interestingly. It is probably as good a book as there is on minorities in the United States.

NOTES

1. Quoted in George Eaton Simpson and J. Milton Yinger, *Racial and Cultural Minorities: An Analysis of Prejudice and Discrimination*, 4th ed. (New York: Harper and Row, 1972), p. 11.
2. David Krech, Richard S. Crutchfield, and Norman Livson, *Elements of Psychology*, 2nd ed. (New York: Knopf, 1969), p. 816.
3. Hiroshi Wagatsuma, "The Social Perception of Skin Color in Japan," *Daedalus*, Vol. 96 (Spring 1967), p. 422.
4. Malcolm X, *The Autobiography of Malcolm X* (New York: Grove Press, 1966), pp. 35–36.
5. For this definition, the authors drew on Robin M. Williams, Jr., *The Reduction of Intergroup Tensions* (New York: Social Science Research Council, 1947), p. 39; and Aaron Antonovsky, "The Social Meaning of Discrimination," *Phylon* (Spring 1960), p. 81.
6. Burton Clark, "The 'Cooling-Out' Function of Higher Education," *American Journal of Sociology*, Vol. 65, No. 6 (May 1969), pp. 569–576.
7. Paul E. Mott, *The Organization of Society* (Englewood Cliffs, N.J.: Prentice-Hall, 1965), p. 270.
8. Mott, *Organization of Society*, pp. 255–256.
9. Peter I. Rose, *They and We: Racial and Ethnic Relations in the United States*, 2nd ed. (New York: Random House, 1974), p. 184.
10. Vittorio Lanternaria, *The Religions of the Oppressed* (New York: New American Library, 1963).
11. V. Gordon Childe, *Man Makes Himself* (New York: Mentor, 1951), p. 109.
12. For a full discussion of power and authority see Robert A. Nisbet, *The Social Bond* (New York: Knopf, 1970), Chapter 6.
13. Barbara W. Tuchman, *A Distant Mirror: The Calamitous 14th Century* (New York: Knopf, 1978), pp. 18–19.
14. Ibid., p. 19.
15. John Beattie, *Other Cultures* (New York: Free Press, 1964), p. 118.
16. Burton Wright and Vernon Fox, *Criminal Justice and the Social Sciences* (Philadelphia: Saunders, 1978), pp. 51–52.
17. Burton Wright, John P. Weiss, and Charles M. Unkovic, *Perspective: An Introduction to Sociology* (Hinsdale, Ill.: Dryden, 1975), pp. 190–191.
18. W. I. Thomas, "The Relation of Research to the Social Process," in *Essays on Research in the Social Sciences* (Washington, D.C.: Brookings Institution, 1931), p. 189.
19. Bureau of the Census, *Statistical Abstract of the United States, 1977* (Washington, D.C.: U.S. Government Printing Office, 1977), p. 452.
20. Bureau of the Census, *Social Indicators, 1976* (Washington, D.C.: U.S. Government Printing Office, 1977), p. 304.
21. For an account of this phenomenon, see Helen Felsing, *Florida Flambeau* (October 30, 1978), p. 1.
22. *Statistical Abstract, 1977*, p. 161.
23. Bureau of the Census, *Historical Statistics of the United States, Colonial Times to 1970*, Part 2 (Washington, D.C.: U.S. Government Printing Office, 1975), p. 382.
24. Elizabeth Janeway, *Man's World, Woman's Place: A Study in Social Mythology* (New York: Dell, 1971), p. 101.
25. Dennis P. Hogan and David L. Featherman, "Racial Stratification and Socioeconomic Change in the American North and South," *American Journal of Sociology*, Vol. 83, No. 1 (July 1977), p. 101.
26. Commission on Civil Rights, *Social Indicators of Equality for Minorities and Women* (Washington, D.C.: U.S. Government Printing Office, 1978), p. 23.
27. *Statistical Abstract, 1977*, p. 30.
28. Ibid., p. 33.
29. Brigitte Mach Erbe, "Race and Socioeconomic Segregation," *American Sociological Review*, Vol. 40, No. 6 (December 1975), p. 809.
30. Ibid., p. 812.
31. Rose, *We and They*, p. 213.
32. See Leo Grebler, Joan W. Moore, and Ralph C. Guzman, *The Mexican-American People: The Nation's Second Largest Minority* (New York: Free Press, 1970), Chapter 22.
33. *Social Indicators, 1976*, p. lxx; and Com-

mission on Civil Rights, *Socio-Economic Profile of American Indians in Arizona and New Mexico* (November 1972).

34. *New York Times* (August 23, 1970), p. 5.

35. For a full discussion of nonviolent strategy see Herbert C. Kelman, "The Relevance of Nonviolent Action," in Edgar A. Schuler et al. (eds.), *Readings in Sociology*, 4th ed. (New York: Crowell, 1971), pp. 253–264.

36. Jean-François Revel, *Without Marx or Jesus: The New American Revolution Has Begun,* trans. J. F. Bernard (Garden City, N.Y.: Doubleday, 1970), pp. 214–215.

7 THE YOUNG AND THE OLD
AGE STRATIFICATION

CHAPTER OVERVIEW

INTRODUCTION

CONCEPTUAL ORIENTATION
The Relationship Between the Problems of Youth and Age
Support of Age Roles by Players
Summary

CROSS-CULTURAL AND HISTORICAL OVERVIEW
Anthropological Conclusions
   The Young in Preliterate Societies
   The Aged in Preliterate Societies
The Impact of the Industrial Revolution
   Changes in the Family
   The Shift to Urban Living
   The Young and the Old as Economic Liabilities
Summary

OBJECTIVE DIMENSIONS OF THE PROBLEM
Delinquency: The Failure of Socialization
Socialization: The Balanced Perspective
Socialization for Retirement
Myths About Aging
   Aging and Learning Ability
   Aging and Personality Change
   Abandonment of Older Persons
   Senility
   Age and Sexual Activity
Summary

ATTEMPTS AT DEALING WITH THE PROBLEM
Iatrogenic Effects of the Education System
Iatrogenic Effects of Social Security

PROSPECTS FOR SOLVING THE PROBLEM
The Problem of Youth
The Problem of the Aged
The Future of Life Cycle Problems

IMPORTANT WORDS AND TERMS

QUESTIONS FOR DISCUSSION

SUGGESTED READING

NOTES

He who is of a calm and happy nature will hardly feel the pressure of age, but to him who is of an opposite disposition, youth and age are equally a burden.

Plato, *The Republic*

Crabbed age and youth cannot live together,
Youth is full of pleasure, age is full of care.

William Shakespeare, *The Passionate Pilgrim*

CHAPTER OVERVIEW

In this chapter, the problems of youth and old age are both discussed to highlight the contrasts but also to demonstrate the considerable similarities between these two groups. One important difference is that while youth has been a social problem for centuries, old age became a problem fairly recently. Two significant similarities are that both the young and the old suffer various discriminations and the problems of both stem from socialization. In addition, traditional conceptions of youth and old age are rife with myths and misconceptions, which are both causes and symptoms of the groups' problems.

The social structure supports and exacerbates the problems of youth and old age. The modern social structure, formed by industrialization and urbanization, created the problem of the elderly and cast the problem of the young in its present form. After demonstrating the extent of these problems, we will again turn to consider the future. Will the problems of youth and old age lessen with time, or will they worsen?

INTRODUCTION

All human societies have some concept of *life cycles*, various stages through which people pass as a function of biological maturation.

Humans are born, attain sexual maturity, and eventually die, just like other animals. But life cycles are not inherent in nature. They are a human invention. The reason is that they are social, not biological, phenomena. Although they are based on biological changes, the stages of the life cycle are changes in social status. Think of the terms for these stages — infant, child, adolescent, adult, and senior citizen are ascriptive statuses. These terms are the product of human invention, part of language. The importance of stressing this is that what humans have made they can change.

Age statuses are useful in societies. But these statuses are also a source of the problems of youth and old age. All statuses have associated with them roles and norms governing behavior. But the roles and norms for age statuses contain contradictions and ambiguities. For example, college students are supposed to be reasonably mature and concerned with the serious work of obtaining a college education. Yet a few years back, a generally tolerant eye was turned on what were called panty raids, and more recently, the short-lived fad of streaking was indulgently allowed. These behaviors were permitted because we anticipate high-spiritedness from youth. But high spirits are occasionally discharged in the form of vandalism or other deviant acts, and these behaviors are punished. When society expects certain behavior from a particular group, they will get that behavior, sometimes to excess. Youth is troublesome because social norms dictate that young people will be energetic and mischievous. Because young people have learned their role but do not fully know society's limits, they will occasionally act with such energy and mischief that their actions will be seen as deviant. Youth is a time of testing limits.

Socialization is also a problem for the old. Our society values youth highly and people of all ages are encouraged to be and act young. Yet there is a certain hypocrisy here. Old people can only act young within certain restrictions. If an old person had joined college students in panty raids or streaking, he would have been subject, at a minimum, to severe censure. Such behavior is considered inappropriate for old people. While it exalts youthfulness, our society really does not permit older persons to act young. And the old face another problem. After a lifetime of socialization to work hard, they are denied employment. How do they adjust to this sudden loss?

CONCEPTUAL ORIENTATION

To understand who we are talking about, we must define our terms. *Youth* is that period of life falling between the ages of eleven and twenty-five. *Old age* means those people sixty-five years of age and older. We chose eleven as the starting point for youth because the ages of eleven or twelve ordinarily mark the end of childhood and the onset of *puberty*, the physical changes that mark sexual maturity. And there are logical reasons for selecting twenty-five as marking the passage from youth to adulthood. Twenty-five is the age by which most college students have graduated and entered the world of work; it is also the age at which the cost of automobile insurance becomes significantly lower. As both facts indicate, that is the age when society assumes that the recklessness we associate with youth has supposedly changed to the greater caution of maturity. There seems to be some reason for that assumption. As Figure 7.1 illustrates, after age twenty-four, people are much less likely to suffer a fatal accident, at least until about age sixty-five.

We chose sixty-five as the starting point for old age because it is the age when most people retire. In 1978, the mandatory retirement age for most occupations was raised from sixty-five to seventy. This change re-

FIGURE 7.1 Rate of Accidental Deaths by Sex and Age, 1953–1975 Average

Sources: Adapted from Bureau of the Census, *Social Indicators, 1976* (Washington, D.C.: U.S. Government Printing Office, 1977), p. 195; and Bureau of the Census, *Statistical Abstract of the United States, 1977* (Washington, D.C.: U.S. Government Printing Office, 1977), p. 71.

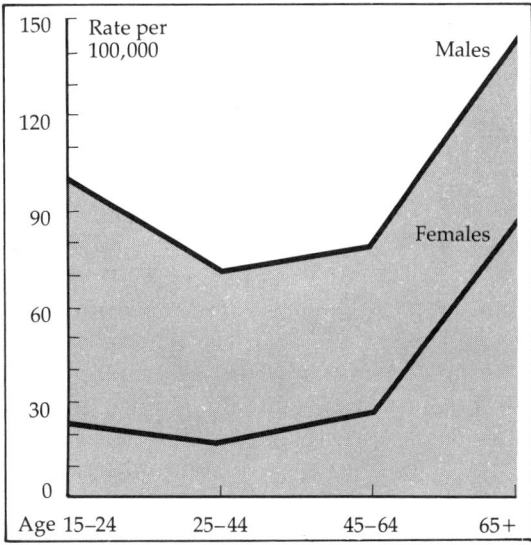

flects the physiological and psychological fact that people age at different rates. Many persons are capable of working productively well past the age of sixty-five, or even of seventy. However, the later retirement age is not yet widespread. Most workers retire at sixty-five, and many leave work earlier, enabled to do so by various retirement programs. As yet we do not know what impact the higher retirement age will have on opportunities for younger workers. However if the current low fertility rate continues (see Chapter 11), our society may actually encourage people to work beyond the age of sixty-five or seventy in order to augment a shrinking work force.

The Relationship Between the Problems of Youth and Age

Youth and old age are of direct, personal concern to nearly all members of our society. The reason is clearly shown in Figure 7.2, the life expectancy at birth is now such that the great majority of Americans will live to be old. Obviously, then, the concern for these problems is personal. All adults have suffered the problems of youth and the great majority will eventually suffer the problems of age. In this case, and given that most people experience the aging of their parents, the 1971 White House Conference on Aging was correct to conclude that "aging is one circumstance that affects every individual."[1]

On the surface, it would appear that youth and old age are separate problems and should be treated as such. But despite the obvious differences, they are comparable in important ways. Youth and old age are both part of the life cycle. Both, while resting on a physiological base, are social in origin. Both groups lack significant power. Both lack occupational identification; most young people

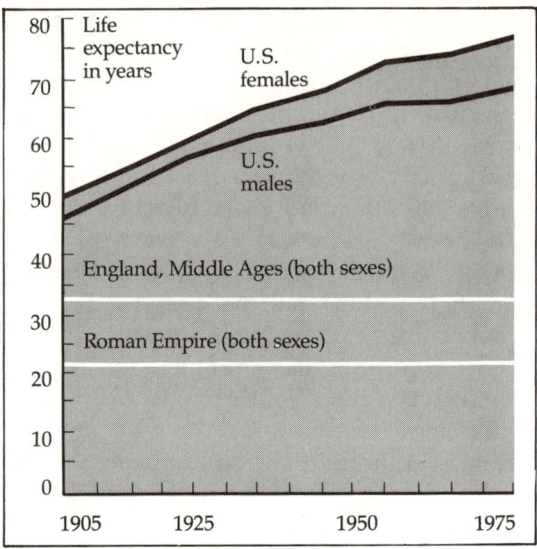

FIGURE 7.2 Life Expectancy at Birth in United States, 1905–1975, Compared to Past

Sources: Adapted from Bureau of the Census, *Social Indicators, 1976* (Washington, D.C.: U.S. Government Printing Office, 1977), p. 190; and Bureau of the Census, *Statistical Abstract of the United States, 1977* (Washington, D.C.: U.S. Government Printing Office, 1977), p. 65.

have not acquired occupational identity and most old people have lost theirs. As social problems, youth and old age are a function of public misconceptions, misunderstandings, and misinformation. Most important, both problems are created and maintained by the social structure.

Support of Age Roles by Players

How the social structure creates problems for these groups will become clear when we discuss the history and objective dimensions of these problems. For now we only need note that the major factor is the way society socializes these groups into their roles.

The young and old have learned their social roles so well that they support the maintenance of youth and old age as social problems. They do this by playing the roles of youth and old age as these roles are socially defined. For example, a widow aged sixty-five or older may have a powerful sex drive. Yet when playing the role assigned to her, she cannot freely seek sexual contacts for two reasons. First, women of any age are not supposed to be sexually aggressive, but more important, women sixty-five and older are supposed to have lost what little sexual urges they had, to concentrate on the higher things of life, whatever those are. For another example, the man who dedicates his life to his job finds himself with no direction when he retires.

The young also play their socially defined roles. For example, a mature, conventional youth is under considerable pressure to participate in the activities of his peer group, even when those activities are deviant. Failure to conform to group pressures may lead to social ostracism, and even adults may wonder what is wrong with the individual concerned. Ironically, when youngsters do engage in serious misbehavior, the reaction of many adults is to treat them like adults. The paradox facing youth is that it is acceptable for them to behave deviantly within certain bounds. Understandably, some young persons have difficulty knowing just when deviance really becomes deviance.

Summary

We have discussed why youth and old age are social problems. The roles dictated by socialization create confusion by forcing contradictory demands on youth and asking the old to abandon their lifelong values. As we will see in the next section, one reason for these problems is the great social changes caused by the Industrial Revolution.

CROSS-CULTURAL AND HISTORICAL OVERVIEW

Before we can analyze the impact of the Industrial Revolution we need to know what conditions were like in agrarian societies. We know very little of the history of societies prior to the invention of writing about 4000 B.C. But the work of anthropologists can help us develop an idea of how people used to view the various stages of the life cycle.

Anthropological Conclusions

THE YOUNG IN PRELITERATE SOCIETIES

All human societies provide for the care of infants and children. Furthermore, all human societies are concerned with preparing their young to become reasonably competent members of society. "The human community and its culture have come to depend on the effectiveness of socialization — i.e., how well the child acquires the values, attitudes, or behavior of his community and family. Consequently, the community must shape or guide the unit that passes on the values to its next generation."[2] The alternative to effective socialization is some form of absolute coercion, which is manifestly impracticable on a wide scale: "To a large degree, each individual must assume responsibility for policing his own conduct. This is achieved through *socialization*."[3] But humans are all individuals and some of the time will act as they want to and not as their social roles dictate. Thus socialization is never fully successful. But every society must socialize with a certain degree of success, or there will be no society, and no human life, at all.

As a culture's values and behaviors are passed from generation to generation by socialization, ethnic traditions play an essential role. For Cuban Americans, one of those customs is the quince, *an extravagant combination fifteenth birthday party and coming-out ball that marks the passage out of girlhood. Families willingly go into debt in order to provide their daughters with this lavish affair, the beginning of their social life.*

Most human societies last for a long time, indicating that they perform socialization well enough. But the concept of just functioning well enough contributes in no small measure to the fact that no society, however simple, is free of deviation.

This deviation will often be found among the young for, as we pointed out, they have not learned the limits of their roles and norms and often act outside them. As a result, concern with youth is as old as human societies. For example, the following was inscribed on stone tablets some 3,700 years ago in ancient Sumeria:

> "Where did you go?"
> "I didn't go anywhere."
> "If you didn't go anywhere, why do you idle about? Go to school! Stand before your school father, recite your assignment, report it to your monitor; then come to me, and do not wander about in the street! Come now, do you

know what I said? Come now, be a man! Don't stand about in the public square and wander about in the boulevards. And when you walk in the street, don't look around! Be humble! You wander about in the public square! You want to achieve success? Then look at the first generation and learn from your elders! . . . Night and day I'm tortured because of you. Night and day you waste yourself in pleasures.[4]

The complaints and exhortations in this exchange have a familiar ring to many of us. Youth is indeed an ancient social problem.

THE AGED IN PRELITERATE SOCIETIES

Until very recent times, the elderly were not a social problem. Before the nineteenth and twentieth centuries, only a small proportion of people lived long enough to reach old age. No particular burden is laid on a society if only a few members attain the age of fifty, let alone sixty or seventy. As Figure 7.2 shows, even ancient Rome and medieval England, highly organized societies, had very low life expectancies. The same is true of preliterate, agrarian societies.

In primarily agrarian societies, *extended families* — in which grandparents, aunts and uncles, and cousins all may live with the husband, wife, and children — are common. These families provide the only social security people in such societies have. In such an arrangement children are expected to take care of their aged parents. But the significance of the extended family goes beyond that. More important, *"age* [is] . . . usually an advantage in simple horticultural societies, at least up to the point where senility sets in."[5]

One manifestation of this high status is that the advice of the elderly "is sought even when little attention is paid to their wishes. This custom has a sound practical basis, for the individual who contrives to live to old age in [such groups] has usually been a person of ability and his or her memory constitutes a sort of reference library to which one can turn for help under all sorts of circumstances."[6] Tradition is powerful in technologically simpler societies and with no written records, the memory of older tribe members is counted on to maintain tradition. Another reason for the high status of the aged is that adults are better organized than the younger members of society and a fundamental source of real power *is* organization.[7]

But to say that most preliterate societies value age is not to say that all are alike. Each culture "not only categorizes the 'ages of man' in different ways and associates different plans for behavior with these ages but it also values various age roles differently."[8] Among the Arunta of Australia, "older members of the society are treated with great respect. The very aged and the ill and the helpless are provided for with care and kindness."[9] The same kind of solicitude is found in many societies, including ours. But the reverse is also found. Among the Siriono of Bolivia, "when the individual becomes too feeble to keep up with the rest in their migrations, or when serious illness overtakes him, he is abandoned and left to die."[10]

The Impact of the Industrial Revolution

American and European society began to change markedly around 1750, with the onset of the Industrial Revolution. The introduction of the factory system brought a shift from essentially agricultural economies to the industrialization we see today. The change had three significant effects on the young and the old:

1. It changed the family.
2. It led to a shift from rural to urban living.
3. It made the young and the old into *economic liabilities* instead of economic assets.

CHANGES IN THE FAMILY

Although there are many variations and many other forms, in our society families are generally *nuclear families*, that is, a man, a woman, and their children live under one roof. While the nuclear family, with its mobility and adaptability, is well suited to industrial societies, it is fragile. If an adult member dies or is incapacitated severe disruption occurs.

In less technologically advanced societies, the extended family is the norm. Kinship ties are thus stronger and supports are available in a crisis. This family type minimizes several facets of the social problems of youth and old age. It means that children and young people are under more continuous observation by their elders. Closely supervised young people and children are less likely to engage in deviant behavior. In this family socialization is more completely under the aegis of the family than it is in modern societies. Social control is more informal and, hence, more effective. It provides a place for old people. The extended family has more resources to care for them when they become ill or weak.

Industrialization has done away with many of these benefits by altering the family structure. As a result, children have much less supervision and, being less under family control, are more subject to the pressures of peers and society. But while the contrast between young people in agrarian and industrial societies is considerable, it is even more marked with respect to the aging and aged.

Alexander Leaf, who has studied the elderly in Ecuador, Pakistan, and the Soviet Union, observes:

> It is characteristic of each of these areas I visited that the old people continue to be contributing, productive members of their society. The economy in all three areas is agrarian, there is no fixed retirement age and the elderly make themselves useful doing many necessary tasks around the farm or home. Moreover, increased age is accompanied by increased social [prestige]. The old people, with their accumulated experience of life are expected to be wise and they respond accordingly.[11]

This perception of the old as repositories of wisdom does not appear common in modern societies. Margaret Mead, an anthropologist, comments:

> The acceptance of the distinction between right and wrong by the child is a consequence of his dependence on parental figures who are trusted, feared and loved, who hold the child's very life in their hands. But today the elders can no longer present with certainty moral imperatives to the young.[12]

The late Professor Mead's words highlight a profound change that has occurred in modern countries. Parents and grandparents do not automatically receive respect, deference, and obedience from their children and grandchildren. The family, once highly authoritarian, is no longer. These changes are not necessarily dysfunctional. But they do contribute to two important facts: (1) they weaken social control over the young, contributing to youthful deviance; and (2) they rob older citizens of important social and psychological supports.

The net result of changes in the family have been to severely worsen the problems of the young and the old. Whereas youth and old age are less serious and more easily handled problems in agrarian societies, they are massive and serious problems in modern, industrial societies. Table 7.1 summarizes the salient differences, showing that the modern nuclear family, so necessary in an industrialized society, is a direct cause of many problems facing the young and the old.

THE SHIFT TO URBAN LIVING

A century ago, some 10 million Americans (26.3 percent) lived in urban areas and 28 million (73.7 percent) were rural dwellers.[13] Today the proportions are reversed. Less than 27 percent of the population of 220 million is rural.[14] As the changes in the family have most affected the old, this population shift has most affected the young.

Urban and suburban living today go hand in hand with two important and useful inventions — the automobile and the telephone. But while the automobile and telephone have made modern life possible, they have also had a negative effect. They have combined with the high population density of the urban area and with the concentration of young people in school to foster the development of a distinct subculture of youth. This subculture serves as an important socializing agent for young people. It sets the life-style for youth and provides both the satisfactions of association with peers and mutual support against what is viewed as the

TABLE 7.1 Contrasts Between Agrarian and Industrial Societies with Respect to the Young and the Old

Agrarian	Industrial
Virtually full-time supervision of the young by their elders.	Limited, part-time supervision of the young by their elders.
Socialization of the young significantly under the control of the family.	Socialization of the young shared with schools, peer groups, and the mass media.
Little need for formal agencies for supervision and control of the young.	Dependence on formal agencies for supervision and control of the young.
Children and young people are economic assets.	Children and young people still in school are economic liabilities.
Crises such as illness or death are handled informally by family and kin.	Crises such as illness and death frequently involve intervention and assistance by formal agencies.
The old contribute to their own support; they are economic assets.	Some substantial proportion of the old rely on formal agencies for their economic support and are economic liabilities both to their families and society at large.
Old age tends to be an honored status.	Old age tends to be accorded very low prestige.
The old do not retire in any formal sense and, thus, retain their occupational identities.	The old formally retire and lose their occupational identities.

tyranny of parents, school, and society. Some of the norms of this subculture are considered deviant by older persons and thus contribute to the youth problem. For example, many adolescents consider going steady as more or less a license to engage in sexual intercourse. They are not promiscuous and are living up to youthful norms. But fornication is against adult norms and parents, along with others, are greatly concerned with the sexual freedom granted by adolescent norms but ideally forbidden by other norms.

This youth subculture is supported by another characteristic of modern urban and suburban living that makes social control of the young more difficult. Modern communities are not like those in agrarian societies. The tendency of people to live away from their place of work means that they are not as involved in their community as their children. They also have little contact with other parents, who go off to work somewhere else. James A. Coleman explains the result:

> The formation of gangs in cities, and most recently in suburbs, is facilitated by the . . . lack of community among parents. The parents do not know what their children are doing for two reasons: first, much of the parents' lives occur outside the local community, while the children's lives take place almost totally within it. Second, in the traditional community, the network of relations gives every parent, in a sense, a community of sentries who can keep him informed of his child's activities. In modern living places (city or suburban) where such a network is attenuated, he no longer has such sentries. He is a lone agent facing a highly organized community of adolescents.[15]

The first intimation that a child is in trouble comes to some parents when they receive a call from the police informing them that their son or daughter is in custody. In agrarian societies, this would not happen because of the network of sentries.

Urban and suburban living makes the problem of youth worse. First, direct continuous supervision of young people by their parents is difficult. For example, the automobile makes youngsters of driving age highly mobile. Second, modern communities are not communities in the traditional sense. Adults take little or no personal responsibility for supervising youth in general. Third, control of serious delinquency is left largely to the formal agencies of social control. These, of course, are engaged for the most part in dealing with delinquent behavior after it has already occurred. Fourth, population density, the educational segregation of youth, and the automobile and the telephone have combined to form a youth subculture, which presents a united front to individual parents. Modern mothers and fathers are only too familiar with the teenage comment, "But that's what everybody else does!"

THE YOUNG AND THE OLD
AS ECONOMIC LIABILITIES

Perhaps the most important change affecting the young and the old is the alteration in their economic status. Nearly 80 percent of all people aged twenty-five and older have had some high school education.[16] Around 27 percent have some college education and a substantial number earn master's degrees and doctorates. In 1976, for example, 316,000 received a master's degree and 35,000 earned the doctorate.[17] But for young people to receive this education, parents and society must subsidize youth for twenty years or more, during which time the students provide little in return. Part of the problem of youth, then, is the fact that young people must be educated and trained. Youthful deviance, while dramatic and newsworthy, is only one aspect of the problem. Of course, preliterate societies also faced that problem,

However long the period of dependency for youth, it eventually ends when they begin working. The prospect for the aging and aged is, in contrast, often grim, unpleasant, and hopeless. For more than a few older persons, "the golden years of retirement" is probably one of the cruelest myths of our time. As we saw in Chapter 5, many retired persons have incomes below the poverty line and have little opportunity for mitigating their economic condition. Those without jobs often must live on social security alone. But even maximum social security benefits are sufficient for only the most frugal lifestyle, and compounding the problem is the fact that the majority of persons on social security do not draw maximum benefits. The lack of jobs is the crux of the matter for both the young and the old. Neither is given the opportunity for full employment.

That the old are economic liabilities is a function of forced retirement, a relatively recent phenomenon, as Bernice L. Neugarten comments:

> we should note that in the year 1900, roughly 65 percent of all males over the age of 65 were in the labor force. But this figure has dropped to just over 35 percent 70 years later and, currently, appears to be still dropping.[18]

"I have my bachelor's and my master's and my Ph.D.—but my parents abandoned me before I could complete my second doctorate."

Over the past few decades, the traditional parent-centered family has become a child-centered family, in which children expect and demand that the family accommodate them rather than vice versa. No longer economic assets, children are economic liabilities, and parents, out of an obligation that would have been ridiculed a century ago, may support their offspring long beyond the normal age of dependence.

but it was not as severe. The key point is that as technology becomes more complex, longer training and more formal training are required to understand it. In preliterate societies, with low technology, children learned from their parents to do the things their parents did. While it is by no means easy to learn how to make a fishing net, it can be learned more quickly than can programming a computer. This meant that the child's apprenticeship, or training period, was shorter and she could contribute economically to the family sooner.

Forced retirement appears to stem from two propositions that are socially eufunctional, or useful. The first is that those who have worked hard during their younger years are entitled to retire and to enjoy recreation during the years remaining to them. This obviously seems to benefit the elderly, who get to rest, but it also benefits society because it motivates people to work harder, knowing that they will be able to rest later. The second social advantage is that forced retirement creates vacancies for younger persons so that they will have reasonable opportunities for good jobs and upward mobility. This helps keep them happy. But while the well-earned rest seems appealing and while society benefits from removing the old from the labor force, the elderly themselves often suffer, as they are pulled away from their life's work and left with nothing to do.

Summary

This brief history of the two life cycle problems indicates how industrialization has caused dramatic shifts in life patterns that had been in effect for thousands of years. Modern industrial society has exacerbated the problems of youth, such as the problem of social control, and has relegated youth to the status of an economic liability, the same status it has given to the elderly.

The mass media have given enormous amounts of publicity to life cycle problems, although they overemphasize such features as juvenile delinquency and underemphasize the problems of the old. Out of this publicity have arisen general perceptions of youth and old age, which view the young as troublemakers in gangs and the old as abandoned victims of heartless families. But how correct are these views? To answer this question, at least in part, we need to examine the objective dimensions of life cycle problems.

OBJECTIVE DIMENSIONS OF THE PROBLEM

The problem of youth revolves around socialization. How well are young people taught to accept society's values and obey society's norms? The primary concern is socialization. How well are young people taught to take a role as adults in society? Similarly, the problem of aging revolves around socialization. How well are old people prepared to adjust to retirement? How well are old people prepared for the mental and physical changes that accompany aging?

There are many myths associated with both age groups. The common view is that youths are juvenile delinquents, constantly breaking laws. But what are the facts? Are young people not being effectively socialized? Is retirement at age seventy or earlier arbitrary or is it a logical cultural device recognizing some decline in physiological and psychological functioning. Does such a decline occur, and is it inevitable? Are the elderly really cut off from contact with other persons, including their families? Fortunately, we have objective evidence that helps us answer these questions. Let us consider this evidence.

Delinquency:
The Failure of Socialization

Every society must solve the problem of ensuring the survival or continuity of the society. "The problem of continuity can be solved only when children are reared to become productive adult members of the society," that is, when they are socialized.[19] A society that fails to accomplish socialization well enough is doomed to disorganization and possibly extinction. But the concept of well enough is situational; what is well enough depends on circumstances. What is productive and what is adult are matters of social definition, which depends on values. In the United States, the perfectly socialized young person incorporates such modern values as individualism, equality, democracy, and achievement and success.

But can American society realistically attempt to socialize young people along the lines of this ideal? Table 7.2 provides a means of answering that question. In addi-

TABLE 7.2 Contrasts Between Culture of Traditional and Modern Youth

	Traditional Youth	Modern Youth
Values	Ascribed status Maintaining status quo Unequal status Constraints on behavior External conformity Religion Authoritarianism	Achieved status Progress Equality Freedom Individualism Secularism Democracy
Family	Extended or joint families Large families Parent-centered families Extended and active kinship Close supervision of young Strong parental authority Little freedom for young Has primary responsibility for socialization of young	Nuclear families Small families Child-centered families Smaller and less active kinship systems Little supervision of young Lessened parental authority Considerable freedom for young Some socialization responsibility borne by other institutions and agencies
Education	Informal Largely practical training Formal education limited to the privileged Lasts short time Low level of public support Low level of literacy Educational materials limited	Formal Massive, complex, and includes education as well as practical matters Mass education including higher level education Lasts long time High level of public support High level of literacy Educational materials abundant, including mass media
Demographic characteristics — Economics	Early entry into adult work Young are economic assets Young are social security for aged parents	Late entry into adult work Young are economic liabilities Public support for the aged
Demographic characteristics	Balance between young and old persons Short life expectancy Deference to elders	Imbalance between young and old persons Long life expectancy Deference not automatically accorded to older persons
Status characteristics	Acceptance of traditional authority Emphasis on early assumption of adult responsibilities Youth viewed as a time of life Youth as high-spirited but in need of close supervision and control	Rejection of traditional authority Emphasis on delayed assumption of adult responsibilities Youth viewed as the most desirable time of life Indulgence for high-spiritedness

tion to listing the modern ideal, the table shows the values of a traditional society, many of which are the values that ensure social continuity. Deference to elders, acceptance of tradition, and obedience to authority all contribute to a smooth transfer of power from one generation to the next. But these values, which adults wish the young to accept, directly contradict the modern values that the young are socialized to believe in. Modern America also emphasizes equality, individuality, and democracy, but these values and inequality, conformity, and authoritarianism are mutually exclusive. Young people imbued with the values of equality and individualism are not likely to meekly accept traditional authority nor automatically defer to their elders. Adults who deplore youthful rebellion and insistence on equality with adults fail to take into account that our society socializes young people to behave that way.

Probably what most adults prefer is some combination of both the traditional and modern model. Certainly, most adults want young people to achieve, make progress, and exert their individuality. But at the same time, they are concerned about allowing too much indulgence of youth. Part of the problem, then, appears to be that we want to have our cake and eat it too. That is, people think that youth can be socialized to be individualistic, skeptical, egalitarian, and democratic but, at the same time, respecting traditional authority, not questioning the status quo, and accepting hierarchical authority. Obviously to internalize these sets of values requires a considerable achievement of balance. To accomplish this task, youth must continuously test the values by seeing what limits society places on behavior. This means that while the values are being adopted by the young, they are breaking the norms established by those values and are labeled deviant.

Deviance is endemic in all societies. But if socialization were maximally effective, we would find no significant differences in the crime or arrest rate on the basis of age alone. That is, we would predict some deviance but we would anticipate finding it equally likely in each of the various age groups. But as Figure 7.3 shows, as people grow older they become increasingly less likely to be arrested. Those data must be used cautiously. As we point out in the following chapter, arrest data are not satisfactory means of determining the actual extent of crime and delinquency. All we can conclude from this information is that the younger a person is, the more likely he or she is to be arrested.

However, the difference in arrest rates by age is so great — a drop from around 60 percent at age seventeen to around 15 percent at age thirty — that it more than accounts for the inaccuracies of reporting crime. And the difference leaves us with a suggestion about socialization. Youthful deviant behavior is greater because socialization is not occurring fast enough. How to balance the traditional values that maintain society and the individualistic values of modern society takes a long time to learn. In a sense, the label for youthful deviance — delinquency — is appropriate. Just as a loan is delinquent when payment is delayed, these youths are delinquent when they have difficulty balancing society's contradictory values.

Socialization:
The Balanced Perspective

When we speak of the youth problem, we almost automatically think in terms of juvenile delinquency or juvenile crime. But, as a

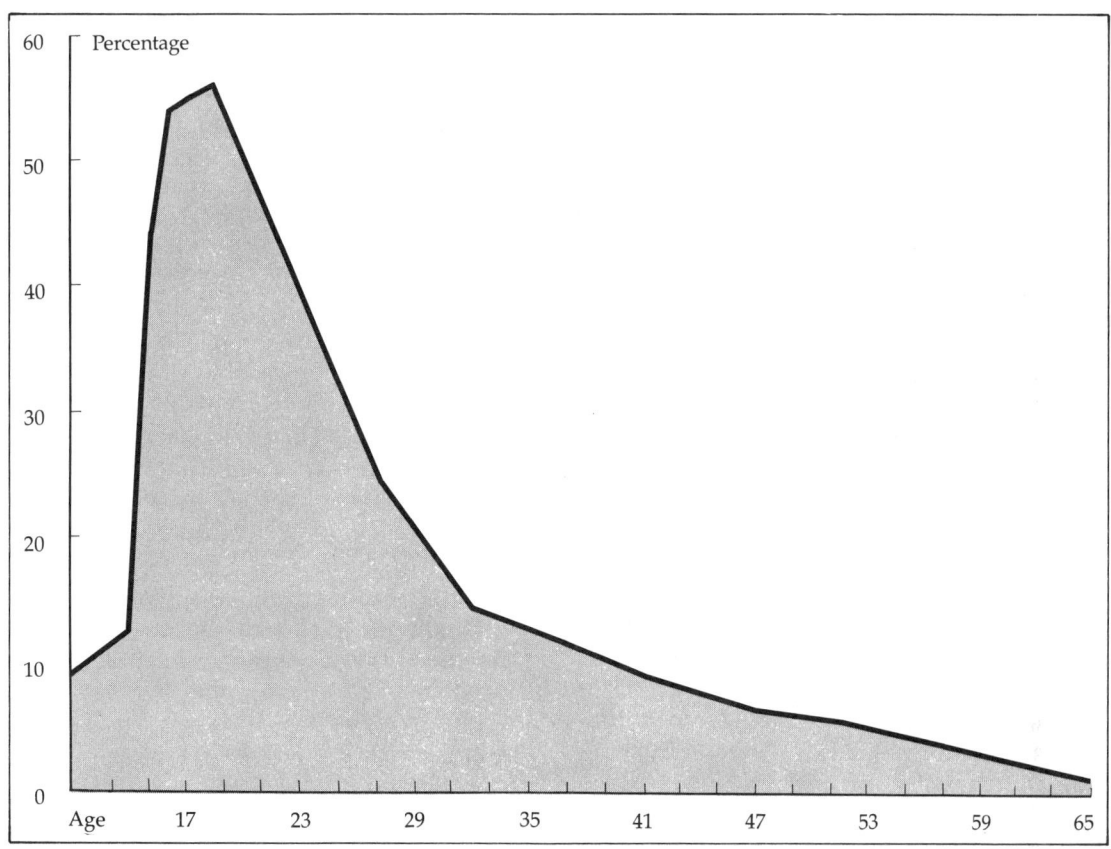

FIGURE 7.3 Probability of Being Arrested at Various Ages

Source: Adapted from Federal Bureau of Investigation, *Uniform Crime Reports: Crime in the United States, 1977* (Washington, D.C.: U.S. Government Printing Office, 1978), pp. 180–181.

problem, youth involves much larger issues. Certainly, the overriding problem is how to prepare young people to take their places as adults in society. And despite the mass media's emphasis on delinquency, our society's actions show that we recognize that youthful misbehavior is the lesser part of the problem of youth.

In 1977, the estimated federal government outlay for the prevention of crime, including juvenile delinquency, was approximately $307 million. In the same year, the federal government spent $131.1 *billion* on education. The differential emphasis is made clearer when we realize that the total federal monies spent to support the criminal justice system was only an estimated $3.2 billion.[20] On the basis of this considerable disparity in the public expenditures, we can say that society clearly regards educating and training young people as much more significant and important than dealing with crime.

We can also say that this emphasis has succeeded. To evaluate socialization fairly we must also determine the degree to which it is working. Young people seem to have been socialized effectively to enter the work force and to be performing well, as evidenced in the rise in the gross national product over the past sixteen years. And the actual rise is remarkable. Holding dollars at a constant value to remove the effects of inflation, from 1960 to 1976 the GNP jumped from $534 billion to $1265 billion, a tremendous increase of 237 percent.[21]

This highly productive work force is the result of socialization. Effective socialization is evaluated on the criterion of the overall efficiency and cohesion of a society. All members of the American work force are either young people now or were at one time. From the standpoint of the survival of our society as it is presently structured (disregarding for now the question of whether it should be restructured), it would appear that the socialization of the young is working well enough. It is not working as well as we might like, but this disparity between ideals and reality helps to define social problems.

Socialization for Retirement

In a society that values work, progress, achievement and success, the realities of retirement are rarely considered ahead of time. Some people attempt to prepare financially, through savings, annuity plans, and retirement programs. Most, however, give little thought to what they will do with their free time when retirement actually arrives. This lack of preparation for retirement can be harmful, as noted in the following statement from the 1971 White House Conference on Aging:

> Comes a time when a man retires from his work and a whole new ball game begins for [him and his wife]. He may feel like a fifth wheel around the house where his wife has been in charge for so long. Unless he has prepared well for his retirement, he may find that the leisure so long anticipated when he would be free to go fishing or spend more time at home fails to satisfy as fully as he dreamed it might.[22]

Worse than the lack of preparation is the fact that previous socialization serves to make adjustments even more difficult. People who have been prepared for lives of work and recreation find it difficult to adjust to recreation alone.

And what about the housewife? It is frequently assumed that she has no retirement problems: after all, whether her husband is retired or not, her work goes on. But is she prepared for her husband's retirement? Can she cope with the problems arising out of a reduced income? Most important, is she prepared for the death of her husband, which, because the male life span is around seven years shorter than the female, will probably come before her own? The result of this longer life span is shown in Figure 7.4; women are much more likely to be widowed than men. And widows have a much smaller chance of remarrying than widowers, if for no other reason than that there are far more widows in the population.

Socialization for retirement is inadequate. To complicate the problem, what socialization does take place is in the form of the myth of a golden time of leisure and also of misconceptions, misinformation, and erroneous beliefs about aging as a physiological, psychological, and social process.

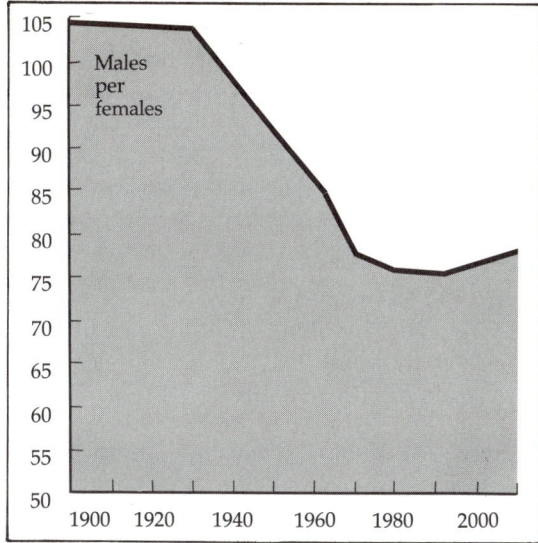

FIGURE 7.4 Sex Ratios for Ages 65 to 74, 1900–2010

Source: Adapted from Bureau of the Census, *Current Population Reports*, "Demographic Aspects of Aging and the Older Population in the United States," Series P–29, No. 59, rev. (Washington, D.C.: U.S. Government Printing Office, January 1978), p. 13.

Myths About Aging

Part of the problem of aging and old age lies in what people believe about this period of life. As we will see, a number of common beliefs about aging are false, myths that do harm to both the elderly and society as a whole.

AGING AND LEARNING ABILITY

Poor learning performance among older persons is assumed to be a function of advancing age. It is widely believed that one of the *dyspacts*, or harmful effects, of advancing age is a decrease in the ability to learn. A serious consequence of this belief is that many older people literally prevent themselves from learning as well as they did when younger.[23] As W. I. Thomas observed, "If people believe certain things to be real, then they are real in their consequences."[24]

Psychologists tell us that the belief that learning ability decreases markedly in later years is in error. "The evidence that has been accumulating on both animal and human aging suggests that changes with age in the primary ability to learn are small under most circumstances."[25] With respect to verbal intelligence, investigators have found individuals who actually show increases in test scores in their eighties and nineties. However, older persons are less able to perform those kinds of tasks requiring a high rate of speed of response.[26]

In fact, far from intelligence decreasing with age, there is a positive correlation between performance on intelligence tests and life span.[27] The more intelligent people are (at least, as determined by intelligence tests), the more likely they are to live to a ripe old age. In general, those over age sixty-five represent a group whose average tested intelligence is higher than that of younger persons. The social implications of this are profound. Our society mandates that the age group with the greatest average intelligence must spend the balance of their lives in enforced retirement. No society can afford so prodigal a waste of talent.

AGING AND PERSONALITY CHANGE

As with the young, part of the social problem of the old relates to personality disturbances. But there is a difference in how these problems are seen. When young people become unstable, disoriented, highly neurotic, or psychotic, psychiatrists, clinical psychologists, and counselors are involved. The implication of their attention is that personality problems in the young are amenable to diagnosis and treatment. "But when these symptoms appear in elderly people, they are considered par for the course of old age. We rarely consider the possibility that elderly people who have had a breakdown can recover."[28]

Since personality problems occur at all ages, we should expect to find such disturbances in older persons. Whether or not such problems continue or disappear depends on how aging and status changes are handled by the individuals concerned and those in their immediate environment. But our society has made it extremely difficult for older persons to make fully satisfactory personality adjustments. We have taken away their right to work; reduced their incomes significantly; robbed them of their occupational sources of self-identity; downgraded their status; deprived them of a considerable measure of self-respect; and, in diverse ways, informed them that they exist only on sufferance in a society enamoured of youth. Under the circumstances, it is surprising that so many retired people function as effectively as they do. If people upon retirement exhibit signs of personality disturbance, so do younger persons who have lost their jobs. The chief difference is that younger individuals have at least the hope and expectation of finding another position; the old are deprived of such hope.

It is a common observation that older people tend to be irascible or short-tempered. This appears to constitute a personality change. But it may merely mean that older persons, particularly those who are retired, no longer have "to beware of offending those whose opinions were critical to [their] . . . advancement in early life."[29] Irascibility may be honesty; the freedom to speak candidly without fear of reprisal may represent a situational adjustment, not a personality change.

Another point needs to be made about these personality disturbances — they may not be disturbances, they could just be changes.

ABANDONMENT OF OLDER PERSONS

There is a grim and widely held stereotype that the aged are alone and living in institutions, abandoned by their families while they wait for the merciful release of death. But the facts are quite different. For example in 1976, there were approximately 21.3 million persons sixty-five and older in the population, but only around 1.4 million were actually hospitalized or in convalescent homes.[30] Thus, the belief that the elderly are largely institutionalized is incorrect.

We cannot doubt that some old people have been abandoned by or have outlived their families. Nor can we question the statement that some old people are virtually friendless. For that matter, it cannot be doubted that some young people are in a similar situation: children deserted by parents and relatives constitute part of the social problem of youth. But the stereotype that old people are largely deserted by their families is not borne out by the facts. Research finds a great deal of face-to-face visiting, telephoning, letter writing, and close association between aging and aged parents and their grown children.[31] The realities of being old in modern American society have many unpleasant features, but they do not include massive institutionalization and abandonment.

SENILITY

Most dictionaries define *senility* as the state of being old or exhibiting the characteristics of old age. But this definition, though straightforward, is vague. Senility has other connotations, or associated meanings. When people speak of senility they mean more than simply old age. The common view is that senility entails a physical deterioration, marked by such things as wrinkles and false teeth, that reflects serious mental impairment, including poor memory and loss of intelligence.

Medically speaking, mental impairment in old age is thought to be caused by hardening of the arteries (*arteriosclerosis*) accompanied by damage to the large and medium sized arteries of the brain (*atherosclerosis*). But brain damage does not occur in everyone, and when it does it by no means automatically produces senility. Senile behavior has been observed in persons having few or no indications of brain damage.[32]

The implications of this are important to the problem of aging. As we have pointed out, personal idiosyncracies, disorientation, hallucinations, and suspiciousness, when observed in the young, are not regarded as signs of senility but as symptoms to be treated. But identical symptoms among the aged are seen as signs of brain damage and considered irreversible. If senility were an invariable accompaniment of old age, we would have the vast majority of older persons institutionalized. But as we noted earlier, less than 6 percent of those sixty-five or older are actually in institutions, negating the common stereotype that the aged are senile and must be institutionalized.

Social beliefs inculcated early in life are powerful determinants of whether or not a person retains physical and mental vigor with advancing years.[33] Those who accept the stereotype of senility anticipate a loss of ability and these expectations frequently become realities. Some older people become senile because they expect to become senile. Symptoms of senility may then result in institutionalization. Once institutionalized, the decay in abilities is accelerated because segregation of the aged in institutions creates a climate in which deterioration of behavior is more likely a result of being institutionalized than it is the result of the aging process.[34]

A part of the problem of old age, then, arises out of learned expectations that growing old is invariably accompanied by serious impairment in functioning. That is, the problem is a social rather than psychological matter. The removal of this myth from American and other cultures would have considerable positive consequences for the aging.

AGE AND SEXUAL ACTIVITY

The young and the elderly have something in common in their sex lives. Young unmarried people — a majority of teenagers — are not supposed to indulge in sexual activity, from intercourse to masturbation. The elderly, married or not, aren't either. They are assumed to be past the age for active sexual involvement. Both young people and adults often express the belief that sex is unimportant or negligible for the elderly.[35] And while both the young and the old are, at least verbally, prohibited from sex, they are alike in another way. Large numbers of both groups engage in sexual activity, from intercourse to masturbation, regardless of popular expectations.

There are two important sexual changes that occur with aging. For the female, a decline in the production of estrogen causes a hormonal imbalance, which leads to less lubrication of the vagina and can result in painful intercourse. For males, the *refractory period* becomes longer. That is, after orgasm the length of time required for the arousal of sexual interest and the ability to gain and maintain an erection increases. For females, there is little if any refractory period at any age and the ability to have multiple orgasms apparently continues indefinitely.

Although there are clearly physical changes that accompany advancing age, Masters and Johnson have concluded that there is no apparent age that, when attained, marks the end of sexual activity. Sexual capacity appears to resemble other types of physical functioning. The individual who exercises regularly for several hours each week retains physical vigor. It is the same with the ability to have sexual relations. The general rule seems to be, "If you don't use it, you lose it."[36]

Problems associated with sexuality are seen as afflicting males more than females. Males of all ages experience sexual failures. Cases of *impotence*, the inability to achieve or maintain an erection, are reported even for the very young but are more common in elderly males and, as such, constitute part of the problem of aging and old age. But the problem is not inevitable; it arises largely from an acceptance of the stereotype that sex and old age are mutually exclusive. Belief in this stereotype reduces sexual capabilities in older males. For those who have consciously or unconsciously internalized the sexual stereotype of the elderly, a failure at any time signals the onset of a decline in sexual functioning that has been anticipated. A few such failures and the result is *psychical impotence*, that is, the inability to copulate because the person believes he cannot do so. Like senility, impotence is often a socially created problem.

Love, affection, and desire do not fade away at age sixty-five. The needs of the elderly for social, intellectual, and sexual companionship are sadly misunderstood, and too often the myths about old age become self-fulfilling prophecies.

Summary

We are all born, progress from infancy through childhood, adolescence, maturity, middle age, and old age, and finally die. Some of us do not live long enough to pass through all the stages of the life cycle, but a high proportion do. The life cycle, as such, and the social problems related to its extremes, youth and old age, are socially defined, socially caused, and socially maintained. These problems revolve around certain social stereotypes and myths.

The crux of the social problem of youth is how to effectively socialize young people to take their roles as adults in society. The vast sums spent on the training and education of young people and the multitude of laws governing the treatment and behavior of youth, provide compelling evidence that this socialization for adulthood is what society considers the most important segment of the youth problem. Contrary to this actual social emphasis, the mass media have concentrated public attention on the more dramatic matter of juvenile delinquency and crime. Although important, this remains a lesser part of the youth problem, but one suggesting that socialization is working more slowly than would be desirable.

Enforced retirement at age seventy or earlier coupled with serious misconceptions about aging and the aged have contributed significantly to the social problem of old age. Rather than being decrepit slow learners whose intelligence is slipping, older persons represent a select group whose intelligence is superior to that of the general population.

As the American society is structured, both the young and the old are viewed as incompetent. The young, until they reach eighteen, cannot vote, enter into business contracts, drink in public, or be held accountable for serious crimes, except in unusual cases. Similarly, those past seventy are prevented in most cases from working at their occupations, and their ability and judgment are viewed as suspect. Neither the young nor the old are granted full membership in American society. While both de jure and de facto discrimination deprive the young and old of many things, including self-respect and identity, they also serve as self-fulfilling prophecies. When a society labels any particular group as undeserving of full membership, the group may accept society's evaluation and behave in accordance with the stereotyped view.

ATTEMPTS AT DEALING WITH THE PROBLEM

In Chapter 2 we observed that actions taken to alleviate or remedy social ills do not necessarily work out as anticipated. Some measures may and frequently do have what we call *iatrogenic effects,* creating new problems. In this section, we discuss the iatrogenic effects of the two principal solutions for life cycle problems: changes in education to better socialize the young, and economic supports for the aged.

Iatrogenic Effects of the Education System

Modern industrial states require a literate work force. More than that, modern economies need a host of specialists, ranging from well-trained technicians to professionals. To provide people with these skills, all modern societies have massive systems of education, which include elementary schools, high schools, technical schools, and colleges and universities.

The enormous growth in mass education has had one obvious iatrogenic effect. The authority of parents over their children has been weakened. Implicit in the establishment of formal schooling has been a division of authority between parents and schools. Also creating problems is the fact that modern education teaches some values and concepts that undermine not merely the authority of parents but the schools as well. Even young children are taught about the scientific attitude, to be skeptical of authority. We do not argue that young people should be taught to blindly accept authority, but given that this skepticism is taught it is hardly surprising that the young do not defer to authority. Teaching these values helps create conflict between these values and traditional values, as we discussed earlier. It also delays socialization.

The main objectives of education appear straightforward enough: (1) to socialize students for taking adult roles in a competent and responsible manner, and (2) to prepare students to take a productive role in the economy. There are additional goals, to help individuals to improve their economic lot in life and to be better adjusted and happier. Education performs these three functions well enough, but many see this "well enough" as falling far short of the ideal.

For Theodore Roszak, the ideal product of education would be a creative, innovative person for whom life and work have meaning.[37] For others, the ideal is a conforming person thoroughly imbued with traditional American values and eager to compete for the rewards available in American society. The push-pull between these mutually exclusive ideals has resulted in another iatrogenic effect, a system of education that can be aptly described as a normative crazy-quilt. For example, the vast majority of schools at whatever level give lip service to individuality, but how much individuality is permitted students? This normative confusion has helped create deviant behavior. Students are taught the values of democracy, equality, and universalism. But when they try to put these values into practice, they find themselves locked in a struggle with a basically authoritarian system.

Another iatrogenic effect comes out of the universality of universal education. Unless officially suspended or expelled, all young people are required to attend school until they attain the age of sixteen or graduate from high school. These legal requirements are a recognition of the importance with which American society views education, but they also create a dilemma for educators. If they graduate only those students whose performance is satisfactory, there would be a sharp rise in the proportion of students not receiving diplomas. But this would invite serious and possibly violent reactions from parents. To more than a few parents, schools constitute not centers for learning, but tax-supported custodial centers for their children. How have the schools responded to these pressures?

First, there exists throughout virtually all school systems the practice of *social promotion,* promoting students for social not academic reasons. It is held that failing, not being promoted, is likely to result in serious personality damage. To avoid this possible problem and to avoid the criticism of parents, educators have instituted social promotions. But that creates new problems. The higher the socially promoted student goes in the school system, the less well-equipped he or she is to master more difficult subjects. Serious boredom and classroom disruption can occur when all students — those socially promoted and those promoted on merit — are lumped together.

Some schools have set up *track systems* in an effort to segregate competent from less competent students. Based on ability, performance, or both, students are placed in one track or another. But the students, themselves, are well aware of the invidious distinctions between the various tracks. Students placed in lower tracks suffer from both the knowledge of their inferiority and the taunts of other students. The track system has some advantages — it does focus special attention on those most in need of it — but it also compounds differences between groups of students.

Iatrogenic Effects of Social Security

The original Social Security Act of 1935 established certain economic supports for citizens upon retirement. Financed by payments from workers and employers, it provides for regular income for eligible persons upon retirement. This act and later modifications of it represent the modern expression of a concern that dates as far back as the end of the seventeenth century in this country.[38]

But these aid programs are not without problems. Social legislation providing assistance and benefits to retired persons has at least three iatrogenic effects: (1) it partially frees the family and close relatives of old people from their traditional obligations; (2) it is based on the fallacious assumption that chronological age is the criterion for determining when people should cease work; and (3) it encourages people not to work past age sixty-five, although they can now legally do so and are quite capable of doing so.

The latter two points we have already discussed. We have shown that the physical and mental collapse that supposedly accompanies age is largely a matter of myth. Not only are old people still highly functional, they have valuable experience that younger people do not possess and may even be the most intelligent age group in society. The other problem is the arbitrary retirement age of sixty-five years. In the more than forty years since social security was instituted, this age has become the common retirement age for workers, first because coverage under social security has been extended to include almost all workers, second because most pension programs have adopted the same age. The result is that most workers are influenced not to retire when they are sixty-two, even if they wish to, and not to work when they are sixty-six, even if they wish to. This may change. Congress has recently passed a law stipulating that retirement cannot be forced on people when they reach sixty-five. Although this law has undoubtedly made a difference in individual cases, it has not been in force long enough to make later retirement a widespread practice. But even this law has drawbacks. It does allow forced retirement at age seventy — but why is that age any less arbitrary than sixty-five?

The major iatrogenic effect of social security is the one we mentioned first. By instituting a system of government support, the legislation removed the burden of responsibility for the welfare of the aged from the family. But the support provided by the government is insufficient to maintain a reasonable life-style. Implicit in social security legislation is the belief that the assistance payments are supplementary. That is, they are not intended to be the sole support of retired persons, for even maximum benefits are insufficient to maintain all but the most frugal life-style. However while meant to be supplementary, they are not. A large proportion of retired persons are totally dependent on social security for support. And because most retired people draw less than the maximum, many live at or below the poverty line. Their hopelessness is shown in the fact that if they do work, even part-time, in an effort to attain a modest standard of living, their benefits are reduced accordingly. If they do not work, they are condemned to eke out an existence well below the one they enjoyed prior to retirement.

Social security may be adequate when it supplements other sources of income, but as the single source of income it is woefully inadequate. This is true in spite of the fact that in constant dollars, all public income maintenance programs have increased by six and one-half times during the 1950–1975 period — from $20.4 billion to $132.1 billion per year. The problem is that the increase in the number of social security beneficiaries has been even larger — from 3.5 million in 1950 to 32.1 million in 1975 (from 2.3 percent to 15.0 percent of the total population).[39]

PROSPECTS FOR SOLVING THE PROBLEM

The social problems of the life cycle appear almost insoluble. Practically speaking, our society has solved them sufficiently well to permit its continuance. But do we have it within our power to provide and implement improvements? The answer is clearly yes. The real question is will we?

The Problem of Youth

The general problem of youth is to make socialization more efficient and to accelerate the process. But this general problem is composed of a number of lesser problems. How do we improve socialization within American families? Family life and childrearing are relatively immune to interference by society. And little in the way of formal education and training in family life is offered in high schools or colleges. Although much conflict within families is concerned with economics, one looks in vain for courses in family economics.

While we cannot expect the family to socialize young people any better than in the past, formal education probably will not either. The social institution of education, a complex of loosely interacting bureaucracies, is inherently conservative. Teaching methods and curricula remain much the same from year to year. In the face of a declining fertility rate, colleges of education continue to turn out thousands of individuals each year prepared to teach elementary school. In effect, young people are being prepared for jobs which will not exist when they graduate. Education has failed in another respect. Our society will very likely require increased numbers of technically trained persons in the future. But vocational training continues to be avoided by many young people. It has less prestige and the onus of implying inferior ability. At the same time, colleges and universities annually admit thousands of students who are ill-prepared for college work on the basis of aptitude, previous preparation, or both. The waste of human resources and the psychological and social damage from the many almost inevitable failures is beyond computation.

College is not for everyone. Even our affluent society could not afford to give all young people a college education if they all possessed the requisite aptitudes, but that is irrelevant, for they do not. But the limited opportunity for a college education is not distributed equally. The chance for college falls mainly to the children of middle- and upper-class parents while the social structure denies these opportunities to less affluent people who have the aptitude to succeed. What can we do? Should the United States adopt mass testing, as prevails in France and Japan to determine who goes on to college?

The American Dream notwithstanding, college is not for everyone. Many young people lack the desire, aptitude, finances, or preparation for a university education. Vocational schools are becoming an appropriate alternative, offering training for trades — from automotive repair to food preparation — essential to the marketplace.

We doubt that this would be acceptable. But one thing surely can and should be done. Young people should be provided with forecasts about the future of as many occupations and professions as possible. Further, they need to be informed as realistically as possible about the actual requirements and duties of various occupations. As college faculty can testify, even upperclassmen very frequently have only the most cursory knowledge of the requirements and duties of the profession or occupation they expect to enter when they graduate.

The Problem of the Aged

We may be entering the *age of the adult*.[40] If so, one cause is the increasing number and proportion of persons aged sixty-five and older in American society. As of 1979, about 11.5 percent of the population was in this age group. Using a conservative projection of population growth, that proportion will rise to nearly 13 percent by 1990. By the end of this century, our society will include more than 29 million persons aged sixty-five and older.

Considering that the aging and elderly in American society represent a group of higher than average intelligence and millions of person-years of experience, it is inconceivable that changes in the social structure to improve the condition of the aged will not occur. These changes, some of which have already begun, fall into three areas: (1) there will be increasing resistance to the imposition of any mandatory retirement age; (2) social security and other retirement programs will be altered to provide greater benefits for the retired; and (3) services and industries devoted to satisfying the needs of older citizens will proliferate.

The first two changes will very likely be the most dramatic. Part of the reason for this is economic. In 1979, there were about thirty-three beneficiaries of social security for every one hundred persons in the full-time work force. It is difficult to estimate costs for social insurance in the future, but even discounting inflation the total amount will be high. Thus economic pressures alone will relax mandatory retirement rules and permit an increasing number of persons to continue working past what is now considered the proper age for retirement. And the demographic changes caused by a lower birthrate will require older people to stay in the work force rather than retire so that industry can maintain the level of production. This explains why we expect that benefits will go up even as the number of old people increases, a seeming contradiction given the limitations on funds. But while there will be more old people, there will also be fewer retired old people. The abandonment of mandatory retirement will mean that many more will be working.

As the elderly take on a greater role as producers, so will they as consumers. The American economy already has many services and some industries catering to the wants and needs of older citizens. Communities built for older persons, a growing number of physicians specializing in geriatrics, organizations devoted to lobbying on behalf of the aged, and magazines focusing on the special interests, problems, and needs of the aged are prevalent and will increase. Numerically, economically, and politically, older citizens will become increasingly more powerful every year. This will not only affect the position of the elderly, but that of youth as well. We may see a lessening of the emphasis on youth as the most desirable period of life. We may also see increased supervision of young people by the community. Because there will be fewer young people than there were in the 1960s and 1970s, toleration will decrease and standards of conduct will be more strictly enforced.

The Future of Life Cycle Problems

The problems covered in this chapter will remain problems. The reader will remember that social problems, among other things, represent gaps between ideals and realities. Even if conditions improve, a gap will remain. A peculiarity of humans is that, as realities change for the better, ideals are also modified. Almost invariably, ideals stay well ahead of the realities. As we improve our condition, our ideals and aspirations likewise move constantly ahead.

With respect to the problems of youth, no dramatic changes appear on the horizon. If our present fertility rate of approximately 1.79 continues into the future, there will be fewer people than there were in the past. If behavioral standards are more rigidly en-

Prospects for Solving the Problem 229

Old people are organizing to lobby for their special interests. Perhaps the best known national group is the Gray Panthers, who, under the spirited leadership of Maggie Kuhn (far right), fight discrimination against the elderly wherever it appears.

forced for children, they should be followed more closely by young people. This, combined with the smaller population of young people, indicates that arrests for juvenile delinquency and juvenile crime will probably decrease. If so, youth as a behavioral problem will tend to recede from public consciousness.

More funds may become available to concentrate on the quality of education, as recent spending should assure adequate physical facilities — buildings and classrooms. To the degree that this takes place, youth will be aided and some of the serious waste of human resources reduced. The teacher–student ratio should decrease, permitting closer attention to each individual student.

We also feel safe to predict greater satisfaction for older Americans. Because of the reduction in the earlier high fertility rate, older persons will derive increased power and influence from their higher proportion of society. They will be aided in increasing their influence by their tendency to organize. The American Association of Retired Persons, founded in 1950 and with as few as 1000 members as recently as 1970, had jumped to 11.5 million members by 1979.[41] As we saw in discussing minorities, when a group organizes to protect its interests and rights it has a good chance of success.

The old possess strengths that the young do not. A principal strength is organization. While there are youth groups, virtually all of them are not formed or run by young people. Instead, they are controlled by adults. And it is not likely that young people will organize effectively to do anything about the youth problem. Youth qua youth is unlikely to organize to change the general lot of youth for the same reason that the so-called proletariat in this country has not organized. In the first place, there must be some general consciousness of kind — a recognition that youth are tied by certain common oppressions. Second, organization requires knowledge of how to organize. Third, such a movement demands financial support. One cannot imagine any of these conditions being met, much less all three. Of course, there *are* youth organizations but, as was noted in this chapter, they are almost invariably run by older persons. In sum, youth lacks the principal requirements for any kind of effective organization: (1) consciousness of kind, (2) organizational knowledge, (3) financial resources — in short, the kind of power required to make protests meaningful. When social movements drawing youthful support are in motion (recent examples were the widespread protests against the Vietnam war), these movements are often fueled and led largely by older persons.

In contrast, older persons have had considerable experience with organizations of all kinds. Thus, they know how to organize. This is dramatically illustrated by the American Association of Retired Persons, mentioned earlier. The extensive lobbying of this organization was at least instrumental in raising the retirement age from sixty-five to seventy in 1978. It is unlikely that its efforts to alleviate the problems of the retired will stop there.

We can anticipate that both youth and old age, as *major* social problems, will recede from public consciousness in future years. This will happen to youth because their proportionate representation in the population will be smaller. It will happen to the elderly because they will organize and reduce the magnitude of their problems. As we have said, the major improvement will be the end of retirement at age sixty-five. As former Secretary of Health, Education, and Welfare Joseph Califano wrote, "There are reasons to wonder aloud whether the trend toward even earlier retirement is a trend in the right direction. A 1974 poll, for example, indicated that four million people 65 and over wanted to work but were not doing so."[42] With time, the trend toward early retirement will reverse. Those 4 million people, and countless others, will find themselves not only wanting to work, but able to, as society will once again value the contributions of the old.

IMPORTANT WORDS AND TERMS

age peers	dyspact	old age	social promotion
age status	economic liabilities	psychical impotence	social security
alienation	extended family	puberty	stereotype
arteriosclerosis	impotence	refractory period	subculture of youth
atherosclerosis	invidious distinctions	senility	track system
de facto	life cycle	sentries	youth
de jure	nuclear family		

QUESTIONS FOR DISCUSSION

1. The fatal accident rate is lower for females in our society at all ages. Why is this so? Are females inherently more cautious and careful or do they have better judgment?
2. Speed of reaction and keenness of sensory perception decline with age, which could explain the higher accident rate among people over sixty-five years of age. But could any social or psychological factors be involved? Explain your answer.
3. Your text observes that "absolute coercive control of humans is manifestly impossible." Do you agree? Why or why not?
4. Authenticated cases of many persons living more than one hundred years have been found in the Soviet Union. These people subsist by agriculture and live in rural areas. Do you think that their life-style has much to do with their long life span? Why or why not?
5. How significant a part of the social problem of youth is the subculture of youth? What are the chief social factors contributing to this particular subculture?
6. Can society socialize youth to be individualistic, skeptical, egalitarian, and democratic but also respectful of traditional authority? Explain your answer.
7. Should federal, state, and local governments spend more money to control juvenile delinquency and juvenile crime? If no, why not? If yes, how would you suggest that additional funds be spent?
8. At what age should people be preparing for retirement? How can they prepare?
9. Why do you think there is a positive correlation between advanced age and intelligence test scores?
10. The text claims that people who think they will suffer a loss of ability as they grow older will lose ability because of that belief. Do you agree?
11. On the evidence, juvenile delinquency is not the most important aspect of the social problem of youth. Yet, most people believe it is. How has this misconception come about?
12. Will raising the retirement age from sixty-five to seventy have any iatrogenic effects? What will they be?
13. Most of us agree that parents have some right to question how a school deals with their children. However, we would all also agree that this right is not unlimited. What guidelines would you set up for parents with respect to actively intervening with teachers or school authorities?
14. Should high schools offer courses in such things as sexual behavior and the economics of family life? Why is it that such courses, particularly in the area of sexuality, are rarely offered in high school?
15. Would you favor mass testing of high school students to determine who does or does not go on to higher education in this country? Why or why not?

SUGGESTED READING

Janet Shibley Hyde, *Understanding Human Sexuality* (New York: McGraw-Hill, 1979).

Sexuality is one of the problems of youth and old age. Two chapters in Hyde's book deal closely with these problems and help shed some light on the sexual difficulties of the young and the aged. Chapter 10 emphasizes childhood and adolescent sex. Chapter 11, concerned with adult sex, contains a particularly good section on sex and the senior citizen. These two chapters, indeed the entire book, contain much useful information on an important topic to most people.

Solomon H. Katz, "Anthropological Perspectives on Aging," *The Annals of the American Academy of Political and Social Science,* Vol. 438 (July 1978), pp. 1–12.

Students should examine social problems from the broadest possible perspective. Anthropology is particularly helpful in this respect because anthropologists study a wide range of different cultures and bring high objectivity to their work. Their detachment enables them to ask questions that might not occur to someone limited to a single cultural perspective. In this light, Professor Katz notes that it is only the human female who lives well beyond her reproductive years, and in modern societies beyond her husband. He wonders whether this fact reveals the evolutionary significance of the existence of grandmothers. This short but provocative article also directs attention, among other things, to health and medical care for the aging in American society and makes insightful comment on the pros and cons of preventive medicine. Professor Katz, whose approach is humanistic, maintains that we need a much more mature appraisal of the needs and potential contributions of the elderly to our society.

Matilda White Riley, "Aging, Social Change, and the Power of Ideas," *Daedalus,* Vol. 107, No. 4 (Fall 1978), pp. 39–52.

In this article, Professor Riley argues that there is no precise process of aging. Her contention is that each age group ages somewhat differently. She discusses aging and social change, myths and fallacies about aging, and the power of ideas and everyday life. While Professor White is fully cognizant of the physiological aspects of aging, her article focuses on the sociological dynamics of aging, emphasizing the meanings we attach to aging. One of her conclusions is that aging is a process that is, to some extent, under our control.

NOTES

1. 1971 White House Conference on Aging, *Toward A National Policy on Aging,* Vol. 2 (Washington, D.C.: U.S. Government Printing Office, 1972), p. 93.
2. William J. Goode, *The Family* (Englewood Cliffs, N.J.: Prentice-Hall, 1964), pp. 19–20.
3. Gerhard E. Lenski, *Human Societies* (New York: McGraw-Hill, 1970), p. 30.
4. Quoted by Marvin E. Wolfgang in "Crime in Urban America," in *The Threat of Crime in America* (Newark: University of Delaware, 1969), p. 24.
5. Gerhard E. Lenski, *Power and Privilege* (New York: McGraw-Hill, 1966), p. 136.
6. Ralph Linton, *The Study of Man* (New York: Appleton-Century-Crofts, 1936), p. 120.
7. Lenski, *Power and Privilege.*
8. Philip K. Bock, *Modern Cultural Anthropology* (New York: Knopf, 1969), p. 105.
9. Elman R. Service, *Profiles in Ethnology* (New York: Harper and Row, 1963), p. 23.
10. Allan Holmberg, *Nomads of the Long Bow: The Siriono of Eastern Bolivia,* Vol. 10 (Washington, D.C.: Smithsonian Institution, Institute of Social Anthropology, 1950), p. 85.

11. Alexander Leaf, "Getting Old," *Scientific American* (September 1973), pp. 45–52.

12. Margaret Mead, *Culture and Commitment: A Study of the Generation Gap* (Garden City, N.Y.: Doubleday, 1970), p. 64.

13. U.S. Bureau of the Census, *Historical Statistics of the United States, Colonial Times to 1957* (Washington, D.C., 1960), Series A 195–209, p. 14.

14. Francis R. Allen, *Socio-Cultural Dynamics: An Introduction to Social Change* (New York: Macmillan, 1971), p. 9.

15. James A. Coleman, "Community Disorganization," in Robert K. Merton and Robert A. Nisbet (eds.), *Contemporary Social Problems*, 2nd ed. (New York: Harcourt, Brace and World, 1966), p. 705.

16. Bureau of the Census, *Statistical Abstract of the United States, 1977* (Washington, D.C.: U.S. Government Printing Office, 1977), p. 137.

17. Bureau of the Census, *Social Indicators, 1976* (Washington, D.C.: U.S. Government Printing Office, 1977), p. 304.

18. Bernice L. Neugarten, "The Aged in American Society," in Howard S. Becker (ed.), *Social Problems* (New York: Wiley, 1966), p. 180.

19. Burton Wright, John P. Weiss, and Charles M. Unkovic, *Perspective: An Introduction to Sociology* (Hinsdale, Ill.: Dryden Press, 1975), p. 129.

20. *Statistical Abstract, 1977*, pp. 129 and 179.

21. *Statistical Abstract, 1977*, p. 429.

22. Conference on Aging, *Toward a National Policy on Aging*, p. 214.

23. David Krech, Richard S. Crutchfield, and Norman Livson, with the collaboration of William A. Wilson, Jr., *Elements of Psychology* (New York: Knopf, 1974), p. 193.

24. W. I. Thomas, "The Relation of Research to the Social Process," in *Essays on Research in the Social Sciences* (Washington, D.C.: Brookings Institution, 1931), p. 189.

25. James G. Birren, *The Psychology of Aging* (Englewood Cliffs, N.J.: Prentice-Hall, 1964), p. 110.

26. Krech et al., *Elements of Psychology*, p. 194.

27. Lissy F. Jarvik, "Thoughts on the Psychobiology of Aging," *American Psychologist*, Vol. 30, No. 5 (May 1975), p. 580.

28. "The Old in the Country of the Young," *Time Magazine* (August 3, 1970), p. 51.

29. Jarvik, "Psychobiology of Aging," p. 579.

30. *Social Indicators, 1976*, p. 201.

31. Conference on Aging, *Toward a National Policy on Aging*, p. 210. See also Joan Aldous, "Intergeneration Visiting Patterns: Variations in Boundary Maintenance as an Explanation," *Family Process*, Vol. 29, No. 2 (1967), pp. 277–281.

32. David Rothchild, "Senile Psychoses and Psychoses with Arteriosclerosis," in Oscar J. Kaplan (ed.), *Mental Disorders in Later Life*, 2nd ed. (Stanford, Calif.: Stanford University Press, 1956), pp. 71–72.

33. Jarvik, "Psychobiology of Aging," p. 578.

34. Richard N. Filer and Desmond D. O'Connell, "Motivation of Aging Persons in an Institutional Setting," in Sheila M. Chown (ed.), *Human Aging* (Middlesex, England: Penguin, 1972), p. 364.

35. Peggy Golde and Nathan Kogan, "A Sentence Completion Procedure for Assessing Attitudes Toward Old People," *Journal of Gerentology*, Vol. 14 (1959), pp. 355–364.

36. Janet Shibley Hyde, *Understanding Human Sexuality* (New York: McGraw-Hill, 1979), p. 272.

37. Theodore Roszak, *The Making of a Counter Culture* (Garden City, N.Y.: Doubleday, 1969), pp. 31–32.

38. John D. Hogan and Francis A. J. Ianni, *American Social Legislation* (New York: Harper, 1956), p. 490.

39. *Social Indicators, 1976*, p. 102.

40. Stephen R. Graubard, "Preface to the Issue 'Adulthood,' " *Daedalus*, Vol. 105, No. 2 (Spring 1976), p. v.

41. Furnished by Lloyd Wright, Associate Director of Public Relations, AARP.

42. Joseph Califano, Jr., "The Aging of America: Questions for the Four-Generation Society," *The Annals of the American Academy of Political and Social Science*, Vol. 438 (July 1978), p. 100.

PART III
PROBLEMS OF DEVIANCE

8 CRIME AND JUSTICE
LAWBREAKERS IN A FLAWED SYSTEM

CHAPTER OVERVIEW

INTRODUCTION

CONCEPTUAL ORIENTATION
The Value of Achievement
Informal Norms and the Law
The Lawbreakers
Summary

CROSS-CULTURAL AND HISTORICAL
  OVERVIEW
Crime in Preliterate Societies
*The Social Consequences of
  Population Growth*
  The Creation of Agencies for Social Control
  Affluence
  Social Stratification
  Autonomy
Criminal Justice in England
  Rising Concern over Crime
Toward a Professional Police Force
  The Thief-Takers
  The Bow Street Runners
  English Tradition and Professional Police
  The Metropolitan Police Force
Summary

OBJECTIVE DIMENSIONS OF THE PROBLEM
How Much Crime?
  The Uniform Crime Reports
  Self-Reports and Victimization Studies

The Criminal Justice System
  A Crime Is Committed
  The Judicial System
  Prisons
Political Aspects of Crime
  The Politics of Making Laws
  The Politics of Enforcing Laws
Summary

ATTEMPTS AT DEALING WITH THE PROBLEM
Biological Theories
  Atavism and Cesare Lombroso
  Somatotypes
  The Extra Y Chromosome
Psychological Theories
  Learning Theory
  Applying Learning Theory to Crime and Justice
Sociological Theories
  The Theory of Anomie
  Differential Association Theory
  Labeling Theory
Iatrogenic Effects

PROSPECTS FOR SOLVING THE PROBLEM

IMPORTANT WORDS AND TERMS

QUESTIONS FOR DISCUSSION

SUGGESTED READING

NOTES

Insofar as social rewards come solely or chiefly from the achievement of goals rather than from conformity to the rules of the game, there is a long-run pressure toward high rates of individual deviation and nonconformity.

Robin M. Williams, Jr., *American Society*

The law in its majestic equality forbids the rich as well as the poor to sleep under bridges, to beg in the street and to steal bread.

Anatole France

CHAPTER OVERVIEW

Do we have too much crime in the United States? Most people think so. What causes crime? There are a variety of answers. Some say that crime is caused by the desperation of the poor. Others say it is caused by the greed of the rich. Some maintain that parents are far too permissive and need to institute old-fashioned discipline. Others claim that it results from children rebelling. All these hypotheses are limited. The causes of crime and the way justice is administered can be understood to some extent by studying: (1) the history of criminal justice and (2) the social structure within which crime flourishes and justice is administered.

The first part of this chapter presents a conceptual picture of crime and justice, explaining the importance of such cultural traits as the emphasis on achievement and the great power of informal norms.

Next, we give a brief history of crime and justice, focusing on the development of the English system of criminal justice and English legislation because they provided the model for the modern American system. We then turn to consider how that system functions today, explaining that its functioning is primarily political. This leads us to ask how good crime data is. We will see that the figures given in the mass media are unrealistically low.

We then discuss what we have tried to do about crime and justice by discussing the various theories about the origin of crime and the attempted solutions based on them. Finally, we will consider the prospects for the future: can an end be put to crime or will it always be with us?

INTRODUCTION

Judging from mass media reports, crime is becoming an ever more serious problem. For some years, we have been treated every year to headlines in our local papers announcing that crime has increased by some frightening proportion. Judging from the mass media, it is easy to conclude that our society is entering some final phase of dissolution and degeneracy, as Oswald Spengler prophesied many years ago.[1]

Are things really getting worse? The answer to this question is not easy because it involves making value judgments rather than depending strictly on objective data. One thing is clear, however. We cannot rely on the mass media for the information we need to decide. In order to attract readers, viewers, and listeners, newspapers, television, and radio must emphasize the sensational and dramatic. But there is a great deal more to social living than that; our everyday lives are dominated by the mundane rather than the exciting. But even if we discount the sensationalism of the mass media, we can tell that something is wrong about crime and justice. The question then becomes, exactly what? What is wrong about crime? Why does the criminal justice system seem to be failing?

Initially, it is possible to make a general statement about crime and justice. Both problems have their genesis in the social structure, as we emphasized in Chapter 2. Our society is designed so as to produce thousands of new criminals each year as well as to guarantee that many persons already criminal will continue in their criminal careers. The way our society is structured and functions is fundamental to the prevalence not only of crime but also of injustice in dealing with it. If we are to reduce the amount of crime and promote justice, then, we must understand how our system works to promote crime and injustice and to prevent significant improvements in these areas. This chapter will provide the information necessary to such an understanding.

CONCEPTUAL ORIENTATION

A peculiarity of the problem of crime is the heavy burden placed on the criminal justice system. We do not expect our schools to educate everyone to receive a doctorate nor do we require our politicians to be all-wise and all-knowing. Those in the military are even forgiven occasional strategic or tactical lapses provided they are brave. But the police, the judiciary, and the penal system are viewed as problematical because, despite their work, there is still crime. The police, frequently underpaid and often poorly trained, are expected to perform without failure. Unfortunately even if the police were superbly trained and highly paid, they could not stamp out crime. The nature of society makes this impossible. Deviance and crime are literally created by values, laws, and norms — formal and informal. The result of this is to make deviance and crime literally impossible to cure, for almost everyone violates norms, behaves contrary to values, or breaks laws — at least from time to time.

The Value of Achievement

There are many reasons underlying violations of the law, that is, the commission of crimes. Some people steal because they need food or lodging. Others because they like nice things. But the traditional American values of achievement and success have important consequences for much criminal activity. Because of these values, there is great emphasis on goal attainment in our society, with a frequent disregard for the particular ways goals are attained. The interpretation of the value as meaning success or achievement at any cost contributes much to crime. This is particularly true of *white-collar crime*, the primarily economic offenses (such as false advertising or violations of labor law) committed by people with high social status. It is against the law, for example, to act in restraint of trade or cooperate in price fixing. Yet a good deal of this goes on, undetected and unpunished. Advertisers are forbidden by law to deal in untruths or to distort the truth. Yet, as we know, they do it all the time.

Informal Norms and the Law

Legislators at all levels seem to cherish a delusion. They appear to believe that all they have to do to control or direct human behavior is to pass a law. They are either unaware of or grossly underplay the significance of *informal norms*. Such laws might be called *betwixt and between laws*, because, though not *mala per se* (bad in themselves), they are not quite *mala quia prohibita* (bad because the law defines them as bad) — or at least not everyone sees them as such. The result is chaos. Laws against abortion are an example.

Abortion was defined as criminal for a long time. Although the laws varied from state to state, most outlawed abortion. Yet in the face of such laws, which carried severe penalties, abortion was for many years a thriving illegal business in the United States. Even when abortions are performed in hospitals by properly trained physicians, there is some element of risk to the woman, yet thousands of women annually resorted to quacks or otherwise poorly qualified persons and had abortions performed under conditions that multiplied the risks. Apparently the motives pushing women to obtain abortions were powerful enough to override both fear of legal consequences and the real dangers to their own lives and health. This was the case until abortion was largely decriminalized by a Supreme Court decision handed down in 1973, ruling that the states may prohibit abortions only in the last ten weeks of pregnancy.[2]

The most striking and immediate effect of decriminalizing abortion was to reduce the number of crimes committed. As critics of criminal justice often point out, the best way to reduce the number of crimes is to reduce the number of laws. It seems particularly desirable to decriminalize those acts that are supported by informal norms. Most of such laws prohibit what are called *victimless crimes*, so named because the person committing the crime is harming no other person.[3] Despite the arguments against these laws, all political entities have laws against a wide variety of victimless crimes, from prohibitions against certain sexual behaviors to laws against drug use. The argument behind such legislation is that the crimes have victims — the person committing the crime and society at large.

A major argument for decriminalizing these laws is the impossibility of enforcing them. Because so many people break these laws the police cannot arrest everyone who does. As a result, enforcement must be selective and thus engenders widespread resentment. The irony lies in who gets blamed for the poor enforcement of these laws. Oddly enough, the onus for the failure of these laws is rarely laid at the door of the legislature, which should be blamed. Rather, the police and judiciary are blamed, by some because they attempt to enforce what are seen as bad laws, by others because they fail to enforce what are seen as good laws.

The Lawbreakers

Who are the lawbreakers? What are their characteristics? What do they look like? The answer requires only a look in a mirror. All of us are *lawbreakers* — perhaps not habitually or continuously, but at least occasionally. One reason is that the legislatures have passed so many laws that it is quite literally impossible to go through life without committing several felonies or misdemeanors.

But while we are all *lawbreakers*, we are not all criminals. Our laws give those in criminal justice great power, a situation that lends itself to arbitrary or even capricious use of power. Criminal justice officials are in a position to decide which laws they will enforce and which laws they will disregard. Since all of us break a law from time to time, we might well find ourselves in custody because of some chance circumstance, perhaps a run-in with a zealous police officer who chooses to recognize, label as criminal, and react formally to a behavior that might otherwise go unnoticed, unlabeled, or unarrested.

Every crime should be detected and punished. All citizens should be treated equally in court and accorded full opportunities to defend themselves. For those found guilty, the punishment awarded should fit the crime. Punishment ought to act as a deterrent to future crime by the person convicted and others in the society. But it would be naive to believe that this ideal is even approximated by reality. If we were to choose a single word to describe the criminal justice system in our country, that word would be *selective*.

Policemen are selective in terms of which laws they enforce and selective in deciding whether or not to arrest. The judiciary is selective as well in terms of the treatment accorded those arrested, in deciding, for instance, whether to release a person on bail or on personal recognizance. Further, the severity of sentences is often left to the discretion of judges. Even in prison, the treatment of convicts can depend on their status when they were free citizens. There is no question that our criminal justice system is discretionary and that the exercise of that discretion is at the heart of many of its most serious flaws.

This selectivity explains why all lawbreakers are not labeled *criminals* — only those who are apprehended, arrested, convicted, and sentenced are. But the stigma of being a criminal does not end with sentencing, or even with serving time. Punishment goes on even though a convicted person has been released. Once a person acquires the label of criminal — or even ex-criminal — many occupational and social doors slam shut and remain closed for the rest of that person's life. In Florida, for example, a convicted felon cannot hold a state government position of any kind. What better guarantee of *recidivism* (a return to crime) than to make certain that, for the criminal, opportunities for a conventional occupation are closed or nearly closed on a more or less permanent basis.

Summary

The criminal justice system cannot eradicate crime because crime is supported by cultural values and by informal norms. But how did the criminal justice system become so unrelated to the reality of crime. To understand this we must understand how this system developed. We now turn to a brief history of crime and justice to see if some insights into present problems can be gleaned from the past.

CROSS-CULTURAL AND HISTORICAL OVERVIEW

Crime in Preliterate Societies

Strictly speaking, crime does not and did not exist in preliterate societies because there are and were no formal laws. But these societies do recognize something like what we call the law. All such societies have mores and informal norms; the violations of them are dealt with, in varying degrees of severity. As anthropologist Marvin Harris observed: "man has lived in orderly social groups for . . . thousands of years with only the most rudimentary forms of law and virtually no provisions for law enforcement."[4]

By this, Harris meant that these societies have no body of laws or formal agencies of social control such as a police force. He does not mean that social rules were not enforced, because they were. For example, three deviant acts are regarded with concern in most preliterate societies, murder, incest, and adultery, and anyone committing them is punished. Among the Ashanti of West Africa, murder — even suicide — is symbolically punished by the decapitation of the offender, or the offender's corpse in the case of suicide.[5] *Incest,* sexual relations between kin, usually restricted to mean intercourse between parents and children or between siblings, is a prevalent taboo, although some societies permit or encourage marriage between closely related individuals. But other societies, such as the Dobu Islanders of the Western Pacific, extend the taboo to include sexual relations between a man and his sister's son's wife. In this society incest is punished by killing the offending male.[6] Often, as among the Kaoka Speakers of Guadalcanal, it is considered a grounds for divorce.[7]

Preliterate societies, then, do have something like laws; what makes them distinct from modern societies is that the laws are not written and enforcing them is a community matter. In a sense, all the adult members of these societies act somewhat automatically to preserve the social order. There is considerable social cohesion and frequent use of informal sanctions to ensure obedience to norms. But this also means that there is very little of the freedom and autonomy that marks modern societies. Living in a preliterate society is similar to being a member of a large family. It is satisfying to have close support from other persons, but less satisfying to be constantly under the scrutiny of others and subject to their control.

But the success of preliterate societies in maintaining social control makes us wonder why we need the vast formal apparatus of social control that we have in modern societies. Could we go back to those days when such systems were unnecessary? It is highly improbable. To see why, let us consider the history of our criminal justice system.

The Social Consequences of Population Growth

The informal norms and community control of preliterate societies became insufficient to maintain order when societies became larger. The introduction of agricultural technology and the domestication of animals enlarged the food supply greatly, resulting in greatly increased human populations. This revolution occurred about six thousand years ago and marked the beginning of civilization and recorded history. As long as human societies had been small, they could rely on informal means for maintaining social control. But even in the beginning of civilization, around 2000 or 3000 B.C., some cities had populations in excess of 100,000.[8]

THE CREATION OF AGENCIES FOR SOCIAL CONTROL

Size creates many problems. No society, once it has become larger than a few hundred persons, can function effectively or even at all without centralized leadership. Further, the efficient food production that precipitated this growth brings with it the creation of many specialists — individuals who work at activities other than agriculture — whose work must be coordinated. This requires the development of political specialists, government officials of various kinds.

Among these officials would be those charged with overseeing crime and justice. In small societies, crime and justice were handled by the community as a whole. With larger and more complex societies, this became impossible. Larger societies had two distinct kinds of enemies: (a) those outside the society, that is, other societies motivated by conquest; and (b) those inside the society, elements who ignored or flouted its laws, including some individuals or groups who wished to seize power. Monarchs who remained in power created official agencies for dealing with external control problems; forces for defense or offense. Of course, these could also be used against internal enemies.

Specialization also meant that simple rules of conduct and principles of justice would no longer suffice. Gradually, formal codes of law evolved, the most famous being the Code of Hammurabi, named after the king of Babylonia who ruled from 1792 to 1750 B.C. This code was based on *retributive justice*, the idea that a crime should be punished (rather than the criminal reformed), often in a manner appropriate to the crime. A boy who struck his father, for instance, had his hand cut off.[9] We have some similar punishments today; the death penalty, for instance, is used to punish murder.

But why did size bring about all these changes? Couldn't people live together in a civilized manner respecting each other's rights, lives, and property without any necessity for formal agencies of social control? This did not happen, for three major reasons: (a) increased productivity meant affluence; (b) affluence created a new basis for social stratification; and (c) increased size meant individual autonomy.

AFFLUENCE

In small societies, theft is uncommon, although it occasionally occurs. Under normal conditions in such societies, theft is generally unprofitable. Items of personal property are well-known to group members, making it impossible for a thief to keep and use what he might steal. Foods, which can be consumed quickly, are about the only items that can be stolen successfully. In preliterate societies, the actual basic needs of members are frequently provided for by informal charity or reciprocal giving. Thus, there is little necessity for theft which is made hazardous by the fact that people are under the observation of others most of the time in these societies.

But larger societies are more affluent. With the development of specialties that accompanies size, many things begin to be manufactured and are no longer identifiable as a particular person's property. Growing affluence also fostered the development of monetary systems and few things are more anonymous than money. With increasing productivity and the appearance of money, there was much more around to steal and crimes against property are invariably far more numerous than crimes against persons.

SOCIAL STRATIFICATION

Another result of affluence was *social stratification*, the ranking of persons in a social system in terms of differences in affluence, authority, prestige, privileges, and influence. Those high up in the social system wished to protect their desirable status. They perceived that some of those further down in the system envied and coveted their status and privilege. And these people with status and privileges also had influence with those in power, which they used to get politicians to establish formal agencies of social control or to turn those established already to protect the government from external threats to also protect the wealthy. An important reason for the establishment of formal agencies of social control, then, was to protect the privileged in their positions, lives, and property.

The public reason given for the existence of formal agencies of social control is to protect the lives and property of all citizens. While this is true, in that each citizen does have a life and some property to protect, some citizens have more property than others. Because those in the higher levels of society had the resources and the authority, they could establish criminal justice systems and define crime and punishment. We find in the Code of Hammurabi, for instance, that the punishment for a crime varied with the offender's social position: those higher up were punished less.[10] Fear of competition from below, fear of the mob, and concern about lives and property were powerful incentives for them to take steps for self-protection.

AUTONOMY

The last change caused by greater size was mentioned earlier. People had more *autonomy*, more freedom. They could act as they wished, with less direct control. Supervision was only minimal and choices of behavior increased. With the breakdown of community control, the increase in population, and the establishment of formal agencies of social control, two significant results occurred. Individuals were less closely supervised by kinfolk and neighbors. And individuals had more *anonymity* — they could hide in a crowd — creating for them more autonomy. Therefore, criminals could operate more freely.

The same is true today. A good part of the autonomy enjoyed by citizens in modern states is a direct result of the breakdown of informal community controls. People in modern societies do not know each other and their neighbors as well as they once did. Kinfolk, often scattered about the territory of the state, are not in a position to exercise direct informal control. With an assist from formal agencies of social control, the principal influence to maintain social order is individual self-control. As we are well aware, this combination is not fully effective.

Criminal Justice in England

The Industrial Revolution that began in the eighteenth century brought with it marked and rapid social changes, which had a considerable influence on crime and the administration of justice.[11] We have already cited population growth as a development contributing to crime and have pointed to the role of affluence, stratification, and autonomy in the rise of crime and criminal justice. These factors accelerated in the Industrial Revolution, as prosperity increased even more and population shot upward. This revolution also introduced two new factors. It marked the breakdown of the old feudal system of landed gentry. And it initiated urbanization, the movement of a considerable proportion of a population from rural areas to cities.

These two developments made the problem worse. Crime and justice had been largely matters for local authorities, under the supervision of the landed gentry. With their loss of power they could no longer maintain order. Further, cities like London and Manchester were growing tremendously. The industrializing cities quickly exceeded the established means of controlling crime and administering justice. The result was growing dismay over crime.

RISING CONCERN
OVER CRIME

During the eighteenth century crime control and the administration of justice were largely uncoordinated, merely a patchwork. Each city parish had constables who were buttressed by night watchmen chosen by lot from among the citizens. Since it was possible for those chosen to obtain paid substitutes, the watchmen who served were often

Eighteenth-century England saw the beginnings of public outcry and outrage over crime, especially the increasing threat of mob violence, a largely class-based phenomenon. Mob action was not confined to the lower classes, however; the 1780 Gordon riots, depicted here, were a short-lived but virulent anti-Catholic protest led by landed gentry.

less than competent. Frequently they were the old and infirm, whose motivation, considering their low pay and the risks involved, was not the highest. Public protection was virtually nonexistent.

Although the system was clearly inefficient, it was accepted without too much question until London grew so large that the deficiencies of the watchmen became apparent. As the city passed the million population mark around the beginning of the eighteenth century, the sheer number of people invited attention to the shortcomings of the constable-watch system. Complaints were constantly made about the increase in crime. While it is undoubtedly true that crime increased, simply because there were more people, we do not know which crimes increased or by how much. There is very little data available on the amount and types of crime committed in London in the seventeenth and eighteenth centuries. One thing is clear, though. However much crime increased, the rise seemed tremendous to those who felt victimized by it.

Throughout the eighteenth century, lip service was given to the concept that all citizens ought to be secure in their persons and property, but there is no question that complaints about rising crime were more specific. What we know about crime in industrializing England comes largely from the writings of middle- and upper-class persons. Their focus is class oriented. They feared the lower classes and the threat the poor posed to the persons and property of themselves. Many of the privileged perceived the lower class as immoral, untrustworthy, and leading lives of sin and debauchery.

The fears of lower-class rebellion were sharpened by the ever-present threat of mob violence.[12] This fear of mob violence was not without foundation. There were numerous riots in the seventeenth and eighteenth centuries, in which mobs of lower-class persons temporarily upended the social order. But these mobs were often led by upper-class individuals with a political motive. For example, the Gordon Riots of June 1780 were led by Lord George Gordon to protest laws removing restrictions from Catholics. After a week of very serious disorder, the riot was ended by troops who fired upon the mob killing or injuring some 300 people.[13] But the riot never would have occurred without Gordon.

The threat of riots was not the only reason that complaints about crime grew. Another factor was the rise of the middle class. As the middle class gained in prosperity and grew in size, it became as protective of its privileges as the landed gentry had been. Because it was primarily an urban class, it felt the ill effects of urbanization strongly. The crowding of people took space from it; the increase in crime, largely an urban phenomenon, was crime against its property. Crime touched the middle class more acutely than it ever had the rural gentry. Finally, the middle class cried out in protest and set about to change things.

Toward a Professional Police Force

THE THIEF-TAKERS

There was no question that something needed to be done. Not only was crime seemingly increasing, but there was considerable corruption in both the traditional constable-watch system and the judiciary. City magistrates often had close and mutually beneficial contacts with professional criminals and some made large amounts of money from these associations to the detriment of justice. To do so, they took advantage of the institution of *thief-takers*.

Followers of Western movies are familiar with a similar term, the bounty hunter. Thief-takers were, in effect, bounty hunters. They were private individuals who, for a fee, apprehended criminals and recovered stolen property. The government paid some fees, ranging from forty pounds for apprehending a robber to only one pound for nabbing a deserter from the army or navy.[14] If the thief-taker was recovering stolen property, the fee was paid by the victim of the theft. Obviously, such an arrangement was available only to the more affluent.

THE BOW STREET RUNNERS

To combat the corruption of this system the first professional police force, the *Bow Street Runners,* was created by Henry and John Fielding in the middle of the eighteenth century. (Henry, who was a judge, should be familiar to modern readers as the author of *Tom Jones*.) Instead of providing only local protection, the Bow Street Runners covered the entire metropolitan area. These men were paid by a combination of funds from the treasury and a fee system. Although the force was augmented after a time by a force on horseback to patrol the highways and a group of foot patrolmen in the central part of London, it was never extremely effective, simply because of size. The total strength of the runners never exceeded 160 men. The creation of the runners does show, however, a willingness to try a full-time professional police.

ENGLISH TRADITION AND PROFESSIONAL POLICE

Both Paris and Munich had professional police forces by the late seventeenth century but the English were less open to the idea. These forces were independent of the civil law to a considerable extent and English tradition was strongly in favor of protecting individual rights. As a result, the English deeply feared an independent police and its power over citizens. They did, however, recognize that both the Paris and Munich police were more efficient than the English system.[15]

In Paris and Munich, the professional force prevented crime by relying on *deterrence*. That is, an example was set for all citizens by apprehending and punishing criminals. While many in England in positions of authority and power were concerned about crime, they were also concerned about the uses to which this deterrent power would be put. Jealous of their rights, the English also wished to improve social order. They thought it necessary that any established police force come under civil control, and local control at that. This English fear of a too-strong and potentially capricious central government, with power to enforce obedience by using the police, is reflected in the structure chosen for the English police system.

THE METROPOLITAN POLICE FORCE

In 1829, the Metropolitan Police Force was created by an act of Parliament. The act established a model for English and American professional police forces followed to this day. First, the new force was paramilitary, or formed on a military pattern. It was organized in a hierarchy from top to bottom. Members had to meet certain strict physical standards and submit to military discipline. It was responsive to the orders of its officers in much the same way as a purely military organization.

But there were also differences between this force and the military. Titles were civilian and members were not armed except under unusual circumstances. Most important, the police were subject to local authority and were held responsible for their conduct. A police officer could not plead, as a defense against charges of misconduct, that he had merely been obeying the orders of his superiors.

As we observed earlier, the British system was used as a model for the professional police of the United States. By and large, American police forces are local matters, police officers are responsible for their actions, and police forces are paramilitary. Of course, the United States did eventually adopt a central police authority — the Federal Bureau of Investigation (FBI). But this organization only has jurisdiction over certain crimes; social control is still largely a matter left up to local forces. The English fear of a centralized police may be supported by recent revelations about the misconduct of the FBI, as we have learned that the agency has undertaken some political suppression. And while this demonstration of the costs of unchecked centralized power is disturbing, it is also true that local police have often suppressed rights as well. We can only conclude that regardless of the nature of any organization or its ultimate control, some citizens will seek to subvert the system.

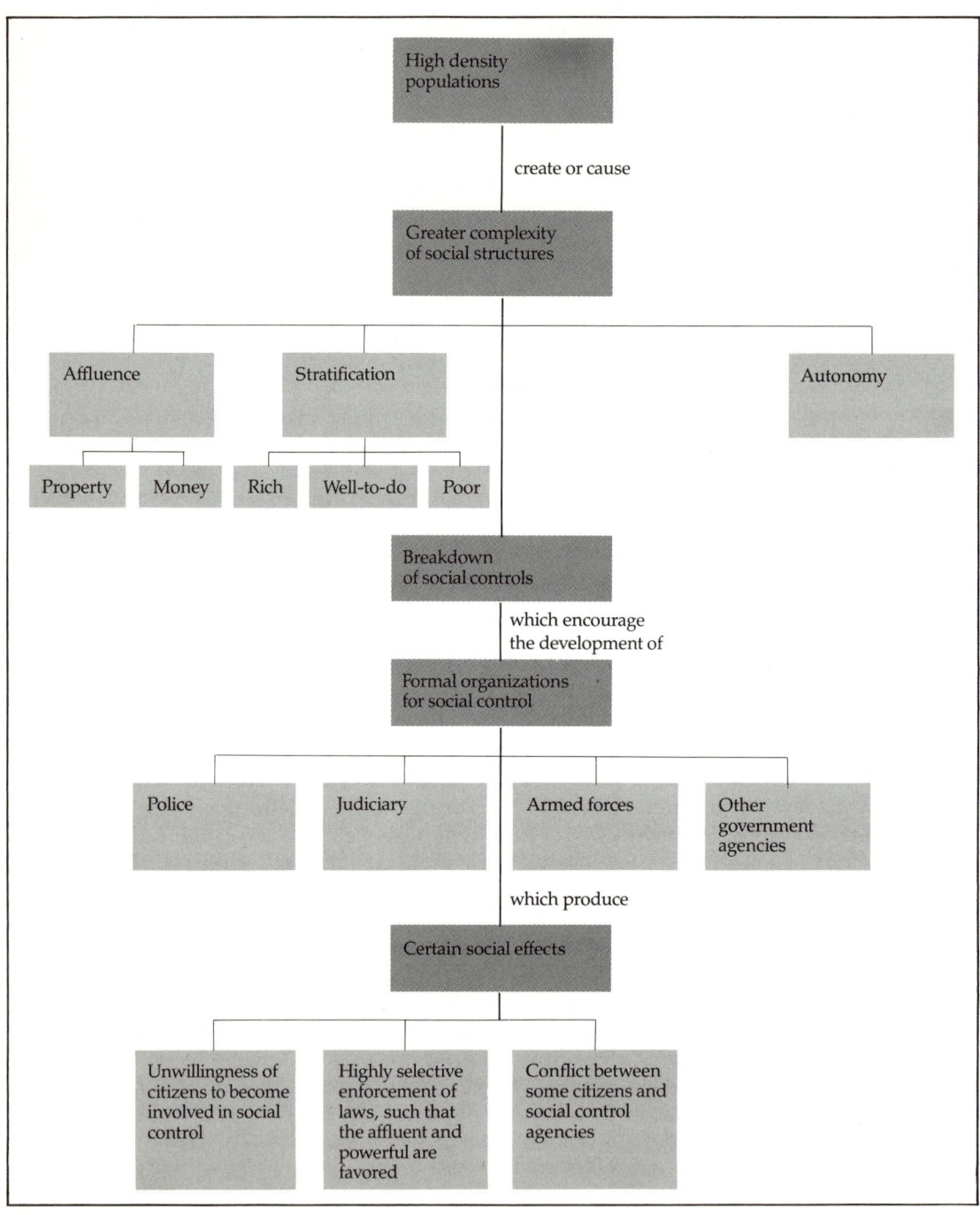

FIGURE 8.1 A Paradigm of the Effects of Population Growth on Crime and Justice

Summary

This brief historical overview should make it clear that modern police developed slowly and haphazardly (see Figure 8.1 for a schematic view of how this development occurred). The discussion should also make clear a major failing of the police, as they are constituted. The American criminal justice system is not directly oriented toward crime prevention. Like the early police forces in Paris and Munich, the primary thrust is toward detection, apprehension, and punishment of crime to act as a deterrent to future crime. The idea is that swift detection and trial and suitable punishment will influence people not to commit crime. But while the idea has been around for centuries, we have no way of knowing whether or not it would work. It has never been tried on a large scale. As we will see, crime is not always detected or reported; criminals are not brought swiftly to justice; and punishment is hardly suitable, but varies with the social status and affluence of the accused.

OBJECTIVE DIMENSIONS OF THE PROBLEM

The objective dimensions of crime and justice are many and complex. To describe them in detail would require many volumes. Our purpose here is not to cite all the dimensions of crime and justice but to provide the information needed to reach a general understanding of how the criminal justice system functions and why it functions as it does. We will begin by discussing estimates of the extent of crime, then discuss how lawbreakers are treated in the criminal justice system, and finally try to explain why they are treated that way.

How Much Crime?

How much crime is there in the United States? Unfortunately, we do not know. Equally unfortunately, we think we do. For many years we have relied on the *Uniform Crime Reports,* published annually by the FBI, which contain data on the number of crimes reported by the police and the number of arrests made. There are other sources of information on crime, which are probably more accurate, but these are largely unknown to the general public and, more significantly, unknown or ignored by the mass media. The result is that the figures we know come from the *Uniform Crime Reports;* those are the data the mass media report; those are the data used to tell us how serious crime is in this country. Let us see how reliable the FBI reports are.

THE UNIFORM CRIME REPORTS

The annual issuance of the *Uniform Crime Reports* generally causes alarm. On a superficial level, there appears to be some basis for this alarm. As Figure 8.2 shows, the number of arrests has risen steadily in this country since 1960, reaching a total of 9,029,335 in 1977. In other words, arrests have increased 221 percent in eighteen years. This enormous jump makes it appear that people are becoming increasingly lawless.

In years when the number of arrests increased, the mass media have given these changes the widest possible publicity. Politicians, understandably eager for campaign issues, have not hesitated to leap on the bandwagon and come out foursquare against crime. Ironically, crime was emphasized in the 1968 and 1972 campaigns of Richard Nixon, who was forced to resign because of White House crimes. But what these media reports ignore is a joker in the FBI data. The FBI data contain two bits of information that

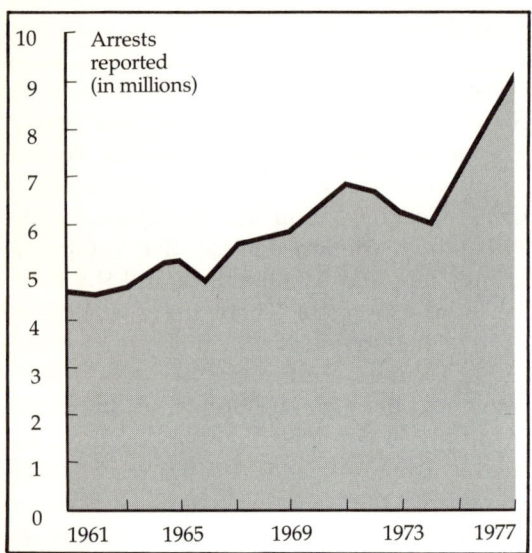

FIGURE 8.2 Arrests Reported to the FBI, 1960–1977

Source: Adapted from Federal Bureau of Investigation, *Uniform Crime Reports: Crime in the United States, 1960* through *Uniform Crime Reports: Crime in the United States, 1977* (Washington, D.C.: U.S. Government Printing Office, 1961–1978).

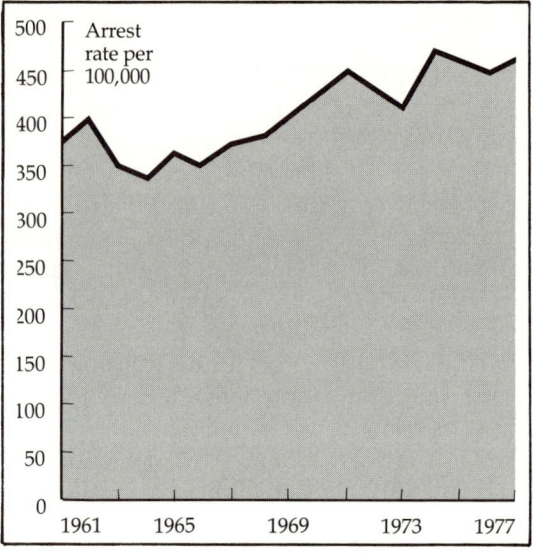

FIGURE 8.3 Arrest Rate Per 100,000 Population as Reported to the FBI, 1960–1977

Source: Adapted from Federal Bureau of Investigation, *Uniform Crime Reports: Crime in the United States, 1960* through *Uniform Crime Reports: Crime in the United States, 1977* (Washington, D.C.: U.S. Government Printing Office, 1961–1978).

should have been considered: (a) the number of agencies sending in arrest data to the FBI; and (b) the total population of those areas with agencies reporting data. The greater the number of reporting agencies and the larger the population concerned, the more arrests will be reported. In fact, this is the case.

A more reliable statistic is obtained by holding these figures constant, by calculating the *arrest rate*, or number of arrests per 100,000 people. As we can see in Figure 8.3, a different picture is revealed. The arrest rate went up, but it was a small rise. The 1977 arrest rate was 460.1, contrasted with 383.4 in 1960. This increase — just 18 percent — is a far cry from the increase in total arrests of 221 percent.

But does even this increase mean that there is greater lawlessness in this country? We have no way of knowing. The only thing that arrest data tell us is the number of persons actually arrested. We must turn to other sources of information to determine the number of crimes committed.

SELF-REPORTS AND
VICTIMIZATION STUDIES

A serious weakness of the *Uniform Crime Reports* is that they provide us with no information on the successful criminal, the one who isn't caught. Who are these persons? The best answer is that this category includes most of us, as is made clear by *self-report* studies. These studies consist of questionnaires asking respondents to check off on a list those crimes that they have committed. These studies have found that crime is very prevalent. The National Council on Crime and Delinquency reports that "a large number of self-report studies conclude that close to 100 percent of all persons have committed some kind of offense, although few have been arrested."[16]

Victimization studies also supplement official crime data by trying to determine how much crime is unreported to the police. One elaborate study of eight cities was conducted by the Criminal Justice Research Center in 1972. Between ten and twelve thousand households were selected in each city by the Bureau of the Census. Within each household, interviews were attempted with all persons fourteen years of age and older. In addition, information about persons twelve and thirteen years old was gotten "by having a knowledgeable household member answer questions for these respondents."[17] The magnitude of this survey can be appreciated in this fact: some 21,000 interviews were conducted in each of the eight cities, totalling approximately 168,000 interviews. We can have some confidence, therefore, that the number of unreported crimes is at least as high as shown in this study, with some allowance for respondents' forgetting a crime or being reluctant to tell of one.

The results are about what would be expected. Very high numbers of offenses of various kinds were never reported to the police. Table 8.1 shows a comparison between the data collected by the survey and the data contained in the *Uniform Crime Reports*. Except for vehicle theft, which is generally well reported, there is a considerable discrepancy for several types of crime. The actual incidence of many crimes is considerably higher than the FBI data indicate.

Self-report and victimization surveys allow us to draw only one conclusion about the amount of crime in the United States. It is at least two-and-one-half times higher than the data in the *Annual Crime Reports* show. This is not the fault of the FBI. Their data are dependent on the cooperation of reporting agencies. Of course, this is not the fault of local police either. Their data are dependent on citizens reporting crimes committed against them. As we have seen, citizen cooperation is far from total.

The Criminal Justice System

The *criminal justice system* of the United States, the complex of institutions and agents from police to courts to prisons, is marked by a high degree of selectivity. Despite considerable emphasis on the rights of the individual, accused individuals have sometimes had no rights at all. It is possible for accused persons to languish in prison for years without even a formal hearing, much less a trial. Law enforcement officials have evaded constitutional protections to behave in arbitrary and capricious ways and to ride roughshod over the rights of private citizens. Even when the system acts in accordance with these protections, it often turns out that people are wrongfully and illegally treated.

The most serious problem with the system arises from its great complexity and from the discretion given those who are a part of it. At each step of the complex process, those enforcing or administering the law are able to choose whether they will do so and with what degree of severity. The discretion that ideally grants flexibility has deteriorated to a selectivity that continually favors the privileged and punishes those without influence. We will examine the criminal justice system,

TABLE 8.1 Comparing Results from Victimization Study and the *Uniform Crime Reports* on Crime in Eight Cities

Crime	Uniform Crime Reports	Victimization Study	Ratio of Victim Survey to Uniform Crime Reports
Rape	3,090	6,340[a]	2.05
Aggravated assault	24,095	49,580	2.06
Robbery	34,274	76,502[b]	2.23
Burglary	119,984	325,581[c]	2.71
Larceny	161,799	487,870[d]	3.02
Vehicle theft	65,966	65,690	1.00

[a]Excludes male rapes.
[b]Includes personal and commercial robbery.
[c]Includes household and commercial burglary.
[d]Includes personal and household larceny.

Sources: Adapted from Criminal Justice Research Center, "An Analysis of Victimization Survey Results From the Eight Impact Cities: Summary Report," (1974), p. 102; and Federal Bureau of Investigation, *Uniform Crime Reports: Crime in the United States* (Washington, D.C.: U.S. Government Printing Office, 1972), Table 76.

from its beginning in the commission of a crime to its end result in the punishment of the criminal.

A CRIME IS COMMITTED

Between the commission of a crime and the first appearance in court, the offender has four possible escapes from the criminal justice system. As we know, a great many crimes go unreported or undetected, meaning that the first point of escape is when the crime remains unknown to the authorities. The second comes with police failure or inability to apprehend the criminal. Once a crime is reported or otherwise detected, much depends on such circumstances as the skill of the police and the availability of witnesses. If there is reasonable evidence pointing to a suspect, the police obtain a warrant and attempt to arrest those concerned. But if no evidence can be found or the warrant cannot be served, no arrest is made.

The third escape may occur when police apprehend the criminal. They have the discretionary authority to either make an arrest or release the individual. There are many reasons for police to do the latter, but probably the most significant is that the police sometimes determine that making an arrest would harm the offender more than it would benefit society. This decision is generally based on the offender's status (age or occupation) and is most common in nonstreet crimes such as shoplifting. The police may decide that, rather than suffering arrest and trial, a teenage shoplifter would be better deterred from further shoplifting by a warning. The importance of this discretion is that the decision to release the offender is rarely made in favor of "those segments of society stereotypically linked with serious crime, the poor and the relatively powerless."[18] Just as the Code of Hammurabi gave different punishments according to social status, and just as a professional police force was originally established to protect middle-class interests, so do modern police treat criminals differently according to class.

Finally, even persons once they are arrested can escape a court appearance. Under further questioning, or with the receipt of new evidence, the police may decide that the suspect is innocent. If so, he is released. If not, if the evidence points toward guilt, the suspect is *booked*, or formally charged with a crime.

THE JUDICIAL SYSTEM

Once arrested and booked, a suspect must be brought within a reasonable time to a magistrate for an *initial appearance* and for setting of bail. At this appearance there is another opportunity for escape from the system. The prosecution, which handles the case at this point, can drop the charges or the judge can dismiss them, for instance, because the police used illegal procedures to apprehend the criminal or gather evidence. If the charges are not dropped and the offender is charged with a minor offense — traffic violation or public drunkenness — he can plead guilty and receive the sentence, usually a fine. For more serious crimes, a guilty plea is not allowed at this point. Instead, the judge sets the amount of *bail*. If the suspect can pay this amount, she can return to her normal activities, although she will still have to face the remaining steps of the system, including possibly a trial. If the suspect cannot pay this bail, she will be kept by the police under pretrial detention. Again, the system works to the detriment of the underprivileged, who cannot raise the money to pay the bail. It is not essential for them to pay the full amount. They could resort to a bail bondsman, who pays the court the bail amount on receipt of 10 to 20 percent of the amount from the suspect. But even this smaller amount is difficult for the underprivileged to raise, and the result is that many remain in the custody of the police.[19]

In some areas, some suspects are caught up in what is called a *pretrial intervention program*. These programs involve a period of time, usually ninety days, in which the suspect is studied by paid workers and volunteers and participates in mutual efforts to work out his or her problems. At the conclusion of the ninety-day period, the counselor in charge of a case may make several recommendations, ranging from dismissal of the charges to the return of the accused to regular court proceedings.[20]

Once held for trial, the defendant then faces a grand jury. Grand juries do not attempt to determine guilt or innocence, but only whether or not there is sufficient evidence to bring a person to trial. "Grand juries were intended to allow the defendant to avoid a public accusation and the trouble and expense of a public trial before establishing the likelihood of his having committed a crime. They were also intended to prevent hasty, oppressive, and malicious prosecutions."[21] If the grand jury returns what is called a true bill it indicts the suspect of the crime. If it decides that the evidence is not sufficient, the defendant may be released, although the prosecution may decide to press a lesser charge.

At this point, the defendant appears before a judge to make his plea. If he pleads guilty, the judge sets a date for sentencing; if not guilty, she sets a date for trial. The judge has to accept a not guilty plea, but can reject a guilty plea. If, for instance, the judge feels that the defendant received bad advice from counsel in making this plea, she can reject it and send the case to trial. Prior to coming to trial, a defendant may engage in *plea bargaining*. This means that the defendant agrees to plead guilty in exchange for the prosecutor reducing the original charge to a lesser one, presumably carrying a lighter sentence.

There are many advantages to plea bargaining for both defendants and the judicial system, at least ideally. For the guilty individual facing a mass of evidence, plea bargaining affords an opportunity to get off with a lighter sentence. For the judicial system, the time, effort, and expense of a public trial is avoided. Then too, public prosecutors are judged on their scores, that is, the number of convictions they obtain, and a plea of guilty counts as a conviction. Reflecting this perception of the advantages of plea bargaining is a startling fact: the overwhelming majority of defendants never go to trial. Around 90 percent of all criminal convictions result from guilty pleas.[22] While not all are the result of plea bargaining, most assuredly are.

There are many objections to plea bargaining, however. The *Harvard Law Review* notes that "plea bargaining nullifies constitutional guarantees for a substantial number of criminal defendants, yet it is a key element of the existing criminal justice bureaucracy."[23] Defendants automatically deprive themselves of the possibility, however slight, that they might be judged not guilty. Even more serious, from the standpoint of the accused, is the fact that "many offenders plead guilty to charges out of fear of conviction for greater offenses, when in fact no charges could be sustained."[24]

In spite of criticism, the judicial system defends plea bargaining. There are sound reasons for this, some not without considerable self-interest. If plea bargaining is done away with, the burden on the courts and public prosecutors would be unbearable. Unless hundreds, perhaps thousands, of new judgeships were established and public prosecutor staffs vastly augmented, defendants would necessarily be deprived of the right to a speedy trial. The right to a speedy trial has been reinforced by both law and court decisions. When a trial is unnecessarily delayed, a defendant may and can be released because the prosecution has not afforded the accused a trial within a reasonable period of time.

A defendant who does not plea bargain faces trial and can benefit from the next possible escape: a verdict of not guilty. When a person is found guilty or pleads guilty, he has to undergo sentencing. The judge can sentence the guilty person to go to prison or pay a fine. Or the sentence can be suspended if the judge determines (like the police in releasing someone they arrested) that a sentence would harm the defendant more than is necessary.

Whatever the decision, the judge does not act alone in making it. In some jurisdictions, the jury recommends or even sets the penalty although, for the most part, it is the judge's concern. But the decision is made with the help of others. There is often a presentencing investigation, in which the probation department analyzes the accused's social background and other relevant factors, including the state of physical and mental health, and then makes its recommendation to the trial judge. In some states, sentences are set by law, although most simply stipulate minimums and maximums, allowing judges wide discretion.

Numerous studies demonstrate that judges vary widely in terms of the sentences handed down for the same or highly similar offenses.[25] As criminologist Richard Quinney has observed:

> The criminal sanctions that are ultimately imposed on the convicted defendant are influenced by such extralegal factors as the personalities of the judges who assign the sentences,

the norms that regulate sentencing, the judiciary's social organization, the attorney's activities, the responses and cues provided by the defendant, and the socioeconomic and racial characteristics of the defendant.[26]

None of these factors has anything to do with justice, as such. But these are very much the realities of crime and punishment here and elsewhere. Selectivity and variability of recommended punishment even differs widely with respect to probation officers. In a study of nineteen such officials, recommendations of probation varied from a high of nearly 89 percent of all cases to a low of 40 percent for the same or similar offenses.[27]

Those who are convicted have not exhausted all avenues of escape from the criminal justice system. They can appeal their case to a higher court. The vast majority of appeals are based on legal technicalities. If a defendant has a competent attorney, there is almost always the possibility of that attorney detecting a technical error made by the police or prosecution sometime between arrest and conviction. A higher court can almost always find some grounds for reversing a lower court decision.[28] Those already in prison also have the right of appeal. In the past, such appeals were based on what happened prior to incarceration. But, in very recent years, the right of appeal has come to include treatment in prison. In a celebrated decision, *Mempa* v. *Rhay* in 1969, the Supreme Court gave prisoners the right to counsel in probation revocation hearings and opened the possibility of appeals based on rights in prison.[29]

Appeals are also useful in other ways. For instance, filing an appeal delays execution of the sentence pending the appeal's outcome. Those with considerable resources are thus enabled to avoid going to prison for very long periods of time. Again, selectivity works against the underprivileged. To be able to make an effective appeal with a highly skilled lawyer requires much time and money, which the poor do not have.

Figure 8.4 recapitulates the judicial process, showing the ten points whereby a person can escape punishment. On the basis of this model, it would generally seem poor strategy for a defendant to plead guilty unless the evidence is overwhelmingly against him. A plea of guilty automatically eliminates half of the possible escape routes. As we will see, the selectivity of the criminal justice system has meant that a disproportionate number of those punished come from the lower classes.

PRISONS

Imprisonment is meant to have four separate but related functions: (1) protection of the

These inmates exercising in a prison courtyard certainly suffer the isolation and punishment that imprisonment is supposed to impose. It is questionable, though, whether their detention deters them from returning to criminal behavior or rehabilitates them for successful reentry into society.

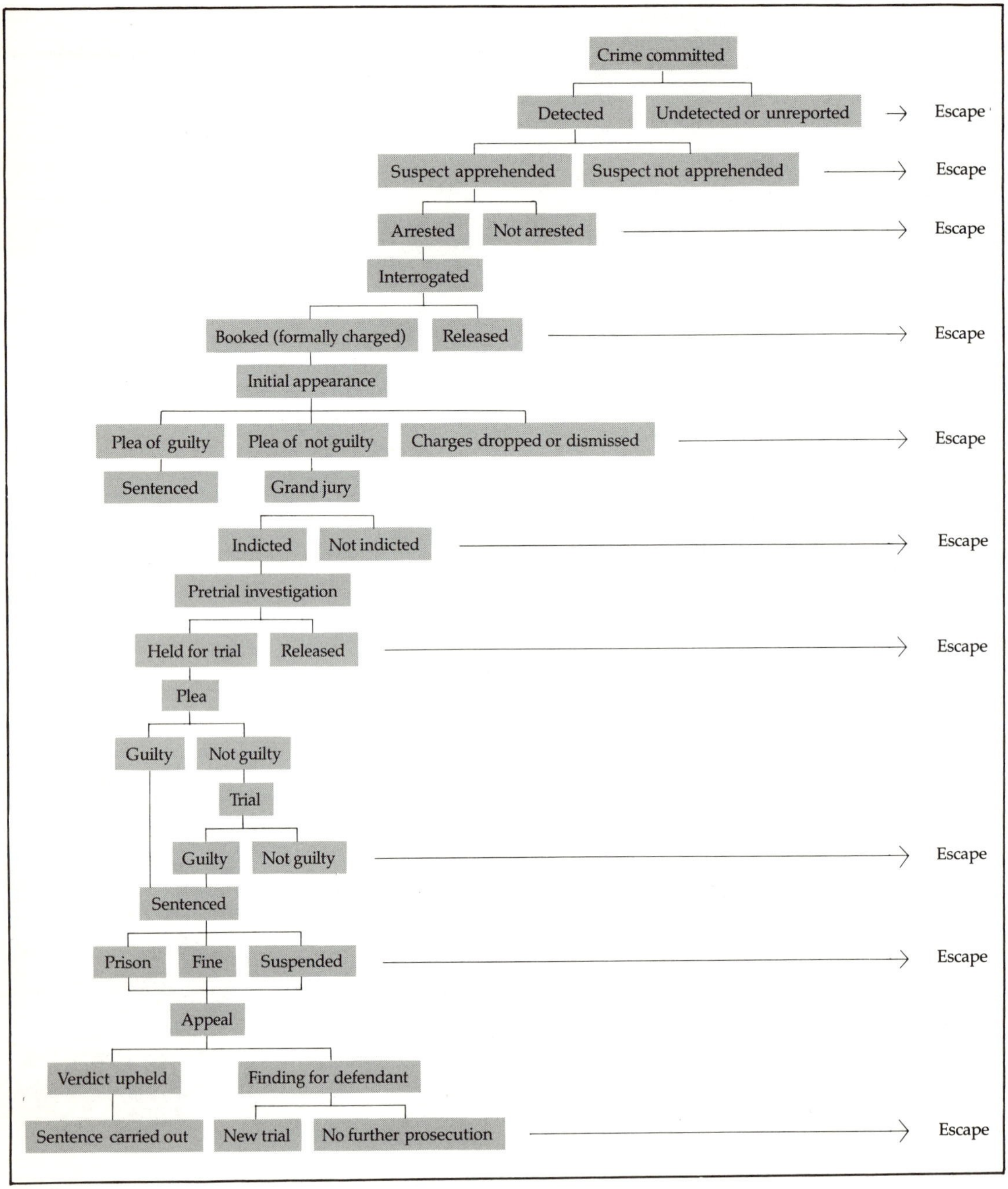

256 CRIME AND JUSTICE: *Lawbreakers in a Flawed System*

FIGURE 8.4 The Criminal Justice System and Points of Escape

public from lawless or dangerous persons, (2) punishment of the guilty, (3) deterrence from further crime, and (4) rehabilitation of criminals. Of these four, only the first two are met to any appreciable degree. The deterrent effect of prisons is difficult to estimate. Assuredly anyone who has spent time in a jail or a prison would hardly wish to return, yet many do return. Lumping all criminals together results in prisons serving as a school for crime. And as we mentioned earlier, once out of prison, ex-convicts often find other opportunities closed to them and feel that crime is the only thing they can turn to. As for rehabilitation, American prisons have accomplished little.

The selective nature of the criminal justice system is clearly evidenced by the characteristics of persons in prisons. Black persons, the young, the poorly educated, and the poor are heavily over-represented in the prison population, as Table 8.2 shows. Blacks comprise about 11.5 percent of the U.S. population but 46 percent of those in state prisons are black. More than half of the prison population did not graduate from high school and about the same proportion had incomes below the current poverty line.

The reasons for this imbalance are plain. The young, the black, the poorly educated, and the poor have inadequate resources, including knowledge for dealing successfully with the system. The poor and less well educated are also more likely to be involved in crimes of violence, which increases the probability of a prison sentence, and a severe one at that. There is strong middle-class disapproval of such crimes and, because the criminal justice system is run largely by persons from the middle class, those who commit such crimes are treated less leniently than crimes not involving violence.

TABLE 8.2 Demographic Characteristics of Inmates of State Correctional Facilities, 1974

Characteristics	Number of Inmates	Percent of Inmates
Race		
White	97,700	51
Black	89,700	47
Other	3,400	2
Not reported	600	—[a]
Age		
Under 18	1,800	1
18	5,500	3
19	7,900	3
20–24	57,100	30
25–29	44,900	23
30–34	27,300	14
35–39	16,300	9
40–49	19,600	10
50 and over	10,300	5
Not reported	600	—[a]
Education		
Eight grade or less	49,000	26
1–3 years high school	65,900	35
High school	52,200	28
1–3 years college	14,300	8
4 years or more of college	1,500	1
Not reported	4,700	2
Personal income prior to arrest		
Less than $2,000	32,400	19
$2,000–$3,999	30,700	18
$4,000–$5,999	30,400	18
$6,000–$9,999	29,900	18
$10,000 or more	23,000	14
Not reported	1,800	1

[a]Less than 0.05 percent.

Source: Adapted from Michael R. Gottfredson, et al., *Sourcebook of Criminal Justice Statistics 1977 United States* (Washington, D.C.: National Criminal Justice Information and Statistics Service, 1977), p. 616.

Black convicts argue that they are political prisoners. This is not entirely correct in the sense that the term usually means — they are not imprisoned for their political views. In another sense, however, it is true. Most poor people, including blacks, are imprisoned because they were convicted of committing crimes and because they lacked the resources to capitalize on one or more of the escape routes from the system. It is also true because they lack political power.

Political Aspects of Crime

All crime is political. Crime is defined as a violation of a law or laws and laws are made by political bodies. Also, the criminal justice system is under political control. Paul Tappan, a sociologist, maintains that an individual is a criminal only because his behavior has been legally defined as criminal. Tappan holds that "only those are criminals who have been adjudicated as such by the courts."[30] Tappan's contention appears to fly in the face of common sense; surely any person who violates a law is a criminal. But if this were true, virtually all adults would be criminals in the technical sense. Remember the distinction we made earlier between lawbreakers and criminals. Nearly all states have laws against fornication, or sexual intercourse between two people not married. But as a small-scale study showed (see Table 8.3), more than 75 percent of our young people would be classed as criminals if breaking these laws were the sole criterion for acquiring the label of criminal.

Sociologically speaking, what is significant about committing a crime and getting caught is the application of the label of criminal. This is not to say that anyone who commits a crime and escapes detection does not or may not suffer some unpleasant consequences. British novelist W. Somerset Maugham wrote: "Conscience is the guardian in the individual of the rules which the community has evolved for its own preservation."[31] That is, we know when we have done wrong and we punish ourselves.

THE POLITICS OF MAKING LAWS

Ideally, elected officials, including legislators, are servants of the people. All should be responsive to the wishes of the public. But do these ideals apply in the real political arena? The answer is no. The primary allegiance of many elected officials is to themselves; their focus is on getting reelected. This means that most public officials are particularly sensitive to the opinions and wishes

TABLE 8.3 The Incidence of Fornication: Technical Sexual Crime

First Intercourse with	Males[a]	Females[a]
Prostitute or casual pickup	14.1	0.9
Casual date	18.2	2.7
Friend	13.2	7.3
Steady date	32.2	49.1
Engaged partner	2.5	7.3
Spouse[b]	10.6	23.3
Other	1.6	0.9
No sexual experience[c]	23.0	19.4

[a]There were 121 male and 110 female respondents in this study.
[b]Based on married or previously married respondents' replies only.
[c]Based on single respondents' replies only.

Source: Adapted from Cheryl Gilland, Kathy Fanning, William Brown, and Thomas Tichnor, "Sexual Attitudes and Behavior of Social Science Students." A paper presented at the Seventh Annual Alpha Kappa Delta Sociology and Research Symposium, 1976.

of those who are in a position to further their careers. This means that the rich and powerful have a good chance of influencing political action, including the passage of legislation. But organization is another factor to which politicians are sensitive and responsive.

A prime example of the effectiveness of organization is the passage of the Eighteenth Amendment to the Constitution, which was law from 1919 until its repeal in 1933. As we discussed in Chapter 1, the Eighteenth Amendment enacted prohibition, making it illegal to manufacture, sell, import, or export intoxicating liquors. Was this constitutional amendment really the will of the people? Judging from the consequences it was not. The law proved unenforceable. It created millions of technical criminals; demonstrated that a billion-dollar-a-year industry could flourish outside the law; engendered a general contempt for the law; and served to corrupt agents and agencies of law enforcement. Despite the unpopularity of the law, it had been passed. That, as we've discussed, was due to the power of organization.

Of course not all laws passed are a matter of group pressures. Many laws have a large proportion of citizens supporting them. Laws against murder, rape, burglary, and larceny are hardly unpopular. What is significant is that even these agreed-upon laws are not enforced equally.

THE POLITICS OF ENFORCING LAWS
We have pointed out that the criminal justice system operates selectively. The police do not and cannot fearlessly and without favor enforce the law against all citizens. First, there are practical reasons: there are too many lawbreakers and not enough police. But what would happen if that problem was removed and the police ceased being selective and started doing what they are supposed to do? The answer was revealed in Chicago in September of 1972.

A group of dedicated police officers went on what the newspapers called a "ticket blitz." Instead of following the informal norms, that is, enforcing the law selectively, this small group of police officers began plastering tickets on the cars of all violators — including the Cadillac of an alderman. The alderman decried their actions as "crucifying the people of Chicago." An unbelievable wave of protest arose, including outraged protests from most of the local police organizations. Informally, the superintendent of police promised to discipline officers guilty of writing too many tickets. The crusading officers quickly yielded to the pressure and the ticket blitz came to an end after only four days.[32]

Being a police officer is not easy. He or she must not only know the law, but when to enforce it. Under pressure from those who make the laws and the voters who elected them, the police are compelled to focus on enforcing certain kinds of laws. They concentrate on such major crimes as property crimes — burglary and theft — and interpersonal violence — murder, mugging, and rape. This is not to say that these crimes are not serious; they unquestionably are. However, it is also true that such crimes, particularly property crimes, are most often committed by lower-class people and often take from middle-class and upper-class people. To protect their interests, the middle class — which supports the politicians who control the police — ensures that the crimes against it are prosecuted. Remember the point we made earlier about white-collar crime, the economic crimes primarily committed by people

White-collar crimes are usually economic crimes committed by upper status individuals who are seldom detected, rarely prosecuted, and even more rarely convicted. White-collar crimes may also be political crimes whose victim is society at large. The Watergate scandal was the 1970s ultimate symbol of white-collar crime and still stings our memory.

with higher status. These crimes are often not prosecuted and when they are, the criminals suffer less than lower-class criminals: "The penalties assigned by law to predominantly lower-class crimes (robbery, burglary, assault, heroin pushing) are in general higher than those for predominantly upper-class crimes (corporate fraud, misrepresentation in advertising, restraint of trade, environmental crimes)."[33]

Summary

When he wrote the draft for the Massachusetts Constitution, John Adams stated the ideal: "A government of laws, and not of men." The idea underlying Adams's words is that humans are given to prejudice, misjudgment, and self-interest rather than objectivity and justice. A government of laws would be absolutely impartial; free from the adverse effects of human emotions and thus administered equitably to all those coming before the bar of justice. As we have seen, however, a government of laws does not exist in this country. The criminal justice system treats criminals differently, from the definition of crimes to the punishment for them. This is true because the criminal justice system is controlled by those with political power, the middle and upper class, who use the system to maintain their power.

ATTEMPTS AT DEALING WITH THE PROBLEM

Down through the ages, people have wondered why it is that some men and women do not obey laws. Answering that question, and the related one of what to do with those who commit crimes, have troubled many for millenia. Today, while the focus of the criminal justice system is on what to do after crimes are committed, there is increasing interest in the question of how to prevent crime. To be able to prevent crime, our society must answer that age-old question, what causes crime?

In this section, we will consider three classes of theories about the origin of crime. All efforts to deal specifically, efficiently, and concretely with crime and justice rest on one of these theories or a combination of them.

These three theoretical approaches are biological, psychological, and sociological. These theories have profound implications for the administration of the criminal justice system.

Biological Theories

Do some of us inherit tendencies toward criminality? Is there any relationship between one's general body build and the likelihood that one will be involved in criminal acts? These questions have aroused the interest of many persons and are still widely believed to be of importance.

ATAVISM AND CESARE LOMBROSO
In a famous work, *L'uomo delinquente* (*The Human Criminal*), a three-volume exposition running into five editions, Cesare Lombroso (1835–1909) set forth his concept of *atavism,* or a throwback to an earlier evolutionary state. Lombroso believed that he had detected among criminal populations a preponderance of individuals who represented throwbacks to earlier forms of our species. Lombroso wrote of certain signs of degeneracy, such as a low sloping forehead, snaggly teeth, a receding chin, and protruding ears, painting a picture of a creature like such early humans as Neanderthal.

Lombroso's hypothesis about atavism was largely subjective, however, and certainly highly speculative. His ideas were largely negated by the work of Charles Goring, an English physician who did a reasonably scientific study of a large sample of both criminals and noncriminals. Goring concluded that there was "no such thing as a physical criminal type."[34]

If Lombroso's conclusions had turned out to be accurate, they would have raised serious problems for law enforcement and justice. If criminals were born and not made, they could not be held responsible for their actions. By the same token, they could not be expected to behave any other way. It would be expedient to lock up those persons possessing those physical characteristics even though they had committed no crimes.

Most people today recognize that Lombroso's ideas lacked scientific foundation. But old ideas die slowly. Some thirty years after Lombroso's death, Ernest Hooton, an anthropologist, performed a study and published findings that seemed to support Lombroso. It was Hooton's conclusion that people of different body types tended to commit different types of crimes. For example, he said that short heavy men are more likely to engage in sex crimes.[35] Hooton's work caused a brief flurry, but it quickly subsided when others pointed out serious flaws in his research, including his selection of samples.

SOMATOTYPES

Psychologist William H. Sheldon and his associates performed a very elaborate and sophisticated study attempting to relate personality characteristics to three distinct *somatotypes,* or body types: (a) the *endomorph,* round, plump, and showing a predominance of fatty tissue; (b) the *mesomorph,* well-built, strong, and muscular; and (c) the *ectomorph,* lean, thin, and fragile. Sheldon and his associates concluded that the mesomorphic body type predisposed youths to delinquency.[36]

Later research by Sheldon and Eleanor Glueck appeared to support Sheldon's findings. Using an experimental group of 500 delinquents and a control group of 500 nondelinquents, the Gluecks found a correlation between mesomorphic body build and the incidence of delinquency. But correlation does not necessarily mean causation and the Gluecks recognized this. Instead, they noted the possibility that a mesomorphic body build may predispose a person to delinquency: "We would expect mesomorphs to have a higher 'delinquency potential' for the same reason we would expect them to have a higher 'high school athletic potential.'"[37] That is, mesomorphs would be more likely to be found among delinquents because the body type gives them greater strength and agility, which can be important for some delinquent behavior.

THE EXTRA Y CHROMOSOME

Over a decade ago, excitement was generated by the discovery that some males have an extra Y chromosome, producing an XYY pattern instead of the usual XY combination. Because several persons accused of serious and brutal crimes were found to have this combination, it was believed that some serious crimes could be explained by genetics.

Is there any real substance to this notion? Frankly, we do not know. In order to draw any scientific conclusions, it would be imperative to determine two things: (a) the incidence of the XYY pattern among both criminal and noncriminal male populations; and (b) the linkage between genetic abnormalities and human behavior. Until these two conditions are met, it is necessary to withhold judgment about the relationship between criminal behavior and XYY chromosomes.

Psychological Theories

There are many psychological theories of criminality. Some of these show intuitive promise; they seem to make sense. Those which direct the focus of their attention on the individual, however, all suffer from a practical problem: they require enormous resources in the form of trained therapists to solve the problems of crime and delinquency. A further difficulty is that many of these theories rest on relatively few cases, which do not represent anything like an adequate random sample of the criminal population. In addition, they do not have adequate controls. But one set of theories rests on a scientific basis and has considerable practical applications for human behavior, both criminal and noncriminal. We are referring to *learning theory*.

LEARNING THEORY

Learning theory rests solidly on the concept of *reinforcement*, meaning the positive or negative consequences of behavior. When the consequences of an action are satisfying and rewarding, the behavior becomes learned and tends to be repeated. When the outcomes of behavior are painful and unpleasant, the behavior is learned but tends to be suppressed. If behavior is followed by no pattern of results, it is rarely learned at all.[38]

According to learning theory, since criminal behavior is followed by unpleasant consequences, it should be suppressed. Since humans are capable of thinking ahead in time and symbolically experiencing the effects of being detected and punished, learning can and does take place purely through symbolism. In other words, honest citizens tempted to commit a crime will be aware of the possible punishing consequences and not yield to temptation. This is the argument that punishment deters crime. Paul Tappan's analysis of the evidence leads him to believe that punishment does achieve a significant level of general deterrence. Further, Tappan contends that punishment of lawbreakers serves to buttress society's moral code, that is, it serves notice on citizens that the code is enforced and should be taken seriously.[39]

But as we have seen, detection, apprehension, and punishment are by no means certain. This fact leads to another concept having a bearing on crime and justice. Under the theory of deterrence, people would refrain from committing a crime to avoid punishment. Yet people do commit crimes. To explain why they do so, while they are aware of the risks, psychologists have coined the term *hedonistic calculus*. By this they mean that the potential criminal weighs the advantages of committing a crime against the disadvantages of being caught and convicted. He then decides whether or not to engage in the criminal behavior on the basis of relative advantages and disadvantages. If the possible gains from crime outweigh the possible risks, the crime may well be committed.

APPLYING LEARNING THEORY TO CRIME AND JUSTICE

Increasing the probabilities of being punished would improve deterrence. Currently, our flawed criminal justice system does not function with enough efficiency to maximize the deterrent effects of punishment. What would happen if our criminal justice system were suddenly to become completely efficient? The result would be that everyone, including those working in criminal justice, would wind up behind bars. The impossibility of this makes it manifest that the criminal justice system can never operate at a very high level of effectiveness, which means that from the standpoint of learning theory, our system can never provide maximum deterrence. Fortunately, learning theory works very well on another level.

Criminal justice systems are designed to exert direct social control over only a very small segment of our population. By far, the

greater part of social control is informal. First there is self-control — we all control ourselves to a considerable extent. Other potent controls are maintained by those around us — our family, our friends, and our close associates. Reinforcement, positive and negative, is constantly being applied to us by those with whom we are in close, continual contact. The praise and criticism we hear from others provide powerful incentives for socially approved behavior.

Furthermore, each of us applies positive and negative sanctions to ourselves. Of all the agents of social control, the human conscience is probably the most powerful and it functions in accordance with learning theory, that is, we reward and punish ourselves. What becomes important, then, is socialization. If society socializes its members well, their consciences — and informal control — will be in accordance with society's values and goals.

Sociological Theories

Sociological explanations of crime seek causes not within individuals but in factors external to individuals and outside their control.[40] As is the case with psychological theories, there are many sociological explanations that illuminate crime. Three particularly useful ones are the anomie concept of Robert K. Merton, the differential association theory of Edwin H. Sutherland, and the labeling theory of Howard S. Becker.

Learning theory contends that if a certain behavior is positively reinforced, it will be repeated for continual social approval. Children's toys, games, and television favorites are often cited as vehicles for reinforcing violence.

THE THEORY OF ANOMIE

The majority of Americans have internalized society's emphasis on the values of achievement and success. This particular value is constantly emphasized in many ways in the mass media. The boy gets the girl or vice versa; the hard-working person gets a well-deserved promotion and so on. Onward and upward is an enduring theme of American life. But what about the person who does not find the ordinary avenues of upward mobility and success open to her? And what of those who are not particularly motivated for the struggle or those who are turned off by society? Robert V. Merton explains what happens to them by pointing to the relationship between society's goals and the approved ways of attaining these goals.

Table 8.4 shows a model of Merton's theory of *anomie*, meaning a state in which social norms of conduct or belief are weak.

TABLE 8.4 Adaptation to Cultural Means and Goals

Method of Adaptation	Culturally Prescribed Goals	Culturally Prescribed Means
Conformist	Accepts	Accepts
Ritualist	Rejects or is unmotivated	Accepts
Innovator	Accepts	Rejects or finds unavailable
Retreatist	Rejects	Rejects
Rebel	Rejects but attempts to change	Rejects but attempts to change

Source: Drawn from Robert K. Merton, *Social Theory and Social Structure*, enl. ed. (New York: Free Press, 1968), Chapter 7.

Merton divides the members of society into five groups, according to how they react to society's goals and society's norms for achieving them.[41] To begin with, those who accept society's goals and use approved ways of attaining them are categorized as *conformists*. Such individuals are no problem for the criminal justice system.

Also not a problem are *ritualists*, people who have lost sight of or are uninterested in socially approved goals. But ritualists are like conformists because they follow culturally approved behavior. They simply go through the motions without really trying to reach goals. As the name implies, ritualists are obsessed with ritual. For example, they may attend church or synagogue services without ever really practicing the tenets of their religion. Because they behave conventionally for the most part, ritualists pose no particular problems for the criminal justice system.

Three of the groups Merton describes are problems for the criminal justice system, however. First are *innovators*, those people who desire socially acceptable goals but feel they are blocked from attaining them in acceptable ways. Because they are strongly motivated to achieve those goals they seek other means, which may be deviant. Whether or not the socially approved means are actually unavailable to innovators is a moot point. The important thing is that innovators believe that the acceptable pathways to success are not open to them. The pimp provides a good example of the innovator. Desiring the material rewards society defines as good, he resorts to the business of prostitution and makes his living off the earnings of a stable of prostitutes.

But this is not the only kind of innovator. Almost all of us fall into the innovator category from time to time. Circumstances arise to block us from a goal we desire. Under such circumstances, the temptation to behave deviantly is difficult to resist. For example, the NCAA has a number of rules regarding the recruitment of athletes for football and other intercollegiate sports. Strict adherence to these rules would make it difficult for a coach to obtain needed talent. Coaches, if they wish to remain employed, must win more games than they lose. The situation is such as to pressure them to become innovators, to "bend the rules," as we all call it. As the annual list of penalized colleges and universities indicates, much innovation goes on in coaching ranks.

Retreatists are epitomized by that phenomenon of the 1960s, hippies. Retreatists reject both society's goals and its means. Generally harmless and inoffensive, the hippies attempted to withdraw from society and lead their own lives. Retreatists can cause some problems of law and order, however. The hippies, for instance, broke social norms for drug use and sexual conduct.

Rebels are those who reject society's goals and attempt to change them. When they try to bring about changes by sanctioned means, they are not a particular source of trouble. But often they reject the means as well, advocating violent rebellion. Planting bombs or killing or wounding persons who represent (to the rebels at least) the government or society have been and will be used by such rebels as a means of affecting social change. Such persons represent a singular and difficult problem for law enforcement agencies.

DIFFERENTIAL ASSOCIATION THEORY

Formulated by Edwin H. Sutherland, *differential association theory* explains, in part, how individuals learn innovative ways rather than the socially approved means for attaining goals.[42] Recalling what we said about learning theory, imagine the results of individuals being placed in situations where they are likely to receive positive reinforcement for deviant behavior. Such situations are those where persons are in regular contact with delinquent or criminal subcultures. While criminal and noncriminal behavior are directed toward the same general goals — achievement, success, and affluence — the difference between criminals and noncriminals is that noncriminals generally associate with other noncriminals while criminals often learn their values and behaviors by associating with criminals.

Prison and reformatory systems are designed, unintentionally, to ensure that the kinds of learning that Sutherland describes will take place. Reformatories and prisons are schools for crime. Although there are some efforts to keep first offenders separated from so-called hardened criminals, prison overcrowding and budgetary limitations make such separation difficult to achieve in practice. This enforced association between first-time and multiple offenders helps to explain the high incidence of recidivism, of ex-convicts again committing crimes. As Table 8.5 shows, the amount of such behavior is significant.

Aside from being congruent with learning theory, differential association is consonant with what we know about other social processes, particularly socialization. Much of our everyday behavior, from eating habits to manner of dress, is learned through those who socialize us. It is not surprising then, that criminally innovative behaviors are acquired in the same fashion.

LABELING THEORY

Howard S. Becker's *labeling theory* has considerable application for most of us.[43] Becker distinguishes between primary and second-

TABLE 8.5 First and Repeat Offenders Among Inmates of State Correctional Facilities, 1974

Number of Sentences Served	Number of Inmates	Percent of Inmates
None (first offenders)	500	0.26%
1	55,700	29.0
2	43,900	23.0
3	36,000	19.0
4	23,800	12.0
5 or more	31,400	16.0
Total	191,400	

Source: Adapted from Michael R. Gottfredson et al., *Sourcebook of Criminal Justice Statistics 1977 United States* (Washington, D.C.: National Criminal Justice Information and Statistics Service, 1977), p. 620.

ary deviance. *Primary deviance* refers to occasional deviant behavior on the part of individuals who are generally conforming. *Secondary deviance* takes place when a deviant act is discovered by others and the individual concerned is given the label of deviant. Labeling theory does not tell us why people are deviant originally but explains what happens to them after they acquire the label of deviant. Not only are individuals punished formally by law but powerful informal punishments continue to be imposed on people after they have finished their sentences.

First, labeled individuals find themselves increasingly isolated from the conventional world. They experience difficulty in finding jobs, at least the better ones. It is not easy for them to make friends or cultivate a circle of informal social relationships among people who have not been labeled and even their families may abandon them. Thus, they are driven to seek associations with others who also bear the stigma of the deviant label. Denied access to socially acceptable ways of earning a living, they may and often do return to crime.

A primary effect of labeling is to organize various kinds of deviation. Certain bars and other social centers become known as hangouts for groups of labeled individuals. This puts stigmatized individuals in touch with one another and provides a network of informal relationships and communications that sets off labeled individuals from the rest of society, thus increasing deviant behavior. For example, information about local law enforcement and how to evade police attention is exchanged as well as such technical knowledge as how to commit successful burglaries or where to obtain weapons for holdups. The possibilities for increasing the efficiency of lawbreakers is considerable. It is ironic that this system is a creation of society.

Can a labeled individual rid himself of the stigma? Possibly, but it is much more difficult today than it was in the past. Upon arrest and booking, suspects are photographed and fingerprinted with copies sent to the FBI in Washington. Many jobs, particularly those in factories engaged in defense work, require security clearances before hiring, which involves a fingerprint check. The result is discovery of the prior arrest and no job. The chance of evading the discovery of a previous arrest or conviction is virtually nonexistent. Of course, the problem goes beyond such cases. Almost all employment application forms ask if the applicant has ever been arrested and convicted. The applicant can lie, but there is always the chance of detection, which can carry severe penalties. And credit bureau files often have information on individual arrests and convictions and many firms ask for credit checks prior to hiring an applicant. For these reasons, we can expect more individuals, rather than less, to be to some degree barred from conventional society and forced to seek not only social interaction but economic support among deviants and in deviant ways.

Iatrogenic Effects

Many solutions to crime have been attempted on the basis of the biological, psychological, and sociological theories just outlined. Among them, those based on biological theories are the most dangerous for they open the way to frightful abuses of power. On the surface links between biology and crime are attractive. Presumably if such correlations were fully established, we would be able to identify potential criminals and deal with them prior to their actually committing a crime. This might be done, initially at least, by separating them from the rest of the population. However, our principles of justice make this possibility unpalatable and unlikely to occur.

The other means of dealing with inherited criminal tendencies would be the institution of a program of *eugenics*, which would bring under state control the decision of who could or could not have children. But this possibility is totally unacceptable and goes against all our values on individual rights and freedom of choice. It also creates tremendous opportunities for the authorities to abuse their power. They would, of course, always decide in favor of themselves. In addition, they could deal with their enemies by denying them the right to have children. And this power could also be turned against entire social groups, being the most effective means of extinguishing a minority. It is clear that this solution cannot even be considered.

More satisfying and acceptable are psychological theories to explain the origin of crime. Of course here too we need to avoid those solutions that would entail psychological testing to locate potential criminals so they can be segregated. But there are other theories that are less distasteful. For instance, learning theory offers much in the way of dealing more successfully with crime. Some programs related to learning theory have been in operation for a long time, for example, the policy of granting *parole* or time off a prison sentence for good behavior. Extensions of this concept are represented by programs releasing convicts from prison to work and then returning to prisons in the evening and on weekends. Furloughs are also granted to persons in some systems as a reward for exemplary conduct. These programs are all based on learning principles because they use positive reinforcement to induce socially approved behavior.

But while these programs seem to benefit the person in prison, there is no question that they still suffer, that they are still subjected to the persecution resulting from labeling. First, we find that only the most exemplary behavior in prison will make someone eligible for such a program. Even justifiable complaints about inhuman conditions can cast the prisoner in an unfavorable light. Second, those prisoners in work release or furlough programs must suffer the adjustment from daily freedom to nightly control by others. Returning to prison after working outside must be difficult to bear.

But worse is the humiliation that those on parole must suffer. As we have discussed, as ex-convicts they will already have difficulty in finding a job. A greater problem is their lack of control over their own lives. All parolees must report regularly to their parole officer. In addition to this humiliating need to be checked on, parolees are not allowed to make personal decisions. They cannot move, choose their own friends, and have little privacy. The result is ironic: the parolee "has no effective control over his own life, and yet is required to demonstrate that he can in fact control his life. Rather than encourage the development of a favorable self-image, the conditions of parole often undermine the parolee's sense of worth, reduce his status in the eyes of those he cares about, and lock him into a condition of dependency."[44]

The sociological theories have also contributed to our understanding of crime, but solutions are more difficult. Anomie theory tells us that a good deal of deviant behavior and crime is a function of the social structure. Some efforts are being made to solve the problem by opening up conventional channels of upward mobility for the poor and underprivileged. But as we discussed in Chapter 5, these programs are not sufficiently wide in scope to have any appreciable effects. Indeed in looking over some current programs, it is not too cynical to state that they seem to work best in providing well-paying positions for the middle-class persons who run them. Any benefits to the clients are only incidental.

Solutions to the problem based on differential association are subject to many of the same objections as those based on biological theories. Society can restructure patterns of association, so that people do not learn to become innovators and first offenders do not learn to become repeaters. But doing so would entail a serious infringement of personal freedom. Indeed, we have just discussed such problems in connection with parole.

A very serious flaw in the criminal justice system is not so much the fault of the system as of the society. The treatment of those who have acquired the deviant label is self-defeating. The most disheartening aspect of this problem is the little that is being done to solve it. No programs of public education are being conducted to inculcate greater tolerance. No efforts are being made to change even the attitudes of those in authority. There are some employers who are willing to hire ex-convicts, but these are a scarce handful. Until that changes, crime will continue and for some people punishment will never end.

PROSPECTS FOR SOLVING THE PROBLEM

Crime and justice have undergone considerable changes, most of these relatively recently. When we look back only a century or two, when suspects could be imprisoned at the caprice of rulers or tortured to obtain confessions, it is apparent that justice has changed a good deal. It is also good for us to remember that these medieval practices continue in some nations today.

If justice has changed, so has crime. For example, the modern criminal who is part of organized crime is not too much different from his counterpart in conventional business. He serves customers for goods and services and expects to make a profit. And the activities of organized crime demonstrate that it is society that creates crime. Laws make illegal many goods and services that people want, inviting a certain class of entrepreneurs. For example, while Prohibition was the law, bootleggers flourished and made handsome profits. Similarly, dealers in narcotics today find their operations economically rewarding. It appears that marijuana will be decriminalized, decreasing by one the number of these crimes that do not conform to informal norms. But many others will still remain, and the enforcement of these laws — however sporadic — will still use up police time and resources that could benefit more being used elsewhere.

Economically, white-collar crime represents the greatest overall loss to citizens. Dealing with this kind of deviance, however, requires the most sophisticated kind of law enforcement, that is, people with considerable training in the law and in accounting and in technical skills. In 1979, the FBI announced that they were making increasing efforts to combat white-collar crime, but this is a formidable task. Those committing such illegal acts are almost invariably well educated and highly intelligent, possessing the skills, expertise, and knowledge to cover their tracks. More important, to combat this kind of crime effectively will require a change in society, that would view it more seriously.

Some crime is present at all times in all societies. Part of our problem, as we mentioned earlier, arises out of a continuing struggle to protect both the rights of victims and the rights of the accused. Given our value system, most of us would not wish to pursue any other course. But the result of this double pursuit appears to be that the prospects for any marked reduction of crime or more equitable justice are meager indeed.

IMPORTANT WORDS AND TERMS

anomie theory
arrest rate
atavism
autonomy
bail
betwixt and between laws
booked
Bow Street Runners
conformist
criminal
criminal justice system
deterrence
differential association theory
ectomorph
endomorph
eugenics
extra Y chromosome
hedonistic calculus
incest
informal norms
initial appearance
innovator
labeling theory
lawbreaker
learning theory
mesomorph
paramilitary
parole
plea bargaining
pretrial intervention
primary deviance
rebel
recidivism
reinforcement
retreatist
retributive justice
ritualist
secondary deviance
selectivity
self-report studies
social stratification
somatotypes
thief-takers
Uniform Crime Reports
victimization studies
victimless crimes
white-collar crime

QUESTIONS FOR DISCUSSION

1. Do you think parental permissiveness is an important cause of juvenile delinquency, or even adult crime? Why?
2. Do you think that the mass media ought to do more reporting of desirable behavior? Is this likely to happen? Why or why not?
3. Why is it so difficult to detect and legally prove cases of price-fixing?
4. As we know, advertisers sometimes exaggerate or lie about their products. Does such behavior on the part of respectable business people influence others to engage in criminal activities? Explain your answer.
5. If you were a police officer, would you attempt to enforce all laws rigorously and equally? Why or why not?

6. Police officials do not encourage private citizens to become involved in crime detection. Why?
7. The text maintains that the most important social control in our society is self-control. Do you agree? Why or why not?
8. Think carefully before answering this question. Virtually all states have laws against fornication. Since this particular kind of law cannot be enforced, every state should probably repeal their antifornication laws. Why don't they? To answer, put yourself in the place of a state legislator contemplating presenting a bill to repeal his state's antifornication law.
9. We appear to have quite a few betwixt and between laws. Can you think of some laws that do not fit this category? Be specific.
10. Whose interests are better served by plea bargaining — the accused's or the judiciary's? Why?
11. We know that the sentences judges hand down for the same or highly similar offenses vary greatly. What can or should be done about this?
12. Imagine that you are a twenty-year-old black male with less than a high school education coming from a family with an income well below the poverty line. You stole a car, were caught, and are now serving a prison sentence. Make a case that you are a political prisoner.
13. Explain how a college student might use the hedonistic calculus in attempting to decide whether or not to cheat on a test for which she is woefully unprepared.
14. Can differential association theory be used to explain white-collar crime? How?
15. If a person has been busted for marijuana possession, should he lie about having been arrested when applying for employment? Why or why not?

SUGGESTED READING

A REPORT BY THE PRESIDENT'S COMMISSION ON LAW ENFORCEMENT AND ADMINISTRATION OF JUSTICE, *The Challenge of Crime in a Free Society* (Washington, D.C.: U.S. Government Printing Office, 1967).

Government documents often make heavy reading but this particular publication is different. Although it has some deficiencies — one of which is that it is now somewhat out of date — it remains an important statement on crime in our society. In many ways, it is a total social document. It presents data on crime but, at the same time, probes the social structure and attempts to shed light on the causes of crime, with considerable success.

RICHARD QUINNEY, *Criminology: Analysis and Critique of Crime in America* (Boston: Little, Brown, 1975).

Professor Quinney provides a sociological analysis of crime in America, taking into account the social forces underlying both crime and justice in this country. As he remarks in his preface, "Crime is ultimately related to the political economy of the nation." Two attractive features of this book are that the author does not assume any extensive previous knowledge on the part of readers and that he has organized it in such a way that the reader is led easily from simpler to more complex considerations. An additional desirable feature is his excellent writing, with an occasional felicitous touch of mild humor.

THOMAS A. REPPETTO, *The Blue Parade* (New York: Free Press, 1978).

This is a colorful history of American police. Recognizing that our criminal justice system had its roots in England, the author traces the rise of organized police forces from England to the United States. Professor Reppetto is an excellent historian whose love for his subject makes his book highly readable and informative. Dr. Reppetto is particularly well-qualified to write such a book. Not only is his experience in police work impressive (he was a commander of detectives in the Chicago Police) but he also holds a doctorate in public administration. Readers will be struck by the fact that the author is a staunch idealist who manages to have both feet firmly on the ground of the realities of crime and justice. Although primarily a history, *The Blue Parade* provides many sociological insights of great value.

NOTES

1. Oswald Spengler, *Decline of the West*, Vol. I (New York: Knopf, 1926).
2. *New York Times* (January 23, 1973), p. 1.
3. See Edwin M. Schur, *Crimes Without Victims* (Englewood Cliffs, N.J.: Prentice-Hall, 1965).
4. Marvin Harris, *Culture, Man and Nature* (New York: Crowell, 1971), p. 370.
5. Elman R. Service, *Profiles in Ethnology* (New York: Harper and Row, 1963), p. 735.
6. R. F. Fortune, *Sorcerers of Dobu* (New York: Dutton, 1959), p. 61.
7. Ian Hogbin, *A Guadalcanal Society: The Kaoka Speakers* (New York: Holt, Rinehart and Winston, 1964), p. 29.
8. Leo Oppenheim, *Ancient Mesopotamia: Portrait of a Dead Civilization* (Chicago: University of Chicago Press, 1964), p. 140.
9. Hugh D. Barlow, *Introduction to Criminology* (Boston: Little, Brown, 1978), p. 108.
10. Ibid., p. 108.
11. See Thomas A. Reppetto, *The Blue Parade* (New York: Free Press, 1978), Chapter 1.
12. Captain W. L. Melville-Lee, *A History of Police in England and Wales* (London: Methuen, 1901), p. 133.
13. For accounts of this and other riots, see T. A. Critchley, *The Conquest of Violence* (London: Constable, 1970), pp. 81–87; and George Rudé, *Hanoverian London, 1714–1808* (Berkeley: University of California Press, 1971), pp. 222–224.
14. Sir Leon Radzinowicz, *A History of English Criminal Law and Its Administration from 1750* (London: Stevens and Sons, 1948), Chapter 3.
15. See Philip J. Stead, *The Police of Paris* (London: Staples, 1957), pp. 45–48.
16. Eugene Doleschal and Nora Klapmuts, *Toward a New Criminology* (Hackensack, N.J.: National Council on Crime and Delinquency, 1973), p. 4.
17. Criminal Justice Research Center, "An Analysis of Victimization Survey Results from the Eight Impact Cities: Summary Report" (1974), pp. 3–4.
18. Barlow, *Introduction to Criminology*, p. 393.
19. Ibid., pp. 411–412.
20. Harold J. Vetter and Clifford E. Simonsen, *Criminal Justice in America* (Philadelphia: Saunders, 1976), pp. 323–324.
21. H. A. Bloch and G. Geis, *Crime and the Legal Process* (New York: McGraw-Hill, 1962), p. 481.
22. Barlow, *Introduction to Criminology*, p. 416.
23. "Plea Bargaining," *Harvard Law Review*, Vol. 83 (April 1970), p. 1410.
24. Bloch and Geis, *Crime and the Legal Process*, p. 477.
25. See Frederick J. Gaudet, "The Differences Between Judges in Granting Sentences of Probation," *Temple Law Quarterly*, Vol. 19 (April 1946), pp. 471–478.
26. Richard Quinney, *Criminology: Analysis and Critique of Crime in America* (Boston: Little, Brown, 1975), p. 219.
27. Robert M. Carter and Leslie T. Wilkins, "Some Factors in Sentencing Policy," *Journal of Criminal Law, Criminology and Police Science*, Vol. 58 (December 1967), p. 512.
28. Vetter and Simonsen, *Criminal Justice in America*, pp. 244–246.
29. Ibid., p. 248.

30. Paul W. Tappan, "Who Is The Criminal?" *American Sociological Review*, Vol. 12 (February 1947), p. 100.

31. W. Somerset Maugham, *The Moon and Sixpence* (New York: Modern Library, 1919), p. 14.

32. Described in William M. Hastings, *How to Think About Social Problems* (New York: Oxford University Press, 1979), pp. 75–76.

33. Barlow, *Introduction to Criminology*, p. 429.

34. Quoted in D. G. Hardman, "The Case of Eclecticism," *Crime and Delinquency*, Vol. 10 (1913), p. 202.

35. Ernest A. Hooton, *Crime and the Man* (Cambridge: Harvard University Press, 1939), p. 376.

36. William H. Sheldon et al., *Varieties of Delinquent Youth* (New York: Harper, 1949).

37. Quoted in Albert K. Cohen, *Deviance and Control* (Englewood Cliffs, N.J.: Prentice-Hall, 1966), p. 52.

38. There is evidence that mere contiguity in time, space, or both may result in learning. On this point, see: Edwin R. Guthrie, *The Psychology of Learning*, rev. ed. (New York: Harper, 1952).

39. Paul W. Tappan, *Crime, Justice and Corrections* (New York: McGraw-Hill, 1960), p. 246.

40. Gwynn Nettler, *Explaining Crime* (New York: McGraw-Hill, 1974), p. 138.

41. Robert K. Merton, *Social Theory and Social Structure*, enl. ed. (New York: Free Press, 1968), Chapter 7.

42. Edwin H. Sutherland and Donald R. Cressey, *Principles of Criminology*, 6th ed. (Philadelphia: Lippincott, 1960), pp. 77–79.

43. For a full discussion see Howard S. Becker, *Outsiders* (New York: Free Press, 1963).

44. Barlow, *Introduction to Criminology*, pp. 451–452.

9 HUMAN SEXUALITY
CHANGING STANDARDS AND BEHAVIOR

CHAPTER OVERVIEW

INTRODUCTION

HISTORICAL AND
   CROSS-CULTURAL OVERVIEW
The Ancient Heritage
The Christian View of Sex
  and Morality
Cross-Cultural Perspectives
Summary

CONCEPTUAL ORIENTATION
The Meaning of Sexuality in
  American Society
The Sexual Revolution
Summary

OBJECTIVE DIMENSIONS OF
   THE PROBLEM
Extramarital Sex
Homosexuality

Prostitution
Pornography and Obscenity
Paraphilias
Rape
Summary

ATTEMPTS AT DEALING WITH
   THE PROBLEM
New Attitudes
Iatrogenic Effects

PROSPECTS FOR SOLVING
   THE PROBLEM

IMPORTANT WORDS AND TERMS

QUESTIONS FOR DISCUSSION

SUGGESTED READING

NOTES

> *An openness in exposures of the human body, an openness in public intimacy and an openness in the dramatic arts (in exposing to public view two or more humans engaging in public intimacy while nude) has become more commonplace in the Western world than at any time in the past 1600 years.*
> Vance Packard, quoted in *Sexual Latitude*

> *To create guilt for doing something as natural as breathing by instilling the notion that this act is an ugly vice rather than a beautiful and fulfilling communication between two people is to me the worst sin of all.*
> Ruth Dickson, quoted in *Sexual Latitude*

CHAPTER OVERVIEW

Human sexual expression is rooted in physiology, but is channeled and directed by the normative structures of the groups within which it occurs. As with other kinds of human behavior, sexuality is a learned response, capable of being shaped into a variety of different forms. What is deviant in one society may be quite acceptable in another, but all societies define some behaviors as normal and others as deviant. We will discuss these differences and then look at changes in our culture. We will see that in heterosexual relationships the major change has been in female sexuality. But changes have recently occurred in other areas as well, with many forms of sexual behavior considered to be immoral a generation ago now widely tolerated and permitted.

INTRODUCTION

The streets of every large city and many smaller ones are filled with massage parlors, porno shops, hookers, and gay bars. As God once destroyed the ancient cities of Sodom and Gomorrah for their wickedness, some people feel the same thing should happen in our own society. The police have instead settled for isolating these businesses in combat zones, then leaving hands off this sexual activity, much of which was considered illegal as well as immoral a decade ago. The reason for this attitude is that change has come to sexual behavior, as part of the greater freedom permitted people in their private lives. In the past decade the discussion of sex has come much more out in the open. Many older people are dismayed by this new openness about sexual matters, seeing it as casualness toward taboo topics. Ironically, sexual attitudes may have changed faster than behavior, and that even with the increasing availability of sexually oriented materials, students today still ask many of the same questions their own parents asked as young people a generation ago.

It may seem obvious to note, but sex is, first of all, a physiological process. People engaging in some sort of sexual encounter are expressing a basic physical need. But the way we choose to meet this need is directed by a given cultural, social, and psychological context. People act in terms of the prevailing norms and values of the groups to which they belong. Human sexual responses, like all the other aspects of our behavior, are not well developed at birth, humans have only vaguely defined biological needs, not the sharp instincts of other animals. Sexual response, then, is learned as the person is socialized, not only as a child but throughout his or her entire life.

In addition, as humans develop, sexual behavior becomes conditioned in accordance with a wide variety of other concerns, such as those about power, morality, religion, and the law. Also, how we act sexually is a product of the ideas transmitted to us by past generations. Some observers, like sociologist Peter Berger, describe this as being almost a "tyranny of the dead," for in many societies tradition is an extremely strong force to be reckoned with.[1] In our society traditional ideas *are* changing, but what is seen as being problematical about sexuality is based in part on traditional understanding of the nature, purpose, and role of sexual activity in life. Because traditional beliefs are still strong among a large segment of the American population, the historical context must be considered if we are to understand what is seen as problematical about sexuality in American society.

HISTORICAL AND CROSS-CULTURAL OVERVIEW

In order to understand and appreciate some of the changes occurring in our basic sexual attitudes, we will focus on the changing roles and statuses of women, as we did in Chapter 3. We do this because it has been mainly female sexuality that has been restricted in accord with prevailing norms and values. This does not mean sexual expression for men has never been regulated; it has been, as our review will indicate. But in virtually all societies much greater attention has been paid to the suppression and control of females in expressing their sexual needs. The entire range of erotic behavior allowed in any society depends in large measure on the power and privileges distributed to women. As this has changed, so have notions of what kind of sexual response is appropriate for women. This obviously has major consequences for sexuality in general, because the control of female sexuality has major implications for what men can do. Since so many societies of the past have been male-dominated, men have hardly ever been the prime target of these restrictions.

The Ancient Heritage

Our heritage, in terms of the range of issues connected with sexuality, can be traced back to the ancient Hebrews. In marked contrast to more recent Christian teachings, ancient Hebrew attitudes toward sex were characterized by a naturalistic view of the world. For ancient Hebrews, every aspect of daily life was sacred and holy and all human activities were viewed as existing within the covenant made between God and his chosen people. Their religion did not make a distinction between the sacred and profane, but saw the love of God and every variety of human love as being in the same category. This included the love between parents and their children, a husband and his wife, and even the love between a man and his mistress. As Robert Francoeur has stated: "It is very hard for us, as sophisticated cultured Westerners, to admit that the Ancient Hebrew view of sexuality and morals in many ways far surpasses our contemporary images in maturity, basic humanness and moral depth. But the evidence appears very solid that this is indeed the case."[2]

Hebrew culture did not have the dualistic view of the world so prevalent in Christian theology, which divides the world into good and evil, light and darkness, or sacred and profane. The ideas of the ancient Hebrews were quite opposite to the Christian theology that emerged during the early days of the church, for they held a much more wholesome and mature view. They saw human sexual expression as a natural and integral part of life.

The ancient Greeks had somewhat similar views about sexuality, seeing it positively. But because of ideas about male dominance during the classical period, this favorable view applied primarily to men. Monogamy had been established and wives were expected to be sexually faithful to their husbands, although sex outside marriage was seen as both a man's right and necessary for his health. These views led to two distinct kinds of prostitution — the hetairai and the prostitutes of the temples. The *hetairai* were well-educated, beautiful, and intelligent women who were expected to be part of a man's public life, able to go where wives were forbidden. The other groups consisted of women who worked in the temples and gave the money paid for their services for the upkeep and decoration of the houses of worship. Many pieces of Greek temple art show the atmosphere of their work, with men and women fornicating in every possible way. The Greeks believed sexual gratification was one way to appease their gods and the walls of their temples were adorned with art work that today would be labeled pornographic.

Male prostitution was also quite prevalent and homosexuality flourished. The Greeks held women in a certain contempt and felt male homosexuality to be a far superior form of sexual expression. However, female homosexuality was also found, with the word *lesbian* being taken from the name of the Greek island Lesbos, where the female homosexual poet Sappho formed a circle of intimates. As can be seen from the remains of Greek civilization, sexual expression was freely and openly enjoyed. But as the Greek author Demosthenes said: "We marry a woman in order to obtain legitimate children and to have a faithful warden in the house; we keep concubines for our service and daily care; and Hetairai for the enjoyment of love."[3]

Many similarities exist between the Greeks and early Romans in terms of the general status held by women. Men were free to turn to prostitutes and lovers for sexual expression and in records homosexuality appears frequently. However, Roman women were held in greater respect than Greek women as wives and mothers, although male authority still prevailed. Unlike Greek women, Roman wives were allowed to share their husbands' social lives. While in later Roman times women attained a greater degree of freedom, men were generally allowed even more freedom to express themselves sexually. Much of the poetry that survives this period speaks of love in all its forms and is filled with tales of adultery, prostitution, and frequent divorce. As the art historian Verena Zinserling has said: "Rome became the Roman Empire through its wars which made husbands legionnaires and kept them away from hearth and home for years.

Loneliness and war-widowhood were the regular fate of Roman women."[4] In light of the turmoil brought by constant military campaigns, many families were torn apart. And while the legionnaires took prostitutes along with them, the poetry of the time tells many stories of their lonely wives taking lovers to satisfy their sexual and emotional needs. Despite these hardships, and like the Greeks and Hebrews before them, the Romans viewed sex as a natural and pleasurable aspect of being human and engaged in a wide variety of sexual practices frowned on today.

The Christian View of Sex and Morality

The almost two thousand years that have passed since the founding of Christianity have witnessed many changes in Christian attitudes toward human sexuality. There is no single Christian position on sexual behavior, but a series of ideas changing over the centuries. The actual teachings of Christ make no mention of sexual behavior, so it has been up to churches to make clear what implications other Christian teachings might have for sexual expression. Wayland Young, in *Eros Denied,* has outlined the result, talking about the general suppression of sexuality in the Western world.[5] Since its beginning, according to Young, the teachings central to Christianity stress that the love of God for man is greater than the greatest possible love of man for his fellow man. While this widely recognized tenet of the church is innocent enough, it has had important ramifications for notions of sexual morality. If God's love of man was so great, then anything interfering with man's love of God was sinful. As a result, major concern of the early church in working out sexual morality focused on the problem the human orgasm created for man's ability to love God.

Sex researcher Alfred Kinsey has shown it is possible to fire a pistol in a room where two lovers are at a point of orgasm without disturbing them in their pleasure.[6] In light of this, the early church was probably right in fearing that an orgasm did prove distracting to a person's thoughts of God. As Young has said, "It is the one moment of forgetfulness, of total oblivion for all things, including God," and the early church fathers knew it.[7] These ideas, developed before the fifth century, are the basis of many other Christian views on sexual expression. The early church felt love of God was much more important than the love between a man and woman and that sexual love threatened this highest and best form of love. Therefore, they determined chastity to be more virtuous than marriage, virgins to be better than wives, and celibacy to be preferable to sexual intercourse. However, the early church realized that most men were unable to live a sexless existence; it also realized sex was necessary for the continuation of the species. Sex was therefore to be confined to marriage and used specifically for procreation rather than pleasure. Notable in their condemnation of human sexuality were Saint Augustine, Saint Paul, and Saint Jerome, all of whom helped to structure early Christian ideas about sex. As Young concludes:

> Among the great religions of the world and of history, Christianity must be squarely qualified as anti-life. . . . Only when it [sex] is done in marriage and with the desire to have children can it be "excused," or even hallowed.[8]

In accordance with this view, nuns were expected to be virgins and the wives of

Christ. But even though there was a move to limit the marriage of priests beginning around the fourth century, it took nearly twelve hundred more years to establish the celibacy that characterizes the Catholic priesthood today. There were always tensions between the ideal and the actual, but during the Renaissance the leadership of the church moved farthest away from the views held by the early church. In the year 1492, a Spanish cardinal, Rodrigo Borgia, became Pope Alexander VI and according to the sociologist R. E. L. Masters he "converted the Vatican, already no stranger to such revels, to a brothel. There he frolicked with harlots, staged erotic exhibitions for the entertainment of himself, and looked benignly on upon the orgies sponsored by his son."[9] And according to Masters, Pope John XXIII had been ousted earlier in the fifteenth century for having committed incest, adultery and homocide.* "Like Pope Benedict IX, John XXIII was a renowned drunkard, trafficking with demons to abet his seductions and improve his potency; and like Popes Paul II, Sextus IV and Julius II, he practiced sodomy with boys."[10]

It was this kind of moral climate within the church that led Martin Luther and others to begin the Protestant Reformation, originally a movement to clean up the church in the sixteenth century. His chief target was the selling of indulgences that allowed people to contribute money to the church to have their sins removed, which promoted sin. Since most of these sins were sexual, Luther felt compelled to deal harshly with what he saw as the loose moral code of the day. His attempt at a greater restriction of human sexuality was carried on to its ultimate conclusion by the followers of another Protestant leader, John Calvin. As noted in Chapter 4, Calvinists believed in predestination and, anxious to know if they had been chosen for heaven, were always looking for some sign of their salvation. For Calvinists, sin was seen as being primarily sexual, creating some rather bizarre attempts to completely desexualize the world. All images, words, and thoughts of a sexual nature were seen as temptations from the devil, and were to be avoided like the plague.

This brings us to early colonial America and to Massachusetts Bay Colony where Puritans, heirs of the Calvinists, dominated. Drawing on Saint Paul, Saint Augustine, and Thomas Aquinas, the Puritan colonists were determined not to let sex rear its ugly head and get in the way of their building a society dedicated to God. With their lives dominated by Puritan theology, the founding fathers of America thought that the best way to get all thoughts of sex out of their minds was through the discipline provided by hard work. Only through a life of hard work and the material rewards stemming from it, they thought, that one could know if one was chosen to be saved. Women were seen by the early male colonists as presenting temptations that might interfere with their overriding purpose. They were intent on setting up a theocratic state where men could work, serve God, and carve out a new life for themselves. Human sexuality could only get in their way of accomplishing this and so, as two modern feminists have noted, "Sexuality, which would have threatened the single-minded drive of the community, indeed sensuality of any kind, was condemned as sinful."[11]

The attempt at extinguishing sexual desire and placing severe limits on sexual activity

---

*This pope should not be confused with John XXIII who served from 1958 to 1963. The earlier one was one of the so-called antipopes, whose claim to the papacy was disputed.

continued in both this country and in England up through the Victorian period of the nineteenth century. American *blue laws* prohibiting sinful activity have traditionally reflected these Puritan and Victorian attitudes. During the Victorian period, one major way to regulate sexual behavior was to control the sexual activity of women. Chaperones supervised meetings between single males and females and girls were taught the importance of virginity for making a good marriage. Sexual behavior of all sorts was described as dirty, something a wife did only because her husband demanded it. Ironically, pornography and prostitution flourished during this time, because men were free from these rigid standards.

Many of our sex laws, based on these values, were written to reinforce the institution of heterosexual marriage. Marriage was the way sexual relationships were regulated between men and women and the law provided

Victorian morals continued in the Puritan model to suppress the sexual role of proper young ladies. Meanwhile, on the other side of the tracks, prostitutes coyly advertised their services, which were much in demand by men free under the double standard.

for the setting up of a stable family unit based on legitimate sexual access between husband and wife. All other forms of sexual activity, including premarital intercourse and extramarital intercourse, were defined as illegal and immoral. In the United States, the system of law has usually reflected the morality of the times where the sexual behavior appropriate for men and women was based on their roles as seen in a larger political and economic context.

Cross-Cultural Perspectives

In addition to understanding the history behind our current ideas about sexual behavior, we can gain some insight into our own culture by looking at how other societies regulate and control human sexuality. In what is still an excellent reference, social scientists Clellan Ford and Frank Beach published *Patterns of Sexual Behavior*. In it they outline the vast variety of sexual expression found among human beings in other cultures and deal with the sexual behavior in the animals most closely related to man. From their work a number of basic ideas of importance to understanding human sexuality emerge. First, they present a variety of sexual customs of other societies in which virtually all the forms of sexual expression we consider deviant are found acceptable and normal. For example, "Examination of the societies in our sample reveals that formal restrictions to single mateships characterizes 29 (less than 16 percent) of the 185 groups on which this information could be obtained. Furthermore, of these 29 societies, less than one-third wholly disapprove of both premarital and extramarital liason."[12] They go on to note that in 84 percent of the societies in their sample, men were permitted to have more than one mate at a time if they could afford it. In only about a third of the societies for which Ford and Beach had data was homosexuality either absent or rare, with the rest considering it moral and acceptable for at least certain males of the society. A few examples of what they found will illustrate the variety of homosexual customs. "Among the Siberian Chukchee such an individual puts on women's clothing, assumes feminine mannerisms, and may become the 'wife' of another man. . . . Among the Koniag, some male children are reared from infancy to accept the female role. . . . Keraki bachelors of New Guinea universally practice sodomy. . . . This practice is believed by the natives to be necessary for the growing boy."[13]

While it is possible to go on with the details of all the different ways sexual expression is channeled by the world's cultures, a number of general conclusions can be reached from Ford and Beach's work. First, there is virtually no sexual behavior considered abnormal or deviant by all cultures. Homosexuality, prostitution, incest, masturbation, and premarital and extramarital sex are all normal in many societies. Second, no society fails to regulate in some way the sexual behavior of its members. This regulation varies from the poles of extreme restriction to extreme permissiveness, but in all groups sexual expression is channeled into socially defined appropriate outlets. All societies have notions of deviant sexuality, and this may include notions we consider quite normal, including the positions used for intercourse, the attainment of orgasm by women, or the presence of foreplay before coitus. On a scale of sexual permissiveness, American society historically would be placed well toward the more restrictive end, especially that part based on traditional Puritan ideas of appropriate conduct. Cross-cultural comparisons do indicate the importance of early sexual experience as major influences on a person's sexual tastes. And Ford and Beach conclude that the smoothest heterosexual adjustments are made in societies where young boys and girls are both allowed and encouraged to have premarital sexual play with each other.

Summary

The range of behaviors presented and discussed by anthropologists interested in sexual expression in other cultures becomes an important commentary on what is basic to understanding human sexuality. Unlike the sexual behavior of animals, human sexuality is learned and is based on conditioning done in a social context. When the context is changed, different behavior results. In order to understand what has been happening in American society in the past quarter century, this fact must be kept clearly in mind. Human sexual behavior never occurs in an unregulated context, and the larger cultural context defines what is acceptable and appropriate for both sexes. The roles men and women play in society are closely associated with the way their sexual behavior is channeled and conditioned; status and power relations between individuals and groups are very influential in defining appropriate sexual behavior. And as these ideas about power, authority, and status have changed over time, so have people's ideas about what is normal or deviant sexual behavior. More will be said of this later.

CONCEPTUAL ORIENTATION

Sexual expression in humans has more variety than in any other species, which makes it impossible to say with any certainty what is a normal form of human sexuality. Because of this, we must base our understanding of human sexuality in American society on the sociological concepts developed in Chapter 2. As with the process of defining deviance in many different areas, groups with power influence socialization to make their ideas the ones defined as normal. And for many years, the groups with power in this country were largely white, Anglo-Saxon, and Protestant, which meant that the prevailing view of sexual morality was focused on males and followed Christian teaching. In contrast to traditional teaching, American popular culture seems to have become highly sexually oriented. The increased emphasis on sex can be seen in all aspects of today's music, films, and mass media. The late Harvard sociologist Pitrim Sorokin noted this trend over twenty years ago, and predicted the decline in American power and influence and the general decay of our society as a result. He drew an analogy between contemporary events and those which supposedly occurred as part of the decline of Rome, and saw America as a "sensate plum" ready to fall from the tree.[14] Still other observers have claimed we are today living in a sexual wilderness, with no standards to guide our behavior. All of these charges are an outgrowth of something usually called the sexual revolution. A major question many sociologists have been trying to answer over the past decade is whether there really has been a sexual revolution or just a minor change in behavior. Perhaps today people only talk more about sex, while acting as they always have. Let us examine the evidence on this question to sketch out some sort of an answer.

The evidence usually presented by sociologists focuses on several different factors, most of which are related to the liberation of female sexuality. As noted in Chapters 3 and 4, the roles of women have been changing rapidly in the family, education, and work.

As women have achieved more education, have entered the labor force in ever greater numbers, and have limited their fertility, their general independence and freedom has increased greatly. As their access to other social resources has increased, they have been freed from many of the restraints governing their sexual behavior as well. And the technological breakthrough in contraception known as the *pill* has had an important effect, giving women themselves for the first time almost complete control over their chances for pregnancy. Fear of pregnancy, once used to keep women in their traditional roles, has been partly overcome by the birth control pill.

The pill and other forms of effective contraception like the *intrauterine device* (or IUD) have not in themselves changed our system of morality. This can be clearly seen from the difficulty these new methods have had in being accepted in other cultures, like India and Pakistan. The pill and the IUD have had an impact in the United States because they came in the context of other changes involving the role and status of women in American society. They use these devices to control their reproductive capacity in order to be able to control other aspects of their lives as well. Procreation, the traditional purpose of sexuality in Western culture, has become separated from sexuality, in accordance with women's other needs and desires. A growing number of American women, then, no longer center their lives around their roles as wives and mothers. Sex for pleasure and personal satisfaction both within and outside of marriage has now become possible and has reinforced demands for greater freedom in other areas as well, which in turn reinforced demands for greater sexual freedom. In every society, human sexual activity is inextricably bound with the prevailing worldview that shapes behavior.

The Meaning of Sexuality in American Society

While in other cultures religious or political institutions have predominated, American society has given primacy to economic activity as organized in the capitalist mode of production. As noted in the chapter on work, many American workers apparently confront problems of alienation on their job because they are required to sell their labor to the people who manage or own the means of production. In such a society, people transform themselves into "personalities" sold as any other commodity on the open market. While show business is the most obvious example of this, it also occurs in the appearance and conduct of waitresses, teachers, and corporate executives on their jobs. And if much of the literature on job satisfaction is correct, many American workers seek the major sources of satisfaction in their lives not from their jobs but from their personal lives. One of these activities, obviously, is sexual expression both within and outside of marriage.

Much of what is characteristic of the American approach to sexuality can be traced to the way people deal with each other. Instead of treating people as people, we too often see them as objects to be manipulated for personal profit or advantage. The stereotypical successful man is surrounded by the symbols of success, including beautiful sexy women as wives or girlfriends. Access to desirable sexual partners comes from success in the marketplace and is bargained for like any other commodity. Today, sex itself has become a commodity to be consumed or used to motivate people to buy a range of goods, from cars to sunglasses. Our views on sex, as with those found in other cultures, are rooted in the social structure that regulates our political and economic activity.

In American society, it is hard for many

Products from shampoos to summer vacations can and do carry the same advertising theme — sex appeal. The unabashed use of sex for promotion reveals a great deal about our sexual views and values.

people to make the shift away from this way of thinking. Some changes have recently occurred, however. Ironically, the demand for social change made by young people during the 1960s has not resulted in an alteration of the political structure, in a transformation of the military, or in a basic change in the workplace, all of which appeared to be central themes to the protestors. It has had an effect on their personal lives, however. Yet a decade later, we do see greater freedom in the enjoyment of personal pleasures, such as in the recreational use of drugs and sex. This is another demonstration that ways of thinking developed and reinforced in our public lives spill over into our private lives, including our ideas about human sexuality.[15]

The Sexual Revolution

So far we have discussed the attitudes behind much of the inter-personal behavior we engage in each day. This brings us to our next question, namely, has there actually been a *sexual revolution,* a dramatic change in the way people behave? Or are we simply talking more openly about sex while behaving as we have for the past fifty years? Let us examine the latest evidence on changes in American sexual behavior.

As noted earlier, the focus of almost all current research is on the behavioral changes of women, for their sexuality has traditionally been the more repressed in American society. In the past this led to the *double stan-*

dard, which permitted men to engage in certain sexual behavior but condemned women who engaged in the same behavior. During the Victorian period, women were divided into two categories: the nice girls remained pure and chaste before marriage and sexually repressed in marriage, and the bad girls enjoyed sexual expression and engaged in it for pleasure. While the Victorian period produced a great deal of hypocrisy in sexual matters, the double standard derived from this era seems to have prevailed until at least the mid-1960s. Let us examine what has happened in terms of behavior since then, using the famous Kinsey studies as the best available indicator of behavior before 1960.

In 1948, zoologist-turned-sex-researcher Alfred Kinsey published his landmark study on male sexuality. In 1953, his volume on women followed. For a generation these studies were the standard for saying anything about human sexuality, even though they were criticized on a variety of counts. Two of the more telling criticisms were that the studies overrepresented prisoners among the lower-class respondents and the ability to generalize to the whole population from the sample was questionable. Regardless, his data were used to support the following conclusions about sexual behavior in America in the 1950s. In comparing males and females, men were shown to have had sexual experiences at an earlier age, more homosexual contacts, a higher level of sexual experimentation with forms considered deviant, higher rates of masturbation, more extramarital sex outlets, and in general a higher level of sexual activity. These were probably the most valid conclusions Kinsey reached, although the differences he found may have been somewhat exaggerated. Still, his figures are the best we have for that period, and show that a double standard did exist in sexual behavior.

Research on the sexual revolution has focused primarily on the sexual activities of young women prior to marriage—this group has been analyzed more than all others combined. In essence, going back to the late 1950s and continuing up until about 1970 there were two conflicting sides taken on the issue of whether sexual behavior was changing. On the one side is Ira Reiss, a leading researcher on this topic for almost a decade, who said in 1968: "The popular notion that America is undergoing a sexual revolution is a myth. The belief that our more permissive sexual code is a sign of a general breakdown of morality is also a myth."[16] Reiss used large and representative samples as the basis of his work; in his opinion, as of 1968, the changes were occurring slowly enough so they could not be called a revolution. Reiss noted that there had been more of a change in attitude than in behavior: "The greater change actually is in sexual attitudes rather than in behavior. If behavior has not altered in the last century as much as we seem to think, attitudes have—and attitudes and behavior seem closer today than for many generations."[17]

On the other side was Vance Packard, who also published his examination of changes in sexual attitudes and behavior in 1968. Packard said: "For whatever they are worth, the clues offered by trends in illegitimacy, pregnant brides, and venereal disease in the U.S.A., all suggest the incidence of premarital coitus has been rising in the past quarter century."[18] While he felt that major changes in sexual behavior had occurred since the end of World War II, Packard found no single study done between 1940 and 1968 adequate in allowing a conclusion to be reached about the entire American population. What Packard and others began to understand was that premarital sexual activity varies directly with the social class, educa-

TABLE 9.1 Percentage with Premarital Intercourse Experience[a]

	Sample Culture					
	Intermountain		Midwestern		Danish	
Samples and years	Males	Females	Males	Females	Males	Females
Total samples						
1958	39	10	51	21	64	60
1968	37	32	50	34	95	97
Difference	−2	+22	−1	+13	+31	+37

[a]Based on number answering. The number who failed to answer in any group varied from 0 to 4.

Source: Harold Christensen and Christina Gregg, "Changing Sex Norms in America and Scandinavia" in Arlene Skolnick and Jerome H. Skolnick, (eds.), *Intimacy, Family, and Society* (Boston: Little, Brown, 1974), p. 184.

tion level, and region of the country of the samples used for the studies. No general conclusion could possibly be reached about changes in behavior unless the size and diversity of the population were taken into account. Unfortunately, most early studies often cited as the base line from which to measure change did not do this.

One exception was the work of Harold Christensen, who headed family study seminars at meetings of the American Sociological Association. In 1970 Christensen and his coworker Christina Gregg published the most sophisticated study yet done, which today serves as a model for the approach taken for other studies. Briefly, Christensen and Gregg compared samples drawn both from different groups within this country and several in Denmark. They had data on sexual behavior and attitudes for their groups in 1958 and did a ten-year follow-up. One group was religious young Mormons from Utah (called the Intermountain group); another was drawn from the Midwest and thought to be somewhat liberal in both behavior and attitudes. The third group, from Denmark, was thought to be more permissive than the other two.

A number of comparisons were made, with the following results. The authors found that when asked about the acceptability of a nonvirgin as a marital partner, the "permissive attitudes increased for both sexes and in both sample years from lows in the Inter-mountain to highs in the permissive Danish; and increased between 1958 and 1968 for both sexes in each of the three cultures."[19] Both males and females showed more approval of premarital intercourse in 1968; the more permissive Danes were more approving than the other groups. Among the Danes the differences between males and females were lowest, suggesting that as permissiveness increases, many differences between male and female attitudes will decrease. Females in the two American groups still had more restrictive attitudes than males, but in all three groups females moved more toward approving premarital sexual intercourse than did the males.

This set of results is not surprising in terms of what many authors had been saying. But Christensen and Gregg went one step further. They also investigated the relationship between attitudes and actual behavior. As Table 9.1 shows, the incidence of premarital intercourse increased for each of the three groups for females between 1958 and 1968, but only in the Danish group did it increase for both men and women. For the

Danes, in the 1968 sample, 95 percent of the females and 97 percent of the males had engaged in premarital intercourse; in a decade the Danes had completely abolished the double standard. For the Midwestern group, the percentage of females having intercourse increased 13 percent and in the more traditional Intermountain group the percentage increased by 22 percent. For males it remained relatively constant except among the Danes. It is interesting to note that the greatest change in behavior occurred among females, with the girls living in a restrictive and a permissive culture changing the most. But the single greatest change in premarital sexual activity occurred among females living in the permissive culture of Denmark.

Christensen and Gregg also found that there tended to be more sexual activity taking place in 1968 without the demands for commitment that marked behavior earlier. They used the term "promiscuous" to say that intercourse took place without either partner having made a long-term commitment to the other (it was not meant to be an evaluation) and stated that "Danes appear to be more promiscuous than Americans, males more promiscuous than females, and 1968 respondents more promiscuous than 1958 respondents."[20] These results show that there probably was a change in the 1960s in sexual activity in our society and that this has resulted largely from changes in both attitudes and behavior found among young women. There still seemed to be somewhat of a double standard at work concerning both attitude and behavior, but the evidence suggests that male and female sexual standards have recently begun to converge.

In the most recent work of this sort, published in 1977 (but unfortunately limited only to a sample of college students), the results were quite similar to those of Christensen and Gregg. As the authors concluded, "Liberalization was accelerated in the early 1970s. Second, due to the greater liberalization in female premarital sexual behavior and attitudes, the difference between male and female behavior and attitudes has greatly diminished."[21] Additional work on cohabitation (discussed in Chapter 3) among all segments of the population shows that a dramatic increase has occurred in this phenomena as well in recent years.

Summary

A generation of studies have shown that rates of pre-marital sexual intercourse among young unmarried people increased dramatically, especially on the part of females. Female sexuality has been liberated from many of the traditional pressures that had restricted it. This is an inescapable conclusion, suggesting that by the time young women reach twenty, many are not virgins. These studies also indicate that the double standard seems dead, a single sexual standard is now seen as appropriate for both young men and women. It may not have been a revolution, but real behavioral change has occurred during the past ten years.

OBJECTIVE DIMENSIONS OF THE PROBLEM

We have already examined the evidence on the changing sexual behavior among young unmarried people in our society. In addition to the great changes in the sexual behavior permitted to young unmarried females, our society has become more permissive in our attitudes toward other sexual behaviors as well. We don't seem justified in calling this a revolution though. The authors of an extensive study on cohabitation concluded that most young people were conventional in their expectations about marriage and that most would end up in more or less traditional marriages by the time they had reached thirty. It would be more accurate to view the increased rates of premarital sex and cohabitation as part of a changing pattern of courtship and not as a serious challenge to marriage as an institution. On the other hand, extramarital sex challenges traditional notions about monogamy and is still considered by many people unacceptable. It is to this and some other forms of sexual expression still considered deviant that we now turn our attention.

Extramarital Sex

Much less attention than that showered on premarital sex has been devoted to extramarital sex, or *adultery*. With our growing permissiveness, extramarital sex is no longer talked about in totally negative terms; instead of being called adultery, it is now referred to as having an affair. The change in terminology represents a basic change in attitude. But as with premarital sex, in talking about extramarital sex it is important to distinguish between behavior and attitudes. Unfortunately, the data upon which to base any comparisons with the past are even more sparse than was the case with premarital sex. This is partly because of a greater problem of gaining accessibility to those people who have affairs. Disclosures of extramarital sex are threatening to the marriage or to a person's ability to maintain status in the eyes of an employer or neighbors. As a result, we do not have very good data on which to build a theory of change in this activity. Read the following statements about extramarital sex with these cautions in mind.

In the early 1950s, Kinsey found that by age forty, about half of the American males and about one-quarter of the females had engaged in extramarital sex.[22] More recent research has made pretty much the same findings on premarital sex. On the attitudinal level it has been found that permissiveness toward extramarital sex varies from one group to the next within American society. One recent study found that "the best explanation of extramarital sexual permissiveness is offered by premarital sexual permissiveness."[23] This, of course, is not surprising but some other results were unexpected. The researchers found that social class, age, and degree of family satisfaction did not make a difference in explaining attitudes toward extramarital sex, although these variables are important in understanding attitudes toward premarital sex. Marital status, race, and the degree of religious involvement all were related to feelings about extramarital sex. Overall, the sample disapproved of it. About three-quarters of the almost 1500 respondents in this study said extramarital sex was always wrong; only about fourteen percent said it was wrong sometimes or not at all.

In another recent study, Shirley Glass and Thomas Wright reviewed many previous studies of extramarital sex and then analyzed a sample taken from a poll conducted by *Psychology Today*, which had over 10,000 responses.[24] While their sample is not representative of the entire population, Glass and Wright found that about 40 percent of the males and 36 percent of the females reported that they had engaged in extramarital affairs. This was in a sample where the median age was about thirty for both sexes, where 92 percent had gone to college, and in which about half had done some graduate work. While this group was relatively young and much more highly educated than the average American, the results do show that this behavior occurs among more women than Kinsey reported and that the differences in the incidence of this behavior among men and women are no longer significant. Other recent studies, some using the same methodology and some using a different kind, tend to reach the same conclusions about the frequency of this behavior. They have also almost unanimously shown no large difference in rates between men and women.[25]

The research done on premarital and extramarital sex shows an increase in their frequency. But although it seems widespread, especially among the younger and better educated parts of the population, extramarital sex is still not generally approved of. However, these two behaviors are undoubtedly considered the least deviant by American society and are ones the law virtually never becomes involved in. All the other areas discussed in this chapter still evoke responses from the police and court systems, at least occasionally. Because of this, research on the actual extent of these behaviors is even harder to do. As was noted by early critics of Kinsey's work, "where sex is concerned, the typical attitude has grown out of the problem of shame, concealment, prevarication, and perversion of the truth. This can be clinically proved."[26] With this constantly in mind, let us look at those patterns of sexual behavior still socially defined as deviant.

Homosexuality

The late 1970s will be remembered as the time when homosexuals came out of the closet and into the open. This was partly due to a more permissive social climate toward all forms of sexuality and partly due to a number of legal decisions giving homosexuals the same civil rights as other persons. Yet there continues to be heated controversy over this behavior. As Anita Bryant's anti-homosexual crusade recently demonstrated, there continues to be an aversion and fear of the homosexual in American society. Behind the overt discrimination practiced against them, homosexuals must suffer the stigma of being mentally sick, sex criminals, and child molesters. Playing on these stereotypes, Anita Bryant had little trouble whipping up public sentiment against homosexuals in the Miami area, where the issue revolved around their right to teach in public schools. In a number of recent test cases in Oregon, New Jersey, Washington, and Maryland, teachers found to be homosexuals have either been fired or forced to resign. Such discrimination extends to the military services. Air Force Sergeant Leonard Matlovich received an involuntary discharge for admitting to being a homosexual.

Homosexuality, the preference for sex partners of one's own sex, has long been found among all-male institutions like armies or prisons, causing Winston Churchill once to remark that the three finest traditions of the British Navy were "rum, sodomy, and the whip." Kinsey, from his work with males, estimated that about 4 percent of the male population was exclusively homosexual and that about 37 percent had some form of homosexual experience at least once. He also estimated about 13 percent of the population had more homosexual than heterosexual experience, a figure considered much too high by more contemporary researchers.[27] Morton Hunt more recently put the figure at about 3 percent with 1 percent openly active in a gay community.[28] If this is accurate, there are about 7 million male homosexuals in the United States today and a largely undetermined number of female homosexuals.

Like those who engage in other behaviors society labels as deviant, homosexuals have formed relatively closed communities where their contacts are primarily with other homosexuals. There are homosexual areas in virtually every large city, with gay bars and public baths catering to an almost exclusively homosexual trade. During "gay pride week" in June 1977, marches for homosexual rights drew about 150,000 persons in San Francisco, 50,000 in New York City, and 20,000 in Los Angeles. Clearly, San Francisco is the center of homosexual life in the United States; it has become a haven for both men and women preferring this form of sexual behavior. The reason is that police have kept hands off for the past decade. The result is that homosexuals have shown that, when left alone, they can be good workers, lawabiding citizens, and responsible parents. San Francisco has avoided what is elsewhere the problem of homosexuality, that is, the creation of a hostile subculture through labeling and harassment. Faced with a constant fear of arrest and a general paranoia about their life-style, homosexuals have created an atmosphere of distrust, guilt, and fear within the gay community itself. Where homosexuality is accepted, permitted, or at least tolerated by the larger society, these elements seem to be completely absent.

These findings tie in with those of the largest study ever done on homosexuals, published by Alan Bell and Martin Weinberg in late 1978.[29] Their project involved about 1500 four-hour interviews with Bay Area homosexuals. Bell and Weinberg found that in some respects, homosexuals were like heterosexuals. While most male homosexuals cruised the gay bars for partners, about 40 percent did so only about once a month or not at all. Rather than searching for a brief physical encounter, both male and female homosexuals were looking for love, warmth, affection, and understanding. The majority of male homosexuals had sex only about two or three times a week, while for females it was only about once a week. Bell and Weinberg report other, quite unexpected, results. In terms of numbers of different sexual partners, the single largest group in the male sample estimated they had had sex with be-

Lesbians differ in many ways from male homosexuals, especially in the tendency for couples like this one to establish long-term relationships. It is impossible to estimate the number of lesbians in the United States, because most female homosexuality is less easy to recognize and less frequently discussed than male homosexuality.

tween one hundred and five hundred other men since they had become homosexual. And among white males, 28 percent claimed to have had more than one thousand different partners, with most contacts lasting only a short time. As a possible result, almost two-thirds of all male homosexuals have had venereal disease during the course of their sexual careers.

Bell and Weinberg found the vast majority of homosexuals do not fit the stereotyped images many people hold of the homosexual. Most homosexuals are not riddled with compulsive desires or filled with emotional conflicts based on guilt and paranoia. The majority accept their sexual inclination as simply a different preference from that of straights and they live out their lives in a stable manner. The authors feel that the picture most people have of homosexuals is derived from the way the police have dealt with the gay community rather than from the way homosexuals behave if they are not harassed. In many areas, homosexuals are herded into the worst parts of cities, where they are forced to mix with other deviants and social outcasts. Without these external pressures, homosexuals behave virtually the same as heterosexuals as far as their jobs, neighbors, and the general community are concerned. When not rejected as a deviant subgroup, homosexuals do not take on any of the negative behaviors characteristic of one.

As far as female homosexuality is concerned, little is known about the rates of lesbianism within the general population. Kinsey put the figure at about one-third the rate for males, but this was at a time when the overall sexuality of women was more repressed than it is today.[30] In addition to the repression of behavior, women have traditionally been less willing to talk about their sexual lives, especially to teams of all-male sex researchers. According to some writers the lesbian minority in America may run as high as 10 million women.

One difference between lesbians and male homosexuals is that women seem to establish longer lasting homosexual relationships than men do. These more stable relationships among females may be founded on different attitudes held by men and women about the nature of the sex act itself. Males in our culture are still pressured to learn dominance, aggressiveness, and a lack of sentimentality in most behavior, including sex. Female roles include an emphasis on opposite attributes, stressing affection, love, submission, and emotional release. The two different patterns of homosexuality clearly reflect the different masculine and feminine roles still prevalent.

Many groups of female homosexuals have become quite militant in preferring lesbianism to heterosexual relationships, which, they claim, are almost always male-dominated. As the feminist Martha Shelly has said: "Lesbianism is one road to freedom, freedom from oppression by men. Through her ability to obtain love and sexual satisfaction from other women, the lesbian is freed of dependence on men for love, sex and money."[31] The women's rights movement's protest of male political dominance, and the lesbians' desire to free themselves of dependence on men are closely related ideas. Most of the women in the feminist movement are not lesbians. However, when these two groups of women discuss their common problems of living in a male-oriented society, the logic of their arguments is often parallel. As Shelly has noted, "I have never met a lesbian who believed that she was innately less rational or capable than a man; who swallowed one word of the 'woman's role' horse-shit."[32]

Prostitution

Prostitution, or sex for hire, is wide open in large cities like New York; laws against it are rarely enforced unless incidents of violence become too frequent. It is legal only in Nevada, where it is controlled and taxed by the state. Other states still seem to feel that the legalization of prostitution would have a negative effect on general moral standards, although this would be hard to prove one way or the other. It is also seen as an evil because, like gambling, prostitution is connected with organized crime.

There have been few attempts to assess the extent of prostitution in our society and none have been successful enough to produce comprehensive and valid data. Kinsey's work in 1948 showed that about sixty-nine percent of the males in his sample had frequented prostitutes.[33] But this figure is not representative of the general population, for it contained a disproportionate number of lower class men and prisoners. Other studies have shown a dramatic decrease in recent years from the data in Kinsey's work, and the latest figures seem to show only about 5 percent of college males have gone to prostitutes.[34]

This decrease is attributed to the recent opening of other avenues of sexual gratification as a result of the far-reaching changes in attitudes and behavior that are part of the sexual revolution. Today, there is greater emphasis on female sexuality, with marriage manuals suggesting anything goes between husband and wife, rather than endorsing only a few sex acts, as in the past. Partners who do not find gratification within their marriage often get out of it; in the past, the husband may have gone regularly to prostitutes. We are not saying that formerly only unmarried men or those with poor marriages would frequent prostitutes; but prostitution, like other forms of sexual deviance, is closely related to sexual standards and to notions of what is appropriate behavior for both sexes. With the increase in sexual behaviors deemed acceptable, there may be less of a need for men to go to prostitutes.

As sexual attitudes have become more liberal in general during the past decade, prostitution has become more accepted. However, a growing area of present concern centers on the prostitution of young girls who have run away from home and are forced into prostitution by older men acting as pimps. As part of a general emphasis on youth in our culture, the age of prostitutes is getting younger. The flesh market is demanding younger and younger goods. Runaways provide an accessible group, powerless to fight back against a well-organized prostitution racket using violence and drug addiction to keep them in line. As a result, prostitutes of twelve and thirteen are not uncommon in the large cities. By the time a girl reaches the age of twenty, she may have been in the business for a long time. In Boston, in the winter of 1978, police broke up a child prostitution ring specializing in young boys, some as young as nine.

The problem of runaways has become severe. A federal study estimated there to be more than half a million youths age ten to seventeen who ran away from home for at least one night in 1976.[35] Many authorities place the number much higher, usually in the area of 1 million runaways per year. Police estimate that 20,000 runaways may be living in New York City, with Los Angeles having more than 10,000. Studies have found that about 70 percent of female runaways get into prostitution.[36] Police have reported that there are currently more than 3,000 young people under the age of fourteen being sexually exploited in Los Angeles alone and other estimates are that there are well over a quarter of a million youngsters under seventeen involved in some kind of prostitution in the New York City area alone.

The breakdown of parental control, the increased freedom given to young people, and our changing sexual standards have all worked together to produce what appears to be an alarming increase in the number of young people who have become involved in prostitution. Changes in family structure have created a climate where young people are pretty much on their own at an early age. But, unlike earlier times in our history, these free teenagers are not thought of or treated as adults; they are kept in the nebulous status of adolescence. In years past, many males entered the job market at age fifteen and females married and had children by the time they were sixteen. As we have changed from a rural to an urban society, become more highly educated, and experienced profound changes in the job market, problems facing adolescents have greatly increased. And in no place are the ramifications seen more clearly than in the growing number of children who run away from home. This problem of the family also contributes to a worsening problem in sexuality, for the result of running away is often prostitution.

Pornography and Obscenity

Pornography literally means to write about whores and prostitutes and includes any material specifically designed to be sexually arousing. *Obscenity,* on the other hand, refers to language, written material, and actions that violate standards of decency.

There have been numerous attempts to define pornography, but there has been little success in reaching agreement in our culture.

Some notion of what was pornographic in the 1880s and 1890s can be derived from old pictures of the beach attire of both sexes. Women literally wore a full suit of clothes into the water, with only the ankles and wrists exposed. Today there have been many attempts to institute nude sunbathing in the United States, while nude beaches are fairly common in Europe. Standards have changed greatly in the past 75 years but our society has not fallen completely apart as some had predicted would happen if more of the human body was shown in public.

Other societies seem to be able to function with few sexual taboos, but in American culture with its puritan heritage, sexual denial serves a variety of larger purposes. As John Money, co-founder of the Johns Hopkins Gender Identity Clinic, has said: "We have become dependent on tabooing and punishing the natural erotic functions of sexuality in childhood as the means of establishing a sense of guilt and a mechanism for the control of behavior. Once established, a sense of guilt can be played upon to control behavior far removed from sex."[37] Money notes that politicians sense this when they vote on censorship laws, often rejecting the liberalization of existing obscenity laws because of the larger social purposes such laws serve. Socialization in American culture has long involved the suppression of erotic impulses in favor of the discipline of work, and while this is changing, the vestiges of these attitudes are still with us.

Great literary works of major authors have sometimes been banned as obscene, including *Alice in Wonderland, Robinson Crusoe,* and *Huckleberry Finn*. Part of the problem in defining what is pornographic and obscene lies in determining what are current standards, which is usually done in the courts. Some local ordinance will be broken, the police will act, and a jury will be selected to try the case. Community standards are usually inferred from the jury's decisions.

The sale of sexually explicit material, leaving nothing to the imagination, is more tolerated in large urban areas. New York City is considered the "porn capital" of the United States, although most domestic explicit magazines and movies are produced in California, but compared to Copenhagen, Denmark, New York is prudish. The Danes have abolished censorship of any sort, and pornography flourishes, although much of it is reportedly purchased by German, British, and American tourists, who eagerly buy what is not as widely available in their own countries. With no censorship, Denmark provides a model for what could happen here if censorship were lifted. The Danes have gotten used to it and no one makes a big fuss over pornography any more.

A major fear of some people who favor strict codes of censorship is that widespread pornography would lead to a drastic increase in the number of sex crimes. In the late 1960s Lyndon Johnson appointed a presidential commission to make a series of recommendations about what should be done about pornography and obscenity. Their findings about the effects of pornography on behavior are quite interesting. This commission, using the techniques of social science, tried both to gauge public opinion on pornography and to assess its effects on human behavior. To determine the latter they interviewed a variety of people, from sex educators to chiefs of police. These experts were split in their views. Most psychiatrists, social workers, counselors, and other professionals felt that pornography had no harmful effects on adolescent or adult behavior. But of the police chiefs, 58 percent believed that pornographic material was a major factor in causing juvenile delinquency.[38]

The commission also examined some experiments in which carefully chosen groups of men and women were shown erotic material. In the commission's words:

> Experimental and survey studies show that exposure to erotic stimuli produces sexual arousal in substantial portions of both males and females. Recent research casts doubt on the common belief that women are vastly less aroused by erotic stimuli than are men.[39]

The Commission found that any major differences between men and women are due to cultural conditioning, which stresses greater modesty and sexual restraint for females. It is true that most erotic material is oriented toward males, but new magazines like *Playgirl* and older ones like *Cosmopolitan* are aiming explicit sexual material at middle-class females.

It is interesting to note that the majority of the people (56 percent) questioned by the commission felt that widespread pornography will lead to a breakdown of morals, but only 1 percent said it had some effect on their own morals. Thirty-seven percent felt that this material would "make people sex crazy," but only one half of 1 percent said it had done so for them. The effects of this material always appeared to be greater when talking about someone else, not about one's self.[40]

Turning to Denmark as an example, growing availability of explicit sexual materials there has been accompanied by a decrease in sex crimes. Police records from Copenhagen for a twelve-year period show a dramatic decrease in reported sex crimes, which coincided with the lifting of censorship. It is important to note that this decrease in offenses could not be attributed to changes in the legal or social definition of sex crimes or in public readiness to report such crimes.

On the basis of a wide range of evidence the commission recommended that censorship against obscene and pornographic material be dropped in this country. But by the time the group finished its report, in 1970, the president was Richard Nixon, who refused to implement the commission's recommendations. Liberalization of pornography laws was dealt another blow in 1973. The Supreme Court ruled that lower courts could simply assume that sexually explicit material had negative effects and that these effects need not be proved in every case. This ruling made it possible for states to enact censorship laws. This has meant that states and localities were given the right to prosecute theaters and book stores marketing sexually explicit material, if the material was seen as violating community standards. Although communities had this ability, a rash of convictions did not result. It is becoming increasingly difficult to prove pornography or obscenity to a jury, because tolerance is greater.

This greater tolerance has also meant a relaxation of enforcement against *soft-core pornography*, the graphic depiction of widely accepted behaviors. But enforcement does occur, and that means that the Supreme Court occasionally becomes involved, for there is a fine dividing line between censorship of obscene materials and preserving the freedom of speech guaranteed by the Constitution. A pertinent case was *Miller* vs. *California* in 1973, which introduced the matter of *community standards*. The Court ruled that if an average person applying community standards would find the material patently offensive, the community could ban it as obscene. The issue soon became unsettled, however. Ruling against the censorship of the film *Carnal Knowledge* by a Georgia court only a year later, the Court reversed itself and said that localities do not have the final say after all. And in light of the inability of the Supreme Court to make a definitive ruling, the best we can say is that law enforcement will gradually follow society's move to greater tolerance.

But what about material considered *hard-core pornography*? This means material about sexual behaviors still considered by many people to be deviant such as sadomasochistic sex, bestiality, and sex acts involving young children (called kiddie porn). Standards of most communities are clearly violated by most of these films and pictures. When law enforcement officials become sufficiently outraged by an instance, they will probably try to prosecute. But these efforts have never and probably will never rid society of pornography completely.

Paraphilias

Instead of speaking of "unnatural forms of sexual expression" or "acts against God" as past generations have, sex researchers now call some deviant sex acts *paraphilias*. These acts include such things as sadomasochism, oral sex, anal sex, and fetishism. These acts are usually referred as "kinky sex" in anything but scholarly journals, but paraphilia is preferable because it avoids the value judgments implicit in evaluating these acts as perversions. Because what we know about these sexual behaviors is mostly taken from work with people who have had problems in their sexual functioning and sought professional help, these forms have also been labeled as abnormal. This approach is incorrect and has been part of the generally distorted image we have of these behaviors. We discuss these behaviors here because they still arouse strong negative feelings among some parts of the population.

Needless to say, we do not have a good idea of the extent to which these behaviors occur within the general population. But like other forms of sexuality considered to be deviant, we know they are far more widespread than most people assume. Almost every large city has a magazine or newspaper where people who prefer these kinds of sex advertise for what they want, using a code most people would not understand. Oral sex is referred to as "French," sodomy is called "Greek," and sadomasochism has picked up the label of "English."

With the liberation of sexuality for women in our society, many paraphilias are now being added to the range of sexual expressions considered as permissible. Whereas prostitutes were once about the only source for gratifying the impulses behind these acts, now many women are apparently engaging in them. In a widely read and much criticized book called *The Hite Report* over 3,000 women spoke about their feelings on a wide range of sexual topics.[41] Many spoke of their profound enjoyment of oral sex, previously thought of as aberrant behavior, but though these women were far from representative of the general population, they were not abnormal either. Many movies depicting the kinds of sex acts being discussed here, such as *Deep Throat*, *The Opening of Misty Beethoven*, *The Story of O*, and *The Devil in Miss Jones*, have been seen by millions of people in recent years, making it safe to say that the interest in these once forbidden forms of human sexuality is on the increase.

No psychological explanation of this fascination is demanded, as once may have been. This greater interest simply shows that, as in other forms of sexuality, when a culture defines certain sex acts as normal, normal people engage in them. As with explanations of homosexuality, our understanding of this phenomena has changed radically in recent years, and today focuses

Nympho w/male needs to please a lady with fun sex. I'm 34, 6', 170, 8" long, love oral. Answer all. Box 7667, Van Nuys 91409 (072-076)	W/M, 57, generous seeks female over 35 avg lk few hours week for fun/sex. Mark 11325 Blix No Hollywood Ca 91602 answer all.
USC. COED Wants nightlife guy, mar/sgl. Steele Agcy. (Est. 1967) 12-9 PM	**SEXY BLACK NYMPH** seeks men of all ages for day & evening fun. *Hollywood Dating Service*
Girls wanted, any age (18 plus) race or shape, smart, dumb, ugly, pretty for psychological study. Bob. (075-079)	**IF YOU LIKE BROWN SUGAR GIVE ME A CALL. I'LL CUM OVER FOR 3-6 HRS. O.C. ONLY. PAM**
I BEG YOU Don't call me if you have a weak heart outcall (066-067)	**COUPLE OR FEMALES** Yng W/M seeks adventurous-kinky people 25-45 photo a must to John POB 128 Calimesa CA 92320 (075-078)
BROWN SWEETNESS Your imagination is my pleasure. Petite chocolate. Outcall	**BI INTRODUCTION** For girls curious and discreet. Boxholder, POB 215, Hawthorne, California 90250 (075-078)
HANDICAPPED LADY Sexy swinger wants nice people Karen's Dating Club or Orange Co. (070-071)	**WM 23 BLONDE** sks sincere cpls for oral & greek fun ask for Terry & leave message (075-076)
DAYTIME AFFAIR WOMEN Gdlkg W/M 26 marr looking for a sincere discreet affair must enjoy oral sex POB 602 91789 (071-077)	**ORIENTAL LADY 24** Seeks men for a night on the town and? *Hollywood Dating Service*
BLACK BEAUTY 23 Let me satisfy your desires, I'm sweet, sexy, discreet	**MAN OF PLEASURE** Handsome blk male 27 wishes to meet generous women for good times
HOUSE OF CORRECTIONS Men if your mate is wild & you want her tamed & or you both seek to fulfill erotic desires together through expert B&D S/M in privacy w/discretion & all is legit	**MILLIONAIRE 37** Very successful motion picture attorney, large Beverly Hills House, yacht, seeks cult., attr.

The term paraphilias refers to what has in the past been considered deviant or perverse sexual conduct. Personal classified advertisements like the ones reprinted here appear regularly in thousands of newspapers; they indicate both the range of sexual expression and gratification being sought and the great numbers of persons doing the seeking.

not on the so-called abnormal psychological processes of individuals but on changing social tastes, norms, and customs. Our ideas about what constitutes appropriate sexual expression have changed greatly in the past twenty-five years, and with this rethinking has come the understanding that no forms of sexual behavior are abnormal, especially when we take a cross-cultural perspective. This way of looking at these forms of sexual expression has relieved much of the guilt and anxiety people once felt about them. The growing willingness to talk openly about paraphilias and the long lines at the theaters indicate a fascination with and curiosity about these forms of sexual expression. While these may be examples of ideas changing before behavior, in light of the more permissive attitude toward sexual expression behavioral changes are probably also occurring.

Rape

While some ideas about deviant forms of human sexuality have changed, rape continues to be totally unacceptable to the American population. Both males and females can be victims of a rape, but the majority of cases are committed against females. Cases of male rape are frequently reported in the diaries and journals of men who have served time in prisons, where a rape is used as an expression of dominance. Obviously, these cases do not become public knowledge, and in most instances they are ignored by prison officials. We will focus on the rape of women, a matter of growing concern.

There are two different types of rape, statutory and forcible. In *statutory rape*, the female may have consented to sexual intercourse but was younger than the age of consent. The male is then charged with raping her. Each state sets its own age of consent at the level it feels is most appropriate; as a result the age varies widely from state to state. Statutory rape is not as frequent as forcible rape and does not seem to be as great a concern today as it once was, except in cases of preadolescent children. This is primarily because of changing standards for premarital sex. With this in mind, let us focus on the kind of rape most frequently encountered and the form receiving most attention today, *forcible rape*.

Forcible rape is the fastest growing crime in the country, and estimates by criminologists indicate it is the violent crime most frequently committed in America today. According to official statistics, one rape occurs on the average of every nine minutes, but the actual occurrence of rape is undoubtedly higher than this because official statistics are inaccurate, for a number of reasons.[42] First, women are often very reluctant to report that they were raped because of the stigma attached to this act by their family, friends, or spouse. Second, they may wish to avoid an often unpleasant situation when the police and doctors, usually males, question and examine them. Third, once they report it, they may be pressured to testify against the rapist, leading to a confrontation with the assailant, his lawyers, and the court system. This experience can be humiliating. A standard defense practice has been to question not only the accuracy of testimony given by the victim but also her integrity, honor, and character. In the past, rape victims have been forced to disclose details of their prior sexual activity as part of the attempt to imply they may have invited or agreed to the sex acts in question. The reluctance of women to report rape leads most experts to suggest the actual rate of forcible rape is at least four times higher than official figures indicate.

An interesting thing being learned from studies of rape cases, is that forcible rape is not primarily an act of sexual expression. Rape appears to be done not for sexual satisfaction, but to act out male hostility. The rapist wishes to make the woman submit to and be humiliated by the sexual encounter. The satisfaction for the rapist comes from a feeling of power created by making someone submit to his will. The violence or threats of violence accompanying the act of rape are central to understanding this behavior. To focus on sexual satisfaction as the prime motivation of rapists is to miss the most important dimension of this crime.

As with other deviants, the rapist has long been thought of as either insane or psychopathic. According to many studies, particularly Menachem Amir's research on 646 rape cases, this is not true. Amir says, "Studies indicate that sex offenders do not constitute a unique or psychopathological type, nor are they a group invariably more disturbed than the control groups to which they have been compared."[43] Men convicted of rape have a normal sexual personality; the difference between them and nonrapists is that they have a greater tendency to act out and express their pent-up rage in a violent manner.

Because of this, some sociologists are beginning to consider rape as only an extreme form of the relations between men and women traditionally found in our society. American men are taught to be aggressive and to dominate in their relations with women; according to this argument, the rapist simply carries this one step beyond what is considered acceptable. As a result of this view, many feminists interested in the larger issue of sexual politics have seen rape as epitomizing the essential nature of most male-female sexual encounters. For them, rape is simply a more visible form of the way men act toward women and they use rape as a model for discussing the power differences between men and women in American society. While the analogy between rape and other forms of heterosexual behavior may seem farfetched, it has proved useful in sensitizing people to the problem of the relative powerlessness of women.

Besides research findings in the characteristics of rapists, these feminists draw support for their argument from the way rape victims have traditionally been treated by the legal system. If a victim's prior sexual activity can be shown to have involved a number of males instead of just one, the courts traditionally have been more willing to acquit the defendant. This has led to the claim that the courts see women as the sexual property of some man (father or husband) and that in essence, rape is a property crime committed by one man against another. As the feminist Susan Griffen has said, "The laws against rape exist to protect rights of the male as possessors over the female body, and not the right of the female over her own body."[44] Given the way defense and prosecution both have acted in rape cases in the past, it is hard to argue against this view. As Griffen points out, even the prestigious *Yale Law Journal* reflected this rationale in an article published in 1953, when it pointed out that rape decreases the value of a sexual possession because the female becomes used by another man.[45] This kind of thinking was followed in Bangladesh a few years ago when many women were raped by the invading Indian army. When these women returned to their husbands and families, they were cast out on threats of death because they had been raped. They were viewed as spoiled sexual property violated by other men and were deemed to have lost all value in their status as women. Clearly, American thinking does not go this far, but our treatment of rape shows how we think about women and the power men have over them. Like other forms of sexual deviance, rape is deeply rooted in the social structure; to understand it we need to know about the norms, values, and attitudes prevailing in a wide variety of social and sexual relationships between men and women.

Summary

The sexual revolution we described in terms of premarital sex may be said to be occurring in other behaviors as well. There seems to be a growing incidence of extramarital sex, homosexuality, and the paraphilias; and a growing willingness to discuss these matters openly, creating new legal questions connected with sexuality. "How should society treat prostitution?" and "What should be done about pornography in an atmosphere of greater tolerance?" are only two of today's more important questions. Less of a question — and more of a problem — is the question of what should be done about rape, the fastest growing crime. In the next section, we will discuss the various social responses to these problems.

ATTEMPTS AT DEALING WITH THE PROBLEM

New Attitudes

A wide range of sexual behavior has been discussed in this chapter, from premarital sex to rape. Clearly, there is no consistent attitude toward all these acts, some are seen as more deviant than are others. In generations past, the distinctions we now make weren't made. If a boy was caught having sexual intercourse with a girl or was known to have had, a wedding was arranged. Today our attitudes have changed dramatically. Much of what was considered immoral in the past is today seen as within the range of acceptability. This is not true among all segments of the population, for conservatives, certain religious groups, and many older people still feel sex is primarily for reproduction and should be confined to marital partners.

But among the general population and in the legal system, many behaviors once punishable by law are now considered the business of the consenting adults involved. This has led people to say that statutes against certain acts create victimless crimes, such as prostitution, homosexuality, and some of the paraphilias. In trying to ease up on enforcement of laws, for instance, the best the police seem able to do is to localize prostitution, confining it to a particular area of town. In doing so we are right back to the strategy followed by New Orleans before the turn of the century. The infamous district of Storyville was the city's answer to controlling vice; almost a century later, many cities are now reverting to this method of dealing with it.

Based on a changing consciousness of the power available to men and women in our society, many feminists have sought to change how rape is dealt with by the police and courts. They have pressured police departments to hire more female officers and to set up special units to examine rape victims, in an effort to lessen the trauma women encountered in dealing with the police. Women have lobbied to change the notions of acceptable evidence, so that a woman's prior sexual activities are no longer relevant. As a result of these efforts, women who have been rape victims no longer face the ordeal once encountered in confronting their assailant. Also, as feminist ideas spread throughout the population, many more women are willing to acknowledge a rape when it happens to them and bring the matter to the police. With these changes, a greater percentage of rapes is probably being reported to the police.

In other areas of sexual activity, recent changes in the way problems are handled has led to a seeming increase in the activity itself. Homosexuality is perhaps the best example, for with the move to decriminalize this form of sexual expression, it would seem as if there was a great increase in it. Most important for homosexuals is their increasing political organization. In San Francisco, for example, because the homosexual community is politically organized, a candidate for mayor is usually endorsed by gay activists. Getting their endorsement often means picking up an additional 50,000 or more votes, not to be taken lightly by a candidate. Homosexuals are developing a changed self-image and, through their actions, many cities have repealed antihomosexual legislation and have written laws to protect homosexuals against discrimination in employment. And recently the federal government has seemed to change its discrimination against them in both employment and immigration. The case of Air Force Sergeant Leonard Matlovich, who admitted to being a homosexual, caused a change in some of these federal statutes. Matlovich was court martialed and forced to resign from the military, but the Supreme Court decided his dismissal was unconstitutional. In future cases, the military will have to prove a person's homosexuality has interfered with the operation of his unit before he can be forced to resign.

Another recent attempt to resolve the homosexual issue was begun by Anita Bryant, a former beauty queen and a well-known spokeswoman for the Florida citrus industry. Early in 1977 Bryant began a struggle against homosexuals in the Miami area, and became the prime mover behind a group called Save Our Children, organized to get gays out of teaching positions in the public schools. She had little trouble getting an ordinance passed to this effect. Because of her outspoken and sharp attacks on homosexuals, however, she seems to have aroused a political reaction by gays in other parts of the country, where they are better organized. There have been attempts to force President Carter into a stand on the issue of homosexual rights, and there was a short-lived attempt to boycott Florida orange juice at gay bars across the country. But for the most part, the major accomplishment of Bryant has been to politicize the homosexual community more than ever before and to legitimize homosexuals' claims to being an oppressed minority.

Like the feminists, homosexuals are now adopting a more militant stance regarding their civil rights. These two movements are closely related — both challenge the way our society is organized in terms of sex roles. Although their membership does not overlap to any great extent, both groups recognize a central problem to be the issue of male dominance; and each has devised a different strategy to deal with it. Rather than seeing either women's rights activists or male or female homosexuals as sick people, we are beginning to realize that the most basic issue is whether one group in society has the right to dominate another. Politically active homosexual groups as well as groups like the National Organization for Women see the problem as one of limitations placed on individual freedom. Both are intent on trying to change this as rapidly as possible.

Our ideas about prostitution have also changed in recent years. Today there is considerable disagreement over whether prostitution should even be considered a crime. While still illegal, prostitution is usually considered a victimless crime, unless the client is robbed or blackmailed. This view is perhaps the predominant one among judges throughout the large urban areas of the country, where many kinds of sexual deviance are not punished as much as they are in smaller towns. In New York City, some of the more militant prostitutes have formed an organization called Prostitutes of New York. Their aim is not so much to get prostitution legalized but to get male police, judges, lawyers, and pimps off their backs.

Prostitution has been linked to the women's movement. Some women's writings state that, when a woman is willing to play up to a man and use her sexuality as a means of obtaining what she wants, she is essentially acting like a prostitute. There are many variations in selling oneself, including selling one's sexual services for a price. These writers are saying that what constitutes illegal prostitution and what goes on in many heterosexual relationships may not be very different. The past president of NOW, Gloria Steinem, has gone so far as to discuss marriage as a modified form of prostitution. While this is an extreme view, it reflects the kind of concerns some women have when they discuss the problems of living in a male-dominated society. Some radical feminists feel that prostitution compares favorably to marriage because it is more open and honest.

In recent years, another area of controversy has been the definition of what is pornographic or obscene. The courts around the country have bounced from one side to the other in this debate, going from putting actor Harry Reems in jail in Tennessee for his part in *Deep Throat* to allowing kiddie porn to be sold openly in New York City. The debate over community standards of sexual conduct seems to focus on pornography as the major issue, rather than obscenity, probably because of the enormous distribution of the mass media. Magazines like *Penthouse, Hustler,* and *Screw* have huge monthly circulations and their publishers have on occasion been jailed. With pornography becoming even more open in its exposure of human sexual organs and activity, each new issue of these magazines seems to stir up the controversy anew. The issue has become whether a community can set its own standards and what role the law plays in regulating or reinforcing moral notions.

Most of the laws against oral or anal sexual intercourse date back to the turn of the century, and reflect the attitudes of that time. About twenty years ago, the American Law Institute drafted a Model Penal Code to be used by the various states as a guide for the revision of their existing statutes. It provided for the decriminalization of all sexual acts between consenting adults in private. At this writing, nineteen states have adopted this approach; the majority still have laws on the books that make almost all forms of sexual behavior, except heterosexual monogamous intercourse, crimes even for persons married to each other. Needless to say, most of these laws are never enforced.

Iatrogenic Effects

Attempts at dealing with the problem of sexual deviance have not always resulted in a decrease of this behavior, but have often made it appear that there is more of the behavior. For example, the politicization of the gay community has meant homosexuals now have a clearer sense of themselves as being a repressed minority and they are more vocal and willing to fight for their rights. On the other hand, as they become more outspoken and public in their life-style, a backlash is created. Even the most conservative person knows that these behaviors always existed (the Bible is full of incest, adultery, paraphilias), but they could ignore them if they were kept hidden. Once prostitutes and homosexuals became politically active and called for changes in the law, a response was required.

One response is calling for the law to be

vigorously enforced, which can cause an apparent crime wave of a particular undesirable activity. Because of the backlash effect, many cities that were previously lenient are now beginning to crack down on these behaviors. With prostitution, this has meant, in many cities, that the police are arresting male clients as well as the prostitutes. This can have a disastrous effect on the careers or private lives of those men, and the police know it. But with the prostitutes being harder and harder to deal with, arresting and prosecuting the clients seems the best chance to come to grips with the problem.

As our attitudes toward sex behavior have become more liberal, ideas about what constitutes deviance have begun to change. Today we have become blasé about many things that were highly erotic to past generations. In light of this, some people seem to be needing to go to ever greater extremes to become sexually stimulated. Today there is a search for new and ever more bizarre forms of sex, which can be clearly seen in the change in what is considered pornographic or obscene. During World War II, *Esquire* featured daring pin-ups of women in bathing suits; in the early postwar period *Playboy* made millions by showing naked females. Today the more open magazines like *Penthouse* and *Hustler* have seriously cut into *Playboy*'s hold on the market, so much so that Playboy clubs are closing and circulation is dropping. But in the wings await magazines like *Screw* and those publishing kiddie porn, which has been alluded to in popular films like *Taxi Driver* and *Pretty Baby*.

The search for new excesses is also evident in film. X-rated movies once made millions by featuring oral sex, but as that became commonplace, other forms of sexuality were needed to keep the audiences buying tickets. Sadomasochism is now widely featured, with the most bizarre forms of torture and sadism being thought up for each new film. This finally culminated in the supposed appearance of *snuff films*, where an actress was put through the usual array of sex acts common to these films and then finally murdered as part of the grand climax. While no concrete evidence has been found for the existence of these films, that they are even spoken of indicates that at some point, the line of acceptable behavior will have to be drawn again. But until then it is clear that more liberal attitudes have almost forced pornographers into a search for more bizarre kinds of sexuality to sell to the public. As our standards have changed, new definitions of what is deviant have emerged which make past obscenity and pornography appear the epitome of good taste in comparison.

Since the police are the ones who usually become involved in the attempt to keep sexual deviance under control, an additional problem is the drain on the resources available to fight other forms of crime. As with our drug laws, and as happened in the past with prostitution, the police are spending a large amount of their time and effort on problems that do not have great social or economic impact. At the same time they are almost totally unable to come to grips with the major forms of crime in our society. For example, while organized crime is involved in prostitution and pornography, its greatest source of income is gambling. And in light of what we are beginning to find out about the infiltration of organized crime into labor unions, these other activities seem small by comparison.

The law enforcement process misdirects much of its energies into policing relatively harmless forms of behavior while other forms of deviance that are more important go virtually unchecked. In addition, the attempt to control forms of deviance in high demand has always resulted in the corruption of law

Liberal attitudes toward sex mean relaxed standards on pornography and obscenity. Porn shops displaying bizarre gadgets and gimmicks for sexual stimulation are a measure of our obsession with the erotic.

enforcement and has greatly reduced the general respect for the entire legal process. This was obvious from Prohibition in the 1920s, but we never seem to learn that the random and sporadic enforcement of unpopular laws does more to harm social control than it does to eliminate the deviant behavior itself.

PROSPECTS FOR SOLVING THE PROBLEM

As noted at the beginning of this chapter, American sexuality has an adolescent character to it, with a high degree of guilt and anxiety over sexual expression. There also seems to be a lack of understanding that sexuality occurs in the context of human relationships, resulting in a continued attempt to divorce sexual expression from other means of communication. Our understanding of this issue is sharpened by the distinction some authors now make between sexuality and sensuality in our culture. *Sexuality* has to do primarily with genital expression and release, whereas *sensuality* involves a broader range of erotic behavior. A walk through the woods or the smelling of freshly cut hay delights the senses erotically, and is part of the sensuality so lacking in American life. Good food, served in a relaxed and friendly atmosphere adds to the enjoyment of life and is made very much a part of the erotic in other cultures. Instead, in American culture we have a proliferation of McDonald's and porno-shops, both of which have been labeled as equally obscene. In other words, American society has been very good at separating out the sexual from the sensual, commercializing sex, and using it to motivate people to fill their other social roles.

To become sensual, people would have to decompartmentalize their existence and to integrate their lives in a way presently impossible. This was outlined by the political philosopher Herbert Marcuse when he described how the erotic impulses of Americans are repressed and channeled into socially useful ends.[46] The problem is that how these impulses are shaped and structured may not be satisfying to the individuals themselves. Marcuse calls this the process of *repressive desublimation:* sexual impulses are allowed more direct expression than ever before but the gratification of these impulses is used to control behavior in other areas. The idea is complex, but the ramifications of what he is saying can be seen around us. There is little sensuality in a porno shop or in many other forms of sexual expression now allowed. Pornographic movies epitomize what we are talking about, for with very few exceptions they deal with the actors only in terms of their genitals and totally neglect other dimensions of being human.

As we are now beginning to understand, the impulses behind human sexuality are only a small part of the total erotic impulses of life. Sensuality needs expression as well, so that sexuality does not become an overriding concern as the only outlet for our erotic impulses and does not become distorted by being expressed out of context with other aspects of the human condition.

Today we acknowledge that previous standards were too repressive, but many Americans are without any solid idea about what to put in their place. People find themselves with greater freedom, which is hard for many to handle without some guidelines. This is what the great French sociologist Emile Durkheim referred to as anomie, a concept central to his understanding of the paradoxes of a modern society. *Anomie,* a state of general normlessness where ends and the means to achieve them are not clearly defined, creates genuine problems for people. People can no longer rely on standards to guide their actions; and while they have achieved a freedom from control, they are left without goals or limits to direct their behavior. They become confused about how to act, find themselves at odds with past convictions, and have problems in giving meaning to their existence. Some even commit suicide, but excesses of behavior also result from anomie.

A man who saw firsthand the results of anomie is the German-born sociologist Ernest Van den Haag. He spells out his ideas as part of a debate over whether a community should have the right to censor things it finds obscene and pornographic. As part of his position, Van den Haag stressed the fact that communities are bound together by sets of commonly shared norms and values, and that these are essential elements of an integrated social structure. He argues that pornography depersonalized sex, removing the human element and reducing the person to his genitals. This was the kind of thinking, says Van den Haag, which allowed Hitler to move against the Jews and to turn their bodies into soap, their hair into cloth, and the gold from their teeth into money. His main argument is that pornography is a way of thinking that turns people into means to be used simply for pleasure, with all other considerations of their humanness removed.

> Human solidarity is based on our ability to think of each other not purely as means but as ends in ourselves. Now the point of all pornography in my opinion is that it invites us to regard the other person purely as an object of exploitation for sexual pleasures.[47]

Many pornography films reflect this kind of thinking. The problem is that if film and magazine producers have their freedom limited only to those ideas acceptable by today's standards, their right of self-expression is surely being violated. Because of this contradiction between action and our principles of freedom, a new set of acceptable standards may not be developed for some time.

This discussion reflects the most important matter, how people are socialized to treat each other. In pornography people are reduced to their genitals and used for the sexual pleasure they afford. They are not treated as total human beings, but simply as mean to ends. In fact, in many social relations people are treated this way — by the schools, their employers, or even their families. The ability to relate to the total person is largely missing in American society because of the way our work has been structured and by the widespread use of bureaucratic structures by all major institutions, except the family. We learn to treat people as objects in order to survive in our society, and the roles we play with others seldom allow getting to know the other person very well.

Because of their occupational involvement, men are subjected to these pressures far more than women. Successful men seem to know how to sell their personalities and motivate others to work for them while they hide their true feelings about what they are doing. For certain activities this behavior works well; but this behavior also creates many of the problems men face. Many men report having no close male friends because of the inability to break out of this way of relating. Other men are essentially seen only as competitors in the search for success. And if we are to listen to women talking about their relationships with men, we know that their key complaint involves the same issue. They resent their manipulation as a source of pleasure. Because of the high degree of interdependence between social institutions, what goes on in one is bound to influence what happens in the others as well.

Until people learn to restructure their ideas and feelings about sex and begin to relate to other people for themselves, we expect little if any real solution to the problem of sexual deviance. Prostitution and pornography fit in with how power, status, and success are distributed. The pornography of American society is not seen in our X-rated movie houses alone, but is reflected in the way we deal with each other on a day-to-day basis. Unless our ideas about these relationships change, it is doubtful that Americans will use their newly found sexual freedom to create a more sensual and gratifying existence.

IMPORTANT WORDS AND TERMS

adultery	community standards	forcible rape	homosexuality
anomie	double standard	hard-core pornography	intrauterine device (IUD)
blue laws	extramarital sex	hetairai	lesbian

obscenity	pornography	sensuality	soft-core pornography
paraphilia	prostitution	sexuality	statutory rape
pill	repressive desublimation	sexual revolution	

QUESTIONS FOR DISCUSSION

1. This chapter is about sexual deviance. What is normal sexual behavior?
2. The birth-control pill and other forms of reliable contraception have removed reproduction from sex. Has this been good or bad in its consequences?
3. Now that women can control their fertility, should they take the same attitude toward sex that men have had?
4. If there are going to be controls over sexual behavior, who should establish them?
5. Should prostitution be legalized as it has in Nevada? If so, should it be regulated somehow?
6. There is a difference between legalizing a deviant act and decriminalizing it. What is the difference and why is understanding it important?
7. If prostitution were legalized, would the price fall because the costs of doing business would go down?
8. Homosexuals in the military and as classroom teachers are still quite controversial. Take a position on each issue and support it.
9. Does religion still exert an important control over sexual behavior in American society?
10. Can a married man rape his wife, given the way the marriage contract is usually interpreted by the courts?
11. Is deviant sexuality possible between two persons married to each other?
12. What is the age at which sexual intercourse should be legal for girls? Would the age for boys be the same?
13. If a female has sex in return for candy, flowers, dinner, and dancing, is she a prostitute?
14. Male prostitution is not common in American culture. Why?

SUGGESTED READING

RAY RIST (ed.), *The Pornography Controversy; Changing Moral Standards in American Life,* (New Brunswick, N.J.: Transaction Books, 1974).

This collection of articles includes excerpts from the report of the Commission on Pornography and Obscenity and other research articles and position papers. The material assembled aims to shed light on the issues involved in deciding what is pornographic and obscene as well as on the pros and cons of legalizing all sexually explicit material. Comparative studies from Sweden and Denmark are also included. The author has put together a work that is both highly readable and informative.

LESTER KIRKENDALL AND ROBERT N. WHITEHURST (eds.), *The New Sexual Revolution,* (Buffalo, N.Y.: Prometheus Books, 1974).

This collection of articles sheds light on a central theme, the humanist view of sexual morality. The numerous authors have clearly been informed by Kirkendall of his intent, for the articles read as if they were written by a single person working from a single moral position. The authors attempt to formulate a system of morality that does not condemn what many would call deviant sexuality. Instead, each tries to ask when homosexuality, prostitution, and extramarital sex, among other behaviors, can be considered appropriate and acceptable behavior. The articles represent a major contribution to the development of a new system of morality, based not on the religious teachings of the past but rather on a set of principles Kirkendall labels as humanistic. The book is provocative, especially for readers who *might* hold more traditional notions of sexual morality.

ALAN BELL AND MARTIN WEINBERG, *Homosexualities* (New York: Simon and Schuster, 1978).

Based on a large study of homosexual life-styles, this work was sponsored by the Kinsey Institute for Sex Research and represents a major breakthrough in our understanding of gays. While some of the findings were anticipated by earlier studies, this work illustrates the diversity of the life-styles existing within the gay community. By doing so, it breaks down many of the stereotypes about homosexuals and provides good data from which to argue one way or the other about this issue. For those who are interested in being informed on one of the more heated controversies of the day, this book is must reading.

MORTON HUNT, *Sexual Behavior in the 1970s* (New York: Dell, 1975).

Working with a research grant from the Playboy Foundation, Morton Hunt has attempted to update the Kinsey studies of sexual behavior. He tries to determine if there has been a sexual revolution since Kinsey's pioneer work and if so, what is now considered normal sexual behavior. Hunt finds an increase in most kinds of sexual behavior usually considered deviant; in fact, he finds many of these behaviors so common that we must reconsider what we call deviant. For the person interested in reasoning about sexual morality based upon research findings, this book pulls together a lot of statistics not available elsewhere. It is a hard book to dismiss, for while its findings are surprising they seem valid; the research was well done and clearly presented.

WILLIAM MASTERS AND VIRGINIA JOHNSON, *Human Sexual Response* (Boston: Little, Brown, 1966).

While many authors were busy arguing about the morality of human sexuality, this now-famous research team decided to look at sex as it had never been examined before. The physiology of the human sexual response makes for fascinating reading, and while this book is not about deviant sexuality, it should be read by anyone who wishes to be informed in this area. Masters and Johnson have gone on from this basic work to write on problems of human sexual functioning, but this book should be read as the starting point for those interested in the control and expression of human sexuality. While written primarily from a physiological and psychological viewpoint, the book sheds new light on many questions involved in the changing sexual behavior in America.

NOTES

1. Peter Berger, *Invitation to Sociology* (Garden City, New York: Doubleday, 1963).
2. Robert Francoeur, *Eve's New Rib* (New York: Harcourt Brace, 1972), p. 30.
3. Anne Juhasz, *Sexual Development and Behavior* (Homewood, Ill.: Dorsey Press, 1973), p. 195.
4. Verena Zinserling, *Women in Greece and Rome* (New York: Abner Schram, 1972), p. 57.
5. Wayland Young, *Eros Denied* (New York: Grove Press, 1964).
6. Ibid., p. 170.
7. Ibid.
8. Ibid., p. 172.
9. R. E. L. Masters, *Patterns of Incest* (New York: Julian Press, 1963), p. 33.
10. Ibid., p. 34.
11. Connie Brown and Jane Seitz, "You've

Come A Long Way Baby" in Robin Morgan (ed.), *Sisterhood Is Powerful* (New York: Random House, 1970), p. 5.

12. Clellan Ford and Frank Beach, *Patterns of Sexual Behavior* (New York: Harper, 1951), p. 107.

13. Ibid., pp. 130–132.

14. Pitrim Sorokin, *The American Sex Revolution* (Boston: Porter Sargent, 1956), pp. 19 ff.

15. For other examples see Eli Zaretsky, *Capitalism, the Family and Personal Life* (New York: Harper and Row, 1976).

16. Ira Reiss, "How and Why American Sex Standards Are Changing" in J. Ross Eschleman (ed.), *Perspectives in Marriage and the Family* (Boston: Allyn and Bacon, 1969), p. 398.

17. Ibid., p. 401.

18. Vance Packard, *The Sexual Wilderness* (New York: David McKay, 1968), p. 138.

19. Harold Christensen and Christina Gregg, "Changing Sex Norms in America and Scandinavia," in Arlene Skolnick and Jerome H. Skolnick (eds.), *Intimacy, Family, and Society* (Boston: Little, Brown, 1974), p. 180.

20. Ibid., p. 181.

21. Karl King et al., "The Continuing Premarital Sexual Revolution Among College Females," *Journal of Marriage and the Family*, Vol. 39, No. 3, (August 1977), p. 458.

22. Yoon H. Kim, "The Kinsey Findings" in Gerhard Neubeck (ed.), *Extramarital Relations* (Englewood Cliffs, N.J.: Prentice-Hall, 1971), pp. 65–74.

23. B. Krishna Singh et al., "Extramarital Sexual Permissiveness," *Journal of Marriage and the Family* (November 1976), p. 711.

24. Shirley Glass and Thomas Wright, "The Relationship of Extramarital Sex, Length of Marriage, and Sex Differences in Marital Satisfaction and Romanticism: Aghanasious's Data Reanalysed," *Journal of Marriage and the Family*, Vol. 39, No. 6 (November 1977), p. 695 ff.

25. See Minako Maykovich, "Attitudes Versus Behavior in Extramarital Sexual Relations," *Journal of Marriage and the Family*, Vol. 38, No. 3 (November 1976), pp. 601; and R. R. Bell et al., "A Multivariant Analysis of Female Extramarital Coitus," *Journal of Marriage and the Family*, Vol. 37, No. 2 (May 1975), pp. 375.

26. Edmund Bergler and William Kroger, *Kinsey's Myth of Female Sexuality* (New York: Grune and Stratton, 1954), p. 2.

27. Alfred Kinsey et al., *Sexual Behavior in the Human Male* (Phila.: W.B. Saunders, 1949), p. 650.

28. Morton Hunt, *Sexual Behavior in the 1970s* (New York: Playboy Press, 1974).

29. Alan Bell and Martin Weinberg, *Homosexualities* (New York: Simon and Schuster, 1978).

30. Kinsey et al., p. 650.

31. Martha Shelly, "Notes of a Radical Lesbian," in Morgan, *Sisterhood Is Powerful*, pp. 306–307.

32. Ibid., p. 308.

33. Kinsey et al., p. 597.

34. Hunt, *Sexual Behavior in the 1970's*.

35. Department of Health, Education, and Welfare (Office of Human Development), *The Legal Status of Runaway Children* (Washington, D.C.: U.S. Government Printing Office, 1976), p. 7.

36. Ibid., p. 9.

37. John Money, "Imagery in Sexual Hang-ups," *The Humanist* (March-April 1978), p. 14.

38. *The Report of the Commission on Obscenity and Pornography* (Washington, D.C.: U.S. Government Printing Office, 1970).

39. Ibid., p. 24.

40. Ray Rist, *The Pornography Controversy* (New Brunswick, N.J.: Transaction Books), p. 11.

41. Shere Hite, *The Hite Report* (New York: Macmillan, 1976).

42. Federal Bureau of Investigation, "Crime in the United States," *Uniform Crime Reports* (Washington, D.C.: U.S. Government Printing Office, 1977), p. 14.

43. Menachem Amir, *Patterns of Forcible Rape* (Chicago: University of Chicago Press, 1971), p. 314.

44. Susan Griffen, "Rape: the All-American Crime," *Ramparts*, Vol. 10, No. 3 (September 1971), p. 34.

45. Ibid., p. 33.

46. See Herbert Marcuse, *One Dimensional Man* (Boston: Beacon Press, 1964).

47. Quoted in W. Goodman, "The Coming of Bold Pornography," *Current* (February 1977), p. 34.

10 PERSONAL PATHOLOGY
ESCAPE BY MENTAL ILLNESS AND DRUGS

CHAPTER OVERVIEW

INTRODUCTION

HISTORICAL OVERVIEW
Perceptions of Mental Illness
    The Judeo-Christian View
    Institutionalization
    Recent Developments
The Long History of Drugs
    Religious Opposition to Alcohol
    The Failure of Prohibition
Summary

CONCEPTUAL ORIENTATION
Problems in Defining Mental Illness
The Medical Model
    Psychosis
    Neurosis
The Sociocultural Model
    Mental Illness as a Social Role
    The Myth of Mental Illness
The Operational Model
Escape by Drugs
    Defining Drugs
    Defining Drug Abuse
Summary

OBJECTIVE DIMENSIONS OF THE PROBLEM
Who Are the Mentally Ill?
    Social Groups and Mental Illness
    Mental Illness and the Social Structure
    Escaping the Label
Alcohol
    Patterns of Alcohol Consumption
    Perspectives on Alcohol Abuse
Tobacco
Sedatives
Illegal Drugs
    Who Are the Illegal Drug Users?
    Social Costs of Illegal Drug Use
    Perspectives on Illegal Drug Use
Summary

ATTEMPTS AT DEALING WITH THE PROBLEM
Treating Mental Illness
Treating Alcohol Abuse
Treating Drug Abuse
Iatrogenic Effects

PROSPECTS FOR SOLVING THE PROBLEM

IMPORTANT WORDS AND TERMS

QUESTIONS FOR DISCUSSION

SUGGESTED READING

NOTES

This chapter was written by John T. Washington of the University of Central Florida. Copyright © 1980 by John T. Washington.

The greatest blessings come by way of madness, indeed of madness that is heaven sent. It was when they were mad that the prophetess at Delphi and the priestess at Dodona achieved so much for which both states and individuals in Greece are thankful; when sane they did little or nothing.

Plato

It is no longer satisfactory to defend social disapproval of a particular drug on the ground that it is a "mind altering drug" or a "means of escape." For so are they all.

National Commission on Marijuana
and Drug Abuse

CHAPTER OVERVIEW

Mental disorders are considered to be a major health problem in this and other nations as well. Drug abuse is seen as a related and equally grave problem. Since drugs are *psychoactive,* or mind affecting, they influence the mental processes including perception and reasoning. Thus the two are rather closely related problems. Both are essentially *escape mechanisms,* that is, a way of dealing with personal problems by running away.

In this chapter we analyze both mental illness and drug abuse in terms of what makes them social problems. We give a brief historical overview to explain how our society has developed its present perceptions of these problems. Defining mental illness is difficult because different people make different assumptions; we will discuss various definitions and the resulting approaches to the analysis of mental illness. In looking at drug abuse, both legal and illegal drugs are considered. After defining both problems, we will outline their objective dimensions: who is mentally ill and how much drug abuse is there? Finally, we will discuss how attempts at controlling mental illness and drug abuse have led to new problems that some consider to be as serious as the original problems.

INTRODUCTION

Implied in both of the opening quotations is the theme of this chapter, that both mental illness and drugs are means of escape. The question obviously arises: escape from what? The answer is that many people are attempting to get away from what appears to be the deplorable condition of our society. Some groups find themselves poor while living in the world's most prosperous country. The unemployment rate is astronomically high for some segments of the population. The existence of crime, corruption, discrimination, violations of human rights, and various other social conditions contribute to alienate individuals, which provides some motivation for wanting to escape from it all. As we shall see, mental illness and drugs are sometimes used as a way of running away.

Some problems arise when we try to define these two problems. Neither can be defined without subjectivity. With drugs, the subjectivity enters in the decision that one drug is problematical and another is not and in the determination of how much use is a problem and how much is acceptable. With mental illness even more subjectivity is involved. Why are the attempts some individuals make to cope with life a problem and those of others not?

For years this subjectivity was denied. Mental illness was not found in many of our early social problems textbooks. But now we realize that it is one. Societies depend to a considerable extent on their members being at least somewhat predictable and a salient problem with the mentally ill is that they are not. In fact, the components of our definition do fit mental illness. Mental illness represents an observable condition; it is subjectively analyzed; it has been considered by many to be not only undesirable but dangerous, harmful, and even immoral.

It has not been uncommon to attribute the behavior of the mentally ill to possession by an evil spirit. The mentally ill were once perceived as witches, as was discussed in the introductory chapter. For centuries, then, two components of our definitional process were not applicable in the perception of mental illness — mental illness was not regarded as something that could be remedied and it remained a personal condition, not a social problem. The individual was viewed as at least partly responsible because it was widely believed that no evil spirit could possess one's body without one's consent. It was not until the late eighteenth century that we began to reevaluate our perceptions regarding the mentally ill. When Phillippe Pinel took over the Paris Institution for the Insane, he felt that the condition of the mentally ill could be remedied, or at least alleviated. It was at this time that mental illness took on the status of a social problem. Pinel demonstrated his ideas by ordering the chains to be removed from the patients and showing a little kindness toward them. He began the campaign for an environment in which the mentally ill could have the opportunity to recover.

Now, of course, we not only accept the idea that remedy is possible for mental illness, but also believe that at least certain degrees of mental illness can be prevented. For while the behavior is individually exhibited, we find that the roots of that behavior can almost always be located in the social structure in which the individual lives and interacts. Thus, organized efforts have been made to deal with persons suffering from mental illness.

HISTORICAL OVERVIEW

Perceptions of Mental Illness

Throughout human history mental illness has been perceived and treated in a variety of ways. Because of the lack of knowledge regarding the mentally ill, their behavior was frequently misunderstood in ancient times. Many ancient communities regarded the mentally ill as under the influence of unseen supernatural forces. Throughout ancient references to mental illness, there is evidence of this notion that the mentally ill have been possessed by a supernatural power. This notion was apparently widespread. It is this view of the mentally ill — seeing them with a certain awe and mystery — that impelled Plato to write the words that we used as the first epigraph to this chapter.

THE JUDEO-CHRISTIAN VIEW

With the development of the Judeo-Christian tradition, mental illness took on a different connotation. Contrary to being seen as possession by a divine power, mental illness was seen as possession by evil spirits or demons or as a likely result of disobedience. The early Israelites were warned that "if [you] will not obey the voice of the Lord your God or be careful to do all His commandments and His statutes . . . the Lord will smite you with madness and blindness and confusion of mind."[1] Mental illness was clearly undesirable. Instead of evidence of divine presence, it was a punishment or evidence of demonic presence. As a result, the mentally ill were not well treated. We were reminded of the Christian stance on mental illness in the recent movie *The Exorcist*. Exorcism is a ritual designed to drive the evil spirits out of the mentally ill. Various other kinds of treatment have also been used, all reflecting the idea of mental illness as an unnatural possession. In some periods, the mentally ill were branded as heretics and executed.

INSTITUTIONALIZATION

Institutionalization as a form of treatment for mental illness did not come into existence until near the close of the eighteenth century, when segregation replaced execution as a solution to the problem. They were institutionalized by being confined in cells, but were neglected. With the growing secularism of the eighteenth century, the religious view of mental illness was abandoned and cures were thought possible. In the 1790s the French physician Phillippe Pinel began to initiate reforms. Pinel was successful in turning what were prisons for the mentally ill into what later came to be called asylums. In America, Dorothea Lynde Dix was influential in the 1800s in securing better treatment for the mentally ill in institutions. With the founding of the National Committee for Mental Hygiene in 1909, real reforms began to take place. The committee was founded largely as a result of the publicity given the autobiography of Clifford Beers, a former mentally ill patient. Beers's work, *A Mind That Found Itself*, was influential in the refutation of the stereotype of mental illness as incurable. The committee was successful in securing funding for research into mental illness and a new direction was taken to treat this social problem in a more scientific manner.

RECENT DEVELOPMENTS

More recent developments in psychiatry, psychology, psychotherapy, and chemotherapy have arisen out of subjecting the problem of mental illness to serious scientific scrutiny. In the early 1900s, Sigmund Freud and his perspectives on mental illness were given increasing attention and psychology as a science was expanding rapidly. Freud contended that much of mental illness results from the interplay of social and personality factors, indicating the possibility that external social forces play a critical role in determining mental illness. Freud's theories drew criticism from many quarters, and still do, but Freudian psychology influenced changes in many perspectives on mental illness.

With the surfacing of the notion that something could be done about mental illness — with mental illness becoming a social problem — Congress passed the National Mental Health Act in 1946. As a result of this act, the National Institute of Mental Health was established within the United States Public Health Service.[2] Mental illness began to be focused on as a major health problem. The American Psychiatric Association was also growing at this time, and the profession of psychiatry was gaining increasing stature. With the gradual dissemination of more scientific knowledge about mental illness, psychiatrists, psychologists,

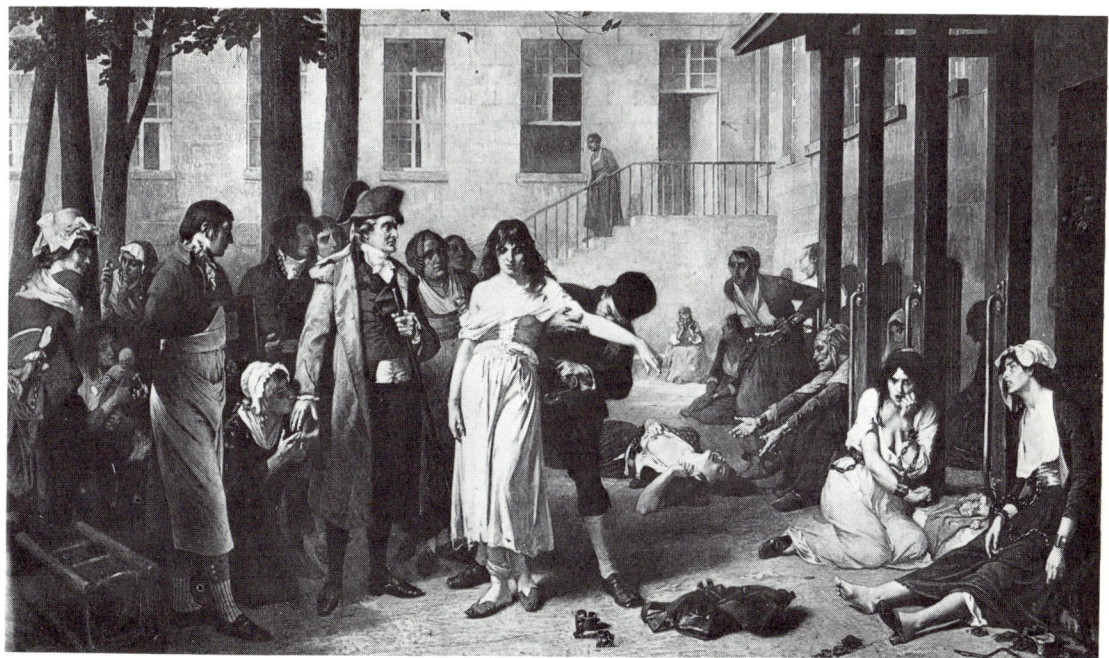

Until the late 1700s, the mentally ill suffered inhumane treatment, even death, at the hands of authorities who believe the affliction was of the devil and incurable. One reformer who introduced decent care for the mentally ill was French physician Phillippe Pinel, shown here removing chains from patients of a Paris insane asylum.

and other professionals began to counter some of the stereotypes held about the nature of mental illness.

The Long History of Drugs

Narcotics — drugs that lull the senses and can lead to addiction — have been used since antiquity, particularly in the Orient. By the mid-1800s, physicians had become aware of the addicting potential of the *opiates*, narcotics derived from the opium poppy such as heroin and morphine. However, since drugs were not illegal or restricted in America, those who had become addicted to opiates could obtain them on a regular basis. Opiates were sold conveniently and at low prices throughout the century; morphine came on the market after the Civil War, and heroin, synthesized in Germany in 1898, was readily available. These drugs could even be purchased by mail order. Opium and its derivatives could be legally imported and drugs such as morphine were manufactured legally within the United States. Historical evidence indicates that there was considerable production of opium in the South during the latter half of the nineteenth century. The nonmedicinal use of opium, while not illegal, was regarded as immoral, although there were few serious social sanctions against its use. Some, pointing at the widespread use of narcotics and the ease with which they could be obtained, have called nineteenth-century America a "dope fiend's paradise."

Twentieth-century America, on the other hand, is the land of the smoker and drinker. On a numerical and proportionate basis, alcohol and tobacco are the most common drugs in America today. Cigarette smoking has undergone a number of changes in America. As far back as 1870, smoking was strongly condemned by many individuals and groups. But during Prohibition in the 1920s, cigarette smoking increased and Americans began to show greater acceptance of this behavior. Alcohol, of course, is an older drug. References to the problems connected with alcohol date back well into ancient times. Despite warnings about the ultimate outcome of excessive use of alcohol, drinking played an important ritualistic and social role in the major ancient civilizations. Because of its longer history and because more efforts have been directed at changing patterns of alcohol use, we will focus on it in our historical survey.

RELIGIOUS OPPOSITION TO ALCOHOL

During the Industrial Revolution's initial phases, drunkenness became widespread, particularly in such cities as London, where many areas of the city were *ginhead* regions where the drinking of gin, which was cheap and readily available, was prevalent. The skid rows of today's large cities provide a modern counterpart. Opposition to this emerging pattern of visible and substantial alcohol use led to the enactment of statutes against drunkenness, the first significant legal reaction to the problem. The campaign for such laws was spearheaded by religious organizations. Religious opposition was based largely on Calvinistic concepts of asceticism and provided the ideological basis for much of the religious opposition to alcohol use today.

It should be noted, however, that for the most part religious opposition is not concerned with alcohol abuse but with the question of whether alcohol should be used at all. Religious and legal opposition to the use of alcohol has contributed to the problem by creating an ambivalence toward alcohol use in societies where drinking has been historically tolerated or even encouraged. Of course, the triumph of the movement to put an end to the use of alcohol was Prohibition, the result of almost one hundred years of campaigning for temperance in the United States.

This struggle had intensified immediately before and during World War I, when much unrest existed with respect to the use of alcoholic beverages. In the South, many states enacted prohibition laws to control alcohol use. By 1916, twenty-four states, or half of all the states at the time, had such laws. Legislation was passed on the federal level also. Laws enacted in 1917 had reduced the alcoholic content of beer and Congress had passed a law outlawing the manufacture of all alcoholic beverages except beer and wine. In January 1918, the issue of complete national prohibition was presented before congress as the Eighteenth Amendment to the Constitution, commonly known as the Volstead Act after its sponsor. After Congress passed the act and overrode a presidential veto, the Supreme Court in June 1920 declared the Eighteenth Amendment constitutional. Prohibition became law. During the twenties further steps were taken to strengthen the law; by 1929, persons convicted of manufacturing, importing, exporting, selling, or transporting alcoholic beverages could be sent to jail for five years and fined $10,000.

Gin, cheap and plentiful, was the drink of the English poor and the target of religious temperance campaigns. This 1829 anti-alcohol cartoon shows a drunken London family, children and infant included, delirious in the jaws of a vicious trap from which the only escapes are workhouse, madhouse, jail, or death.

THE FAILURE OF PROHIBITION

The law's failure became rapidly evident during the twenties, as massive deviance prevailed. People everywhere were drinking, even those who had not drunk before. The Association Against the Prohibition Amendment started compiling data, which indicated that after 1920 there was a steady increase in alcohol-induced insanity and in deaths from alcoholism and alcohol-related diseases. At the same time, organized crime grew rapidly, realizing considerable income in the manufacture, sale, and distribution of illegal alcohol.

The noble experiment, as Prohibition was called, had virtually no effect on the hard-core population who had been alcoholic before the law was enacted. If anything, the widespread flouting of the law made alcohol use more acceptable, enabling alcoholics to hide their behavior more successfully. Thus it did not even deal effectively with the problem it was created to solve. By focusing on alcohol use rather than abuse, it made excessive drinking under certain circumstances entirely legitimate socially, and caused many to question whether laws relating to alcohol consumption had any validity.

This questioning was extended to other drugs as well. Prohibition not only contributed to the increase of the popularity of alcoholic beverages, it also contributed to the popularized use of drugs in general, particularly marijuana, which had been little used before the 1920s.[3] The use of other drugs, such as ether, caffeine, and tobacco also increased.

People began to see that the law was not working and that it helped to legitimize deviance and stimulated the growth of organized crime. Opposition to the law grew rapidly in the late 1920s. By 1932, both major political parties had come out in favor of repealing the law. In 1933, Congress finally passed the Twenty-first Amendment, which repealed the Eighteenth and left the matter of regulating alcohol up to the states. The problem came to be defined as alcohol abuse — not mere use.

Summary

Both the problems of mental illness and drug use have undergone changing definitions in this century. Mental illness was long perceived as a visitation by a supernatural power, first by a benign one, then by a demonic one. With this perception, nothing could be done to help the mentally ill. With a more secular view of the world, we now see mental illness as a condition that is abnormal but that can be treated and cured.

Attitudes toward drug use have also changed. It too was long associated with religious experiences, but such an attitude disappeared in the face of Christian thinking.

The religious opposition to alcohol — the most common drug then as now — rose after the Industrial Revolution and peaked in the United States in Prohibition, which banned all alcohol consumption. The failure of Prohibition has convinced many people that fighting the use of drugs is impossible. Still followed, however, is a policy of opposing and trying to end drug abuse — the excessive use of drugs. This is the focus of efforts against most drugs today.

CONCEPTUAL ORIENTATION

Both mental illness and drug abuse are complex concepts, requiring careful definition. Both seem like personal matters, but entail social definitions, a fact which makes them social problems. The concept of mental illness implies a comparative mental health; because the workings of the mind are less well understood than those of the body, the decision of what is health and what isn't is less objective. Because the criterion for judging is social interaction, the definition is social. Drug abuse implies an acceptable limit for drug use; it is social because that limit is subjectively and variously defined by groups. To understand what we mean by these terms then, we must see how our society defines them.

Problems in Defining Mental Illness

Most everyone agrees that being mentally ill is undesirable. However, what are perceived as the specific characteristics of this undesirable condition will vary from one individual to the next. Our question then becomes how do we know what mental illness is or what causes it? Is the person who becomes too easily enraged suffering from a mental disorder? Is the person who talks with spirits sufficiently odd to merit the label of mentally ill? Is mental illness many different things? Does it really exist?

These questions are not easy to answer. Over the past century, our perceptions of mental illness have changed. We have come to recognize that a serious disorder in one part of the world is regarded with indifference in another. But this is an example of how more knowledge of mental illness has confused us rather than clarified the matter. It is no secret that several psychiatrists examining the same patient may all come up with quite different diagnoses. We may deduce then that despite our familiarity with mental illness as a concept, there is little consensus on the necessary conditions for this label.

John J. Schwab and his associates tell of a highly esteemed psychiatrist in Brazil who was empowered to build a mental hospital. In seeking scientific criteria to determine who should be admitted, he reviewed his medical knowledge and searched the writings of philosophers and theologians. He found that obvious psychopathology, or behavior disorders, was an insufficient criterion and concluded that mental illness is evidenced by a disturbance of reason or of the mental faculties, by a deviation from Aristotle's golden mean. Using this criterion, however, he found he would have to confine most of the population — imbalance was characteristic of the majority. Therefore, he reevaluated his criteria and decided that perhaps the mentally ill were really the remaining few who appeared to be balanced, despite the chaos, revolution, and unrest of the time. Eventually almost everyone in the province would have been hospitalized at one time or another according to various criteria. Realizing that scientific precision had not been achieved, he finally released all the inmates, and with supreme logic, incarcerated himself as the sole patient.[4]

The Brazilian psychiatrist's dilemma is that of all who work with the mentally ill. No single definition of mental illness is fully satisfactory to all. How one defines mental illness is very much a matter of the particular perspective or model one uses in studying the topic. We will concentrate on two such models: the medical and the sociocultural. Both have useful and important things to say about mental illness and they are not necessarily opposed, as we will see.

The Medical Model

Traditionally, mental illness has been approached from the perspective of the medical model. The medical model assumes that mental illness has some organic basis — that it should be defined by traditional medical criteria. Using this perspective, psychiatrists and psychologists generally agree that mental disorders fall into two basic categories: (1) *psychosis,* which is characterized by gross departures from reality; and (2) *neurosis,* which is characterized by a low degree of departure from reality, if any at all.

PSYCHOSIS

Distinguishing between psychosis and neurosis is not always easy. Indeed sometimes it is impossible. The diagnosis of mental illness is a major problem. Many of the symptoms of the severe neurosis may be identical with those of a mild psychosis. Also, characteristics of the patient's social background may influence the diagnosis of his particular illness. This diagnostic confusion adds to the problem of dealing successfully with mental illness.

In an effort to resolve this diagnostic disarray, the American Psychiatric Association (APA) has produced a classification system that attempts to sort out various types of mental illness and disorders. This scheme appears in Table 10.1, with appropriate examples. It embodies a progressive effort to sort out neuroses from psychoses, acute from chronic conditions, and organic from functional disorders. However, a detailed inspection of the system will disclose many areas of overlap, particularly between the neuroses and the personality and nonpsychotic mental disorders. While this classification represents an attempt to define certain types of mental illness more rigidly, the problem is still far from resolved.

Among psychoses, the main differentiation is between organic psychoses and nonorganic psychoses, sometimes called functional psychoses. The *organic psychoses* are those which are the result of some physiological cause, such as damage to the brain tissues or a chemical imbalance. Brain tissue damage may result from physical injury, brain tumors, or alcoholism, among other causes. *Functional psychoses* are thought to have no such clearly defined physical basis. Instead functional psychoses are believed to be either partially or totally psychological. It is these kinds of psychoses that we are particularly concerned with, because it is these that seem to represent an attempt to escape. Also, these are the disorders believed to be most severe.

Schizophrenia is the most common functional psychosis. Schizophrenia includes many different types. *Simple schizophrenia* is characterized by a slow reduction of external interests and attachments and by apathy and indifference, which leads eventually to the deterioration of social relationships. *Hebephrenic schizophrenia* is easily recognizable, as the patient has very disorganized thinking, often giggles inappropriately and for long periods of time, displays silly or regressive mannerisms, and has many hypochondriac complaints. The *paranoid schizophrenic* possesses grandiose or persecutory delusions, often accompanied by interest in or obsession with religion. This type is a common diagnostic category of schizophrenics, and is possibly the closest to popular stereotypes of what constitutes insane behavior. In *catatonia*, another variation of schizophrenia, a patient may spend long periods of time in a comatose state, seemingly cut off from the external world. These patients provide acute problems for the asylums in which they are confined, since they require total care. Because of the identification of these various types, physicians, particularly psychiatrists, are becoming convinced that schizophrenia is not a single illness, but a group of illnesses with substantial variety. This conclusion makes the search for causes extremely difficult.

NEUROSIS

In contrast to the psychotic, who suffers a serious disorder and is often unaware of his illness, the neurotic person suffers a milder disorder and is often aware of the difficulties that he is having and is thus easier to treat. This is particularly true with regard to those patients who voluntarily seek help.

The main symptom of neurosis is anxiety. Some neurotic behavior is more clearly detectable than others. For example, the form referred to as obsessive-compulsive neurosis, in which the person experiences the persistent intrusion of unwanted thoughts, urges, or actions that he is unable to stop, may result in an observable activity out of the ordinary. The person may engage in behaviors intended to drive away the dreaded

TABLE 10.1 The Diagnostic Nomenclature Adopted by the American Psychiatric Association

Condition	Examples
1. Mental retardation	Borderline retardation (IQ of 83) to severe retardation (IQ may be impossible to determine).
2. Organic brain syndromes	Disorders caused by, or associated with, impairment in brain tissue function; psychosis caused by senility, alcoholism, intracranial infection, arteriosclerosis, other physical disorders, poison.
3. Nonorganic psychoses	Schizophrenia of the simple, hebephrenic, paranoid, or undifferentiated type. Different categories exist for whether the condition is acute or chronic. Other disorders include involutional melancholia, manic-depressive illnesses, "pure" paranoia, and depressive reactions that are clearly psychotic.
4. Neuroses	Types: anxiety, hysteria, phobic, obsessive-compulsive, depressive, neurasthenic, depersonalization, and hypochondriacal. There is a residual category of "other."
5. Personality disorders and nonpsychotic mental disorders	Personality disorders: paranoid, schizoid, obsessive-compulsive, antisocial, and hysterical are some examples. Included in this category are sexual deviations: fetishism, pedophilia, transvestism, exhibitionism, voyeurism, sadism, and masochism. Also included are disorders caused by alcoholism and drug dependence.
6. Psychophysiological disorders	Psychologically-caused skin disorders, respiratory, musculoskeletal, cardiovascular, hemic, lymphatic, gastrointestinal, genito-urinary, and endocrine disorders. Other special symptoms with a psychological cause: speech disturbances, learning disorders, tics, excessive insomnia, and other special symptoms.
7. Transient situational disturbances	Adjustment reactions at various transitional stages in the life cycle: infancy, childhood, adolescence, adulthood, old age.
8. Behavior disorders in childhood and adolescence	Withdrawal, overanxiety, runaway, unsocialized aggression, hyperkinetic disorders, and group delinquent reactions.

Source: Adapted from Committee on Nomenclature and Statistics, *DSM-II, Diagnostic and Statistical Manual of Mental Disorders* (Washington, D.C.: American Psychiatric Association, 1968), pp. 5–12.

thoughts or urges. For example, if the obsession is about germs, the patient may attempt to rid himself of them by frequent compulsive handwashing. Sometimes more complicated rituals are employed by persons with such an obsession.

Other identified neuroses include *phobia* (an exaggerated fear of something), *hypochondria* (imagining physical ailments), *neurasthenia* (chronic weakness), and *hysteria* (high excitability or unmanageable fear). Persons who exhibit behavior that fits these labels experience a certain inability to function adequately. The person does not completely break with reality and is able to function on a whole, but he does experience anxiety that makes it difficult to perform some social roles.

The Sociocultural Model

If the assumption of the medical model is correct, we may think of mental illness simply as a form of physical illness. Unfortunately, we cannot be sure that this assumption is correct. There is evidence that much of the behavior labeled mental illness is brought about by social and cultural factors. The weakness of the medical model is that it does not sufficiently account for the influence of these factors. To correct for this lack, we may analyze mental illness from a sociocultural perspective. Some interesting contributions to this view have been made by Thomas Scheff and Thomas Szasz.

MENTAL ILLNESS AS A SOCIAL ROLE

Thomas Scheff presents a theory of mental disorder in which psychiatric symptoms are considered to be labeled violations of social norms and chronic mental illness is a social role.[5] Scheff sees mental illness as a way of escaping from the pressures of reality.

Scheff argues that mental illness may be more usefully considered as a social status than as a disease, because the symptoms are vaguely defined and widely distributed, and the definition of behavior as symptomatic of mental illness usually depends on social rather than medical considerations. He contends that the status of the mental patient is an *ascribed status,* or imposed from outside, with the conditions for gaining and losing the status external to the patient. (In an *achieved status* the conditions for gaining and losing the status depend on the person's own behavior.)

To explain how the label is applied, Scheff posits that the culture of the group provides a vocabulary for categorizing many norm violations: crime, perversion, drunkenness, and bad manners are familiar examples. Each term is derived from the type of norm broken and from the behavior involved. After exhausting these categories, however, there is always a residue of the most divergent violations. For these behaviors the culture provides no explicit label. For the convenience of the society, those instances of unnamable rule-breaking are lumped together into a *residual category:* formerly it was witchcraft or spirit possession, in our society it is mental illness.

What is defined as mental illness is behavior out of consonance with social perceptions of reality. Although there is a great cultural variation in what is defined as real, each culture tends to regard its definition of reality as true and absolute. Society does not always provide an orderly way of handling violations of its expectations. The typical norm governing reality, therefore, goes unstated, but its violation is unthinkable for most members of society. For many in our society, violation of these norms may be frightening. Thus, the violator is perceived to be deviant and accordingly is labeled as mentally ill.

THE MYTH OF MENTAL ILLNESS

The thesis of Thomas Szasz is that mental illness is a myth.[6] Szasz is not suggesting that mental disorders do not exist. Instead, he contends that they are not illnesses as such, but merely problems in coping with life or interacting with others.

According to Szasz, mental illness is an ambiguous label, and those who use it seem to wish to straddle and evade the conflict of interests between the patient and his social environment. Szasz argues that the significance of interpersonal and social conflicts tends to be obscured by traditional definitions, which emphasize conflicts among objects, identifications, or roles within the patient. Szasz is quick to point out that he does not intend to minimize the theoretical significance and therapeutic value of the basic psychoanalytic position concerning the function of internal objects. His thesis is simply that it is as possible for a person to use inner conflicts as an excuse to avoid facing up to interpersonal and sociopolitical difficulties as it is for him to use the latter difficulties to avoid facing up to the former. Thus, in the words of Szasz, "mental illness may be viewed as a manifestation of strain in an individualistic society."[7]

Szasz analyzes mental disorders in terms of what he calls *defective strategies*. He reminds us that all societies have practices that are intended to make life easier for those who are ill, which all members of societies are aware of. Therefore, when some members of society are faced with difficulties or problems that they feel are insurmountable, they simply use mental illness, on an unconscious level, to avoid dealing with their unpleasant situation. In this sense, many people become mentally ill as a result of not having effective strategies for coping with unpleasant situations or demanding conditions. The so-called mental disorder is simply the language of illness, indeed, the myth of mental illness.

The Operational Model

Before leaving the sociocultural approach to mental illness, one final definition should be mentioned. John Schwab, Nancy McGinnis, and George Warheit developed an operational definition for mental impairment. Schwab and his associates operationally define mental impairment as the "degree of disturbance and distress felt by the individual, his capacities as perceived by himself and others, and his subjective sense of failure and dissatisfaction."[8] These authors suggest that substituting *impairment* for *illness* will make study easier in three ways. It will enable researchers to rate respondents on a continuum of severity, without diagnosing them. It will enable researchers to sidestep the question of causes to the extent they wish. And it will open up this study to social scientists who maintain that the nature of mental illness is unclear and therefore unmeasurable.[9]

Measuring impairment, they say, involves rating on each of the following indices:

1. a symptom inventory specifically designed to gauge indicators of health and illness, particularly anxiety and depression, basic human reactions
2. a detailed assessment of functional capabilities pertaining to work, leisure, and family; other relationships; and a wide variety of social interactions
3. an index of aspirations and dissatisfaction that can show the individual's sense of success and failure

The authors point out that these indices are derived from the social science as well as medical models. They also say that such a synthesis is necessary in order to appreciate the sociocultural changes that are altering standards for appraising health, illness, and impairment.

Finally, Schwab and his associates summarize what they believe to be the strength of this definition, by saying that it does not completely reject seeing illness as an entity while it still acknowledges that mental impairment is, to some extent, socially defined. The definition evaluates the individual's interpersonal life and role expectations and performance as well as his capabilities and functions. This model is also valuable because the individual's condition can be viewed in temporal perspective, taking into account whether it is unchanging or changing, and if changing, whether in a satisfactory or unsatisfactory way.

Escape by Drugs

Drugs, in themselves, do not necessarily constitute a social problem. We are a drug-taking society and for the most part always have been. It is safe to say that most human societies engage in some drug use that is accepted as normal. What also should be said is that each society determines which drugs its members may legitimately consume and which they may not. Because norms surround drug taking — both in the acceptability of certain drugs and in the acceptability of certain quantities — drug abuse is made possible. It is drug abuse that is really the social problem.

DEFINING DRUGS

In the broadest sense a *drug* may be defined as any substance that affects or alters any functioning of an organism. Drugs may cause changes in both the bodily processes and behavior.[10] Included in this definition would be many of the substances that are very familiar to most Americans, such as aspirin, tobacco, and caffeine. But it is not these familiar substances that come to the minds of most Americans when we discuss drugs, and certainly not when we talk about drug abuse. When someone mentions drugs, most Americans simply think of those that are considered illegal, such as marijuana, heroin, and cocaine. But although the more familiar substances do not come readily to mind, they are drugs nonetheless and they can be both misused and abused.

DEFINING DRUG ABUSE

Drug abuse refers to three things. It means the use of illegal drugs. It means the illegal use of legal drugs, for example, obtaining narcotics through forged prescriptions or through the unethical connivance of a physician. And it means the excessive use of legal drugs. An important point to remember is that excessive use is recognized by law: for example, there are many laws regarding public drunkenness or driving while under the influence of alcohol.

Summary

Without overlooking the fact that some disorders have an organic origin, more and more social scientists are emphasizing the importance of social and cultural factors in the development of mental illness. The mentally ill are stigmatized because people are afraid of their behavior. They are not treated like other deviant groups and not held responsible for their condition. Society relieves them of responsibility for their behavior, excusing it on the grounds that they are incompetent, and may even care for them. Thus, mental illness can be a tool for escaping unpleasant social conditions.

Also available as a means to escape are drugs. As we have shown, drug abuse has two aspects. When it involves illegality — using or obtaining illegal drugs — it becomes a social problem because it is a crime. But in its other aspect it is also a social problem. Excessive use of drugs, when it occurs often, shows a desire to escape from reality and impairs the person's ability to function socially.

OBJECTIVE DIMENSIONS OF THE PROBLEM

How many people are using these forms of escape? What proportion of the population cannot cope with life and tries to avoid it? What are the characteristics of these people? What are the social consequences of their actions? It is to these questions that we now turn.

Who Are the Mentally Ill?

In 1974, 374,554 persons were admitted to state and county mental hospitals, but 389,094 were released.[11] This trend has been followed for many years, resulting in a steady decline in the number of individuals in state and county institutions. The resident population in 1974 was only 38.5 percent of that in 1955. These data reflect the tendency to treat the mentally ill outside institutions. More admissions are to general hospitals now and when admissions are required, hospitals tend to treat patients and release them more quickly.

SOCIAL GROUPS AND MENTAL ILLNESS

As Figure 10.1 shows, males are more likely than females to be admitted to hospitals for mental illness at all age levels. This is true among whites and nonwhites. However, adult nonwhite females are admitted more often than white males, because nonwhites tend to be overrepresented among those admitted. Nonwhites accounted for 22.1 percent of those admitted to mental hospitals, with the largest percentage in those under twenty-four years old.[12] In addition, those persons with the least education comprised the highest percentage of admissions relative to size of the national population, as shown in Figure 10.2. These data clearly show differences in the patterns of diagnosis and treatment of the mentally ill in different social strata.

As with any social indicators, there are some problems inherent in the collection of mental health data. A number of factors need to be considered in looking at the data on mental illness. We must recognize the possibility that people in the higher social strata are better able to conceal mental illness by seeking private treatment and by being diagnosed as less seriously ill. Recent evidence indicates that the poor are less likely to seek treatment for mental disorders until the condition has become severe.[13] Accordingly, poorer patients are more likely to be diagnosed as seriously ill. Thus, low-income persons are likely to be overrepresented in the group labeled psychotic and underrepresented in the group called neurotic. Higher-status neurotics, by seeking treatment earlier, are less likely to develop psychoses. This pattern of exposure to treatment reflects the tendency of other health statistics to reflect class differences. Moreover, recent evidence suggests that the rate of psychological impairment of all types (neurosis, psychosis, and personality disorders) is highest among the poor.[14] Since the poor do not usually seek treatment until the symptoms are serious, it is evident that the group most in need of treatment actually receives the least amount of early treatment. The gap between need and treatment is a major problem, which is

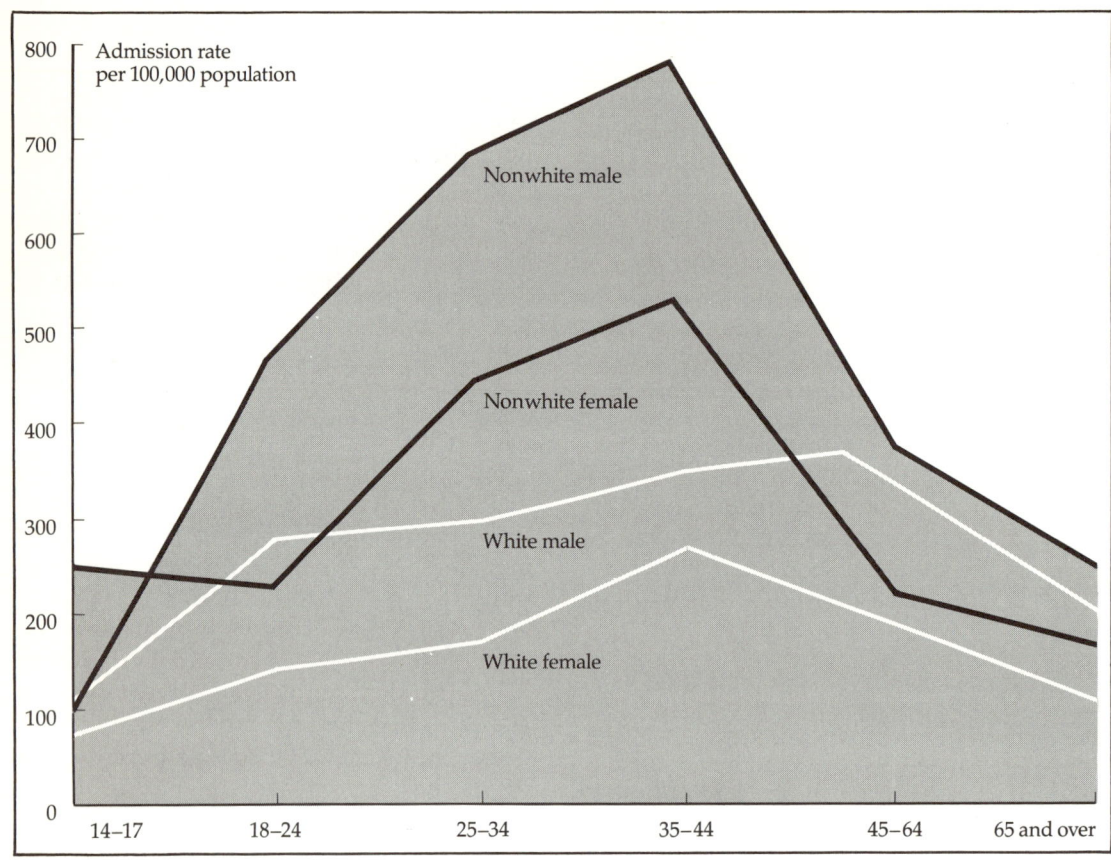

FIGURE 10.1 Admission Rates to State and County Mental Hospitals by Age, Sex, and Race, 1969

Source: Carl A. Taube, *Statistical Note No. 41* (Washington, D.C.: Department of Health, Education, and Welfare, 1971).

produced by social class and by the relative isolation of the poor from the rest of society.

MENTAL ILLNESS AND
THE SOCIAL STRUCTURE

Key aspects of the social structure influence the incidence of mental illness, including the socioeconomic order, urbanization, urban migration, and the type of treatment the mentally ill receive. Social values also have an effect, such as our emphasis on competition, individual initiative, individual responsibility, and success. These values, coupled with the desirability of upward mobility, place many people at a competitive disadvantage and create strains and stresses with which it is difficult, if not impossible, for them to cope with successfully.

Some evidence indicates that mental illness may have a close relationship to other social problems, particularly crime. Stanislav Kasl and Ernest Harburg, in a study of mental illness and residential factors, found that perceived stress was an important factor in

Objective Dimensions of the Problem

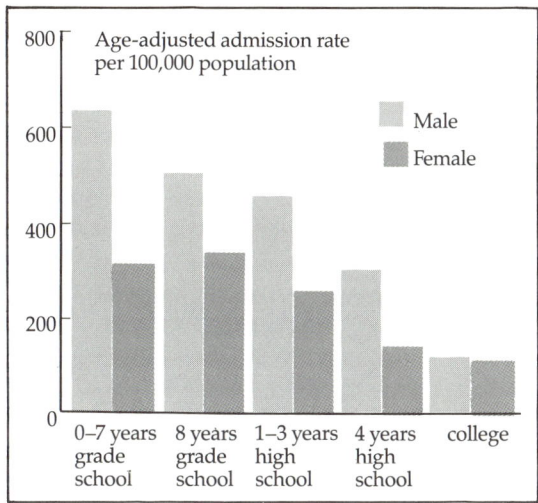

FIGURE 10.2 Admission Rates to State and County Mental Hospitals by Extent of Education, 1969

Source: Carl A. Taube, *Statistical Note No. 34* (Washington, D.C.: Department of Health, Education, and Welfare, 1971).

producing mental illness, and that stress was highest in high crime areas as people felt quite threatened by criminal activities.[15]

As with any form of deviance, mental illness can be viewed as a problem that emerges as a result of how people are labeled and whether their behavior is regarded as threatening or not. Many sociologists, particularly Howard Becker, regard the labeling of deviant behavior as a social process quite independent of the characteristics of the person exhibiting the behavior.[16] This view helps explain the class differences in mental illness also. Lower-class people are likely to be regarded as dangerous, and others are not, even when they exhibit similar behavior. Also, high-status persons can avoid being labeled as deviant, or mentally ill, by hiding their illness or being labeled as less threatening because of their social position.

ESCAPING THE LABEL

Even if a person resists the label of mental illness, it may be hard to discard. If a person violates critical norms, such as disrobing on a public street or bursting into violent fits of temper with no apparent reason, he may still be regarded as deviant even if he claims that there is no impairment. The reason is that one of the characteristics of some kinds of mental illness is a denial by the patient that anything is wrong with him. To modify Scheff's approach somewhat, the person may be forced to accept the sick role, even if he vehemently denies that anything is wrong, because stereotypes of mental illness are such that denials are expected. This differs from Scheff's theory that mental illness is adopted in an effort to relieve pressure. In this instance, however, the person has no control over the labeling process or its consequences.

Alcohol

Abundant evidence suggests that alcohol is the most widely used drug, and is the primary addiction problem in the United States today.[17] However, evidence provided by the National Commission on Marijuana and Drug Abuse showed that few Americans are aware of the extent of alcohol abuse or addiction. In one survey only 7 percent of the respondents recognized alcoholism as a serious social problem.[18]

PATTERNS OF ALCOHOL CONSUMPTION

Most American adults over eighteen drink some form of alcoholic beverage occasionally, and over half of the adult population uses alcoholic beverages on a regular basis.[19] From this information, one might reason that being a drinker, rather than an abstainer, is normative in American society. However, there are wide variations in American drinking practices, as well as some serious value conflicts over alcohol and its use. Such variations make it difficult to perceive any common values or drinking pattern. Consumption patterns are strongly influenced by socioeconomic factors, age, group membership, and individual needs.

Despite this confusion, some generalizations can be made. There has been a slight increase in the proportion of adults who can be considered as drinkers, or those consuming alcohol once a month or more frequently, as shown in Figure 10.3. As Figure 10.4 shows, more males are heavy drinkers. The percentage of male heavy drinkers is 15 percent, compared with 9 percent of the total population. It is also apparent that men exceed women in all age categories, although drinking in general — and heavy drinking in particular — is concentrated among the young (see Figure 10.5). Included within the youthful and early middle-aged male population of heavy drinkers are a large proportion of the nation's alcoholics.

Heavy drinking may be common among adolescents and young adults, but for most persons drinking becomes controlled and tends to taper off as the individuals develop more rigid social controls. For some 9 million or more American adults, however, drinking progresses to the point that it becomes a personal problem, eventually culminating in the pattern that we call alcoholism.[20] Because this happens to one in every ten drinkers, we see that use of an acceptable drug can result in a social problem.

PERSPECTIVES ON ALCOHOL ABUSE

Alcohol abuse on a regular basis, which people call alcoholism, eludes precise definition. Marty Mann, one of the cofounders of Alco-

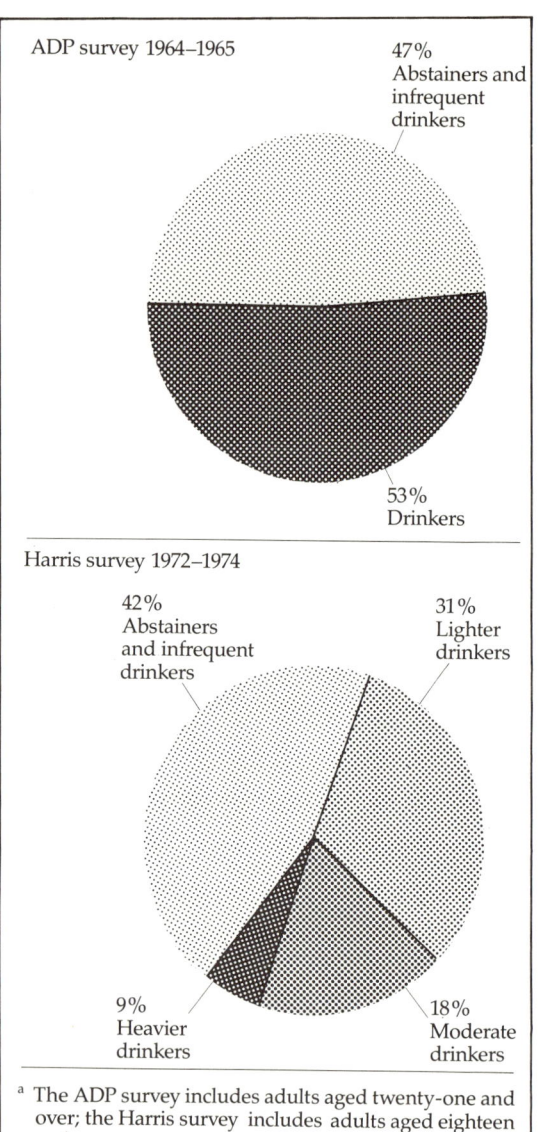

[a] The ADP survey includes adults aged twenty-one and over; the Harris survey includes adults aged eighteen and over.

FIGURE 10.3 Percentage of Drinkers and Types of Drinkers Among Adults, 1964–1974[a]

Source: National Institute on Alcohol Abuse and Alcoholism, *Second Special Report to the U.S. Congress on Alcohol and Health: June, 1974* (Washington, D.C.: U.S. Government Printing Office, 1975), p. 7.

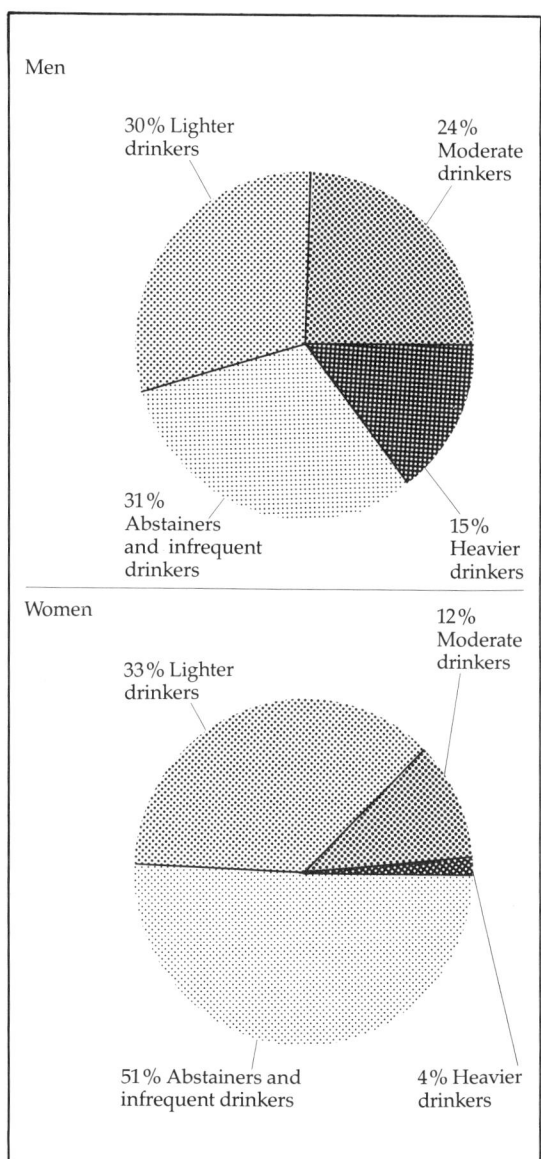

FIGURE 10.4 Percentage of Drinkers by Sex, 1972–1974

Source: National Institute on Alcohol Abuse and Alcoholism, *Second Special Report to the U.S. Congress on Alcohol and Health: June, 1974* (Washington, D.C.: U.S. Government Printing Office, 1975), p. 7.

holics Anonymous, an organization dedicated to rehabilitating alcoholics, defines alcoholism as "a pattern of drinking which causes a continuing and growing problem in any department of the drinker's life."[21] Mann concludes that the alcoholic is a person who is "powerless over alcohol and whose life has become unmanageable."[22] The alcoholic is defined by Mark Keller as the drinker who "continuously drinks to the point of creating adverse economic, social, and psychological consequences for himself and for others," and thereby is considered deviant by others.[23] We may determine from these definitions that alcoholism is not the result of excessive drinking in and of itself. Instead, the problem is the difficulties that arise after a prolonged drinking pattern. Drinking can be a way of forgetting or temporarily getting away from some undesirable condition or situation. Once the individual begins to drink to escape, however, he can get caught up in a vicious circle; the drinking that is done to escape problems creates other problems that are perceived to be solved only by more drinking. With this cycle of drinking, alcoholism develops.

However, the conception of drinking to excess varies drastically among groups in our society, so it is unlikely that a definition for alcoholism can be universally applied. Various groups in society differ in terms of their attitudes toward drinking, how they drink, and how much they drink. If we view alcoholism in terms of the social context in which the drinker resides, we must recognize that these contexts vary. As a result, no precise, quantitative definition of alcoholism is possible. We must regard alcoholism as relative, depending on the values of the group within which the drinking takes place. In other words, alcoholism cannot be defined universally in any sense.

330 PERSONAL PATHOLOGY: *Escape by Mental Illness and Drugs*

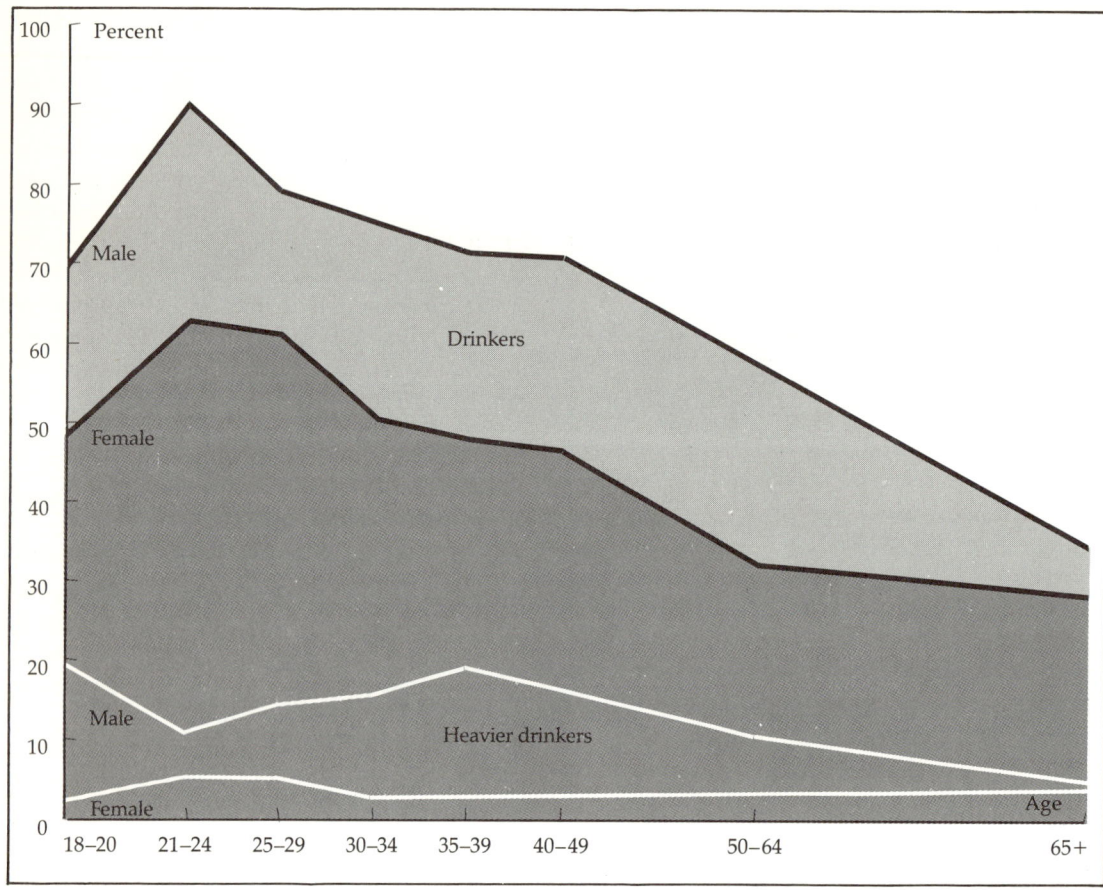

FIGURE 10.5 Percentage of Drinkers and "Heavier" Drinkers Among Adults by Sex and Age, 1972

Source: National Institute on Alcohol Abuse and Alcoholism, *Second Special Report to the U.S. Congress on Alcohol and Health: June, 1974* (Washington, D.C.: U.S. Government Printing Office, 1975), p. 11.

This does not mean that it is not a problem, however. Those who are likely to regard alcoholism as a social problem are the people who are affected directly by it or those who have knowledge of the effects of alcohol abuse. Much publicity is given to the effects of drinking while driving, particularly in the advertising media. Much of this publicity stresses the potential harm that the drinking driver can cause to himself and others, and emphasizes the penalties for such an offense. Rarely, however, is much information given about the social, medical, and economic consequences of alcohol abuse, particularly over the long term. Most information on alcohol abuse and alcoholism never reaches the general public in sufficient quantity to counter some popular myths about alcohol.

Among the questions being debated is whether alcoholism is a physical disease or a mental one. Some rely on the model advocated by the medical profession to explain alcoholism. According to the medical model, alcoholism is like any other disease, it requires medical treatment. There is much disagreement, however, about treating alcoholism or problem drinking as a disease, and whether or not a physician can or should treat the problem.[24]

And opponents of the medical view contend that it does not tell us what causes alcoholism. Although it is generally agreed that the disease involves a loss of control — in the sense that a person cannot refrain either from starting to drink or from continuing to drink once started — no physiological factor has been isolated that accounts for this.[25] It is not too difficult to understand how psychological factors may influence alcoholism, nor is it difficult to see how social and cultural factors can contribute. The pressure our society puts on males to succeed may explain why more heavy drinkers are men than women. And the unsettled nature of adolescence, a time of testing social norms, would contribute to making the younger age groups drink.

Tobacco

After gaining popularity in the 1920s, cigarette smoking became acceptable behavior and socially desirable. No longer. It is now believed that tobacco is probably the most physically damaging of all drugs used in the United States. In the 1960s, as accumulated evidence began to reveal that serious illnesses were associated with smoking, attitudes began to change. More recently, in the 1970s opposition to cigarette smoking reached greater heights. Radio and television advertisements of cigarettes were banned and more and more public places banned smoking. Nonsmokers began proclaiming their rights not to inhale the fumes from cigarette smoking and a number of citizen groups emerged to raise opposition against cigarette smoking and are campaigning for stronger measures against it. Leading these campaigns is the Department of Health, Education, and Welfare. Cigarette smoking has taken on the status of a social problem.

As stated earlier, few drugs, if any, are more physically damaging than tobacco. Data presented by the Department of Health, Education, and Welfare indicate that life expectancy is reduced by cigarette smoking. Smoking contributes greatly to lung cancer and emphysema and increases the likelihood of heart disease. Pregnant women who smoke cigarettes risk birth defects with their unborn babies.[26]

The active ingredient in tobacco is *nicotine*, a unique chemical capable of producing a depressant effect, a stimulant effect, or a tranquilizing effect. It is this addictive chemical that cigarette smokers get hooked on. A tolerance for nicotine is quickly developed by those who smoke. Thus it is not uncommon for smokers to increase their consumption from perhaps a couple of cigarettes a day to more than two packs a day. In the words of Russel Hamilton, "It requires no more than three or four casual cigarettes during adolescence virtually to ensure that a person will become a regular dependent smoker. . . . If we bear in mind that only 15 percent of adolescents who smoke more than one cigarette avoid becoming regular smokers and that only 15 percent of smokers stop before the age of 60, it becomes apparent that of those who smoke more than one cigarette during adolescence, some 70 percent continue smoking for the next 40 years."[27]

Nonsmokers are increasingly becoming antismokers in asserting their right to breathe fresh air. Their more adamant stance is prompted by the flagrant disregard of courtesy and law shown by many smokers.

Like alcohol, tobacco is not generally seen by the public as part of the drug problem. Evidence indicates that the effects of cigarette smoking are similar to the effects of other psychoactive, or mind-altering, drugs. Like all drugs, tobacco provides an escape mechanism for its users. Smokers find it relaxes them, relieving tension and anxiety. So despite its capacity to damage health, it is likely to remain in widespread use. Also contributing to use is its long association with sexual attractiveness and sophistication. And the tobacco industry will unquestionably continue to oppose any measures to discourage cigarette smoking. Despite the recent revelations of the dangers connected with cigarette smoking, then, millions of American citizens continue to use the drug. There is no evidence to indicate that this escape mechanism used by many people to help them cope with anxiety is likely to cease or decrease soon.

Sedatives

Our discussion of legal drugs will end with a note on *sedatives*, drugs like barbiturates and tranquilizers, taken to calm people and relieve anxiety. Sedatives also can be escape mechanisms to withdraw from life's difficulties. In many instances, barbiturates and other sedatives are misused. Despite the fact that laws exist to preclude the obtaining of barbiturates without a prescription, they are not difficult to acquire. It is reported that approximately 11 percent of America's adults use barbiturates, legally or illegally. Many businessmen and housewives feel the need for these sedatives to help them cope with daily realities. These drugs are also used by young people for kicks.

Illegal Drugs

As far as the general public is concerned, the major drug problem is narcotics addiction. This concern is reflected in the fact that this is the major priority of the police enforcing drug laws. Heroin addiction is regarded as the most serious drug-related social problem; at this time it is estimated that there are about 300,000 addicts in the United States.[28] Recent trends in drug use patterns suggest that there may be a decline in the use of heroin, although we must wait for further data before drawing any conclusions. But even if this decrease is true, among the drug-addicted population heroin is still the most common drug used. Reliable information is difficult to obtain on the scope of the use of other drugs, but we know that it is widespread. For example, it is estimated that as many as 20 million Americans have used marijuana, America's most popular illegal drug.

WHO ARE THE ILLEGAL DRUG USERS?

Males are more likely to use drugs than females and are more prone to become addicted. Younger people tend to use and abuse drugs, and addiction to drugs, particularly narcotics, has for a long time been more common in urban than rural areas. More recently narcotics addiction has spread to the white middle class, which helped it be recognized as part of the drug problem. Still, many narcotics addicts tend to be of low socioeconomic status, and many commit crimes to support their habits. In fact, it is estimated that each heroin addict must steal or otherwise acquire as much as $50,000 a year to support his habit.[29]

Although narcotic use is considered by most Americans as the most serious drug-related problem, narcotic use is actually confined to a small segment of the population. The use of other drugs, such as marijuana, may comprise a more serious problem, because the incidence of such use is greater. Also, although these drugs are less serious than narcotics, the law makes no distinction. It describes users as criminals and legally stigmatizes them.

Many of these users — primarily young people — do not regard their behavior as a social problem. The use of some drugs among young people assumes almost a ritualistic function. Turning on becomes a sign of solidarity and of opposition to established norms and institutions. What is a social problem for some is a normative behavior pattern for others.

SOCIAL COSTS OF ILLEGAL DRUG USE

There are many social costs of drug use and abuse. Criminal behavior is possibly the most serious of these. In 1974, 388,154 persons were arrested for violations of the narcotic laws, but these statistics drastically underestimate the overall effects of drug use and abuse on the crime rate.[30] They do not account, for instance, for all users. Nor do

International illicit traffic is a flood that authorities seem powerless to halt. Some reduction in drugs entering into the United States has been accomplished by agreements with foreign countries that are the drug sources. Large scale inspections of incoming freight, sometimes conducted with the aid of specially trained dogs, has resulted in some arrests and seizures. But as long as drug smuggling brings high profits, it will continue to flourish.

they include crimes committed to get money to purchase drugs.

The federal government spends millions of dollars on the drug problem, as Figure 10.6 shows. Most is applied to the prevention of drug traffic into the United States. In order to block this traffic, the United States has had some significant problems in foreign policy, particularly with the nations that supply opium, such as Turkey, Mexico, and some nations in Southeast Asia. It is likely that future foreign aid proposals to these nations may contain provisions designed to have them stop the production of drugs that may eventually reach the illicit drug market.

The social costs of drug use and abuse traceable to individual health problems are hard to measure. We know that drug over-

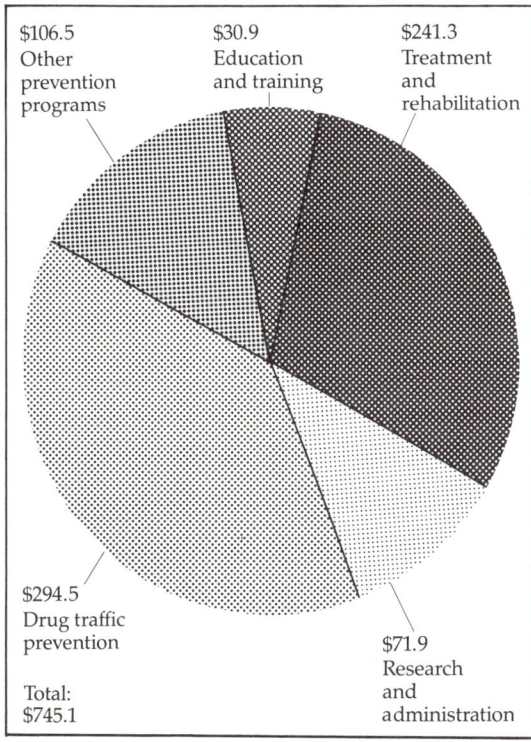

FIGURE 10.6 Estimated Funding of Federal Drug Abuse Programs, 1975 (in Millions)

Source: Strategy Council, *Federal Strategy for Drug Abuse and Drug Traffic Prevention* (Washington, D.C.: U.S. Government Printing Office, 1974), p. 13.

doses result in death, both accidental and planned. Drug dependence may also result in problems for the individual in her occupation, family life, and personal stability. In this sense, the social costs of drug use and abuse are critical.

Another social cost of the use of illegal drugs is organized crime, for the drug trade serves as the basis for some of its existence. The drug traffic into the United States would not be so extensive were there not heavy consumers of illegal drugs. It is quite possible that if some illegal drugs were legalized and their use publicly controlled, organized crime would be significantly curtailed, as a major source of its income would disappear.

PERSPECTIVES ON ILLEGAL DRUG USE

The use of illegal drugs that we have been considering is a problem largely because such behavior is labeled as illegal, and is regarded as a danger to individual users and society. By emphasizing the deleteriousness of certain drugs on health, much support can be generated for legislation controlling drug usage. Such an approach ignores two facts: (a) prohibition is an ineffective way of controlling its use and popularity (as was seen with alcohol); and (b) there is evidence that even hard drugs like heroin can be used on a regular basis without the serious physical deterioration that occurs from the abuse of a legal and acceptable drug, alcohol.[31] Clearly, the popular perspective on drug use and its effects does not reflect accurate medical information. Much of the evidence indicates that with many drugs the major problem is abuse, not mere use. However, the law does not always distinguish between the user and the abuser, and so the drug problem is seriously complicated.

Summary

Because these escape behaviors are private, we encounter methodological problems in trying to establish how many people use them. Statistics are often misleading and different criteria are used to define behavior. Nevertheless, research seems to show that the distribution of mental disorders is not random. Rather, they are more likely to occur in certain social contexts and among certain social groups. The poor and deprived seem more prone to mental illness than those better off. Social class appears to be the central contributing factor to this pattern: persons of higher social status are better able to deal with their mental disorders in that they can obtain early and private treatments.

More common as a means of escape is drug use. America is a drug-prone society. But when we go beyond that statement to consider all of the issues related to drug use and drug abuse, many difficulties arise. Indeed, trying to determine what exactly is meant by drug abuse can be a problem. Traditionally, it has been seen as the use of illegal drugs, primarily a phenomenon of the lower class. Most people have not considered the common legal drugs, such as aspirin, tobacco, and alcohol, as part of the drug problem. However, when we consider how tobacco and alcohol are used and the effects they have, it is clear that both are similar to other psychoactive drugs. And as abuse of these drugs is widespread in the higher social groups and those with more status — more males than females smoke and among those most prone to alcoholism are males of high socioeconomic status and much education — opposition to the use of these drugs has grown and more people consider it a social problem. In light of this change in views, we may conclude that there is little connection between the harmfulness of drugs and the degree to which society reacts negatively to them. What is important is the position of those who use the drug most.

ATTEMPTS AT DEALING WITH THE PROBLEM

As with all social problems, attempts have been made to solve mental illness and drug abuse. Because these problems are matters of individual behavior, the attempts have focused on treating the individual. The aim is to solve the problem by removing the individual's need to escape from social pressures by engaging in the behavior. At its worst, this system relies on the individual alone. Although a mass media campaign against smoking is now being mounted by the government, the Department of Health, Education, and Welfare is not organizing groups to help people quit smoking. Rather, it has concentrated its efforts on educating the general public particularly young children through television and the schools by giving out information on the dangers of smoking and leaving the decision to individuals. But this lack of organized efforts to solve the problem is largely because smoking is a relatively new social problem. Mental illness, alcohol abuse, and illegal drugs have been seen as problems longer and have been the subject of more organized solutions.

Treating Mental Illness

Just as we have always had difficulty in defining mental illness, we have also lacked the knowledge of how to treat it. Our treatment methods have tended to change with our perceptions of mental illness. For example, when the mentally ill were perceived as being possessed by an evil spirit, it was not uncommon to flog or starve them. The aim was to make the individual's body a less inviting dwelling place for the evil spirit. With the advent of more humane perceptions of the mentally ill came more humane treatment. At first facilities were provided by private organizations, followed later by public institutions.

More recently the mentally ill have been treated in a general hospital setting or in a private facility using a private psychiatrist. Since 1963 there has been a movement to provide local mental health centers that allow the mentally ill to be treated in a community environment.

Psychotherapy and chemotherapy have been the most frequently used contemporary treatment techniques. Psychotherapy techniques take many forms, from counseling to psychoanalysis. The primary intent of psychotherapy is to make the individuals more aware of the reasons underlying their condition. With some understanding of the reasons for certain kinds of behavior, it is believed that the individual will be better able to change the behavior.

Psychotherapy can be not only expensive but also time-consuming. Reports indicate that these techniques are most successful when used with people suffering from some form of neurosis.

Since about 1954, chemotherapy has been used frequently to treat mental illness. Tranquilizers and antidepressants are the most common forms of chemotherapy, meant to deal with excitable and depressive symptoms respectively. An intriguing aspect of the use of drugs to treat mental illness is the fact that they seem effective in a majority of the cases, but there is little knowledge of how or why these drugs work. There is also little understanding of why drugs may not work for some people who have symptoms similar to others for whom the drugs have been effective. Effectiveness of drugs does not imply that drugs are a cure for mental illness. They are not; in fact, the strongest criticism of drugs as a treatment of mental illness is that they merely suppress the symptoms rather than cure the illness. Nevertheless, chemotherapy does offer some hope as a treatment that may increase as knowledge about how and why they work increases.

Treating Alcohol Abuse

A wide array of facilities, agencies, programs, and approaches now exist to combat alcoholism. One area of recent progress is the general hospital. The American Hospital Association is beginning a national action program to promote the treatment of alcoholism in all general hospitals, including changing admission policies so that alcoholic patients can be admitted under a diagnosis of alcoholism. Some large urban hospitals are establishing special alcoholism units, with organizational ties to community agencies. While general hospitals cannot provide comprehensive treatment for alcoholism, they can handle the complications of excessive use and provide detoxification and drug therapy.

Possibly the best known organization that treats alcoholics is Alcoholics Anonymous (AA). Founded in 1934, it is dedicated to helping the recovery of alcoholics who voluntarily join. The only membership requirement is a sincere commitment by self-admitted alcoholics to stop drinking. Members follow a program consisting of twelve steps to recovery based on medical, religious, and psychiatric principles, possibly the most important of which is the recognition by the drinker that he is powerless over alcohol and his life has become unmanageable. Two types of regular meetings are held. In the open meeting, to which the public is welcome, self-confessed alcoholics relate the experiences that led them to excessive drinking and to eventual recovery. In closed meetings, a sort of group-therapy session, members help one another with adjustment problems. Other programs offered include Al-Anon, designed for the families of alcoholics, and Ala-Teen, created for teenagers with alcoholic parents, guardians, or other alcoholic relatives.

Treating Drug Abuse

Most of the visible and publicized means of combating drug abuse have been through law enforcement, mostly on the federal level. The effectiveness of this kind of social control is questionable; so other solutions have been attempted, usually focusing on removing the addiction. Many halfway houses for addicts have been set up, using group living and group therapy in order to help the addict adjust to a world without drug dependence. The most famous treatment center was Synanon, an organization established by former addicts for the rehabilitation of drug addicts, mainly heroin users, modeled to some extent after Alcoholics Anonymous.[32]

Synanon was at first a kind of therapeutic community. The basic assumption of its treatment approach fits the theme of this chapter — drugs are escape mechanisms. Synanon, and most therapeutic communities, assume that drug abuse is a learned way of dealing with an underlying emotional disorder. Therefore, the person has to learn new ways of coping.

Persons admitted to Synanon initially gave up all ties to the outside world and entered a period of isolation. The individual acknowledged his problems and gradually began to assume personal responsibility. The person was helped to learn new ways of coping through encounter group therapy.

Methadone is also a widely used means of treating or controlling drug addiction. Indeed, when first introduced in America it was thought to be the solution to the drug abuse problem. We have come to know, however, that no such single answer exists.

Two types of treatment processes are associated with the methadone program: detoxification and maintenance. During the detoxification process addicts receive methadone as a substitute for heroin to help them through a drying-out period of about two to four weeks. During that period, the individual is also exposed to group and individual support services designed to contribute to his rehabilitation. The individual is administered decreasing doses of methadone in the expectation of eventual freedom from addiction.

Methadone maintenance is a continuous program. The addict simply substitutes methadone for whatever kind of illicit narcotics he may have been using. Methadone is provided daily. Properly adjusted doses of methadone are intended to prevent withdrawal discomfort. Perhaps the primary advantage to this process is that although the individual uses a drug, it is inexpensive to him or her and can be administered legally without great costs. At the least, the addict can avoid the criminal activity so frequently needed to support an illicit drug habit.

Iatrogenic Effects

We have already noted that attempts at controlling mental illness and drug use and abuse have not always met with success. Indeed, rather than being successful, some of our efforts at control have produced more of the behavior we were trying to eliminate. And, as with all social problems, these attempted solutions have created new problems.

Treatments for the mentally ill have produced some iatrogenic effects. Mental hospitals can have an atmosphere which Erving Goffman described as a "total institution." Goffman is convinced that mental institutions create an overall environment in which inmates learn to play a sick role. Indeed, the mental hospital is believed by many to create more problems than it solves.

Although drugs have had some significant effect in controlling the behavior of the mentally ill, they have been criticized. Accusers say that drugs simply serve as a "chemical strait jacket" for the mental patient. The individual's real problem is neglected and the individual simply becomes dependent on drug therapy. In that sense, the escape mechanism of mental illness is replaced by drug use, which also can be perceived as an escape mechanism.

Iatrogenic effects are also associated with other attempts at controlling drugs. Therapeutic communities have been criticized for creating a repressive or cult-like environment. The most famous example, Synanon, is generally regarded as having almost completely departed from its original nature. It has been seen as exerting dictatorial control over every aspect of members' lives and its leadership has been implicated in the attempted murder (by poisonous snake) of an outspoken lawyer who represented critics of the group. In view of the 1979 Jonestown incident, this evolution of Synanon appears especially sinister.

Unexpected problems have also resulted from methadone maintenance programs. Some programs have been criticized for creating illicit channels of methadone distribution. Also, some programs have been poorly administered, resulting in the theft of drugs. Finally, we cannot be sure of the long-term medical effects of methadone. We cannot be sure that in the long run the individual will not be worse off.

Prohibition provides an example of iatrogenic effects. Rather than causing a decrease in drinking, the ban on alcohol resulted in an increase. Too, organized crime began manufacturing alcohol and earning great profits by providing it to the many who were willing to pay high prices for it, despite its illegality. With the repeal of Prohibition, organized crime shifted its operations to other illegal drugs and continues to make high profits from their distribution.

The major thrust against drugs has been law enforcement, but enforcing the laws against drug users and drug sellers creates problems also. The many hours law enforcement officers spend trying to enforce drug laws, many argue, would be more usefully spent trying to end more serious crime. And complicated legal issues are involved when they do enforce drug laws. Often, officers are accused of *entrapment* in trying to catch a seller. This practice, luring a suspected criminal into committing a crime, is illegal, and arrests caused by entrapment are thrown out of court.

PROSPECTS FOR SOLVING THE PROBLEM

Mental illness may never be eradicated entirely, but the best possible outlook for dealing with it lies with the development of more effective treatment. Improvements in treatment, such as drug therapy, and changes in how the mentally ill are cared for, such as the development of alternative facilities that supplement the asylum, are the brightest prospects for dealing more successfully with mental illness. Increasingly effective methods of treatment are being developed, including group therapy, encounter groups, psychodrama, and sociodrama, which help by enabling the patient to act out the stress roles causing many of her problems. There is also increasing emphasis on out-patient treatment of the mentally ill. This approach and the use of the community mental health centers should put treatment closer to the persons in need of it.

Quite possibly, however, what is needed most is an alteration in the stereotypes of mental illness, many of which are untenable in an age of scientific reasoning and rational approaches to human problems. In particular, we must redefine the role of the mentally ill without the stigma, or superstition of the past. It is unlikely that our society will begin to deal more effectively with mental illness until our attitudes are altered substantially. We should remember that the mentally ill individual may find this condition a convenient role to play when under stress or strain. With less stigma attached to it, people might be even more willing to adopt the role of the mentally ill patient.

Since Americans make frequent use of many drugs, both legal and illegal, it is unlikely that we will ever be without a drug problem. Since newly publicized drugs tend to be readily used and rapidly abused, this circumstance is more probable. While the punitive approach our society has taken in dealing with the problem of drug use is giving way to an emphasis on rehabilitation, laws against some drugs, such as heroin, are likely to remain. The worldwide drug traffic is well established in many areas, and the lucrative profits it provides will ensure its existence for many decades to come. So long as our society and other Western nations outlaw certain drugs and regard the addict as a person who has committed an illegal act, the drug traffic will remain uncontrolled and unregulated.

In the case of alcohol and tobacco abuse, the fact that the drugs are legal and readily available establishes a high probability that some people will abuse them. Since these behaviors are so difficult to change, it is likely that our future strategy will be to dissuade the young from beginning them. For solving the problem of illegal drugs, many believe that legalization is the best approach. Some advocates of this idea refer to the British system, which is to supply addicts with some drugs. The British do so on the grounds that it may be less difficult and entail fewer problems to supply addicts with drugs than to attempt to cut off their supply. Certainly America's experience with Prohibition supports this idea. It is also argued that providing drugs can undermine organized crime.

We should recognize, however, that deviance is endemic in human societies. Accordingly, these personal pathologies will always remain with us to some degree. Drug abuse and mental illness are associated with many social factors: social disorganization among the poor, lack of treatment for the poor, youthful experimentation, and overemphasis on success. These groups, faced with pressures and conflicts, use these behaviors as escape mechanisms. Some people will continue to do so as long as other social problems remain.

IMPORTANT WORDS AND TERMS

catatonia
defective strategies
drug
drug abuse

entrapment
escape mechanism
exorcism
functional psychosis

ginhead
hebephrenic schizophrenia
hypochondria
hysteria

impairment
narcotics
neurasthenia
neurosis

nicotine	paranoid schizophrenia	psychosis	sedatives
opiates	phobia	psychopathy	simple schizophrenia
organic psychosis	psychoactive		

QUESTIONS FOR DISCUSSION

1. Why is it so difficult to define mental illness accurately? What is the line (diagnostically) between neurosis and psychosis? What social factors may enter into the diagnosis of mental illness? Illustrate with examples.
2. How accurately are we able to report the incidence of mental illness in America at any given time? What are some of the problems researchers encounter when they attempt to measure the rates of mental illness?
3. Which approach to mental disorders do you think best analyzes the condition — the medical model or the sociocultural model? Are these models best seen as contradictory or complementary?
4. What advantages are there in looking at mental illness in terms of degrees of impairment, as suggested by Schwab and his associates?
5. Evaluate the various strategies our society has used to treat mental illness. Who is advantaged and who is disadvantaged? To what extent do the strategies of treating the mentally ill reflect social realities?
6. Is it possible to eliminate mental illness, completely solving the problem? Why or why not?
7. Why is alcoholism likely to be a permanent feature of American society?
8. What do we mean when we describe the American attitude toward alcohol as ambivalent? Illustrate with historical and contemporary examples.
9. What is defined as alcoholism and what factors are relevant in making the distinction? Which factors are more important, quantitative (how much one drinks) or qualitative (under what context drinking occurs)?
10. Why do many believe that tobacco is the most physically damaging of drugs?
11. Despite the recent campaign against smoking by the Department of Health, Education, and Welfare, millions of Americans continue to smoke. Why?
12. What would happen if the currently illegal drugs such as heroin and marijuana were made legal, so that addicts would not be defined as criminals and could use these drugs under medical supervision? Compare the British approach to heroin addiction with our own as an example.
13. Do you think marijuana should be legalized? What about the other drugs presently illegal?
14. How would you evaluate federal drug policy? How could it be improved? What does previous policy against alcohol show us?
15. For what persons and groups are the two social problems discussed in this chapter (mental illness and drug abuse) functional? Can we say that social facts serve as essential barriers to the solution of these problems?

SUGGESTED READING

EDWARD M. BRECHER, *Licit and Illicit Drugs: The Consumers Union Report on Narcotics, Stimulants, Depressants, Inhalants, Hallucinogens, and Marijuana — Including Coffee, Nicotine, and Alcohol* (Boston: Little, Brown, 1972).

This is the most recent and definitive work on the patterns of drug use in the United States today. It covers all facets of drug use, including alcohol abuse and contains historical and contemporary data from a variety of perspectives.

PAUL FUQUA, *Drug Abuse: Investigation and Control* (New York: Gregg, 1978).

This book is written specifically to aid law enforcement officers in avoiding some of the errors in handling drug cases. It describes the drugs most commonly abused in America, what their effects are, and how to recognize the abusers, and it presents the major treatment methods.

ERVING GOFFMAN, *Asylums* (New York: Doubleday, 1961).

Anyone who wishes to obtain a real insight into the mental health establishment and how we treat the mentally ill should read this work. Of particular importance is Goffman's description of the asylum as a total institution.

THOMAS J. SCHEFF, *Being Mentally Ill: A Sociological Theory* (Chicago: Aldine, 1966).

This book approaches mental illness as an escape from the pressures of reality. Rather than seeking a single cause of mental illness the author views mental illness as the violation of residual rules, social norms so taken for granted that they are not explicit.

THOMAS S. SZASZ, *The Myth of Mental Illness* (New York: Delta, 1961).

This book makes fascinating reading for anyone with a serious interest in mental illness. Szasz presents a controversial and novel approach to the study of human behavior. He contends that mental illness is nothing but an ambiguous label.

DEBRA L. ASHBROOK AND LINDA C. SOLLEY, *Women and Heroin Abuse: A Survey of Sexism in Drug Administration* (Palo Alto, California: R and E Research Associates, 1979).

This research fills a significant void and has important implications for the future treatment of addicted women. It also points to the need for further research in this area. This book also includes an extensive review of heroin legislation, the status of women in society, and the treatment of female heroin addicts.

NATIONAL INSTITUTE ON ALCOHOL ABUSE AND ALCOHOLISM, *Second Special Report to the U.S. Congress on Alcohol and Health, June 1974* (Washington, D.C.: U.S. Government Printing Office, 1975).

This work compiles all the recent information on alcohol use and abuse in the United States today, including some data comparing the patterns here with those of other countries. Much data is provided about the social, medical, and economic causes and consequences of alcoholism.

Diagnostic and Statistical Manual of Mental Disorders (Washington, D.C.: American Psychiatric Association).

Although this manual is designed for specialists, the layman could profit considerably by reading the sections describing the various kinds of psychic disorder — since such definitive chaos exists on the issue of defining mental illness. Each kind of disorder is described in brief and objective terms. It reveals why there is such disagreement about what type of behavior constitutes particular forms of mental illness.

National Commission on Marijuana and Drug Abuse, Drug Use in America: Problems in Perspective (Washington, D.C.: U.S. Government Printing Office, 1973).

This report contains much data on alcohol and drug abuse and much about the interrelationship between the two social problems. It is a key source of recent and factual information. In particular, the report contains interesting arguments on the legalization of marijuana, a potent topic of political and social controversy.

NOTES

1. Deuteronomy 28: 15, 28.
2. John A. Clausen, "Mental Disorders," in Robert K. Merton and Robert A. Nisbet (eds.), *Contemporary Social Problems* (New York: Harcourt, Brace and World, 1961), pp. 154–155.
3. Edward M. Brecher, *Licit and Illicit Drugs:*

The Consumers Union Report on Narcotics, Stimulants, Depressants, Inhalants, Hallucinogens, and Marijuana — Including Coffee, Nicotine, and Alcohol (Boston: Little, Brown, 1972), p. 266.

4. John J. Schwab, Nancy H. McGinnis, and George Warheit, "Toward a Social Psychiatric Definition of Impairment," *British Journal of Social Psychiatry*, Vol. 4, No. 1 (1970), p. 1.

5. Thomas J. Scheff, *Being Mentally Ill: A Sociological Theory* (Chicago: Aldine-Atherton, 1966).

6. Thomas S. Szasz, *The Myth of Mental Illness* (New York: Dell, 1961).

7. Ibid., p. 71.

8. Schwab, McGinnis, and Warheit, "Toward a Social Psychiatric Definition of Impairment," p. 2.

9. Ibid, p. 2.

10. Paul Fuqua, *Drug Abuse: Investigations and Control* (Washington, D.C.: McGraw-Hill, 1978), p. 7.

11. *The World Almanac and Book of Facts: 1976* (New York: Newspaper Enterprise Association, 1976), p. 967.

12. Carl A. Taube and Mildred S. Cannon, *Statistical Note, No. 67* (Washington, D.C.: Department of Health, Education, and Welfare, 1971), p. 8.

13. Leo Srole, Thomas Langer, Stanley Michael, Marvin Opler, and Thomas Rennie, *Mental Health in the Metropolis* (New York: McGraw-Hill, 1962).

14. Robert E. L. Faris and H. Warren Dunham, *Mental Disorders in Urban Areas* (Chicago: University of Chicago Press, 1939); see also August B. Hollingshead and Frederick Redlich, *Social Class and Mental Illness* (New York: Wiley, 1958) and Leo Srole, *Mental Health*.

15. Stanislav V. Kasl and Ernest Harburg, "Mental Health and the Urban Environment: Some Doubts and Second Thoughts," *Journal of Health and Social Behavior*, Vol. 16, No. 3 (September 1975), pp. 268–281.

16. Howard S. Becker, *Outsiders: Studies in the Sociology of Deviance* (New York: Free Press, 1963).

17. United Press International, "Alcohol Rated Top Problem," *The Arizona Republic* (December 15, 1972).

18. National Commission on Marijuana and Drug Abuse, *Drug Use in America: Problems in Perspective* (Washington, D.C.: U.S. Government Printing Office, 1973), p. 69.

19. National Institute on Alcohol Abuse and Alcoholism, *Second Special Report to the U.S. Congress on Alcohol and Health: June 1974* (Washington, D.C.: U.S. Government Printing Office, 1975).

20. Robert R. Bell, *Social Deviance* (Homewood, Ill.: Dorsey Press, 1971), p. 178.

21. Marty Mann, *Primer on Alcoholism* (New York: Holt, Rinehart and Winston, 1950), p. 5.

22. Ibid.

23. Mark Keller, "The Definition of Alcoholism and the Estimation of Its Prevalence," in David J. Pittman and Charles R. Snyder (eds.), *Society, Culture and Drinking Patterns* (New York: Wiley, 1962), p. 313.

24. J. Hershon, "Alcoholism and the Concept of Disease," *British Journal of Addictions*, Vol. 69 (1974), pp. 123-132.

25. Charles H. McCaghy, *Deviant Behavior: Crime, Conflict and Interest Groups* (New York: Macmillan, 1976), p. 271.

26. National Commission on Marijuana and Drug Abuse, *Drug Use in America*, pp. 44–45.

27. Russel M. A. Hamilton, "Cigarette Smoking: Natural History of a Dependence Disorder," *British Journal of Medical Psychology*, Vol. 44 (1971), p. 9.

28. National Commission, *Drug Use in America*, p. 69.

29. Ibid., p. 175.

30. Ibid., p. 185.

31. Jerome H. Jaffe, cited in Louis S. Goodman and Alfred Gilman (eds.), *The Pharmacological Basis of Therapeutics*, 4th ed. (New York: Macmillan, 1970), p. 286.

32. Brecher, *Licit and Illicit Drugs*, p. 78.

PART IV
PROBLEMS OF OUR CHANGING WORLD

11 POPULATION
GROWING NUMBERS AND SHRINKING RESOURCES

CHAPTER OVERVIEW

INTRODUCTION

HISTORICAL OVERVIEW
The Neolithic Revolution
The Industrial Revolution
Summary

CONCEPTUAL ORIENTATION
Fertility and Mortality
The Scarcity of Resources
Summary

OBJECTIVE DIMENSIONS OF THE PROBLEM
Population Growth in the World
Population Growth in Developed Countries
Summary

ATTEMPTS AT DEALING WITH THE PROBLEM
The Eufunctions of Zero Population Growth
Iatrogenic Effects

PROSPECTS FOR SOLVING THE PROBLEM
Factors Tending to Reduce Fertility
  Economics
  Careers for Women
  Government and the Law
  Fertility Reduction Factors: A Summary
Factors Tending to Increase Fertility
  Economics
  Religion
  Culture
  Fertility Support Factors: A Summary
A Look Ahead

IMPORTANT WORDS AND TERMS

QUESTIONS FOR DISCUSSION

SUGGESTED READING

NOTES

The most important thing in the world is people.
              T. Lynn Smith and Paul E. Zopf, *Demography*

Drive dangerously — avoid overpopulation.
              Ralph Thomlinson, *Population Dynamics*

CHAPTER OVERVIEW

One of the gravest dilemmas facing humankind is the fact that there are too many people in the world today and there will be millions more in the years to come. In the introduction to this chapter, we explain how overpopulation is an international problem. To understand how it came about, we give a brief history of human population, recounting the factors underlying its relatively rapid growth in recent times. With this historical perspective, we consider the statistics that are essential to studying population, focusing on the birthrate and death rate.

Once we have the historical background and the conceptual framework, we can discuss population in the world today and consider projected future levels. Then we discuss the principal thrust of this chapter: the factors functioning for and against increases in population as an approach to determining the prospects for solving this pressing world problem.

INTRODUCTION

As a social problem, population is not merely a matter of the number of people. If the earth were much larger and had greater resources, population would be no problem at all. Sheer numbers of people do not become a problem until they begin to press upon available space and resources. They are a problem now because precisely that is happening. That resources are insufficient is demonstrated in the need of countries to import food. Many primarily agrarian, heavily overpopulated countries can no longer raise enough food for their people. As a result, they must import food from other countries, bringing in American grain, for instance. What makes the problem even more alarming is the fact that it should get worse. That it will get worse can be shown by an analogy. We are all aware that banks offer saving accounts and pay a regular rate of compound interest. Compound interest means that in each interest period, the earned interest is added to the savings; the next interest amount, then, is computed on the basis of increased savings. Over time, this produces an accelerated rate of growth even though the depositor adds no funds. So it is with population growth. As each year's increase is added to the population, further increases result.

The compound interest analogy applied to the world population is depicted in Figure 11.1. As of 1976, the world population stood at slightly more than 4 billion. Using an annual increase rate of 1.8 percent (a conservative estimate), we calculate that the population will grow to more than 8 billion by 2015. But growth will continue at a faster rate — even assuming the same annual percentage

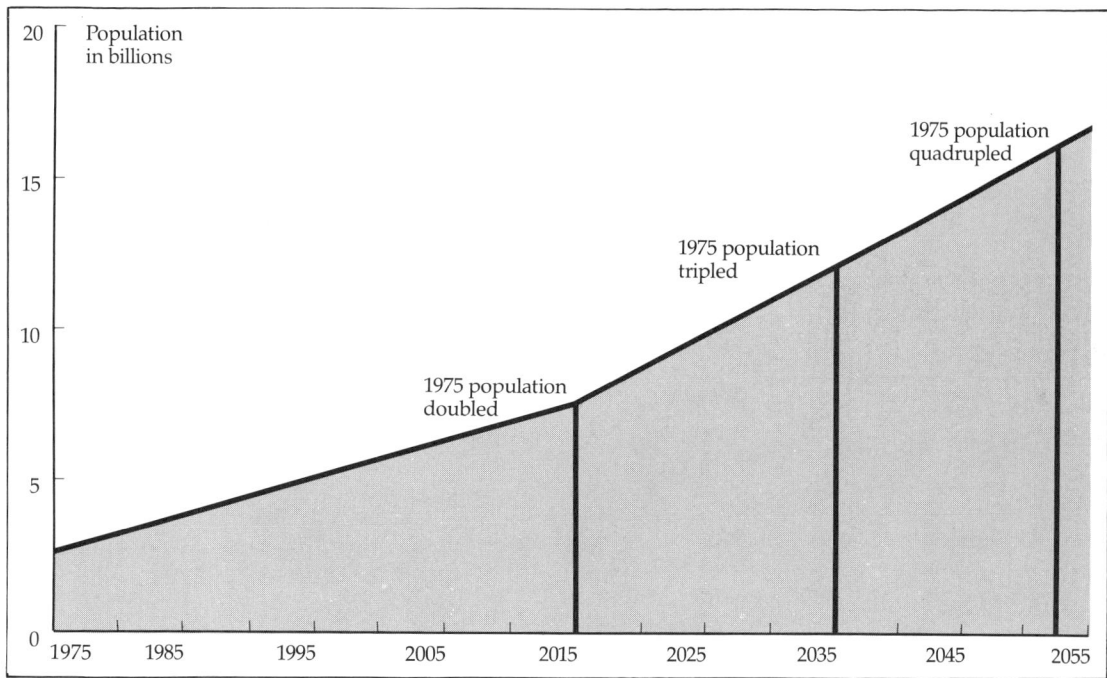

FIGURE 11.1 Projected World Population Using Constant Rate of Annual Increase of 1.8 Percent

increase. We just saw that it would take about forty years for the population to double, to more than 8 billion; but it will only require twenty-three years for it to triple, and less than sixteen more to quadruple. If we cannot adequately feed 4 billion now, how will we provide food for four times that number?

It is plain that our species is in a predicament largely of its own making. We have been wildly successful in meeting the test of survival. In fact, we have been too successful. The question is whether we'll be able to meet it in the future.

If not, if the high rate of population growth continues and food supplies are not increased, the consequences for millions of people will be horrible. The famines and malnutrition that currently plague a large proportion of the population will be intensified. Wars, large and small, will break out as people struggle for living space and dwindling resources. The *developed countries*, with highly industrialized economies, like the United States, will find their standard of living sharply reduced as the resources become scarcer. Can we prevent an accentuation of present conditions to avert this worldwide catastrophe? A meaningful attempt to answer this question begins with answering yet another question: how did this all come about?

HISTORICAL OVERVIEW

What distinguishes humans from animals, allowing us to grow in numbers over the ages while animal populations remain relatively steady or grow extinct, is our biological heritage and what we've done with it. Our large brain, complex nervous system, upright posture, and flexible hands have made the difference. These purely biological attributes have been used to construct an enormous array of tools and other aids to extend our physical capabilities and protect us from the environment. In early days, the spear or bow and arrow enabled humans to remain at a safe distance and slay bigger, stronger animals. People made clothing for protection from the cold. Humans built extensive and elaborate shelters to shield themselves from the elements. All human inventions, material and nonmaterial, have freed our species from the need to rely only on the slow process of biological evolution.

The Neolithic Revolution

The first modern humans, identical to ourselves, appeared about 40,000 years ago. Archaeological remains indicate that early *Homo sapiens* (the Latin name for modern humans) was numerous, but there was nowhere near the volume of people we have now, even as recently as 2,000 years ago. Had humans continued to subsist as hunting and gathering bands of nomads, population would be no problem today. But our species is forever trying to improve its condition and the first great step occurred when people began to do something to make their food supply more certain.

Toward the end of the Upper Paleolithic Age, about 10,000 years ago, there came a gradual change in humankind's struggle to obtain food. Over a period of time, various groups changed from concentrating on hunting and gathering to raising food by the form *agriculture* called horticulture, deliberately planting and tending crops to guarantee a steady food supply. With this *Neolithic Revolution,* humans had developed food producing technology to a point where, "given favorable circumstances, a community . . . [could] produce more food than it need[ed] to consume and [could] increase its production to meet the requirements of an expanding population. A comparison of the number of burials from the Old Stone Age with that from the New in Europe and the Near East shows that, as a result of the Neolithic Revolution, the population had increased enormously."[1]

The Neolithic Revolution marked a change from nomadic life to life in settled communities. No longer were people completely at the mercy of an uncertain food supply. They began to have some measure of control over their food supply. With this control came the first great increase in human populations. We must not, however, imagine that there was a sudden change in the life-styles of our ancient forefathers. The Neolithic Revolution covered several thousand years.

The most important nonmaterial development that grew out of the Neolithic Revolution was the increasing sophistication of language. However clever and resourceful our early ancestors were, it would have made little difference to those who came after them if they had not been able to pass on information to other humans. Language made complex *culture* possible. It also ensured continuity. Because of language, culture is

Hunting and gathering food gave way to agriculture and animal domestication around 10,000 years ago, a gradual change reflected in this contemporary wall painting of a Nile Valley wheat harvest. The immediate results of the shift were twofold: production surpluses led to specialization of labor and trading, and nomadic populations settled down establishing villages and cities.

cumulative. As a generation is born, it inherits the changes of the past; as the next generation is born and grows up, the first passes on improvements it has made. The result is that the improvements of the Neolithic Revolution could be built on and benefit later generations. This created a slow but steady increase in population, from somewhere between 1 million and 10 million in 10,000 B.C. to from 5 to 20 million by 5000 B.C. (see Figure 11.2). From this point onward, human populations began to grow somewhat more rapidly, reaching around 250 million by A.D. 1, and nearly 500 million by 1650, on the eve of the Industrial Revolution. This considerable increase had its origins in culture, a constantly changing and more sophisticated culture that constantly improved the means for keeping people alive.

FIGURE 11.2 Estimates of World Population from 10,000 B.C. to A.D. 1650

Source: A. M. Carr-Saunders, *World Population* (Oxford: Clarendon Press, 1936), p. 42.

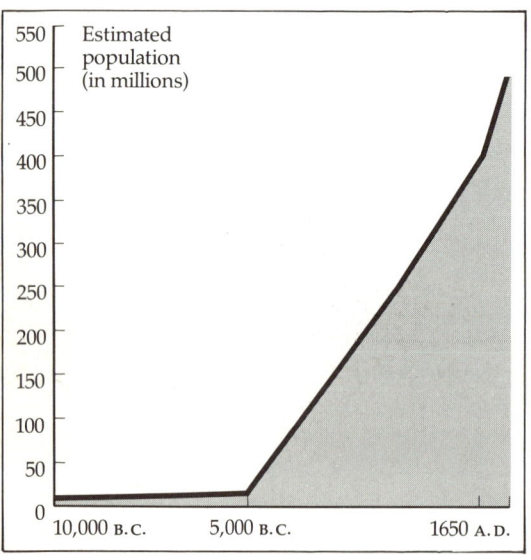

In the early years, this improvement did not so much increase the life span as it increased the chances of survival of the young. An ample supply of food extended the life of more and more infants. More children grew to the age at which they could become parents and add to the human population before dying.

The Industrial Revolution

As much as the population grew from 10,000 B.C. to A.D. 1650, the growth in that period doesn't compare to the phenomenal jump in the number of people in the past three hundred or so years. The population is now eight times higher than it was in 1650 (see Figure 11.3). Part of this increase can be explained by the compound interest analogy described earlier. With more people in one generation, growth in the next generation, barring a disaster, is certain. But more important factors contributing to this growth were improvements in sanitation, medicine, and food production and distribution.

Sanitation always plagued humankind, even in the smaller cities of the first civilizations. For centuries waste removal consisted of using running water to carry waste down city streets. Effective sanitation measures were not widespread until the nineteenth century. And although plumbing systems to supply fresh water were developed to an advanced state by the Romans, they fell into disuse during the Middle Ages. Improvements were not made until the Industrial Revolution. Because of the technological changes brought on by this revolution — such as the use of steam to propel water — the filthy streets and stagnant water supplies that bred disease became things of the past.

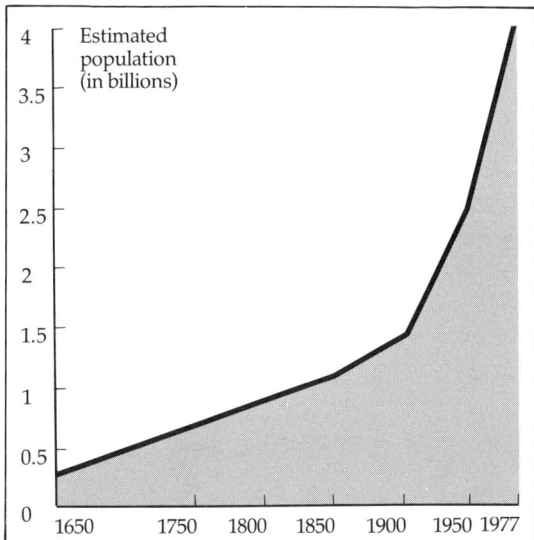

FIGURE 11.3 Estimates of World Population from 1650 to 1977

Sources: A. M. Carr-Saunders, *World Population* (Oxford: Clarendon Press, 1936), p. 42; and United Nations, *Statistical Yearbook, 1961, 1963, 1965, 1966, 1967, 1968, 1969, 1970, 1972, 1973, 1974,* and *1975* (New York: United Nations, 1961–1975).

Contributing to these changes was a better understanding of the cause of disease. During the nineteenth century the *germ theory of disease* was firmly established as medical orthodoxy. Physicians and scientists no longer saw disease as the result of astrological influences or as an imbalance of bodily humors. Rather, disease was viewed as the result of infection caused by microorganisms. This discovery gave impetus to the changes in sanitation and public health. By improving sanitary facilities, people could reduce their chances of contact with germs. Developments in medicine also contributed to population growth in another way. Improvements in treatment of disease meant that more people survived. The smallpox vaccine, developed by Edward Jenner at the end of the eighteenth century, is a good example. Jenner found that giving people cowpox, a disease similar to smallpox but milder, prevented them from catching smallpox. As inoculation spread, death rates decreased, similar discoveries about other diseases, and improved medical techniques, like more sanitary surgical practices, helped make physicians able to cure disease, rather than simply alleviate pain.

But the major change was the tremendous increase in the ability of people to grow and transport food. Largely a product of the nineteenth century, increased production was the result of technological improvement, symbolized by two inventions of the 1830s. First was Cyrus McCormick's mechanical reaper, patented in 1831, which allowed farmers to harvest grain much more quickly than before. The invention of the reaper, in combination with the cultivation of the rich soil of the American Midwest, meant a tremendous increase in the amount of grain grown, a significant development because grain was a staple of most people's diets. Second was the invention of the first mechanical refrigerator, patented in 1834. This invention created the possibility of preserving more varied foods than before. The result, as refrigeration was improved, was an increase in the variety of food people could eat, which meant better nutrition.

The benefits of these two inventions were enhanced by a third, the railroad, which made food more available. Steam-powered locomotives were proven effective in 1830 and rail lines were built in growing numbers throughout the decade. More important, in 1853 the Atlantic Coast was linked by rail with Chicago, opening up the East as a market for the grain and later the beef raised in the Midwest. But this development did not just help the United States. Although most agricultural produce was meant for domestic consumption before the Civil War, after 1870 more and more was exported to Europe, supporting the growth of population there.

Summary

As we have seen, the major increases in human population have occurred as the result of significant technological changes that greatly increased society's ability to produce food. The Neolithic Revolution of about 10,000 B.C. and the Industrial Revolution of the eighteenth and nineteenth centuries allowed societies to produce more children and permitted those children to grow to reproducing age. For thousands of years of human existence, "we were forced to concede the upper hand to nonhuman forces."[2] New technological weapons and tools for use in humankind's battle with the forces of nature helped change that and make life easier. But in doing so, they created a new problem: the problem of too many people.

CONCEPTUAL ORIENTATION

But how can we determine objectively whether there are too many people? To understand the population problem, we must first be able to understand three concepts related to population growth. One is fertility, the rate of births in a society, and another is mortality, the rate of deaths. The third is not actually a measure of population, but of the environment of a society. To understand population, we must also understand that a population is limited by its available resources.

Fertility and Mortality

The arithmetic of population increases or decreases is elementary. "The number of births minus the number of deaths in a given population during a specified length of time (usually one year) gives the *natural increase* of population. This, in turn, is the primary element in the study of population growth."[3] The problem, reduced to its simplest essentials, is to bring births into balance with deaths. Once this is accomplished, human populations will be stable and the spectre of a continuously burgeoning population will be banished.

Demographers, the social scientists who study population trends, define *fertility* as "the actual reproductive performance of a woman or group of women."[4] There are two general ways to approach the measurement of fertility: the period approach and the cohort approach. The period approach expresses fertility as the birthrate over a given period of time, usually a year. The most common example of the period approach is the *crude birthrate*, the number of births occurring per thousand population over a period of one year.

The cohort approach is more involved. It uses successive *cohorts* of women throughout their childbearing years, computing the total fertility of women of various age groups. *Cumulative cohort birthrates* tell us the number of births per one thousand women in a particular age group. This cumulative cohort approach is preferable to the crude rate because it can show trends. It also allows demographers to analyze population characteristics with greater precision. For example, each cohort of women must produce an average of 2.1 births per female during childbearing years (age fifteen through forty-five) if a population is to remain stable. More than this and the population will increase; less and it will go down. If either an increase or a decrease occurs, demographers can identify which cohort is most responsible and then look at other characteristics of that cohort to understand why.

Population growth is not simply a matter of births, however. It is a direct function of an excess of births over deaths. To illustrate, in preindustrial societies, fertility is high but mortality, the rate of deaths, is also high.[5] Under such conditions, population growth is slow. But if mortality is sharply reduced, as is the case in industrial societies, and falls below fertility, the obvious result is a rapidly rising population. As Harold Dorn observed, "It is the combination of a medieval birth rate with a twentieth century mortality rate that is responsible for the current high rate of population increase."[6] The world problem is to bring births, or fertility, into line with deaths, or mortality. *Zero population growth* (ZPG) will result when the two become approximately equal and remain so for an extended time.

In fact, although the world population is growing, fertility rates around the world are lowering (see Figure 11.4). But "declines in birth rates [alone] cannot solve all problems of numbers immediately, or indeed for a very long period of time. But, problems of numbers will not be solved in the long run without declines in birth rates."[7] A declining birthrate can help, but it won't be enough.

FIGURE 11.4 Birthrates in Major World Areas, 1965 and 1976

Source: United Nations, *Statistical Yearbook, 1965* and *1976* (New York: United Nations, 1965, 1976).

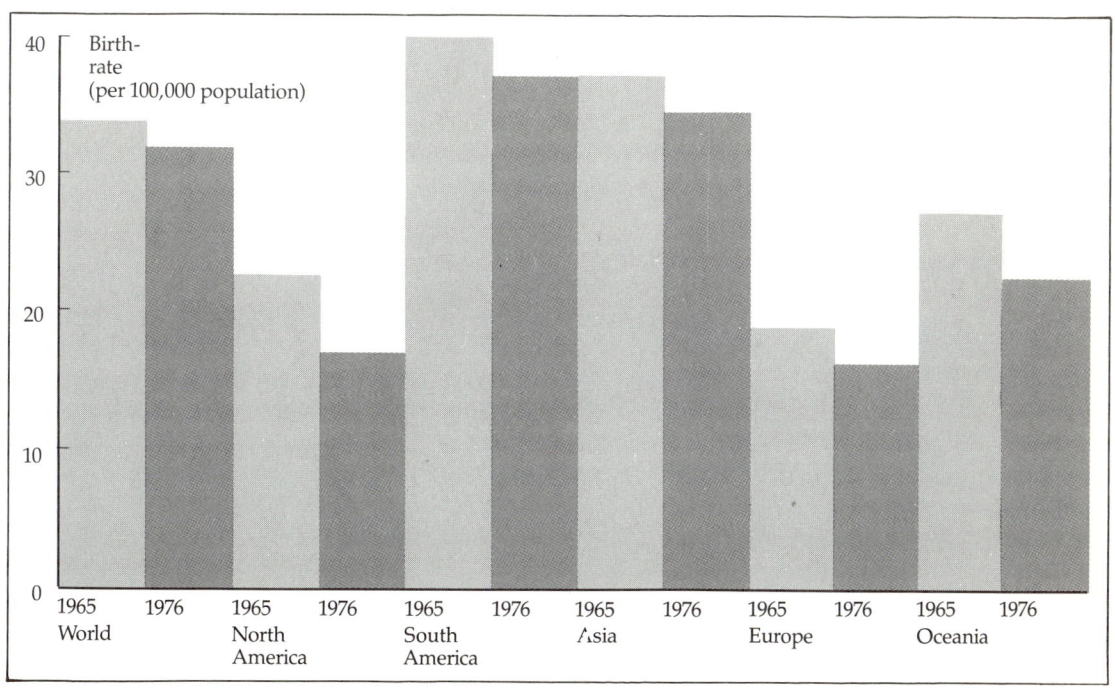

Many people believe that the enormous increase in the world population in the last century is simply a result of rising birthrates. But fertility has not increased in any large part of the world for a century or more, while as Figure 11.5 shows, the death rate in the world is declining. Essentially, the population explosion is a function of the decrease in mortality.[8]

The Scarcity of Resources

A population does not exist by itself. Any society must exist alongside other societies, and humans as a species must live with other species. In fact, to a degree humans live off other species: we eat plants and we eat animals. Other natural resources — coal, oil, wood, air — are consumed in other ways. These facts have a direct bearing on questions of population. Since people consume resources, there can only be as many people as there are resources to consume. Population growth "can be viewed as the result of many individual acts and decisions, made within a framework of biological and environmental constraints."[9] For our purposes here, we can ignore individual biological constraints. The vast majority of humans are capable of reproduction and the number of children any couple has is a function of individual decisions constrained by the bio-

FIGURE 11.5 A Comparison of Death Rates for Major World Areas, 1965 and 1975

Source: United Nations, *Statistical Yearbook, 1965* and *1976* (New York: United Nations, 1965, 1976).

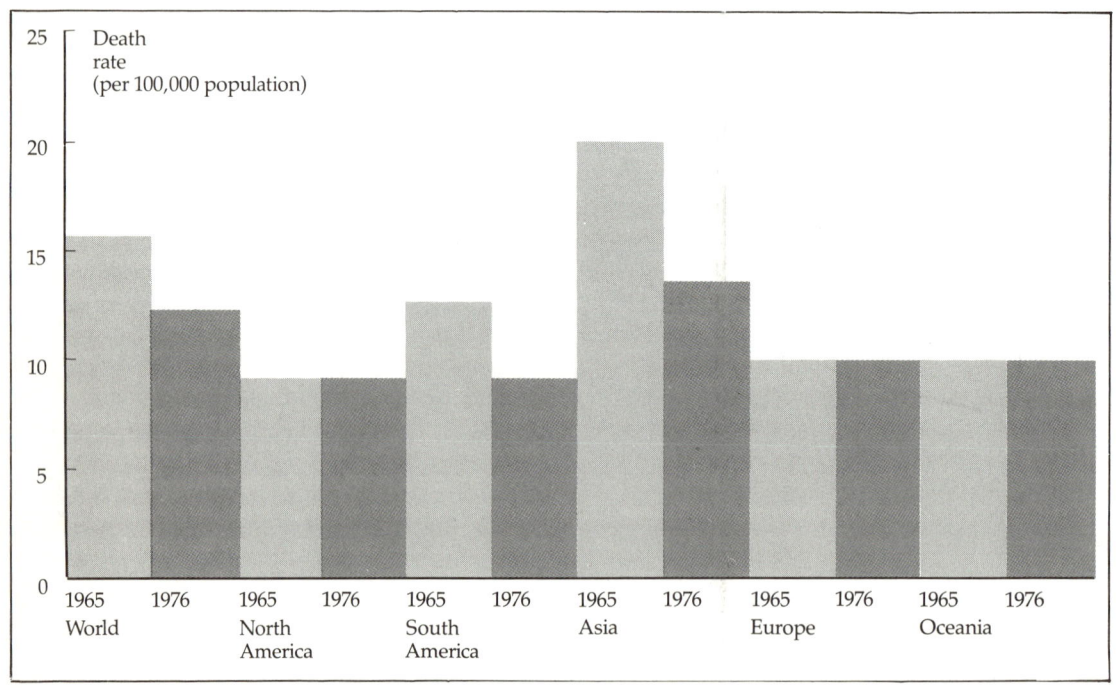

logical and social environment. The social influences on fertility will be discussed at the end of the chapter, when we analyze the factors that inhibit and promote fertility. For now we will focus on what makes overpopulation a problem: the scarcity of resources.

The problem of resources was first identified in 1798, when Thomas Malthus, an English clergyman, published the first edition of *An Essay on the Principle of Population*. Malthus argued that population should grow faster than available food. According to his calculations, human population should increase *geometrically*: 1, 2, 4, 8, 16, 32. At the same time, food supply increases only *arithmetically*: 1, 2, 3, 4, 5, 6. In nine generations, the ratio of population to food supply would be 256 to 9. As is illustrated in Figure 11.6, the result is that the number of human beings will eventually exceed the available food supply.

Malthus saw ways of avoiding this problem. He stated that there were two general ways of ensuring that population did not outstrip resources. One was not having children. This was a *preventive check* — it would prevent the problem from arising. In Malthus's age, with no good method of birth control, the preventive was, as he called it, *moral restraint*, which meant celibacy. This method is unreliable, however. With the exception of a small proportion of people who can live celibate lives, most people seek sexual gratification. In modern times, with the introduction of such effective birth control methods as the pill and the intrauterine de-

FIGURE 11.6 The Malthusian Hypothesis of the Relationship between Increases in Population and Increases in Food Supply

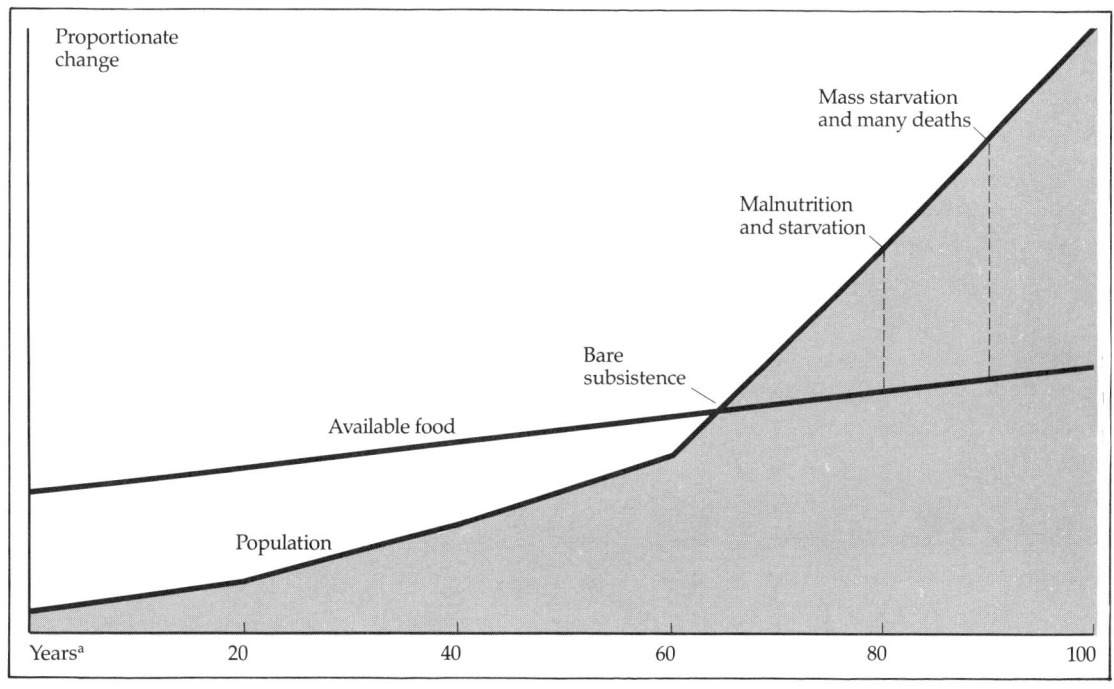

vice, moral restraint needn't be relied on. Mechanical or chemical birth control — far more dependable — can be used.

The other check on population that Malthus saw was war, famine, and disease, which he termed *positive checks*. (He did not call them positive checks because he favored them, but because they were more effective than moral restraint.) Malthus predicted that without enough food for everyone, more people would die from these causes. People would fight over what little food was available, famines would have a more devastating effect because more people would be dependent on each crop, and disease would be more often fatal because people would be weakened by malnutrition.

For many years events showed Malthus to be grimly correct. The Irish potato famine of the 1840s killed one out of eight people in Ireland, for instance. But in the end his predictions were not borne out. What Malthus had not foreseen were the technological innovations outlined earlier, the improvements in medicine that saved more lives from disease and the improvements in food production and distribution that allowed the movement of food from producing countries to countries not producing enough food for their people. Without imported grain, India would probably suffer many deaths from famine. With it, the country avoids the devastation that hit Ireland over one hundred years ago.

Today, however, people are beginning to see the problem Malthus predicted in the ratio of population to food. While impressed by the past achievements of technology, people wonder if food production can be pushed significantly higher than present levels. Certainly some increase is possible, with the introduction of more advanced methods to new areas, but the supply of arable land is limited. Not every place can grow food. The question then becomes, do we rely on famine, disease, and war to keep the population down, coldheartedly condemning some people to death? Or do we make an effort to prevent the problem by practicing birth control?

Summary

The importance of Malthus's preventive checks is not in his methods but in the underlying assumption. Fertility can be controlled by conscious interference. Given that this interference is now possible and can be effective, we need to look at current fertility and mortality to see if population control can be achieved.

OBJECTIVE DIMENSIONS OF THE PROBLEM

To determine the extent of the problem of population, we need to discuss the actual population of the world and its present growth rate. Because we will find that there are differences in nations' tendencies to control population, we will look at the figures by region. Then we will focus on population in one kind of nation, the developed countries of Europe and North America.

Population Growth in the World

The dividing line between high and low fertility groups is a crude birthrate of thirty, that is, thirty births per thousand population per year. As we saw in Figure 11.4, the world as a whole has a high fertility rate of thirty-four births per thousand. This rate is attributable to the very high birthrates in South

America (thirty-eight per thousand) and Asia (thirty-five), the other three regions were below thirty. But as we have pointed out, population growth is a matter of the relationship of births and deaths. Significantly, "in most of the underdeveloped countries, the death rates have been declining quite rapidly since World War II."[10] The result is shown in Figure 11.5. In North America, Europe, and Oceania, the already low death rates remained virtually unchanged; in South America and Asia the reduction in mortality was greater than the reduction in births.

We can be somewhat encouraged by the fact that three out of five major world areas are moving, albeit slowly, toward achieving a balance between fertility and mortality. But for the other two, the picture is not sanguine; the gap between birthrates and death rates is widening rather than narrowing. When we add to this the fact that the three areas with a widening gap contain over 2 billion people, we can see that there is even greater cause for concern. The result is shown in Figure 11.7, which shows the world as a whole evidencing a substantial annual increase in population, with the growth rate rising from 1.8 percent per year to 1.9 percent between 1965 and 1976. Much of this increase is attributable to Asia and South America. As of 1976, the growth rate for Asia was 2.2 percent

FIGURE 11.7 Annual Rates of Population Increase for Major World Areas, 1965 and 1976

Source: United Nations, *Statistical Yearbook, 1965* and *1976* (New York: United Nations, 1965, 1976).

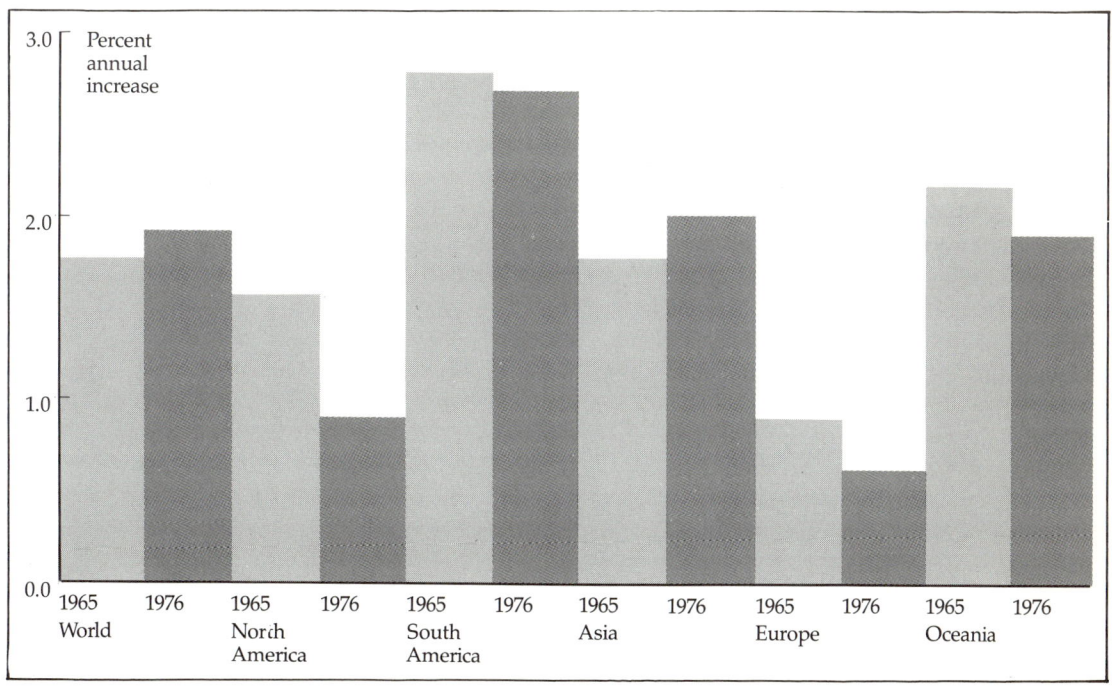

and for South America an alarming 2.8 percent. (Table 11.1 presents the data on which Figures 11.3, 11.4, and 11.5 are based.)

This disparity between fertility and mortality means that "for every two persons on the earth in 1950, there are now three. For every three today, there will probably be five in the year 2000."[11] This estimate may turn out to be conservative. Judging from the past, the best estimate is that the death rate

TABLE 11.1 A Comparison of Birthrates, Death Rates, and Rates of Annual Increase for the World and Major World Areas for the Years 1965 and 1976

	1965	1976
The World		
Population	3.3 billions	3.97 billions
Birthrate	34	32
Death rate	16	13
Annual increase	1.8 percent	1.9 percent
North America		
Population	214 millions	237 millions
Birthrate	23	17
Death rate	9	9
Annual increase	1.6 percent	0.9 percent
South America		
Population	243 millions	324 millions
Birthrate	41	38
Death rate	13	9
Annual increase	2.8 percent	2.8 percent
Asia		
Population	1.83 billions	2.3 billions
Birthrate	38	35
Death rate	20	14
Annual increase	1.8 percent	2.2 percent
Europe		
Population	444 millions	473 millions
Birthrate	19	16
Death rate	10	10
Annual increase	0.9 percent	0.6 percent
Oceania		
Population	175 millions	213 millions
Birthrate	27	23
Death rate	10	10
Annual increase	2.2 percent	2.0 percent

Note: Africa is not included in this table principally because the majority of the developing countries in Africa do not take periodic censuses or maintain accurate data regarding births and deaths.
Source: United Nations (Department of Economic and Social Affairs) *Statistical Yearbooks, 1965* and *1976.*

will continue to fall in Asia and South America in the last two decades of the twentieth century. Unless there is a corresponding reduction in birthrates, which seems unlikely, population increases would then be even greater than this estimate.

Why has mortality decreased, and why will it continue to? "Although a great number of global factors could be cited as affecting mortality, four are of particular relevance in understanding trends in the death rate. These are natural environmental factors, economic development and technological change, advances in public health and medical science, and changing causes of death."[12] Technological and economic development and improvements in public health and medical science, in combination, have enabled people in modern societies to live far pleasanter and much longer lives. They have also enabled people in developing societies to live much longer than in the past.

Economic development and technological change function to give people in modern societies a more than adequate supply of food along with excellent medical care. These in conjunction with public health measures have done away with some of the so-called natural factors — Malthus's famine and disease — which in the past served as a check on population growth by keeping mortality high. As Harold Dorn comments:

> It is difficult to realize today how effectively disease and famine have acted as a check upon the increase of population during the centuries of man's existence and how recently the effectiveness of these checks has been curbed. The last great famine of Western Europe occurred in Ireland about 115 years ago. A severe shortage of food lasted for nearly six years. In spite of assistance from other countries, one out of every eight persons alive at the beginning of the famine in 1846 died during the following five years.[13]

Few of us would advocate a return to the conditions prevailing many years ago when, for example, only 360 children out of every one thousand born were still alive in their fifth year.[14] Clearly, prior to the Industrial Revolution mortality among young children was very high. In this respect, it should be remembered that the first few years of life, particularly the initial two years, are critical for children. If they survive beyond these early years, the odds are that they will live long enough to have children of their own. The better organized humans become in terms of economics, technology, medicine, and public health, the higher the survival rate not only of children but adults as well. As an obvious result, there are more children in the next generation and so on. The larger part of the current population problem lies in the steadily improving organization among our species. To see what solutions might be offered, let us look at the most organized groups, the developed nations.

Population Growth in Developed Countries

In contrast to our life-style, most people living in those large areas termed *developing* — the unindustrialized nations of Africa, Asia, and South America — are neither well fed, well housed, nor well educated. Grinding poverty is the lot of the majority of the world's people. Yet these are the areas in which population is growing the fastest. What are the prospects for at least leveling off population growth? The evidence is mixed, but some encouragement comes from considering population in the developed countries.

It is generally agreed that most of the developed countries are located in Europe and North America. There are several others,

362 POPULATION: *Growing Numbers and Shrinking Resources*

The populations of developing countries are the fastest growing in the world, with little likelihood of tapering off in the foreseeable future. The inability of these nations to feed, clothe, and house their people is a bitter foretaste of how world overpopulation may well affect us all. These Brazilian favelas, urban slums of Rio de Janeiro, are not unlike the living quarters of millions worldwide.

such as Japan and Australia, but we will concentrate on Europe and North America as being representative of modern nations.

As Figure 11.6 and Table 11.1 show, the current annual increase rates for Europe and North America are much smaller than for the rest of the world, at 0.6 and 0.9 percent respectively. This seems a very slow rate of growth and appears to indicate that neither Europe nor North America have any particular growth problems, at least for a long time to come. But, in fact, these slow rates of growth will still mean a tremendous difference in absolute numbers.

Table 11.2 provides a projection of population increases for both Europe and North America, showing what the population will be, using the present rate of annual increase and using the 1965 rate. As can be seen in Table 11.2, a period of almost three-quarters of a century can make quite a difference in terms of absolute numbers, even with a low rate. At the lowest growth rate in the world, the population of Europe would increase from about 444 million people to approximately 716.5 million by 2055.

North America, with a slightly higher rate of 0.9 percent, will also increase greatly. This large an annual increase rate, if continued, will result in the current population of North America more than doubling by the year 2055, with an increase of about 105 percent.

Can North America accommodate a population in excess of 439 million people? Probably, in terms of space. Can North America feed, clothe, and house this many people? Again, the answer is probably yes. But can North America have a population this large and maintain the standard of living we have today? On the basis of what we know about the available resources in the world, the answer is no. If the population of North America continues to increase at the 1976 rate, the results can hardly be other than a sharp reduction in the current standard of living and severe dislocations for society.

But the data in Table 11.2 are encouraging. While we see in it a tremendous jump in the number of people, using the current rates of increase, we need to look at the other two columns, which show the population growth at old rates of increase. Once we do a different picture emerges. A decrease of only 0.3 percent (from Europe's 1965 rate to the 1976 rate) is highly significant in terms of numbers of people. At the lower rate Europe will have 191 million fewer people in 2055 than it would have if the 1965 growth rate had been maintained. The difference in North America is even more dramatic. Instead of dou-

TABLE 11.2 Projected Populations for Europe and North America at Different Rates of Annual Increase (in Millions)

Year	Europe		North America	
	0.9%	0.6%	1.6%	0.9%
1976	444	444	214	214
1980	464.3	457.5	228	223.8
1985	485.6	471.4	246.9	234
1990	507.9	485.7	267.3	244.8
1995	531.1	500.4	289.3	256.5
2000	555.5	515.6	313.2	268.3
2005	580.9	531.3	339.1	280.6
2010	607.5	547.4	367.1	293.4
2015	635.4	564	397.4	306.9
2020	663.4	581.2	432.3	321
2025	693.8	598.8	468	335.7
2030	725.6	617	506.1	351
2035	758.9	635.7	547.9	367.1
2040	793.7	655	593.2	383.9
2045	830	674.9	642.2	401.5
2050	868	695.4	695.2	419.9
2055	907.8	716.5	752.7	439.2

Source: United Nations, *Statistical Yearbook, 1977* (New York: United Nations, 1977).

bling by 2055, as the population will do at the current growth rate, the old growth rate of 1.6 percent would have increased it by more than 3.5 times. The difference between this projected population of over 750 million and the projected total at the present rate is enormous and shows the importance of reducing the rate of population growth by any amount.

We should not be too hopeful about these figures; they do not mean population will no longer be a problem. A reduction in the annual rate to anything above zero is, in effect, merely buying some time for future generations. But any reduction in the prevailing rate of increase anywhere in the world is worthwhile for posterity, not to mention the millions living today. And the developed nations show that a lowered growth rate is possible.

Summary

We have seen that world population is growing at a fast rate, largely because of decreases in mortality in the developing nations. We have also seen that the developed nations show that it is possible to reduce the rate of growth, thus at least delaying the time when we reach enormous numbers. But this delay is not enough — it doesn't solve the population problem, it merely postpones it. It is now time to discuss what would happen if there were no population growth at all.

ATTEMPTS AT DEALING WITH THE PROBLEM

As of the end of the 1970s, an analysis of the available data promotes some optimism and considerable pessimism. North America and Europe both have relatively stable death rates and what appears to be a constantly but slowly lowering fertility. In contrast, Asia and South America are experiencing a decreasing death rate but without a commensurate lowering in fertility. We can see where this will lead. Levels of aspiration continue to rise among Asian and Latin American peoples, but the means to meet these aspirations are not available. An important reason for this is of course the rapid increase in populations. Continuing misery, suffering, and political unrest will characterize Asia and South America for a long time, which will undoubtedly have some adverse consequences for the developed nations. This is the result of continued growth; but suppose the world could achieve zero population growth. What might the consequences be?

The Eufunctions of
Zero Population Growth

The first benefit of zero population growth (ZPG) is obvious. Resources will no longer be consumed at rapidly rising rates. Of course, increases in consumption will still occur, unless there are dramatic changes in life-styles. But these increases would be minor compared to what would happen with unchecked population growth.

Another benefit of ZPG would be the greater possibility of social planning. For example, demographers can now tell us within a small margin of error the number of persons, male and female, in all age groups. When ZPG is a reality, such predictions could be made years ahead. The implications of this for government policy are considerable. For example, school systems would be able to plan more precisely, knowing how many new students they would have. Similarly, colleges of education would know far ahead what the demand for new teachers would be. This would enable them to change their admissions to reflect these more accurate numbers, thus reducing the great fluctuations in the number of teachers trained and unemployed.

This ability for long-range planning would also benefit the federal government. In recent years, the social security system in this country has been experiencing difficulties because of the constantly expanding number of persons eligible for social security and other benefits. If ZPG were achieved, the number of people collecting social security will remain relatively constant. This will permit more accurate assessments of the financial support required. Other federal expenditures, such as aid to education, could also be planned more thoroughly on the basis of more accurate projections of how many will need the help, thus avoiding expensive crash programs.

Business, too, could benefit. All sectors of the economy would be able to gear their operations to reasonably predictable conditions. Rather than facing the problems of a constantly rising demand as the population increases geometrically, the economy can function on the basis of regular demand. Those businesses with age-related products, like diapers and amusements, could plan production more carefully. And long-range planning for the allocation and use of resources would be possible.

Society as a whole would benefit, with the reduction of some social problems. The changing balance of age groups would help increase the value of the aged, so that they would be allowed to contribute more to society. And crime should decrease because there would be an absolute and proportionate decrease in the number of those twelve to twenty-four. It is these age cohorts that contribute disproportionately to much recorded crime. All these changes are highly desirable, but attaining ZPG will also entail certain costs.

Iatrogenic Effects

The United States is entering the third and final stage of what is called the *demographic transition*:

1. Stage 1: high birthrates and high death rates.
2. Stage 2: high birthrates and rapidly falling death rates, resulting in rapid population increase. Much of the world's nations are in this second stage.
3. Stage 3: fertility rates drop to a point approximating death rates and ZPG is achieved, although constant population does not become a fact until women from earlier periods of high fertility have passed through their childbearing years.

ZPG, as such, does not have any significant iatrogenic effects. It is passing through the demographic transition that has iatrogenic effects.

First, as large numbers of women from earlier high birthrate years age, some dislocation is inevitable. For example, the input of high school graduates into colleges and universities around 1989 could well prove to be the highest for many years to come. Providing the current fertility rate is maintained, the number of entering freshmen will then decline yearly until well into the twenty-first century, when ZPG is attained and age groups stabilize. In practical terms, this means that universities will have to plan for fewer students each successive year. The faculty, administration, and space problems resulting are obvious. Figures 11.8 and 11.9 show the changes in each age cohort by sex for the years 1977 and 2000.

Both the mean and median age of the population will continue to rise while the country goes through the third stage of the demographic transition. Consumer goods and services will be affected. The economy will be constantly faced with signficant changes in the kinds of goods and services needed. Even now, diaper services, toy manufacturers, obstetricians, and specialists in childhood diseases face a declining market for their products and services. High-school teachers too are faced with the problem now confronting elementary-school teachers, that is, declining enrollments and reduced opportunities for employment. Again, this problem will end when ZPG is reached and the age groups stabilize.

The sex ratio will become increasingly out of balance until ZPG is attained. At around age thirty, the number of females in the population begins to exceed the number of males (see Figure 11.8). This is because the mortality rate for males is higher at all ages. This means that an increasing number of women age thirty and older are going to be unmarried. In 1977, there were about 5.47 million more females than males. By the year 2000,

FIGURE 11.8 Distribution of United States Population by Age and Sex, 1977

Source: Bureau of the Census, *Current Population Reports,* "Projections of the Population of the United States: 1965 to 2050," Series P–25, No. 601 (Washington, D.C.: U.S. Government Printing Office, 1975), pp. 270–71.

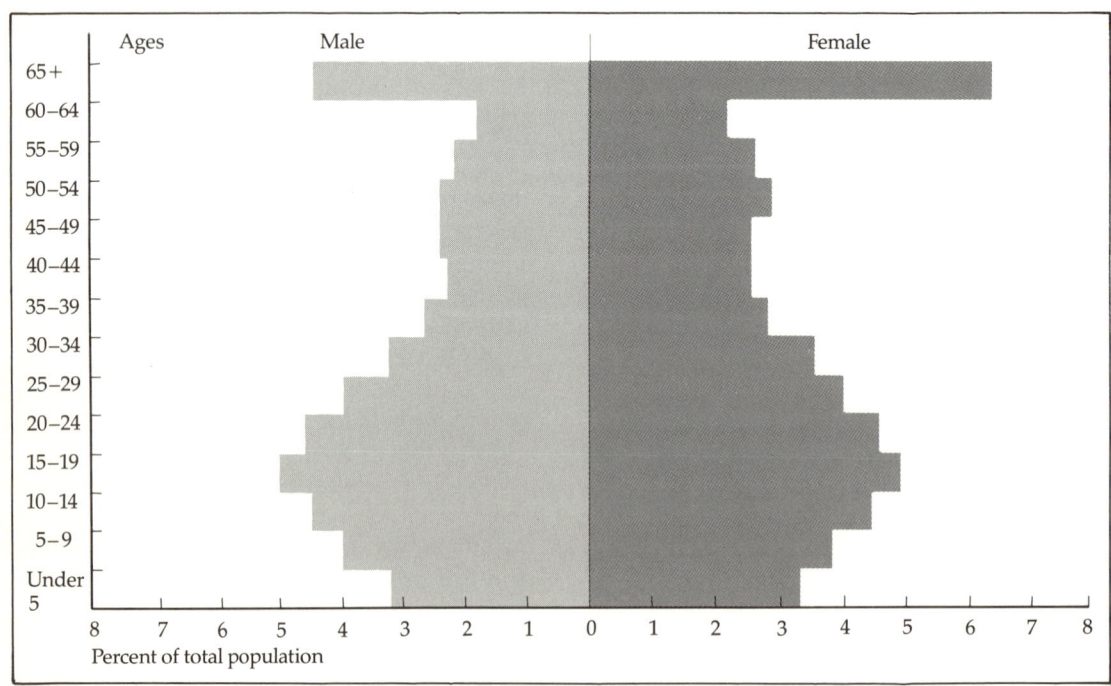

that figure will have increased to around 7.86 million.

The number of persons eligible for social security will increase steadily for many years. Provided the present fertility rate is maintained, the imbalance between those under and those over sixty-five will continue to mount until the start of the twenty-second century. Barring some significant change in the current retirement policies, such as raising the age beyond seventy, a shrinking work force will, of necessity, be supporting a larger and larger part of the population. The drain on social security programs will indeed become greater and so will contributions from the incomes of working people.

The foregoing constitute the principal iatrogenic effects of attaining ZPG and apply, as we have said, to moving through the third stage of the demographic transition. But taking all factors into account, we should be willing to pay these prices. We have the advantage of being armed with advanced knowledge of what is likely to occur. The alternatives rising out of continued increases in our population appear far more disagreeable to contemplate. Further, we also know that these iatrogenic effects are temporary — they will end when zero population growth is attained. On the other hand, not

FIGURE 11.9 Projected Distribution of United States Population by Age and Sex, 2000 (Assuming Continuing Fertility Rate of 1.7)

Source: Bureau of the Census, *Current Population Reports,* "Projections of the Population of the United States: 1965 to 2050," Series P-25, No. 601 (Washington, D.C.: U.S. Government Printing Office, 1975), p. 272.

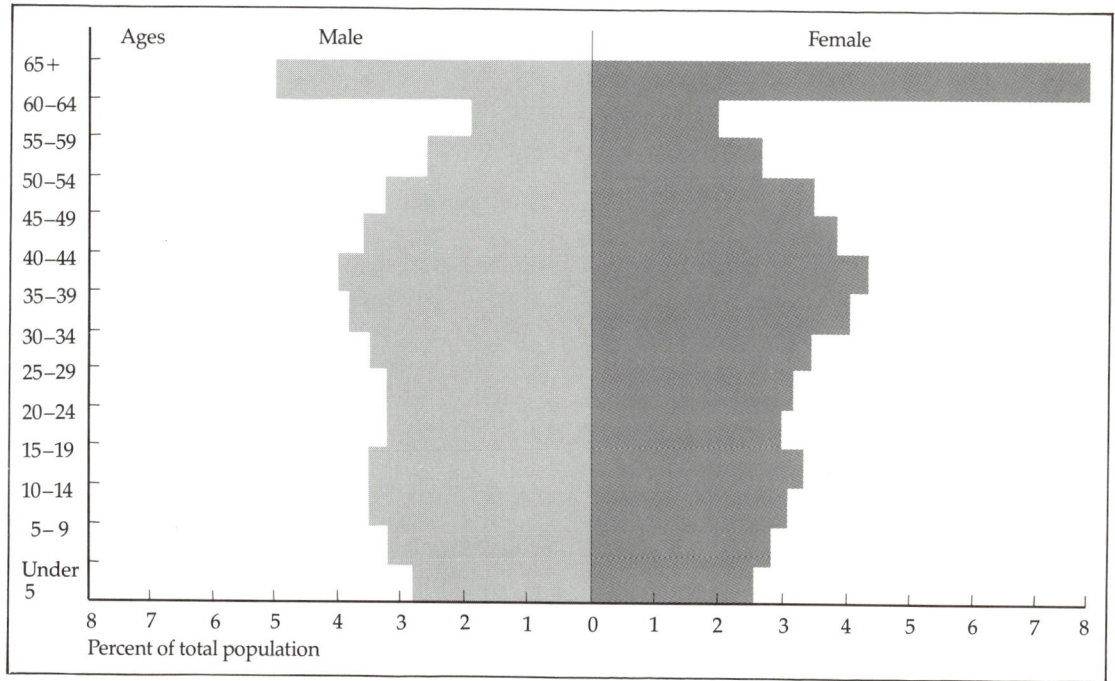

restraining population growth will mean long-term misery.

PROSPECTS FOR SOLVING THE PROBLEM

The likelihood of attaining ZPG is influenced by various subjective factors, some that support fertility and some that support the reduction of fertility. Let us make it clear that by "subjective factors" we do not mean merely emotion or sentiment, although these are also involved. What we mean, though, is the way people look at things. Individual perceptions, as we stressed in Chapter 1, are often at least partially objective. That is, when making decisions, people are influenced by knowledge of objective conditions and by objective considerations. But they are also influenced by subjective factors — the way they perceive things and the judgments and actions they make based on these perceptions.

The objective factors already discussed form the basis for viewing the continued population growth as a serious social problem. It is objectively clear the measures must be taken to achieve ZPG. If all parents and potential parents in the world accepted this point of view and acted on it, population growth would cease to be a problem in a few years. It is an understatement to say that this is not likely to happen.

The fertility of human populations appears to be a function of independent decisions made by couples all over the world. Sometimes fertility is a matter of no decision at all. As Ronald Freeman says, "A rather large proportion of all pregnancies are 'accidents' or otherwise unplanned."[15] But birth control information techniques and materials are available. Granting this, the focus of sociological investigation must turn to two questions: (1) what social and psychological factors encourage reduced fertility? and (2) what social and psychological factors tend to keep fertility high?

Factors Tending to Reduce Fertility

Charles Nam and Susan Gustavus point out that "industrialization, urbanization, and other aspects of modernization are believed to be precipitating agents in, first, the decline of mortality, and, later, the decline of fertility."[16] In other words, modernization is an independent variable of both a decline in mortality and a decline in fertility. Let us consider what factors brought on by modernization influence the lowering of fertility rates.

ECONOMICS
General affluence is not a characteristic of those nations in which a large proportion of the population is engaged in agriculture. In developed countries, however, by far the greater part of the work force is found in industrial and service occupations. For example, by the end of the 1970s, only about 5 percent of the United States population was engaged in farming. When a large part of a population is engaged in industry, the result is a vast outpouring of goods and a consequent increase in general affluence.

It is clear that the general spread of influence to a large part of a nation's citizenry is a function of industrialization. But what has this to do with fertility? One would imagine that when people could afford more children, they would have them. Rising prosperity ought to be accompanied by a rising birthrate. But in fact the reverse is true. As Barbara Ward points out, economic expansion is a cause of a declining birthrate.[17] Why? It appears to fly in the face of logic. David Heer and Eba Turner explain it this way:

> An increase in the level of economic development leads to an increase in fertility as married couples become more optimistic concerning their future economic status. On the other hand, the increase in the level of economic development then sets in motion other forces such as increased knowledge and the use of birth control and increases in net economic costs of children, which tend to reduce fertility. In the long run, the forces depressing fertility tend to be stronger than the forces increasing fertility.[18]

One factor, then, is that birth control measures are known, available, and considered desirable. We know that birth control is more available and more effective now, but why is it desirable?

> Under the old regime of high fertility and high mortality women experienced the drain and danger of pregnancy often to no purpose because a large proportion of the offspring died before reaching maturity. Too much effort was spent in trying to bring each new generation to adulthood; too much energy was lost in sickness, malnutrition and mourning; too much time was taken for mere sustenance. The new type of demographic balance [low mortality and low fertility] released a large part of this energy — a tremendous amount of human energy — for other things.[19]

It is no longer necessary for a couple to have ten or twelve children in order for two or three to survive to maturity. For example, between World War I and World War II, the infant mortality rate decreased from 85 to around 30 per thousand live births — a reduction of nearly 300 percent.[20] This tremendous decrease means that couples in modern countries can expect their children not only to survive to adulthood but to outlive the parents. Thus a married couple does not need to have as many children as used to be the case.

In addition, in modern societies children are largely economic liabilities. In fact, they are economic liabilities for a long time. As modern societies become increasingly complex technologically, the demands for unskilled labor decrease and the need for persons having usable skills and knowledge increases. The net result of this is to place considerable pressure on parents and children to prepare youngsters for entering the world of work by undergoing more and more formal education and training. Even affluent families cannot afford to meet the costs of educating very many children. It is the recognition of this that leads people to use the efficient contraceptives available, thus reducing fertility.

CAREERS FOR WOMEN

Today, increasing numbers of women are seeking lifetime careers in a variety of fields, including many previously considered appropriate only for men. The fact that women find these occupations satisfying and desire to pursue them has consequences for fertility. Clearly, bearing and rearing more than one or two children render full-time employment outside the home difficult.

As the 1970s come to an end, we find that more than 40 percent of the work force is composed of women, some occupying high professional or managerial positions. The loss of income and work satisfaction that might result from having too many children is clearly a reason for limiting family size — and limiting it sharply. As a number of studies show, there is an inverse, or negative,

One of the factors tending to reduce fertility is the increasing number of women, like this university law professor, who choose to pursue full-time, lifetime careers. The higher the proportion of working women — a characteristic of industrialized developed countries rather than agrarian undeveloped countries — the lower the fertility rate.

relationship between fertility and the proportion of employed women and economic opportunities for women.[21] As more women work, they have fewer children.

GOVERNMENT AND THE LAW

For a long time artificial methods of birth control were against the law in many states. Just prior to World War I, Margaret Sanger opened a birth-control clinic and was sentenced to thirty days in jail on the charge of maintaining a public nuisance. Much later, in 1959, we find President Dwight D. Eisenhower saying:

I cannot imagine anything more emphatically a subject that is not a proper political or governmental activity or function or responsibility [than birth control]. This government has not, and will not so long as I am here, have a positive political doctrine in its program that has to do with this problem on birth control. That's not our business.[22]

But times change and it would seem that even Eisenhower came to realize this. Ten years later he became the honorary chairman of Planned Parenthood.

On the whole, the government often lags behind the general public. The official position of the government until recent years was against contraception and abortion. However, the laws ran counter to the informal norms prevalent then and increasingly prevalent today. Contraception was widely practiced and illegal abortions were common.

In recent years, the government has changed its stand. The legalization of both contraception and abortion has unquestionably had some significant effects on fertility. For example, in New York there was a 23 percent decline in births from 1970 to 1972. Christopher Tietze estimated that one-half of this decrease in fertility was a function of legal abortions.[23] The legalization of effective birth-control methods, like the pill, has also had a significant effect. Although abortion and birth control were practiced before they were legalized, as people followed informal norms, their use has probably increased since legalization, for many people would hesitate to deviate from the law, even if others did. And legalization also means more information on these practices, which means that many will know about them who wouldn't otherwise.

FERTILITY REDUCTION
FACTORS: A SUMMARY

Earlier it was noted that the current rate of increase for North America is around 0.9 percent. For the United States alone, the rate of increase in 1976 was 0.73 percent.[24] Figure 11.10 shows the *total fertility rate* from 1920 through 1976. "The total fertility rate for a given year shows how many births a group of 1,000 women would have by the end of their childbearing years if, during their entire reproductive period, they were to experience the age-specific birth rates for the given year."[25]

While the period following World War II was characterized by a great increase in total fertility rates — the so-called baby boom — the general trend since the beginning of the century has been toward lowering fertility. In fact, sometime during 1971, the total fertility rate in this country dropped below the replacement level, as Figure 11.10 shows.

We can ascribe this fertility reduction to the factors we have discussed, which have marked our history in this century. First is modernization in general, including industrialization and urbanization. Second is the rise of general affluence, which means that fewer children are needed and those born need more training, thus becoming economic liabilities. Third is the greater number of women in the work force. Fourth is government support for birth control. And last is the availability and greater effectiveness of birth-control methods, although this factor alone would not have an effect: the others are needed to make birth control desirable.

The fact that the fertility rate in the United States is currently below replacement levels indicates that we may have the recipe for controlling population size and growth. It would seem that we are ready to solve the world's population problem. But the situation is far from being that simple. Other equally strong social factors tend to increase fertility.[26] Let us now examine these influences.

Factors Tending to Increase Fertility

In contrast to the situation in the United States, population in the developing countries is rising at a rapid rate. As we have seen, fertility is declining throughout the world; the major reason for the rapid growth of population is that mortality is going down. Since fertility is declining, we know that a number of people in developing countries are taking steps to prevent conception. This is the only possible explanation. The problem is that the birthrate is going down too slowly. But the reasons commonly given — that people in these nations lack responsibility or have no knowledge of birth-control techniques — cannot be true, or else there would be no reduction in fertility. Let us see why, then.

ECONOMICS

Because most Americans lead urban lives, it is difficult for us to appreciate what life is like in a primarily agricultural society. In the majority of the world's nations, the greater proportion of people make their living directly in agriculture. And by modern standards, it is a primitive form of agriculture.

On all farms, there are a host of chores and duties that must be done, but do not require a full-grown adult to do them. Many things on farms can be done quite well by young children, such as slopping the pigs, collecting eggs, or feeding animals. But because

FIGURE 11.10 Fertility Rate, 1920–1976

Source: Bureau of the Census, *Current Population Reports,* "Population Profile of the United States: 1976," Series P-20, No. 307 (Washington, D.C.: U.S. Government Printing Office, 1977), p. 6.

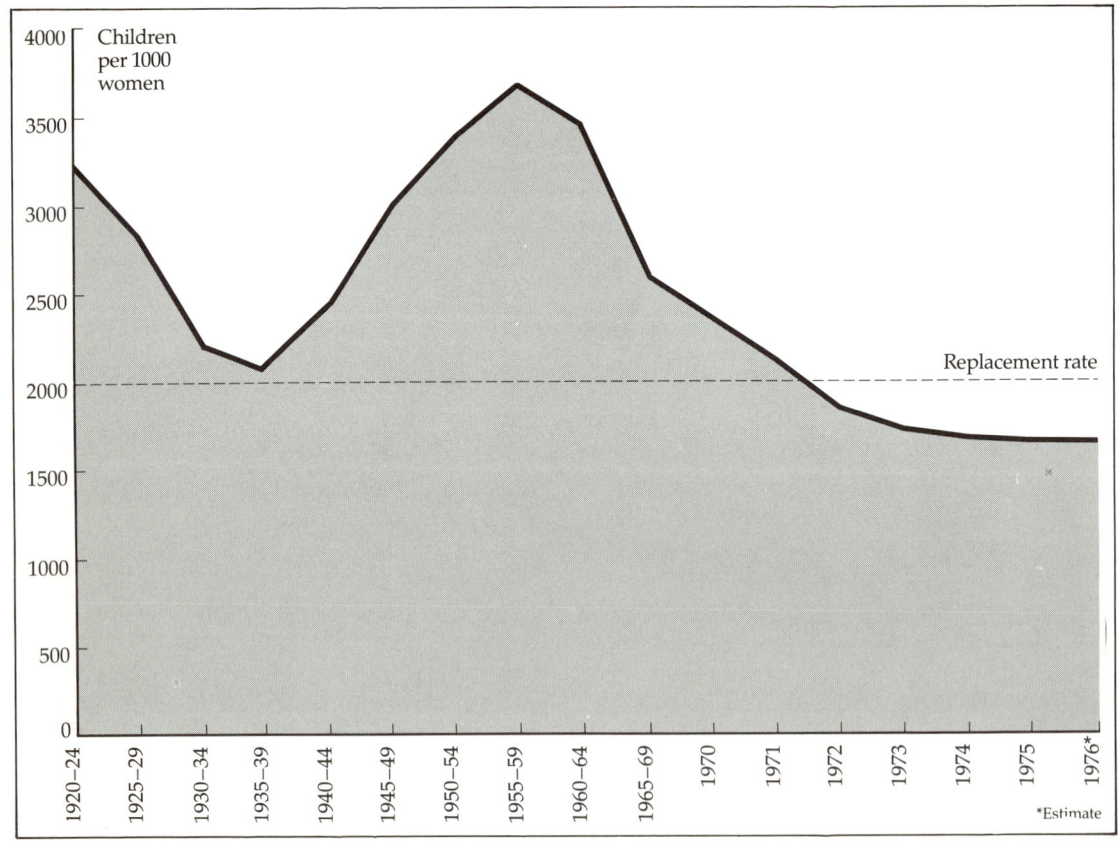

Prospects for Solving the Problem 373

there are many such jobs, many hands are required. Few farmers in developing countries can afford to hire outside labor. The labor problem is met by having large families. As Frank Lorimer writes,

> so long as children are, in an economic sense, capital assets that require relatively small investments and soon yield appreciable returns from their labor — as well as being objects of affection and a source of satisfaction and prestige — parents have no strong reason to limit the number of their offspring.[27]

Another factor that promotes having many children is concern for future security,

Many misinformed people are convinced that irresponsibility and ignorance are the only reasons why large families prevail in certain cultures. On the contrary, great numbers of children are often planned, prayed for, and indulged in, in areas where offspring are lifelong economic assets and where child mortality rates dictate long odds against sons reaching maturity.

both economic and psychological. In developed societies, people are concerned about having enough money to support themselves in illness or in old age and the psychic support afforded by kinfolk, particularly their own children is vital. But with low infant mortality and modern health care, modern parents can usually count on being survived by their own children. Further, government social security systems provide some funds for economic support and medical expenses. Sweden, with its cradle-to-grave social security system, epitomizes the modern welfare state.

In contrast, we need to consider the situation in the developing world. There is no government social security, except in Kuwait. There is no regular income from a government when one reaches retirement age or is unable to work. More important, there is no assurance that any children will survive the parents. Alan Berg has estimated that in many parts of the world parents need to have at least six children to have a reasonably high degree of confidence that a single son will be alive when the father attains his sixty-fifth birthday.[28] A son is particularly important because it is largely to males that parents in the developing countries look for support and assistance when needed. Given these conditions, parents in agricultural countries are doing the intelligent thing to have many children.

RELIGION

The major religions of the world have traditionally supported fertility as an expression of human duty. Even in modern societies, there are fertility differences between Roman Catholics, who hold this view most vigorously, and others. In the United States, Roman Catholics have the highest fertility. But this difference is becoming less with the passage of time. A study by Charles Westoff and Larry Bumpass indicates the possibility that the birth-control practices of non-Catholics and Catholics may well become virtually indistinguishable by the end of the century.[29] This can be attributed to the growing secularism of our country — its turning away from religion — and to the greater strength of the other factors.

In the developing world, however, particularly in those countries dominated by Roman Catholicism or Islam, religion encourages high fertility.[30] Historically, predominantly Moslem countries have been marked by high fertility. However, this is by no means only a matter of religion. We must remember that these now developing nations have primarily agricultural economies. The religious sanction in favor of fertility reinforces its economic benefits.

In one respect religious beliefs can be important, however. Religious sanctions against abortion can be very forceful. We need not concern ourselves with the arguments for or against abortion, these are well known. But we must remember that opposition to abortion is a factor in fertility control. In the past, it was sufficiently influential to make abortions illegal throughout the United States. In recent years, organized groups have gone to the extent of fighting legal battles with abortion clinics and even picketing them. At this time, however, the best estimate is that efforts to make abortions illegal will prove largely ineffective. In fact, we predict that abortion will become an increasingly important means of population control.

CULTURE

Other supports for fertility come from the cultural tradition of a society. Large families have always been favored by culture, even in developed nations until recently. While this cultural support no longer exists in those countries, in the developing countries the sight of parents with five or six children still brings smiles. Similar influence can be seen in the developed world in the pressure on young couples to have children coming from aspiring grandparents.

In the developing countries, cultural tradition is still functioning powerfully to maintain fertility at a high level. "Traditionally, fertility has been a positive value — sanctified by religious dogma and attested to by folk rituals."[31] If it is somewhat difficult for people in modern countries to escape completely from traditional ways, it is nearly impossible for most of those living in developing countries. While this support is not necessarily a primary cause for fertility, it, like religion, can reinforce the economic reasons.

FERTILITY SUPPORT
FACTORS: A SUMMARY

The prospects for solving the population problem decrease when we consider the various factors militating against reduced fertility. These formidable barriers to attaining ZPG include living in a rural area and depending on agriculture, and religious and cultural support for large families.

Although these factors can be found in modern societies, in general they prevail in developing societies. Because the major part of the world's population problem is found in these developing countries, it appears that the supports for high fertility are more powerful than those tending to move the world toward ZPG.

A Look Ahead

If modern industrial nations are marked by lower annual rates of population growth than the developing nations, then a possible solution would be to industrialize all the nations of the world as rapidly as possible. Unfortunately, this is not a realistic solution. Because of a high rate of population growth, the Third World cannot acquire the necessary capital for modernization. When a nation's gross national product increases by 3 percent yearly but the population grows by an equal or nearly equal amount, very little is left over for providing the capital necessary for industrialization.

Perhaps the People's Republic of China has hit upon the only possible practicable solution. In addition to discouraging marriage before the age of twenty-six and prohibiting premarital intercourse, the government of the largest nation on earth has recently moved to restrict families to two children. If this proves successful, other developing nations may be moved to follow suit. There is no question that something needs to be done. Throughout this chapter, we have pointed out the dysfunctions of continued high population growth, but we have not mentioned the eufunctions. What benefits would result from continued growth? None. The evidence shows overwhelmingly that we must control population growth and bring an end to the pattern of geometric increases, particularly in Asia and South America.

In concluding this chapter, it is necessary to issue a warning about the prediction of future population trends. Projections based on present growth rates continuing in the future are risky. All projections depend for their accuracy on conditions continuing to change at the same rate in the future they followed in the past or in the present. But this never happens. Mostly, we are pleased to settle for approximations when we make projections; let us hope, for the sake of our species, that any errors in population projections will be in the right direction. But even if the errors are on the conservative side, and the world's population doesn't double by the

2020s, it may by the 2040s or the 2050s. In this light, Harold F. Dorn's observation is indisputable:

> The results of human reproduction no longer are solely the concern of the two persons immediately involved nor of their families, nor even of the nation of which they are citizens. A state has been reached in the demographic development of the human race when the rate of reproduction in any part of the globe may affect the health and welfare of the rest of the world's population. It is in this sense that there is a world population problem.[32]

IMPORTANT WORDS AND TERMS

agriculture	cumulative cohort	fertility	Neolithic Revolution
arithmetical increase	birthrate	geometric increase	positive checks
cohort	demographer	germ theory of	preventive checks
compound interest	demographic	disease	total fertility rate
analogy	transition	*Homo sapiens*	zero population
crude birthrate	developed countries	moral restraint	growth (ZPG)
culture	developing countries		

QUESTIONS FOR DISCUSSION

1. The heavily populated agrarian nations do not always grow enough food for their own people. Why?
2. Is human fertility really a matter of millions of individual decisions made independently by couples around the world? Why or why not? Explain your answer.
3. The population explosion is, in good part, a product of declining death rates around the world. Some of this decline was brought about by public health measures, instituted in many cases by the industrialized nations of the world, including the United States. An interesting ethical question is this: Has it been a good thing for the industrialized nations to do this, that is, to take steps that have significantly lowered the mortality rate in the developing nations? Be able to defend your answer.
4. Why do you think that the growth rate is higher in South America than it is in Asia?
5. With what we know about the earth's available resources, is it possible to bring all or nearly all the people of the world up to the standard of living enjoyed in American society? Why or why not?
6. Your text maintains that there are not only too many people in the world today, but too many in the United States. Do you agree? Why?
7. What does Ronald Freeman mean when he says that "a rather large proportion of all pregnancies are 'accidents' or otherwise unplanned"? What are the implications of this in terms of the goal of ZPG?
8. Currently in the United States, women are moving toward greater equality with men in the world of work. Can we expect this to have any appreciable effects on the fertility rate in future years? Explain your answer.
9. Why do you think that in the past so many states had laws against the use of artificial

contraceptives and the dissemination of information regarding their use?
10. As we know, people in developing countries tend to have a higher fertility rate than do people in the industrialized countries. Can we correctly conclude that citizens in the less developed nations are irresponsible and irrational? Why or why not?
11. It might help to reduce world population growth rates if all nations were to establish government social security and health programs. Why don't they?
12. Should abortion be legal? If not, what alternatives do you suggest to control population size and growth?
13. If all or nearly all the nations of the world were to industrialize fully, we could expect that a lowering in fertility and growth rates would occur. But there are formidable barriers to accomplishing this. What are they?
14. If the current low fertility rate of 1.799 in the United States continues, can you think of any occupations or professions that people might be advised not to enter? Will this low fertility rate make some other occupations and professions more desirable? Be specific in your answers.
15. Considering the immediate urgency of the world population problem, do you believe that all nations of the world should take steps to limit legally the number of children a couple can have? If you answer no, what alternatives do you suggest? If you answer yes, how would you enforce such laws?

SUGGESTED READING

BERT F. HOSELITZ AND WILBERT E. MOORE (eds.), *Industrialization and Society* (The Hague: Unesco-Mouton, 1966).

This book contains fifteen articles by recognized authorities and covers a wide range of problems confronting the developing and underdeveloped nations of the world in attempting to modernize. It provides considerable help in understanding the many difficulties confronting Latin American nations in particular. We know of no single work that discusses these problems as well as this text.

CHARLES B. NAM AND SUSAN O. GUSTAVUS, *Population: The Dynamics of Demographic Change* (Boston: Houghton Mifflin, 1976).

For those who wish a thorough grounding in the fundamentals of demography, this is a good source. Written with charm and understanding, the text progresses easily and comfortably through the basic concepts of demography. It avoids excessive presentation of data but where data are used, they illuminate rather than confuse.

It is further enlivened by a number of excellent cartoons that help make various points clearer — sometimes with devastating effect. Those who have previously regarded demography as a subject of unsurpassed dullness will be pleasantly surprised by the writing of Professors Nam and Gustavus.

BARBARA WARD, *The Rich Nations and the Poor Nations* (New York: Norton, 1962).

Poverty and high fertility rates appear to go hand in hand. But why? And will this change? Barbara Ward has some provocative and interesting things to tell us in this book about significant social contrasts between the haves and have nots. She sees a great revolution occurring in the world today, the revolution of rising expectations. This great revolution breaks down into four other revolutions. Those revolutions occur in ideas, material affluence, rising populations, and applications of science and capital to economic processes. Those who take time to read this book will be richly rewarded.

NOTES

1. V. Gordon Childe, *Man Makes Himself* (New York: Mentor, 1951), p. 35.
2. Ralph Thomlinson, *Population Dynamics*, 2nd ed. (New York: Random House, 1976), p. 17.
3. T. Lynn Smith and Ralph E. Zopf, Jr., *Demography: Principles and Methods* (Philadelphia: Davis, 1970), p. 3.
4. Warren S. Thompson and David T. Lewis, *Population Problems*, 5th ed. (New York: McGraw-Hill, 1965), p. 11.
5. William Peterson, *Population*, 2nd ed. (New York: Macmillan, 1969), p. 498.
6. Harold F. Dorn, "World Population Growth," in Phillip M. Hauser (ed.), *The Population Dilemma* (Englewood Cliffs, N.J.: Prentice-Hall, 1963), p. 18.
7. Irene B. Taeuber, "Population Growth in Underdeveloped Areas," in Phillip M. Hauser (ed.), *The Population Dilemma* (Englewood Cliffs, N.J.: Prentice-Hall, 1963), p. 32.
8. Thomlinson, *Population Dynamics*, p. 19.
9. M. B. Smith, *Social Psychology and Human Values* (Chicago: Aldine, 1969), p. 292.
10. Thompson and Lewis, *Population Problems*, p. 373.
11. Thomlinson, *Population Dynamics*, p. 19.
12. Charles B. Nam and Susan O. Gustavus, *Population: The Dynamics of Demographic Change* (Boston: Houghton Mifflin, 1976), p. 64.
13. Dorn, "World Population Growth," p. 8.
14. Emile Levasseur, "The Tables of Mortality and Survivorship," *Royal Statistical Society Journal*, Vol. 50, No. 3 (translated from the *Journal de la societé de statistique de Paris*, March 1887).
15. Ronald Freeman, "American Studies of Family Planning and Fertility: A Review of Major Trends and Issues," in Charles B. Nam (ed.), *Population and Society* (Boston: Houghton Mifflin, 1968), pp. 255–265.
16. Nam and Gustavus, *Population*, p. 294.
17. Barbara Ward, *The Rich Nations and the Poor Nations* (New York: Norton, 1962), p. 93.
18. David M. Heer and Eba S. Turner, "Area Differences in Latin American Fertility," *Demography*, Vol. 3 (1966), p. 290.
19. Kingsley Davis, *Human Society* (New York: Macmillan, 1949), pp. 601–602.
20. Thompson and Lewis, *Population Problems*, p. 357.
21. Geraldine B. Terry, "The Interrelationship Between Female Employment and Fertility: A Secondary Analysis of the Growth of American Families Study, 1960." Unpublished doctoral dissertation, Florida State University, 1973.
22. Dwight D. Eisenhower, "The Presidential News Conference of December 2, 1959" (Washington, D.C.: U.S. Government Printing Office, 1960), pp. 787–788.
23. Christopher Tietze, "Two Years' Experience with a Liberal Abortion Law: Its Impact on Fertility Trends in New York City," *Family Planning Perspectives*, Vol. 5 (Winter 1973), pp. 36–41.
24. U.S. Bureau of the Census, *Current Population Reports*, "Population Profile of the United States, 1976," Series P-20, No. 307 (Washington, D.C.: U.S. Government Printing Office, 1977), p. 4.
25. Ibid., p. 4.
26. For a complete discussion of fertility, see Thomlinson, *Population Dynamics*, Chapters 8–11.
27. Frank Lorimer, "Issues of Population Policy" in Phillip M. Hauser (ed.), *The Population Dilemma* (Englewood Cliffs, N.J.: Prentice-Hall, 1963), p. 149.
28. Alan Berg, "Nutrition, Development and Population Growth," *Population Bulletin*, Vol. 29, No. 1 (1964), p. 33.
29. Charles F. Westoff and Larry Bumpass, "The Revolution in Birth Control Practices of U.S. Roman Catholics," *Science*, Vol. 179 (1973), pp. 41–44.
30. Dudley Kirk, "Factors Affecting Moslem Natality," in Bernard Berelson et al. (eds.), *Family Planning and Population Programs* (Chicago: University of Chicago Press, 1966), pp. 31, 34.
31. Robert A. Nisbet, "Introduction: The Study of Social Problems," in Robert K. Merton and Robert A. Nisbet (eds.), *Contemporary Social Problems*, 2nd ed. (New York: Harcourt, Brace and World, 1966), pp. 8–9.
32. Dorn, "World Population Growth," p. 27.

12 THE CITIES
A STUDY IN SENESCENCE

CHAPTER OVERVIEW

INTRODUCTION

HISTORICAL OVERVIEW
The Rise of Ancient Cities
American Cities
Summary

CONCEPTUAL ORIENTATION
Changing Patterns of Urbanization
Demographic Changes
Summary

OBJECTIVE DIMENSIONS OF THE PROBLEM
Race and Politics in the
  American City
City Financing
  Revenues and Debts
  Spending
Education

Employment
Housing
Summary

ATTEMPTS AT DEALING WITH THE PROBLEM
The Changing Federal Role
The Structure of Current
  Welfare Programs
Employment and Education Programs
Iatrogenic Effects

PROSPECTS FOR SOLVING THE PROBLEM

IMPORTANT WORDS AND TERMS

QUESTIONS FOR DISCUSSION

SUGGESTED READING

NOTES

Men come together in cities for security; they stay together for the good life.

Aristotle

In my opinion, policemen should have had instructions to shoot arsonists and looters — arsonists to kill and looters to maim and detain.

Mayor Richard Daley

CHAPTER OVERVIEW

The central cities are today facing problems that are the direct outgrowth of major economic and demographic changes that have taken place since the end of World War II. Local government has been charged with providing basic services, including education, jobs, and housing. Yet in recent years, the people living in the older and larger cities of the Northeast have found their communities deteriorating at a rapid rate, and the services local government provides increasingly inadequate. The problems facing the residents of central cities are the direct result of national trends that have left such areas without the resources to deal with their problems. This is true despite the fact that about ten years ago, the federal government began to play a more significant role in helping the cities. We will discuss what has been the nature of this role and why federal efforts have not worked.

INTRODUCTION

During the late 1960s it became a frequent occurrence for there to be major outbreaks of violence in the central cities, some of which ended as full-scale urban riots. As a result, whole sections of cities such as Detroit, Washington, D.C., and Los Angeles were set ablaze. There was great alarm over whether the fires of discontent could be contained or would spread rapidly throughout the land. Clearly something was wrong. Mayor Daley of Chicago blamed it on communists who brought trouble to the usual peace and quiet of his smooth running Chicago. Numerous other, more serious, government reports provided reasons for all of this violence. These reports contained a blanket condemnation of the employment and educational opportunities available to many residents of our cities. Various government fact-finding commissions also outlined enormous problems in housing and health relating to the widespread poverty found in many central city areas.[1]

These government reports, newspaper articles, and scholarly writings were prompted by the realization that people had actually set fire to and tried to destroy the very parts of the cities where they were living. This destruction seemed close to the ultimate act of desperation, especially when viewed by people who had never done more than pass a ghetto in a locked car or train on their way to and from suburban homes. In the decade or so since the riots occurred, a number of government programs have been designed to make sure that something like this would not happen again. Millions of dollars were spent on equipment designed to allow the police to better investigate and crack down on the urban guerrillas and insurgents, as rioters were called by a government entangled in a war in Vietnam. Increased riot control training was given to the National Guard and army reserve and military contingency plans were drawn up to handle any future outbreaks.² And millions were also spent on education, housing, and job training, fulfilling model cities programs. But this spending seems to have been unfruitful. While much of the obvious large-scale ghetto violence seems to have stopped, the problems that aroused these protests remain. In fact, some have intensified.

In this chapter we will examine these problems facing people living in the central cities, focusing on the problem of paying for public services, the quality of these services, and the overall quality of life. While many suburbs face some of the same problems large cities are encountering, the cities suffer from more of them and more acutely.

HISTORICAL OVERVIEW

The Rise of Ancient Cities

Humankind has not always lived in large cities like those found in the modern world. For many thousands of years humans and human ancestors roamed the land in small bands. It was not until somewhere between 5000 and 3500 B.C. that people first moved into dense settlement patterns. The foundation for this movement into the earliest cities was provided by some elementary but significant changes in agriculture. As part of the struggle for survival during the last Neolithic period, approximately 10,000 years ago humankind began to develop new strains of plants and to domesticate animals to be used for milk and food. The survival advantages of these changes were obviously great; they resulted in rapid growth of the human population.

Most of these ancient civilizations, with their early cities, were located in the river valleys, which ensured continuous refertilization of the land through yearly flooding. The rich soils created by this flooding provided a continuous and dependable agricultural surplus. The effect of this surplus was to free some people from the land and to promote trade with other areas needing food. The result was more centralized living arrangements and considerably more complex social organization. Through the work of archeologists, we now know that many of the basic and important contributions of these civilizations were made necessary by the problems arising from an agricultural surplus.³

For example, surplus grain needed to be stored and kept track of through a system of weights and measures. The need for a way of distributing grain to people who did not produce it led to the creation of a system of exchange. Gradually, as specialization increased and life grew more complex, the people living in these ancient cities gave the world major innovations such as writing, arithmetic, and architectural planning. And these innovations could be used in agriculture, creating even more of a surplus, as rivers were dammed, new varieties of seed developed, and plows invented. As Paul Meadows has observed:

> Cities emerge historically when a technological complex (tools, skill, and theory) creates an economic surplus. The routes and scope of this exchange of the economic surplus develop an ever widening network of communities, and with the growth of trade and transportation

there is a corresponding increase in the size and complexity of the urban net which contains and utilizes the surplus.[4]

But although these civilizations produced a surplus, their technology was still primitive so the number of people who could live in cities was severely limited. It took an estimated one hundred people working on the land to yield enough agricultural surplus to support half a dozen living in the city. Yet it was these early city dwellers who made major advances in writing, mathematics, art, and politics, features we now identify as the contributions of these early civilizations.

With the great diversity of people living in a large and relatively densely populated area, the possibility for creative interaction between them became vastly enlarged. Because of this, all sorts of occupational subgroups began to develop, based on the need for providing specialized services to the larger community. It is this freedom to pursue one's life work, no matter how specialized or deviant, that has long characterized city life.

American Cities

A similar role was played by cities in colonial America, although because of the way much history is written we don't realize it. For example, among the distortions in the history taught to American children has been an overemphasis on the opening of the frontier and the westward movement accompanying it. The picture every schoolchild has of America during its early days is one of woods, Indians, and adventurous farm people living miles from their neighbors. To a degree this is true. Philadelphia was the only city approaching 30,000 people and only one American in twenty-five lived in a city of 8,000 or more inhabitants. But the lack of size doesn't mean cities were unimportant. The actual picture was quite different, which historians are finally coming to realize. At the time of the American Revolution, Boston, Philadelphia, and New York were hotbeds of sedition, treason, and radicalism and served as the basis for violence directed at overthrowing British rule. Both before and after the Revolution the cities led the country, providing the talented people who shaped national goals.

But while these cities, like the ancient and medieval cities, came to both reflect and embellish their cultures, they were also faced with typical urban problems. Dirt, crowding, and disease resulting from unsanitary conditions usually went hand in hand with positive contributions. Garbage removal was often left to swine, goats, and geese who wandered about in the streets; and crime was a problem early on. The problem of noise in Philadelphia was so great that Benjamin Franklin often complained of the need to repeat himself because of the din of outside traffic. He longed for what we call the suburbs where one could get some quiet yet be near the activity of the city itself.

Throughout the early nineteenth century the cities grew gradually, not really solving these problems. Then came the great turning point for American cities, following the Civil War. As a result of a series of technological changes, such as harnessing steam, generating electricity, and beginning mass production, the cities of the late nineteenth century began to change drastically. Commercial activity, trade, and manufacturing activity all intensified in the post-Civil War period. All three contributed to rapid urban growth. By the turn of the twentieth century, New York City had nearly two and a half million people

Mulberry Street, New York City, streamed with mercantile activity in the late 1800s. The population of the city was nearing 2.5 million, including thousands of immigrants for whom crowded tenements like these were home. Cities simply grew too fast to accommodate their own needs, in terms of sanitation, transportation, housing, employment, education, and on and on.

living in its boundaries. Los Angeles gained twenty times in population in the forty years after the Civil War.

The percentage of the population living in cities jumped sharply. The cause was not just internal migration from country to city, but the influx of large numbers of foreign immigrants beginning in the late 1880s and continuing on until the 1920s. But as the urban centers grew their problems proliferated. In housing, for example, by the late 1860s there were 15,000 tenement houses in New York City. Within twenty years this number had doubled, with crowding so bad that these 30,000 housed more than a million people. Urban problems were worse for the immigrants who streamed onto our shores and then crowded into the cities of our land. Coming to this country in search of prosperity, most found miserable housing and abominable sanitary conditions, creating survival problems unheard of today.

The physical environment of the cities, then as now, was also a source of major social concern. In 1886 when New York City set up its first Board of Health, an early task was to remove 160,000 tons of horse manure from the streets and vacant lots of the city. The stench of animal waste was added to by the smell of hundred of dead horses, left to decay where they had dropped from old age or exhaustion. Today, when we worry about the 50,000 cars abandoned in New York City every year, we should perhaps be thankful that these cars do not scent the air as those decaying animals did less than one hundred years ago.

Summary

Once agricultural surpluses were available, permitting some people to do work other than raising food, cities became established. Throughout human history cities have been marked by vigorous economic activity and cultural leadership. They have also always been plagued by the problems that inevitably arise from concentrating many people in one place: dirt, crime, and the need to provide adequate services for vast numbers.

CONCEPTUAL ORIENTATION

To understand the problems facing American cities we must understand the concept of *senescence*. This word, although not often used by sociologists, nicely summarizes the dynamics behind the range of urban problems. Senescence means the process of aging, physical deterioration, and a corresponding decline in vigor and dominance, an accurate picture of what is happening to the older and larger cities of the Northeast and North Central states. Cities like New York, Detroit, Chicago, and Philadelphia face major social, political, and economic crises. Atlanta, Phoenix, San Diego, and Dallas, although they are not free of problems, seem by comparison to have a certain growth and vitality the others lack. The key difference is senescence.

Behind the political and financial issues facing these aging cities is a major economic crisis. The economy of the Northeast is stagnant, and many of the cities have suffered a dramatic economic decline. For example, as the senator from New York, Daniel Moynihan, noted in 1977, New York City has lost 640,000 private sector jobs since 1969 — "enough to sustain a metropolitan area of two million persons . . . [and] Buffalo has lost more than one-fifth of its population in the past twenty years."[5]

The causes of this loss of economic vitality are many and complex. The federal government has for many years sponsored the growth of other parts of the country simply by the way it has allocated funds for federal projects. In addition, Northern states have taxed private corporations at a far higher rate than the Southern ones. When the South combines a lower tax rate with the lure of tax incentives offered by states and localities and cheaper labor because of less unionization, the results are hardly surprising. And given that computers, inexpensive long-distance telephone rates, and the federally sponsored highway system allow for rapid communication and delivery of goods over long distances, the movement of many major companies from the Northeast was easy. As a result, economic decline has reached serious proportions.

Changing Patterns of Urbanization

In 1970 the population of the United States was 73.5 percent urban, with 31.5 percent of the total population living in the central cities of the urbanized areas. This amounted to almost 64 million persons in the central cities compared to 54 million living in rural areas. The remainder of the urban population (about 85 million) lived in the part of the urban area we usually identify as being the *suburbs*. To get a better idea of the relationship between city and suburb, the Census Bureau has recently developed a concept called the *Standard Metropolitan Statistical Area* (SMSA). The SMSAs include basically the same cities that would be on a list of cities of 50,000 people or more, the limit for defining urban areas. But SMSA boundaries are larger; they include suburbs and thus cover entire counties. The county was chosen because it was the smallest territorial unit for which statistical data are regularly gathered.

Using this definition, in 1970 SMSAs contained about 10 million people fewer than had been classified as part of the urban population. This discrepancy is based on problems of definition in terms of the available residential categories.[6] If this all sounds a bit confusing, it may be consoling to know that even urban sociologists who must work with census data on a day-to-day basis find it so. The important part to remember is that we must learn about the SMSA because many statistics are given in terms of it, but those statistics often underestimate the true extent of the urban problem.

If we are to take the broad view of what has been happening to the population of the United States for the last hundred years, it is clear that the trend has been toward greater and greater urbanization. Figure 12.1 clearly shows this trend from 1850 to the present and projects the future of the trend to the year 2000. Since 1850 the number of people classified as living in an urban area has increased sharply, until today almost three-quarters of the population is urban. And interestingly, although the total amount of acreage encompassed by urban areas has been going up slowly, the number of acres per person has been falling off rapidly. There are now more people living in urban areas with less acreage per person; this trend is not expected to change in the near future.

From 1900 to 1920 the central cities were growing faster than their surrounding areas.

FIGURE 12.1 Urbanization of the United States, 1850–2000

Source: John McHale, *World Facts and Trends* (New York: Macmillan, 1972), p. 81.

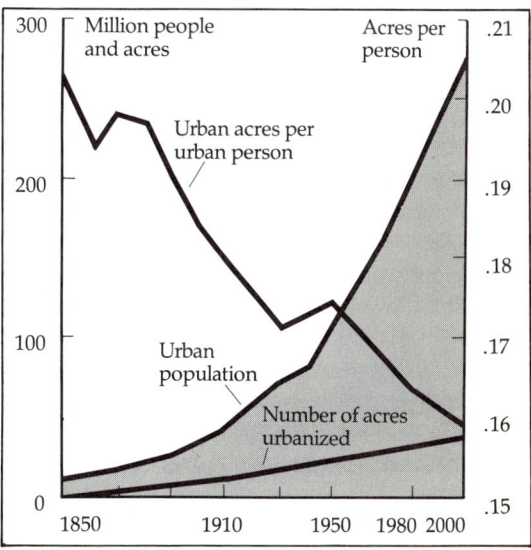

This growth was largely the product of immigration from foreign countries and from the rural areas of this country. But by about 1930 adjoining areas, communities outside the central cities, began to grow at a more rapid rate with a consequent decline in the percentage of the SMSA population living within the central city itself. This occurred largely because of changes in transportation, because of the need for more housing, and because they were cheaper than the central cities. Throughout the United States, central city growth rates have declined rapidly since 1930.

Demographic Changes

As we documented in Chapter 6, the problems facing minority groups in the United States are of great magnitude. These minority problems cannot be divorced from the crisis of the central cities, for the demographic shifts of the past forty years that have been partly responsible for the deterioration of the economic basis of the older and larger central cities have been largely ethnic and racial in character. This is not to say that minorities have been the cause of central city problems. To say so would be completely inaccurate, although such blaming the victim is something people often have a tendency to do. Rather, our point is that certain demographic shifts have occurred in response to the changing allocation of economic resources, and these shifts have involved minority group members.

To oversimplify, the technology of America as it industrialized included the mechanization of agriculture as well as that of other parts of the production process. This meant the displacement of manual laborers in the fields; this displacement has gone on for more than a century now. The result has been that blacks, who a hundred years ago were primarily rural and agricultural, moved to cities looking for jobs. If we examine the distribution of blacks by region and place of residence, certain trends are evident. There has been a steady and continuous shift of the black population from the South to the North and West. In 1940, for example, 77 percent of the black population lived in the South, with 22 percent in the North and 1 percent in the West. By 1970, the percentage of blacks in the North had almost doubled (to 39 percent) while the percentage of blacks in the West went up eightfold.[7]

The trend has not just been from one region to another. Blacks have moved from farm to city. In 1960, 68 percent of all blacks lived in metropolitan areas, with 53 percent of all blacks living in the central cities. By 1975, 75 percent of all blacks lived in metropolitan areas, with almost 60 percent of blacks found in central cities. In absolute numbers, the increase has been from 9.9 million blacks living in central cities in 1960 to 13.8 million in 1975.[8]

Despite this growth in the number of blacks, between 1970 and 1977 the population of central cities has declined by 5 percent. On the other hand suburbs have gained in population, sharing a net gain of about 9 million people due in part to immigration. It is revealing to break the data down by race. Between 1975 and 1977, 4.7 million whites left the central cities and moved to the suburbs and 2.5 million whites left the suburbs and moved to the cities, for a net loss of 2.2 million whites in just two years.

However, with a net migration of 400,000 blacks to the suburbs between 1975 and 1977, the suburbs gained many fewer blacks than whites, continuing a long established pattern.[9] The result is that only about 5 percent of the total suburban population is made up of blacks.

What is significant about this difference is economics. The families who moved to the suburbs between 1970 and 1974 had a higher income than those families who moved to the cities. In the mid-1970s the median income for city families ($11,300) was about $2700 less than the median of suburban families ($14,000). The earnings of suburban men are higher than their central city counterparts, although no such relationship appears to hold for the earnings of women. The number of families receiving some sort of public assistance was about two and a half times greater for the central city than for the suburbs. This may be due in part to the fact that there are almost twice as many families with women as their head in the central cities as in the suburbs.[10] These demographic changes have meant that those groups who are economically worse off are the city dwellers.

Summary

Based on the latest complete census data, almost three quarters of the population lives in urban areas. But the impact of technology, based in part on the automobile, has meant that people are now able to live outside the city and commute back and forth to the central city proper. As a result there has been a continued growth of the areas on the outskirts of the cities at the expense of the central cities' industrial sector and tax base, leaving the central city itself in a state of decline. Contributing to both changes has been a major demographic movement out of the central city by more affluent people. Without the desire or — more likely — the financial resources to move out, other groups have been left behind to face a gradual decline in the services provided to them. To compound the problems there has been a major movement of disadvantaged groups into the cities, filling the space vacated by the middle-class people moving out.

As a result of these major demographic shifts, the central cities are facing a continued decline in the services they can provide their residents. This problem is the direct result of the financial squeeze the cities are now experiencing, which stems from the loss of tax revenues caused by the exodus of industry and the affluent. But the problems dumped into the lap of the cities are next to impossible to deal with not only because of inadequate finances but also because of a sadly outdated political structure. It is to these problems, in politics, finances, and services, that we now turn.

OBJECTIVE DIMENSIONS OF THE PROBLEM

Although they are a level of government, the cities of this country have been systematically ignored by the constitutions that outlined the powers of the state and federal levels. Without going into the complexities involved, it is fair to say that most cities hold an inferior legal position to the other levels of government. Cities have no rights of self-government beyond those granted by state legislatures. The courts have consistently permitted state legislatures to override local authority on a wide variety of important issues including taxation, sewage, and transit systems. Although some freedoms are given to cities, they are held in relatively short rein; city autonomy is severely restricted. Given the large number of city governments within every state, each with a potential to write laws at variance with existing state statutes, this is perhaps as it should be. But the subservience of city to state has also had negative consequences. As a rule, cities cannot use sources of taxation other than the property tax to finance the local services they are called upon to provide. Usually the use of sales tax and income taxes has been preempted by the state and federal governments.[11] This is true despite the fact that cities often provide social and cultural services to their entire region and sometimes nationally and internationally as well. The result of this lack of political power can be seen in the problems we are about to describe.

Race and Politics in the American City

Part of the reason for our focus on political structures is that, in the last analysis, politics determines how the resources are allocated. And the structure of politics in this country works against our coming to grips with basic urban problems since our political system is based on the will of the majority. This reliance does not help the cities. The majority of Americans are white, live above the poverty line, and do not live in the central cities. Basic political decisions generally favor this white middle-class majority.

For instance, most white-dominated suburbs never have to resort to passing laws establishing segregation; they simply pass zoning ordinances that price their housing out of the range that the poor (of both races) can afford. Supreme Court rulings have established that segregation by law is illegal. But sociologists have noted that, since 1970, the Northern cities have become more segregated. With the white movement to the suburbs and the increased resistance by both blacks and whites to integration in the cities, many neighborhoods in the cities of the North are now more segregated than they were at any time in the recent past. This actual segregation (called *de facto segregation* to distinguish it from the *de jure segregation* imposed by law) was brought about by people changing their places of residence, a factor outside the control of the law. It is ironic that in the wake of so many court decisions attempting to strike it down, segregation has spread so rapidly.

The reason for this increase is our relatively open society. The ability to choose where one wishes to live — given one has the money to pay for it — has led to affluent people leaving the cities. This movement out was also made possible by the automobile. The flexible transportation it provides meant people need not live too near where they work. As a result, the residential pattern of many cities has changed drastically in the past decade. The magnitude of this change was described earlier — most suburbs are almost all white while many city areas are almost all black. Neighborhoods have changed color rapidly in many areas, but often without a decrease in the segregation of the races.

What is happening in many Northern cities is a reinforcement of segregation. In fact, if the news media are looking for *apartheid*, or racial segregation, they need not send reporters to South Africa or Rhodesia. They only have to go to the South Bronx, Detroit, and Philadelphia. In contrast to South Africa, where blacks are kept in outlying areas, in America blacks are concentrated in the central cities, surrounded by new, all-white cities organized around growing industries, schools, and shopping centers. And these new cities are so self-sufficient and have such a high density of population, that they cannot really be called suburbs any more. It is these cities on the urban fringe that hold political power.¹²

Relations between these two areas are strained, the mood around the cities can best be described as one of fear and distrust of one race by the other. Whites who feel this way have read endless newspaper stories about crimes committed against whites by blacks, have had to send their children to schools with increasing numbers of blacks, and have seen entire neighborhoods change from white to black. These whites are not racist in the older sense of the word; they are willing to grant blacks many opportunities never even considered by earlier generations. But while not wishing to subjugate blacks, they fear blacks.

On the other side, blacks distrust and fear whites, although the reasons are less publicized. While newspapers play up the crime and violence in the streets, they ignore the failure of the predominantly black urban schools. Nor do they write about the 45 percent unemployment rate among black teenagers or any of the other conditions that breed the distrust blacks feel for whites. Clearly, the crime and violence are symptoms of deeper social ills that are part of the changing political and economic conditions of society. We will now explore these complex and interrelated problems of the cities, looking first at the underlying economic problems.

City Financing

The demographic changes we've discussed have affected the economics behind the financing of city services. Politics was discussed prior to the economics of city problems because politics determines how much money is available to cities to finance their services. With the income tax monopolized by state and federal government, city governments have had to turn increasingly to the property tax as the only major source of revenue available to them. But as the 1978 vote on Proposition 13 in California made clear, the average homeowner is fed up with increasing property taxes. California voters mandated a cut of 50 percent in the property taxes they pay; they did so in such overwhelming numbers as to make politicians around the country shudder. To understand why, let us examine the sources of city revenue in this country and the changing role of the federal government in helping cities meet their financial obligations.

REVENUES AND DEBTS

Starting with the year 1950, there has been a considerable increase in the total revenues collected by all levels of government. In 1950 total governmental revenues were a mere $66.7 billion; by 1975 this figure had skyrocketed to $517.2 billion. Inflation is a significant part of this increase, but there has been a real expansion of governmental expenditures as well. For example, spending on all public welfare programs in constant 1976 dollars went from $54.5 billion in 1950 to $330.6 billion in 1976, a sixfold increase. On a per capita basis, the increase has been great as well, with more than four times the amount per person being spent on social welfare programs in 1976 as in 1950.¹³

While spending has gone up, it has hit state and local governments hardest. In 1950 the federal government contributed 65 percent of the social services budget, with the rest raised by state and local governments. By 1975 the federal share was down to 58.5 percent of the total, meaning an increased tax burden fell on the state and local levels to meet the growing costs. The total burden falling on local government increased almost nine times in twenty-five years. Reflecting this change, property tax revenues increased from $34.1 billion in 1970 to $51.5 billion in 1975, about a 50 percent increase in only five years.[14]

A closer look at the finances of city governments reveals a major problem. In 1960 the total revenue available to city governments was $14.9 billion while by 1975 it had increased to $59.7 billion. The central role of the property tax as a source of revenue for cities continues even though there was a percentage decrease from 35 percent in 1960 to 22 percent in 1975. Each year there has been an increase in the outstanding debt cities have incurred in financing their services. In 1960 the total debt for all cities was over $23 billion; this figure had risen to over $65 billion by 1975, the vast amount of this being in the form of *long-term debt*, which is paid out over many years. Naturally, the more long-term debt the worse a city's finances, for the city will need to make more interest payments. Worse yet, long-term debt may not be guaranteed by banks, making the financing even riskier. The long-term debt not guaranteed in 1960 was about $7.5 billion (one-third of the total long-term debt). This figure more than tripled to almost $24 billion in 1975, becoming 43 percent of the total long-term debt. In 1960 the cities incurred about $1 billion more in debts than they retired, but by 1975 they were issuing about $2 billion more than they retired per year. Clearly, the indebtedness of the cities is rising while the economic base from which to pay off these debts is steadily declining.[15]

Revenues can be compared not only over time but also between cities of different sizes. In 1975 the property taxes per capita for all cities was $96 per year. But in cities of less than 50,000 persons (called small from now on) it was only $57 per year, while for cities of 1 million or more (called large from now on) it was $198, more than three times as much. Small cities had total per capita revenues of $196 while large cities had $922. Small ones had a total tax bill of $87 per person while large ones had $378.

In terms of outstanding debts, small cities are also better off. They had $279 per person compared with $1165 for large cities. While small cities had only $16 per capita short-term debt outstanding, large cities had $301 per person, almost twenty times more short-term debt. Each year short-term debt that piled up from previous years' deficit spending either has to be paid off, refinanced, or restructured as a long-term obligation. And since the per capita short-term debt facing large cities ($301) is half again as much as the total expenditures of small cities ($194), it is no wonder that heads of large cities are haunted by the specter of bankruptcy.[16]

Even though the debt structure of the cities is rising, little appears to have been done to reduce expenditures; in fact, especially for the larger cities, expenditures are increasing rapidly. In 1960, total expenditures for all city governments came to about $12 billion. By 1975 this figure had risen to $48.6 billion. Spending had quadrupled in only fifteen years.

SPENDING

As Table 12.1 makes clear, there have been some changes over the past fifteen years in the percentages of total spending allocated to the most important city government functions. Cities spent the greatest percentage of their revenues on schools in 1960 and in 1975 as well. They also consistently spent the smallest percentage on parks and housing during this time period. However, they are

TABLE 12.1 Percent and Rank of City Expenditures by Function, 1960 and 1975

Function	1960 Percent	1960 Rank	1975 Percent	1975 Rank	Percentage Increase or Decrease
Education	15.2	1	14.6	1	− .6
Highways	13.3	2	7.8	4.5	−5.5
Sewage	11.2	3	10.4	3	− .8
Police	10.7	4	10.8	2	+ .1
Fire	7.4	5	5.9	7	−1.5
Health	6.7	6	7.4	6	+ .7
Welfare	5.1	7	7.8	4.5	+2.7
Parks	4.6	8	4.5	8	− .1
Housing	3.9	9	3.4	9	− .5

Source: Bureau of the Census, *Statistical Abstract of the United States, 1977* (Washington, D.C.: U.S. Government Printing Office, 1977), p. 300.

spending more on welfare (the greatest percentage change on the list), more on health, and slightly more on police protection.

Again, if we compare large and small cities, the differences in expenditures are striking. Large cities spend 163 times the per capita amount small cities do on welfare, 11 times the amount on health care, 8.5 times the amount on education, and 2.9 times the amount on police.[17] Given this massive spending, why is the quality of life more problematic in large cities? Why are the small cities usually seen as being more liveable than the giant metropolitan areas?

Part of the reason is that the cost of living is higher in the large cities than in the small ones. As a result, city services cost more and city employees earn more. In addition, many more of the city employees in the large cities are unionized; while this is beneficial to the union members, it often costs the cities dearly, not only in wages but also in pension plans, early retirement programs, insurance plans, and other fringe benefits. But the increased salaries and other personnel costs cannot alone explain the enormous discrepancy in quality of life between the small and some of the large cities.

The answer lies in understanding the role government plays in the overall life of people living in large and small cities. First, the federal government spends much money on the large cities, but gives more to small ones. The federal government provides 16 percent of small city revenues, but only 10 percent of those for large cities.[18] Second, in the small cities, the private sector or the state or federal government provides many services that city government is called on to provide in the large cities. A few examples may help to clarify this.

In the field of health care, over half of all Americans belong to some form of private prepaid insurance program. When they get sick, the hospital costs are paid not by the city but by their insurance companies. In this case, the private sector's contribution never appears as a cost to the city. Like many large cities, New York City must make a percentage contribution toward welfare costs.

Because the cost of living in these cities is high, these contributions can be significant. But in virtually none of the small cities is the city itself required to provide a percentage. And in the area of housing, many small cities have no low-cost city housing programs, even though there may be a real need for them; large cities, on the other hand, almost always do.

Despite the fact that the large cities are spending far more money on services than the small ones, they seem to be coping less effectively with their problems. Given the greater magnitude of the population of the large cities, the quality of life continues to deteriorate. If simply spending huge sums of money could have solved the crisis of the central cities, their problems would have been over years ago. But as everyone who has been to one of these supercities knows, urban problems are still with us. It is to specific problems in services that we now turn our attention.

Education

Beginning in 1880 when the waves of new immigrants began pouring into the large cities of the North from Europe, the process of assimilation began on a massive scale. The key to accomplishing this assimilation lay in employment and education.

First, jobs were important. The economy was expanding rapidly in the late nineteenth century and large amounts of cheap and unskilled labor were needed in industry. With no other means of survival, millions of unskilled and illiterate immigrants worked their lives away in sweatshops. Most immigrants had no skills, but few skills were needed by the manufacturing processes of the day. In response to economic problems in their quest for better working conditions, more pay, and shorter hours, these workers engaged in a bitter and often violent struggle with the factory owners. Strikes, rioting, and clashes with the police characterized American cities throughout this time period. Urban violence is not a recent phenomena.

As technology became more complex, requiring more training, and as the need to socialize the children of these immigrants grew more acute, the major force for assimilation became not jobs but the schools. Education was also part of a filtering process that made some people eligible for certain jobs and systematically excluded others, who did not have the right background. As part of our ideology, the educational process in our society was supposed to provide equality of opportunity for all individuals. It was supposed to select out the most intelligent and capable individuals for advancement. Thus, if a child did not make it successfully through the school system, it must have been his or her own fault due to some personal defect, or a lack of drive, lower intelligence, or some other deficiency. This point of view, held by a large number of Americans (including the children themselves), is largely at variance with what many sociologists and some educators are now starting to believe. Rather than providing equality of opportunity, educational discrimination held certain groups in a subordinate position by providing unequal educational experiences to different groups.

Today, although the victims are no longer immigrant children but black children, the same inequality plagues the schools and has become the focus of the debate on urban educational policy. No one believes that central city schools provide the same quality of education as suburban schools, but few agree why. Some argue that the amount of money spent makes a difference in the quality of education a child receives. If so, lower spending should explain the large city's poorer education. Ironically, though, because of higher personnel costs and costly programs, the per capita expenditure for many big city schools is above that for some suburban schools. Spending is not the answer, for the greater amount of money is not producing better results. Numerous research reports show that the educational achievements of children who have attended central city schools is far below that of children attending suburban schools.

One such study, funded by the federal government, was carried out as a team effort headed by sociologist James Coleman. His work took several years to complete, had over 600,000 subjects, and led to a landmark report published in 1966 called *Equality of Educational Opportunity*.[19] Coleman argued that the quality of education students received in school was strongly related to the cultural influences of their home environment and was not based on the money spent. The results of Coleman's study were disturbing to the educational community. Coming, as they did, at the same time as legal efforts to end de facto segregation, they were used to support *busing* to achieve desegregation. But many people believe that, instead of narrowing the academic gap between black and white students, busing has perpetuated it, at least in the short run.

The decision to bus children to different schools outside their neighborhoods in order to obtain greater equality of educational opportunity began in the late 1960s. Busing has met with only limited success in the big Northern cities, to put it mildly. The original strategy behind school busing was based on Coleman's study. Coleman had asserted that the socioeconomic background of students was of greater importance to success in school than the money spent on school. The decision was made to mix students from different backgrounds to help diminish the effects of family background factors.

Rather than seeing racial balance in the schools, the 1970s has seen the increasing exodus of whites to the suburbs, called by some *white flight*. Of course, it is impossible to know how much of this migration is due to busing alone. In 1978 nonwhite and Hispanic enrollments were extremely high in some cities: 97 percent in Washington, D.C.; 91 percent in New York; 77 percent in Chicago; 82 percent in Detroit; and 76 percent in Baltimore.[20]

It is clear that no matter how badly these cities want to integrate their schools, the white students are no longer available for them to do so. Other large cities are moving in the direction of those mentioned above, with most today having nonwhites as well over half of their students. Given these figures, busing cannot change the racial composition of the central city schools unless white students living in the urban fringe are bused across county lines and into the central city. But with the social obstacles to this, it seems an unlikely solution.

In light of the failure of busing to achieve racial balance in the schools, many central city parents want a different educational strategy followed. They have recognized that many urban school systems are either in the hands of an all-white school board or under the tight control of white political interests. Rather than believing that school problems can be solved through the existing political structure, many parents want *decentralization* of the school system. Control over education would be taken out of the hands of a monolithic and distant school board and would be placed under the control of local neighbor-

Every September, school systems in the North that are struggling with court busing orders anticipate opening day with more doubts than hopes. In 1979, school buses and schools themselves in several Boston neighborhoods had to be heavily guarded by city and state police to deter or reduce violence. Busing as a means to ensure equal educational opportunities for all children has been plagued by iatrogenic effects; some would say that the remedy has been worse than the illness.

hoods. Many parents, blacks and those from other minority groups, favor community control because they would then be able to remove those administrators and teachers who they feel are insensitive to their own educational objectives. With community control, proponents believe, schools will provide motivation for learning by restructuring teaching; teachers and administrators will be responsible to the parents for what goes on in school; and a greater sense of racial pride and individual worth will be instilled in the children.[21]

This debate has pointed out the educational issues to be faced in the near future. Different strategies must be found to upgrade the quality of education that children in the central cities receive. If one looks behind the rhetoric, it is clear that more money must be pumped into these schools and class size must be reduced to allow for more individualized instruction. But the rhetoric itself makes clear that much of the turmoil in cities today focuses on the basic issue of who the schools are meant to serve and who should control them.

Employment

The failure of education in the cities leads to disadvantages when blacks are out of school. The inequality of education does not end with the end of school; its results, too, are unequal. The teaching provided in school is supposed to train young people to enter the work force, but education in our society works quite differently for blacks than it does for whites and differently for the poor than it does for the affluent.

In a study of twelve central cities, economist Bennett Harrison noted the result of the different ways education works for the two races:

> The weekly wage of white high school graduates in the twelve sets of poverty areas is nearly $25 higher than that of whites who never entered high school. For non-whites, the difference is only $8.83. High school, therefore, has three times as high a marginal payoff for ghetto whites as for ghetto non-whites.[22]

In writing about the relationship of unemployment rates to education, Harrison showed that for whites increased education reduces the possibility of unemployment.

> For non-whites, on the other hand, the average effect of education on unemployment as well as the effect over the 9 to 12 interval is zero! The non-white college graduate faces the same risk of unemployment as the high school dropout.[23]

It is easy to see why nonwhites living in the central cities do not feel as optimistic about their educational opportunities as do whites, particularly suburban whites. Not only are their schools inferior in terms of physical facilities, books, and programs, as pointed out by Coleman, but if they stay in school and graduate, their employment opportunities are far less given the same educational attainment. These two factors, educational quality and job opportunity, are interrelated in a number of subtle ways. When opportunities in both are lowered, the effects are hard for any individual black to overcome.

Earlier, we outlined the role of the cities in providing a warehouse for cheap labor during the early stages of the Industrial Revolution. Given the simpler nature of manufacturing processes at the turn of the century, unskilled and uneducated labor was useful to factory owners. Since the mass of laborers were unorganized and lacked the political tools to push their interests, wages tended to be low, work boring and routine, working conditions miserable, and hours long. But changes occurred because of the shifting nature of employment opportunities brought about by our changing technology. This shift has had profound implications for the problems of central city employment.

It is clear that jobs have changed, with increased levels of skill, expertise, and education now needed. What is significant for this chapter is that the cities have failed to provide access through training and education for certain groups to these new jobs. As a result, long-range and widespread unemployment characterize urban life. It is rather difficult to talk about unemployment in exact terms, for the reasons we outlined in Chapter 4. As we did in that chapter, in this we will accept the government definition of and data on unemployment, keeping in mind that the real figures are undoubtedly higher.

The government figures are startling

enough. According to them, the national unemployment rate rose from 4 percent in the late 1960s to 9 percent in mid 1975. This rise was part of the overall national economic strategy followed for several years in an attempt to cope with inflation. The governmental strategy under both the Nixon and Ford administrations was to let unemployment rise and to keep it at relatively high levels in order to cool off demand for consumer goods and services. Without any income, as their reasoning went, people would be unable to purchase goods and services, which would reduce demand and thus lower prices.

During the period this strategy was pursued, those hardest hit by unemployment were the poor — particularly the nonwhite poor living in the central cities. Government estimates of the unemployment rates for some central city areas were as high as 20 percent, more than twice the national average. As late as 1978 estimates for many central city ghettos put the unemployment rate of nonwhite males between ages eighteen and twenty-five at anything from 45 to 75 percent. But the unemployment rate shows only part of the picture of the employment problems which plague our urban areas.

Another employment related problem which has a negative effect on the quality of life and economic viability of the cities is underemployment. *Underemployment* includes *unemployment*, where people who want work cannot find it, but it also includes four other groups:

1. those working part time and who want to work full time but cannot find jobs
2. those who want to work but have stopped looking for a job out of frustration
3. those who are working full time at unsatisfactory wages
4. those who work but must take jobs far below their capability and training.[24]

Unemployment statistics do not deal with underemployment. For example, people often become so discouraged in looking for work that they give up the search entirely. They are then removed from the potential labor force when the government compiles its statistics; ironically, the unemployment rate actually drops when these people stop looking for work. Several times during the early 1970s, the unemployment rate fell for that reason. Such a change is deceptive.

The underemployment rate, although less often used by the government as a measure of employment problems, provides a better indicator of the magnitude of the difficulties facing central city residents. And the difficulties are huge. The national underemployment rate is usually two to three times the unemployment rate. Underemployment rates for central cities usually follow the same pattern, running several times the unemployment rates. That makes underemployment extremely high, since unemployment figures are already about twice as high for central cities as for the suburbs.

Another factor greatly limiting the employment opportunities open to certain groups is the transportation network now existing in many metropolitan areas. With the growing deterioration of mass transit, it is becoming increasingly difficult for poor people to reach jobs outside their own neighborhoods. Those mass transit lines kept in good repair are usually designed to bring middle-class commuters into the city from the suburbs. Because of their higher wages, suburban workers can usually afford the high price demanded for transportation to and from work in the downtown business district. But with the rising costs of transportation and the deterioration of services to parts of the city where low paying jobs can be found, it becomes increasingly difficult for many people living within the city itself to find and keep jobs.

Housing

Although sociologists continue to be concerned with the effects of crowded and deteriorated housing on the lives of people, we must be cautious about attributing deviant behavior directly to crowding. Some researchers have held that many ill effects suffered by animals who live in crowded conditions are found among humans living in such conditions. But relating findings from animal studies to human behavior is tricky; there is often a tendency to overgeneralize results and disregard the basic assumptions underlying the work done with animals. And humans have developed a technology that can modify the effects often associated with high density and crowding among animals. However, this does not mean that people can eliminate the effects of crowding altogether; it only means that simplistic conclusions based on animal research should not be used as the basis for programs designed to better human living conditions. We prefer the direct study of humans, as yielding more accurate data. In fact, studies of people living in close physical proximity have shown results not noted in animal studies, such as extreme social isolation of one individual from another.

Representative of the research being done is a study on the effects household crowding had on the psychological development of children. Numerous earlier studies had suggested negative effects of crowding on the behavior of children. For example, some researchers had found that the number of appearances in juvenile court was related to household crowding, as was the number of children receiving some sort of welfare assistance. Other studies had shown that parental control is reduced and child withdrawal heightened when household crowding increases; and population density has also been statistically related to infant mortality rates.[25]

But the significance of these findings was limited by the fact that the studies did not control for other social factors known to influence behavior. A more recent study avoided that trap and the researchers, Alan Booth and David Johnson, found some interesting results. Living in a relatively dense neighborhood seemed to have little effect on children's development, but living in a crowded household did. As the authors say:

> Children living in congested households are shorter, weigh less, and are sicker than their uncrowded counterparts. . . . However, it is noteworthy that the effects of crowding are very small. Parental health and socio-economic status, for example, are much more momentous in child health than is household crowding.[26]

Crowded housing, they found, has a negative effect on a wide range of important behaviors. For example, inadequate and crowded housing often undermines the ability of children to do school work and may therefore be a contributing factor in lowered educational achievement. And even if the effects of crowding are small, when joined with other social factors like race or class the problem becomes worse.

In the 1960s, to combat the problems of housing, the major thrust of many government sponsored programs was to tear down slums and put up more adequate housing in their place. This effort was part of the *Model Cities* program of the federal government. Entire neighborhoods had the bulldozer put to them, leaving many American cities looking like a war had been fought in their midst. In fact they had, the War on Poverty. Whole areas were torn down and neighborhoods ripped apart because some government officials had declared the area to be ripe for urban renewal or as it more accurately came to be called, Negro removal. After a neighborhood was leveled to the ground, unanticipated problems in reconstructing it often arose. With a shortage of funds brought on by escalating Vietnam war costs, the mid-1960s found many of these urban renewal programs at a standstill after the first phase, demolition, was completed.

City, state, and federal politics entered the arena when decisions were made about the now-vacant land. In some cases the cleared land became valuable, especially to developers who wanted to build high-rise apartments for the affluent in areas close to the downtown business district. When the government did sponsor public housing it was usually poorly designed and built. The most infamous case, the Pruitt-Igoe project in St. Louis, cost $400 million and was so badly vandalized that it had to be abandoned in less than five years. The huge housing projects were designed more to warehouse poor people than to provide them with decent living facilities, which contributed to the vandalism that doomed the projects in two ways.

First, although the major funding was made available from the federal government, the project was designed to ensure community involvement and control of the projects. From the beginning, this local control cut two ways; it involved the local people in planning for their needs but it also allowed contracts to be let to the friends, family, and business acquaintances of local politicians. This often involved bribing city officials, resulting in substandard construction approved by building inspectors and others on the take. As a result, the newly completed projects began to deteriorate, often in a matter of months. Bathrooms leaked, ceilings fell in, plaster peeled off walls, and tenants soon stopped caring about the rapidly deteriorating buildings.

In addition, since the housing was built without any consideration for the development of a viable community, the social controls necessary to keep vandalism and delinquency under control were noticeably lacking. As numerous urban sociologists have shown, urban planning involves understanding the social dynamics involved with spatial design.[27] Ignoring this fact, the federal government simply made money available to tear down slums and put up gigantic housing projects in their place. The money was spent in violation of all principles of good urban planning, designed to ensure quality of life despite high population density. That the result has been the continuation of the problems of urban housing is not surprising; the money spent was not sufficient to create a habitable environment. The corruption of city officials, poor construction, a lack of adequate planning, and not enough money to do the job right in the first place all combined to create new concrete high-rise slums in the place of the old wooden ones.

Summary

The central cities are suffering from grave problems. The educational system is not working as it should, reflected in poor student performance in school and in the difficulty that people in the central cities have finding work. Also suffering is housing, de-

In 1972, demolition of the Pruitt-Igoe public housing project in St. Louis, Missouri, was the only alternative, given the vandalism that was destroying it from the inside out. The project failed to meet its objective — solid housing for low-income families — because officials turned their backs on shabby construction practices and because the project was built in a vac· um, with no consideration of the community or personal needs it was to serve.

spite the efforts of the government to provide more and better housing, Underlying all these problems is the most disturbing development — the exodus of the middle class to the suburbs and the depletion of the cities' financial resources.

ATTEMPTS AT DEALING WITH THE PROBLEM

The Changing Federal Role

Any look at the strategy which has evolved in post-World War II America for dealing with central city problems must focus strangely enough on the building of the suburbs. The suburban explosion during the past 35 years has, for millions of Americans, meant a better life than they could have found in the city proper. For millions of Americans still residing in the older and larger cities of the Northeast, conditions have steadily worsened. Each year at their annual convention, mayors make a loud and unanimous call for greater involvement from the federal government in alleviating the problems facing the cities.

Yet each year these cries for help seem to fall on deaf ears in the executive branch.

Presidents Nixon and Ford refused outright to help New York City avoid bankruptcy; President Carter, although he campaigned on a platform of more federal help for the cities, has not followed through with the massive programs needed to help the cities meet their financial crises. Although the cities have not yet been helped in solving their financial problems, over the past decade many federal programs have been initiated to attack the other problems of the cities.

Many government officials at all levels feel that money is the key to solving the problems facing the central cities. Based on this view, the federal government has attempted to get into the act of providing the money for a wide range of projects aimed at helping the residents of central city areas. A more basic question has yet to be solved: whether the city can count on the federal government to deal with the fiscal problems keeping many of them on the brink of bankruptcy. But until that question is settled, federal spending on other problems will probably increase.

In 1978 the Carter Administration proposed an urban aid package of $4.4 billion in new funds designed to help the big cities avoid bankruptcy. And ever since 1976 the role of the federal government has increased drastically. In that year, the federal government contributed thirty-one cents for every dollar raised locally; by 1978 federal aid had risen to more than fifty-four cents for every dollar in local funds. As Figure 12.2 shows, it is the big cities of the Northeast that are getting the increased federal aid.

Under the Carter administration, federal aid to the cities amounted to about $11 billion in 1978. This aid went to three programs: one was to help areas slow to recover from an economic recession and another provided for local public works. The third was established by the *Comprehensive Employment and Training Act* (CETA), designed to combat chronic urban unemployment. The impact of these programs has been to cut the national unemployment rate down below 7 percent, the lowest it has been in the past four years.

The Structure of Current Welfare Programs

The number and variety of state and local welfare programs is so great that it is difficult to make a single statement about them. Still, a few things can be noted in respect to these various programs. First, the benefits under the various programs vary considerably from state to state. A comparison shows that three or four times the benefits are available to people in the North than in the South. And while living costs are much higher in the North, the difference in benefits does keep many people in the North Central cities. For example, in 1975, welfare benefits in New York City were the highest in the nation, with a mother and three children receiving $394 per month, not including publicly paid health care and the federal food stamp program. In Houston, the same woman and her children would get only $116 per month. Many urban affairs experts conclude that the disparity in payments encourages the poor to migrate to those cities least able to support more welfare recipients.

Another fact to be noted in looking at welfare expenditures is the different role the federal government plays in picking up welfare costs. In New York City the federal government contributes about half the money for the welfare program, with the remainder split between state and city governments. In Houston, on the other hand, the federal gov-

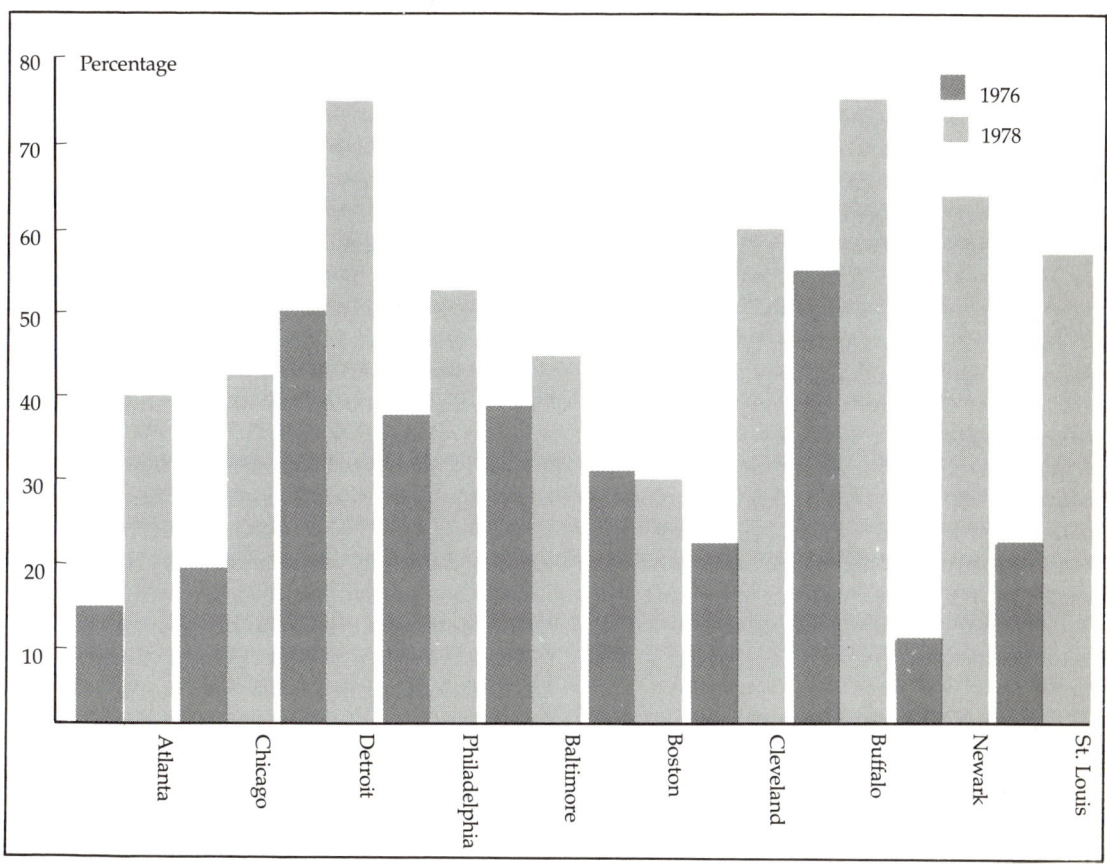

FIGURE 12.2 Federal Aid as a Percentage of City Tax Dollars
Source: Advisory Commission on Intergovernmental Relations.

ernment puts up about two-thirds of the cost and the state pays the rest. The reason for the difference is that federal contributions to city welfare programs are based on a complex formula using per capita income of the state involved. Federal contributions vary from a minimum of about 50 percent to a maximum of about 85 percent. This difference helps explain why mayors demand a federal welfare program that pays uniform benefits from state to state. Many urban analysts feel that a uniform benefit program would, at the very least, spread out the concentrations of unskilled and unemployable persons and force some wealthy suburban areas to pay for more of the total welfare costs.

Employment and Education Programs

For almost a decade the federal government has stayed out of the business of dealing with hard-core, central-city employment problems. This is partly due to the failure of efforts made during the mid-1960s to deal with the problem with the Job Corps. Even though this program continued throughout the 1970s, it barely made a dent in employment problems. Because of this, the Carter administration took a different approach, in the Comprehensive Employment and Training Act. Designed to be temporary, it works by providing funds to create jobs in schools, hospitals, and social services agencies. The employer is expected to provide on-the-job training for the CETA employee in return for work. This program, aimed at avoiding the problems encountered by earlier attempts, has at least had the effect of allowing many local governments, hospitals, and agencies to expand their staffs. Whether the intention was met and the hard-core unemployed did receive practical training still remains to be seen.

Many people realize today just how complex the problem of unemployment is, involving such issues as access to jobs (transportation), labor market discrimination, worker motivation, education, and training. Unless some attention is paid to all of these simultaneously, the long-range problems will probably still remain. A rising level of technology coupled with businesses leaving the cities for better locations in the suburbs has already vastly compounded the problem. Unless the unemployed workers can be educated to cope with the need for increasingly sophisticated job skills and then moved out to where the jobs are, any program will have only limited success. Such action would require government involvement in a variety of different areas where it has to date been extremely reluctant to get involved. Also such a program would probably mean a further decline of the central cities, since it does nothing to check the tendency of business and industry to locate their facilities outside the central cities.

The effort to increase employment by improving training is also evident in the vast amounts spent in an attempt to improve education. The money spent per capita on education increases directly with the size of the city as Figure 12.3 makes clear. Large cities are today spending more than double per capita what most others are spending. Yet all the latest information and research indicates that educational failure in the large cities is still increasing steadily.

The problem is demonstrated by what happened in New York City. Many sociologists believe that a major cause of juvenile delinquency is the way schools handle student behavior. This problem probably becomes more acute as the number of students increases, but the other needs of the school system are forcing administrators to increase class size. New York's strong teachers' union wanted more money for teachers' salaries and threatened to strike if their demands were not met. Since the city was on the verge of bankruptcy, there was no money available for increases in teachers' salaries and the city had decided to hold the line on all expenditures. In order to finance a raise of 20 percent over two years, the administration decided to let 20 percent of the teachers go. Class sizes increased, teaching specialists were laid off, and a whole series of programs were eliminated. This experience provides a model for the actions many other cities may have to take as they run out of money, a likelier prospect as taxpayers become more and more angered by rising tax bills.

What many people now propose is a system of federal education, where the government in Washington foots the bill for the entire school system in the country. The major

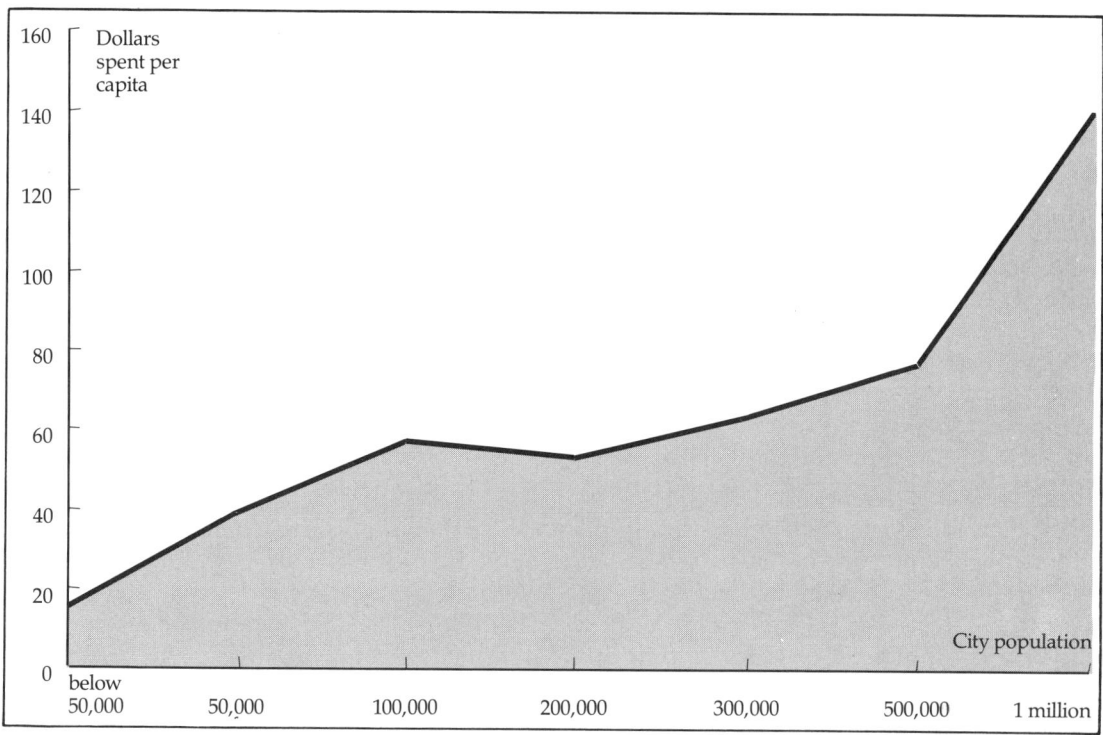

FIGURE 12.3 Per Capita Expenditures on Education by City Size, 1975

Source: *Statistical Abstract of the United States, 1977* (Washington, D.C.: U.S. Government Printing Office, 1977), p. 301.

stumbling block to this plan, besides the issue of money, is the ideology that wants to restrict the involvement and control of the federal government in the affairs of the local community. This financial involvement and the resultant control have been increasing in recent years, and many fear the results. But in light of the problems discussed in this chapter, is there any real alternative for the central city schools? Many parents, educators, and city officials are arguing today that federal control of education is the only realistic alternative. They contend that education more and more has become the key sorting mechanism in American society, and current approaches to financing education have proven ineffective.

Iatrogenic Effects

Obviously, many actions taken to solve the problems we have discussed in this chapter have not been successful. In fact, many programs seem to have compounded the problems, making a real solution more difficult. Since so many of the attempted solutions have involved spending money, perhaps a discussion of the effects of such spending is the logical place to begin.

As services have deteriorated, cities have taken steps to raise additional revenue by increasing taxes. In response, businesses and members of the middle class have found that they would be better off in the suburbs. This white flight has exacerbated the cities' problems, first because it reduces tax revenues and second because the groups that have taken their place have been politically impotent. They are less able to demand an upgrading of city services.

Services like education have deteriorated without there being any group whose voice is politically effective enough to prevent it. And the attempt to solve racial problems through busing has been claimed by some researchers to have hastened the move to the suburbs. Evidence on this issue is hard to evaluate, for other factors, like the expanded highway system, may have done as much to hasten this flight as forced busing. But one thing is clear, whatever effect busing had on migration from the city, forced school integration has contributed much to the antagonisms within local communities. The round of battles in South Boston, fought both in the streets and in the courts, are the direct result of efforts to integrate the schools through forced busing. In the decade or so since busing began, many school systems (especially in the older and larger cities) have become more rather than less segregated. Changing demographic patterns as the result of a complex set of factors have resulted in the cities becoming increasingly populated by the poor and minority groups. The creation of two societies, one urban and poor, the other suburban and affluent, has come about in the wake of such efforts to bridge the gap between the rich and the poor. The failure of these attempts at integration demonstrates the complexity of the problem.

Attempts to improve city financing have been failures too. One attempt has been through *revenue sharing*, in which the federal government gives some of its tax money to cities. But distribution is often unequal; the cities get back less money than their citizens originally paid to Washington. Even if they do get back a sizable share of the revenues collected, there still remains the key political issue of who determines how the returned money will be spent. Most city politics continues to be white-dominated, with business interests having a major say in how money in the city treasury is to be spent. Lack of political power for the poor and minority groups continues to be a problem, and revenue sharing has done nothing to subvert the long-standing pattern of white influence.

This failure became apparent when the Model Cities program of the late 1960s was evaluated. Federal funds had often flowed into the pockets of community leaders who reflected business and other interests of the white community rather than into the hands of the poor and minority groups, as was intended. Much of the money was used to rip apart neighborhoods and to remove poor and minority group people from areas that had become desirable for purposes other than slum housing. Many more buildings and houses were destroyed than were ever built through these federal programs, causing a major increase in the price for housing, which has hardly benefited the poor.

Employment has become a greater problem for the urban poor as many businesses have decided to relocate either in the South or in the urban fringe, both areas that give them tax advantages. With rising demands for increased skills, many poor and minority group persons are falling further behind in their ability to secure good employment. The ranks of the hard-core unemployed in the central cities are growing. Government response to this has not been aimed at the long-range solution of this problem but has usually involved the maintenance of the system by granting welfare or instituting temporary programs like CETA.

Programs aimed at the hard-core unemployed, like the Job Corps, failed for a number of reasons. Because most of the unemployed lacked basic skills, many programs soon had to face the fact that the real problem went beyond anything they were equipped to deal with. In many cases, these programs focused instead on encouraging people to look for jobs and on teaching them how to present themselves to employers when trying to secure employment. The net effect of these efforts was to raise the expectations of the unemployed without increasing the odds of having those expectations met. When they did not get a job because they had no skills, many became even more frustrated and hostile.

The failure of so many government efforts to solve the cities' problems has convinced many people that government cannot solve social problems at all. As a result, there has been a significant backlash against liberal thinking, especially on the range of problems discussed in this chapter. After a decade of liberal failure to solve the problems of the cities, many people are moving in a more conservative direction. The will to try harder, to make more money available, and to try new programs seems to be gone. A souring of the national mood and an increased unwillingness to make an effort on behalf of the people living in the cities is probably the major iatrogenic effect of these programs.

PROSPECTS FOR SOLVING THE PROBLEM

Until now, efforts to solve the problem have not been effective. This is largely the result of not having analyzed the problems to get behind the symptoms. One reason for this failure is American political ideology, which has kept cities subordinate to both the state and federal governments. Another ideological block to solving the problem is a general fear on the part of conservatives of the effects of an expanded role for the federal government. For these two reasons, many efforts to solve the cities' problems have been poorly conceived, inadequately funded, and haphazardly implemented. Federal grants for education have been given on a one-time basis, when the need was for funding with long-range continuity. Much federal money has started programs that have just been allowed to die when funding was turned over to people at the local level.

The cities and states claim they do not have the revenues needed to keep these programs going, and many are right. The key problem, again, is our national priorities and the role government at all levels is to play in determining them. The role of the federal government has grown rapidly in recent years, until today federal expenditures account for almost one quarter of the total dollar output of goods and services in this country. The growth at the federal level has not occurred because of some conspiracy to concentrate power at the top, but largely in response to the changing scale of the problems confronting American society. No one would suggest we could still plan for defense on a state by state basis. National security involves planning of immense scope, requiring a major commitment of national resources; state militias, which were important up through the Civil War, have become obsolete as a form of organizing our basic defense.

Similarly, many problems of education, housing, and employment are of national scope. Since the federal government has access to the resources needed to deal with these problems (through its greater power to tax), it has grown in importance. Yet the federal efforts have been plagued by uncoordinated planning and control. Greater involvement in the lives of people by government at all levels is something many people still fear. This fear is reaching a point where a taxpayers' revolt is becoming increasingly likely, especially on the state level. The implications of this for the federal government and the consequent effect on aid to the central cities are far from clear, but the prospect is gloomy.

During the urban violence of the late 1960s, most government action was aimed at keeping the lid on what many people feared was contagious mass rioting. But little was done to solve the basic problems that led to the riots, causing many to fear more urban violence in the future. Ironically, as long as this violence is contained in the central cities, it will most likely accomplish little. The reason is that most Americans will be isolated from it; the urban poor are a minority.

They are also marginal people, in a number of different senses. Living and being socialized in the ghetto, the urban poor are able to cope with its life-style but are not well equipped to meet the demands of the larger society. The urban poor are, in a way, a subculture. The ghetto culture provides the survival mechanism for central city residents; it is a product of the larger economic and political structure. That is, the ghetto culture is not the cause of poverty but the consequence of it.

The patterns of adjustment worked out by ghetto residents, then, stress values and ways of behaving that are at odds with the larger society. Because of this, the ghetto resident is a marginal person, caught between the national culture on the one hand and the ghetto culture on the other. Any solution to the problem of the central cities must take this into account, along with the need for structural change that will widen opportunities for central city residents. Because of the successful pattern of adjustment many ghetto people have worked out and because of a basic mistrust they feel toward the larger society, just making greater opportunity available to them may not help them overcome problems associated with their poverty. They will be understandably reluctant to give up the safety of the ghetto subculture.

Based on our changing technology, with the development of the highway system, vastly improved communication, and computers, some sociologists are beginning to wonder if there are not valid reasons for the decline of the cities as a form of social organization. Many of the reasons causing people to form cities in the first place seem no longer to exist, as our technology allows for alternative means for communication, innovation, and social interaction. This is not to say that the cities can no longer provide a setting for the innovation, change, and cultural diversity that suburbs sadly lack. As places where great museums, theaters, libraries, and universities are found, they still have much to offer. But as places where people actually want to live, work, and bring up their children, they seem less necessary.

With the majority of Americans suffering from this anticity bias, we must wonder who will supply the incentive to pump the needed billions of dollars into the cities to rebuild substandard housing or to improve education. And we must wonder who at the state and local level will speak for those who remain when they are badly outnumbered by the more affluent. The great strength of our system of government is that decisions made are based on the will of the majority. But what about the rights of the rest?

America is a consumer-oriented society, allowing most individuals great freedom to

New York's Katos Wunchacus gang exemplifies the isolating, survival-oriented nature of the ghetto subculture. These young men have adapted to urban slum life, but the values and behaviors of their culture are at odds with, and opposed to, society at large. To cross the barrier out of their narrowly defined and controlled world is virtually impossible.

choose where they live and how to spend their money. But people in our society make these choices in terms of the options available to them. Sometimes the way those options are limited can be detrimental to a group. A case in point is in transportation, where the private automobile has been glorified. The result is an enormous number of resources going into the production and maintenance of cars and the fuel they consume, and highway building and upkeep. Not all these resources are wasted, for clearly there are some advantages inherent in having a highly flexible transportation system. But this tremendous expenditure of resources may mean that there will be no resources left to do other things, which require collective action. The price of having many cars may be having little mass transit. With all our wealth, we never have enough for everything we want.

The problem is that the rebuilding and revitalization of cities will never be done without collective agreement that this is desirable and without the willingness to forgo some of the things most Americans seem to prefer, like one car for every two people. If this is true, if urban problems require a major cultural redefinition of priorities, then meaningful action may be improbable.

Our solution to city-related problems has been to build an endless number and variety of suburbs. But today many people are arguing that we have just about reached the limits in our ability to spread out. And many of the suburbs themselves have lost their glitter, as many city problems seem strangely to have followed right along with suburban expansion. In fact, the age of innocent belief that the suburbs would solve basic human problems is almost at an end. As a result there is a growing interest in the field of urban planning. The questions then become whether planning will work, whether we are really committed to planning, and whether the cities have already deteriorated too far to rebuild. Perhaps, as some have suggested, our best solution would be simply to tear them down and start fresh. Not as a strategy but simply out of neglect, this process has already begun.

IMPORTANT WORDS AND TERMS

apartheid
busing
Comprehensive Employment and Training Act (CETA)

decentralization
de facto segregation
de jure segregation
long-term debt
Model Cities
property tax

revenue sharing
senescence
short-term debt
Standard Metropolitan Statistical Area (SMSA)

underemployment
unemployment
urban fringe
white flight

QUESTIONS FOR DISCUSSION

1. As you know, California's Proposition 13 set upper limits on property taxes in that state. What do you think the long-term results of this proposition will be — especially once the state reserve is used up? What about the numerous state programs in existence that are threatened by the reduction in taxes? Do you believe that the federal government can or will step in and take over these programs?
2. On the whole, mass transit systems have not done well in the United States. Why? Considering the rising cost of gasoline, do you believe that mass transit systems can or will become more successful in the future? Explain your reasoning.
3. Considering the considerable array of governments at the local level — state, county, and township or city — do you believe that city planning is realistic? Why or why not?
4. Would it be desirable for city governments to have more autonomy, that is, be freer from state and federal influence and control? If cities had more autonomy, what do you believe some of the results might be?

5. Should all social services be centralized and brought under the control of the federal government? What do you see as the advantages and disadvantages?
6. De facto segregation exists in the large cities of the Northeast. Can you think of any procedures, legal or economic, that might reverse this trend and produce integrated cities? Would integrated cities be more desirable? Why?
7. What difficulties face minority group children in our school system? What do you think needs to be done in our educational system to make it function more effectively for minority students?
8. Consider briefly the reasons underlying the blight of our central cities. Are cities outdated as a form of social organization? Why or why not?
9. What do you see as the undesirable features of the quality of life in cities? What would you recommend be done to improve the quality of life?
10. The late 1960s were marked by a number of urban riots. Do you believe that if central cities continue to deteriorate that there will be rioting again? Why or why not? Is rioting productive for the rioters? Does it get them what they want? Why or why not?
11. Given the deterioration of the housing in many central city ghetto areas, should there be a federal program aimed at supplying low cost housing for poor people? What would be a reasonable percentage of the GNP for the federal government to allocate to the program?
12. Is the building of endless suburbs going to provide the answer to central city problems? Consider your answer especially in light of the growing energy crisis.

SUGGESTED READING

JANE JACOBS, *The Death and Life of Great American Cities* (New York: Random House, 1961).

In this work, Jane Jacobs criticizes the attempts at urban planning made during the past quarter century. She feels they have torn neighborhoods apart because they violated principles of urban life. Jacobs outlines these principles, based largely on her experiences in the Greenwich Village section of New York, and shows how planning efforts have brought death instead of life to our urban areas. Once you have read this book, you will wonder how urban planners continue to make the same mistakes year after year.

V. GORDON CHILDE, *Man Makes Himself* (New York: Mentor, 1951).

Childe traces the record of prehistoric humans to determine when the urban revolution began. He examines what life must have been like in the cities of antiquity and looks at the rise of civilization through invention and innovation and the diffusion of ideas. He gives a very readable account of how the need for writing, mathematics, and architecture arose from problems associated with agricultural surplus and shows how the city was an indispensable form of social organization at a crucial time in human history.

MIKE ROYKO, *Boss* (New York: Signet, 1971).

While it is clear Royko is not a fan of the former mayor of Chicago, Richard Daley, he presents a careful and detailed account of how the mayor ran Chicago for almost a quarter century. Royko delves into Daley's habits and style of leadership, showing that Daley's prime motivation was a love of power. While Daley's rule of Chicago was unique in the post-World War II era, Royko helps us to understand how all city politics are organized and work to the advantage of certain interest groups.

HOWARD BECKER (ed.), *Culture and Civility in San Francisco* (New York: Aldine, 1971).

In a collection of articles from *Transaction*, Becker has pulled together some most interesting ideas about life in San Francisco. A seaport located in an ideal natural setting, San Francisco has developed a tolerant culture, where numerous minority groups live in relative harmony. This book looks at the mechanisms used to unite the various communities while keeping them as identifiable entities. Becker's concern is to show how widespread differences in attitudes and behaviors can coexist within a particular city.

CHARLES HAAR (ed.), *The End of Innocence* (Glenview, Ill.: Scott Foresman, 1972).

The authors of the articles in this collection show that the suburbs are now facing many of the same problems confronting the larger cities. Whereas it was once thought that the answer to urban problems would be in spreading out from the cities, these readings show that a lack of planning has caused the same problems to crop up again in the suburbs. This book is important because it is one of the few to question what has become a major strategy for solving a wide range of the social problems.

NOTES

1. National Advisory Commission on Civil Disorders, "Report," in Louis E. Lowenstein (ed.), *Urban Studies* (New York: Free Press, 1971), pp. 146 ff.
2. Ron Ridenhour and Arthur Lublow, "Bringing the War Home," *New Times* (November 28, 1975), pp. 18–24.
3. See V. Gordon Childe, *Man Makes Himself* (New York: Mentor, 1951).
4. Paul Meadows, "The City, Technology and History," *Social Forces*, Vol. 36 (December 1957), p. 143.
5. Daniel P. Moynihan, "The Liberals Dilemma," *The New Republic* (January 22, 1977), p. 58.
6. Bureau of the Census, *Social and Economic Characteristics of the Metropolitan and Non-Metropolitan Population — 1977 and 1970* (Washington, D.C.: U.S. Government Printing Office, 1977).
7. Ibid.
8. Bureau of the Census, *Statistical Abstract of the United States, 1977* (Washington, D.C.: U.S. Government Printing Office, 1977), p. 30.
9. Ibid., p. 7.
10. Ibid.
11. Edward Banfield and James Wilson, *City Politics* (New York: Vintage Books, 1966), p. 68.
12. Irving Howe, "The Cities' Secret," *The New Republic* (January 22, 1977), p. 55.
13. *Statistical Abstract, 1977*, p. 278.
14. *Statistical Abstract, 1977*, pp. 278, 320.
15. Ibid., p. 300.
16. Ibid., p. 301.
17. Ibid.
18. Ibid.
19. James Coleman, *Equality of Educational Opportunity* (Washington, D.C.: U.S. Government Printing Office, 1966).
20. U.S. Commission on Civil Rights, *Desegregation of the Nation's Public Schools: A Status Report* (Washington, D.C.: U.S. Government Printing Office, 1979), pp. 26–71.
21. For a good analysis of these points on urban education, see Marilyn Gittell, "Education: The Decentralization-Community Control Controversy," in Jewell Bellush and David Stephen (eds.), *Race and Politics in New York City* (New York: Praeger, 1971), pp. 134–163.
22. Bennett Harrison, "Education and Underemployment in the Urban Ghetto," in Martin Carnoy (ed.), *Schooling in a Corporate Society* (New York: David McKay, 1975), p. 150.
23. Ibid.
24. See *The Manpower Report of the President*

(Washington, D.C.: U.S. Government Printing Office, 1967), pp. 74–75.

25. Omar Galle et al., "Population Density and Pathology," *Science*, Vol. 176 (April 1972), pp. 23–30.

26. Alan Booth and David Johnson, "the Effects of Crowding and Child Health and Development," *American Behavioral Scientist*, Vol. 18, No. 6 (July–August 1975), p. 746.

27. See Jane Jacobs, *The Death and Life of Great American Cities* (New York: Random House, 1961).

13 HUMAN ECOLOGY
ORGANIZED DESPOLIATION

CHAPTER OVERVIEW

INTRODUCTION

CONCEPTUAL ORIENTATION
The Ecological Perspective
Ecological Concepts
Summary

HISTORICAL OVERVIEW
The Beginning of Human Destructiveness
American Destructiveness
Ideology and Environmental Damage
Summary

OBJECTIVE DIMENSIONS OF
   THE PROBLEM
The Scope of Pollution
Air Pollution
Water Pollution
Pesticides

Other Forms of Pollution
Summary

ATTEMPTS AT DEALING WITH THE PROBLEM
Different Views of the Problem
Environmental Groups
The Politics and Economics
  of Technology
Attempts at Increasing
  Public Awareness
Iatrogenic Effects

PROSPECTS FOR SOLVING THE PROBLEM

IMPORTANT WORDS AND TERMS

QUESTIONS FOR DISCUSSION

SUGGESTED READING

NOTES

Here we are . . . standing knee deep in garbage . . . firing rockets at the moon.

Pete Seeger

A bear needs five square miles of wilderness in which to live. If wilderness is worth $1,000 per acre, is a bear worth $3.2 million?
Edward Hoagland, "Looking for Wilderness"

CHAPTER OVERVIEW

In this chapter we approach ecology from a perspective that looks at man as part of the natural environment and does not view man as dominant over or apart from nature. Problems of water, air, or noise pollution are examined only after the ecological framework is outlined and discussed. Environmental damage is seen as the result of actions taken by our highly industrialized society as it produces the consumer goods we all demand. The politics and economics of our consumer society are viewed as important factors to be considered when looking at ecological problems, and their solutions.

INTRODUCTION

In a recent strike of sanitation workers, New Yorkers found out just how much garbage they create as it piled higher and higher in the city's streets. In this country there are places where people are afraid to drink the water and end up paying high prices to have bottled spring water delivered to their homes. And Tokyo has air so foul people are willing to pay a quarter for a breath of fresh air dispensed by a vending machine. On hearing of such things, we are all prone to fear that where we live may someday be the same. As the above examples point out, we are beginning to find out that clear water and clean air involve not only real costs, but that the costs are often higher than many of us are willing or able to pay.

The growing tragedy of environmental damage is that the human species seems able, on the surface at least, to adjust to and survive despite increasing pollution. When we notice that the birds are dying, the trees shriveling up, and that dead fish are washing up on the shore, the prevailing attitude is that humankind will surely find a way to escape. But can we? This is the central question treated in this chapter. The answer will have a great impact not only on our lives but on the lives of generations to follow.

The strategy used by many people when pollution, crowding, and pace of urban life becomes too great is to pick up and move. The state of California, up until the early 1970s, saw the massive influx of people who were looking for the good life, including an unspoiled environment. But as we look at California today, the noise, dirt, congestion, and filth seemed to follow right along with the new residents, until people finally stopped coming. Parts of California turned out to be just like those crowded and polluted places that emigrants had left and many people again found themselves trapped in an environment almost unfit for human habitation.

Taken individually, these people are like the rest of us: they assume environmental damage is someone else's problem, always caused by the other guy. But it is becoming harder to avoid the fact that we all pollute. It is also becoming apparent that the visible signs of pollution are just the tip of the iceberg, since the larger proportion of all pollution is invisible. We do not see the DDT in our waters, carbon monoxide in the air, the Freon released from aerosol spray cans, or the nitrates running off fertilized land or out of inadequate waste systems into the rivers and lakes. But they are real and are doing great damage to many forms of life crucial to our existence. And the age of easily exploitable resources is over as well, something anyone can see by looking at the price of gasoline. The price of our exploitation of nature may be tied closely to the long-range survival of our species. Yet the perception of the damage we have done to the environment is a recent phenomenon, for the damage was only noticed when it began to punish us for our misuse. This increased awareness is due, in part, to the growth of a new field of study called ecology. In this section we will look at the growth of this field and its related concepts; then we will give an overview of how people have affected their environment over time.

CONCEPTUAL ORIENTATION

The Ecological Perspective

As the environment has become noticeably damaged in many parts of the country, interest in taking steps to save endangered land, water, or air has sharply increased. As people have searched for solutions to these problems, they have become interested in the field of ecology. Actually, the words *ecology* and *economics* derive from a common Greek root, *oikos*, meaning household. *Ecology* was coined in 1873 by the German biologist Ernst Haeckel to mean the study of the economics of plants and animals.

Today we would be more accurate to define it as Paul Shepard has: "Ecology deals with organisms in an environment and with the processes that link organism and place."[1] It might seem from this definition that an ecologist can have two distinct sets of interests: one in the organism and the other emphasizing the environment. But in reality the key concern of the ecologist is in the interaction between organisms and their environments. The major focus of ecology is on how an environment sustains life; that is, how an organism interacts with the environment to survive and how such modes of survival affect the viability of that environment. As Shepard points out, ecology emphasizes the wholeness of the interaction between organism and environment. Although ecology is relatively new, this perspective has been around for quite some time and today is common outside the modern world. But with the growth of the physical sciences and the technologies they produced in the developed nations during the past 300 years, this perspective fell into disuse.

Today this ecological perspective is being rediscovered by scientists interested in looking at the way things actually work out in the real world as opposed to remaining within the strict confines of the laboratory. Because the trend is of relatively recent origin, many of the most prestigious scientists and administrators charged with making policy affecting the environment remain ignorant of basic ecological principles.[2] Scientists trained in specialized fields are not able to approach problems in the *holistic* fashion of the ecological perspective, which tries to understand the whole of a system. Rather than taking that broad view, specialists look at problems from their own narrow field of expertise. But most environmental problems

HUMAN ECOLOGY: Organized Despoliation

are ones of organism and environment interacting with each other.

Ecological Concepts

Within this general perspective, there are certain key ideas important to understanding ecology. The first of these is the concept of an *ecosystem*, a term coined by the British plant ecologist, Tansky, in 1935. In simplest terms, the notion behind an ecosystem is that the whole is greater than the sum of its parts. For example, "a human being is more than the simple addition of its organs, chemical compounds, and tissues." Figure 13.1 should help make this pivotal notion clearer. For the ecologist, the boundaries drawn around any particular ecosystem may vary greatly in size. There are large aquatic ecosystems such as oceans and seas, and smaller ones like lakes, ponds, and estuaries. But regardless of the size of the ecosystem, the ecologist is primarily interested in the kinds of interactions that take place between organisms and their environments.

In an ecosystem, each living organism takes something from the system and in turn gives to the system something of use. In the figure, plants take basic nutrients from the water, and are eaten by the invertebrates, who then supply food for the forage fishes. All the parts of the ecosystem depend in one way or another on the other parts. Any change in one part of the system will have feedback effects on the other parts, because life within an ecosystem is interdependent.

With the above in mind, it is possible to state a number of general ecological laws that will help our understanding of the problem

FIGURE 13.1 The Aquatic Ecosystem

Source: John Clark, "Thermal Pollution and Aquatic Life" in Garrett Hardin (ed.), *Science, Conflict and Society* (San Francisco: Freeman, 1969), p. 263.

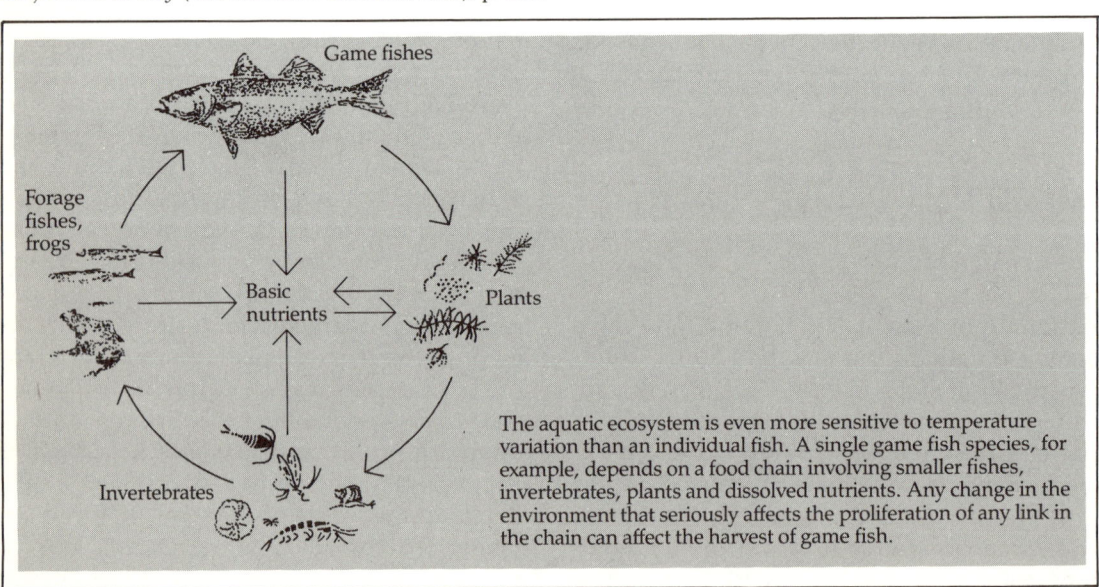

The aquatic ecosystem is even more sensitive to temperature variation than an individual fish. A single game fish species, for example, depends on a food chain involving smaller fishes, invertebrates, plants and dissolved nutrients. Any change in the environment that seriously affects the proliferation of any link in the chain can affect the harvest of game fish.

of environmental damage. These laws, formulated by Barry Commoner, state basic ecological principles.[3] The first law of ecology is that "Everything is connected to everything else." This key to ecology focuses on the interdependence between the species inhabiting an ecosystem. In such a system, if one part is thrown out of balance, other elements will be affected.

The stress an ecosystem can absorb is related to the amount of complexity built into the system. An ecosystem is said to be simple if there are few alternatives available to each of the organisms living within it; it is complex if each organism has many alternatives. Many problems of environmental damage stem from the fact that pollution often simplifies certain aspects of an ecosystem in ways not immediately obvious. When the system is made more vulnerable to stress by continued simplification, it sets the stage for events that could lead to a final collapse.

The simplifying of an ecosystem can be presaged by such an event as the disappearance of a species of fish or animal. But even though an ecosystem does not immediately collapse because a few species of fish leave, the danger signs of an environment being simplified are there. This is essentially an accurate description of what happened to Lake Erie in a series of slow and agonizing stages. A huge lake does not just collapse when it is ecologically abused, but it does become more susceptible to a process ecologists call *aging*, which is a phenomenon of growing simplification. Lake Erie aged at least 5,000 years in the past fifty, as the result of human abuse. The groundwork for a final collapse was laid by a half century of human-made stress. People who thought the danger to Lake Erie was being overstated failed to realize the implication of the first law of ecology. Increasing stress set the stage for the final collapse because, as Commoner states, "the ecological network is an amplifier so that a small perturbation in one place may have large, distant, long delayed effects."[4]

Lake Erie also demonstrates another principle, the second law, which states that "everything must go somewhere." Because so many of our toxic materials are invisible, people don't consider where they all go. The population of New York City knows very well where some types of pollution go, because the bathing beaches often get shut down in the midst of the summer heat when raw sewage washes on them. New York has long operated its garbage and sewer system on the basis of what Philip Slater has called the "toiletbowl assumption."[5] Many people think that getting the problem out of sight is the same as solving it. This way of thinking is followed by many Americans, not only about pollution but about other social problems as well. Thus for some problems, we build prisons; for others, mental hospitals. As for pollution, we either bury it or dump it. But when we discharge and dump wastes into the oceans, they accumulate and sometimes wash back on the beaches. Just because we cannot see it doesn't mean it is not there.

In the age of rapidly increasing scientific knowledge, people have become convinced that humans know best. Our knowledge has brought us power over nature and allowed us to defy natural laws. But this is folly; according to the third law of ecology, "nature knows best." Humans and our ancestors have been around for perhaps 4 million years, which seems like a long time until we see that the earth has sustained life for 2 or 3 billion years. And although humans have existed for only a short time in comparison to life on earth, our ability to damage the environment with chemical compounds that do not exist in nature is only about one hundred years old. In the millions of years before we developed our ability to change drastically our environment, living things had evolved into complex organisms, each compatible to an extent with the others in its ecosystem. These ancient interactions were supportive, rather than destructive, of life.

But although nature knows best, humans inflict damage. As the fourth law states, "there is no such thing as a free lunch." We must be careful in trying to get something for nothing from nature. It appears that for a long time nature can be abused, as it bounces back every spring with a new face hardly distinguishable from the old. But damage has been done, even if no one observes it. We are now beginning to pay the price for the neglect of past generations. The foul water, the depleted soil, and the many changes in the atmosphere we are now beginning to notice did not happen only in our lifetimes. They are, like science itself, part of the legacy we have inherited from past generations who died before we were born. But while our ancestors may not have known any better, we should. We are mortgaging the future of generations yet to come with the wastes we are dumping into the environment, and it is inexcusable because we now know that we are doing it.

Summary

Ecology gives us the perspective from which to view the relationships between organisms and their environment. This perspective has as its central concept the idea of an ecosystem within which each organism occupies its own niche. From this rather straightforward presentation, one would never suspect that ecology has been called the "subversive science." However, after we look at what we have done to our environment and the ideological rationale used for doing so, we will begin to understand why this term was used.

HISTORICAL OVERVIEW

The Beginning of Human Destructiveness

The myriad ways humans have changed the environment are not neatly catalogued in one place. If they were, we would perhaps not be so reluctant to modify our current bent for environmental destruction. Much of the record of the human role has been lost because it went by, unnoticed in an age when record keeping was nonexistent or not well developed. Partly for this reason our treatment of this enormously complex phenomenon will be limited to a few examples that can be presented with reasonable certainty and that illustrate the kinds of things people have done during their tenure on the earth.

In 1956, a massive 1,200-page study of human destructiveness was published, entitled *Man's Role in Changing the Face of the Earth*.[6] The list of indictments contained in this work is long and includes changes in soil composition, climate, and bodies of water, mineral depletion, and other human-made disasters. This book was dedicated to George P. Marsh, who first attempted to catalog the effects of humans on the environment in a book published in 1864. In this pioneering work, Marsh detailed the variety of ways people had modified the environment, including the following:

1. Humans changed plant distribution around the world.
2. Animals domesticated by people, like the goat or camel, overgrazed the land.
3. Agriculture served as a breeding ground for insect life.
4. Deforestation increased climatic contrasts.
5. People have used fire to clear land for agriculture.
6. People have drained bogs.
7. People have fixed sand dunes.

Marsh's ideas proved influential, both in America and in Europe, where he was often called on to help write laws protecting the environment. His catalog of what was then known about the changes wrought by humans led many who read his work to wonder if the fall of many ancient civilizations might not have been the result of damage to their life-support systems.

In a recent version of Marsh's work, Paul Ehrlich and John Holdren have put together an up-to-date inventory of humankind's disastrous effects on the environment. As they say:

> The most startling terrestrial event in the two billion year history of life on the Earth has been the rise of the species *Homo sapiens* to its present position of global preeminence.[7]

About 10,000 years ago, humankind was only one of a large number of species of large land mammals roaming the earth. Erhlich and Holdren put the number of people at less than other species, like the bison, when they estimate a human population of approximately 5 million individuals. But human use of fire and increasing skill as hunters changed all this in a few thousand years, a relatively short time given the age of the earth. But change it humankind did. There is good evidence that in pre-Columbian America, humans caused the extinction of 70 percent of the large mammals; in Africa, they wiped out about 30 percent of such creatures.

Fire made possible the clearing of land on a large scale, which in turn made possible the beginnings of settled agriculture. As the nomadic life of the hunter was slowly abandoned, the agricultural revolution began in earnest. With the increased production of food, the growth of human populations was made possible and the first cities developed wherever there was an agricultural surplus able to support them. In about 10,000 years, the population of the human species increased 700 times. Of course, population growth has become so rapid in today's world that it takes only twenty-six days to add 5 million people to the total (see Chapter 11), but the changes have been occurring since humans settled down. And while this chapter is not about population, these rapidly growing numbers need to be mentioned, for they put growing pressure on the environment. The environment had to be changed, shaped, and molded so it could provide support for more and more humans. That the growing numbers of ancient people had long-range effects is seen in the deserts of the Middle East and northern Africa, thought to stem largely from environmental damage. Today the Fertile Crescent of western Asia is dry and barren, hardly the way this cradle of civilization looked 10,000 years ago.

American Destructiveness

The late 1800s marked the beginnings of an awareness of the damage industrialization had done to natural resources. The work of Marsh spurred the naturalist and conservationist John Muir to write of human damage done to the American continent. One of the original founders of the now famous conservationist group, the Sierra Club, Muir wrote of the glory of the native American forests and described their despoliation by the settlers:

> the invading horde of destroyers called settlers made its fiery way over the broad Rocky Mountains, felling and burning more fiercely than ever, until at last it has reached the wild side of the continent, and entered the last of the great aboriginal forests on the shores of the Pacific.[8]

He wrote of the wanton abandon with which the settlers denuded the forest to make way for farm and orchard, and of people driven to conquer the wilderness in the name of progress.

Along with this progress came the near or total annihilation of some animals, like the buffalo and passenger pigeon. From our view today this annihilation seems senseless. Most buffalo killed in the 1870s and 1880s were slaughtered for their tongues, considered a delicacy in the East. After the tongue was removed, the remainder of these great animals was left to rot where they had fallen. This wasteful slaughter continued until the species was nearly extinct. The work of men like the naturalist John Audubon documented the spoilage done to other species during the 1800s. He writes of the now totally extinct passenger pigeon:

> When they alighted on the trees their weight was so heavy that not only big limbs and branches of the size of a man's thigh were broken straight off, but less firmly rooted trees broke down completely under the load.[9]

Yet by the turn of the century, the passenger pigeon had become extinct, the whole species was hunted to death, every last bird killed.

This kind of destruction had begun when the Europeans first came. The land, like the forests, birds, and animals, has been systematically changed by three hundred years of settlement. Early attempts by the very first settlers to get a cash crop led to a massive clearing of land to plant tobacco, which came to be known as a robber crop. It depleted the soil and resulted in extensive erosion throughout the colony of Virginia. The lands further south and in the West provided a place to go when the soil of the East became exhausted. But as the settlers moved west, they displaced the Indians, who had lived off the land without ruining it for thousands of years, and destroyed the virgin forests. These changes finally aroused concern at the turn of the century. Due to the efforts of men like Muir and Audubon, around 1900, New York took the lead in establishing state forests designed to protect what little virgin territory there was left. While the damage done to the environment by the early settlers was great, in many cases nature seems to have healed itself. But the worst was still to come; the damage done in the twentieth century made much of what had come before look almost like conservation.

From about 1880 onward, the growth of American urban areas was speeded up as the result of both foreign immigration and improved transportation linking city and farm. With the widespread use of the automobile, suburban sprawl began. People were now able to live in one place and work in another, and so they spread out in space more than ever before. Roads were built under public sponsorship and easy credit made it possible for the purchase of both a house and a car, two things central to the American Dream. Expressways, polluted air, parking lots, unplanned land use, and millions of cars have added to the human impact on our environment in ways the axes of the settlers never could have. And today, as industries move out of the central part of the city, they take their pollution with them into areas not yet heavily damaged.

Ideology and Environmental Damage

Our mad pursuit of the production, distribution, and consumption of consumer goods continues in spite of increasing evidence that such demands harm our environment. We do so because we subscribe to a value system and worldview that permits the continued exploitation of the land, air, and water regardless of the consequences. An overriding emphasis on progress, defined in quantitative terms, and a blind faith in the ability of future technologies to right the wrongs or undo the damage of past technologies have made us insensitive to the effects of our actions on the quality of life and have allowed us to ignore our responsibilities to our environment and future generations.

A great deal of environmental misuse happens because of a series of factors Garrett Hardin outlines in a provocative article, "The Tragedy of the Commons."[10] To explain behavior today, Hardin bases his argument on the practice in seventeenth- and eighteenth-century Britain of establishing large tracts of publicly owned land held in common and used freely for the grazing of cattle by all the townspeople. Since the land use was free and without restriction, each person who owned cattle looked at grazing only from his own point of view. As each individual added cattle to his herd, he became wealthier; but as more individuals did this, they all became poorer. The land quickly became overgrazed. And so it is today, when there is little feeling of collective responsibility for the use of commonly held resources, such as air or water. This lack of a common sense of responsibility is an inevitable outgrowth of our values, which stress the uniqueness and worth of the individual. This strong belief in individuality has helped open the way to environmental destruction.

Another common attitude helps promote widespread destruction, the American arrogance toward the environment. Some authors have tried to tie this arrogance to a message in the book of Genesis, in which God gives people domination over the earth. The noted sociologist, Lynn White, Jr., finds a rationale for environmental destruction in the Judeo-Christian view of humankind as separate from the rest of nature. Still other scholars have suggested the presence of the American frontier as being important because it provided Americans with a view of their environment as endless and able to absorb any abuse heaped on it. But as interesting as the search for the historical roots of our contemporary views may be, this work has also been widely criticized. Other authors note how in other times and other places (such as in ancient Greece or China) there were massive amounts of environmental damage done without the support of Judeo-Christian doctrine. And in this century, the Soviet Union seems to be damaging its environment as well, without a thought for the teachings of the Bible.

There may be an element of truth in all these speculations but the origin of our attitudes is not as important as their result, nicely summarized by Henry David Thoreau:

> If a man walks in the woods for love of them half of each day, he is in danger of being regarded as a loafer: but if he spends his whole day as a speculator shearing off those woods and making earth bald before her time, he is esteemed an industrious and enterprising citizen.[11]

Thoreau understood that we have an anticonservationist ethic in this country, which persists strongly today. John Muir noted that we were one of the last nations in the world to feel the necessity to develop a conservationist movement, something the European countries had been doing for quite some time.

Another important attitude is the average American's belief in the ability of science to solve problems. We use electrostatic filters to remove particles from smokestacks and catalytic converters to cut down pollution from cars, showing that we believe that science will provide the cure, if not for all problems, at least for these particular ones. The great contrast between an informed ecological view of the world and the image most Americans have of science was pointed out by Garrett DeBell. He contrasted popular and widely read science magazines with those like *Audubon Magazine* and *Sierra Club Bulletin*. As DeBell notes, the naturalist magazines are concerned about the probability of impending ecological disaster in the form of the death of the oceans, or the extinction of species like whales, pelicans, or eagles. As he says:

> The magazines popularizing science such as *Popular Science* and *Popular Mechanics* speak of the technological Utopia of the future — a television screen attached to every telephone, a helicopter on every rooftop, and sleek supersonic transports for the fortunate few who cannot hear their sonic boom. The two kinds of journals seem oblivious of each other. Yet there is a connection: the more we strive to reach the popular science future, the more likely we are to achieve the ecological disaster.[12]

We live in an age of belief in the omnipotence of science. Most people reflect this with a faith in the ability of science to fix nature after we have broken it.

The scientific discoveries made by the early astronomers changed people's picture of themselves in the universe. The Polish astronomer, Copernicus, was initially branded as a heretic when he suggested that the earth was not the center of the universe. A similar change in perspective has been slow to come in our understanding of our relationship with our environment. We can understand how Copernicus' ideas subverted the way of thinking about the world in his day. The message of ecology is the message of Copernicus: humankind can no longer be seen as the center of the natural universe. This message from the new science of ecology, however, is bucking a popular belief in science itself, which has been used to shape the world to our liking. If ecology is to be taken seriously, it must subvert that basic faith in science and restructure our attitudes and actions. Given our ideology of material comfort and economic gain which is predicated upon a strong belief in "science" as an integral part, how many of us can accept the heretical message of ecology?

Summary

Humankind has changed the environment ever since the species first appeared. Our ideology, with historical roots in the Judeo-Christian view of man and our vast and open frontier, helps explain why we damage nature today. But the most important factor is our belief in science, the basis for our relationship to the environment. Modern people will see nothing wrong with their treatment of nature until they take the message of ecology seriously. One thing ecologists have been trying to point out is the actual damage we have done to the environment. Their findings are a massive indictment of our use of the world around us. To grasp the immensity of the current problem, we will discuss the most recent aspects of this human folly.

OBJECTIVE DIMENSIONS OF THE PROBLEM

The Scope of Pollution

As stated earlier, the past hundred years or so has seen the application of science to problems. The application of scientific principles to the practical needs of people on an everyday basis is called *technology*. While it is possible to separate science and technology in theory, in practice they are interrelated. Pure scientific research is often funded by those in search of profits, which they get by selling new discoveries. The older technology of the past hundred or so years has been dwarfed by recent advances in the production of synthetic materials, which are being used to replace many natural ones. Figure 13.2 represents the direction some of

FIGURE 13.2 A Comparison of the Projected Per Capita Consumption of Materials

Source: John McHale, *World Facts and Trends* (New York: Macmillan, 1972), p. 74.

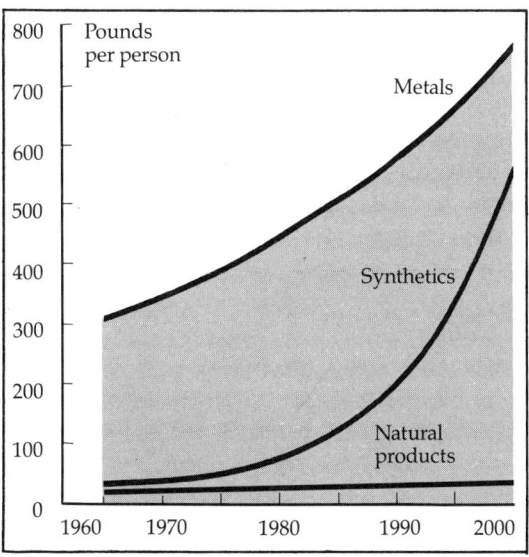

the latest processing technology is expected to take in the near future.

As can be seen, the fastest rising curve is the one representing the use of synthetics. Most of these materials are derived from petroleum and many are new products that have the advantage of being almost indestructible. Of course, this indestructibility is also a disadvantage, as a visit to the beach shows. Even the disposable packaging and cans we produce are around long after their usefulness has been outlived. But this reflects our values. As part of our rising standard of living, Americans have come to expect that they will be able to consume even greater amounts of goods. G. Tyler Miller has estimated that an American baby born in 1973 will use the following:

1. 26 million gallons of water
2. 52 tons of iron and steel
3. 1,200 barrels of petroleum
4. 13,000 pounds of paper
5. 21,000 gallons of gasoline
6. 50 tons of food
7. 10,000 pounds of fertilizer

These enormous amounts of goods will require expanding our use of environmental resources. Worse is the tremendous amount of waste dumped back on the landscape. In the average American's lifetime, he or she will discard:

1. 10,000 no-return bottles
2. 17,500 cans
3. 27,000 bottle caps
4. 2.3 automobiles
5. 126 tons of garbage
6. 9.8 tons of particulate air pollution[13]

The United States standard of living equals the consumption of between 30 and 40 percent of the resources produced by the entire world, although the United States has only about 6 percent of the world's population. This tremendous overconsumption of resources is closely linked to our pollution of the environment. *Pollution* occurs when the carrying capacity of an ecosystem is not able to absorb what is put into it. Some materials like arsenic, mercury, and lead are found very infrequently in nature and infinitesimally small amounts of these elements can massively upset the delicate and complex ecological balance. Yet millions of tons of these materials are dumped each year into an environment which cannot absorb them.

Any concern at all for the effects of dumping polluting substances into the environment is of recent origin. As a result, much data we need for comparison purposes were not kept until recently and some sources remain incomplete, even today. But just taking what we do know about the ability of the earth to handle our pollution, Donella Meadows has suggested four basic conclusions:

1. The few kinds of pollution that have been measured seem to be increasing exponentially.
2. We have almost no knowledge about what the upper limits of this growth might be.
3. The presence of natural delays in ecological processes increases the probability of underestimating the control measures necessary, and therefore of inadvertently reaching these upper limits.
4. Many pollutants are globally distributed; their harmful effects appear long distances from their point of generation.[14]

Despite this warning, year by year we continue to dump contaminants into the atmosphere, water, and land. Many answers prove to be useless in attacking the real problem. A home trash compactor is the only machine ever invented that can take twenty-five pounds of garbage and turn it into twenty-five pounds of garbage. The garbage may be compressed and easier to handle, but its environmental impact will be largely the same. The huge increase in environmental pollution that has occurred, especially since the end of World War I, has resulted from four factors:

1. our rising standard of living
2. the increase in population
3. the great increase in industrial production
4. the use of more sophisticated manufacturing techniques, which are introducing more exotic and often toxic materials into the environment

Keeping in mind that these are the four major contributors to pollution, let us examine what has actually been done to the environment as a consequence of our pollution of air, water, and land.

Air Pollution

Anyone who has flown to New York City notes how on certain days at 35,000 feet, about 150 miles outside of the city, the passenger can see what looks like a bowl placed over the entire area. This bowl is smoke, haze, and other hydrocarbon pollutants rising above the huge metropolitan area. Down in the street, the air is terrible. As Robert and Leona Rienow report:

> A recent scientific analysis of New York City atmosphere concluded that a New Yorker on the street took into his lungs the equivalent in toxic materials of 38 cigarettes a day.[15]

Partly because of conditions like this, emphysema is the fastest growing cause of death in this country. Deaths from this disease have increased more than eight times since 1950. Asthma, acute infections of the upper respiratory tract, common colds, and other health problems have been traced by epidemiological studies to increased air pollution. The city of London has been suffering from contaminated air for over 500 years, and current attempts to pass antipollution laws can trace many of their arguments back to these times. The air over Moscow is reportedly becoming more and more polluted, as Russian industry increased production. Japanese cities suffer from perhaps the worst air in the entire world, but major United States cities also feel the effects daily.

There are many different forms this pollution of the atmosphere can take, including carbon monoxide, sulfur dioxide, nitrogen oxide, unburned hydrocarbons, and particulate matter. The sources of these pollutants are many, but as Table 13.1 clearly shows, the automobile plays a major role. The 90 million American automobiles were, by the late 1960s, putting into the atmosphere an estimated 66 million tons of carbon monoxide, 1 million tons of sulfur dioxide, 12 million tons of hydrocarbons, 1 million tons of particulate matter, and 6 million tons of nitrogen oxides per year. Paul Ehrlich has calculated that, on a daily basis, this amounts to pollutants weighing more than a line of cars placed bumper to bumper stretching from Chicago to New York.[16]

As a result of this garbage in the air, there are estimated to be about 110,000 deaths per year due partly to air pollution. And about 50,000 people die each year from cancer of the respiratory tract. In addition, there are direct costs borne by the places where air pollution is intense. For instance, steel deteriorates more quickly due to the influence of some pollutants; thus the train cars and rails

TABLE 13.1 Air Pollution in the United States by Source, 1976

Pollutant	Total Emissions (mil. tons)	Controllable Emissions (mil. tons)						Misc. Uncontrollable (mil. tons)	Percent of Total		
		Transportation		Fuel Combustion		Industrial Processes	Solid Waste Disposal		Transportation	Fuel Combustion	Industrial
		Total	Road Vehicles	Total	Electric Utilities						
Carbon monoxide	96.1	76.8	67.7	1.3	.3	8.6	3.1	6.3	80.0	1.4	8.9
Sulfur oxides	29.6	.9	.4	24.1	19.4	4.5	—	.1	3.0	81.4	15.2
Hydrocarbons	30.7	11.9	10.2	1.5	.1	10.4	.9	6.1	38.7	5.0	33.7
Particulates	14.8	1.3	.9	5.1	3.5	6.9	.4	1.0	9.0	34.3	47.0
Nitrogen oxides	25.3	11.1	8.6	13.0	7.3	.8	.1	.3	43.9	51.3	3.0

Source: Bureau of the Census, *Statistical Abstract of the United States, 1978* (Washington, D.C.: U.S. Government Printing Office, 1978), p. 215.

in England need to be replaced more often because of sulfur pollution. Rubber also deteriorates when exposed to certain pollutants, which crack the walls of tires. And women walking in downtown Chicago have reported that their nylon stockings disintegrate.[17] The Public Health Service surveyed the effects of air pollution on expenditures for the cleaning and repair of residences and the health care of people who have been exposed to dirty air (see Table 13.2). The total costs, amounting to about $12 billion per year are largely the result of automobile emissions, which create a brownish smog composed of unburned gasoline and nitrogen oxides.

Los Angeles has the worst air pollution problem of any American city, exacerbated by another problem, *atmospheric inversion*. In many places, air pollutants are carried off quickly by the wind; in Los Angeles, a layer of warm air above the cooler ground air prevents any pollutants from escaping. This smog imperils human life, due to factors we are only beginning to realize. For example, genetic damage as a result of smog is beginning to be of concern to many scientists. Laboratory studies done with mice show that reproduction may be endangered:

> When male and female mice were made to breathe chemically produced "smog," a striking decrease in reproductive capacity occurred. Females conceived less often and when they did the size of the litters was smaller than average.[18]

Furthermore, pollutants in the air interact in complex ways with each other and with other elements in our ecosystem. While it is hard to pinpoint short-run effects, mounting evidence indicates that air pollution is a major cause of human health problems. That

TABLE 13.2 Cost of Cleaning a Residence in an Industrial Town

Outside maintenance of house	$ 17.00
Inside maintenance of house	32.00
Laundry	25.00
Hair, facial care, etc.	10.00
	$ 84.00

Source: A. J. Haagen-Smit, "Air Conservation," in Arthur Boughey (ed.), *Man and the Environment* (New York: Macmillan, 1971), p. 320.

many are potential victims of pollution is indicated in that the concentration of certain automobile exhaust hydrocarbons is 50 million times greater in New York City, Chicago, and Los Angeles — our largest cities — than it is in the Grand Canyon.[19]

Industrial processors and power plants also add to the problem, producing a greyish smog rather than the brownish one associated with pollution from automobiles. Power plants produce large amounts of sulfur oxides, which are quite damaging. Although efforts have been made to burn fuels with low sulfur content or to use desulfurated oil in the cities with major problems, the total output of energy from these plants and the total amount of such fuels used have been steadily increasing. This has caused many scientists to be concerned with an air pollution problem that had not been regarded as a problem before. Carbon dioxide released by the burning of fossil fuels over the past hundred years has been accumulating in the atmosphere at a steadily increasing rate. The amount of oxygen needed to burn all the fuel consumed in the United States has been estimated to be about 3.8 billion tons annually. On a massive scale, then, the balance between carbon dioxide and oxygen is being slowly upset.

There appears to be two other major negative effects accruing from increased release of carbon monoxide into the atmosphere. Carbon dioxide traps surface heat created because of infrared radiation from the sun's rays. Carbon dioxide has what is called a *greenhouse effect,* acting much like glass window panes that trap heat inside. As more carbon dioxide accumulates, then, the world's climates may be changed. The second potentially catastrophic effect carbon dioxide has is that it interferes with the ability of ocean bacteria to maintain the acidity of seawater, a process of vital importance for the reproduction of bacteria. These bacteria are important because they fit in a complex process that produces most of the oxygen released into the atmosphere by plants. If there are no longer plants to replenish oxygen, we will undoubtedly suffer.

The long-range effects of releasing large amounts of carbon dioxide into the atmosphere are open to debate. It has been hypothesized that the ice caps may melt as the temperature of the earth rises because of the greenhouse effect. If this occurred, there could be massive flooding of coastal plains. Since 15 percent of the United States population lives in coastal states, this result would clearly be damaging. As for the acidity of water, "The effects of altered acidity on marine life under laboratory conditions are well known to experimental biologists. Marine fish (herring for example) can tolerate only minute alterations in the acidity of seawater."[20] Even if these two dangerous results are challenged in a scientific debate, why are we willing to take the chance of endangering our life-support system after it has been around for millions of years? The wholesale release of carbon dioxide may prove to be the most damaging air pollutant yet. If we simply wait for scientists to agree on the global effects, the series of disastrous events may be impossible to reverse.

Water Pollution

A person can go for a considerable time without food, but can live only a short time without water. Life on this planet is so dependent upon water that the two are inseparable. In the United States, the average rainfall amounts to about thirty inches per year. Multiplying this by the nation's land area means that the total daily rainfall is about 4,300 billion gallons. Of this, 1,300 billion gallons run off or remain as ground water, while the remainder evaporates from the soil or is used by plants and then released into the atmosphere. Of the 1,300 billion gallons available for use, the United States currently is using about one quarter. This is probably the upper limit of what we can expect to use, for two major reasons. First, the water table is dropping in parts of the United States; this indicates we are already overusing the available water supply.[21]

Second, most of the water not being used is so polluted as to be unsuitable for drinking or cooking. The ecologist Paul Ehrlich tells of some grafitti he saw scribbled in a public restroom along the upper Mississippi River: "Flush the toilet, they need the water in St. Louis." This bit of sarcastic humor may, however, contain more truth than the people in St. Louis would care to admit.[22] The Public Health Service has released a list of sixty cities whose water supplies were rated as unsatisfactory or a potential health hazard. As towns and cities have grown, their sewage treatment facilities have failed to keep pace. Such facilities are seldom built in anticipation of growth. Money is not appropriated for expanded sewage treatment until demand has created a catch-up problem. Often in areas under development, septic tanks are installed, which can discharge waste water into the same water table used for drinking.

And as industry grows in an area, plant owners look for some place to dump their waste products at the lowest possible cost. Nothing works quite so well as a river for making your waste problems belong to somebody else. The major rivers of this country today contain large amounts of lead, sulfuric acid, hydrofloric acid, and ammonia, dumped there as part of many different manufacturing processes. Because of present bans on dumping waste into public waterways, some firms have started dumping their pollutants into underground wells. In one part of New Jersey, this practice is thought to have contaminated the well water of people living over forty miles away from the dumping site.

Many problems of water pollution are related to agricultural practices, as well as those created by industry. Nitrates from fertilizers have become serious problems in parts of the Midwest. For example, the city of Elgin, Minnesota had to find a new water supply after its wells were contaminated by nitrate runoff. However, the classic case of water pollution in the United States has to be the damage done to Lake Erie by the 13 million people who live along its shores.

As part of the Great Lakes, Lake Erie is one of a series of lakes made by a great advancing ice sheet during the last Ice Age. Its age has been put at about 20,000 years and when first discovered by American settlers, it was filled with clear water. Lake Erie used to support a large and varied population of fish, and had a complex ecosystem capable of supporting many different kinds of life. "Before 1900, Lake Erie yielded a million pound annual crop of sturgeon . . . in 1964, only 4,000 pounds of sturgeon were taken. In 1920, northern pike which had until then yielded million pound catches, all but disappeared."[23]

Other species of fish have also vanished, their disappearance traced to the process called *eutrophication*. This means the overfertilization of a lake, which reduces the oxygen available to the complex chain of marine organisms on which fish depend. Each year, the cities along the borders of Lake Erie dump their waste into the lake or rivers leading to it. One of the rivers feeding into the lake, the Cuyahoga, has become so polluted that it caught fire. Although that fire was put out by the fire department, the river remains a fire hazard. While many of these cities and towns have ordinances preventing citizens from dumping wastes in public waters, it is often the cities and towns themselves that do so.

Phosphates from industrial processes, fertilizers, and laundry detergents are dumped by the river into the lake at the rate of 174,000 pounds per day. At the other end of the lake, via the Niagara River, only 24,000 pounds leave the lake each day. Commoner has calculated then that about 55 million pounds of pollutants remain in the lake each year. What happens to all these phosphates is complex, but Commoner summarized what has happened to the lake:

> Thus, instead of Lake Erie forming a waterway for sending wastes to the sea, it has become a trap that is gradually collecting on its bottom much of the waste material dumped into it over the years — a kind of huge underwater cesspool.[24]

Additionally, the lake is characterized by an increasingly high oxygen debt, which had

The rivers that flow into Lake Erie make deadly contributions to the destructive aging of that Great Lake. One of those rivers, the Cuyahoga, pours in thousands of pounds of pollutants, invisible and all too visible, each day. In its role as a carrier of filth, the Cuyahoga itself became a fire hazard, burning furiously. The spectacle of the burning river spurred a vigorous clean-up program.

previously gone unnoticed. Certain forms of iron have combined with the bottom mud to form a layer of material protecting the surface water from the oxygen-demanding sludge buried below it. But in a critical absence of oxygen, the iron compound itself breaks down, releasing what has accumulated during the last century, with the potential outcome being the killing of the lake in a short time. This has not happened yet, but as the lake becomes more polluted, on top of a century's neglect, the final great collapse is imminent. Lake Erie typifies what has happened to many bodies of water in the United States. They have aged because of the pollutants being pumped and dumped into them, until they age 5,000 years in the space of only fifty.

Pesticides

The rivers and streams of this country carry to the oceans heavy metals, phosphates, nitrates, and other industrial and agricultural chemicals. They have also carried DDT by the hundreds of thousands of tons. Traces of DDT have been found in the eggs of the penguins of Antarctica, while the milk of human mothers has been found to contain levels of DDT above that deemed safe for the milk of cows. As Paul Ehrlich has pointed out, "Most mothers' milk in the United States contains so much DDT that it would be declared illegal in interstate commerce if it were sold as cows' milk."[25] And around the world, the daily DDT intake of infants is about twice the maximum considered safe by the World Health Organization.

DDT was originally discovered in the 1870s, but its value as a pesticide was only realized during the late 1930s. It was primarily used to kill the mosquito that transmits malaria, and seemed only beneficial until its damaging environmental effects were publicized by Rachel Carson in her book *Silent Spring*.[26] Her concern grew out of certain side effects associated with the growing use of DDT, although it was only one of a number of pesticides American manufacturers produced at the rate of one billion pounds per year.[27] Carson focused on DDT because, during the 1960s, it was used at the rate of about 100,000 tons per year because it was quite inexpensive (at seventeen cents per pound) and effective. Within a few years after the publication of Carson's book, it was estimated that 1 million tons of DDT had accumulated in the earth's surface. Carson's fears were valid.

Many problems are associated with the widespread use of DDT. First, it kills in a nonselective way. It was aimed at the 1 percent of all insects people have labeled as pests, but it is equally effective in killing those insects vital to ecosystems. Second, its use has not been careful or well regulated, for people thought that the greater the size of the target and its population, the more DDT should be used. This was a mistake because its effectiveness is not influenced at all by the size of the target population. Third, DDT accumulates in animals and fishes as they feed on the organisms that inadvertently pick it up from the water and soil, and as it accumulates it becomes more potent. McHale has estimated that the DDT is concentrated by a factor of 10 million times by the time it reaches certain birds at the end of the food chain.[28]

Finally, in terms of the target population, insects, the effectiveness of DDT has recently diminished, while it still damages higher animals. Insects that used to be killed by DDT are now developing an immunity to it. This is possible because many generations of target species have reproduced since DDT spraying started. Genetic changes are made easier by having large numbers of short-lived generations; thus, mosquitos and cockroaches have become relatively immune. Yet in birds and animals who breed more slowly (such as the brown pelican), the effect on reproductive ability has been disastrous. Decreases in egg weight and thin shells have been traced directly to the interference of DDT with calcium metabolism in these birds. The list of species endangered by DDT poisoning grows as we begin to understand how this deadly chemical undercuts the ecosystem of all animals, including humans.

Now that we are becoming aware of the level and amount of DDT poisoning, it would seem likely that a major attempt would be made to move away from the production of chemical pesticides. This is especially true given that many being considered as replacements for DDT also have negative side effects of their own, and we know much less about many of these than we do about DDT. However, according to government figures, the total output of pesticides is increasing at a rapid rate (see Figure 13.3). As can be seen from this data, we continue to produce and use pesticides at an alarming rate. None of these occur in nature in very large quantities, but eventually these pesticides will find their way into our water and air, where their effects on animal and plant life, now not well understood, can only be feared.

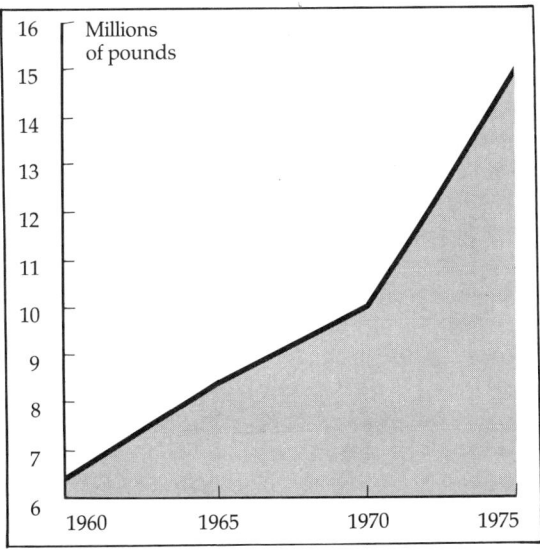

FIGURE 13.3 Production of Pesticides, 1960–1975

Source: Bureau of the Census, *Statistical Abstract of the United States, 1977* (Washington, D.C.: U.S. Government Printing Office, 1977), p. 207.

Other Forms of Pollution

Each year, people in the United States junk 7 million automobiles. They also scrap some 10 million tons of iron and steel and some 3 million tons of waste rock and other byproducts of the industrial process. Add to these major forms of solid waste all the bits and pieces of garbage, from broken bottles to pop tops, and the damage to the environment staggers the imagination. Fifty-five billion cans, 26 billion bottles and jars, 65 billion bottle caps, and one-half billion dollars worth of packaging material add up to a major problem for every city and town in the land. In some places it is buried, usually adding to the pollution of underground waters; in other places it is burned, fouling the air. According to Edward Gross:

1. The total amount of all types of solid waste is 3.5 billion tons.
2. The amount of refuse collected per person per day is about five pounds, totaling 190 million tons each year.
3. By 1980, this will reach 340 million tons.
4. The country's total annual trash bill is $4.5 billion.[29]

The Department of Health, Education and Welfare has reported that 94 percent of all waste disposal sites are unacceptable because they are unsanitary, ugly, or pollute the environment. Many attempts have been made to solve this aspect of the problem, ranging from burning these waste to generate electricity to turning them into compost and returning them to the soil as fertilizer. However, none seem to work profitably with current methods of collection and sorting; and while these problems are being attacked, the mountain of garbage and trash grows higher with each passing day.

The catalog of things man has injected into this environment is almost endless.

Heavy metals like lead, cadmium, arsenic, and mercury have been systematically dumped wherever water would carry them quickly out of sight. Another dangerous pollutant not mentioned above, which has entered both the atmosphere and water, is *asbestos fiber*. Asbestos is found wherever a highly heat resistant and virtually indestructible coating is needed. The brake linings of cars, insulation for furnaces, and many building materials contain asbestos fiber. When any of this material is inhaled, as it often is by people working on automobiles or walking by an area where old buildings are being demolished, the effects can be serious. The natural cleaning action of the lungs is helpless to deal with asbestos material and the chances of cancer developing increase greatly. Lung cancer was found to be seven times more frequent in people whose occupations exposed them to asbestos than in a control group. When dead bodies have been examined in large urban areas, the results have been surprising. In Pittsburgh, 41 percent of all autopsies were found to have growths due to asbestos in their lungs; in Montreal, the total was 48 percent. In three New York City hospitals, nearly half of all lung tissue samples showed asbestos.[30] Something that affects half our urban population and has been directly connected to the development of cancer must be considered a major health hazard. It can no longer be ignored.

While there are numerous other environmental problems, including thermal pollution and resource depletion, the last one we will deal with is the problem of noise. With over 75 percent of our population now living in urban areas, it often seems that there is no longer any quiet place to go. Even the large national parks are crowded now, with noisy motorcycles and people watching televisions or listening to radios. *Noise*, defined as unwanted sound, comes from every imaginable source. Sound levels are measured in *decibels*, with a classroom being about 35 decibles, 55 in a restaurant, and 60 or higher for a football game. Levels above 90 decibels can be tolerated for only a short time, and levels of about 130 are at the threshold of pain. Anyone who has been close to a jet airplane revving its motors before takeoff has experienced noise at decibel levels where pain occurs.

Yet people continue to live around city airports, where they often must tolerate noise levels above 100 decibels. As a result of this kind of exposure, older people in our society suffer from a higher loss of hearing than do people in other societies. Reactions to noise may manifest themselves in various ways, including gastrointestinal upset that can lead to ulcers. Hypertension, altered responses to allergic material, and migraine headaches may all one day be directly traced to increased exposure to noise. Work in this area has just begun and because of the complexity of the problem, it is often very difficult to trace the direct effects of increased noise levels on human behavior. However, as we are learning more about the effects of noise, we are beginning to realize that some quiet is important to our health, particularly when a person is trying to sleep. It seems fair to say that with growing urbanization and increased use of lawn mowers, motorcycles, jet aircraft, and stereo sets, noise pollution will become an increasingly severe problem in the future.

Summary

Over the years, because of changes in technology, increases in production, and growth in population, we have gradually dirtied the environment. Similarly, in an effort to benefit people by removing the insects that cause disease, we have spread harmful pesticides throughout the world. The result is damage that can hardly be assessed. We have caused lakes to die, animals to become extinct, and cities to sit in clouds of dirt. The question now is whether we can do anything about it, or if it's already too late.

ATTEMPTS AT DEALING WITH THE PROBLEM

Different Views of the Problem

There are a wide variety of ideas of what should be done about the problems outlined above. Basically, these ideas can be put into two major schools of thought. One school believes in a *technological fix* becoming available, in which technological solutions are found for whatever problems we create. The other school contains those who believe that technology not only is a false god, but that it is the villain. For these people, technological solutions only compound the environmental effects. Kenneth Boulding has coined the concept, "Space Ship Earth," to reflect the view that our environment is finite. Let us examine both sides to see the arguments each marshalls in support.

Some of the arguments came to a head as an outgrowth of work done by Donella Meadows and her colleages in a study called *The Limits to Growth*. Her conclusions were published as a report on the present predicament of humankind. Given the nature of environmental damage, this report asked some significant questions and came up with some interesting answers. But as soon as they were published, Meadows was charged with being biased and inaccurate and with basing her work on false assumptions.

Meadows started out with a set of assumptions about the nature of future changes in technology, the extent of the depletion of resources, population growth, and pollution, based on long-range trends. She then used a computer to work out a series of models of the future in which these factors interacted with each other in different ways. Her conclusions were that even with a greatly increased resource base and rapid changes in the development of new technology, at present rates the upper levels of industrial and population growth will be reached before the year 2100. In other words, given the finite size of our planet and the way the various factors have been growing recently, they reach the limits of their growth in just over 100 years. At that point, because of increases in population, pollution levels, and the lack of available resources, the world economic system will collapse, producing widespread starvation, with no ability to do anything about it. The central point of Meadows's work is the inability of technology to solve or fix problems caused by trying to maintain infinite growth.

If these are the ideas one group of scholars has developed about the role of technology in solving the environmental problems, what about the other side? Many of the leading spokesmen for the school which does believe in the ability of technology to solve the problems of the future usually base their arguments on the following points:

1. Nuclear fuel promises inexhaustible, cheap energy.
2. One resource can be substituted for another as it becomes depleted.
3. Population problems can be solved, through technology.

4. Economics will be the only factor governing the future availability of resources.

In the past, it has seemed that technology could solve whatever problems arose in the course of relating man to his environment. Skyscrapers solved the problem of urban space by using the technology of the elevator; this school argues that through traffic engineering, major problems of transportation will be solved in like fashion. People who have continued faith in technology point to other examples of technological success. Lower and lower grade copper ores are now being used because of advances in processing technology. In 1880, according to LaMont Cole, the lowest grade of copper ore that could be economically refined was about 3 percent; by 1906, it was 2.1 percent; today, it is only 0.4 percent. Increased technology has allowed the use of materials that at another level of technology were close to being depleted.[31]

A short examination of the role government has played in developing technological solutions to human problems might shed some light on this debate over technology. A great deal of the funding for research to develop new technologies has come from the federal government. Government funding has given space exploration high priority, putting this one aspect of our technology far ahead of other areas. In a penetrating article, Julian McCaull reported that from 1961 to 1967 the government funded 2 million human-years of research and development activity for the Defense Department, 1 million for the space program, and 175,000 for nuclear products related to military needs. By comparison, only 53,000 was dedicated to environmental knowledge or improvement.[32] This demonstrates why there is a good reason to expect we have not progressed far in our understanding of the problems of ecology.

The other major source of funding for technology comes from the private sector, industrial firms in search of a profit. While there has been continuing debate on the role of corporate responsibility toward society, clearly the company unable to turn a profit will not be around long. The biologist Rene Dubos points out why we probably shouldn't look to the private sector for pollution control: "But the tendency at present is to determine the use of lands and waters, mountains and valleys only on the basis of short-range economic benefits."[33]

The growing awareness of the fact that some individuals and groups profit from environmental damage while others foot the bill has raised many serious questions about our political and economic system. Decisions will need to be made in the future about which is the greater right, that to enjoy a livable environment or that to profit from creating and satisfying certain needs using technologies with severe environmental impact. Technology cannot tell us whether the cities should be rebuilt or whether the flight to suburbia should be allowed to continue. Whether it is better to send a man to the moon or spend equivalent funds for new housing for urban poor is not a scientific question. Such questions involve value judgments.

Massive environmental damage and pollution have raised many of the same questions as those involved in other social problems. Who benefits? Who pays? What is the legitimate role of government in maintaining a balance between the two? Environmental damage and quality have become political issues, something that may help to set up new political coalitions between groups formerly very much at odds with each other.

Environmental Groups

Based on their different perceptions of the essential nature of the problem, distinct groups have formed throughout the country. These have ranged from ultraconservative sportsman's clubs to women in Florida who joined together to get laundry detergents containing phosphates banned from the supermarket shelves. The Sierra Club and the Audubon Society were the first of a series of ecologically minded organizations to be established on a permanent basis. More recently, however, a series of loosely confederated groups have formed, focusing on particular environmental issues. One of these, the Clamshell Alliance, has tried to get a ban on nuclear power reactors. Another militant group, Greenpeace, has become involved in a wide range of environmental issues, from the killing of whales by the Russians to the testing of nuclear devices in Alaska by the United States. A movement like this one, willing to cross international boundaries, reflects a recognition that political boundaries often shield those doing ecological damage.

But still, for many Americans, the need to

Decisions that affect the environment are made in Congress and in corporate boardrooms. But groups of concerned citizens are organizing to pressure those decision makers and to awaken the power of the general public. One of the most visible and influential environmental groups is Greenpeace, shown here protesting the annual slaughter of baby Canadian seals for their fur.

take the environment into account interferes with our ability to exploit the environment for profit and for progress. The federal government now requires all federal projects to complete an *environmental impact statement* outlining the effect the undertaking will have on the natural world. One such statement focused conservation arguments on a small fish named the snail darter. Construction was halted on a dam being built because it was determined that completion would threaten the snail darter, designated an endangered species and thus accorded government protection. Many congressmen and senators who supported the legislation creating the endangered species list felt this concern for the snail darter was not in keeping with the intention of Congress. But others argue that once a species disappears it will never exist again, and that disappearance cannot be allowed. The debate over the snail darter has once again brought to a head the opposing sides of the debate over environmental protection.

Pollution, involving the air, water, and wildlife, is a problem for us all. But as so often happens, we figure that once the pollution crosses some political boundary, it becomes someone else's problem. Oil spills off the coast of France and water pollution in Japan do not arouse the same responses as oil spills off the Texas gulf coast. But they should, because they reflect a dangerous attitude toward the environment. Eventually that attitude will hit home; it may then be too late to do anything but clean up the mess, if that is even possible.

The government seems to recognize this. The Environmental Protection Agency (EPA) has been formed as part of the government's attempt to get into the act of environmental concern. In addition to requiring the environmental impact statement, the EPA has begun to make funds available for pollution

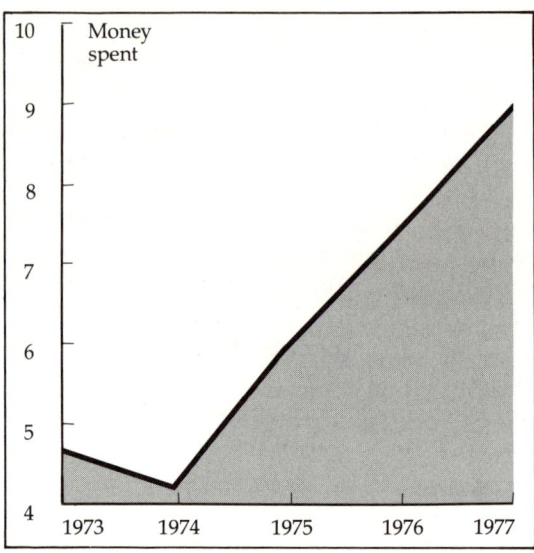

FIGURE 13.4 Federal Funds for Pollution Control, 1973–1977 (in Billions of Dollars)

Source: Bureau of the Census, *Statistical Abstract of the United States, 1977* (Washington, D.C.: U.S. Government Printing Office, 1977), p. 203.

control. As Figure 13.4 shows clearly, there has been a sharp increase in these funds since 1974.

But in contrast to the government efforts, we find many groups of varying interests whose actions deeply affect environmental issues. The National Association of Manufacturers, thousands of local chambers of commerce, graduate schools of business, and the boards of directors of every large corporation make plans on a day-to-day basis for the further use of the environment. Unfortunately, many of these plans will not be ecologically sound.

The Politics and Economics of Technology

The environmental crisis translates quickly into the economics and politics of technology. In many future environmental battles, corporate attorneys will face attorneys hired by groups who want the environment protected. But while they are a significant part of the problem, the corporations who hire those attorneys and use the air, rivers, and land in profitable ways are not the whole of the problem. We must remember that corporations produce whatever they do in order to satisfy demand. And a large percentage of the total output of goods and services falls into the category of consumer goods we all purchase.

In a society like ours, it is not possible to separate economics from politics. Many persons in the ecology movement realize that at the heart of both economics and ecology lie basic political issues. Laws passed through the political process can cost billions of dollars to giant corporations and affect their profit margins substantially. This does not mean that the economies of noncapitalistic countries are not also subject to political pressures; based on the damage done to both Soviet and American environments, Marshall Goldman has concluded that it may be harder to prevent environmental damage in a socialistic society.[34] However, the point is that the politics of our society have had enormous ramifications on ecology, as the following examples will make clear.

The Santa Barbara oil spill of 1969 provides one example of the political dimensions of the environmental crisis and illustrates the types of actions undertaken to cope with the problem. Before offshore oil drilling was to proceed, federal regulations were drawn up providing for safety procedures to be followed and a course of action to be taken in the event of an accident, with a penalty stipulated for noncompliance. When a Union Oil well began to pour oil into the sea, it became obvious the regulations in force at the time were totally inadequate to cope with the massive amounts of environmental damage that followed. The reason was simple; in writing the regulations the government had turned to the oil companies for wording. The government also had turned to experts in universities for help in drawing up regulations, but many of the university experts were from departments that got extensive grants and subsidies from the oil companies. Much reluctance to recommend more stringent guidelines by the California universities' experts has been traced to the influence of oil money on the operation of university departments of geology and other closely related natural sciences.

Since the Santa Barbara spill, the amount of oil consumed by Americans has steadily increased. The reluctance to do anything serious to cut back on the use of fossil fuels has led to our importing an ever-increasing supply of the oil we consume. Because of this we have an unfavorable balance of payments, which has resulted in the dollar plummeting to record lows against other more stable currencies. Also a result, and more to the point of this chapter, there has been a sharp increase in the amount of oil spilled in United States waters by tankers and barges (see Figure 13.5).

Government itself, both at the state and federal levels, is often reluctant to take steps needed to reduce environmental damage, for this usually means reducing profits. When government is committed to financing wars and domestic social projects, it desperately needs future economic growth to pay the bills for its programs. Ensuring an ever-increasing gross national product is part of the complex process of establishing budgetary policy. In our society, taxes on corporate profits make up a large proportion of the monies the government gets to run its programs. To reduce profits by requiring ecological responsibility is to undercut government revenues.

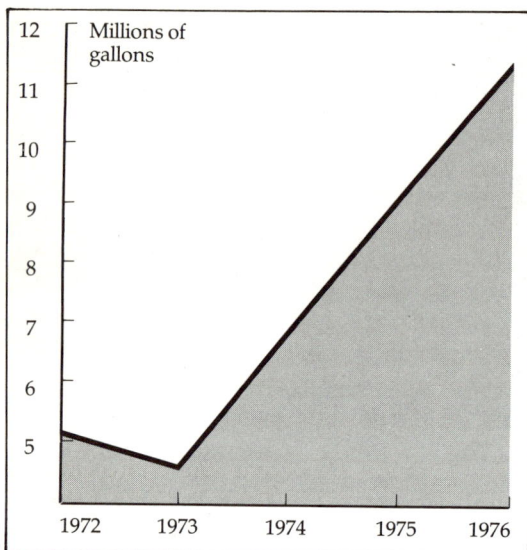

FIGURE 13.5 Oil Spilled from Tankers and Barges in U.S. Waters, 1972–1976

Source: Bureau of the Census, *Statistical Abstract of the United States, 1977* (Washington, D.C.: U.S. Government Printing Office, 1977), p. 206.

One other reason why government has failed to act decisively on environmental issues is of importance. Since the 1940s, the strategy for solving many social problems has been to expand the economy. Cures for poverty, racism, housing, and educational problems have all been based on the strategy of increasing affluence for all Americans. Rather than attacking many of these problems directly — for example, redistributing income to reduce poverty — government policy has been directed at ensuring steady growth in the GNP. It is hoped that with this growth of our economic resources, some will filter down to the bottom levels of the society. But with this growth has come greater and greater environmental damage, and that damage will continue as long as those solutions are attempted.

The Sierra Club and the Audubon Society do not make the decisions affecting environmental quality. These decisions are made in corporate directors' meetings, in government economic conferences, and by untold millions of people when they do their daily shopping. We are not saying that the conservation and ecologically minded organizations have not done a good deal to bring about recognition of the problem. But many of the actual solutions require legal changes, and in more than a few courtroom fights, the power and influence of corporate America has been overwhelming. The skill of a David is needed against the Goliath-like power of economic growth. The major question to be raised is whether or not this skill will ever be forthcoming.

Attempts at Increasing Public Awareness

In the late 1960s, as the environmental movement became fashionable among middle-class people, there was an attempt to awaken the rest of the population to the problems of ecology. This effort culminated in 1970 with the celebration of Earth Day, an attempt to get the message across to a larger segment of the population to foster political pressure for environmental protection. In retrospect, many changes of the early 1970s can be seen as a product of increased public awareness of the problem. But it is also clear that in the time between the first Earth Day and now, the environmental movement has waned. The systematic and organized despoliation of the environment has not abated. Environmental damage has continued on at the same levels in almost all areas, partly as the result of increasing consumption accompanying general prosperity. There has been a move to smaller cars, but people are driving more than ever before. The environmental movement has simply not caught on.

In fact, the movement has been transformed. With the onset of the energy crisis, many who were involved in environmentalism have advocated *solar energy* as the solution. The appeal of solar energy is enormous. The sun promises a source of power that is more economical, inexhaustible, and not subject to embargo. Because solar technology is clean it appeals to the environmentalist concerned with air pollution, nuclear waste, and thermal pollution.

But the solar energy movement has a serious drawback. It has never questioned what is basic to the American standard of living in the first place, the amount of energy we consume. America is the most wasteful of nations, using at least four times more energy per capita than the next closest competitors. While the standard of living in Sweden, Switzerland, or Denmark is roughly comparable with our own, on a total quantity basis, our per capita energy consumption level is at least four times greater than any other nation in the world. This overconsumption is the product of the ethic we described earlier, which values the traditional single-family suburban household relying on the private automobile for transportation.

The essential trouble with efforts like Sun Day, the 1978 day meant to promote solar energy, is that they promise us more of the same without facing the inadequacies in a way of life based on materialism. Such issues as the need for different residential patterns or the need to move toward mass transit are largely ignored. In other words, Americans have responded so well to Sun Day because they are fed up with increasing utility bills that leave them with cold swimming pools and growing winter heating costs. These are reasonable objections, given our basic cultural assumptions. But if the central problem is our standard of living in general, our styles of life, and our level of consumption, which the environment had better not stand in the way of, what effect has Sun Day had on environmental issues? Unless our way of life changes, future Sun Days will only glorify an ever-increasing standard of living for an ever-greater number of Americans, leaving untouched the question of the quality of life. But that is the question that should be at the heart of the environmental issue.

Iatrogenic Effects

Back in the early 1950s, noted scientists were becoming alarmed over the growing pollution of the atmosphere by the automobile engine. The Ford Motor Company was approached in 1953 by a Los Angeles county supervisor who objected to the increased smog levels beginning to appear. Ford's response was this statement:

> The Ford engineering staff, although mindful that automobile engines produce gases, feel that these waste vapors are dissipated in the atmosphere quickly and do not present an air pollution problem.[35]

Ford was then asked to do something about the problem, a request it did not respond to for over three years. Then, California took the lead in writing legislation for antipollution devices, the first law being adopted in 1963. But compliance by industry proved to be too little, too late, for while numerous devices were being added piecemeal, the problem became steadily worse.

Although by 1970 each individual new car polluted a little less, there were so many more cars on the road that the smog problem had worsened significantly. In 1970 a series

Solar energy is, as far as we know, clean, reusable, and economical—qualities that fossil fuels cannot claim. The south-facing solar collector panels of this house, designed and built by students at Pittsburgh's Carnegie-Mellon University, allow it to be heated by the sun.

of amendments to the Clear Air Act set emission standards for the entire automobile industry. Carbon monoxide, nitrogen oxides, and underburned hydrocarbons would be allowed to be emitted only at or below certain established levels. The automobile industry said that it did not have the technology available to meet these standards; at the same time, Ralph Nader noted that General Motors reportedly had spent $250 million changing their slogan. Couldn't some of this money have been spent on research to lessen pollution? Since these 1970 amendments included a timetable for implementation, each year the automobile companies put up a major effort to get the dates moved back. And only reluctantly did they develop the *catalytic converter,* to abate the problem of unburned hydrocarbons and carbon monoxide.

Despite the auto companies' reluctance, they finally acted, and one step seems to have been taken toward solving the problem. But like so many other solutions to social problems, the catalytic converter has iatrogenic effects. In addition to using up large amounts of platinum, an increasingly scarce metal, the new converters require the use of unleaded gasoline. On the surface, this seems to be a fine idea, for the lead in gasoline was a known pollutant. But the element used to replace it, phosphorus, may prove to be an even greater health hazard than lead. Some scientists hypothesize that when these new phosphorus compounds are released in the same quantity as lead has been, the environment will suffer more. While some effects do remain speculative, it illustrates well what we face in expecting technology to solve any environmental problem. A technological fix, even if it works, may compound the problem.

Iatrogenic effects can also be found in the advance of *nuclear power,* on which great hope is pinned. This has been billed as pollution-free power, able to avoid the environmental damage resulting from burning fossil fuels. But that claim ignores the potential hazards. First, there is the problem of where to get the fuel to run nuclear reactors. A basic fuel, uranium, is not found in concentrated amounts anywhere. At our present level of scientific knowledge, finding it will mean extensive new mining operations, processing millions of tons of waste rock to get at small amounts of uranium. New Hampshire, containing extensive amounts of granite in which uranium is often found, may be defaced to air condition Boston or New York.

In addition to the problem of fuel, there is another problem raised by nuclear power, *thermal pollution,* unnatural heating of water. The only efficient way to cool a nuclear reactor is through vast amounts of water. With power plants located on rivers, estuaries, or along the coast, major changes in marine ecology can be expected because the water used to cool the reactor becomes heated and is simply pumped back into the source it came from. If present trends continue, by 1985 one-quarter of the annual water runoff in the United States will be from cooling power plants.[36] The effect on marine life would be devastating.

Finally, pollution-free electricity does not appear possible from nuclear power because of the problem of radiation. Although the safety record of nuclear power plants was good for many years, as more are built the probability of an incident triggering a nuclear disaster grows with each year. Early in 1979 we were confronted with just such an occurrence, when the nuclear power plant at Three Mile Island, near Harrisburg, Pennsylvania, malfunctioned. While the accident did not immediately destroy anything, the potential for devastation was high enough that the governor of Pennsylvania ordered the evacuation of all people living within ninety miles of the plant. And though no one died immediately afterward, the long-term effects of the radiation leaked into the atmosphere are still being debated. The number of people who will suffer from this accident is unknown.

And besides the possibility of a reactor breakdown, another problem remains over what to do with nuclear wastes. Enormous numbers of barrels of radioactive waste have already been dumped off the coast of California. Incredibly many of these barrels have a life span of twenty years, whereas the half-life of the nuclear waste inside is hundreds of years. We have only a short while to wait until these barrels burst open, and we must pay for our carelessness during the beginning of this so-called pollution-free nuclear age.

Nuclear power, while holding enormous long-range promise, does not offer something for nothing. It contains many elements of risk to human life and well being, which are understated by some experts. New forms of pollution will go hand in hand with the desire to consume more and more energy, even if it comes from nuclear reactors. No solution is simple.

That the environmental problem is complex can be seen in the iatrogenic effects of another attempted solution. The use and production of DDT was halted in the United States about 1970, but stopping production may have more serious effects than DDT poisoning itself. The problem can be seen in how effective DDT had been on the island of Ceylon. After an extensive campaign of spraying during the late 1950s and early 1960s, the number of cases of malaria reported in 1962 was thirty-one. In 1963 it was seventeen. The program was eliminated in 1964; the number of cases rose to 150. There were 308 in 1965, 499 in 1966, and 3,466 in 1967. By 1968, a full fledged-epidemic was underway, with almost 60,000 cases reported in January and February alone. The total for 1968 was over 1 million cases, out of a total population of 12 million. The spraying of DDT was effective, and when the spraying was banned the disease increased 25,000-fold in a few short years.[37]

In judging whether the end of DDT use as a victory for humankind or for the mosquito, one must take into account these facts. Are 1 million cases of malaria worse than the side effects of DDT? This is a difficult question to answer, for it depends on many political and economic considerations. In treating our environment more kindly, we are slowly beginning to learn that there are costs involved. And because our key environmental decisions are always made with an eye on economics, many of the actions taken to solve environmental problems, based on new technology, may end up doing greater long-range damage to the environment than what we are now doing. Solutions often have a way of working in the short run, only to leave hidden long-range effects for future generations to face. We must decide whether we are willing to mortgage generations yet unborn so that we can continue to enjoy the luxuries most of us have come to see as part of our birthright. From the evidence we seem willing to do so, and no technology likely to be developed in the foreseeable future promises to change it.

PROSPECTS FOR SOLVING THE PROBLEM

One major component of the popular belief in the use of science to solve all our problems is summarized in the tenet that knowledge is power. It is claimed that if we only knew a little more, we could probably accomplish miraculous cures. But the key message of ecology is that this thinking is inapplicable to environmental problems. Until the complete faith which people have in science is moderated, there will be little change in how we view the environment that supports our lives. That there are problems that do not respond to a technological fix is not likely to be accepted by most Americans. There is real tragedy in our scientific accomplishments.

The propaganda of the space program or the traveling displays designed by the Atomic Energy Commission to sell people nuclear power subvert the kind of thinking we will need to do if we are to come to grips with the long-range effects of environmental damage. It has been suggested that we do future environmental planning not for next year, or even next decade, but that we should keep an eye on what things might look like in the year 8000 if we continue on as we have for the past one hundred years. From that sort of perspective, it becomes clear that we must change our ways. There are too many environmental limitations to it. We must then confront the other stumbling blocks likely to stand in the way of long-range solutions.

The first stems in part from programs designed to assure people that something is already being done about the problem. For example, plans were proposed in a Midwest industrial area to use only one stream for dumping waste materials, reserving others for recreational purposes. But even if the plan was adopted, 300 pounds of mercury would still reach Lake Erie every day. Similar to pretending the problem is being solved is the strategy of sending it somewhere else. A second proposed way to solve our environmental problem has been to turn to the greater use of imported goods. Then we, the importing country, would be spared the hazards of pollution, which would be transferred to some other part of the world. The cruelty and shortsightedness of the plan is obvious. It is no solution; it merely places the lives and health of strangers in jeopardy rather than Americans.

Another often used solution to the environmental problem is to spend considerable funds which give the appearance of solving the problem while continuing on in the same old fashion. A favorite way that oil, gas, electric, and automobile companies do this is through a flashy advertising campaign based on ecological concepts. Pacific Gas and Electric was advertising that it "Keeps a smile on Mother Nature's face" even while it fought conservationists in the courts. The aluminum industry has made a great effort to present themselves as ecologically minded because their products can be recycled. Atlantic Richfield advertised it was planting grasses in Alaska to heal damage done to North Slope tundra by the pipeline before it was known whether or not the grasses would actually grow. And nuclear power plants producing increased amounts of thermal pollution have even advertised this as a means of drawing fish to an area. If words alone would make the problems go away, they would all have been solved long ago.

While the tactics described above diverted attention from the essential problem, there have been genuine efforts to do something about environmental quality. DDT has been banned, even though many other chlorinated hydrocarbon poisons are still found on the shelves of hardware stores. And the environmental impact statements required for any project involving federal money are a positive step, even though they only require that potential environmental problems be described, not solved. Fortunately, too, the dumping of materials into streams and rivers has been halted in a number of places through state and federal regulations. Many innovative ways of conserving materials and energy have been developed, some of which can probably be made economical. The use of solar energy to heat homes can economically compete with other forms of heating in certain parts of the country. And some cities are doing what a few years ago would have been considered a minor miracle with their garbage, by sorting it, reclaiming the glass, iron, and aluminum, and burning the rest to generate electricity.

In the area of energy, some communities now draw nonpolluting steam from deep within the earth. This *geothermal power* is already in use in Italy, New Zealand, and Japan and is also being tried in California. The large oil companies have actually become energy companies and are hedging their bets in the event that oil runs out or becomes only a secondary source of power. Thirty miles under the earth's crust, the inner core of molten lava reaches some 2000 degrees; deeper down, temperatures top 3500 degrees. This intense heat, combined with the ability to use laser beams for deep hole drilling has made geothermal power of increased interest, especially in a time of rising oil prices. Lawrence Lessing has calculated that so much energy is stored inside the earth that "if the earth's crust could be cooled by only 1°F., it would release enough heat energy to run all existent power plants for 20 million years."[38] He has calculated that the energy stored only six miles under the ground in the United States is equivalent to burning 900 trillion tons of coal. This may be an even more promising alternative energy resource than solar power.

Once again, the message is that ecology is a problem that cannot be solved by a technological fix. The sooner we recognize that, the better off we and our environment will be. Each attempted technological solution only beclouds the central problems and postpones the time when they will have to be faced. In the interim, the ecological damage mounts in ways that cannot be easily cured. Imagine how much worse it will be if all people of the world suddenly attained the standard of living of the average American. While this goal may be desirable, we have already damaged the environment badly and nothing indicates that, as they industrialize, other countries would not do the same. The problem then is not necessarily to increase energy; it is much more complex. As the noted scientist and author, Arthur C. Clarke, said, "In this inconceivably enormous universe, we can never run out of energy or matter. But we can all too easily run out of brains."[39]

IMPORTANT WORDS AND TERMS

aging	ecology	geothermal power	pollution
asbestos fiber	ecosystem	greenhouse effect	solar energy
atmospheric inversion	environmental impact statement	holistic	technological fix
catalytic converter		noise	technology
DDT	eutrophication	nuclear power	thermal pollution
decibel			

QUESTIONS FOR DISCUSSION

1. Ecology is seen by many people as the subversive science. Why?
2. What are the implications of the concept of the ecosystem for understanding the problem of water pollution?
3. What are Commoner's four laws and how do

they represent a departure from many common sense assumptions we all make in our daily lives?
4. How have people changed the face of the earth, including the continent of North America?
5. American ideology stresses many ideas that are antithetical to the basic ideas of ecology. What are some of them?
6. Many think that air pollution can be solved with a technological fix. From experience, what seems to be wrong with this kind of solution?
7. What would be wrong with the popular advertisement "People start pollution, therefore people can stop it"?
8. Certain groups would inevitably lose if we really cleaned up the environment. Which ones?
9. The environmental crisis may cause a crisis in our institutions. Which ones? How?
10. What do you think the environment will be like a thousand years from now?
11. What is wrong with using the GNP as an indicator of the quality of life in our country?
12. The oil spill at Santa Barbara started many people thinking about the role of government in protecting the environment. What are the dilemmas the government faces in taking any action in this area?
13. Do you agree with the generally pessimistic conclusion this chapter reaches about our ability to solve the problem?
14. The nuclear accident at Three Mile Island caused many to doubt the feasibility of nuclear power. What are your views on this issue, and what should be done with the existing nuclear power plants?

SUGGESTED READING

BARRY COMMONER, *The Closing Circle* (New York: Alfred A. Knopf, 1971).

Commoner is universally regarded as one of the leading ecological pioneers and one of its current experts. His virtue over other authors is his ability to explain difficult concepts with great clarity. This book is wide ranging, touching on water, air and land pollution. Especially good is a chapter on Lake Erie and one on the economic impact of trying to end environmental damage.

G. TYLER MILLER, *Living in the Environment* (Belmont, Calif.: Wadsworth, 1975).

This book, designed as a text to be used in an ecology course, is comprehensive. There are a number of short guest editorials written especially for this volume by people who are noted experts in their respective fields. On top of being readable, this book contains some of the best illustrated material to be found on the subject. Many graphs, illustrations, and pictures help the student understand the problem.

WILLIAM OPHULS, *Ecology and the Politics of Scarcity* (San Francisco: Freeman, 1977).

The world of the future will not be the same as it was in the past in respect to the availability of resources if current trends continue. And according to Ophuls, either we learn to limit our growth now and buy some time to deal with scarcity or we will face major calamities later when resources run out. His work contains the necessary background data to back up his arguments about resource depletion, and his discussion of the politics and economics of a no-growth society synthesizes current thinking in this area.

THEODORE ROSZAK, *Where the Wasteland Ends* (New York: Doubleday, 1973).

This book offers some heavy reading, but it is important because it attempts to look at the growth of science as the cause of the environmental crisis, as well as other contemporary social problems. A glimpse into the future is also provided, in which Roszak predicts that we must change many elements of our social organization if we are going to solve this problem.

PAUL SHEPARD AND DANIEL MCKINLEY (eds.), *The Subversive Science* (Boston: Houghton Mifflin, 1967).

The authors have assembled a series of articles dealing with how human progress, in the form of population growth and the development of technology, have altered our relationship with the environment. Numerous case studies are included to show the impact people have had on the environment. The authors show through these studies that any attempt to solve environmental problems means subverting the kinds of human activity now taken for granted. The development of a new ethic to replace the current emphasis on production and consumption is discussed, and revolutions in thinking are suggested as necessary for our future survival.

NOTES

1. Paul Shepard and David McKinley, *The Subversive Science* (Boston: Houghton Mifflin, 1969), p. 1.
2. LaMont Cole, "Man's Ecosystem" in Arthur Boughey (ed.), *Readings in Man, the Environment and Human Ecology* (New York: Macmillan, 1973), p. 13.
3. Barry Commoner, *The Closing Circle* (New York: Knopf, 1971).
4. Ibid., p. 39.
5. Philip Slater, *The Pursuit of Loneliness* (Boston: Beacon Press, 1971), p. 15.
6. William Thomas (ed.), *Man's Role in Changing the Face of the Earth* (Chicago, Ill.: University of Chicago Press, 1956).
7. Paul Ehrlich and John Holdren, "An Inventory of Disaster" in Clifton Fadiman and Jean White (eds.), *Ecocide* (Palo Alto, Calif.: James Freel and Associates, 1971), p. 21.
8. John Muir, "The American Forest" in Thomas Jones (ed.), *The Environment of America* (Chicago, Ill.: Ferguson, 1971), p. 298.
9. Pehr Kalm and John Audubon, "The Passenger Pigeon" in Thomas Jones (ed.), *The Environment of America* (Chicago, Ill.: Ferguson, 1971), p. 246.
10. Garrett Hardin, "The Tragedy of the Commons," *Science*, Vol. 162, No. 1243 (1968), pp. 1243–1248.
11. Henry Thoreau, "Life Without Principle," in Bruce Wallace (ed.), *Essays in Social Biology* (Englewood Cliffs, N.J.: Prentice-Hall, 1972), p. 32.
12. Garrett DeBell, "A Future That Makes Ecological Sense," in Garrett DeBell (ed.), *The Environmental Handbook* (New York: Ballantine Books, 1970), p. 153.
13. G. Tyler Miller, *Living in the Environment* (Belmont, Calif.: Wadsworth, 1975), p. 15.
14. Donella Meadows et al., *The Limits to Growth* (New York: Universe Books, 1972), p. 69.
15. Robert Rienow and Leona Rienow, "38 Cigarettes a Day," in Garrett DeBell (ed.), *The Environmental Handbook* (New York: Ballantine Books, 1970), p. 113.
16. Paul Ehrlich and Anne Ehrlich, *Population, Resources, Environment* (San Francisco: Freeman, 1970), p. 118.
17. Daniel Bruhl, "Air Pollution," in George Frakes and Curtis Solberg (eds.), *Pollution Papers* (New York: Appleton-Century-Crofts, 1971), p. 113.
18. John Esposito, "The Threat to Human Life and Health," in George Frakes and Curtis Solberg, *Pollution Papers* (New York: Appleton-Century-Crofts, 1971), p. 113.
19. Ibid., p. 115.
20. Bruce Wallace, *Essays in Social Biology* (Englewood Cliffs, N.J.: Prentice-Hall, 1972), p. 73.
21. Ibid., p. 59.
22. Ehrlich and Ehrlich, *Population, Resources, and Environment*, p. 126.
23. Commoner, *Closing Circle*, p. 96.

24. Ibid., p. 104.

25. Ehrlich and Ehrlich, *Population, Resources, and Environment*, p. 129.

26. Rachel Carson, *Silent Spring* (Boston: Houghton Mifflin, 1962).

27. Martin Jezer, "How Many Harvests Have We Left?" in George Frakes and Curtis Solberg (eds.), *Pollution Papers* (New York: Appleton-Century-Crofts, 1971), p. 146.

28. John McHale, *World Facts and Trends* (New York: Collier Books, 1972), p. 21.

29. Edward Gross, "Digging Out From Under," in Arthur Boughey (ed.), *Man and the Environment* (New York: Macmillan, 1971), p. 478.

30. Esposito, "Threat to Human Life," p. 116.

31. Cole, "Man's Ecosystem," p. 39.

32. Julian McCaull, "The Politics of Technology," *Environment*, Vol. 14, No. 2 (March 1972), p. 2.

33. Rene DuBois, "A Theology of the Earth," in George Frakes and Curtis Solberg (eds.), *Pollution Papers* (New York: Appleton-Century-Crofts, 1971), p. 22.

34. Marshall Goldman, *The Spoils of Progress* (Cambridge, Mass.: MIT Press, 1972), p. 74.

35. Theodore Jacobs, "Pollution, Consumerism, Accountability," *The Center Magazine* (January-February 1972), p. 44.

36. Ehrlich and Holdren, "Inventory of Disaster," p. 31.

37. Rita Beatty, *The DDT Myth* (New York: John Day, 1973), p. 12.

38. Lawrence Lessing, "Power from the Earth's Own Heat," in Arthur Boughey (ed.), *Man and the Environment* (New York: Macmillan, 1971), p. 525.

39. Quoted in Stuart Chase, *The Most Probable World* (New York: Harper and Row, 1968), p. 90.

14 HEALTH PRESCRIPTIONS AND PROSCRIPTIONS

CHAPTER OVERVIEW

INTRODUCTION

CONCEPTUAL ORIENTATION
Medical Sociology
    Epidemiology
    Organizational Theory
    Professionalization
    Health Support Systems
    Social Change
Summary

HISTORICAL OVERVIEW
The Origins of Medicine
Medicine in the Middle Ages
Modern Medicine
Summary

OBJECTIVE DIMENSIONS OF THE PROBLEM
Systems of Health Care
Health Care in the United States
    Costs of Health Care
    Components of the Health Care System
Medical Professionals:
    The Non-Western Perspective
Summary

ATTEMPTS AT DEALING WITH THE PROBLEM
Iatrogenic Effects
    The Power of Physicians
    Drugs and Health
    Diet and Fitness
Alternative Medical Perspectives

PROSPECTS FOR SOLVING THE PROBLEM

IMPORTANT WORDS AND TERMS

QUESTIONS FOR DISCUSSION

SUGGESTED READING

NOTES

This chapter was written by Ida Cook of the University of Central Florida. Copyright © 1980 by Ida Cook.

Medical care in this country is like a pay toilet. You take a biological necessity and then charge to have it satisfied.
Richard Kunnes, *Your Money or Your Life*

The methods of quackery are merely a theft from the most ancient phases of folk-medicine.
Karl Sudhoff

CHAPTER OVERVIEW

Health is unquestionably a social problem, because society determines how health care will be structured. Formulating a reasonable definition of health requires consideration of the sociological approaches to health and the health care system, embracing such factors as epidemiology, organizational analysis, professionalization, and social change. After we've established these definitions, we will examine the development of medical practices from antiquity, emphasizing the recent significant social and medical advances. We will then analyze the various types of health care systems in the world and compare the United States system with those of other countries.

Iatrogenic effects related to health care are then discussed, focusing on such results of professionalization as unnecessary surgery, improper prescribing by physicians, and overreliance on drugs. The burgeoning numbers of individuals who seek to treat and medicate themselves is also considered. Finally, we recommend the revision of the Western approach to medicine to allow for expansion of available information and techniques and the creation of a broader umbrella of protection providing more equitable payment for health care, supervision of medication, and increased flexibility on the part of the medical profession.

INTRODUCTION

Among their other concerns, most members of society desire good health. When we talk with people who have lived long lives, we find ourselves asking them for the secret to their longevity and continued health, and perhaps adjusting our exercise or dietary practices according to their comments. All choices on health care are made by the consuming public with definite self-interest in mind, but society also plays a role. We make choices with an awareness that both society and its selected authorities — physicians, shamans, or priests — agree or disagree with these recommendations. And we accept or reject the long-lived person's recipe for success, depending on such social factors as our own training, experience, and perceptions.

Health has been a problem since people first appeared. First, it involves questions about simple survival or subsistence; when that basic goal is reached, it turns to questions concerning the quality of health and survival. Menander, a Greek comic playwright, maintained that health and intellect are the two blessings of life. We cannot be certain that there would be any overwhelming consensus with respect to intellect, but health is certainly a matter of timeless universal concern. But what is health? Is it simply a matter of feeling good? Is it only physiological or does it also include mental well-being?

The definition of health provided by the preamble to the Constitution of the World Health Organization (WHO) acknowledges that health is more than the absence of disease. Health, it says, "is a state of physical, mental, and social well-being and not merely the absence of disease and infirmity."[1] Note that health is defined in social as well as physical terms, for we cannot determine well-being without referring to the culture in which it is found. According to René Dubos, a noted biologist, "A healthy society is one in which the natural adaptability of the species is enhanced and not one in which disease does not exist. Health is maximum adaptability to the inevitability of disease."[2] If we consider this definition from the social standpoint, it is clear that it refers to the ability of society and its members in social and physical terms to adjust to various types of illness and disease. Gerhard and Jean Lenski suggest that much of social development is the result of adaptation of society to environmental factors and natural selection.[3]

As suggested by the above definitions, health is both physical and social in origin and explanation. As it is a problem confronting society and its members, we shall examine the social context and consequences of health and health care. In order to approach health in an informed way, several sociological concepts need to be considered and defined.

CONCEPTUAL ORIENTATION

As sociologists examining health as a social problem, we must examine the structural and institutional configurations that arise in societies out of attempts to deal with problems of health and medicine. The structure of health and medical care is strongly influenced by the economics, politics, and values of society. Those responsible for health care can vary from physicians to medicine men to herbalists; institutions in which health care takes place can range from medicine lodges to complex, highly specialized hospitals. In taking a sociological approach, we will aim to answer certain questions. How is health or illness legitimated in a society, that is, how does society define and view illness? Who is seen as a legitimate healer, and how does a member of society become one? Who determines when a healer exceeds her legitimate purpose? In what social institutions is healing meant to take place? Does illness afflict certain groups, and is health care delivered equally throughout society? These questions are a few of the most important that come to mind when we regard health as a social problem.

Medical Sociology

The sociological study of health, called *medical sociology*, includes five major topics: epidemiology, organizational theory, professionalization, health support systems, and social change.

EPIDEMIOLOGY

Epidemiology has to do with the existence, prevalence, and extent of disease and illness in countries and populations of the world. This topic is closely related to demography because both involve the use and analysis of population data. Before the origin of illness was discovered and accepted by medical practitioners, the control of the spread of diseases was almost impossible. The situation

Three milestones stand out in the history of epidemiology: the discovery of contagion by a sixteenth-century Italian physician, Fracastoro; the development of the smallpox vaccine and subsequently of inoculation in the eighteenth century by Edward Jenner; and, in the nineteenth century, Louis Pasteur's introduction of the germ theory of disease. The efforts of these and other pioneers have made it possible to control the spread of deadly diseases. Here, a World Health Organization team immunizes African children against cholera.

changed when medical science reached an understanding of the *germ theory of disease* — which traced disease to the presence of bacteria or viruses — and became aware of the problem of *contagion* — the transmission of disease from an ill to a well person. That knowledge, coupled with the discovery of *inoculation* (purposely causing a controlled disease to prevent the contraction of a worse disease) has made the question of the spread of health a concern of epidemiology.

ORGANIZATIONAL THEORY

One of the broader areas in the field of medical sociology is *organizational theory*, which examines how health care is structured. This would include the decision to use licensed practitioners as opposed to religious or magical healers. It also evaluates the structure and form of different locations for treatment, whether it is medicine lodges or specialized hospitals. In this area, it examines the effects of and interactions between institutions and their patients.[4]

PROFESSIONALIZATION

The topic of *professionalization* is a central concern of medical sociologists, partly because the activities and behavior associated with it are readily observable. Ronald Pavalko has defined professionalism by citing specific characteristics which differentiate professions from occupations, as illustrated in Table 14.1. According to Pavalko, the "profession refers to an extreme end of the continuum of work characteristics, and professions are those work activities that exhibit this complex of work characteristics to a high degree."[5] Physicians and nurses, then, are more formally involved in the pursuit of their profession than persons in other occupations.

TABLE 14.1 The Occupation-Profession Model

Dimensions	Occupation	Profession
Theory, intellectual technique	Absent	Present
Relevance to social values	Not relevent	Relevant
Training period		
A	Short	Long
B	Nonspecialized	Specialized
C	Involves things	Involves symbols
D	Subculture unimportant	Subculture important
Motivation	Self-interest	Service
Autonomy	Absent	Present
Commitment	Short term	Long term
Sense of community	Low	High
Code of ethics	Undeveloped	Highly developed

Source: Ronald M. Pavalko, *Sociology of Occupations and Professions* (Itasca, Ill.: Peacock, 1971), p. 17.

Another important part of professionalization, in addition to work characteristics, is the profession's longitudinal development. A profession does not appear full-blown, but accumulates these characteristics over a long time. Harold Wilensky saw the following events developing as an occupation moves toward becoming a full-fledged profession:

1. A substantial number of people begin doing full-time some activity that needs doing.
2. A training school is established.
3. A professional association is formed.
4. The association engages in political agitation to win the support of law for the protection of the group.
5. A code of ethics is developed.[6]

There is no question that these characteristics, as well as those in Pavalko's table, describe the health care professions.

HEALTH SUPPORT SYSTEMS

The sociological view of health care also considers *health support systems,* the different types of organizations that provide health coverage for citizens. As organizations in modern industrial societies, health support systems have been the target of attacks for inadequacy on one hand and have been defended by systematic attempts to deny public scrutiny of possible alternatives on the other. In some countries the structure of the health support system is simply decided by the government. In others, its structure and funding are part of political controversy and discussion, with leaders of various political factions and representatives of private enterprise attempting to persuade the public of the merits of those problems.

The structures of these health support systems and their sources of support cover a range of types:

1. National, state or provincial, county, or municipal governments guarantee health care for all, funding it by general taxation.
2. Governmental or quasi-governmental health insurance, social security, or sick-

ness funds provide health care, based on specifically earmarked financial contributions.
3. Large, private organizations, such as mines, factories, and plantations, provide care for their own workers.
4. Prepaid member-supported nonprofit organizations are formed.
5. Charitable and voluntary organizations provide supplementary care.
6. The private practice of medicine, with private health insurance companies, provides health care as a profit-making business.
7. Indigenous, traditional, spiritual, empirical, or magical healers provide care while observing specific cultural practices.[7]

The proper structure and funding of health care in the United States will be in the forefront of health issues in the 1980s. With large numbers of the total population vulnerable to costs related to both minor and catastrophic illness and with increasing and highly organized and financed opposition to publicly funded programs, the debate on the issue promises to be intense.

SOCIAL CHANGE

Finally, sociological analysis of health care includes consideration of *social change*, the various approaches explaining and solving health problems from ancient history to the present. Preeminent in the twentieth century has been the positivistic, Western model of illness, which deals with health basically in a dichotomous fashion. Texts on the topic suggest that Western medical practice has focused on the physical, biological nature of humankind. And due to scientific advances, the medical profession assumed that the human body is like a machine; when it breaks down, it requires the replacement or repair of parts, without necessarily referring to any other systems interacting with that machine or its environment.[8]

An alternative approach, a non-Western approach, takes a more *holistic* view of illness and health, rejecting the view that humankind can be split into mental and physical parts or that people are separate from their environment. The trends of today's medical practice involve the juxtaposition of these two divergent approaches. We are seeing the beginning of tentative attempts at sharing hypotheses, theories, and techniques. Because this sharing involves changes in both values and technology, the analysis of social change is crucial.

Summary

Medical sociology — the sociological approach to health and health care — involves five areas of study, which will be the focus of our discussion. We will need to study the extent of disease, to get an idea of general health. To understand who cares for the ill, we will look at the characteristics of the medical profession. To see how that profession works in society, we will discuss the structure of health care and how it is paid for. And to understand how modern health care grew to have its present shape, we must look at how it developed over time. It is to that topic that we turn our attention first.

HISTORICAL OVERVIEW

The Origins of Medicine

The history of medicine is a mirror of humankind's attempts to answer the questions regarding the basis of health, whether it is religious, scientific, or magical. There is evidence that even in prehistoric times, people made attempts at dealing with health problems. Archaeological finds indicate that crude attempts at trephining (boring holes in the skull) were made, resulting in the survival of the patient.[9] The purposes of such surgical procedures may have been to relieve pressure on the brain from skull fractures; that it occurred indicates the concern of early humans with problems of health. It seems reasonable to conclude that other medical practices, such as the use of herbs and incantations, were also used.

With the development of literate societies our search for evidence of medical and health practices is made easier. Artifacts from earlier civilizations such as Egypt (dated around 2500 B.C.), Mesopotamia, and Minoa show that surgery was practiced, and hygiene and pharmaceuticals were part of medical practice in China around 2700 B.C. As early as 800 B.C., Indian records point to Brahminic medicine, which was a combination of both religious and medical practices.[10] By the fourth century B.C., the Hippocratic oath, pledging physicians to honorable care of their patients, was widespread in Greek civilization.

About the same time that the Hippocratic oath was becoming prominent, southeast Asian and Chinese physicians were developing similar codes and practices. In China an extensive bureaucratic system was developed to instruct and examine physicians. Records also show that health and medical information were characterized by magic and religious themes. For example, Greek physicians referred to the zodiac for guidance in treating patients, and they also attempted to determine the basic nature of matter.[11] Health was thought to consist of a balance of the four basic elements: fire, water, air, and earth, and their conditions, hotness or coldness, wetness or dryness. Asian physicians arrived at similar basic elements, although they were given different names.

Public health probably became more of a concern along with the development of dense population settlements. The first Roman aqueduct was completed in 312 B.C., to be followed in A.D. 50 by Athenaeus of Attila's development of a method for filtering water.[12] By the second century A.D., Galen was active in the medical field, pursuing questions of anatomy and physiology. He made some major contributions to medicine, improving knowledge of the brain, nerves, spinal cord, and pulse. He became the authority for medical practices, but some of his writings were lost to the West after the fall of the Roman Empire in the fifth century. His efforts and information were assimilated by Arabic scientists and physicians, however, who recorded and preserved many medical practices and procedures unheeded by European physicians in the early Middle Ages.

Medicine in the Middle Ages

Medical practices remained basically unchanged after Galen for many hundreds of years. Changes were gradually made in institutional developments, however, often by the impetus of Catholic church councils and leaders. In 1131, the Council of Rheims forbade clerics to practice medicine, and in 1139, the Lateran Council prohibited surgery by higher clergy.[13] As early as 1162 the city of Arles, France, issued a series of medical ordinances. In addition to municipalities setting rules for health practices, rulers also were involved in determining the behavior of medical practitioners. In 1224 and 1240, Frederick II of the Holy Roman Empire (modern Germany) issued laws regulating the study of medicine and favoring dissection, surgery, and pharmacy. The concern on the part of established religion for interference on the part of magicians and alchemists can be seen in the proclamations by Pope John XXII in 1317 and 1326 prohibiting alchemy and magic. These acts indicate the involvement of both religious and governmental institutions with the conduct of medical practices.

These developing institutional arrangements were totally unable to handle the devastation of the great bubonic plague of the 1340s, called the Black Death. The social, economic, political, and ecclesiastical structure of Europe was almost destroyed. Europe alone lost perhaps 25 million people, and in the Middle East, India, and China, additional tens of millions died.[14] Up to that time physicians had no conception of the cause of disease and instead ascribed it to conjunction of planets or other cosmic or divine causes. The spread of the plague helped foster the recognition of contagion. Venice, for

This 1349 woodcut illustrates the devastation of bubonic plague, or Black Death, which ravaged much of the known world in the mid-fourteenth century. To the survivors of that killer that claimed millions of victims, as to this artist, there seemed to be more coffins than pallbearers. The plague was transmitted by fleas from infected rats, a fact not understood in the 1340s.

instance, excluded plague-ridden ships for forty days, and the term and practice of quarantine (from the Italian word for forty) was introduced.

In the Middle Ages other diseases were also epidemic, including smallpox, diphtheria, measles, influenza, and tuberculosis. During the same time, but some eight hundred or more years after such institutions and practices were developed in Rome, hospitals were founded and public sanitation practices were developed in Europe.[15]

From the time of the Middle Ages to the 1800s medical practices showed a mixture of obstacles and great leaps forward. Interspersed between edicts dealing with bloodletting (1514) and witch burning (1484) are great discoveries and inventions such as Galileo's development of the microscope (1610).[16] Artists such as Vesalius, da Vinci, and others made great contributions to medical knowledge by studying skeletal structure and musculature. But associated with these advancements was the unwillingness of society to accept them. Vesalius was criticized by the established church and forced to reject his own works describing anatomy.[17]

During this time medicine and religious belief were uneasy travellers on the road to scientific advancement. Society at that time was virtually synonymous with the church. The religious teaching that disease and illness were the result of divine will or punishment left little place for human efforts to deal scientifically with health. Additionally, dissections of the human body were prohibited by religious order in Europe, just as they had been in Arab medicine. The Arab physicians had the foresight to preserve Galen's works on anatomy, which were the result of dissection, but their own laws prohibited going further. In the Arab and Christian worlds, the search for knowledge stagnated.[18]

Modern Medicine

As the Western world entered the early modern age, health care became more regulated and training more available. In the United States during the colonial period, Maryland and Virginia passed laws to limit charges for medical services. Massachusetts in 1649 and New York in 1665 passed laws restricting the practice of medicine, surgery and midwifery. The first hospital in what is now the United States was established on Manhattan Island in 1663. Between 1765 and 1790 there were medical schools set up at Columbia, Harvard, the University of Pennsylvania, and the College of Philadelphia.[19] Hospitals of the early period were the Pennsylvania Hospital of Philadelphia, organized in 1751; the Philadelphia Dispensary, founded in 1786; and the New York Dispensary, begun in 1791. The first mental hospital was the Eastern Lunatic Asylum at Williamsburg, Virginia, opened in 1773.[20]

With the advent of the Industrial Revolution and the increased density of population in urban centers, medical and public health programs proliferated. Working conditions in the newly developed factories were far below present-day standards and increased the likelihood of injury and disease. Awareness of these conditions on the part of the general public and a drive for improving health standards were accentuated by the high incidence of death, illness, injury, and disease among small children employed in the factories.

Associated with this awareness came the creation and support for public health standards enacted by national and state governments. By 1873 there were 134 cities in the United States with boards of health. Two years later, in 1875, England passed the Public Health Act, establishing a governing board of health and authorizing the post of medical officer of health to local boards.[21] In 1879, the United States had its first national board of health. These enactments were not the first attempts on the part of municipalities and governments of industrialized nations to protect the health of their citizens, but they symbolized the new awareness of health problems. Considering that almost all of the United States was still predominantly rural, this fact was important. By 1906 the first regulation of food and drugs in the United States was legislated, primarily because of a concern for the health of the public.

By and large early physicians learned their craft by being apprenticed to other doctors. In 1847, the American Medical Association was organized as a result of a national convention of medical societies and colleges. Early goals of the organization included establishment of medical ethics, the "direction of public opinion with reference to public hygiene and medical education, and checking through the Council of Pharmacists and Chemists, the exploitation of the medical profession by patent medicine makers and the swindling of people by quacks and quackery."[22]

While these changes in public health were significant, the most important change in the nineteenth century was in the understanding of the causes of disease.

> Although some important work on disease control had been done in the eighteenth century, for instance, Lind's demonstration of the prevention of scurvy and Jenner's work on cowpox vaccination, the rise of microbiology depended upon the chemical and technological base provided by the Industrial Revolution. Refinements in microscope design, the chemistry of dye manufacture, developed for the textile industry, were incorporated into histology and bacteriology. From such a shaky foundation, through a remarkably concerted achievement of human intellect, a flood of discoveries poured from the world's laboratories in the latter half of the nineteenth century and established the cause and basic means of transmission of many major bacterial and parasitic diseases of man and domestic animals. . . . Knowledge of physiology, nutrition, and many other aspects of medical science advanced during this period.[23]

Significant developments also occurred in the twentieth century, particularly the discovery of antibiotics and advances in medical technology. *Antibiotics* are microorganisms used to destroy other microorganisms. The ability of some adverse microorganisms to inhibit the effects of other organisms was first discovered by Louis Pasteur in the nineteenth century, but the discovery and development of many specific antibiotics are a twentieth-century phenomenon. The massive production of such antibiotics as penicillin, tyrothricin, and streptomycin has resulted in a considerable decrease in disease and death. Technological changes have made medical practice, particularly surgery, more effective. The discovery of X-rays led to surer diagnosis, advances in blood transfusion allowed safer surgery, and the improvement of anesthetics and the adoption of antiseptic conditions helped reduce fatalities.

Summary

Medicine has grown over the years to become a science, with emphasis on research and the use of sophisticated technology. Physicians are guided by a tradition of service to the patient established by the Hippocratic oath. This fact, coupled with long training and control, has resulted in the evolution of medicine as a profession. Associated with the medical profession are the service institutions, such as hospitals and health insurance providers. This is the medical system we know. Let us now consider how that system is paid for.

OBJECTIVE DIMENSIONS OF THE PROBLEM

Systems of Health Care

The different types of health care systems were briefly described in the conceptual orientation section. Here we will provide a cursory description of each type, so they can be compared to the United States system.

The first type of health care system, governmental support, consists of the government assuming full responsibility for the health of citizens at no or trivial cost to the user. This has often been described as socialized medicine and can be found in the Soviet Union, the Scandinavian countries, Cuba, and the United Kingdom. Despite political differences, all these governments attempt to "divorce the care of health from questions of personal means or other factors unrelated to it and thus encourage the obtaining of early advice and promise of good health rather than treatment of ill health."[24]

The second type of health support system is the social security and quasi-governmental health insurance system. In Belgium, France, Greece, the Netherlands, Italy, and Japan, insurance schemes were merged into national programs after World War II. In some countries membership is compulsory for persons below a certain minimum wage; in others, like Austria, West Germany, and the Netherlands, it is voluntary. In Denmark benefits are graduated based on ability to pay. In Switzerland the area of residence determines the form of membership and governmental support. In China eligibility is determined by the nature of one's work area and in rural districts subscription is voluntary with governmental supplement for those unable to pay. In Europe specific sickness funds are organized around occupational categories. Latin America is characterized by both social security plans and governmental health ministries. In the United States most of the population is covered by private insurance plans and governmental subsidies are uncommon, but since 1965 specific benefits are available for certain disabilities such as kidney failure, and for certain groups like the elderly.

The next three systems are smaller in scale than the first two, rarely covering the entire population of a country. Private organizations in such countries as Malaysia, Liberia, and South Africa provide medical care to all employees and their dependents. Prepaid member-supported plans, or health maintenance organizations, offer a different form, in which participating members are charged a flat monthly fee in return for comprehensive medical care. In the United States the largest such program is the Kaiser Permanent Health Plan. Charitable and voluntary organizations consist of mission hospitals and the like, and rely on donations, often collected away from where they actually provide care.

Private practice of medicine as a profit-making business best describes the predominant health care system in the United States. It consists of private medical practice and large numbers of independent, profit-making health insurance companies. A similar situation exists in Brazil, and some such care is also found in Europe. With the 1974 reorganization of the British National Health

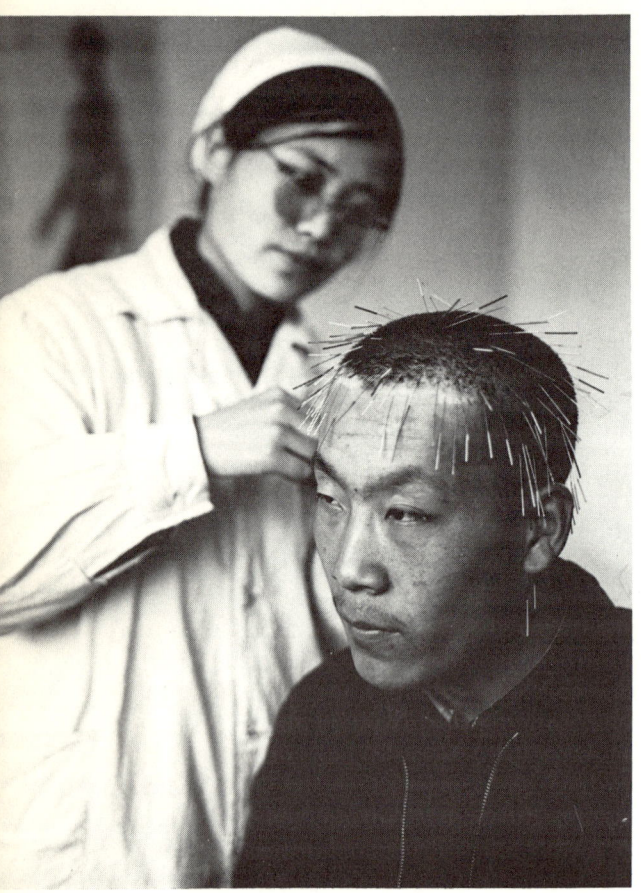

Acupuncture is a traditional medical practice that involves inserting needles at certain points on a patient's body. While it has long been common in the Orient, acupuncture is slowly becoming more accepted in the West, especially for its remarkable ability to relieve chronic pain.

Service, for instance, private practice was retained for those preferring to supplement their health care with it.

Indigenous and traditional healers is the last form of health support systems. "The usership of traditional medical care systems probably exceeds that of scientific or Western medicine by a factor of at least two to one."[25] In India and China efforts have been made to integrate indigenous medical practices with modern medicine. Persons may elect to receive treatment by traditional medicine, using herbs, or acupuncture, or modern medicine, or both.[26]

Health Care in the United States

Comparatively speaking, the health care system in the United States is loosely organized. It consists of several of the above components, but coordination of efforts and function between these components is almost nonexistent. Some people receive government aid. One such program is Medicare, which is designed for the elderly. Medicaid is medical funding that supplements other welfare programs. In only a few places do health maintenance organizations exist, although they are slowly increasing in subscription. The remainder of the United States health care is in the private, profit-making sector. Profits motivate the insurance industry that finances health care and the private agencies such as hospitals and pharmacies that supply it. It has been estimated that only 70 percent of the population is covered by private health insurance. This means that 30 percent of the population is served by the government or has no protection.[27]

As Table 14.2 suggests, Medicaid is ever increasing. Both costs and number of recipients have been rising steadily. The growth of this program far exceeded initial expectations of planners, who underestimated the costs and enrollment. Based on these figures and the growing proportion of old people in the population, the trend is unlikely to slow down in the near future.

COSTS OF HEALTH CARE

As evidence of the debilitating effects on health of one's place in the social structure, see Table 14.3. Differences in level of family income clearly affect the presence of certain types of illnesses. The table suggests that low-income families experience at least double or triple the amount of some illnesses. Comparing all people with those over sixty-five dramatizes the difference. Within the older age groups, the effects of level of income are also important.

Using the concept of income in another context, Table 14.4 shows the proportion of the family income that is spent for health care services. In this case a far greater proportion of the total family income is spent by the low-income families for health services than by the higher-income families. The crucial importance of the statistics found in Tables 14.3 and 14.4 is that while a far greater number of low-income families are crippled by illnesses, they are also faced with the necessity of giving up more of their meager earnings to pay for these illnesses. That is, those least able to pay for health care pay the greatest proportion of their income for it.

The situation may be worsening. It is instructive to consider the increased expenditures for health care. When figured as a percentage of the gross national product, we see in Table 14.5 that the amount devoted to health care has grown from 4.5 percent in 1950 to 8.8 percent in 1975. This doubling of

TABLE 14.2 Number of Recipients, Total Payments, and Payments per Recipient under Medicaid, Fiscal Years 1968-1977

Fiscal Year	Number of Recipients[a] (Millions)	Total Federal and State Payments[b] (Billions of Dollars)	Payments per Recipient (Dollars)	Medical Care Price Index[c] (1968=100)	Payments per Recipient (Constant 1968 Dollars)
1968	11.5	3.45	300	100.0	300
1969	12.1	4.35	361	106.9	338
1970	14.5	5.09	351	113.7	309
1971	18.0	6.35	353	121.0	292
1972	18.0	7.35	408	124.9	327
1973	18.8	8.71	463	129.8	357
1974	20.8	9.74	467	141.8	329
1975	22.1	12.09	547	158.9	344
1976	23.9	13.98	585	173.9	336
1977[d]	24.7	17.16	696	192.9	361

[a] Includes some recipients of aid under assistance programs that do not receive federal matching funds.

[b] Includes payments in 1968–1970 for medical care programs enacted under the Social Security Amendments of 1960.

[c] U.S. Bureau of Labor Statistics medical care price index adjusted to make 1968=100, estimated for fiscal year 1977 and for November and December 1976.

[d] Figures for 1977 estimated by HEW, Medical Services Administration, Budget Office.

Source: U.S. Department of Health, Education and Welfare Financing Administration, *Data on the Medicaid Program: Eligibility, Services, Fiscal Years 1966-77* (Institute for Medicaid Management, 1977), p. 34.

health care costs suggests that the average citizen is paying more now for basic health care than in the past. In light of these data, it appears that the heavier burden will be felt by the poor.

In terms of what kind of health care money is buying, Table 14.6 separates the costs for hospitals, physicians, and other related expenses for three different years. It should be noted that the lowest amount is

TABLE 14.3 Prevalence of Selected Chronic Conditions by Family Income Class, Fiscal Years 1964 and 1965 and Calendar Year 1971[a]

Chronic Condition and Income Class[b]	All Ages		65 and Over	
	1964 and 1965	1971	1964 and 1965	1971
Visual impairment				
All incomes	28.8	47.4	145.6	204.6
Lowest	71.2	96.3	177.5	232.1
Lowest middle	21.7	37.7	115.4	163.2
Upper middle	14.3	28.9	110.1	181.3
Highest	15.2	34.5	105.7	169.2
Hearing impairment				
All incomes	45.7	71.6	216.3	294.3
Lowest	90.0	132.9	242.5	323.0
Lower middle	38.2	63.3	199.4	271.4
Upper middle	30.4	49.4	173.3	247.3
Highest	32.4	48.6	190.4	259.2
Impairment of back or spine[c]				
All incomes	34.7	39.6	55.4	67.1
Lowest	45.0	57.6	67.1	78.6
Lower middle	33.1	37.7	52.2	51.2
Upper middle	32.5	34.0	34.3	30.0
Highest	31.4	32.1	25.6	27.7

[a] Data in the first and third column based on interviews conducted from July 1963 through June 1965; data in the second and fourth columns based on interviews conducted during 1971.

[b] Income classes (in dollars) are as follows:

	1964 and 1965	1971
Lowest	Under 3,000	Under 5,000
Lower middle	3,000–6,999	5,000–9,999
Upper middle	7,000–9,999	10,000–14,999
Highest	10,000 and over	15,000 and over

[c] Excludes paralysis

Sources: Karen Davis and Cathy Shoen, *Health and the War on Poverty: A Ten-Year Appraisal* (Washington, D.C.: Brookings Institution, 1978); HEW, National Center for Health Statistics, *Prevalence of Selected Impairments, United States, July 1963–June 1965*; Vital and Health Statistics, series 10, no. 48 (Washington, D.C.: U.S. Government Printing Office, 1968), pp. 28, 34, 55; and NCHS, *Prevalence of Social Impairments, United States, 1971*, Vital and Health Statistics, series 10, no. 99, DHEW (HRA) 75-1526 (Washington, D.C.: U.S. Government Printing Office, 1975), pp. 24, 27, 32, 36.

TABLE 14.4 Expenditures for Personal Health Services as a Percentage of Family Income, by Income Group and Age of Oldest Member, 1970

Family Income Group (Dollars)	Expenditures as Percent of Family Income	
	Families Whose Oldest Member is 65 or Over	Families Whose Oldest Member is Under 65
Under 2,000	14.1	15.2
2,000–3,499	11.3	6.9
3,500–4,999	9.4	7.0
5,000–7,499	9.5	5.4
7,500–9,999	5.6	4.5
10,000–14,999	5.0	3.8
15,000 and over	3.8	3.2
All income groups	7.6	4.0
Addenda		
Below near-poverty level [a]	12.9	6.9
Above near-poverty level [a]	6.0	3.8

[a] Near-poverty level is $2,600 for a single person, $3,700 for a family of two, and $5,700 for a family of four.

Source: Ronald Andersen and others, *Expenditures for Personal Health Services: National Trends and Variations, 1953–1970*, DHEW (HRA) 74-3105 (Washington, D.C.: Department of Health, Education, and Welfare, 1973), table 6, p. 13.

used to pay physicians and that the greatest amount is related to hospital costs. This reflects the expensive medical technology found in hospitals and also shows the increased burden on the poor, who are more likely to have hospital care rather than attention from a personal physician. The trend of costs is alarming when we note the percentage change between 1950 and 1975 — a 854 percent increase. Even between 1965 and 1975, the percentage increase was 279 percent.

The result of this tremendous growth in spending is shown by comparing United States figures to those of other countries. Table 14.7 ranks spending by various industrialized nations and lists the mortality rates for children and adults. The table shows that the United States spends the most for health care and yet ranks third from the highest in infant mortality and fifth highest in maternal mortality. Even more serious is the fact that despite the greatest expenditure for health care, the United States has the highest mortality rates for women and is second only to Finland in mortality rates for men. Higher expenditures are not bringing better health. It is not surprising, then, that Senator Edward Kennedy questions why the United States is unable to care for its citizens' medical needs and recommends national health insurance to solve this problem. He further recommends that the health care delivery

TABLE 14.5 National Health Expenditures as a Percentage of Gross National Product

Year	Percentage of GNP
1950	4.5
1955	4.5
1960	5.2
1965	5.9
1970	7.2
1975	8.5
1977	8.8

Source: *Social Security Bulletin* (July 1978), p. 5.

system be reorganized to assure better care for rural populations.

COMPONENTS OF THE HEALTH CARE SYSTEM

As we have mentioned, the hospital is an important medical institution that is part of the health care problem. Hospitals are both publicly and privately supported, but more important to their functioning, the American

One of the most potent arguments for national health insurance is the fact that the average middle-income family, let alone the poor family, cannot afford hospital care without comprehensive protection. Catastrophic illness or accident inevitably erases a patient's entire assets. Cost containment legislation may help, but considering that hospitalization costs have tripled in the last decade, it may be a case of too little too late.

Medical Association monitors standards and practices, as do government health boards. The data suggest that hospital costs are a major source of rising medical costs, partly because of the high cost of medical innovations and other expenses mandated by these overseeing organizations.

It is also interesting to note that because of the oversight responsibility of the medical associations and the constant interaction of physicians and administrators, the hospitals have joined forces with the American Medical Association to resist national health insurance. Millions of dollars have been spent on advertisements as part of a campaign being waged to resist government support of health care. As part of this approach, national health care is equated with socialized medicine, which is presented as an evil. With the major providers of health care working together to control decisions on the structure and costs of health care, the opportunity for public input on those decisions is minimal at best. The powerful medical lobbyists speak with a louder voice and the end result may well be a decline in care available to those less able to pay — the poor and the elderly.

While hospitals are the major institutions in the health care system, the most prominent components are probably the professionals, physicians and related staff, such as nurses, pharmacists, and so on. Most of these persons choose their profession because of similar motivations. According to Ronald Pavalko, the values of idealism, dedication, and high purpose are initially held by prospective physicians. He then describes the change in these values due to medical students' experience in medical school. First, due to the pressure to get high grades, idealism is replaced by a sense of expediency and utilitarianism. Second, it is

TABLE 14.6 Aggregate and Per Capita Amount of Personal Health Care Expenditures by Type

Type	Aggregate Expenses (in Millions)		
	1950	1965	1977
Hospital	3,698 (35.6%)	13,152 (39.3%)	65,627 (46.0%)
Physician	2,689 (25.8%)	8,405 (25.1%)	32,184 (22.6%)
Other	4,013 (38.6%)	11,941 (35.6%)	44,775 (31.4%)
Total	10,400 (100.0%)	33,498 (100.0%)	142,586 (100.0%)
	Per Capita		
Hospital	$24.09	$66.87	$297.38
Physician	17.52	42.74	145.84
Other	26.24	60.71	202.89
Total	$67.85	$170.32	$646.11
	Percent change per capita		
	1950–77	1950–65	1965–77
Hospital	1134%	177	345
Physician	732%	143	241
Other	673%	131	234
Total	854%	151	279

Source: Social Security Bulletin (July 1978), p. 15.

TABLE 14.7 Rank Order of Health Expenditure and of Selected Mortality Rates, Ten Countries, Around 1968–1979

	Expenditures		Mortality Rates[a]					
	Per Capita Amount	As Percentage of GNP	Infant	Maternal	Men 35–44	Men 45–54	Women 35–44	Women 45–54
United States	1	1	7	5	9	9	10	10
Sweden	2	2	1	1	2	1	2	1
Netherlands	5	3	2	3	1	2	1	2
West Germany	3	4	8	9	6	5	9	6
France	4	4	5	6	8	8	6	4
Austria	b	6	9	8	7	7	8	8
Italy	7	7	10	10	5	3	3	3
Finland	b	8	3	2	10	10	4	5
United Kingdom[c]	6	9	4	3	3	4	5	7
Ireland	8	s	6	7	4	6	7	9

[a] Lower number=lower rate
[b] Unavailable.
[c] Expenditures are for United Kingdom; mortality rates for England and Wales.

Sources: Adapted from Maxwell, 1974; from Paul F. Basch, *International Health* (New York: Oxford University Press, 1978), p. 249.

made clear to students that they are not doctors by continually denying them clinical responsibility. This change in attitude appears to be short-term, Pavalko reports, and a more informed type of idealism returns to the students at the end of training.[28]

A similar change has been discovered by Ida Harper Simpson to occur in nurses.[29] She found that as nurses are socialized, they pass through three stages. First, the nurse shifts attention from broad, socially derived goals to a choice of professional goals in specific work tasks. Second, significant others in the work milieu become the nurse's reference group. Finally, the nurse internalizes the values of the group and adopts the behavior it prescribes.

The result of socialization, both of physicians and nurses, is the inculcation of the view that the profession is the proper sphere of health activity and judgment. It is highly autonomous, and in this is one of the problems related to health: the physician is insulated from society, even if he fails to perform properly. Professional examining and review boards certify the qualifications of prospective physicians, nurses, dentists, and other medical practitioners, and later review complaints if malpractice or misbehavior is alleged to have occurred. One problem with this process is that, partly due to the collegiality of the professionals, they are often unwilling to participate actively in censuring an erring colleague, except in cases of extreme negligence. In addition, since the profession serves as a peer group, justification and rationalization of fees and practices are reinforced.

Medical Professionals:
The Non-Western Perspective

We have thus far dealt with the health care professions according to Western medicine. Some attention needs to be given to those practitioners of health care who do not fit precisely into the stated characteristics of a professional as described by Pavalko, although considering the rigorous system of training and ethics, they approximate the characteristics of a professional. These are the folk curers or healers, including bone setters, herbalists, midwives, shamans, and some others. Often these healers are guided by principles of body equilibrium based on humoral theories from antiquity. Their therapies range from physical manipulations to modification of diet and surroundings to medication. Diagnoses require skill in observing and correlating physical symptoms and environment. For many of them, human anatomy and physiology are seen as intimately bound to other physical systems.[30]

This approach is often beneficial to patients and, as suggested by Erwin Ackerknecht, "the successes of the medicine man cannot be fully understood unless one realizes that, acting in small communities, he possesses a more perfect personal knowledge of his patient than most of the other physicians do."[31] Non-Western or folk medicine is effective in many cases, partly because the practitioner and patient believe in the symbolic effect of the act. A Western equivalent is the use of placebos by physicians. *Placebos* are inert substances prescribed by physicians that have no physical benefits for the patient but lead to better health because the patient believes they will work. Placebos may be far more than symbols. The expectations of some patients about a treatment can alter or even reverse the action of a pharmacological agent.[32]

The system of the folk healer is a creation of society. The strength of the folk healer and his own belief in himself is the consequence of the belief of the community.[33] Since this form of health care is twice as common worldwide than the Western form of medicine, its basis and conduct must be given credence. From the perspective of modern industrial society, we tend to discount its practice as superstition and quackery, but we are prejudiced by our acceptance of the tools and theories of positivistic science. Devotion to one orientation creates intolerance for other methods. "Western medicine's position today is akin to that of state religion yesterday — it has an officially approved *monopoly* on the right to define health and illness and to treat illness."[34]

The above discussion does not mean to suggest that quackery and fake healers do not exist and attempt to dupe the public. Obviously the occurrence of such fraud is abhorrent and immoral, but as Carlson has suggested, the creation of barriers based on rigorous professionalism on the model of Western medicine has "succeeded in barring or at least constraining practitioners [from] employing alternate therapies and techniques, such as acupuncture and chiropractic. The opportunities to learn from alternative practices would be lost if prevailing barriers to practice remain."[35] He cites the work of Sister Justa Smith, a biochemist, who has studied the relationship between enzyme activity and the healing process. Her research indicates that "those who claim to be healers and appear to have had success in healing can dramatically elevate enzyme activity in controlled experiments."[36]

Summary

Health care in the United States combines many types of systems, and lacks a coordinated health care system such as those found in other industrialized nations. This lack causes problems with the cost of care, particularly as it affects subgroups of the population like the elderly and poor. The major fact of health care in the United States is the domination of professionals, suggesting the inability of individuals to influence the system. A look at the continued existence of non-Western medical practitioners indicates that they could have a place in the industrialized world. Before we evaluate that possibility, we will discuss in greater detail the disadvantages of Western health care.

ATTEMPTS AT DEALING WITH THE PROBLEM

The problem of health is twofold. First is the problem of achieving a healthy society; second are the problems created by the way a healthy society is achieved. In the last section, we outlined some of the drawbacks in the way health care is structured and paid for. In this section, we will begin by pointing out other iatrogenic effects — problems created by solutions to the original problem — of American health care, and then mention some alternative solutions.

With regard to health itself, the problem is to ensure good health and to provide health care for as many citizens as possible. The American system of doing so has created problems we've discussed: the professionalization of health care means that physicians are beyond control; costs are skyrocketing; and the poor and elderly suffer lack of care. These matters are widely known and are the subject of heated political debate. What people are less aware of is that the health of people also suffers as a result of the kind of care being provided. It is to these problems that we now turn our attention.

Iatrogenic Effects

It is especially fitting for this chapter that the term iatrogenesis is used to describe the neg-

ative effects of attempts to solve social problems, for the word has a medical origin. *Iatros* is the Greek word for physician and *genesis* means origin; the word describes the harmful side effects associated with some cures for sickness.

THE POWER OF PHYSICIANS

Just as there are iatrogenic effects for individual patients resulting from medical care, so there are for society as a whole. One is the overreliance our society places on physicians. In attempting to reduce anxieties and pain, persons look first to a physician for assistance. "In our society, the physician validates his power by prescribing medication, just as a shaman in a primitive tribe may validate his by spitting out a bit of bloodstained down at the proper moment."[37] A short essay by Horace Miner elaborates this view, suggesting that we view doctors as priests or magicians, and hospitals as temples where special people minister to the needs of the sick.[38]

Although the essay overstates the case, there is a danger in the status given to physicians. We need to view our visits to the hospital with more wariness than we have in the past. Often unnecessary operations and treatments are prescribed for patients. A United States government report in 1973 concluded that at least 7 percent of all patients who undergo surgery or treatment in a hospital suffer injuries while being hospitalized, but few of the patients do anything about it.[39] Two common unnecessary operations are the removal of tonsils and of ovaries. In only 54.9 percent of the ovarian surgeries was surgery justified, based on postoperative or pathological examination.[40] Evidence to support these data was found when several physicians went on strike in large metropolitan areas of the United States. Mortality statistics for the duration of the strike for hospitals involved in the strike showed that the death rate dropped significantly. Fewer patients died in those hospitals where physicians refused to go to work. That some of this decrease is due to the cessation of dangerous, unnecessary surgery seems likely. We are not suggesting that physicians cease practicing, but we are suggesting that greater caution be exercised before needless surgeries and treatments are performed.

Another danger of the professionalization of medicine is that social labeling can become medicalized; all deviance then has to have a medical label.[41] While this reaches extremes in other societies, it is also true in a sense in ours: one cannot be said to be sick without certification by a doctor. Society has come to expect translation of social and psychological ills into medical categories. Associated with this responsibility is a kind of power apart from law and religion. As discussed in Chapter 10, both Thomas Szasz and Thomas Scheff have dealt with the labeling involved in identifying mental illness, suggesting that it involves a normative element. Social conceptions of proper and improper behavior are pressed onto individual conduct. There is an inherent danger and possible damage in classifying behavior incorrectly in the service of public sentiment.[42]

DRUGS AND HEALTH

Another danger of overreliance on physicians is that they are pressured to solve all health problems. A result is the problem of overprescription of drugs. Many people become too dependent on drugs to assist them in dealing with anxieties and problems. About 20,000 tons of aspirin are consumed every year, almost 225 tablets per person. Obviously, the American public feels the need to medicate itself with great frequency.

Another kind of drug abuse stems from drug misuse, encouraged by the advertising of pharmaceutical companies. One example is the use of a milk substitute for babies. This substitute milk includes the necessary vitamin and mineral requirements for newborns and growing babies, and has been successful when used by mothers in the United States and other industrialized countries. The difficulty is that these products have been offered to mothers in less developed countries where education is minimal, and where money to buy adequate amounts is not available. Enterprising pharmaceutical companies have ignored these hazards and have provided free samples to mothers urging them to be modern mothers like women in the West. Unfortunately, the free samples are used long enough so that the mothers' own milk-producing ability ceases. Thus the mothers must rely solely on the milk substitute. As a result, children lose the immunity factors of human milk. Worse, because the mothers cannot afford enough milk substitute, they dilute the formulas and the babies become malnourished and in many cases die.

Added to the problem of overprescribing is the problem of harmful side effects of drugs. We have come to realize that drugs are not always helpful. Thalidomide had devastating effects on unborn European children. In a recent example, death and paralysis were sometimes associated with the flu shots of 1975. The problem in these two cases seems to have been validation, the approval of the drug for use. In everyone's desire to get the drugs on the market quickly, thorough study of the drug was neglected.

Associated with the need for the physician to reinforce his or her self-worth by prescribing drugs for patients and the belief on the part of the patient that drugs solve most ills is the desire on the part of the drug manufacturer to sell the drugs and realize a profit. The competition among drug manufacturers is great and for good reason, as can be seen in Table 14.8. The profit to be gained from marketing such products is higher than that of other manufacturers. In addition, the drug manufacturers have been successful in encouraging physicians to prescribe brand name drugs instead of generic drugs, which are cheaper, and for the most part the drug manufacturers have succeeded. Tables 14.9 and 14.10 provide a measure of how many generic drugs are prescribed as part of the total and the relative cost of the brand name drugs.

The problem of testing a drug is not simple. A long chain of events must be considered with some new products, such as sugar substitutes and insecticides. Partly because of plentiful food and higher living standards, many Americans become overweight. Medicine was developed to serve as a substitute sweetener (saccharin), which would reduce caloric intake. Widespread use of saccharin followed, but scientific findings showed that excessive amounts of saccharin could cause cancer. As a result many persons have ceased using it, without a suitable substitute; others continue using it, taking a chance that they won't develop cancer. Clearly, both are taking risks. The problem seems to be one of determining long-term effects, which are difficult to assess.

The issue of validation is confused by yet another factor: the choice is not simply more testing. Validation can be established in several ways. Besides empirical testing, the beneficial effects of a drug can be demonstrated simply in the belief that the procedure or medicine works. In the case of the drug Laetrile in the treatment of cancer, empirical tests by many labs indicated that the drug has no effect and cited the potential danger of cyanide poisoning. Yet people have used the drug and profess that it is effective. We saw in discussing non-Western medicine that belief in a remedy can sometimes be the cure.

TABLE 14.8 Average Net Profits After Taxes As a Percentage of Net Stockholders' Equity

Year	Drug Manufacturers	All Manufacturers
1960	17.0%	9.3%
1965	20.5	13.1
1970	18.2	9.4
1971	19.3	9.7
1972	18.8	10.7
1973	19.0	12.9
1974	18.8	15.1

Source: *Quarterly Financial Report for Manufacturing Corporations* FTC-SEC.

TABLE 14.9 New Generic Drug Prescriptions As a Percentage of Total New Prescriptions

Year	New Generic Drugs
1966	6.4%
1967	7.0
1968	8.2
1969	8.8
1970	9.0
1971	9.2
1972	9.7
1973	10.6
1974	10.7
1975	11.1

Source: *Pharmacy Times* (April 1976).

DIET AND FITNESS

Before the twentieth century the American diet was geared to providing energy and sustenance needed for manual labor. The high caloric content was expended by human effort in work, and little excess intake occurred, except among the higher classes. With more sophisticated technology, including labor-saving devices, the necessity for high calorie diets decreased, but the dietary emphasis on full plates and stomachs did not change. The result was that many people became overweight, and the incidence of related health problems increased.

Once the problems of being overweight became widespread, the medical profession sought to inform the public of the potential dangers, such as heart disease, diabetes, and pulmonary disorders. Over time the public accepted the admonitions of physicians and embarked on a new phase of health treatment, beginning various diets and starting to exercise. Unfortunately, both practices are as fraught with dangers as the high-calorie, low-activity life they are meant to replace. A good diet is an integral part of good health, and this shift in public attitudes is commendable. In fact, more and more Americans are becoming interested in good diet as they see positive results in those around them. The problems arise when the slenderizing diet omits necessary vitamins and minerals or basic nutritional requirements. Unless the dieter is careful, any diet used has potential

TABLE 14.10 Multiple-Source Drug-Price Comparisons

Product	Major Brand Price	Generic Price
Propoxyphene HCL 65 mg 100	$7.02 Darvon Eli Lilly	$3.60 SK 65 Smith Klein Corp.
Meprobamate 400 mg 100	$6.00 Equanil Wyeth	$1.49 Kessobamate McKesson Pharmaceuticals
Reserpine .25 mg 1000	$39.50 Serpasil Ciba	$9.76 Sandril Eli Lilly
Nitrofurantoin 50 mg 100	$10.26 Furandantin Eaton Laboratories	$1.75 Nurofurantoin Ketchum Labs
Sulfisoxazole .5 gm 1000	$26.60 Gantrisin Roche	$10.64 Sulfisoxazole Purepac

Source: *Drug Topics Red Book* (Oradell, N.J.: Medical Economics Company, 1976).

for harm. Quick weight loss methods can cause systemic shock, and may not actually change the poor eating habits that brought on the need to diet. Fasting when taken to extremes causes the pancreas to overproduce insulin, which is associated with diabetes. High protein, low carbohydrate diets often omit certain minerals necessary for metabolizing chemicals in the body. One recent high-protein diet uses predigested protein as the main source of nourishment for as long as a month. This practice causes extreme systemic shock and in several cases has led to death. Vegetarianism, another popular diet though not a weight-loss diet, can be harmful if the dieter, in foregoing meat, does not find another source of protein. Dieting without direction and information almost automatically leads to harmful side effects.

The same is true of exercise. The new and widespread concern for good health has led to sometimes frantic searches for the right exercise program. Exercise has been endorsed by advertisements and by the President's Council on Physical Fitness. Reports of medical research on exercise and its relationship to mental and physical well-being have appeared. Persons of all ages are being encouraged to keep active by exercising. The existence of a Senior Olympics attests to the interest of older citizens to exercise and their ability to profit from it. An advertisement for one life insurance company shows an older woman who jogs five miles a day after having suffered almost total disability due to heart problems. News reports describe people in their eighties and nineties who jog twenty miles a day. Add to this the reports that runners experience a kind of mental high from jogging, and many seeking a new experience rush to try it.

Again, the problem is extremes. Older people, whose bodies are less flexible and who may have been inactive for years, may attempt to make up for lost time too quickly. Tennis enthusiasts visit their physicians for treatment of tennis elbows or sprained or broken ankles. Joggers share the same waiting rooms with the tennis buffs, complaining of fallen arches, traumatized heels, and sore backs. Both groups can suffer from overexertion, as a result of poor preparation or lack of moderation. If exercise continues unsupervised, it can lead to serious consequences such as heart failure. As with dieting, the problem is not exercise per se. It is simply that both are done too often with little guidance from persons trained to measure capacities for exertion and to monitor progress. What is needed is a more informed public and better balance, tying fitness and diet to good health.

Alternative Medical Perspectives

The many problems associated with Western medicine have persuaded some people to explore new approaches to health care. Partly because expertise in medicine has become broken into smaller and smaller parts where distinct types of analysis can be performed, the overall picture of the general health of the patient can be lost.

Some medical approaches appear to try to eliminate symptoms too hastily, without considering and analyzing them to see if they indicate a much greater physical problem or illness. This approach called *allopathic medicine* aims primarily at the cure of ailments at the time of complaint. For example, if a patient has a fever, sore throat and chills, the diagnosis that relies most heavily on the patient's present condition may be flu and the possible solution would be bed rest and fever-reducing medication. Allopathic medicine is in contrast with *holistic* medicine, which argues that past events and experiences are relevant to the physical and emotional state of the individual. This perspective leads the practitioner to seek extensive information about the patient's life and medical history. Presented with the symptoms mentioned, the physician would evaluate the patient's background, recent experience, dietary habits, etc., to establish that the problem was indeed simply a cold. Treatment would also require follow-up to determine that the condition was not chronic or symptomatic of a more serious problem.

At the end of the spectrum of treatments are alternative medical methods, which are inaccessible to empirical testing but which have many adherents. Among these methods are ritual or psychic healing, acupuncture, and biofeedback.

Ritual or *psychic healing* attempts to cure by, for example, psychic removal of damaged or diseased tissue without surgical incision. Often the patient is shown a substance representing the diseased tissue; examination after psychic healing indicates an associated decrease in the size of the tumors or healing of an injury. In modern Western scientific terms this is not possible and yet the change occurs.

Acupuncture consists of healing by insertion of needles at different points on the body. There is considerable evidence to show that this technique has been effective. Most widely used in the Orient, it is now practiced in the United States.

Biofeedback presumes the ability of individuals to generate electroencephalographic brain waves at will. Persons subject to severe stress and anxiety are trained to monitor

If you asked these Central Park joggers why they jog, their answer would probably not be for fun, or for sport, or for adventure. Instead, it is likely to be to keep in shape. Running has been shown to be excellent for the heart and lungs and muscle tone, for overall physical fitness. But it must be done correctly, at a pace geared to each individual, or it can be harmful.

brain impulses and to control them so as to reduce their physical symptoms. Biofeedback reflects the holistic approach in that it encourages an increased awareness of one's body as an interrelated system. Western medicine has been unable to verify changes or cures obtained by the biofeedback process. Depending on the perspective of the observer, the patient is either the victim of a charlatan who is duping the public, or the beneficiary of a valid form of treatment.

PROSPECTS FOR SOLVING THE PROBLEM

When the problem of fair and equal distribution of medical care to the general public is considered, a series of possible solutions come to mind. The first possibility is to improve existing programs like Medicare and Medicaid, so that more people can be covered, and to support such facilities as neighborhood health centers. Another alternative is to expand programs like those of the Health Maintenance Organization, a group formed to protect people financially against unforeseen and unpreventable disaster. At this time participation in HMOs is voluntary, so government action can only make such plans more attractive; it cannot force membership.

Another alternative is to nationalize medicine, giving the government the responsibility of determining the prices, supply, and quality of medical care. The ninety-third Congress, elected in 1974, produced a plethora of plans for health care. We cannot discuss them in detail, but the outlines can be shown. The Kennedy-Corman bill (named for cosponsors Senator Edward Kennedy of Massachusetts and Representative James Corman of California) proposed a comprehensive health insurance program. As a countermeasure, the American Medical Association Medicredit Plan was introduced, which essentially provided health care in the private sector. Another bill proposed to retain health care as it presently exists with the addition of government protection in catastrophic health situations such as multiple operations or extensive treatment. As a result of the above proposals, Senator Kennedy and former Representative Wilbur Mills of Arkansas offered a compromise program, providing national health insurance and a revision of Medicare. It was a compromise in that instead of health insurance being applied universally to all citizens, it would be applied on the basis of need, for which the association in Medicare would provide a measurement. In addition, the private insurance systems could still operate but would be controlled by the government via the Medicare program. This last program was designed to be more acceptable to various factions. The question was neglected for many years, until 1979, when competing proposals from President Carter and Senator Kennedy were made. The Kennedy program would institute full national health insurance, phasing in full coverage over a period of years. The Carter program would introduce federal funding for catastrophic illness as the first step toward full government coverage of health care. Although the Carter plan is not yet completed, it is expected to allow a greater role for existing private health insurance arrangements than the Kennedy program.

Other possible solutions to problems with health care would address other areas than health support systems. First is the increased involvement of the general public in overseeing the activities of doctors and the medical system. In this way decisions will be viewed and tested by disinterested parties. Because of the complexity of modern life, examination of procedures, costs, and practices is extremely important, but at present formal medical organizations like the American Medical Association resist public involvement.

A similar process is suggested by Carlson to review the performance of *quacks,* or incompetent physicians. He recommends developing information on the outcome of treatment of all of a doctor's patients, to be made available to prospective customers. This information could also be used "to bar some practitioners from regional health centers when it is clear that harm is being done to patients."[43] He also suggests that some practitioners could be barred from association with hospitals. It appears that increased participation by the general public would allow for a more open health care system. In addition, those government agencies, such as the Food and Drug Administration, which were created to protect the people, should be made to represent the people and respond to their needs more diligently. This would involve a shift from serving the interests of medical businesses and practitioners to serving the consumers.

Another proposed solution, requiring extensive reeducation, involves a change in perspective and basic philosophy on the part of patients and physicians. This change would be to monitor health instead of waiting for and monitoring sickness. In this approach, the doctor and patient would be partners in attempting to maintain health, rather than assigning sole responsibility to the physician to attend to symptoms and effect cures. This move from allopathic to preventive medicine should be supplemented by the adoption of non-Western medical practices that have proven effective for many generations.

Whether society will make these changes, to provide health care for all its members and open the medical system to public scrutiny, is difficult to predict. It is clear that the powers in medicine will fight to maintain the status quo. Doctors, through their associations, will wish to maintain their oversight authority over each other, which allows them greater freedom in their work. The insurance and pharmaceutical companies, hospitals, and doctors will all oppose the establishment of national health insurance, which will probably be the main battleground of reform of the health care system. It is possible that for any comprehensive program to be instituted, greater public pressure will be needed on Congress and the health care industry. Such pressure will be difficult to arouse, however, for the issue is complex and such debates rarely excite widespread participation.

The prospects for the adoption of newer, non-Western techniques, however, seem good, although not at first glance. A formalized medical structure has evolved, where governments and the physicians are the primary source of authority on health questions. With the recent introduction of other health care perspectives, the formal structure has initially taken a hardline view of these approaches. If the advocates of these new practices persist, the health care system will then attempt to incorporate many of them into the existing structure. Since the essential concern of medical practitioners is to care for the sick, they will seek the best possible methods and knowledge to do so, whatever the source.

IMPORTANT WORDS AND TERMS

acupuncture
allopathic medicine
antibiotics
biofeedback
contagion
epidemiology
generic drug
germ theory of disease
health
health support systems
generic
holistic medicine
innoculation
medical sociology
organizational theory
placebo
professionalization
quack
social change

QUESTIONS FOR DISCUSSION

1. Discuss the differences in health care systems in the United States and England. Should the United States have nationalized health care?
2. What are some ways of determining whether or not a medical practice is acceptable to society? Consider what agencies or individuals decide what is acceptable and what the end result must be for an outcome to be identified as a cure.
3. Give your overall impression of how medicine developed from ancient to modern times. What social conditions hindered or encouraged medical advances? How did members of society respond to epidemics and plague? Would the same thing happen today?
4. It has been said that shamans and medicine men are also professionals. Do you agree or disagree with this? Why?
5. Why do you think that the United States has not passed a national health insurance plan? What social conditions are involved in this situation? How does the label "socialized medicine" affect the possibility of passage? What are the problems of cost?
6. Discuss Laetrile as a treatment of cancer. Should it be made available to members of society who believe it works? Can you think of other drugs that also should be made available to citizens if they believe they work?
7. In cases where evidence of medical malpractice or quackery has been discovered, which group should consider and evaluate these cases, members of the American Medical Association? Legislators and public officials? A combination? Why?
8. What should the Food and Drug Administration do to ensure quality of prepared drugs and medicines and the proper preparation of foods?
9. Why have Americans become concerned about diet and exercise? Is this concern warranted or overemphasized?
10. Why is the cost of medicine so high in the United States? How can this be changed?
11. The cost of health care in the United States is higher than in most other parts of the world, and yet U.S. mortality rates are worse. What are some of the possible reasons for this situation?
12. The health care system in the United States is complex. Are there alternative ways that this system could be constructed and coordinated that would result in better health care for citizens? Consider this question in terms of the various professions, the types of treatment available, and the locations of treatment.
13. Why does the density of population relate to health care problems?
14. A typical image of a caring physician could be found in the media portrayal of the family doctor. Compare the ideal characteristics to the criteria and standards of professionalism suggested by Pavalko.

SUGGESTED READING

Rick J. Carlson, *The End of Medicine* (New York: Wiley, 1975).

Carlson traces the development of medical history and considers its relative impact on health in the United States, which he finds wanting. The two points are substantiated by important data. Finally, he proposes the necessity for medicine, as we know it, to end in order to allow for new approaches. In this regard he makes specific recommendations for change.

Karen Davis and Cathy Shoen, *Health and the War on Poverty: A Ten-Year Appraisal* (Washington, D.C.: The Brookings Institution, 1978).

An excellent example of evaluation research. The data allow for comparison of the costs and benefits of the poverty program's health services to various segments of the population. The data are shocking, but invaluable to the analyst attempting to find better solutions.

Kenneth M. Friedman and Stuart H. Rakoff, *Toward a National Health Policy* (Lexington, Mass.: Lexington Books, 1977).

A good resource for information in various segments of the health care system. Discusses public policy and specific programs. Provides a good comparison of national health care proposals and their alternatives.

Fielding H. Garrison, *An Introduction to the History of Medicine* (Philadelphia: Saunders, 1929).

This excellent book helps to place scientific developments in proper temporal and intellectual context. Its history of medicine emphasizes influential people.

Ivan Illich, *Medical Nemesis: The Expropriation of Health* (New York: Pantheon, 1976).

A strong critic of health care in the United States, Illich makes a scathing attack on the medical system, advancing the idea that health should be in the hands of the people. He is especially concerned about the political power of the medical care system. He uses the concept of iatrogenesis to substantiate his proposals.

Charles Leslie, *Asian Medical Systems: A Comparative Study* (Los Angeles: University of California Press, 1976).

A delightful and enlightening book that provides great insight into the background and practice of non-Western medicine. The material in this book allows for greater understanding of the possibilities of alternative approaches to medicine.

Charles Singer and E. Ashworth Underwood, *A Short History of Medicine* (New York: Oxford University Press, 1962).

A fine history of the development of medicine in the world, which treats the material through the development of practices. It has less of an emphasis on people than Garrison's book.

NOTES

1. World Health Organization, *Constitution of the World Health Organization* (New York: United Nations, 1957), p. 1.
2. René Dubos, *Man Adapting* (New Haven: Yale University Press, 1965), p. 346.
3. Gerhard Lenski and Jean Lenski, *Human Societies* (New York: McGraw-Hill, 1974).
4. For an excellent book see Carol Taylor, *In Horizontal Orbit: Hospitals and the Cult of Efficiency* (New York: Holt, Rinehart and Winston, 1970).

5. Ronald M. Pavalko, *Sociology of Occupations and Professions* (Itasca, Ill.: Peacock, 1971), p. 17.

6. Harold L. Wilensky, "The Professionalization of Everyone?" *American Journal of Sociology*, Vol. 70 (September 1964), pp. 137–158.

7. Paul F. Basch, *International Health* (New York: Oxford University Press, 1978), p. 272.

8. Rick J. Carlson, *The End of Medicine* (New York: Wiley, 1975). See also Charles Leslie, *Asian Medical Systems: A Comparative Study* (Los Angeles: University of California Press, 1976); and Charles Singer and E. Ashworth Underwood, *A Short History of Medicine* (New York: Oxford University Press, 1962).

9. Singer and Underwood, *Short History of Medicine*, p. 1.

10. Leslie, *Asian Medical Systems*, p. 7.

11. Singer and Underwood, *Short History of Medicine*, p. 46.

12. Fielding H. Garrison, *History of Medicine* (Philadelphia: Saunders, 1929), Appendix 1.

13. Ibid., p. 812.

14. Basch, *International Health*, p. 57.

15. Garrison, *History of Medicine*, p. 176.

16. Ibid., p. 882.

17. Singer and Underwood, *Short History of Medicine*, p. 218.

18. Ibid., p. 113.

19. Garrison, *History of Medicine*, p. 405.

20. Ibid., p. 770.

21. Basch, *International Medicine*, p. 71.

22. Garrison, *History of Medicine*, p. 785.

23. Basch, *International Medicine*, p. 74.

24. Department of Health and Social Security, *British National Service*, quoted in ibid., p. 274.

25. Basch, *International Medicine*, p. 283.

26. Ibid., p. 284.

27. Carlson, *End of Medicine*, p. 47.

28. Pavalko, *Sociology of Occupations*, pp. 90–92.

29. Ida Harper Simpson, "Patterns of Socialization into Professions: The Case of Student Nurses," *Sociological Inquiry*, Vol. 37 (Winter 1967), pp. 47–54.

30. Leslie, *Asian Medical Systems*. An excellent example of the rigorous training required and the application of these principles can be found in D. E. Jones, *Sanapia: Comanche Medicine Woman* (New York: Holt, Rinehart and Winston, 1972).

31. Erwin H. Ackernecht, *Medicine and Ethnology* (Baltimore: Johns Hopkins University Press, 1971).

32. Jerome Frank, *Persuasion and Healing* (New York: Schocken, 1961), p. 67.

33. Ackernecht, *Medicine and Ethnology*, p. 131.

34. Eliot Friedson, *The Profession of Medicine: A Study of the Sociology of Applied Knowledge* (New York: Dodd, Mead, 1970), p. 5.

35. Carlson, *End of Medicine*, p. 224.

36. Sister Justa Smith, "Paranormal Effects on Enzyme Activity," *Human Dimensions*, Vol. 1 (Spring 1972), p. 2.

37. Frank, *Persuasion and Healing*, p. 66.

38. Horace Miner, "The Body Ritual Among the Nacirema," *American Anthropologist*, Vol. 58 (1966), pp. 503–507.

39. U.S. Department of Health, Education, and Welfare, *Report of the Secretary's Commission on Medical Malpractice* (Washington, D.C.: U.S. Government Printing Office, 1973).

40. James C. Doyle, "Unnecessary Ovariectomies," *Journal of the American Medical Association*, Vol. 148 (1952), p. 13.

41. Ivan Illich, *Medical Nemesis: The Expropriation of Health* (New York: Pantheon Books, 1976), p. 47.

42. Thomas Szasz, *The Myth of Mental Illness* (New York: Harper and Row, 1961); and Thomas J. Scheff, *Being Mentally Ill: A Sociological Theory* (Chicago: Aldine, 1966).

43. Carlson, *End of Medicine*, p. 225.

15 INTERNATIONAL CONFLICT
SOPHISTICATED WEAPONRY AND STONE AGE MENTALITY

CHAPTER OVERVIEW

INTRODUCTION

CONCEPTUAL ORIENTATION
The Nature of Human Aggression
War in Primitive Societies
Defining War
Summary

HISTORICAL OVERVIEW
Primitive and Early Warfare
Modern Warfare
    Democracy on the Battlefield
    Industrialization and Mass Production
    The Managerial Revolution
    The Scientific Revolution
Summary

OBJECTIVE DIMENSIONS OF THE PROBLEM
Technological Advances
Contemporary Military Organization
The Military-Industrial Complex
The Military Budget
Worldwide Arms Expenditures
The Economics of Defense Procurement
Summary

ATTEMPTS AT DEALING WITH THE PROBLEM
American Ideology and International Conflict
The Rise of Anticommunism
America and Vietnam
Iatrogenic Effects

PROSPECTS FOR SOLVING THE PROBLEM
The Domestic Structure
The Superpowers and the International Community
The Role of the United Nations
Summary

IMPORTANT WORDS AND TERMS

QUESTIONS FOR DISCUSSION

SUGGESTED READING

NOTES

The American eagle is portrayed as holding an olive branch in one claw and a sheaf of arrows in the other. What kind of policy is it that weighs down the one claw with 90 billion dollars worth of arrows and provides the other with a minute, wilted, olive branch on which we spend practically nothing?
  Kenneth Boulding, "The Effects of the War Industry"

We are now the most martial people on the globe and our history, which runs exactly concurrent with the annals of modern arms, demonstrates we are perhaps the "fightingest" society since Rome.
  Robert Leckie, Warfare

CHAPTER OVERVIEW

In this chapter, we will begin by examining the nature of international conflict, finding that modern war is a product of modern political institutions. We will discuss how an ever-increasing level of technology has revolutionized the nature of conflict between nations, especially in terms of the intensity and scale on which wars are fought. Based on a series of changes in social structure, technology, and ideology, conflict today between different countries, especially the superpowers, has the potential for destroying civilization and obliterating humankind. The development of a permanent military establishment, the resources it consumes, and the continuing change in military organization are all discussed, to allow us to assess the prospects for avoiding armed conflict in the future.

INTRODUCTION

In August 1945, the Japanese cities of Hiroshima and Nagasaki were incinerated. In two blinding flashes, each lasting only a few seconds, the dawn of a new age of warfare was ushered onto the stage of world affairs. The search for the ultimate weapon, begun thousands of years ago, was ended. Or so it seemed, as it has each time some technological breakthrough revolutionized human warfare. But this time was different, people said, for who could imagine worse than this? Yet imagined they have. In the decades since 1945, the United States has spent more than one and one-half trillion dollars continually updating its arsenal. Each year the American military wants more resources because, like Alice in Wonderland, they must run at a furious pace just to keep up. With all the furious running they are doing, we have finally reached the point where the United States alone now has the equivalent of at least 12,000 pounds of dynamite for every man, woman, and child in the entire world.[1]

To understand the dilemma inherent in trying to work toward a lasting peace, we must look at how war as a social phenomenon has evolved throughout human history. To set the stage for our understanding of the contemporary aspects of the problem, let us first discuss the work done by anthropologists on the nature of human aggression and the role it has played in warfare. From this review we can more precisely define the concept of war and then go on to consider how war has changed during the past 500 years.

CONCEPTUAL ORIENTATION

The Nature of Human Aggression

Conflicts between human individuals and groups apparently existed prior to the dawn of civilization itself, according to archaeological findings. Physical anthropologists have found skulls from about a half million years ago that appear to have been smashed, perhaps by a rock, providing us with possible evidence that our earliest ancestors were not always peaceful.[2] Aggression resulting in human conflict is thought by many people to be part of human nature. A number of recent books have been published that support this view, and use it to attempt to understand human warfare, the armed aggression of one group against another. Konrad Lorenz's *On Aggression* and Robert Ardrey's *The Territorial Imperative* have become popular because of their claim to help us understand the role warfare has played in human life.

The view exemplified by Lorenz and Ardrey assumes that human aggression is inherited from our animal ancestors, retained deep beneath our veneer of civilization.

> Man is a predator whose natural instinct is to kill with a weapon. . . . The primate has instincts demanding the maintenance and defense of territories; an attitude of perpetual hostility for the territorial neighbor. . . . Our history reveals the development and contest of superior weapons as Homo sapiens' single universal cultural preoccupation.[3]

If so, then studies of aggression in lower animals should shed a great deal of light on aggression in humans. Lorenz makes the connection explicit:

> Like the triumphal ceremony of the greylag goose, militant enthusiasm (for war) in man is a true autonomous instinct; it has its own appetite behavior, its own releasing mechanism, and like the sexual urge or any other strong instinct, it engenders a specific feeling of intense satisfaction.[4]

This view is not widely held, however. While it may be interesting to think about these parallels in everyday behavior between humans and other animal species, most anthropologists reject using them to explain aggression. The noted anthropologist, Ralph Holloway, Jr., understanding that all human aggression must be discussed in a socioeconomic context, summarizes the counterargument to Ardrey and Lorenz:

Human aggression: innate or learned? There are persuasive arguments for each answer, but most people, including anthropologists, believe that aggression must be examined and understood in its socioeconomic context, and not as a purely instinctual, biological phenomenon.

'No, Madam, as a child I was not permitted so much as a water pistol.'

Human aggression cannot be discussed without reference to kinds of socioeconomic conditions under which men live or, better, try to live. This is one of the most disappointing and infuriating aspects of the recent attempts by a few biologists and dramatists to explain human aggression by reference to animal studies, instincts, death drives, and the like.[5]

According to Holloway, those who suggest the need for worldwide games, like the Olympics, or some other activity to displace war as an outlet for aggression, completely overlook an important difference between humans and animals. Human *aggression*, behavior intended to injure some person or object, is an individual act based on some individual emotional state. The decision to go to war involves more than this. It is essentially a political act involving the social organization.

War in Primitive Societies

The realities of human aggression must always be seen in the context of the social framework. Even in the most technologically primitive societies, people live in social structures where they learn the ingredients necessary for their survival. As part of ensuring survival, they set up political organizations, ranging from relatively simple to the highly complex. As they come into contact with other tribes or societies, there is often conflict. When seen from our viewpoint, this resembles organized warfare. Let us examine the conflicts between primitive societies to see if they do, in fact, resemble the warfare we are familiar with.

In the above discussion, we rejected the assumption that innate, instinctual, and inherited aggression is a major explanation for human warfare. We are able to take this position because, while we must recognize conflict and aggression as existing in all human societies, there is a good deal of evidence that warfare, as we know it, is virtually nonexistent among a number of primitive societies. Among the Andaman Islanders, the Arunta, the Eskimos, the Mission Indians, and several other primitive societies, the concept of war is even absent from their language. These people cannot conceive of any sort of organized battle that pits tribe against tribe.

The reason is that small, preliterate societies, with less complex division of labor and little specialization, lack the well-developed or well-defined political entity we call the state. Preliterate societies do have forms of armed aggression and conflict between and among individuals. There is often fighting and even killing, where the motivation is highly individual and the personal involvement is great. As Alexander Lesser comments, "Fighting does occur among these and other primitive peoples, and we find a manifestation of armed aggression, homicide, vengeance, and feud."[6] But what is lacking in these societies is the impersonal involvement and motivation that seem characteristic of modern war, especially as it has been fought in the twentieth century.

If not all kinds of aggressive behavior can be lumped together and labeled as war, where does one draw the dividing line? Feuds, raids, killings, and fighting are found in all societies on which there is any data, but we must differentiate war from these other forms of aggressive behavior.

Defining War

With what we have seen, we can now define *war* with the following words:

War is legal, aggressive behavior with lethal weapons carried out as a part of a national policy by a relatively large, impersonal, and specialized institution aimed at the conquest of people or territory or at the expansion of influence in an area.

While the reason for war — the goal of conquest — is familiar, two other parts of the definition may need explaining. War is defined as "legal aggressive behavior" because the use of weapons to kill people outside the social group is sanctioned by law. Rather than the soldiers being punished for their actual or potential killing, they are often hailed as heroes and are paid salaries, given medals, recognition, and other rewards. While all societies have laws against killing, most do not prohibit all killing, but only some kinds (which are called murder). Two kinds are frequently allowed — that directed against deviant members of the society, called punishment, and that directed against another society, called warfare.

By defining war as a part of national policy we stress the emergence of a separate political entity with a conception of itself, a nation clearly distinguishable from other political entities. Prior to the emergence of a more or less specific political entity within a society, warfare as we know it today did not exist. Aggressive behavior and conflict between individuals and groups of individuals within the society did occur; but this should be labeled as conflict, not as war.

As the famous German military author, Karl von Clausewitz, wrote long ago, war is an organized extension of the political process, carrying diplomacy to a more extreme level. In the 1820s, Clausewitz wrote about war not as being part of either the arts or sciences, as many at the time saw it, but as an integral part of the social fabric of any society. In his own words, "We say . . . war belongs not to the province of Arts and Sciences but to the province of social life. It is a conflict of great interests which is settled by bloodshed and only in that is it different from others. It would be better, instead of comparing it with any Art, to liken it to business competition, which is also a conflict of human interest and activities."[7]

Warfare cannot be understood without comprehending political processes. It cannot be analyzed on the basis of either individual psychology or pent-up emotion. War occurs when the political entity in charge of establishing and carrying out national policy determines that the advantages of waging war outweigh the disadvantages. While it is true that pent-up hatreds and emotions are often present as part of any decision, we must not lose sight of the rational element in the decision to go to war.

Summary

We have differentiated warfare from other types of aggression because it is a phenomenon of the complex social phenomenon called the nation. Having defined war in reference to social processes and not to individual aggressions or emotions, we now need to turn our attention to the question of how warfare has developed during the course of history to possess the characteristics it has today.

HISTORICAL OVERVIEW

In looking at people's technologically more sophisticated ways of killing other people, it is hard not to think that technology causes war. Almost every important scientific discovery has been rapidly transformed into military usage, and wartime pressures have helped speed up certain kinds of scientific research. This rapid incorporation of every new technological breakthrough has led to one key characteristic of modern warfare, its impersonality. Today's technology has made modern warfare capable of pitting people against each other, not in hand-to-hand combat, but using electronic images on radar scopes and pushing buttons to kill each other. Even with the reversion to conventional warfare, resulting from the nuclear standoff between the superpowers, military technology continues to be advanced by the developed nations. Warfare has not always been as impersonal or as destructive as it is today, and to appreciate how warfare has changed, we should review what war used to be like. What we see today is the result of a series of developments over many centuries. In the following analysis we will follow the plan Robert Leckie established in his book *Warfare*, using a series of stages to examine the evolution of the human warfare culture.[8]

Primitive and Early Warfare

Evidence of people fighting other people is older than written history. However, the organization of people into the kinds of armies we are familiar with today is a relatively recent occurrence. Early attempts at warfare were probably related to the way game was hunted for food. With some minor modification, the same weapons were used and the tactics of stalking and pouncing upon an enemy in an unsuspecting moment were commonplace. When weapons were primitive, people fought each other on foot and combat largely involved the physical prowess of one opponent over another.

The next stage of warfare, beginning with the earliest recorded history, covers a 6,000-year period from about 4500 B.C. to about A.D. 1500. During this time, while war was becoming more efficient and destructive, it still remained essentially local in nature. Over this period, the size of armies was increased and tactics used in battle changed to maneuvering and massing more troops, but actual fighting remained highly personal, consisting of individual combat. Warriors of the contending armies usually confronted each other face to face and often fought hand to hand. Combat was, in fact, so highly personal that Alexander, the Macedonian conqueror of the fourth century B.C., supposedly ordered his men to shave closely so that their beards would not offer handholds to the enemy.

In addition to being highly personal, combat was also limited in time and space, even with the increased mobility provided by horses. Most warfare was essentially landlocked and any battles at sea were usually fought close to land, using the tactics derived from land combat.

Modern Warfare

While it is difficult to mark the precise beginning of modern warfare, it is clear that the scientific advances of the fourteenth and fifteenth centuries made war more destructive and made the destruction more widespread. One key change was the European discovery of gunpowder early in the fourteenth century. (Gunpowder had been known in China as early as the first century A.D., but its use in warfare was a European phenomenon.) In the fourteenth century, the French began firing the first cannons; their frequent foes, the English, commenced firing theirs from ships at about the same time. During the fourteenth century, the use of firearms began to emerge, but they were not used effectively until after 1450. However, when gunpowder was coupled with major scientific advances, including those in navigation, mapping, and shipbuilding, the stage was set for the enormous worldwide increase in the power and influence of European nations.

We must be careful not to overemphasize the technological dimensions of the revolution that occurred during this time. For, along with technological change came a revolution in the arts, philosophy, and religion. It was the drastic change in patterns of thought occurring simultaneously with the greatly expanded means of destruction provided by scientific discoveries that laid the groundwork for exploration and conquest by the European powers. It is impossible to say which was more important, the revolution in idea systems or the revolution in science, for each reinforced the other. It was the revolution in idea systems which prompted many of the inventors of this period to apply scientific advancements to create the revolution in exploration, trade, and ultimately in warfare.

Subsequent to this first revolution, four more revolutions have taken place and led to the development of warfare as we know it today. At times these revolutions occurred simultaneously, at other times they were grafted onto changes that had already taken place. Let us look at these four revolutions to see how each changed the face of war and produced the warfare we know today.

DEMOCRACY ON THE BATTLEFIELD

The French Revolution, following closely on the heels of the American, revolutionized the conduct of wars. No longer was war fought largely by small groups of professional warriors, or mercenaries, led by an aristocracy whose principal vocation was the practice of arms. In 1793, the French nation was placed on a total war footing by the famous *levée en masse*, conscripted service for all ablebodied men. As the historian Roger Leonard states, "War became, under Napoleon, an affair of the people and of the nation. The participation of the people made available means and effort limited only by the energy and resources of the nation and the objectives of policy."[9] This dramatic revolution meant that massed armies, in size unlike anything seen before, could be used as part of the emerging military tactics. The masses were compelled to join, supported by their belief in political freedom and the equality of every human. Conscription on a mass scale made soldiers cheap when once they had been expensive.

INDUSTRIALIZATION AND MASS PRODUCTION

Before the mid-1800s, the time of the American Civil War, the application of technology to the mass production of goods was rather limited. But from about 1860 onward, basic industrial processes using new techniques to harness energy and process raw materials were able to place in the hands of troops weapons of even greater destructive power. Advances made in the industrial ability to process and work steel produced rifled gun barrels, which had greater range and accuracy. As Henry Kissinger wrote before he became Secretary of State in the Nixon administration, the Industrial Revolution changed warfare: "Until the Industrial Revolution, total war in the modern sense of fully mobilizing all national resources was impossible. Subsistence economies simply could not spare the manpower or the resources for protracted large-scale operations. . . . The Industrial Revolution made possible the total mobilization of modern war."[10]

The Industrial Revolution had the effect of

increasing the range and accuracy of weapons, making killing less the result of chance. It also made resources and energy available in such large amounts that they could be expended lavishly on a large scale, resulting in a high casualty rate among the combatants. It also changed the focus of fighting; no longer was the purpose necessarily to kill enemy soldiers. Once production capacity is harnessed to manufacture war goods, defeating an enemy requires damaging or destroying his production facilities in order to cut off the flow of supplies. Strategy is then to fight a war of attrition. Not only is the military defeat of an opponent necessary, but the civilian population must suffer as well. The result is that the line between civilian and military personnel in any modern war has become blurred. Whole populations organized to produce the material for conducting warfare have become prime targets in modern war.

THE MANAGERIAL REVOLUTION

As warfare has become increasingly complex, it has required greater administrative skills. Basic managerial techniques have been used in running the military, resulting in a greater efficiency in planning and executing war. From a sociological point of view, it is no longer possible to distinguish between the military's complex bureaucratic organization and those of large business firms — the parallels are too overwhelming. The incorporation of modern business practices into the running of the military services by staff officers has transformed all modern armies. The establishment of a highly trained staff to apply businesslike thinking to procuring shells or counting the enemy dead has become a striking characteristic of modern war.

THE SCIENTIFIC REVOLUTION

The impact of science has been continuous and has drastically altered the nature of warfare. Part of the influence of technology has been to increase the mobility and destructiveness of weapons and to make the soldiers fighting more vulnerable to their effects. Tanks, airplanes, submarines, and numerous other weapons have been made possible by the wedding of the internal combustion engine to various kinds of gun platforms. The transportation of troops and supplies has also made war more fluid, allowing it to cover great stretches of territory and involve still more troops.

Of all technological innovations, however, the decision to construct atomic devices has probably most changed warfare. Today people have weapons capable of ending human civilization. Although nuclear war has not yet occurred, these weapons may well be used as a last desperate attempt to ward off defeat. Surely any beginning exchange would escalate rapidly, until the mindless destruction of some distant enemy becomes the only possibility. This hardly represents the rational element in war defined by von Clausewitz.

Summary

Each of the revolutions discussed above has made the use of war to settle disputes between nations more problematic. The democratic revolution meant that people now had an obligation to fight for the country they lived in and were subject to being drafted on a mass scale. The vast standing armies that faced each other in World War I and World War II were made possible by the belief in a national spirit, ironically based on an in-

Our involvement on an enormous scale in World War II was possible not so much because the draft forced civilians into front lines but because citizens were proud and willing to fight for their nation and its interests. Crowds like this one in Times Square celebrating V-J Day sent off and welcomed back soldiers with a patriotic zest that has had no match since.

creased popular basis for government. No longer did the nation represent only the royalty and their interests; elected representatives of the people became the supporters of the decisions to go to war. Men allowed themselves to be conscripted into the military service to uphold what was seen as their national interest.

While the democracy made larger armies possible, coordinating and controlling these forces were made possible by the managerial revolution. With the mass conscription of modern armies, the enormous productive capacity of industrialized states was turned to the manufacture of instruments of death, producing slaughter on an increasingly terrible scale. But even the millions of people killed in World War I did little to reduce the desire to wage war in the future. Up until the advent of atomic weapons, the killing of millions of people in war had little long-range effect on population growth. In every modern war, the vast numbers killed in any country have only been a small percentage (usually much less than 10 percent) of the national population. The year 1945 changed this potential, with the advent of atomic weapons.

Today the entire human species is threatened by any large-scale nuclear exchange. As weapons become more and more efficient, in the sense of being smaller yet more accurate and more powerful, many observers feel that a resort to full-scale warfare in the future would result in human annihilation. This is the legacy of our increasingly successful attempts to kill other humans. To break the chain of events set in motion by these four revolutions, we need to do more than simply put wiser people in positions of power. As Liddell Hart commented in 1935, years before the atomic bomb was even conceived:

> It is not that generals and admirals are incompetent, but that the task has passed from their competence. Their limitations are due not to a congenital stupidity as a disillusioned public is apt to assume, but to the growth of science, which has upset the foundations of their techniques.[11]

OBJECTIVE DIMENSIONS OF THE PROBLEM

The nations of this world have persisted in building even more powerful weapons since 1945 in anticipation of the need to fight some future war. The need to continue to do this is very much tied up with basic political processes which have occurred since the end of World War II. As part of our discussion, let us examine what the United States has done during the past thirty years to keep itself ready to use military force.

Technological Advances

With the atomic explosions in 1945, most Americans felt relieved that World War II had ended. These blasts signalled peace. But a scant three years later, with the coming of the Berlin blockade and the explosion of the first Russian atomic device in October 1948, a new era in world politics commenced. The Cold War had begun, producing the four significant facts of military technology of the past few decades. First, American monopoly on nuclear weapons was over. Second was the development of a successful hydrogen bomb, even more destructive than the atomic bomb, produced by both the Soviets and the Americans within a year of each other. Third was the enlargement of the nuclear club, with France and Britain joining in the fifties and China and India in the sixties. Fourth was the development of nuclear missiles with ranges up to 6,000 miles.[12]

These missiles were coupled with other technological advances, such as the ability to carry more than one warhead on a missile and the improvement of tracking and aiming systems to provide both the Soviets and the Americans with a force against which there is hardly a defense. Each nation now had the power to destroy its opponent, but risked almost certain self-destruction in the process. Each became caught up in the deadly game called the *arms race* to provide new ways to defeat the enemy defenses and establish surer defenses for itself. The arms race with its constant development, testing, obsolescence, and further development of new weapons has become a dangerous fact of life confronting all of humankind. Threats to use nuclear power against an opponent have only limited credibility because of the enormous chances of self-destruction. The nuclear standoff, then, has not ended the arms race; the search for a way to harm an opponent without being annihilated continues. And rather than eliminating the threat of warfare of any kind, the nuclear standoff has made conventional war (nonnuclear war) limited in scope and fought against a backdrop of possible nuclear holocaust. The war in Vietnam showed that, rather than making warfare obsolete, the nuclear standoff still allows each side in a dispute to battle it out, within the limitations of the nuclear capabilities of the other side.

This set of facts was recognized by the military long before Vietnam and was used by them to justify the increases in the defense budget, which has grown so dramatically since the end of World War II. As Thomas Plate has written, in analyzing the effect of the nuclear standoff on the defense budget, "essentially, to justify the 1,522,000-man Army, the 869,000-man and 7,000-aircraft Air Force, and the 761,000-man and countless vessel Navy, the Pentagon has said that the country must be able to conduct full-scale engagements in Europe and Asia, a minor land war somewhere else (like Latin America) and, of course, a nuclear war."[13] Defense requests after American involvement in the Vietnam War ended did not go down, as many had expected, for four reasons:

1. Each new generation of weapons systems has become more sophisticated and much more expensive.
2. The amount spent on conventional weapons during the war drained money away from new weapons systems, so the military saw the need for catching up after the war.
3. The all-volunteer army is costly because of the higher salaries offered to attract volunteers.
4. Severe inflation has hit the defense industries, as well as the rest of society.

To prepare for all these contingencies requires tremendous amounts of money. The outcome of the fight for this money may be that the goal of preparing a sound national defense is almost impossible.

Contemporary Military Organization

To understand modern war, we must understand how the military has changed in its organization and in what it actually does. The military's function has always been to fight. But military organizations closely reflect the available technology of fighting and the new weapons of mass destruction have created a real crisis among the military itself. As a leading student of the American military establishment, Morris Janowitz, has noted:

> In the contemporary scene, the military profession must face the political imperative that the outbreak of general war is no longer defined as inevitable or in the national interest. General war continues to be a contingency and an undesirable one at that, and it is recognized as such by a significant proportion of the military profession.[14]

Military goals have undergone tremendous change, as a result of the technology of atomic weapons. The line between offense and defense has become increasingly blurred so that now the chief military mission is the *deterrence* of violence rather than the use of it. With the needs for research, development, procurement, and maintenance of modern weapons, the military has had to rely on the private sector. As a result, the boundary between military and nonmilitary activities has been greatly weakened. And given the permanent threat of war, politics has had to incorporate military experts and advisors into the decision-making process, so that plans are kept realistic in terms of the military capacity to implement them. The result, Janowitz feels, is that these new weapons systems have narrowed the gap between military and civilian, and civilian decision-making groups have become militarized.

This is not to say, however, that there are no longer any important differences between military and civilian in our society. The need to fight limited wars under the umbrella of atomic weapons has required the military to retain an image of itself as ready for serious combat. The warrior self-image, however, has been augmented by the images of the military manager and military technologist, because the growing concern is to accomplish goals with technologically sophisticated means. This argument does not mean that the military has the major role in determining United States foreign policy. It only notes that many traditional distinctions between military and civilian have become blurred, making it increasingly hard to know what steps to take to eliminate the problem of war. The blurred distinction is best exemplified in the close association called the military-industrial complex.

The Military-Industrial Complex

Military influence on domestic society has come, in part, from the development of the industries designed to supply the material needed to maintain our armaments. With the billions of dollars spent on the arms race in the last decades, many business firms have grown that derive all their profits, or a substantial proportion, from government defense work. This group of firms interacts closely with the military services, so that together they are said to comprise a *military-industrial complex*.

Those who believe in such a complex point to its tremendous size in industry. The number of people producing war-related goods is enormous. As Jack Raymond states:

> Some 22,000 prime contractors and 100,000 subcontractors enjoy the defense business that is generated in different military programs. A total of 76 industries, from aircraft to X-ray apparatus, is classed as defense-oriented. Plane makers and shipbuilders derive more than half their income from defense contracts. About 5,300 U.S. cities and towns boast at least one defense plant or company doing business with the Armed Forces.[15]

But although there are many employees, they work for few firms. There is a relatively high concentration of firms, with a hundred or so doing more than two-thirds of the total defense-oriented business and a dozen getting about one-third the total business.[16] In addition to the concentration of firms, there is a strong regional concentration. Ten states receive two-thirds of all the contracts let for the production of defense-related goods. Of the money spent, one-third of all contracts went to corporations located in California, Texas, and New York.[17] Military spending, in addition to the people actually in the armed forces,[18] keeps about 4 million others either directly or indirectly employed. The total of all people working for the war effort, then, accounts for nearly 10 percent of the entire labor force.

While we know that the military and the defense-related industries work harmoniously together, do they represent a complex, with goals different from those of other groups in society? Answering this question depends on how a "complex" is defined. The economist John Kenneth Galbraith has argued that the label is appropriate, using a limited definition: "One must not think of the military power — the association of the military and the defense firms — in conspiratorial terms. It reflects an intimate but largely open association based on a solid community of bureaucratic and pecuniary interest. The services seek the weapons; the suppliers find it profitable to supply them."[19]

Some argue that there is no readily identifiable complex sharing common goals and ends, and even if there was one, it is not terribly important because it does not conspire against efforts to establish a lasting peace. While it may be simplistic to label diverse elements as part of a single military-industrial complex, we also feel that denying a connection ignores the facts. Significantly, former Secretary of Defense Robert McNamara seemed to believe there is one. As Raymond notes:

> It may be simplistic to bundle diverse elements of the military-industrial complex into a single "it," but it is very real, as former Secretary of Defense Robert McNamara attested after years in the post. Characteristically, McNamara asserted he rarely lost to "it." He told an interviewer, "I'd say in this area we haven't lost more than two percent of the cases to the so-called military-industrial complex — and in these instances we failed to present our case properly."[20]

Some authors have gone so far as to view the military-industrial complex as a monolithic *elite*. They have charged that this elite establishes policy based on their own self-interest, even if that means undermining the establishment of peace. C. Wright Mills, the proponent of the theory of elites controlling American society, wrote that the military has come to influence more and more of the important decisions made in our society. He says that the military leaders

> are now more powerful than they ever have been in the history of the American elite; they have now more means of exerting power in many areas of American life which were previously civilian domains; they now have more connections; and they are now operating in a nation whose elite and whose underlying population have accepted what can only be called a military definition of reality.[21]

Mills, however, failed to show that the institutional complex is monolithic, coordinated, or self-conscious. He also failed to demonstrate how the elite can impose its decisions on others in society, regardless of external conditions. A more accurate picture of decision-making in American society is the idea of countervailing power, which sees no one group as able to impose its will on all others and points out the existence of consensus.

Different groups compete with each other for advantage on the one hand, while on the other hand they agree on the crucial elements of the American system. Constant competition over who will exercise power prevents the dominance of any one group for an extended period of time. No group could be labeled *the* elite. But along with the conflict between different groups is a considerable degree of consensus over a number of core beliefs. This includes a belief in democracy, as it is structured and practiced in the United States, and a belief in capitalism, the system of privately owned property. This consensus enters into questions of war because it also includes the belief that it is not only right but moral to use violence to preserve our superior way of life. With no counterassumptions to direct American foreign policy, it is hardly surprising that foreign policy since World War II has been fundamentally the same under Republicans and Democrats alike. Even today most Americans probably continue to feel the same ethnocentric way about the rest of the world, regardless of the bitter lessons of Vietnam. If this is true, then how much has really changed since Vietnam? And does the debate over an elite military-industrial complex really make sense when so many Americans share these basic assumptions and would support actions taken to preserve the American economic and political system?

Nor are we the only country in the world that has such a consensus. The Soviet Union is characterized by a parallel set of beliefs, which has helped to create a military-industrial complex there. As a result of Russia's massive losses during World War II, the Russian leadership has become convinced of the necessity to build up its strength so history will not repeat itself. They too have a basic belief in the superiority of their political and economic system and feel as threatened by outside influences on their system as we do. The result is a high priority being placed on the production of armaments and in the competition between the two countries' complexes, the arms race.

The Military Budget

With the coming of the Cold War and its increasingly expensive arms race, the nation has come to assume the need of a large, permanent, professional military. The financial dimensions of this assumption are considerable:

Since 1945, military expenditures have averaged approximately 50 per cent of the annual federal budget. If we add space expenditures and the interest charges on the national debt (mainly war-incurred), seventy-seven cents of each budget dollar is spent on the cost of war, past, present, and future. The Department of Defense controls property in excess of 160 billion: it is the wealthiest economic organization in the nation and in the world. Between 25 and 30 per cent of all economic activity hinges upon military spending.[22]

Since 1967, the Department of Defense has had available for military expenditures well over one trillion dollars. The willingness of Congress to appropriate this kind of money year after year is based on the consensus discussed earlier.

It should be noted that the defense budget, even though it has almost doubled since 1965, has not become a larger part of the gross national product (GNP). Robert Mayo, writing in 1969 as Director of the Bureau of the Budget, noted that while the absolute increases in military expenditures since 1965 were large, increases for civilian programs were even larger.

> Outlays for civilian programs have increased by $53.4 billion from $40.6 billion in 1959 to $94.1 billion in 1969. Over 70 per cent of the increase has been for human resources programs: health, income maintenance, education, manpower, housing, and community development. The percentage increase for civilian programs has been nearly twice as great as that for national defense. As a result, spending for civilian programs has risen from 44 per cent to 51 per cent of total budget outlays.[23]

Since 1965 the amount of money the military has spent has increased from $48.6 billion to $100.0 billion (see Figure 15.1). For fiscal year 1979, the defense budget was better than $120 billion. But if we correct for

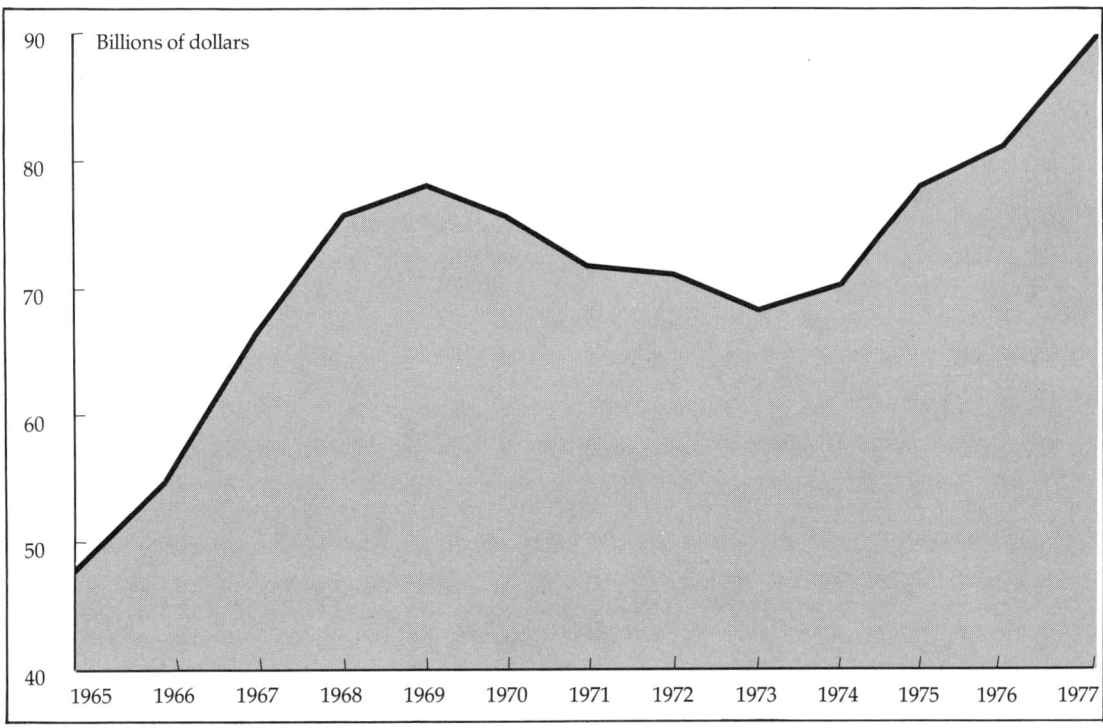

FIGURE 15.1 Defense Spending, 1965–1977 (in Current Dollars)

Source: Bureau of the Census, *Statistical Abstract of the United States, 1977* (Washington, D.C.: U.S. Government Printing Office, 1977), p. 358.

inflation by using constant 1977 dollars as the basis for comparison, we see that spending rose sharply during the Vietnam War years (late 1960s) and decreased sharply afterwards (see Figure 15.2). And an even more interesting set of comparisons looks at defense spending as a percentage of total federal spending and of the total GNP (see Figure 15.3). Between 1965 and 1970 defense spending took a slightly larger share of total federal spending, because of Vietnam. But since 1970 the Defense Department's share of spending has decreased by about 40 percent. The same pattern is seen in looking at defense spending as part of the GNP: the percentage rose between 1965 and 1970 and dropped afterward.

In other words, although in absolute terms we are spending more dollars each year on defense than we did the year before, the proportion we are spending on defense is steadily declining. As Mayo noted, federal health, education, and social welfare programs are increasingly rapidly and taking a larger share of the budget and of the GNP. The old argument that the money spent for defense could be better spent on other things seems to be invalid, given this dramatic growth in federally funded social programs. The American military no longer receives al-

498 INTERNATIONAL CONFLICT: *Sophisticated Weaponry and Stone Age Mentality*

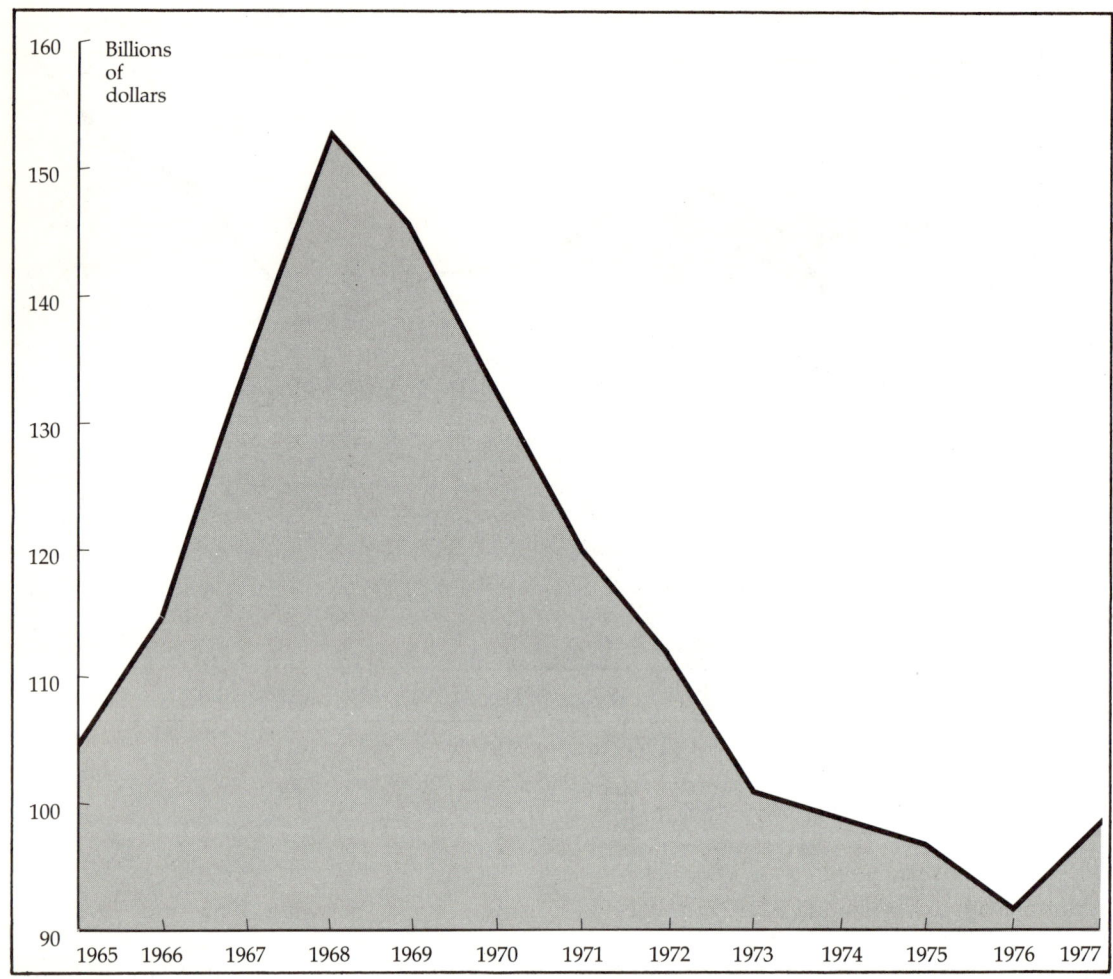

FIGURE 15.2 Defense Spending, 1965–1977 (in 1977 Dollars)

Source: Bureau of the Census, *Statistical Abstract of the United States, 1977* (Washington, D.C.: U.S. Government Printing Office, 1977), p. 358.

most 60 percent of the federal budget as it did in 1955. Rather, today it receives slightly less than one-quarter of total federal outlays.

But in examining the defense budget for any given year, we have to exercise a certain amount of care. There are many hidden costs of war, past, present, and future, which are not included in Defense Department requests. International aid programs, including military aid, veterans' benefits, and space research and technology (including research on military space systems) are all included under other budget categories. And there are other costs as well — the cost of lost

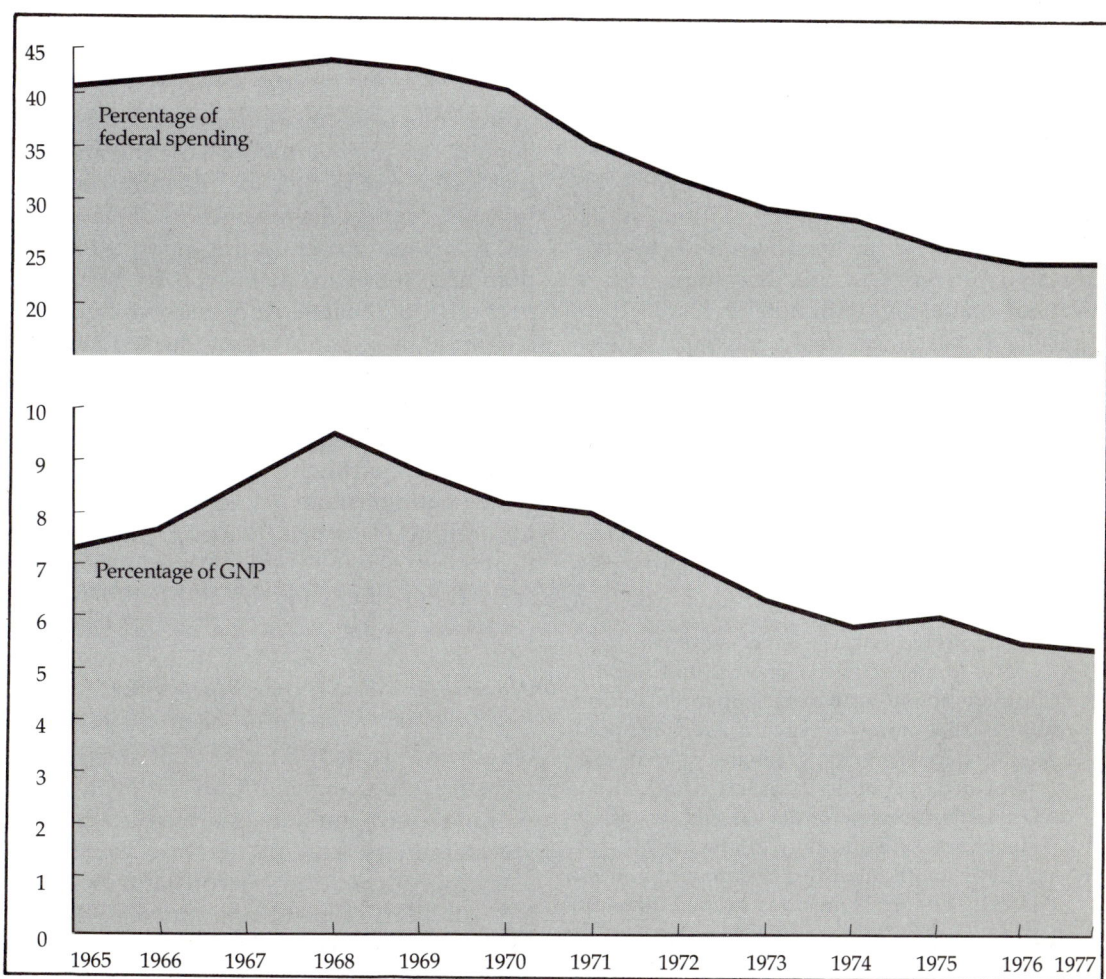

FIGURE 15.3 Defense Spending as Percentage of all Federal Spending and as Percentage of GNP, 1965–1977

Source: Bureau of the Census, *Statistical Abstract of the United States, 1977* (Washington, D.C.: U.S. Government Printing Office, 1977), p. 358.

resources. Even though spending in other programs has increased, many contend that defense spending still drains away needed money. Perhaps the most complete effort in the field was an analysis done by Bruce Russett. He calculated the effect of defense spending on a wide range of civilian activities in the United States from 1939–1968. He looked at the public expenditures on health, hospitals, education, and welfare, among other things, then asked to what extent these changed as defense spending went up. He concluded, in summarizing an enormous amount of data, that military spending increases at the expense of our ability to accomplish other social goals. As Russett states, "It seems fair to conclude from these data that America's most expensive wars have severely hampered the nation in its attempt to build a healthier and better-educated citizenry. . . . A long-term effort has been made, and with notable results, but typically it has been badly cut back whenever military needs pressed unusually hard."[24]

Former Senator J. William Fulbright has long been a critic of defense policy, but his greatest outrage seems to concern the question of alternatives for which this money could be used. Writing in 1969, Fulbright stated:

> It is not until we look at what is left to take care of unmet domestic needs that the full impact of military spending becomes apparent. Education is an example of such a need. Schools from kindergarten to graduate school are overcrowded and underfinanced. Nine billion dollars are authorized for the various programs of the Office of Education in the next fiscal year. Only about one-third the amount authorized, $3.2 billion, is included in the budget.[25]

Economist Kenneth Boulding elaborates on Fulbright's concerns, calculating that the economic burden of defense spending represents a withdrawal of funds from the economy that could be used for household consumption. According to Boulding, in 1929, when the spending on war-related items was only 1 percent of the GNP, household consumption was about 75 percent of all spending. By 1969, Boulding estimated, "household consumption [was] down to about 62 percent of the gross national product. This means in effect that the rise of the war industry in the last generation now deprives the average household of something like 15 to 20 percent of its potential purchases."[26]

The decline in the proportion of GNP going into consumer purchases is due to a general rise in government expenditures, not just to the rise in defense spending. But defense is clearly a major contributor, and even today defense expenditures amount to more than $500 for every man, woman, and child in the United States. And even while the social programs sponsored by the federal government are allowed an ever-increasing part of the federal budget, defense spending is still high and many of the needs outlined by Defense Department critics a decade ago remain unmet. Poor schools, the steady deterioration of urban housing, and unmet health care needs are still with us, as we have seen in the other chapters of this book.

Worldwide Arms Expenditures

On a world scale the problem of steadily increasing arms expenditures is even more striking. With millions starving each year, world military expenditures are even more alarming. Since 1966 (in constant 1974 dollars), military expenditures increased from $279 billion to $340 billion. For the developed countries, spending increased about 10 percent from $237 billion in 1966 to $265 billion dollars in 1975. However, for the developing countries, where the majority of the poor, sick, illiterate, and starving people of the world live, the increase has been more than 50 percent, from $42 billion dollars to $75 billion. When contrasted with the money spent for health care, irrigation, and land development and education by these same countries which have extremely low per capita incomes, these military expenditures represent an enormous drain of the resources

How can countries whose inhabitants are starving and diseased and whose economies are falling apart justify exorbitant arms expenditures? They usually insist that they must defend themselves against hostile neighbors when in fact the arms are used for internal control of a discontented populace. Here, in a familiar encounter, a Nicaraguan national guard trooper forbids a woman from entering her own home.

potentially available for human development. And as each year passes, these nations are spending more and more of their resources on arms.

As the United States' percentage of the total world military expenditures has dropped from 34.6 percent in 1966 to 24.5 percent in 1975, the developing countries, which can least afford it, have poured their resources into ever more sophisticated and expensive weapons systems. In spite of the vast sums spent by all sides, it would be wrong to conclude that the world is a safer place than it was a decade ago. For in that decade all the nations of the world spent in constant 1974 dollars a total of almost $3 trillion on military expenditures.[27] In fact, the scales seem to be tipping in favor of the likelihood of armed conflict increasing rather than decreasing in the near future.

The Economics of Defense Procurement

In addition to the question of alternatives for the money spent on the military, critics have challenged how the Pentagon uses the money allocated to it. Much of the data presented to Congress by the Defense Department is not analyzed in Congress as carefully as the information presented to support budget requests by other agencies. What goes to Congress each year as defense requests is the result of a complex process, the main feature of which is that the Department of Defense works in conjunction with the defense corporations. Although the military and industry always desire to add new weapons systems, both insist on at least maintaining the status quo. "The intense battle to maintain force structures is in fact an industrial battle, since the maintenance of a particular military function — such as strategic bombing — supports a whole host of weapons systems, which in turn keeps the industry alive."[28]

One result of this close cooperation is the lack of competition between different corporations. Although the military is supposed to buy from the lowest bidder, each service will often buy from the same supplier: "Grumman is a Navy corporation; Boeing is an Air Force corporation."[29] Part of the reasons is the virtual monopoly some firms have over technical and intelligence information. This information, most of it classified because of supposed military import, is developed by defense suppliers as research and development and used by them in putting a new weapons system into production. As John Kenneth Galbraith points out:

> One cannot let out the MIRV to competitive bidding in the manner of mules and muskets. In fiscal year 1968, as the work of the Joint Economic Committee has revealed, 60 percent of defense contracts were with firms that were the sole source of supply. Most of the remainder were awarded by negotiated bidding. Competitive bidding — 11.5 per cent of the total — was nearly negligible.[30]

The ability to classify information as top secret means that other sellers of the equipment to be purchased are virtually excluded from the bidding. It also allows greater freedom of action for the Pentagon and industry. It avoids scrutiny from others. The purpose of stamping a top secret classification on, for example, the MIRV project was not to deprive the Russians of knowledge about the system, the Pentagon says they have it anyway. Rather, it was meant to deprive the American people of the opportunity to question (through their representatives in Congress) whether they really needed to or wanted to spend the money on this new weapon. Withholding information has long been part of the process of effectively manipulating people. Given the way bids for military hardware are let, the military is often overcharged for what it purchases. The lack of competitive price mechanisms almost guarantees that costs will be higher. As Roland McKean states, "The price mechanism in government performs most imperfectly. . . . The 'pricetags' that become attached to various actions are far from the 'right' mark."[31]

Many contracts are awarded on a *cost-reimbursement* basis, meaning that the contractor can receive more than the contracted price if the expenses go up. This has resulted in *cost overruns* (bills in excess of the contracted price) of between 300 and 700 percent in some cases, simply because the greater the cost, the greater the profits. According to Assistant Secretary of the Air Force Robert Charles, "a substantial amount [of cost overruns] was due to the fact that most contracts for major systems were of the cost-reimbursement type."[32] These contracts provided little incentive for economy.

Sometimes, inexplicably, defense contractors are faced with the grim specter of competitive bidding. To surmount the problem, they often submit a ridiculously low bid on a weapons system to ensure getting the contract. Then, because the wording of many defense contracts allows companies to pass on to the government any additional costs, the company produces the product at a higher cost, with more profits. The Defense Department must then make supplementary budget requests in Congress, but since billions of dollars have already been invested in the project, more money is approved. An exception to the general rule was President Carter's 1977 decision to discontinue work on the B-1 bomber. Estimates using overrun figures from past projects placed the cost of each bomber at more than $100 million. And at the time of the president's decision, it was said that if the cost estimates could have been held to about $70 million each, the project would have been approved. But given the past record of grossly understated initial costs, the president apparently determined that the project could not be justified on a cost-benefit basis. Since this plane would have been superior to the aging B-52s, the cost alone killed the project. While Pentagon officials have worked hard to eliminate talk about cost overruns, the president apparently had seen too much evidence of them.

Another problem of defense costs is the poor performance record of some of the systems on which large amounts of money have been spent. Rather than being more powerful than their predecessors, many new weapons systems have delivered no bang for the buck at all. A budget bureau specialist, Richard Stubbings, reported that major weapons systems purchased during the 1950s and 1960s at a cost of billions of dollars failed systematically to meet specifications. Less than 25 percent of the weapons systems begun during the 1960s performed up to standards expected of them. Six, or the majority of them, performed "at a level 25 percent or less than the standards and specifications set for them."[33]

Summary

Today there seems to be rather widespread concern that the money spent on national defense has not purchased any additional security. Yet defense spending continues at record high levels, regardless of the other uses the money could be put to or the poor performance of weapons systems. This problem has no easy solutions, but something must be done. The growing recognition that our resources are not infinite is the first step toward solving the problems of excessive costs and substandard performance. Some solution is essential, for with more expensive and sophisticated weapons systems waiting in the wings, the problems of future generations of military planners will be more difficult than those of today.

ATTEMPTS AT DEALING WITH THE PROBLEM

During the past several years there has been little public interest or debate on the issue of nuclear weapons or war. Those who struggled against the development and deployment of nuclear weapons and who want a sane nuclear policy seem to have become exhausted, their energy spent on the protest against the Vietnam War and defused by détente with the Russians. But while détente has meant that neither side has been able to achieve overwhelming nuclear superiority, each has continued to build weapons and attempted, through technological breakthroughs, to gain a superiority over the other. Despite the ongoing negotiations to end the arms race in the Strategic Arms Limitation Talks (SALT), each side is stockpiling more and more weaponry. The warhead count of the United States alone is now approaching 8,000 and according to Leonard Rodberg, "the Defense Department finds itself with more missiles than it knows what to do with . . . so it looks around for additional targets and for new ways of justifying its arsenal."[34]

People can think about alternative uses for these monies, and they can calculate the social costs for such a high priority on defense related spending. What they cannot really conceive of are the effects of a nuclear holocaust and the destruction that would follow. This is one reason why so little of the criticism against the plans for nuclear war takes the form of questioning "doomsday" and why so much time is spent in looking at other uses for the money.

American Ideology and International Conflict

If all that has been said above is true, why do we continue to spend the kind of money we do on military preparedness, especially on nuclear arms? The reason is another set of perceptions about defense, which stresses the positive role defense spending has had in providing the United States with the military force it needs in a hostile world.

American expansionist desires have a long history, dating back to before the Revolutionary War. These desires, up until the late nineteenth century, centered on occupying the territory in North America. But around the turn of this century, when the area became unified, the expansionist goals began to change. Americans looked abroad and saw countries with raw materials and undeveloped markets for American manufactured goods. American expansion then took on an economic and international character.

Expansion into other parts of the world has resulted in at least $60 billion in direct American investment going abroad, producing about $120 billion in goods each year. Some 4,200 American companies do business abroad, and they control over 14,000 foreign businesses. These multinational corporations, as they are called, consist of many of the largest and most powerful corporations and financial institutions in the world. These corporations need a world secure from revolution and revolt in order to carry on orderly and predictable profit-making enterprises. Our nation's foreign policy, then, has attempted to stabilize problem areas of the world by direct economic and military aid and by direct military intervention when considered necessary. As Irons states,

> to protect our foreign investment, we have spread the cloak of the "Free World" wide enough to cover every dictatorial and authoritative government which will allow American capital to extract profit from the toil and sweat of its people. We have provided the ruling classes of these countries with some $32 billion in arms in the last quarter century, arms whose functions are the perpetuation of the rule of a privileged elite.[35]

The need for access to stable foreign markets, both for import and export, is real, and has important consequences. Our foreign policy toward Iran, for example, meant that we were willing to support a repressive and undemocratic regime as long as it allowed us access to desirable resources. The American standard of living, envied by every other nation in the world, is largely dependent on our free and ready access to the raw materials of the rest of the world. Margaret Mead noted that "we are 6 percent of the world's population and are estimated to be using up to 50 percent of the earth's irreplaceable natural resources. It is also estimated that each child born and raised in the United States produces one hundred times the pollution of a child born in India by our use of cars, powers, synthetic materials, etc."[36] As a result, our foreign policy is determined by our need for easy and cheap access to supplies of raw materials. Economist Harry Magdoff outlines how, with the shift from being an exporter to an importer of minerals and metals, American foreign policy has changed.[37] With our dependence on foreign resources, what matters most to many corporations is that the option of foreign investment remains open.

One can fully understand the money we have spent on the military, both at home and as foreign military aid, only in the context of our broader economic objectives. The great corporations of today, which dominate domestic markets in oil, computers, metals, automobiles, and electronics also have extensive holdings in foreign countries. These holdings must be protected by the military, since there may be strong pressures for the foreign country to take control. This need helps to explain why so many key figures in the determining of American foreign policy since World War II have come from the ranks of the business community.

The decision to go to war has become more risky and costly as world politics have changed and the destructiveness of armaments has increased. But for some people war still represents a way of protecting the sphere of influence American business relies on. This attitude may not be realistic, however. Given the complexity of world politics today, it could be that much of our vast military power can no longer protect our interests abroad. The Arab oil embargo and seizures of American plants and equipment abroad did not result in a new round of gunboat diplomacy; such a response would have been futile. This might even be used as an argument against the continuation of large military expenditures.

If the military seems unlikely to or incapable of defending economic interests, then another reason must be found to explain continued military spending. Such a factor is our strong belief in capitalism. As a result of this belief, we have developed an ideology of anticommunism that both motivates and justifies our international actions. It is impossible to understand the continued spending of enormous amounts of money on defense or the continued willingness of American leaders to see war as a useful political tool without understanding this ideology.

The Rise of Anticommunism

In this country during the 1920s and 1930s, there was a growing distrust of the Soviet Union. This was partly because of the reports of much bloodshed and strife within Russia, but was primarily due to communist opposition to capitalism and the presumed desire of Russian leaders to bring the entire world under communism. With the rise of Adolf Hitler in Germany, it seemed better to ally ourselves with the Soviet Union, so differences were temporarily ignored. After the defeat of Germany in 1945, however, an unstable peace developed as both Russians and Americans pursued conflicting goals. Trouble in the Balkan countries, the Berlin blockade of 1948, the communist takeover of China in 1949, the stealing of American atomic secrets by Russian spies from 1945 to 1952, and the invasion of South Korea by the communist North in 1950 convinced most Americans that communism, driven on by its anticapitalist ideology, was a threat to our way of life. As John K. Fairbank noted in

1947, "our fear of Communism, partly as an expression of our general fear of the future, will continue to inspire us to aggressive anti-communist policies in Asia and elsewhere."[38]

Fairbank accurately forecast what happened in Indochina, because he recognized that the general belief in the superiority of one's own system does more than simply rationalize the pursuit of basic economic interests. The men who have shaped American foreign policy, like most of the rest of the population, held a strong and abiding faith in our system of government and the economic base which supports it. They have been distrustful of other systems, even including those of our allies. Immediately after World War II, this belief produced a kind of strict moralism centering on the conviction that the American way was best.

Because of the way World War II was sold to Americans, many came to see the international politics during the 1950s and 1960s as a life-or-death struggle between good and evil. American leaders and the American public, nurtured for over a quarter of a century on distrust of and conflict with communism, internalized a fear of communist intentions. This fear easily translated into an us-or-them attitude — a nation was either for us or against us. The fear was deep enough that it drove leaders to oppose any action that seemed to change where another country stood, thus the American involvement in the Vietnam War.

America and Vietnam

The belief in the righteousness of any political or economic system beclouds the issues at stake in any international confrontation. Noam Chomsky, in his examination of the long process that finally led to our massive intervention in Vietnam, comments on the dangers inherent in the uncritical acceptance of any ideology:

> Twenty years of intensive cold-war indoctrination and seventy years of myth regarding our international role make it difficult to face those issues in a serious way. There is a great deal of intellectual debris to be cleared away. Ideological pressures so overpowering that even their existence was denied must be examined and understood.[39]

Because it underlies many of the conflicts of the twentieth century, the power of ideology is important. There is every indication that this country will continue to react according to the ideology we have described when its interests are threatened. Yet the search for alternatives to war must involve learning how to live in a world where the morality of one nation is not imposed on others. This fact must be recognized. From 1945 until about 1965, it wasn't. The power of ideology held sway, and there were few widespread attempts at cutting the military budget or at pressuring the government to change its foreign policy. However, the escalation of the war in Vietnam, resulting in 500,000 troops fighting there, changed all this drastically. Men began dying in the jungle at the rate of 500 per week, fighting in a war brought into the homes of Americans every day by their television sets. We found that a guerrilla war can be extremely costly.

In 1965, when American involvement was being increased on a large scale in Indonesia, President Lyndon Johnson promised the American people both guns and butter — military success and domestic prosperity. His total budget, because of deficit spending, did not seem to require any real sacrifice from the American people, especially since we were only fighting bands of guerrillas far away in Vietnam. Although President Johnson was totally wrong about the costs, he probably believed what he told the American people. For a time government spending on Vietnam did not seem too costly, and did stimulate the American economy. As Raymond commented at the time, "In the past two years alone (1966–1967), the intensification of the war in Vietnam has created more than a million jobs in the United States. The sharp rise in employment amounted to 23 per cent of the total increase of more than four million jobs in the economy during 1966 and 1967."[40]

But the economy was stimulated at a heavy cost. More than 50,000 American soldiers eventually died in the jungles of Vietnam. Disillusionment set in when it became obvious that the half million troops were not going to be able to accomplish their mission. The costs of the war began to escalate drastically and the objectives always seemed to slip through our fingers. The protest movement came into existence for these and many other reasons.

In response to these protests, which mounted rapidly during 1967 and 1968, President Johnson decided not to run for reelection, popular sentiment against the war increased, and a majority of Congress finally wanted American withdrawal. But a lot of the steam was taken out of the protest movement when President Richard Nixon did two things. He ended the draft, beginning the movement toward an all-volunteer army, and he gradually withdrew American troops from Vietnam.

Iatrogenic Effects

In their attempt to overcome the problem of being prepared for guerrilla war in the future, the military has pushed for what Paul Dickson terms *electronic battlefields*. There are hundreds of projects included in this concept, such as laser-guided bombs, remote-controlled aircraft, electronic surveillance, and new fire control systems. Some of these devices were used with limited success during the later stages of American involvement in Vietnam, but the big push to perfect these inventions came later.

Aside from the problems already discussed — the enormous costs involved and the question of their effectiveness — a unique problem is introduced by this new electronic equipment. Some members in Congress have become very concerned about the inability of the electronic devices to discriminate civilians from soldiers, who are often difficult to identify in a guerrilla war. The difficulty in separating the two groups is a problem for soldiers, but when a more efficient method of killing is developed, often allowing greater distance between the person killing and the person being killed, the difficulty is made greater. The inevitable result is more suffering for innocent civilians, as the *depersonalization* of fighting has always produced. An example can be seen in one of the defoliation programs that Americans instituted in Vietnam. The chemical named agent orange was sprayed in Vietnamese jungles to kill plants and thus remove the hiding places for Vietcong guerrillas. But the chemical also maimed adults and children and caused birth defects. The danger of these methods is that

> by creating a way of warfare that depends on fewer and fewer "American boys," the military is making it easier to win public acceptance for getting into fights around the globe. . . . There would be much less anger against a war in which we were putting hardware, not men, on the line and casualty lists were dominated by decimated sensors, downed RPVs, and inoperative computers.[41]

A central problem in looking at war in the near future is whether American scientific

Electronic battlefields and pushbutton warfare have not eliminated the bottom line in combat: people kill people. In guerrilla warfare, costly technology cannot even distinguish friend from foe. These American soldiers had to judge whether this Vietcong suspect was indeed the enemy in a scene that was repeated countless times in countless villages.

and technological skill will be used for the more automated killing of our enemies, and sometimes our friends, or for alleviating the problems that lead to guerrilla warfare in the first place. According to Dickson, most Americans were outraged over Vietnam not because our presence and actions there were immoral, but because the mounting costs proved that we did not accomplish our stated goals in an efficient manner. The new automated battlefield, designed for greater efficiency and less danger to American soldiers may increase the likelihood of future Vietnams, rather than decrease it.

While the attack on Pearl Harbor welded the country together, the war in Vietnam fractured it. Many combat units were almost torn apart by racial conflict. Further, debate over the war increased the belief of many soldiers that the United States involvement in Vietnam was basically unjust. The upshot of this resentment over the war, especially by those asked to fight it, was the movement to an all-volunteer army. While the all-volunteer army has at least removed the problem of forcing unwilling people to fight, other problems remain.

One problem that has not yet been solved is the fact that the volunteer force is far from representative of our total population. General William Westmoreland said in a 1974 interview, "From a social standpoint it seemed to me that our armed forces should represent a cross-section of Americans from the standpoint of economic status and ethnic and racial [make-up] of our society."[42] But the trend has been toward more black enlistments, with about twice the proportion of blacks enlisting each month as there are blacks in the population. Many combat units are already more than two-thirds black. If current trends continue future wars will be fought by a disproportionate number of black soldiers. Racial antagonism was part of the ineffectiveness of many combat units in the latter stages of the war in Vietnam and it could be a factor in the future as well.

Another problem with the all-volunteer army is that a president would be able to use American troops without worrying about any protest from those who would have to fight. The resistance to the Vietnam war came at first from a group more or less directly affected by the draft, students on college campuses. The all-volunteer army, many fear, will put the president in a position where civilian resistance to the use of combat troops will be low. Further, civilian participation in a war may decrease — benefiting the civilians but possibly creating a more isolated American military force, with a culture and identity of its own. The existence of such a force will not make lasting peace in the world more likely.

PROSPECTS FOR SOLVING THE PROBLEM

War, as a social problem, has two sets of components: those related to the domestic structure, and those affecting the international situation. In order for us to look at the possibility of solving this problem, we must consider each group separately, although in the last analysis, the two components are linked.

The Domestic Structure

As the result of a series of conferences held in 1967 to discuss the problems of peace, a book called *Report from Iron Mountain* was published.[43] Considerable controversy surrounded this report, some critics suggesting it was only a spoof of the think-tank conclusions that have recently helped determine government policy. But some suggestions contained in this report must be considered seriously, because they reflect genuine problems that would arise from dramatically altering defense policy.

The report took as its starting point total and general disarmament, not the Cold War or armed peace we have learned to accept in today's world. The authors suggest that modern society may have moved past Clausewitz's understanding of war. Whereas Clausewitz stressed the civilian responsibility to decide to go to war, the report suggests that the reverse may be true today. The authors feel that it is incorrect to assume that the military is subordinate to the economic and political system it is supposed to serve.

If this point is true, the transition to lasting peace will be more difficult than many people would like to believe. In fact, the nonmilitary functions of the military are so strong that the authors of the report feel the transition to peace will be next to impossible.

> The non-military functions of war are more basic. They exist not merely to justify themselves but to serve broader social purposes. If war is eliminated, the military functions it has served will end with it. But its non-military function will not.[44]

The report divides the nonmilitary functions, which are essential to the maintenance of a society, into five categories:

1. *Economic.* War has provided both ancient and modern societies with a dependable system for stabilizing and controlling their national economies.
2. *Political.* The permanent possibility of war is the foundation for stable government; it supplies a strong basis for general acceptance of political authority.
3. *Sociological.* War provides the machinery through which the motivations governing human behavior have been translated into binding social allegiance. It ensures the degree of social cohesion necessary to the viability of nations.

4. *Ecological.* War has been the principal evolutionary device for maintaining a satisfactory ecological balance between the total human population and the supplies available for its survival.
5. *Cultural and scientific.* War has determined the basic standards of value in the creative arts and has provided the fundamental motivation for scientific and technological progress.[45]

Each of these points contains enough half-truths to make it a dangerous diversion from the real issues. For example, while war does work to motivate people to support political leaders, surely economic self-interest also has a central place. While nationalism has been of great importance in some political campaigns, the permanent possibility of war is not the only basis for all political legitimacy. The same critique can be leveled at all five points. For each point the report raises, facts argue against the conclusions it draws.

Another view comes from Seymour Melman, who has compared what our country has spent on defense with what it has invested in capital equipment. He shows that our large investment in military equipment has seriously hurt our economic position in a number of different ways.[46] First, there is the sheer amount of capital that has been drawn off for military purposes, which has hurt private industry's ability to invest in new machinery. This has amounted to about one and one-half trillion dollars, the total spent on the military since World War II. Second, there is the loss in our position compared to other countries. The Japanese have been plowing 30 percent of their national income into capital equipment in the past few years and Germany has put back in about 20 percent, partly because of a perceived necessity to invest heavily in armaments. The American share has only been 11 percent.

Third, Melman feels the heavy defense investment has, over the years, caused American manufacturing equipment to fall into a relatively poor condition. The economic recession of the 1970s may be due to the decline in American productivity, which is partly the result of heavy defense spending that allows the neglect of other industries.

Many proponents of defense spending see great payoffs in scientific progress coming from military spending. However, while one cannot deny that progress in computers, lasers, aircraft, and space exploration has been partly the result of military research, this may not be the most efficient way of subsidizing scientific progress. Basic research and development budgets represent only a tiny part of total defense expenditures; the lion's share goes to paying soldiers and providing them with military equipment.

The Superpowers and the International Community

In Asia, Africa, and Latin America, people live in conditions most Americans cannot even begin to comprehend. Best estimates of current population trends show that by the year 2000, there could be almost twice as many human beings in the world to feed, shelter, and clothe as there were in 1970. Estimates have also been made that about 10,000 persons are starving to death every day, while the mental and physical development of countless others is being damaged by disease and malnutrition.[47] The governments in power in these countries seem able to do nothing to prevent this suffering.

The misery of the people in these countries is heightened by the fact that the two powers most able to help, the United States and the Soviet Union, have chosen to use these developing nations as pawns in the struggle between themselves.

Instead of confronting each other openly and directly, the United States and the Soviet Union have chosen to oppose and compete with each other through third parties. The internal weakness of most new and emerging nations, requiring foreign support, and the revolutionary situation in many of them give the opportunity of doing so.[48]

In many of these underdeveloped countries, America is primarily interested in continued political stability so our access to raw materials can be assured. The United States is also interested in promoting change, but only if this change will lead to greater stability or if it will disrupt the control of resources by the other side. For millions of people caught in the grip of malnutrition, disease, and outright starvation, the power play between the superpowers has no appeal.

Regardless of the feelings of the people caught in the middle, the struggle between superpowers continues, with ever-present risks of confrontation, escalation, and nuclear holocaust. What begins as a revolutionary civil war may escalate until the major nuclear powers are in open conflict. The prospect has made attempts by both sides to meddle in the internal affairs of other countries dangerous, possibly risking any détente achieved between the Russians and the Americans. With nuclear weapons threatening the entire human species, what happens thousands of miles from our shores in a small developing nation may have a greater effect on our lives than we imagine. The situation in Iran in late 1979 is an example.

The Role of the United Nations

The United Nations exists as the outgrowth of efforts made at the end of World War II to found an international political system. However, the United Nations is not an effective organization for preventing war, for a number of reasons. In the Cold War the superpowers saw the United Nations as one more tool in the game of power politics. And all nations feared that the United Nations might become too effective, meaning that each member nation would have to give up some of its sovereignty, including the decision to resort to war to settle political disputes. The voting in both the General Assembly and the Security Council has for many years reflected the antagonism between East and West, so many issues crucial to world peace were never brought to the United Nations. The Vietnam War is a good example, for the United Nations never really became involved in this major challenge to world peace. Partly this was because the United States was unwilling to follow certain guidelines the United Nations had set up as part of the 1964 Geneva Accords, but other factors contributed.

In attempting to build a forum where all nations would be represented as equals, the United Nations has admitted on an equal footing to the major industrial powers a host of new nations from Africa, Asia, and South America, called the Third World countries. These countries have often voted against the United States and the Soviet Union on many central issues, causing serious divisions within the United Nations. As a result, international cooperation has been rendered largely impossible when war seemed imminent. The attempt to stop war by establishing a democratic world order did not take into account the fact that all nations are not equally powerful in their ability to carry out their desires.

As a result of the inability of the United Nations to act decisively, it has become nothing more than a sounding board for world public opinion. Although such an international forum for discussion is desirable,

The United Nations has not fulfilled the hopes on which it was established; in many respects, it has become another arena of conflict, but in diplomatic maneuvering rather than armed combat. The organization has actively pursued peace, however, by means of its peacekeeping troops dispatched to calm troubled areas, most recently the Middle East. Here, a woman guerrilla trains her Soviet-made machine gun on a French contingent of the U.N. force.

it is not enough. One used to see signs saying "Get us out of the United Nations!"; today one never does. The absence of such signs does not reflect a change in attitude, but the general realization that the United Nations is irrelevant to world politics.

Summary

A basic shift in American foreign policy is needed, recognizing that we are only 6 percent of humankind and we cannot control the destiny of the rest. This is part of what it will take to avoid using war as a solution to foreign policy problems. History teaches us that war is the natural state of affairs. But with the coming of the nuclear age, war has taken on the ability to wipe out the entire species; and it can also be used to prevent the material progress of millions of people in the developing world. In the words of the noted historian Henry Steele Commager:

> Our problem is not primarily one of material resources or material power. It is possible that if we were to use for peaceful purposes all of the wealth we now use for war, we would, in-

deed, have the resources to lift the standards of living in Latin America, Asia, and Africa as well as at home.[49]

Too often Americans assume that the economic progress of the rest of the world will be at our expense. If this view continues, the likelihood of future wars like Vietnam, with rich Americans fighting against the poor of the world, will grow. And if any of these wars escalate out of control, the effort made at détente by Soviet and American diplomats will only have brought some breathing time between the wars of the past and those that promise to annihilate our future. If so, in a flash, 4 billion years of evolution could be destroyed. The possibility of nuclear war is why international conflict is the greatest social problem facing humankind today.

IMPORTANT WORDS AND TERMS

aggression
all-volunteer army
arms race
cost overrun
cost reimbursement
depersonalization
deterrence
electronic battlefield
elite
levée en masse
military-industrial complex
multinational corporations
war

QUESTIONS FOR DISCUSSION

1. What items should an adequate defense budget contain?
2. How much should Americans spend on defense as a percentage of the total GNP?
3. Did the United States win in Vietnam? How do you know?
4. Should the United States abolish the all-volunteer army? Defend your answer.
5. If another war were to be declared, should women be drafted on an equal basis with men?
6. "Technology is not the cause of the problems discussed in this chapter." Take a position on this statement and support your answer.
7. What are the implications of what von Clausewitz said about war for today's world?
8. Many people continue to think that Ardrey and Lorenz are right, and that aggression is instinctive. Do you? Support your answer.
9. To avoid the problems of military aggression in the future, some observers feel we will have to cut back on our level of consumption. Do you agree? Would you be willing to do this in order to prevent possible future wars?
10. Some observers feel we now should be devoting a sizeable percentage of our GNP to help the people in the developing nations. Do you agree? Would you be willing to cut back on personal consumption in order to do this if it meant preventing a possible future war?
11. Many people feel the United States should be spending more money to develop military technology. Do you agree or disagree?

SUGGESTED READING

ALEXANDER ALLANDE, *The Human Imperative* (New York: Columbia University Press, 1972).

A serious anthropological treatise aimed at refuting theories linking human and animal aggression. The author refutes the notion that territory and human aggression cause war. Heavy reading, but a must for the student who wants to move past the work of Ardrey and Lorenz.

Gabriel Kolko, *The Roots of American Foreign Policy* (Boston: Beacon Press, 1969).

A very important book, written from a radical position that tries to look at the determinants of our foreign policy going back to before World War II. Professor Kolko presents the reader with some revealing chapters on who exercises power in our society and the mechanisms used to have their desires translated into foreign policy decisions. The use of war as an instrument of foreign policy can be understood far better after reading Kolko.

Seymour Melman, *The Permanent War Economy* (New York: Simon and Schuster, 1974).

Perhaps the most important book yet written about the impact of military spending on our economy. Melman seeks also to look at what might be involved in trying to move from massive military spending to spending on peace.

Martin Oppenheimer, *The American Military* (New York: Aldine, 1971).

This series of essays looks at the military establishment in terms of its recruitment patterns and impact on domestic society, and at the motivation of soldiers to fight. Written in the post-Vietnam era, it asks what lessons have been learned by our involvement in that war.

Thomas Plate, *Understanding Doomsday* (New York: Simon and Schuster, 1971).

This book describes the arms race and what created our potential to blow up the world many times over. The politics and economics of the United States and the Soviet Union are discussed, highlighting those factors that got both of the superpowers into the arms race and fuel the continued growth of it.

NOTES

1. Seymour Melman, *Our Depleted Society* (New York: Holt, Rinehart and Winston, 1965), p. 13. The data used by Melman are now over ten years old, and given the great effort made to increase our armament, this number has probably at least doubled by now.
2. Robert Ardrey, *African Genesis* (New York: Dell, 1961), p. 32.
3. Robert Ardrey, *The Territorial Imperative* (New York: Dell, 1966), pp. 322–324.
4. Konrad Lorenz, *On Aggression* (New York: Harcourt, Brace, and World, 1966), p. 271.
5. Ralph Holloway, Jr., "Human Aggression: The Need for a Species Specific Framework" in Morton Fried (ed.), *War: The Anthropology of Armed Conflict and Aggression* (Garden City, New York: Natural History Press, 1968), p. 30.
6. Alexander Lesser, "War and the State" in Morton Fried (ed.), *War: The Anthropology of Armed Conflict and Aggression*, p. 30.
7. Quoted in Roger Leonard, *Clausewitz* (New York: Putnam's, 1967), p. 213.
8. Robert Leckie, *Warfare* (New York: Harper and Row, 1970), pp. 3–66.
9. Leonard, *Clausewitz*, p. 11.
10. Henry Kissinger, *Problems of National Strategy* (New York: Praeger, 1965), p. 405.
11. Quoted in Bernard Brodie, *From Crossbow to H-Bomb* (Bloomington, Indiana: Indiana University Press, 1973), p. 12.
12. Ibid., p. 257.
13. Thomas Plate, *Understanding Doomsday* (New York: Simon and Schuster, 1971), p. 50.
14. Morris Janowitz, "Military Organization" in Roger Little (ed.), *Handbook of Military Institutions* (Beverly Hills, Calif.: Sage Publications, 1971), p. 14.
15. Jack Raymond, "Growing Trends of Our Military-Industrial Complex" in Martin Hickman (ed.), *The Military and American Society* (Beverly Hills, Calif.: Glencoe Press, 1971), pp. 73–74.
16. Ibid., p. 74.
17. Ibid.
18. The number of people in the armed forces varies from one time to another, but there have usually been at least 2 million constantly under arms in the United States since 1960.
19. John Kenneth Galbraith, "Testimony Be-

fore the Subcommitee on Economy in Government, Joint Economic Committee" in Martin Hickman (ed.), *The Military and American Society*, p. 161.

20. Raymond, "Growing Trends," p. 73.

21. C. Wright Mills, *The Power Elite* (New York: Oxford University Press, 1956), p. 198.

22. John Clark, *The New Economics of National Defense* (New York: Random House, 1966), preface.

23. Robert Mayo, "Budgetary Considerations" in William Proxmire et al., *National Priorities* (Washington, D.C.: Public Affairs, 1969), p. 5.

24. Bruce Russett, "The Price of War" in Martin Oppenheimer (ed.), *The American Military* (New York: Aldine, 1971), p. 84.

25. William J. Fulbright, "Values in Crisis" in William Proxmire et al., *National Priorities*, p. 2.

26. Kenneth Boulding, "The Effects of the War Industry" in William Proxmire et al., *National Priorities*, p. 135.

27. All data on military expenditures are taken from *Statistical Abstract of the United States, 1977* (Washington, D.C.: U.S. Government Printing Office, 1978), pp. 358–364.

28. Mary Kaldor and Alexander Cockburn, "The Defense Confidence Game," *The New York Review of Books* (June 13, 1974), p. 28.

29. Ibid.

30. John Kenneth Galbraith, "The Role of Military Power" in William Proxmire et al., *National Priorities*, p. 116.

31. Roland McKean, "Divergencies Between Individual and Total Costs Within Government," *American Economic Review*, Vol. 14, No. 3 (March 1964), p. 24.

32. William Proxmire, "Pentagon Accountability" in William Proxmire et al., *National Priorities*, p. 125.

33. Ibid., p. 126.

34. Leonard Rodberg, "The Great American Doom Machine," *Ramparts* (May 1974), p. 13.

35. Peter Irons, "On Repressive Institutions and the American Empire" in Priscilla Long (ed.), *The New Left* (Boston: Porter Sargent, 1969), p. 118.

36. Margaret Mead, "Population Control" in Harold Hart, *Population Control: For and Against* (New York: Hart Publishing Company, 1973), p. 55.

37. Harry Magdoff, *The Age of Imperialism* (New York: Monthly Review Press, 1969), p. 49.

38. John K. Fairbank, cited in Noam Chomsky, *At War with Asia* (New York: Pantheon, 1970), p. 3.

39. Noam Chomsky, *American Power and the New Mandarins* (New York: Random House, 1969), p. 4.

40. Raymond, "Growing Trends," p. 72.

41. Paul Dickson, "Tomorrow's Automated Battlefield," *The Progressive* (August 1974), p. 17.

42. Quoted in Donald Smith, "The Volunteer Army," *Atlantic* (July 1974), p. 7.

43. Leonard Levin, *Report from Iron Mountain* (New York: Dial Press, 1967).

44. Ibid., p. 34.

45. Ibid., pp. 80–82.

46. Seymour Melman, *The Permanent War Economy* (New York: Simon and Schuster, 1974).

47. Robert Heilbroner, "Making a Rational Foreign Policy," *Harpers* (September 1968), p. 67.

48. Hans Morgenthau, *A New Foreign Policy for the United States* (New York: Praeger, 1969), p. 119.

49. Henry Steele Commager, "The Limits of American Power" in Leonard Freedman (ed.), *Issues of the Seventies* (Belmont, Calif.: Wadsworth, 1970), p. 383.

GLOSSARY

absolute definition of poverty. Defining poverty as income below a fixed point, the minimum subsistence level. Government definitions of poverty are absolute. See *relative definition of poverty*.

achieved status. A status acquired through the efforts of the individual concerned, such as occupation or educational level. See *ascribed status*.

acupuncture. An ancient Chinese medical practice in which fine metal needles are inserted into the skin at particular places. Acupuncture is used as an anesthetic and in the treatment of illnesses ranging from blindness to ulcers.

adultery. Sexual intercourse by a married person with someone other than his or her spouse. Because adultery connotes disapproval, many now prefer the more neutral term *extramarital sex*.

affirmative action. Efforts to hire and promote minority group members to compensate for the disadvantages of the group. The goal is equality of opportunity. Affirmative action is termed *reverse discrimination* by its opponents.

age peers. Any status assigned chiefly on the basis of chronological age: infant, child, adolescent, adult.

aggression. The use of force or the threat of force toward another person or group.

aging. Getting older. In referring to ecosystems, aging means a growing simplification, resulting in a reduction in the number and variety of species that an ecosystem can support.

agricultural societies. Those societies in which the principal economic activity is agriculture or related to agriculture. Agricultural societies can and do have industrial production, but such production is not as important as farming.

agriculture. A planned, intensive, cultivation of domesticated plants in which the soil is prepared for planting with a plow. See *horticulture*.

alcohol. Perhaps the most widely used drug and the primary addiction problem in the United States. The extent of addiction to alcohol (called *alcoholism*) is unknown because definitions of addiction vary. See *Prohibition*.

alienation. The subjective feeling of being estranged from one's own society or some part of it. Many claim that alienation from work results from automation.

allopathic medicine. Conventional medicine, which aims at diagnosing ailments by observing symptoms and at curing ailments at the time of complaint. See *holistic medicine*.

all-volunteer army. An army of persons who have entered it voluntarily rather than through conscription.

alternative norms. A situation in which several different norms are applicable. Alternative norms provide flexibility, allowing people choices among socially permissible actions.

anomie. A state of normlessness. Since complete lack of norms is impossible, anomie can mean temporary indecision over how to proceed or act.

anomie theory. Robert Merton's theory that attempts to explain at least some deviance. Merton divides people into five types according to how they react to society's goals and norms. Society is not troubled by the first two groups: *conformists* accept society's goals and the socially approved means for obtaining them; *ritualists,* although they cannot possibly attain the goals, also accept the approved means. Deviance results from the action of three other groups: *innovators,* who accept a society's goals but use deviant means to achieve them; *retreatists,* who reject society's goals and, as a result, can break social norms; and *rebels,* who reject society's goals and sometimes break social norms in trying to change those goals.

antibiotics. Chemical substances produced by various organisms that are used to stop the growth of infectious bacteria. One example is penicillin.

apartheid. An Afrikaan's word meaning "apartness." The term refers to the caste system maintained in the Republic of South Africa in which a small minority of whites severely restricts the lives of the blacks who outnumber them.

arithmetical increase. A simple increase by units of one, the rate of increase Malthus postulated for food resources. See *geometric increase.*

arms race. A competition in which two or more nations attempt to gain and maintain a preponderance of military forces and military power over rival nations. Such competition usually involves stockpiling weapons, devising and building ever more potent weaponry, and devising effective defenses against known enemy weapons.

arrest rate. The number of arrests per thousand of a given population.

arteriosclerosis. Abnormal thickening and hardening of the walls of arteries.

asbestos fiber. Any of a group of silicate minerals that are fibrous in structure and highly resistant to fire and acid. Asbestos was widely used as a fire retardant until it was recently determined that inhaling asbestos particles can be hazardous to health.

ascribed status. Characteristics arbitrarily assigned to individuals or groups. In minority-majority systems, the dominant sector assigns characteristics, largely unfavorable, to minority group members. See *achieved status.*

assimilation. A social process whereby immigrants or members of existing minority groups adopt the dress, language, and customs of the host or dominant group in a society and become, to all intents and purposes, members of the dominant group.

atavism. The reappearance or recurrence in an organism of characteristics found in earlier forms of the organism's species. Cesare Lombroso's nineteenth-century theory of criminality postulated that criminals were atavistic, throwbacks to early humans like Neanderthal.

atherosclerosis. A lesion or lesions of large and medium-sized arteries brought about by deposits of yellowish plaques containing cholesterol, pipoid material, and lipophages.

atmospheric inversion. A climatic condition in which a layer of warm air above a layer of cooler air closer to the ground prevents air pollutants from being dissipated.

authority. Power that is recognized by those subject to it as just, right, and proper.

automation. Machines doing work previously done by people. Machines can work faster and cheaper than people can, but people are usually needed to work with the machines. As a result, the people's work is dull and repetitive and, some claim, alienating.

autonomy. The condition or quality of being self-governing or self-controlling, rather than controlled by others.

baby boom. A period of an unusually high birthrate in the United States, occurring roughly between 1946 and 1955.

backlash. The negative reaction of some whites, particularly members of ethnic groups and the working class, to the successes of the civil rights movement.

bail. A sum of money held by authorities as a condition for releasing an accused person from jail prior to his or her coming to trial. If the person fails to appear at trial, the money or property deposited as bail is forfeited.

beliefs. Somewhat strong convictions of the truth, accuracy, and validity of something. Beliefs are more strongly held than opinions but not as strongly held as faiths.

betwixt and between laws. Laws that have some support in a culture but also have active opposition because they violate certain cultural norms.

bilingual. Having a usable knowledge of two languages.

biofeedback. A relatively recent concept in medical psychology based on the fact that brain activity generates characteristic electrical impulses. Through a complex system of training, people learn to control these brain waves so as to reduce certain physical symptoms such as high blood pressure.

birth control. See *contraception.*

black. A person who identifies himself or herself and is identified by others as a person of Negro ancestry.

black English. A grammatical variant on the English language spoken by some black Americans.

blue-collar worker. A person other than a farm worker whose work is primarily manual. See *white-collar work.*

blue laws. Legislation relating to public and private conduct, particularly laws concerning the observance of the Sabbath.

booked. A person is booked when his or her arrest is formally recorded by the police.

bourgeoisie. Narrowly, the segment of a capitalistic system that owns the means of production. More broadly, the term is used to include a wide range of persons, including small shop owners. See *proletariat.*

Bow-Street Runners. The name of England's first professional police force, created in the middle of the eighteenth century.

bureaucracy. A large organization structured in a hierarchical fashion that operates on specific rules, regulations, and precedents and is geared to meeting long-range and continuing functions of a highly complex nature.

busing. Desegregating public schools by busing students from one school to another. Whether busing should be used only in cases of de jure segregation, and not de facto, is a matter of heated debate.

capitalism. An economic system in which certain individuals accumulate surpluses and use them to acquire ownership and control of the means of production.

caste system. A system of closed social classes characterized by: (1) membership is by birth, (2) membership is permanent — i.e., no chance to change castes, (3) marriage is endogamous, and (4) the division of labor is based on caste. Caste systems often receive powerful support from religious beliefs.

catalytic converter. A device now required on all new cars sold in this country that reduces the amount of unburned hydrocarbons and carbon monoxide released into the atmosphere.

catatonia. A variety of schizophrenia, a psychotic state in which the patient is unresponsive to external stimuli.

Chicano. A term applied to Mexican-Americans.

civil rights movement. An organized movement by blacks for the purpose of obtaining equality in American society.

cohabitation. Living together by two sexually mature persons of the opposite sex who have not gone through either a religious or civil marriage.

cohort. An aggregate of persons having a characteristic in common; for example, an age cohort is composed of persons of the same age.

cohort approach to fertility. Calculating fertility by dividing women between the ages of fifteen and forty-five into age cohorts and following each cohort's reproductive performance throughout the normal childbearing years, fifteen through forty-five.

collective definition. A definition agreed upon by a large number of people, usually a society.

community standards. The prevailing norms of a single community.

compound interest analogy. An analogy used to explain the rapid increase in human population, likening that increase to the compound interest paid by banks, in which interest is paid on the original amount plus any accrued interest. The effect is to greatly accelerate growth in bank accounts, or human populations, over time.

Comprehensive Training and Employment Act (CETA). A federal program designed to combat chronic urban unemployment by having the federal government pay for on-the-job training conducted by private business or local government.

conformist. See *anomie theory.*

conjugal family. See *family.*

conquest. The subjugation of persons, ranging from a single individual to an entire nation by another individual or group. One way to create a minority.

consanguinal family. See *family.*

consensus. Agreement among people on some topic or matter of concern. There is a consensus on a society's norms and values.

contagion. The spreading of disease from one person to another or others by contact.

contraception. Any device or technique used to prevent sexual intercourse from resulting in pregnancy.

cooling-out. A phrase used to describe the workings of a social structure such that individuals who fail in competition or who do not even compete are led to place the blame on themselves rather than their society.

cost overrun. An increase in the cost of providing goods and services over the estimated costs upon which a contract was signed. When bidding on government contracts, some companies underestimate their costs to win the contract and then apply for reimbursement for the higher costs incurred.

cost reimbursement. A federal government policy that allows a contractor to receive more than the original bid when costs exceeding the amount of the contracted price are found justifiable. See *cost overrun.*

criminal. Any person to whom the label of criminal has been successfully applied; someone who has broken the law and been arrested. See *lawbreaker.*

criminal justice system. A group of official agencies charged with maintaining social order and dealing with offenders in societies. It includes the police, the judiciary, and the penal system, as well as associated agencies and officials.

crude birthrate. The number of live births per thousand of a population in a given year.

crude death rate. The number of deaths per thousand of a population in a given year.

crude divorce rate. The number of divorces per thousand of a population in a given year.

cultural trait. Any value, norm, status, or role peculiar to a particular society and its culture.

culture. There are many definitions, but a good short one is Edward B. Tylor's: "that complex whole which includes knowledge, beliefs, art, morals, law, custom and any other capabilities and habits acquired by persons as members of societies."

culture of poverty. A controversial concept put forth by Oscar Lewis in his *La Vida,* which attributes different cultural traits to people living in poverty. While this culture helps people adjust to the problems of poverty, it inhibits upward mobility.

cumulative cohort birthrate. The number of births per one thousand women in a particular age cohort when they have completed their normal childbearing years, normally age forty-five.

DDT. A short term for 2,2-bis(p-chlorophenyl)-1,1,1-trichloroethane, chlorinated hydrocarbon compound, a pesticide used almost indiscriminately after the 1930s because it was cheaper than others and more powerful. DDT has proven to be highly toxic to many forms of insect life not harmful or annoying to humans. Because of its slow deterioration rate, it remains potent and is capable of passing through higher and higher life forms until it reaches humans, in whom unsafe concentrations have been found. Attention was first attracted to the hazards of indiscriminate use of DDT by the late Rachel Carson in her book *The Silent Spring*.

decentralization. The transference of authority from a central government to local government.

decibel. One tenth of a bel. A unit used to measure the loudness of sound.

de facto. In fact. In sociology, de facto is often used to describe something, like a norm, which lacks legality but is nonetheless operative.

de facto discrimination. Discrimination that actually takes place even though forbidden by law. De facto discrimination has the support of powerful informal norms. See *de jure discrimination*.

defective strategies. Behavior that is inadequate in some way or ways for dealing with life. The behaviors of mentally-ill persons are frequently termed defective strategies because they are both inappropriate and ineffective ways of confronting life.

definitional errors. Errors in defining something that are brought about by such circumstances as cultural bias, prejudice, belief, opinion, or physiological errors in perception.

de jure. Legal or of legal effect.

de jure segregation. Segregation established by law. In the United States, there is no more de jure segregation, although de facto segregation continues to exist. See *de facto discrimination*.

demographer. A sociologist who studies the size, growth rate, and geographical distribution of human populations.

demographic transition. A theory that sees world population changes as involving three stages: (1) a stage of high birthrates and high death rates with little population growth, (2) a stage of high birthrates and low death rates with rapid population increases, and (3) a stage of low birthrates and low death rates which, if continued, would result in zero population growth.

depersonalization. The removal of the human elements from a behavior that usually includes such elements. Among the depersonalizing influences of modern life are bureaucracy and automation.

deterrence. Anything that functions in such a way as to reduce the probability of someone performing an unwanted behavior.

developed countries. Those nations with extensive industrial and technological development, characterized by a high and varied productive capacity and a relatively small part of the work force engaged in agriculture. See *developing countries*.

developing countries. Those countries with a low level of industrial and technological development, in which a major portion of the working population is involved in agriculture. See *developed countries*.

differential association theory. A theory that humans are socialized and interact with specific groups and individuals and thus learn the values, norms, statuses, and roles appropriate to these groups from this association. The salient point of the theory is that many deviants are simply following the values and norms of the deviant subculture in which they were socialized.

discrimination. The effective barring from equal and full participation in a society of members of minority groups on grounds that are totally irrelevant to such participation.

divorce rate. See *crude divorce rate*.

double standard. A cultural trait involving one standard of sexual behavior for males and another for females. Usually the standard for females is far more restrictive and repressive.

drug. Any substance introduced into an organism for medical purposes, as with antibiotics, or to affect the central nervous system, as with alcohol, tobacco, and narcotics. The word more frequently refers to the latter group.

drug abuse. The use of illegal drugs or the excessive use of legal drugs.

dysfunction. A useless, inefficient, harmful, or undesirable function.

dyspact. An inefficient or harmful effect of some action or behavior.

ecology. A branch of natural science that studies organisms in their environments and what links organisms and place. See *ecosystem.*

economic liabilities. Someone incurring an economic cost without providing commensurate economic returns. In modern societies children are economic liabilities because they must be supported, trained, and educated for long periods of time, during which they provide no economic benefits to the family.

ecosystem. A space in which organisms live and intereact with each other and their environment. The relationship among organisms and between organisms and the environment is assumed to be reciprocally beneficial. Thus, the basic concepts underlying ecosystems are reciprocity and equilibrium.

ectomorph. See *somatotypes.*

egalitarianism. A political and economic philosophy maintaining that all humans should be treated equally.

electronic battlefields. Areas of battle in which the contenders are not human soldiers but highly sophisticated weaponry including laser-guided bombs and remote-controlled aircraft, and such intelligence devices as sensors and remote-controlled television cameras. In a word, combat between machines rather than people.

elite. A self-conscious, powerful, and coordinated group having a monopoly of economic and political power in some society, or some part of it.

embourgeoisment of the proletariat. Increasing affluence of the proletariat, keeping workers from developing class consciousness. Instead, they develop bourgeois attitudes and values.

emergent norms. Norms that appear in situations usually described as chaotic or confused, such as action by mobs. Emergent norms are norms that guide behavior in unusual or chaotic situations.

endogamous. Marriage within some specified group. Caste members, for instance, are bound to marry only other members of their caste.

endomorph. See *somatotypes.*

entrapment. An illegal technique for catching criminals, in which a person or persons is lured into committing a crime so that the authorities can then make an arrest and obtain a conviction.

environmental impact statement. A paper required by the federal government before a construction project can begin. The paper should summarize the results of an objective study of the effects the project will have on the environment where it will be built.

epidemiology. Knowledge and study of the occurrence and spread of diseases among populations.

Equal Rights Amendment. A proposed amendment to the Constitution that extends protection against discrimination to include women. The amendment was passed by Congress in March 1972 but lacks ratification by the required thirty-eight states.

escape mechanism. Any of a number of psychological devices used by individuals in order to avoid unpleasantness or the intrusion of disturbing ideas.

estate system. A social system common in primarily agricultural countries, which characterized England from late Roman to relatively recent times. In the estate system, society is composed of three estates: (1) nobility, (2) clergy, and (3) bourgeoisie, plus a forth and much larger group of peasants, who were not classified as an estate. See *feudal system.*

ethnicity. The cultural characteristics that differentiate and make identifiable various cultural groups.

ethnocentricism. A general orientation held by all human groups that members of their particular group are somehow inherently superior to all other groups and their members. Ethnocentricism can range from mild ethnic pride to virulent racism.

eufunction. A useful, good, efficient, or desirable function.

eugenics. A branch of biology that deals with controlled breeding in order to improve a species.

eutrophication. The addition of dissolved nutrients to bodies of water, reducing the amount of oxygen available to marine life.

exorcism. Any ritual, usually religious, the purpose of which is to rid persons or things of the evil spirits assumed to be inhabiting or controlling them.

exploitation. The gaining of advantages from people or groups without those people or groups yielding the advantages gaining equivalent ones. In other words, a one-sided exchange.

extended family. See *family.*

extramarital sex. See *adultery.*

extra Y chromosome. Most males have X and Y chromosomes, but some have an XYY combination. For a time, it was thought that having the extra Y chromosome predisposed males to crime. Sufficiently detailed and controlled scientific studies have not yet been conducted, so it is impossible to reach any conclusion.

family. A social unit linking people by common ancestry and marriage. Sociologists discuss family in two senses. The first differentiates types according to the ties bonding the family together. If the primary tie is marriage, the family is said to be *conjugal.* If, however, the primary tie is to blood relatives, the family is *consanguinal.* The second focus of sociological study is the family as a household. If daily interactions between family members are confined to the husband, wife, and children, the family is said to be *nuclear.* If daily interactions include blood relatives outside the nuclear unit — grandparents, aunts and uncles, and cousins — the family is said to be *extended.*

fatalism. An acceptance of the status quo based on the belief that nothing people can do will bring any change for the better.

feminist movement. A social movement to obtain political, educational, and social equality for women.

fertility. The actual reproductive performance of a woman or group of women.

fertility rate. The average number of children born to women of a particular cohort or all women in a particular society during their childbearing years, from fifteen to forty-five.

feudal system. A society in which a very ıl proportion of landowning aristocrats hold all the political power and exploit the greater mass of people, who are classified as serfs or peasants. In a feudal system, virtually all statuses are ascribed. See *estate system.*

forcible rape. See *rape.*

formal agencies of social control. See *social control, agencies of.*

functional psychosis. Any psychosis the origin of which lies in thought processes and does not have some physiological cause. See *organic psychosis.*

gay. See *homosexuality.*

gender identity. Self-identification as a male or female.

general norms. All those social rules not having the force of mores but which direct much behavior in human societies.

generic. A word meaning the same thing as *general;* related to a class.

generic drug. A drug carrying the generally agreed upon scientific name for a particular drug, rather than a brand name. Generic drugs are less expensive than comparable brand name drugs.

geometric increase. A progression in which each element increases by doubling: 1, 2, 4, 8, and so on. Malthus predicted that population would increase geometrically, while food would only increase arithmetically.

geothermal power. The enormous pressures be-

neath the surface of the earth generate considerable heat. When this heat is used to produce steam the resulting power is called geothermal.
germ theory of disease. A well-established theory that certain diseases are caused by microorganisms.
ginhead. A person addicted to gin. Many areas of eighteenth-century London were jammed with ginheads; these areas were similar to modern skid rows.
Great Depression. A period of worldwide economic stagnation falling roughly between 1930 and 1940, marked by very high unemployment, severe inflation in some countries, and a general industrial slowdown.
greenhouse effect. As increasing amounts of carbon dioxide are released into the atmosphere, the accumulation of gas traps surface heat. This trapping of heat is similar to what occurs in a greenhouse, hence it is called the greenhouse effect.
gross national product (GNP). The total value, expressed in a national medium of exchange, of all the goods and services produced in a nation in a given time, usually one year.
guild. An association of people having a common occupation. In medieval times, certain craftsmen organized themselves into guilds, which established rules for conduct for guild members and outlined how the guild could be entered.

hard-core pornography. The written or pictoral presentation of sexual behavior and acts in which the chief purpose is sexual excitation and which lacks any redeeming social value. The line between erotic realism and hard-core pornography is difficult to determine, particularly legally. See *soft-core pornography.*
health. Good health has been defined by the World Health Organization as "a state of physical, mental, and social well-being and not merely the absence of disease and infirmity."
health support system. Any system that provides health care for citizens.

hebephrenic schizophrenia. See *schizophrenia.*
hedonistic calculus. The hypothetical process whereby a person contemplating the commission of a deviant or criminal act weighs the possible gains against the possible risks and decides whether or not to perform the act by seeing which weighs more.
held values. Those values that people have internalized, which guide them in a wide variety of situations.
hetairai. Well-educated women who provide sexual favors for the well-to-do and powerful; courtesans.
heterogeneity. The quality or state of being different, unlike, or dissimilar.
heterosexuality. Sexual attraction to members of the opposite sex. See *homosexuality.*
holistic. The perception of anything from a total rather than a fragmentary point of view.
holistic medicine. An approach to medicine that considers the entire organism in cases of illness or malfunctioning, rather than merely treating symptoms. Holistic medicine takes the position that all events and experiences are relevant to the physical and emotional state of patients.
homeostasis. The tendency of living organisms to maintain a state of internal balance. The characteristic has been attributed to human organizations of all sizes.
Homo sapiens. Our own biological species, from Latin for man the knowing or wise.
homosexuality. Sexual attraction to members of the same sex. Also, the complex of statuses, roles, and norms surrounding homosexual behavior. Female homosexuals are called *lesbians*; the slang term for homosexual is *gay*. See *heterosexuality.*
hunters and gatherers. An economic system practiced by small bands of people in which food is obtained by hunting and fishing, and gathering edible vegetation.
hypochondria. A morbid preoccupation with the state of one's health. The hypochondriac believes that he or she has physical illnesses that he or she does not really have.

hysteria. A neurotic state or neurosis marked by high susceptibility to suggestions and dissociation.

iatrogenic effects. In medicine, used to describe a patholgical condition caused by a medicine or therapy administered to alleviate or cure another condition. In sociology, used to describe social problems caused by attempts to alleviate or remedy some other social problem. Iatrogenic effects are a kind of latent effect. Latent effects can be either eufunctional or dysfunctional, but iatrogenic effects are always dysfunctional.

ideal culture. What people wish and sometimes believe that their cultures were in the past. Also, imagined cultures in which all members are healthy and happy.

immigration. People moving out of one society and into another society, intending to settle permanently in the society to which they are moving.

impairment. Any condition, physiological or mental, that results in functioning at less than some reasonably effective level. Some authors suggest that *mental illness* should be termed *mental impairment.*

impotence. A condition in males in which an individual is unable to gain and maintain an erection, thereby rendering him incapable of having coitus.

incest. Sexual intercourse between persons in socially defined consanguinal relationships with each other. What constitutes incest varies from society to society, but it usually includes at least sexual relations between father and daughter, mother and son, and brother and sister.

income distribution. The proportion of national income received by various segments of a society. If income was distributed equally, the top 20 percent and bottom 20 percent of people would each receive 20 percent of income.

indentured servants. In colonial days, people who obtained passage to the New World by selling themselves into servitude for a period of time, usually seven years. When the time was up, they obtained their liberty and sometimes some land.

Industrial Revolution. That period of history between 1750 and 1850 during which England, and to some extent the United States and European nations, changed from an agrarian to an industrial economy.

influential people. Individuals capable of exerting power or authority in some way so that others will agree with their views. Influential people do not, themselves, have power or authority, but rather some access to other persons possessing power or authority. The category includes those who control or have ready access to the mass media, government officials of a high enough level to influence policy, and various other persons in society whose ideas and recommendations carry weight beyond that of the average citizen.

informal norms. Norms that have been institutionalized into the culture of a society but are not represented in laws or regulations. The sanctions used to enforce informal norms are also informal.

informal agencies of social controls. See *social control, agencies of.*

information chain. The processual chain by and through which information is disseminated to a large number of people. At each step the information is subject to distortion, whether conscious or unconscious.

initial appearance. The first appearance of an accused person before a court official.

inoculation. The introduction of moribund bacteria into an organism for the purpose of activating bodily defenses and thereby rendering the organism immune to a disease for some period of time.

innovator. See *anomie theory.*

integration. The coalescing of different cultures or racial groups into a single new culture. Once the new culture is formed, members will be culturally indistinguishable from one another. Unlike assimilation, in which one group must adopt another group's culture, integration means using aspects of both cultures.

interchangeable parts. In mass production, the

various parts of a finished product are manufactured to be identical. Therefore, any one part of a product is interchangeable with all other parts fulfilling the same function. This speeds up manufacturing time and permits easy repair.

intrauterine device. Frequently called *IUD,* this contraceptive device is placed in the vagina at the mouth of the uterus to prevent fertilization.

invidious distinction. Distinguishing between the characteristics of individuals or groups and attaching a stigma to one set of traits.

Jim Crow laws. A complex of laws, generally from the South, that supported segregation and discrimination against blacks. All such laws have been declared unconstitutional.

knowledge explosion. The tremendous increase in knowledge, particularly scientific knowledge, of recent times, which has resulted in an increase in the objectivity with which we view conditions, meaning that more conditions are defined as problems to be solved rather than miseries to be endured. There has also been an increase in faith in our ability to solve these problems.

labeling theory. Howard S. Becker's theory to explain what happens once a person is labeled as deviant. According to Becker, all people occasionally exhibit deviant behavior, called *primary deviance.* Only some of those deviant actions are discovered by others and labeled as deviant, however. Once a person's actions are labeled deviant, the person is treated differently — segregated from the rest of society, punished, and stigmatized. This treatment can force the person to commit further acts of deviance, called *secondary deviance.*

labor theory of value. Karl Marx's concept that what determines the value of a manufactured article is the amount of human labor put into making it. He argued that capitalism ignores this truth because the profits from selling the product go not to the workers who produced it, but to the factory owners.

lawbreaker. Anyone who commits an act disallowed by the laws of his society. Almost all people are lawbreakers occasionally. What distinguishes a lawbreaker from a criminal is that criminals are caught, that is, their behavior is labeled as deviant by the criminal justice system. Lawbreakers' behavior is also deviant, but goes undetected or ignored.

leisure. Pleasurable activity that involves a person's self-expression, leading to an increased understanding of self and the world. See also *recreation, work.*

lesbian. See *homosexuality.*

levée en masse. A French phrase meaning conscription, the legal impressment of civilians, usually male, into the armed forces of a country. First started on a large scale by Napoleon, this practice radically changed warfare from engagements fought by small bodies of professional warriors to large-scale battles fought by huge conscripted armies.

life cycle. The life span of humans, from infancy through childhood, adolescence, and adulthood to old age.

long-term debt. Debt that will continue well into the foreseeable future, often incurred by governments from deficit spending (spending more than they collect in taxes). The problem with such debt is that the interest becomes a fixed cost increasing government budgets even though the government and its people derive no benefit from the portion of taxes used to meet the interest payments. See *short-term debt.*

mala per se. A Latin phrase meaning "bad as such," referring to laws prohibiting actions that are undesirable in themselves. These laws support the society's norms. See *mala quia prohibita.*

mala quia prohibita. A Latin phrase meaning "bad because forbidden," referring to laws supported by ideal norms but without widespread *support in the society. A good example is the Eighteenth Amendment to the Constitution, which initiated Prohibition. See* mala per se.

marriage. A complex of social norms sanctioning a relationship between (in our society) one man and one woman and outlining the two person's mutual obligations and rights.

median family income. Median refers to that point in a distribution of variables that exactly divides the distribution into two equal parts. Thus, median family income is that amount of income that precisely divides a population into two equal halves in terms of income.

medical sociology. A subfield of sociology concerned with the various social aspects of medicine. Included are such topics as: (1) epidemiology, (2) organizational theory, (3) professionalization, (4) health systems, and (5) social change, as it affects medicine and medical practices.

militance. Active, aggressive, and assertive behavior. Militance can involve physical force or threats of physical force, but does not necessarily: nonviolent protest is a form of militance.

military-industrial complex. Interlocking and mutually cooperative interaction between the military and the civilian suppliers of goods and services required by the military.

minimum subsistence income. The yearly income for a family sufficient to permit them to maintain a standard of living consistent with good health. The figure is used by the government to determine the number of people living in poverty (those earning less than the minimum subsistence income), but the figure is too subjective to be useful.

minority. A group of people who because of physical or cultural characteristics are singled out for discrimination. The word tends to be misleading in that it implies numerical inferiority when, in fact, some minorities constitute the larger part of a population, such as women, and blacks in South Africa.

miscegenation. The intermarriage or interbreeding of persons of different races.

Model Cities. An urban renewal program of the 1960s meant to tear down blighted city areas and replace them with new housing. In some cases, unfortunately, only demolition occurred before funds ran out.

modern functionalism. A sociological orientation that accepts the existence of social conflict (which structural functionalism downplays) and concentrates on trying to ascertain how a particular system or subsystem actually works and what the consequences are of such functioning.

moral restraint. Restraining from sexual intercourse, as a methods of controlling population growth, as originally put forward by Thomas Malthus in the eighteenth century. A not very reliable method of contraception.

mores. Norms that have a sacred or near-sacred quality and express rules considered to be of very great importance to members of societies, such as the norms against murder or incest.

multinational corporations. Corporations that do business in more than one nation, and thus have economic and political interests that go beyond those of particular countries.

narcotics. Drugs that function to relieve pain or in other ways affect the central nervous system.

negative income tax. A proposal to alleviate poverty by exempting from taxes and making payments out of tax monies to persons whose incomes are below some officially determined level.

neofunctionalism. See *modern functionalism.*

Neolithic Revolution. The shift, beginning about 10,000 B.C. and continuing for several thousand years, from nomadic hunting and gathering to horticulture, agriculture, and the domestication of animals. The effect was to increase the number of people that could be fed by a given community.

neurasthenia. A mental state in which the patient lacks physical and mental vigor, frequently accompanied by hypochondria.

neurosis. Any one of several mild mental disorders. Unlike someone with a psychosis, someone with a neurosis can usually function well enough to get by in life, and knows that he or she has a problem.

nicotine. A colorless, soluble alkaloid commonly found in tobacco. Because it functions as a vasodilator and accelerates heartbeat, it provides users with feelings of well-being and contentment. It is highly addictive.

no-fault divorce. A recent alternative to the old form of divorce, in which one party to the divorce had to be blamed for the dissolution of the marriage. Now divorce is available on the grounds of incompatibility, meaning simply that the two persons cannot live in reasonable harmony.

noise. Unwanted sound. Noise pollution — bombardment of the ears by high levels of sound — may be more than just annoying. It may be proven to have detrimental physical and psychological effects.

nonviolent protest. A method of protesting injustice and undesirable policies by assembling masses of people to demonstrate their opposition with marches and boycotts. The major technique of the civil rights movement under Martin Luther King, Jr.

norm. A rule of human behavior.

nuclear family. See *family.*

nuclear power. Power produced by steam produced by the heat generated by nuclear fission.

obscenity. Any object, utterance, or act judged as morally abhorrent or disgusting. The definition varies from culture to culture, from place to place within a culture, and from person to person within a place.

observable conditions. Empirical evidence; facts that can be verified. No social problem exists without there being observable conditions, aspects of life that can be seen and verified.

old age. Generally (though arbitrarily) defined as the period of life from age sixty-five onward.

opiates. Any of several narcotics — particularly heroin and morphine — derived from opium. The drugs dull the senses, and can be addictive.

oppression. Any condition or circumstances under which people are denied totally or partially a voice in their own destinies.

organic analogy. The comparison of societies to organisms. Just as organisms are composed of dissimilar organs each performing specialized functions, so is society composed of different institutions each performing a specialized function for society. The analogy has limited usefulness, however.

organic psychosis. Any psychosis the cause of which is principally organic. See *functional psychosis.*

organizational theory. A substantial body of sociological theory concerned with the genesis, structure, values, statuses, roles, norms, and changes in organizations.

overqualification. Having a job for which the jobholder has more education or experience or both than is necessary for satisfactory performance of the job.

paramilitary. Any organization that is military in organization, such as the police.

paranoid schizophrenia. See *schizophrenia.*

paraphilia. A neutral term referring to the sexual behaviors that were formerly called perversions, such acts as sadomasochism, oral sex, anal sex, and fetishism.

parole. The release of prisoners without their serving out a full sentence in return for requiring them to meet certain conditions, including supervision by a parole officer and prohibitions against associating with known criminals. Violations of the conditions of parole result in the parolee being arrested and confined for the duration of the original sentence.

period approach to fertility. The expression of fertility as births in a given time, usually one year.

phobia. A neurosis, a morbid and frequently irrational dread or dislike of something.

physiological error. An error in perception with a physiological cause.

pill. A chemical contraceptive that affects the endocrine system so as to prevent ovulation, thus inhibiting the possibility of pregnancy.

placebo. Any substances without appreciable medical effects given to a patient for psychological rather than physiological reasons.

plea bargaining. Bargaining between a defendant's attorney and the public prosecutor resulting in the exchange of a plea of guilty for a charge involving a lesser offense than the original charge.

pluralism. Characteristic of a society in which different groups retain their identities and distinctive cultural traits. In a pluralistic society there are no dominant or minority groups, simply a number of different, equal groups.

pollution. Putting more of something into an ecosystem than it has the carrying capacity to absorb.

population explosion. The extremely rapid increase in the world's human population in the twentieth century.

pornography. Written or pictorial materials containing descriptions or depictions of sexual behavior. The definitions of what is or is not pornography vary both within and between societies. Many prefer to use the more neutral term *sexually explicit material.*

positive checks. Checks on population growth such as war, famine, and disease. Called positive checks by Thomas Malthus largely because he considered them more effective as a means of population control than moral restraint. See *moral restraint* and *preventive checks.*

poverty. Poverty is difficult to define objectively, but one definition may be having an income insufficient to maintain reasonable health and security. See *absolute definition of poverty* and *relative definition of poverty.*

poverty line. An annual income figure determined by the government to be used as a cutoff point in defining poverty. The poor are those with incomes below this income figure.

power. The ability to impose one's will on another.

prejudice. From the Latin *prejudicum,* meaning a prejudgement. Prejudice is a complex of negative attitudes and beliefs about members of another group.

pretend rules. These are norms representing ideal behavior to which people give lip service, but which are generally not observed.

pretrial intervention. Analyzing the problems of accused persons between the time of indictment and trial. A thorough background investigation is made and the accused cooperates with counselors and others. Upon completion of this program, those in charge make a recommendation for the disposition of the case, from release from custody to going to trial.

preventive checks. Malthus's concept that population growth could be restricted by conscious human action, such as moral restraint.

primary deviance. See *labeling theory.*

professionalization. The process by which neophytes are socialized into the values, norms, knowledge, and skills of a particular profession. Also, the process by which certain vocations attempt to move toward professional status.

Prohibition. Beginning in the 1830s, the campaign to outlaw the manufacture and consumption of alcohol finally succeeded in 1920, with the ratification of the Eighteenth Amendment. From 1920 to 1933, when Prohibition was repealed, the consumption of alcohol increased tremendously and the law was flouted across the nation.

proletariat. Workers; those who work for wages and do not own or otherwise control the means of production. See *bourgeoisie.*

property tax. A tax on property paid by property owners. Ordinarily the amount of property tax is based on an assessed valuation of property. This is the major tax of municipalities.

prostitution. The exchange of sexual favors for money or something of value.

Protestant work ethic. A set of attitudes toward work arising out of early Calvinistic doctrine that made work an end in itself and maintained that hard work, frugality, and asectism were pleasing to God.

psychical impotence. The inability of males to maintain an erection, for psychological rather than physical reasons.

psychoactive. Generally used to refer to drugs that affect the central nervous system and alter perceptions and reactions.

psychopathy. A variety of mental disorders characterized by difficulty in making conventional social adjustments.

psychosexual. A combination of psychological and sexual, in the sense of biological. Sex roles are ascribed according to sex, but are psychological and social constructs, hence they are said to be psychosexual categories.

psychosis. A serious mental illness characterized by gross departures from reality.

puberty. The time of life, usually around ten to twelve years of age, when sexual maturation occurs.

quack. An individual lacking in accepted medical training and skills who nonetheless practices medicine.

racism. An extreme form of ethnocentricism in which one's own race is exalted and all others denigrated. An individual with such views is called a *racist*.

rape. Sexual intercourse forced on someone unwilling to participate, sometimes called *forcible rape*. *Statutory rape* refers to sexual intercourse with an underage person, who is defined by statute as too young to be able to give consent.

rationalization. The justification of an irrational act or belief by the use of illogic disguised as logic.

real culture. Culture as expressed by the actual behavior of people.

rebel. See *anomie theory*.

recidivism. A return to criminal activity after having been previously caught and punished.

recreation. Voluntary participation in nonwork activities for the purpose of relieving tension, frequently involving the expenditure of considerable amounts of energy. See *leisure, work*.

refractory period. The length of time between a male's orgasm and his ability to regain and maintain an erection.

reinforcement. The consequences of behavior, either reward, punishment, or neutral. These consequences have an effect on learning.

relative definition of poverty. Defining poverty not in terms of a minimum subsistence income, but by comparing the relative economic standing of groups. See *absolute definition of poverty*.

repressive desublimation. A term coined by the late Herbert Marcuse to mean a process whereby sexual impulses are allowed more direct expression than previously but gratification of these impulses is used to control behavior in nonsexual areas.

retreatist. See *anomie theory*.

retributive justice. The kind of punishment in which the culprit is made to suffer in accordance with the magnitude or seriousness of the crime.

revenue sharing. A federal government policy in which some tax money collected by the federal government is returned to local political units for their own use.

reverse discrimination. The label given to such employment practices as affirmative action by those who believe that such practices discriminate against the dominant group in society.

ritualist. See *anomie theory*.

role. A set of norms defining behavioral expectations associated with every status in all societies. Roles are the action components of statuses, outlining what behavior is expected of people and what behavior they can expect from others.

role overload. A condition occurring when wives who are working full time also perform all the household and child-care tasks without assistance from their husbands.

sanction. Social reinforcements for a behavior, by which people are induced to act in socially approved ways.

sanction incongruence. The conflict when a sanction supports the social order but is opposed by yet another sanction. For example, our society has sanctions against vandalism. Yet the adolescent gang member who refuses to vandalize a building with the gang may suffer sanctions from the group.

schizophrenia. The most common functional psychosis. *Simple schizophrenia* consists of withdrawal and apathy, resulting in a deterioration of social relationships. *Hebephrenic schizophrenia* is marked by disorganized thinking, inappropriate behavior, and hypochondria. *Paranoid schizophrenia* is revealed in delusions of persecution or grandeur.

secondary deviance. See *labeling theory*.

sedatives. Drugs that calm and relax people.

segregation. The voluntary or involuntary separation of persons on the basis of race, religion, or ethnicity. Such separation occurs in terms of places of residence, occupation, places of worship, and even places of amusement.

selectivity. The most descriptive word for the criminal justice system. The people in the system have discretion, so at each step — from deciding whether to investigate a crime to deciding how to punish the guilty person — criminal justice officials act selectively.

self-report studies. Studies in which respondents are requested, usually anonymously, to report on various aspects of their behavior. Numerous self-report research studies make it clear that virtually all adults have committed one or more felonies in their lifetimes.

senescence. The process of physical deterioration and a corresponding decline in vigor and dominance. As applied to cities, senescence implies that certain cities are failing to meet their own needs and those of their inhabitants.

senility. A condition marked by loss of memory, poor motor coordination, impaired functioning, and physical weakness; associated with advancing age.

sensuality. The enjoyment of things physical, including but not limited to things sexual.

sentries. Sociologically, people in a community who maintain a lookout for situations, including deviance, requiring action and who take action to remedy such situations as come to their attention. Modern communities rely largely on official agencies for performing this activity.

separatism. A full and complete physical separation of different groups. Also a stated policy of some members of minority groups, who advocate complete separation as a way to end discrimination.

serf. Peasants in the feudal system, who, while not slaves, were not free citizens. Serfs were bound to the land, owed fealty to their local lord, and could not leave their lord's domain without permission. In turn, they were supposed to receive protection. Ideally, the arrangement between lord and serf was one of reciprocal obligations, but actually lords frequently failed to fulfill theirs.

sexist. Someone holding unfavorable stereotypes of the opposite sex. Also, behavior that is overtly or covertly discriminatory against one sex or the other.

sex roles. Any role socially defined as more appropriate for one sex than the other.

sexuality. Behavior and feelings associated with expressions of the sex drive.

sexually-explicit material. See *pornography*.

sexual revolution. The presumed great changes that have taken place in this century in sexual attitudes and behavior.

short-term debt. Debts of organizations that are met out of current income. See *long-term debt.*

simple schizophrenia. See *schizophrenia.*

slave. A person whose labor is controlled by another and who cannot legally end that control unilaterally.

social change. One part of the sociological analysis of health care, which studies the various approaches to explaining and solving health problems throughout history.

social control, agencies of. Individuals or institutions that act to induce socially acceptable behavior. *Informal agencies* are unorganized, but still effective, including such things as peer pressure. *Formal agencies* are organized and officially designated, including such things as all the components of the criminal justice system.

social disorganization. A condition or circumstance wherein norms have lost some of their force and members of a society are uncertain about how to act or behave. Although such conditions do occur, they are generally temporary, so social disorganization does not adequately explain social problems.

social fact. An abstraction from observing human interaction that, when identified, can be said to have some power to influence or coerce human behavior.

social indicators. Data of many kinds that provide objective information as to the state of a society, such as mortality rate, gross national product, or unemployment rate.

social institution. A complex of values, statuses, roles, and norms centered on a function or functions of importance to human societies. Modern societies have at least nine social institutions: (1) art or aesthetics, (2) economics, (3) education, (4) the family, (5) the military, (6) politics, (7) recreation, (8) religion, and (9) science.

socialization. The process by which humans acquire knowledge of the norms, roles, and statuses of the society in which they live.

social learning. Learning that takes place in a social milieu and is social in nature.

social mobility. Upward or downward movement from one class or status to another.

social promotion. A widespread practice in American schools of promoting students to the next level even though they are performing unsatisfactorily, apparently based on the belief that failing a student is more harmful than unjustified promotion.

social security. A system of government payments to persons of retirement age to which eligible individuals and their employers have contributed during the time the retired persons were working.

social stratification. The ranking of persons in a social system in terms of differences in affluence, authority, prestige, priviliges, and influence.

society. A group of persons having a common culture, consciousness of membership in the society, and living within some delimited territory.

soft-core pornography. Material that is highly suggestive of sexual acts but is not explicit. See *hard-core pornography.*

solar energy. Using the sun as a means of furnishing energy.

somatotypes. William H. Sheldon's system of classifying people by body type. *Ectomorphs* were said to have a fragile bone structure and be lean; *endomorphs* were characterized by roundness and softness; and *mesomorphs* were said to have a moderate to heavy bone structure and well developed muscles. Mesomorphs were said to be more inclined to juvenile delinquency.

Standard Metropolitan Statistical Area (SMSA). Defined by the Bureau of the Census as an area including a central city of at least 50,000 persons, the county in which the city is located, and one or more adjacent counties for which the central city provides goods and services.

statutory rape. See *rape.*

status. A social category such as man, woman, child, professor, student. Status is not a synonym for prestige although all statuses carry with them greater or lesser prestige.

status lock. A characteristic of all statuses and

their associated roles, which locks people into behavior in accordance with the norms for their particular status.
stereotype. An overly simplified and usually erroneous characteristic attributed to some group.
stigma. Any mark of infamy or disgrace.
stimuli. Any factors or events that arouse responses in living organisms.
subculture of youth. That complex of attitudes and behaviors of young persons in a society that, although part of the total culture, differs from the total culture in certain ways.
subjective evaluation. Judgments made by people, which are necessarily subjective, influenced by the evaluator's beliefs, knowledge, and experience.
suffrage. The right of voting in political elections. The goal of the feminist movement for almost one hundred years, until the right was achieved with the ratification of the Nineteenth Amendment in 1920.
surplus value. That part of the value of work extracted from the workers and claimed as legitimate reward by the owners of the means of production.

technicways. A term coined by Howard Odum to mean those norms associated with job-related tasks.
technological fix. The remedying of adverse or undesirable conditions or situations through the application of technology and technological knowledge.
technology. The application of science to solutions of human problems.
thermal pollution. The pollution of natural waterways by discharging water at temperatures higher than normal into them. Many marine organisms can survive only within a narrow range of temperatures. When water temperature rises above a certain point, some marine life is killed.
thief-takers. Men who operated in early eighteenth-century England as quasi-official police, apprehending criminals and restoring lost property for fees. Akin to what were known in the United States as bounty hunters.
tobacco. See *nicotine.*
total fertility rate. The mean or average fertility rate for a population of humans.
track system. A school policy of grouping students by ability. For example, superior students are placed in a college preparatory track while those of lesser ability might be placed in a vocational track.
tradition. Values, norms, statuses, opinions, or beliefs that have been handed down to people in a society from the past and remain viable in a society.
trickle-down theory. The economic theory that if the upper classes gain in affluence, some of these gains will trickle down to the lower classes.

underemployment. One or all of three conditions: (1) people working only part-time when they desire full-time employment, (2) people engaged in work calling for a lower level of education, training, or skills than they possess, and (3) people working for wages that place them below the poverty line.
unemployment. Being out of work unvoluntarily.
Uniform Crime Reports. An annual publication of the Federal Bureau of Investigation, which provides comprehensive data on reported crime in the United States.
urban fringe. That area surrounding a central city characterized by largely affluent residential communities and shopping and amusement centers, and possibly light industry.

values. Broad, general guidelines that humans use as a basis for selecting among a range of possible courses of actions and by which actions are judged.
victimization studies. Research in which people are asked, in confidence, if they have ever been the victim of a crime. The purpose of such studies is to account for unreported crime. As a means of determining actual crime rates, carefully per-

formed victimization studies are superior to official crime statistics.

victimless crimes. Crimes in which no harm comes to anyone but the perpetrators of the crime.

visibility. The degree to which some characteristic is capable of being seen by direct observation and thus can be used to differentiate between groups. *Physical visibility* refers to easily recognizable physical traits, such as sex and skin color. *Ethnic visibility* refers to cultural characteristics that distinguish groups and are easily observed, such as language and dress.

war. Aggression involving the use of lethal weapons between two political units or groups.

wealth fare. The various government programs that benefit the affluent, such as crop subsidies.

welfare. The various government programs designed to provide some assistance to the poor and indigent.

white-collar crime. Job-related crime committed by relatively high status persons in the course of their occupations, such as embezzlement or price-fixing.

white-collar work. Usually thought of as those occupations involving principally mental work and not requiring any appreciable degree of manual labor. See *blue-collar worker.*

white flight. A term describing the mass movement of whites from central cities to the suburbs to avoid integration.

witchcraft. The use of supernatural power to affect human events, long thought to be the cause of dire events from individual suffering to natural disasters, but no longer widely believed in.

work. Purposeful physical or mental activities or both directed toward specific and usually utilitarian goals. See *leisure, recreation.*

youth. That period of life between the ages of eleven and twenty-five.

zero population growth (ZPG). A condition in which a population ceases to increase in numbers. This is eventually but not immediately achieved when the crude birthrate and the crude death rate are equal.

TEXT CREDITS (*continued from page iv*)

Table 6.2. Data from Robert Merton, "Discrimination and the American Creed" in *Discrimination and the National Welfare* edited by Robert M. MacIver, pp. 99–126. Copyright 1949 by Institute for Religious and Social Studies. Reprinted by permission of Harper & Row, Publishers, Inc.

Page 195. Excerpted from Angela Davis article, *The New York Times* (August 23, 1970), p. 5. © 1970 by The New York Times Company. Reprinted by permission.

Table 8.1. Adapted from Michael J. Hindelang, *Criminal Victimization in Eight Cities: A Descriptive Analysis of Common Theft and Assault*, p. 399. Copyright 1976, Ballinger Publishing Company. Reprinted by permission.

Table 8.3. Adapted from Cheryl L. Gilland, Kathy D. Fanning, William R. Brown, and Thomas Tichnor, "Sexual Attitudes and Behavior of Social Science Students," a paper presented at the Seventh Annual Alpha Kappa Delta Sociology and Research Symposium, 1976. Reprinted by permission.

Table 8.4. Reprinted with permission of Macmillan Publishing Co., Inc. from Robert K. Merton, *Social Theory and Social Structure*, Chapter VI, p. 194. Copyright 1968, 1967, Robert K. Merton.

Table 9.1. From Harold T. Christensen and Christina F. Gregg, "Changing Sex Norms in America and Scandinavia," *Journal of Marriage and the Family* (November 1970), p. 621. Copyrighted 1970 by the National Council on Family Relations. Reprinted by permission.

Figure 11.2. From A. M. Carr-Saunders, *World Population* (Oxford: Clarendon Press, 1936), p. 42. Reprinted by permission of Oxford University Press.

Figure 11.3. From A. M. Carr-Saunders, *World Population* (Oxford: Clarendon Press, 1936), p. 42. Reprinted by permission of Oxford University Press.

Figure 11.4. From United Nations, Department of Economic and Social Affairs, *Statistical Yearbook*, 1965 and 1976. Copyright, United Nations 1965, 1976. Reproduced by permission.

Figure 11.5. From United Nations, Department of Economic and Social Affairs, *Statistical Yearbook*, 1965 and 1976. Copyright, United Nations 1965, 1976. Reproduced by permission.

Figure 11.7. From United Nations, Department of Economic and Social Affairs, *Statistical Yearbook*, 1965 and 1976. Copyright, United Nations 1965, 1976. Reproduced by permission.

Table 11.1. From United Nations, Department of Economic and Social Affairs, *Statistical Yearbook*, 1965 and 1976. Copyright, United Nations 1965, 1976. Reproduced by permission.

Table 11.2. From United Nations, Department of Economic and Social Affairs, *Statistical Yearbook*, 1977. Copyright, United Nations 1977. Reproduced by permission.

Figure 12.1. From John McHale, *World Facts and Trends*, 2nd ed. (New York: Macmillan Publishing Co.), p. 81. Copyright © 1971, 1972 by John McHale. This figure also appeared in Hans Landsbert, Leonard Fishman and Joseph Fisher, *Resources in America's Future*, a Resources for the Future book (Baltimore: The Johns Hopkins University Press), p. 37. Copyright © 1963, The Johns Hopkins Press. Reprinted by permission of Macmillan Publishing Co., Inc. and The Johns Hopkins University Press.

Page 416. Excerpt from a song by Pete Seeger. Used by permission of Pete Seeger.

Figure 13.2. From John McHale, *World Facts and Trends*, 2nd ed. (New York: Macmillan Publishing Co.), p. 74. Copyright © 1971, 1972 by John McHale. This figure also appeared in R. Houwink, "The Synthetics Age," *Modern Plastics* (August 1966), p. 99, published by McGraw-Hill, Inc. Reprinted by permission of Macmillan Publishing Co., Inc. and McGraw-Hill, Inc.

Page 425. From G. Tyler Miller, Jr., *Living in the Environment*, p. 15. © 1975 by Wadsworth Publishing Company, Inc., Belmont, California 94002. Reprinted by permission of the publisher.

Table 13.2. From A. J. Haagen-Smit, "Air Conservation" in Arthur Boughey, *Readings in Man, the Environment, and Human Ecology*, p. 320. Reprinted by permission of Scientia.

Pages 484–503. Excerpts from Kenneth Boulding, "The Effects of the War Industry"; Robert Mayo, "Budgetary Considerations"; J. William Fulbright, "Values in Crisis"; John Kenneth Galbraith, "The Role of Military Power"; and William Proxmire, "Pentagon Accountability" in William Proxmire, et al., *National Priorities* (Washington, D.C.: Public Affairs Press, 1969). Reprinted by permission.

ILLUSTRATION CREDITS

Facing Title Page. Page ii, Owen Franken/Stock, Boston.

Part I. Page xvi, Terry McKoy/The Picture Cube.

Chapter 1. Page 2, George E. Jones III/Photo Researchers; page 6, Struan Robertson/Magnum; page 11, © Sidney Harris from *Saturday Review World*, 1974; page 14, The Granger Collection; page 15, Courtesy, Transit Advertising and The Advertising Council; page 18, The Granger Collection; page 21, Wide World Photos.

Chapter 2. Page 28, Wide World Photos; page 34, Courtesy Louisiana Tourist Development Commission; page 41, Courtesy DKG, Inc. and Westinghouse Learning Corporation; page 52, UPI Photo.

Part II. Page 60, Leslie Starobin/The Picture Cube.

Chapter 3. Page 62, Ken Heyman; page 70, The Bettmann Archive; page 77, William E. Sauro/The New York Times; page 79, Jean Claude Lejeune; page 84, UPI Photo; page 90, Charles Gatewood.

Chapter 4. Page 96, Ken Heyman; page 106, Gerhard E. Gscheidle/Peter Arnold; page 108, Mimi Forsyth/Monkmeyer; page 113, Wide World Photos; page 119, Arthur Grace/Sygma; page 120, From *Easyriders Magazine*.

Chapter 5. Page 130, Ken Heyman; page 134, The Bettmann Archive; page 140, UPI Photo; page 147, Burk Uzzle/Magnum; page 153, Wide World Photos.

Chapter 6. Page 160, Ray Ellis/Photo Researchers; page 166, Wide World Photos; page 169, UPI Photo; page 173, UPI Photo; page 187, George W. Gardner; page 193, © John A. Ruge from *Saturday Review*, 1976.

Chapter 7. Page 202, Jim Jowers/Nancy Palmer Photo Agency; page 208, Marta Kesa/Liason Photo Agency; page 213, © Leo Garel from *Saturday Review*, 1975; page 222, Myron Wood/Photo Researchers; page 227, Abram G. Schoenfeld/Photo Researchers; page 229, Wide World Photos.

Part III. Page 234, Andrew Brilliant/The Picture Cube.

Chapter 8. Page 236, Martin J. Dain/Magnum; page 245, The Mansell Collection; page 255, Danny Lyon/Magnum; page 260, Fred J. Maroon/Louis Mercier; page 264, Paul Sequeira/Photo Researchers.

Chapter 9. Page 274, Ellis Herwig/Stock, Boston; page 281, The Bettmann Archive; page 285, Joel Gordon; page 291, Joel Gordon; page 297, From *Free Press*, Vol. 2, No. 24; page 304, Frank Siteman.

Chapter 10. Page 310, Tracy Ecclesine; page 315, The Bettmann Archive; page 317, The Mansell Collection; page 332, Getsug Anderson/Photo Researchers; page 334, Michael Hanulak/Photo Researchers.

Part IV. Page 344, UPI Photo.

Chapter 11. Page 321, John Muller/Time, Inc.; page 351, Michael Holford; page 362, Ken Heyman; page 370, Frank Siteman/The Picture Cube; page 373, Robert Azzi/Woodfin Camp.

Chapter 12. Page 381, Sepp Zeitz/Woodfin Camp; page 385, The Bettmann Archive; page 396, Wide World Photos; page 401, UPI Photo; page 409, UPI Photo.

Chapter 13. Page 414, Frank Siteman/Stock, Boston; page 431, *The Plain Dealer*, Cleveland; page 437, B. Kliewe/Jeroboam; page 442, UPI Photo.

Chapter 14. Page 450, James Foote/Photo Researchers; page 454, J. Abcede/WHO Photo; page 458, Giraudon; page 462, Paolo Koch/Photo Researchers; page 466, Copyright 1979 by Herblock in *The Washington Post*; page 470, Drawing by Richter; © 1973 *The New Yorker Magazine*, Inc; page 475, Hugh Rogers/Monkmeyer.

Chapter 15. Page 482, UPI Photo; page 485, © John A. Ruge from *Saturday Review*, 1975; page 491, UPI Photo; page 501, UPI Photo; page 508, UPI Photo; page 512, UPI Photo.

INDEX OF NAMES

Abudu, Margaret J. G., 59n
Ackerknecht, Erwin, 468, 480n
Adams, John, 261
Aldous, Joan, 233n
Alexander VI (pope), 280
Alexander the Great, 488
Allande, Alexander, 513
Allen, Francis R., 233n
Allen, Frederick Lewis, 25
Amir, Menachem, 299, 309n
Amundsen, Tristen, 75, 93n
Andenaes, Johannes, 49, 50, 59n
Anglo, Sydney, 57
Anthony, Susan B., 13
Antonio, Robert, 94n
Antonovsky, Aaron, 200n
Ardrey, Robert, 4, 5, 26n, 485, 514n
Arendt, Hannah, 14
Aschenbrenner, Joyce, 92, 94n
Ashbrook, Debra L., 342
Athenaeus of Attila, 457
Audubon, John, 422, 448n
Augustine, Saint, 17, 279

Banfield, Edward, 412n
Barlow, Hugh D., 272n, 273n
Basch, Paul F., 480n
Beach, Frank, 282, 283, 308n
Beam, Robert, 128n
Beattie, John, 177, 200n
Beatty, John, 26n
Beatty, Rita, 449n

Becker, Howard S., 233, 264, 266, 273n, 327, 343n, 412
Beers, Clifford, 314
Bell, Alan, 201, 292, 308, 309n
Bell, Daniel, 58
Bell, Robert R., 309n, 343n
Bellush, Jewell, 412n
Benedict IX (pope), 280
Berelson, Bernard, 378n
Berg, Alan, 374, 378n
Berg, Ivar, 108, 128n
Berger, Peter, 277, 308n
Bergler, Edmund, 309n
Bernard, J. F., 201n
Biesanz, John, 58n, 59n
Biesanz, Mavis H., 58n, 59n
Bird, Caroline, 94n
Birren, James G., 233n
Blau, Peter M., 59n
Bloch, H. A., 272n
Bock, Philip K., 59n, 232n
Booth, Alan, 399, 413n
Borgia, Rodrigo. *See* Alexander VI (pope)
Boughey, Arthur, 448n, 449n
Boulding, Kenneth, 435, 500, 515n
Braverman, Harry, 107, 108, 128n
Brecher, Edward, 341, 342n
Brodie, Bernard, 514n
Brown, Connie, 308n
Bruhl, Daniel, 448n
Bryant, Anita, 290, 301
Bumpass, Larry, 374, 378n
Butler, Robert, 141

Califano, Joseph, Jr., 230, 233n
Calvin, John, 280
Cannon, Mildred S., 343n
Carlson, Rick J., 477, 479, 480n
Carnoy, Martin, 412n
Carson, Rachel, 13, 432, 449n
Carter, Jimmy, 301, 402, 404, 476, 503
Carter, Robert M., 272n
Casalino, Larry, 147, 159n
Catlin, George E. G., 26n, 58n
Charles, Robert, 502
Chase, Stuart, 449n
Chavez, Cesar, 191
Childe, V. Gordon, 200n, 378n, 411, 412n
Chinoy, Eli, 111, 129n
Chomsky, Noam, 506, 515n
Chown, Sheila M., 233n
Christensen, Harold, 287, 288, 309n
Churchill, Winston, 290
Cisler, Lucinda, 78, 94n
Clark, Burton, 171, 200n
Clark, John, 515n
Clarke, Arthur C., 446
Clausen, John A., 342n
Clausewitz, Karl von, 487, 509
Cloward, Richard, 158
Cockburn, Alexander, 515n
Cohen, Albert K., 49, 59n, 273n
Cole, LaMont, 436, 448n
Coleman, James A., 212, 233n, 395, 397, 412n
Commager, Henry Steele, 512, 515n
Commoner, Barry, 419, 430, 447, 448n
Copernicus, Nicolaus, 424
Corman, James, 476
Coser, Lewis, 32, 58n, 59n, 128n
Cressey, Donald R., 273n
Critchley, T. A., 272n
Crutchfield, Richard S., 200n, 233n
Cuzzort, R. P., 9, 26n

Dahlstrom, Edmund, 94n
Daley, Richard, 382
da Vinci, Leonardo, 459

Davis, Angela, 195
Davis, Karen, 479
Davis, Kingsley, 378n
DeBell, Garrett, 424, 448n
Demosthenes, 278
DeMuth, Jerry, 129n
Dickson, Paul, 507, 508, 515n
Dickson, William, 128n
Diebold, John, 11, 25, 26n
Dix, Dorothea Lynde, 314
Dorn, Harold F., 355, 361, 376, 378n
Doyle, James C., 480n
Dreyfus, C., 94n
Dubois, Rene, 436, 449n
Dubos, René, 14, 453, 479n
Dunham, H. Warren, 343
Durkheim, Emile, 5–6, 26n, 35, 54, 58n, 305
Dynes, Russell, 158n

Ehrlich, Anne, 448n, 449n
Ehrlich, Paul, 13, 421, 427, 429, 432, 448n, 449n
Eisenhower, Dwight D., 371, 378n
Ellul, Jacques, 14
Erbe, Brigitee Mach, 189, 200n
Eschleman, J. Ross, 309n
Esposito, John, 448n
Etzioni, Amitai, 58

Fadiman, Clifton, 448n
Fairbank, John K., 505–506, 515n
Faris, Robert E. L., 59n, 343n
Farrell, Warren, 93, 94n
Featherman, David L., 200n
Federbush, Marcia, 93n
Felsing, Helen, 200n
Fielding, Henry, 246
Fielding, John, 246
Filer, Richard N., 233n
Flaming, Karl, 158n
Ford, Clellan, 282, 283, 308n
Ford, Gerald, 146, 152, 402
Fortune, R. F., 272
Fox, Vernon, 200n

Frakes, George, 448n, 449n
Francoeur, Robert, 277–278, 308n
Frank, Jerome, 480n
Franklin, Benjamin, 384
Frederick II, Holy Roman emperor, 458
Freedman, Leonard, 515n
Freeman, Ronald, 368, 378n
Freud, Sigmund, 86, 314
Fried, Morton, 514n
Friedan, Betty, 72, 88
Friedman, Kenneth M., 479
Friedman, Milton, 152
Friedson, Eliot, 480n
Fuchs, Estelle, 144, 159n
Fulbright, J. William, 500, 515n
Fuller, Richard C., 58n
Fuqua, Paul, 342, 343n

Galbraith, John Kenneth, 495, 502, 514n, 515n
Galen, 457
Galileo, 459
Galle, Omar, 412n
Gans, Herbert J., 58n, 149, 150, 151, 157, 159n
Garrison, Fielding H., 479, 480n
Gaudet, Frederick J., 272n
Geis, G., 272n
Gilman, Alfred, 343n
Gittell, Marilyn, 412n
Glass, Shirley, 289, 309n
Glick, Paul, 79, 80
Glueck, Eleanor, 262
Glueck, Sheldon, 262
Goffman, Erving, 338, 342
Golde, Peggy, 233n
Goldman, Marshall, 439, 449n
Goode, William J., 21, 27n, 232n
Goodman, Louis S., 343n
Goodman, W., 309n
Goodwin, Leonard, 143, 144, 158, 159n
Gordon, David, 128, 129n, 158, 159n
Gordon, George, 246
Gordon, Kermit, 159n
Goring, Charles, 261

Gouldner, Alvin, 58n
Gracchi brothers, 13
Graubard, Stephen R., 233n
Grebler, Leo, 200n
Green, Christopher, 148, 159n
Gregg, Christina, 287, 288, 309n
Griffen, Susan, 299, 309n
Gross, Edward, 433, 449n
Gustavus, Susan, 368, 377, 378n
Guthrie, Edwin R., 273n
Guzman, Ralph C., 200n

Haar, Charles, 412
Haeckel, Ernst, 417
Hahn, Emily, 70, 93n, 94n
Harburg, Ernest, 326, 343n
Hardin, Garrett, 423, 448n
Hardman, D. G., 273n
Hardy, Oliver, 171
Harrington, Michael, 13, 132, 136, 145, 158n
Harris, Marvin, 7, 19, 25, 26n, 27n, 58n, 241, 272n
Harrison, Bennett, 397, 412n
Harrison, James, 26n
Hart, Liddell, 492
Hastings, William M., 273n
Hauser, Philip M., 44, 58n, 378n
Havemann, Ernest, 26n
Heer, David M., 369, 378n
Heilbroner, Robert, 515n
Hershon, J., 343n
Hickman, Martin, 514n, 515n
Higham, John, 158n
Hite, Shere, 309n
Hitler, Adolf, 505
Hoebel, Adamson E., 47, 59n
Hogan, Dennis P., 200n
Hogan, John D., 233n
Hogbin, Ian, 272n
Holdren, John, 421, 448n
Hollingshead, August B., 343n
Holloway, Ralph, Jr., 485–486, 514n
Holmberg, Allan, 232n
Hooton, Ernest A., 262, 273n

Hopkins, Anne, 70
Horton, Paul, 158n
Hoselitz, Bert F., 377
House, James, 129n
Howe, Irving, 412n
Hunt, Morton, 290, 309n
Hyde, Janet Shirley, 232, 233n
Hymes, Dell, 26n

Ianni, Francis A. J., 233n
Illich, Ivan, 479, 480n
Inciardi, James A., 58n
Irons, Peter, 504, 515n

Jacobs, Jane, 411, 413n
Jacobs, Theodore, 449n
Jaffe, Jerome H., 343n
Janeway, Elizabeth, 200n
Janowitz, Morris, 493, 494, 514n
Jarvik, Lissy F., 233n
Jenner, Edward, 353
Jerome, Saint, 279
Jezer, Martin, 449n
Joachim, 102
Job, 4
John XXII (pope), 458
John XXIII (antipope), 280
Johnson, David, 399, 413n
Johnson, Lyndon B., 146, 295, 506–507
Johnson, Virginia, 222, 308
Jones, D. E., 480n
Jones, Thomas, 448n
Juhasz, Anne, 308n
Julius II (pope), 280

Kagan, Jerome, 26n
Kaldor, Mary, 515
Kalm, Pehr, 448n
Kamiat, A. H., 94n
Kaplan, Oscar J., 233
Kasl, Stanislav V., 326, 343n
Katz, Fred E., 58n
Katz, Solomon H., 232

Keller, Mark, 329, 343n
Kelman, Herbert C., 58n, 201n
Kemble, Frances Anne, 199
Kennedy, Edward M., 465, 476
Kennedy, Florynce, 76
Keyserling, Leon, 137
Kim, Yoon H., 309
King, Karl, 309n
King, Martin Luther, Jr., 180, 195
Kinsey, Alfred, 279, 286, 289, 290, 292, 293, 309n
Kirk, Dudley, 378n
Kirkendall, Lester, 307
Kissinger, Henry, 489, 514n
Klapmuts, Nora, 272n
Kogan, Nathan, 233n
Kolko, Gabriel, 514
Komarovsky, Mirra, 73, 93n
Kornhauser, Arthur, 111, 129n
Krech, David, 200n, 233n
Kroger, William, 309n

Langer, Thomas, 343n
Lanternaria, Vittorio, 200n
Larrick, Donald, 59n
Lawrenson, Helen, 86, 94n
Leach, Edmund R., 26n
Leacock, Eleanor, 143, 144, 159n
Leaf, Alexander, 210, 233n
Leckie, Robert, 488, 514n
Lenski, Gerhard E., 26n, 58n, 59n, 232n, 453, 479n
Lenski, Jan, 454, 479n
Leonard, Roger, 489, 514n
Leslie, Charles, 479, 480n
Leslie, Gerald, 158n
Lesser, Alexander, 486, 514n
Lessing, Laurence, 446, 449n
Levasseur, Emile, 378n
Levin, Leonard, 515n
Lewis, David T., 378
Lincoln, Abraham, 178
Linnaeus, Carolus, 168
Linton, Ralph, 232n

Little, Roger, 514n
Livson, Norman, 200n, 233n
Loleschal, Eugene, 272n
Lombroso, Cesare, 261
Lorenz, Konrad, 5, 485, 514n
Lorimer, Frank, 373, 378n
Lublow, Arthur, 412n
Luther, Martin, 280

McCaghy, Charles H., 343n
McCaull, Julian, 436, 449n
McCord, Carey, 113, 129n
McCormick, Cyrus, 353
McDougall, William, 4–5, 26n
McGee, Reece, 44, 59n
McGinnis, Nancy, 323, 343n
McHale, John, 432, 449n
McKean, Roland, 502, 515n
McKinley, Daniel, 448, 448n
McNamara, Robert, 495
Magdoff, Harry, 505, 515n
Magid, Alvin, 159n
Malcolm X, 168–169, 200n
Malthus, Thomas, 133, 158n, 357, 358
Mann, Mary, 328, 329, 343n
Marcuse, Herbert, 14, 305, 309n
Marsh, George P., 420–421
Marx, Karl, 5, 103–104, 106, 128n
Masters, R. E. L., 280, 308n
Masters, William, 222, 308
Matlovich, Leonard, 290, 301
Maugham, W. Somerset, 258, 273n
Maykovich, Minako, 309n
Mayo, Robert, 496, 497, 515n
Mead, Margaret, 68, 69, 73, 93n, 210, 233n, 504, 515n
Meadows, Donella, 426, 435, 448n
Meadows, Paul, 383, 412n
Melman, Seymour, 510, 514, 515n
Melville-Lee, W. L., 272n
Menander, 452
Merton, Robert K., 55, 58n, 59n, 233n, 264, 265, 273n, 342n, 378n

Meyer, Marshall M., 59n
Michael, Stanley, 343n
Miller, G. Tyler, 425, 447, 448n
Miller, Herman P., 137, 159n
Miller, Walter B., 50, 59n
Mills, C. Wright, 110, 128n, 495, 515n
Mills, Wilbur, 476
Miner, Horace, 480n
Money, John, 294, 309n
Montagu, Ashley, 26n
Moore, Barrington, 21, 27n
Moore, Joan W., 200n
Moore, Wilbert E., 377
Morgan, Robin, 93, 94n, 309n
Morgenthau, Hans, 515n
Morris, Charles W., 58n
Mott, Lucretia, 70
Mott, Paul E., 59n, 200n
Mowry, George E., 26n, 59n
Moynihan, Daniel P., 136, 158n, 386, 412n
Mueller, John H., 26n, 58n
Muir, John, 421–422, 424, 448n
Myers, Richard R., 58n

Nader, Ralph, 111–112, 442
Nam, Charles, 368, 377, 378n
Neff, Walter, 99, 100, 128n
Nettler, Gwynn, 273n
Neubeck, Gerhard, 309n
Neugarten, Bernice L., 213, 233n
Nichols, Albert, 129n
Nisbet, Robert A., 200n, 233n, 342n, 378n
Nixon, Richard M., 118, 146, 147, 249, 296, 402, 507
Norton, Arthur, 79, 80

O'Connell, Desmond D., 233n
Ophuls, William, 447
Opler, Marvin, 343n
Oppenheim, Leo, 272n
Oppenheimer, Martin, 514, 515n
Orshansky, Mollie, 137, 159n
O'Toole, James, 129n

Packard, Vance, 286, 309n
Palen, John, 158n
Parks, Rosa, 180
Pasteur, Louis, 460
Paul, Saint, 279
Paul II (pope), 280
Pavalko, Ronald, 454–455, 466, 468, 480n
Perrucci, Robert, 5, 26n
Peterson, Richard A., 58n
Peterson, William, 378
Phillips, Wendell, 13
Pilisuk, Marc, 5, 26n
Pinel, Phillippe, 313, 314
Pittman, David J., 343n
Piven, Francis, 158
Plate, Thomas, 493, 514, 514n
Plato, 5
Proxmire, William, 515n

Quinney, Richard, 254–255, 271, 272n

Radzinowicz, Leon, 272n
Rakoff, Stuart H., 479
Raymond, Jack, 494, 507, 514n, 515n
Reagan, Ronald, 147
Redlich, Frederick, 343n
Reems, Harry, 302
Reiss, Ira, 286, 309n
Rennie, Thomas, 343n
Reppetto, Thomas A., 271, 272n
Revel, Jean-François, 198, 199, 201n
Ridenhour, Ron, 412n
Rienow, Leona, 448n
Rienow, Robert, 426, 448n
Riley, Matilda White, 232
Rist, Ray, 307, 309n
Ritzer, George, 94n, 99, 127, 128n
Robinson, James A., 58n
Rodberg, Leonard, 504, 515n
Rodbill, Samuel, 94n
Roosevelt, Franklin D., 137
Rose, Arnold M., 26n, 34, 58n
Rose, Peter I., 27n, 190, 199, 200n

Rosenberg, Bernard, 59n, 128n
Roszak, Theodore, 224, 233n, 447
Rothchild, David, 233n
Rothlisberger, Fritz, 128n
Royko, Mike, 411
Rude, George, 272n
Russel, Hamilton, 331
Russell, 27n
Russett, Bruce, 499–500, 515n

Sanger, Margaret, 371
Sapir, Edward, 26n
Sappho, 278
Scanzoni, John, 80, 92, 94n
Scarpitti, Frank, 53, 59n
Scheff, Thomas J., 322, 327, 342, 343n, 470, 480n
Schlesinger, Arthur, 134, 158n
Schuler, Edgar A., 58n, 201n
Schur, Edwin M., 272n
Schwab, John J., 319, 323, 324, 343n
Scott, W. Richard, 58
Seitz, Jane, 308n
Senn, Peter R., 39, 58n
Service, Elman R., 26n, 232n, 272n
Seth, Ronald, 17, 27n
Sextus IV (pope), 280
Sharer, Lloyd, 159n
Sheldon, William H., 262, 273n
Shelly, Martha, 292, 309n
Shepard, Paul, 417, 448, 448n
Shoen, Cathy, 479
Shostak, Arthur B., 136, 159n
Siegal, Harvey M., 58n
Silberman, Charles, 108
Simonsen, Clifford E., 272n
Simpson, George Eaton, 200n
Simpson, Ida Harper, 468, 480n
Singer, Charles, 479, 480n
Singh, B. Krishna, 309n
Skolnick, Arlene, 309n
Skolnick, Jerome H., 309n
Slater, Philip, 419, 448n
Smith, Donald, 515n

Smith, Justa, 469, 480n
Smith, M. B., 378n
Smith, T. Lynn, 378
Snyder, Charles R., 343n
Snyder, Richard C., 58n
Solberg, Curtis, 448n, 449n
Solley, Linda C., 342
Solovay, Sarah A., 58n
Solovay, Sarah W., 26n
Sorokin, Pitrim, 283, 308n
Spengler, Oswald, 238, 272n
Srole, Leo, 343n
Stambler, Sookie, 94n
Stanton, Elizabeth Cady, 70
Starnes, Charles, 158, 159n
Stead, Philip J., 272
Steinem, Gloria, 302
Steinmetz, Susanne, 93, 94n
Stephen, David, 412n
Stephens, William, 65, 93n
Stewart, Omer C., 26n
Stone, Lucy, 13
Stopes, Marie C., 13
Straus, Murray, 93, 94n
Strauss, Robert, 142, 159n
Stubbings, Richard, 503
Sutherland, Edwin H., 264, 266, 273n
Szasz, Thomas, 52–53, 59n, 322–323, 342, 343n, 470, 480n

Taeuber, Irene B., 378
Tansky, 418
Tappan, Paul, 258, 263, 273n
Taube, Carl A., 343n
Taylor, Carol, 479n
Terkel, Studs, 111, 127, 129n
Terry, Geraldine B., 378n
Thayer, Frederick, 127, 128n
Thomas, W. I., 182, 200n, 219, 233n
Thomas, William, 448n
Thomlinson, Ralph, 378n
Thompson, Warren S., 378
Thoreau, David, 423, 448n

Tietze, Christopher, 370, 378n
Tijerina, Reies Lopez, 191
Tobin, James, 152, 159n
Tocqueville, Alexis de, 12, 26n, 67
Torbert, William, 105, 128, 128n
Trecker, Janice Law, 69, 93n
Truman, Harry, 180
Tuchman, Barbara W., 200n
Turner, Eba, 369, 378n
Turner, Jonathan, 158, 159n
Turner, Ralph, 55, 59n

Underwood, E. Ashworth, 479, 480n
Unkovic, Charles M., 27n, 200n, 233n

Van den Haag, Ernest, 305
Vesalius, Andreas, 459
Vetter, Harold J., 272n

Wagatsuma, Hiroshi, 167, 200n
Wallace, Bruce, 448n
Ward, Barbara, 369, 377, 378n
Warheit, George, 323, 343n
Washington, Booker T., 173
Weaver, Thomas, 159n
Weber, Max, 101, 104, 106, 128n
Weinberg, Martin, 291, 292, 308, 309n
Weiss, John P., 27n, 200n, 233n
Westmoreland, William, 508
Westoff, Charles, 374, 378n
White, Jean, 448n
White, Lynn, Jr., 423
Whitehurst, Robert N., 307
Wilensky, Harold, 455, 480n
Wilkins, Leslie T., 272n
Williams, Robin M., Jr., 27n, 37, 58n, 200n
Wilson, James, 412n
Wilson, William A., Jr., 233n
Winthrop, John, 70
Wirth, Louis, 163
Wolfgang, Marvin E., 232n

Wright, Burton, 27n, 200n, 233n
Wright, Thomas, 289, 309n

Yinger, J. Milton, 200n
Young, Wayland, 279, 308n

Zaretsky, Eli, 309n
Zeckhauser, Richard, 129n
Zinserling, Verena, 278, 308n
Zopf, Ralph G., Jr., 378

INDEX OF SUBJECTS

Abolition movement, 70
Abortion, 162
   incidence, 64, 76–77
   legislating, 76, 78, 240, 370
Absolute definition, poverty, 136–138, 146
Achieved status, 51, 322
Acupuncture, 469, 475
Adultery, 289
Affairs, 289
Affirmative action, 120, 124, 195–196, 197
Age peers, 207
Age status, 204
Aggression, human, 485–486
Aging, Lake Erie, 419
Agricultural society, 100
Agriculture, 350, 383, 421
   government aid to, 147–148
Al-Anon, 337
Ala-Teen, 337
Alcohol, 84, 316.
   abuse, 328–331, 337
   consumption, 327–328
   opposition to, 316 (*See also* Prohibition)
   treating abuse, 337
Alcoholic, defined, 329
Alcoholics Anonymous, 329, 337
Alianza Federal de Mercedes, 191
Alianza Hispano Americana, La, 191
Alice in Wonderland (Carroll), 294
Alienation, 103–104, 105
Allopathic medicine, 474–475
All-volunteer army, 493, 507, 508
Alternative norms, 47

American Academy of Pediatrics, 85
American Association of Retired Persons, 230
American Hospital Association, 337
American Humane Society, 85
American Indian Movement, 174
American Indians
   discrimination and, 192–194
   pluralism and, 173–174
American Law Institute, 302
American Medical Association, 460, 466, 476
American Psychiatric Association, 314, 320
Anal sex, 296, 302
Andaman Island people, 486
   sexual permissiveness, 10
Anomie, 265, 305
Anomie theory, 265–266
Anonymity, opportunity for and crime, 244
Antibiotics, use of, 460
Anticommunism, 505–506
Anxiety, neuroses and, 320
Apartheid, 390
Arapesh people, sex roles, 68–69
Arithmetical increase, 357
Arms race, 492, 504
Arrest rate, 250
Arteriosclerosis, 221
Arunta people, 486
   respect for aged, 209
Asbestos fiber, pollutant, 434
Ascribed characteristics, prejudice and, 167
Ascribed status, 51, 322
Ashanti people, punishment of deviance, 242
Assimilation, 173, 394

INDEX OF SUBJECTS

Association Against the Prohibition Amendment, 317
Atherosclerosis, 221
Atlantic Richfield, 445
Atmospheric inversion, Los Angeles, 428
Audubon Society, 437, 440
Authority
   within family, 67
   parental weakened, 223–224
   power and, 176–177
Autobiography of Malcolm X, The, (Malcolm X), 168–169
Automation, 107, 123, 126
Automobile
   importance of, 145, 211, 390
   and pollution, 422, 427, 441, 442–443
Autonomy, and crime, 244
Aztec people, human sacrifice, 36

Backlash, against minorities, 196
Bail, 253
Bakke case, 197
Beliefs, 20–22
Betwixt and between laws, 240
Biofeedback, 475–476
Birthrates, 81–82
Black English, 165
Black middle class, 173
Black Muslims, separatism of, 172, 195
Blacks
   defined, 185
   and discrimination, 185–190
   as a minority, 178–181
   negative connotation of label, 165
   population migration, 388
   poverty and, 142
Blue-collar work, 108, 110, 111
Blue laws, 281
Booked, criminal suspect, 253
Bourgeoisie, 103
Bow Street Runners, 246–247
British National Health Service, 461–462
Bureaucracy, in work structures, 104–105

Bureau of Indian Affairs, U.S., 193
Busing, 395, 406

Capitalism, 101, 103, 125, 505
Carnal Knowledge (film), 296
Caste system, 178–179
Catalytic converter, development of, 443
Catatonia, 320
Censorship, 295
Chicanos, 191
Children
   abuse of, 84–85
   divorce and, 80
   poverty and, 140–141
   and sex roles, 73
Chukchee people, homosexuality among, 282
Cities
   ancient, 383–384
   and education, 394–397
   financing, 391–394
   government and, 399–400, 401–402, 406
   history of, 383–386, 422
   housing, 399–400
   population growth, 384–386
   race issue, 390–391
   unemployment, 397–399, 404
Civil disorder, 133, 195, 246, 382, 408
Civil rights movement, 179–181
Clamshell Alliance, 437
Code of Hammurabi, 243, 244
Cohabitation, 78–79, 289
Cohort approach to fertility, 354–355
Cohorts, 354, 365
Coitus, 286
Cold war, 492
Collective definition, social problems, 6
Comunidad Latin, La, 192
Communist Manifesto, The (Marx), 104
Community standards, obscenity test, 294, 296, 302
Competitive bidding, defense contracts, 502
Compound interest analogy, population growth, 348

Comprehensive Training and Employment Act (CETA), 402, 404
Conformists, 265
Conjugal family, 67
Conquest, source of minority status, 164
Consanguinal family, 67
Consensus, 13
Constitution, U.S.
   Equal Rights Amendment, proposed, 72, 87–88
   13th Amendment, 71, 178
   14th Amendment, 71
   15th Amendment, 71
   18th Amendment, 13, 49, 259, 316
   21st Amendment, 318
Contagion, discovery of, 454, 458
Contraception, 75–76
Cooling-out, discrimination and, 171–172
Cosmopolitan, 295
Cost overruns, defense contracts, 502
Cost reimbursement, defense contracts, 502
Council of Pharmacists and Chemists, 460
Council of Rheims, 457
Crime. *See also* Organized crime
   anomie theory and, 265–266
   atavism and, 261–262
   costs, 217
   differential association theory, 266
   in England, 244–247
   extra Y chromosome, 262
   labeling theory and, 266–268
   learning theory and, 263
   political aspects, 258–261
   population growth and, 242–244
   poverty and, 19
   preliterate societies, 241–242
   somatotypes, 262
Criminal justice system, 239, 251–258, 263–264
   selectivity, 241, 251, 254–255
Criminals, 240
   label, 258
   lawbreakers distinguished, 240
Crude birthrate, 81, 354
Cultural trait, 20

Cultural universal, organization as, 55
Culture, 10, 36, 350–352
   and values, 20
Culture of poverty, 142–144
Cumulative cohort birthrate, 354
Cunnilingus, 48

Dawes Act, 193
DDT, 432–433, 444, 445
Decentralization, school districts, 395–396
Decibels, noise pollution, 434
Decriminalization, proposed re drugs, 340
Deep Throat (film), 297, 302
De facto discrimination, 171, 189, 196, 390
Defective strategies, 323
Defense spending, 496–501
   nonmilitary functions, 509–510
   procurement process, 502–503
Definitional errors, 18–19
De jure discrimination, 170
De jure segregation, 390
Demographers, 354
Demographic transition, 365
Denmark, censorship abolished, 295
Department of Defense, 496–497, 498, 502–503
Department of Health, Education, and Welfare, 331, 336, 433
Depersonalization, of war, 507
Deterrence
   military, 494
   punishment of criminals, 241, 247
Developed countries, population growth and, 349, 361–364
Developing countries, 361, 500–501, 510–511
Deviance, as social disorganization, 54, 216
Devil in Miss Jones, The (film), 297
Differential association theory, 266
Discrimination, 169, 170–172, 181
   blacks, 185–190
   Chicanos, 191
   Jews, 191
   Orientals, 192
   Puerto Ricans, 191–192

Discrimination (*cont.*)
    sanction incongruence and, 50–51
    women, 182–185
Divorce rate, 64, 71, 79–81
Dobu Islanders, and incest, 242
Double standard, 285–286
Drug abuse, 22, 23
    defined, 324
    legal drugs, 470–472
    social costs, 333–335
    treating, 338
Drugs. *See also* Sedatives
    defined, 324
    history of use, 315–318
    illegal, 333–335
    validation, 472
Dysfunctional consequences, 33
Dyspacts, 219

ecology, 417–420. *See also* Pollution
    concepts, 418–420
    defined, 417
    environmental groups, 437–438
    historical review, 420–424
    politics and, 438–440
Economic liabilities, young and elderly as, 212–214, 369
Ecosystems, 418
    in stress, 419, 430–431, 445
Ectomorph, 262
Education
    costs of, 212–213, 217
    discrimination in, 184–185, 187–189
    iatrogenic effects, 223–226
    and sex roles, 73–74
    work and, 107–109, 123
Education Act of 1968, Title IX, 88
Egalitarianism, in family, 67
Elderly
    abandomment of, 220
    as economic liability, 213–214
    myths re, 219–222
    old age defined, 205

    poverty and, 141–142
    status, 204, 209
Electronic battlefields, 507
Elizabethan Witchcraft Act, 17
Embourgeoisment of the proletariat, 104
Emergency Tenants Council, 192
Emergent norms, 55
Endogamous marriage, 179
Endomorph, 262
Entrapment, 339
Environmental impact statement, new construction and, 438, 445
Environmental Protection Agency, U.S., 438
Epidemiology, 453–454
Equality, valued, 42
Equal Rights Amendment, proposed, 72, 87–88
Erotic, 303
Escape mechanisms, 312
Eskimos, 486
Esquire, 303
Estate system, 176–177
Ethnicity, source of minority status, 164–165
Ethnocentrism, as prejudice, 167
Eufunctional consequences, 33
Eugenics, 268
Eutrophication, water pollution, 430
Exorcism, 314
Exploitation, economic, 103, 119, 124
Extended family, 66, 209, 210
Extramarital sex, 289–290
Extra Y chromosome, 262

Family, 20–21, 64
    cross-cultural evidence, 68–69
    defined, 65–66
    forms, 66–67
    history, 69–72
    violence within, 83–85
Farm Subsidy Program, 147
Fatalism, 11
FBI (Federal Bureau of Investigation), 247
Fellatio, 48
Feminine Mystique, The (Friedan), 72

Feminist movement, 70–72, 73, 302
Fertility, 82–83, 354
   factors tending to reduce, 368–370
   factors tending to increase, 370–375
Fertility rate, 7, 140
Fetishes, 296
Feudal system, 101
Food and Drug Administration, U.S., 477
Forcible rape, 298–299
Ford Motor Company, 441
Fornication, 48, 212
French Revolution, 489
Functional psychoses, 320

Gay bars, 291
Gay community, 291–292, 301
Gender identity, 68, 73
General norms
   functions of, 45–47
   types, 47–48
Generic drugs, 472
Geometric increase, 357
Geothermal power, nonpolluting, 446
Germ theory of disease, 12, 353, 454
GI Forum, 191
Ginhead regions, 316
Gordon Riots (Eng.), 246
Grand jury, 253
Great Depression, 146
   poverty and, 135
Greece, sex attitudes in ancient, 278
Greenhouse effect, atmosphere, 429
Greenpeace, 437
Guilds, 101
Guilt, 294, 304
Gunpowder, 488

Hard-core pornography, 296
Harvard Law Review, 254
Hayes-Tilden Compromise, 178
Health
   defined, 453
   historical survey, 456–461
   medical sociology, 453–456
   systems of care, 459, 461–462, 466–468
Health care
   costs, 463–466
   diet and exercise, 473–474
   poor and, 151
   systems, 459, 461–462, 466–468
Health care systems
   components, 466–468
   government and, 461
   indigenous, 462
   and insurance, 465, 466, 476
   Medicare/Medicaid, 462, 476
   physicians, 461–462, 468, 470
   private, 461
   profit-making, 461–462
Health maintenance organizations, 461, 476
Health support systems, 455–456
Hebephrenic schizophrenia, 320
Hebrews, sex attitudes of ancient, 277–278
Hedonistic calculus, 263
Held values, 39
Heroin, 315, 335
Hetairai, 278
Heterogeneity, 23
Hite Report, The (Hite), 297
Holistic approach, ecology, 417
Holistic medicine, 456, 475
Homeostasis, 31–32
Homo sapiens, 5, 350
Homosexuality, 282, 290–292, 300–301
Horticulture, 350
Housing
   discrimination in, 189–190
   single-family dwellings valued, 441
   urban, 399–400
Huckleberry Finn (Twain), 294
Humphrey-Hawkins bill, 122
Hunters and gatherers, 99
Hustler, 302, 303
Hypochondria, 322
Hysteria, 322

Iatrogenic effects, 16, 223, 469
Ideal culture, 48
Immigration
  to cities, 385, 394
  and poverty, 134–135
  source of minority status, 164, 165
Impairment, mental, 323–324
Impotence, 222
Incest, 242
Incidence
  crime, 249–251
  mental illness, 325–327
  poverty, 137, 138–139
Income distribution, 138, 149, 151
Indentured servants, 178
Individualism, 146
Industrial Revolution, 133
  impact on family, 209–211
  and population growth, 352–354
  and warfare, 489–490
  and work, 102
Inequality, 162–163
Inflation, poverty and, 146, 151
Influential people, catalysts to defining social problems, 13–16
Informal norms, 239–240, 241, 259
Information chain, 22–23
Initial appearance, criminal process, 253
Inoculation, control of disease by, 454
Innovators, 265–266
Instinct, human behavior and, 4–5
Integration, 173
Interchangeable parts, 102
Intrauterine device (IUD), 76, 284

Jacquerie, peasants' rebellion, 177
Jim Crow laws, 170, 179
Job Corps, 122, 404
Job satisfaction, 109–111
J.P. Stevens Company, 113, 119–120

Kaiser Permanent Health Plan, 461
Kaoka Speakers, and incest, 242

Kennedy-Corman bill, 476
Keraki people, and homosexuality, 282
Kiddie porn, 296, 302, 303
Knowledge explosion, 11
Koniag people, and homosexuality, 282

Labeling theory, 266–268, 470
Labor theory of value, 103
Laetrile, 472
Lake Erie, ecosystem under stress, 419, 430–431, 445
Language
  and culture, 350
  limits of, 10
  and social interaction, 35
Lateran Council, 457
Lawbreakers, 240–241
  criminals distinguished, 240
Laws
  informal norms and, 239–240
  norms and, 48–49
  politics re, 258–261
Learning ability, age and, 219
Learning theory, and crime, 263–264
Leisure, 105–106, 125
Lesbians, 278, 292
Levée en masse, 489
Liberia, separatism, 172
Life cycles, 204, 228–230
Limits to Growth, The (Meadows et al.), 435
Long-term debt, 392
L'uomo delinquente (Lombroso), 261
Lyons (France), peasants riot in, 133

Machismo, 52
Mala per se laws, 49, 50, 240
Mala quia prohibita laws, 48–49, 240
Man's Role in Changing the Face of the Earth (Thomas), 420
Manu people, sex roles, 69
Marijuana, 318, 335
Marriage
  defined, 65

endogamous, 179
proscribed, 170
rates, 78–79
Mass media
awareness of social problems, 14–15, 17
and women's movement, 72
Mass transit, deterioration, 398, 441
Median family income, 138–139
Medical sociology, 453–456
Mempa v. *Rhay*, 255
Mental illness
defined, 318–319
historical perspective, 313–315
incidence, 325–327
medical model, 319–322
myth of, 322–323
operational model, 323–324
sociocultural model, 322–323
treating, 336–337
Mesomorph, 262
Metals, pollution from heavy, 434
Methadone treatment, 338
Mexican-American Political Association (MAPA), 191
Mexican-American Youth Organization (MAYO), 191
Middle Ages
church and poor, 133
estate system, 176–177
medicine in, 457–459
Migration, 7
Militance, 195
Military-industrial complex, 494–496
Miller v. *California*, 296
Minimum subsistence income, 137
Minorities, 42, 43, 163–198
blacks, 178–181, 185–190
defined, 163–164
discrimination and, 170–172, 181–194
ending status, 172–174
historical view, 174–181
prejudice and, 165–169, 170
visibility, 164–165
women as, 177–178, 182–185

Miscegenation, proscriptions against, 170
Mission Indians, 486
Model Cities programs, 399–400, 406
Modern functionalism, approach to sociology, 32–33
Monolithic elite, military, 495
Montgomery Improvement Association, 180
Moral restraint, population, 357
More Equality (Gans), 149
Mores, 44–45, 241
defined, 44
Morphine, 315
Mortality rate, infants, 369, 465
Multinational corporations, 124, 504
Mundugumor people, sex roles, 69

Narcotics, 315
National Association for the Advancement of Colored People, 179
National Association of Manufacturers, 438
National Commission on Marijuana and Drug Abuse, 327, 342
National Committee for Mental Hygiene, 314
National Council on Crime and Delinquency, 251
National Farm Workers Association, 191
National Indian Youth Council (NIYC), 174
National Institute on Alcohol Abuse and Alcoholism, 342
National Institute of Mental Health, U.S., 314
National Mental Health Act, 314
National Opinion Research Center, 109
National Organization for Women (NOW), 88, 301
National Safety Council, 113
National Women's Suffrage Association (NAWSA), 71
Natural increase of population, 354
Natural population checks, 357–358
Neanderthal type, 261
Negative income tax, 148–149
Neofunctionalism. *See* Modern functionalism, approach to sociology
Neolithic Revolution, 350–352
Neurasthenia, 322

Neurosis, 319, 320–322
Niagara River, pollution, 430
Nicotine, 331
No-fault divorce, 81
Noise, 434
Nonviolent protest, 180
Norms, 44–49
  for breaking norms, 47–48
  defined, 44
  emergent, 55
  general, 45–47
  and laws, 48–49, 239–240
  mores, 44–45
  youth and, 45–47, 212
NOW, 88, 301
Nuclear family, 66, 210
Nuclear power, risks of, 443–444
Nuclear weapons, 484, 490, 492–493, 503

Obscenity, 294
Observable conditions, defining social problems with, 7–9
Occupational Safety and Health Administration (OSHA), U.S., 121, 123
Office of Economic Opportunity, U.S., 146
Old age. *See also* Elderly
  defined, 205
  myths re, 219–222
  and sexual activity, 207, 221–222
On Aggression (Lorenz), 485
Opening of Misty Beethoven, The (film), 297
Opiates, 315
Oppression, 103
Oral sex, 296, 297, 302
Organic analogy, social problem model, 31–32
Organic psychoses, 320
Organizational theory, 454
Organized crime, 303, 317, 335, 339
Orgasm, 279
OSHA (Occupational Safety and Health Administration), U.S., 121, 123
Other America, The (Harrington), 132, 145

Overqualification, minorities and education level, 187, 189
Overweight, 472, 473–474

Pacific Gas and Electric, 445
Paramilitary, police organization, 247
Paranoid schizophrenia, 320
Paraphilia, 296
Parole, 268–269
Pathology, and social problems, 32
Pawns, developing nations as, 510–511
Pentagon Papers, 52
Penthouse, 302, 303
People's Republic of China, population control, 375
Personality change, age and, 219–220
Phobia, 322
Physiological error, 19–20
Pill, birth-control, 16, 76, 284
Pimps, 293
Placebos, use of, 468
Playboy, 303
Playgirl, 295
Plea bargaining, 253–254
Pluralism, 173–174
Police, 239
  discretion, 241, 259
  origins, 246–249
  paramilitary organization, 247
  rape cases and, 300
  and sexual deviance, 303–304
Political Association of Spanish-Speaking Americans (PASSA), 191
Politicization, 301–302
Pollution, 6, 32
  of air, 426–429
  health costs, 426–427
  nuclear risks, 443–444
  pesticides, 432–433
  scope of, 425–426
  solid wastes disposal, 433–434
  of waters, 429–432

Population explosion, 7, 8–9, 358–364, 421
  cities, 384–386
  compound interest analogy, 348
  social consequences, 242–244
Pornography, 10, 294–296, 306
Positive checks, population, 358
Poverty, 6, 16, 132–156. *See also* Culture of poverty
  and crime, 19
  defined, 136–139
  and direct political action, 154
  in Europe, 132–134
  functions of poor, 149
  government role, 134–135, 145–148
  incidence, 137, 138–139
  and population growth, 361
  Scandinavia, 155–156
  in U.S., 134–135
Poverty line, 137
Power, and authority, 176–177
Predestination, 101, 280
Prejudice, toward minorities, 165–169
President's Commission on Income Maintenance, 152
President's Commission on Law Enforcement and Administration of Justice, 271
President's Council on Physical Fitness, 474
Pretend rules, 48
Pretrial intervention program, 253
Preventive checks, population, 357
Price fixing, 239
Primary deviance, 267
Prison, 255–258, 266
  functions, 255–257
Probation, 254
"Problem of Conceptualizing Poverty, The" (Strauss), 142
Professionalization, 454–455
Prohibition, 49, 316–318
Proletariat, 103
Promiscuity, 288
Property tax, 391
Prostitutes of New York, 302
Prostitution, 48, 293–294, 301–302
Protestant Reformation, 101, 280
Protestant work ethic, 102
Psychical impotence, 222
Psychic healing, 475
Psychoactive, 312
Psychology, 314
Psychology Today, 289
Psychosexual categories, 69
Psychosis, 319–320
Puberty, 205
Public Health Act, Eng., 459
Puritans, 280

Quacks, controlling, 460, 477

Race
  and fertility rate, 140–141
  and poverty, 155
Racism, 42, 168–169
Racists, 167
Rape, 298–299, 300
Rationalization, 19, 43
Real culture, 48
Rebels, 266
Recidivism, 241, 266
Recreation, 105, 125, 126
Refractory period, 221–222
Reinforcement, learning theory, 263
Relative definition, poverty, 138–139
Report from Iron Mountain (Levin), 509
Repressive desublimation, 305
Resources, scarcity of, 505
  and pollution, 434, 435
  population growth and, 356–358
Retirement, 213
  forced, 213, 223
  increased age, 206
  socialization for, 218
Retreatists, 266
Retributive justice, 243
Revenue sharing, 406
Reverse discrimination, 172, 196–197

Rich Man, Poor Man (Miller), 137
Ritualists, 265
Robinson Crusoe (Defoe), 294
Role overload, 114
Roles, 51
   elderly, 207
   family, 65–66
   machismo, 52
   sex (*see* Sex roles)
   work, 98
   young, 207
Rome, sexual attitudes in ancient, 278–279

Sadomasochism, 296, 297, 303
Sanction incongruence, 50–51
Sanctions, 49–51
Santa Barbara (Calif.), 1969 oil spill, 439
Schools
   control over, 395–397
   costs, 392, 404
   declining enrollments, 366
   segregation, 180, 395
Screw, 302, 303
Secondary deviance, 267
Sedatives, 332–333
Segregation, 172
   housing, 189–190
   schools, 180, 395
Selectivity, criminal justice system, 241, 251, 254–255
Self-report studies, crime, 250–251
Senescence, cities, 386
Senility, 220–221
Sensuality, 304–305
Separatism, 172
Serfs, 101
Sexism, in texts, 74
Sex roles, 68–69, 87, 178
   American, 69–72
   changing, 89–91
   education and, 73–74
   stereotyping, 114–115

Sexual deviance
   police and, 303–304
   regulating, 48
Sexuality, 304–305
   ancient cultures, 277–279
   Christianity and, 279–282
   learned, 276, 277, 283
   other cultures, 282–283
   prejudice and, 167
   suppressed, 279, 294
Sexually explicit materials, 296
Sexual revolution, 276, 285–288
Short-term debt, 392
Sierra Club, 422, 437, 440
Silent Spring (Carson), 432
Simple schizophrenia, 320
Siriono people, treatment of aged, 209
Skid-row areas, 316
Slavery, 100, 174–176, 178
Slaves, 100, 176, 178
Snuff films, 303
Social change, 456
Social control, origin of agents of, 242–243
Social disorganization, 53–56
   defining, 53–54
   relativity of, 54–55
Social facts, 35, 40
Social institution, 36–38
Socialization, 9, 11, 19, 294
   controlling agents of, 103
   elderly, 205, 218
   failure of, 214–216
   medical personnel, 466–468
   sex roles, 91
   young, 207, 211, 214–218, 226–227
Social learning, and sex roles, 73
Social mobility, 125
Social problems
   causes, 30–31
   defining, 4, 5–17
   models, 31–33
   values and, 40–44
Social promotion, 224

Social security, 225–226, 461
Social stratification, 243
Society, 35
Society for the Prevention of Cruelty to Children, 84
Sociology, defining, 34
Sodomy, 282, 297
Soft-core pornography, 296
Solar energy, appeal of, 441, 445
Somatotypes, personality and, 262
Soviet Union, competition with, 492, 503, 505, 511
Standard Metropolitan Statistical Area (SMSA), 387
Statutory rape, 298
Status, 51–53, 66
  ascribed/achieved, 51
  defined, 51
Status lock, 53
Stereotype
  senility, 221
  sex roles, 114–115
Stigma, labeling, 267, 298, 333
Stimuli, 9
Story of O, The (film), 297
Strategic Arms Limitation Talks (SALT), 504
Stratification. *See* Social stratification
Subculture of youth, 211–212
Subjective evaluation, social problems, 9–11, 313
Suburbs, 387, 390
  white flight, 395
Suffrage, 71
Suicide, elderly, 141, 142
Supreme Court, U.S.
  and abortion, 240
  and pornography, 296
  and right to counsel, 255
  and school segregation, 180
Surplus value, 103
Survey Research Center, University of Michigan, 109
Synanon, 338, 339

Tax policy, 149–150, 155–156
  and trickle-down theory, 145
Tchambuli people, sex roles, 69
Technicways, 47
Technological fix, 435, 443
Technology
  and ecological harm, 425
  faith in, 423, 424, 436, 444
  Industrial Revolution, 353
  politics and, 438–440
  and population growth, 353, 358, 361
  as a social problem, 14
  and warfare, 487–488, 489, 490, 492–493
  and work, 99–102, 126
Telephone, importance of, 211
Territorial Imperative, The (Ardrey), 485
Thalidomide, 472
Thermal pollution, 434, 443
Thief takers, 246
Three Mile Island (Pa.), nuclear plant malfunction, 443
Tiwi people, women's role, 177
Tobacco, 316, 331–332
Toda people, sex roles, 69
Total fertility rate, 370
Track systems, 224–225
Tradition, 177, 209
Trickle-down theory, tax policy, 146

Underemployment, 116, 123, 398
Unemployment, 16, 115–116, 121–122, 146
  blacks, 186
  Great Depression, 135
  urban, 396–399, 404
Uniform Crime Reports, 37, 249, 250, 251
United Nations, 511–512
Urban areas, Industrial Revolution and, 211–212. *See also* Cities
Urban fringe, 391

Values, 20
  defined, 39–40
  held, 39

Values (*cont.*)
  and social problems, 40–44
  traditional, 40–42
Venereal disease, 10, 292
Victimization studies, crime, 251
Victimless crimes, 240, 300
Victorian period, 281, 286
Vietnam war, 493, 506–507, 508, 511
  costs of, 400, 497, 507
Violence. *See also* Civil disorder
  in family, 83–85
  fear of and backlash, 196
  rape and, 298–299
Virgin, 279
Visibility, minorities and, 164–165
Volstead Act, 316
Voting Rights Act of 1965, 180

War
  conscription, 489
  costs, 494, 496–503
  defined, 486–487
  management of, 490
  nuclear, 484, 490, 492–493
  primitive societies, 486, 488
  technology and, 487–488, 489, 490, 492–493
Warfare (Leckie), 488
WCTU (Women's Christian Temperance Union), 13
Wealth-fare, 147–148, 149
Welfare, 135
  costs, 122, 151–154
  defined, 146
  food stamps, 152, 153
  government role, 146–148
  urban burden, 402–403
  "wealth-fare" distinguished, 147–148
Western Electric study, 110
Wheeler-Howard Act, 193–194
White-collar crime, 19, 239, 259–260, 270
White-collar work, 107, 110
White flight, 395

White House Conference on Aging, 218
Witchcraft, as social problem, 7–8, 17–19
Women's Christian Temperance Union (WCTU), 13
Women
  as a minority, 177–178, 182–185
  sexual independence, 284, 285, 288
  suffrage, 70–71 (*see also* Feminist movement)
  and work, 64, 74–75, 114–115, 369–370
Work, 98–126
  defined, 105
  education and, 107–109, 123
  government role, 120–121, 124
  impact on health, 112–114
  job satisfaction, 109–111
  labor unions, 118–120, 125
  management, 117–118
  Marx on, 103–104
  minorities and, 182–184, 185–187
  roles, 98
  and safety, 120–121
specialization, 99–100
  technology and, 99–102
  wages, 111–112, 115
  Weber on, 104–105
  women and, 64, 74–75, 114–115, 182–184
World Health Organization (WHO), 453

XYY chromosome pattern, 262
Yale Law Journal, 299
Youth, 204, 226–227
  defined, 205
  delinquency, 214–217, 404
  as economic liability, 212–214, 369
  and norms, 45–47, 212
  preliterate societies, 207–209
  runaways, 293–294
  subculture of, 211–212

Zero population growth (ZPG), 355, 364–368
ZPG. *See* zero population growth